Rational Leadership

Developing and Redeveloping Corporations

Second Edition

Paul Brooker
Margaret Hayward

OXFORD
UNIVERSITY PRESS

Great Clarendon Street, Oxford, OX2 6DP,
United Kingdom

Oxford University Press is a department of the University of Oxford.
It furthers the University's objective of excellence in research, scholarship,
and education by publishing worldwide. Oxford is a registered trade mark of
Oxford University Press in the UK and in certain other countries

First Edition published in 2018
Second Edition published in 2023

Published in the United States of America by Oxford University Press
198 Madison Avenue, New York, NY 10016, United States of America

British Library Cataloguing in Publication Data

Data available

Library of Congress Control Number: 2023938862

ISBN 9780198894643

DOI: 10.1093/oso/9780198894643.001.0001

Printed and bound by
CPI Group (UK) Ltd, Croydon, CR0 4YY

MIX
Paper | Supporting
responsible forestry
FSC® C013604

For Fred Brooker 1918–2021

Preface to the Second Edition

Several years ago, we co-authored a book about a version of rational leadership that develops business corporations. *Rational Leadership: Developing Iconic Corporations* presented several cases of rational leaders who have developed a corporation so successfully that it has attained iconic status. But the book's analysis of corporation development did not include rational leaders who have *re*developed corporations: who have remedially renewed a corporation. A redeveloping leader tries to solve the problems of a troubled, stagnating, or declining corporation and give it a bright new future, propelling it forward to perhaps even iconic status. The most prominent example is Steve Jobs redeveloping Apple into an iconic corporation during the 2000s. Redeveloping is therefore a special and important form of corporation development. And redeveloping has become more important in recent times, due to the need for problem solving and to a decline in the establishing and enhancing of corporations. So this second edition of the book has been expanded to include not only new material on development but also seven additional chapters, a Part II, on the *re*developing of corporations.

Part I comprises the eight chapters of the first edition, plus a new chapter that looks at another iconic case of corporation development. This additional chapter describes Jeff Bezos's development of Amazon into an iconic and multifaceted high-tech corporation. Some other new material on development is included in a chapter-like Addendum on the Volkswagen case of 'reconstructive' development, which is problem-solving rational leadership in the very early stages of developing a corporation.

The new Part II has five chapters that each present a classic case of redeveloping from the 1980s–2010s era. In these five cases, rational leaders are redeveloping well-known corporations and in industries that range from Nike's sneakers to Apple's smartphones. Part II also has chapters that focus on the rational means of redeveloping and on the relationship between charismatic leadership and rational redevelopment. The key conceptual point of Part II, though, is that redeveloping uses a specialized, distinctive set of rational means to achieve its special objective of remedial renewal. Specifically, redevelopers' appropriate rational means are a distinctive 'tool kit' of five change-making organizational processes, such as cultural transformation or diversifying the range of products. These five tools are very different from the seven rational methods that are used by developers and are discussed in Part I. Redeveloping a corporation is therefore a distinctive version of rational leadership that differs from the standard corporation-developing version. This 'finding' has some practical implications as well as adding to knowledge about rational leadership—the most modern, complex, and important type of leadership.

Finally, we would like to acknowledge the support we have received from several people during this edition's years of research, writing, and publication. We owe many thanks to Adam Swallow, Jenny King, and Jade Dixon at Oxford University Press. Many thanks are also owed to family and friends, especially Fred Brooker, Margaret Clark, and Kang Tan.

Contents

List of Abbreviations

1G	first-generation analogue mobile-phone technology
2G	second-generation digital mobile-phone technology
3G	third-generation mobile-phone technology
4G	fourth-generation wireless broadband
5G	fifth-generation wireless broadband
AI	artificial intelligence
AJ II	Air Jordan II sneakers
AMC	American Motors Corporation
AOL	America Online
AWS	Amazon Web Services
B&BW	Bath & Body Works
BH	Bachelor of Hamburgerology
CDB	centralized database
CFO	chief financial officer
CIA	Central Intelligence Agency
COO	chief operating officer
CPU	central processing unit
CRM	customer-relations management
CSP	cloud services provider
CTO	chief technology officer
DFM	design for manufacture
EBITDA	earnings before interest, taxes, depreciation, and amortization
EDLC	'Everyday Low Cost'
ERC	Employers Reinsurance Corporation
FAQ	frequently asked questions
FBA	'Fulfillment by Amazon'
GE	General Electric
GM	General Motors
GSM	Global System for Mobile communications
HDR	hybridized development-redevelopment
HP	Hewlett-Packard
HU	Hamburger University
IaaS	Infrastructure as a Service
IBM	International Business Machines
IPO	initial public offering
ISP	Internet service provider
IT	information technology
KdF	Nazi Labour Front's leisure organization, 'Strength through Joy'
MaVeNS	Mobile apps, Video, Native advertising, and Social networks
MBWA	Managing by walking around
NSN	Nokia Siemens Networks

OS	operating system
PCs	most personal computers but not Apple's
PR	press release
PwC	PricewaterhouseCoopers
QSC&V	Quality, Service, Cleanliness, and Value
R&D	research and development
RILD	rapid-initiation lengthy development
SaaS	software-as-a-service
STB	Server and Tools Business
SUV	sport utility vehicle
TLGP	Temporary Liquidity Guarantee Programme
TQC	Total Quality Control
VIT	voice information technology
VW	Volkswagen
WBR	Weekly Business Review
WMC	Weyerhaeuser Mortgage Company

PART I
DEVELOPING ICONIC CORPORATIONS

1

Rational Business Leadership

Developing Corporations through Rational Leadership

This book highlights and illustrates how various business leaders have developed a corporation in a rational way. They are examples of a rational, modern type of inspirational leader who inspires his or her followers with a modern, rational kind of confidence. Such confidence arises from the fact that the leader is capably using the appropriate rational means of achieving an objective, such as developing a business corporation. Some remarkable examples of this achievement will be described in the following eight chapters, which illustrate how business leaders have established or enhanced iconic corporations.

These examples confirm that rational leadership is the most modern, relevant type of leadership for twenty-first century society and organizations. Rational leadership is nothing new, and it has been discussed by theorists for more than a century. Their pioneering contributions have recently been restructured, though, into a more widely applicable concept of rational leadership, as is described in Appendix 1. This new concept acknowledges that there are many different versions of rational leadership, each with its own kind of objective and its own appropriate means of achieving that objective.

If there are so many versions of the rational type of leadership, why focus solely on the corporation-developing business version? There are at least three important reasons for focusing on examples of this highly specialized version of rational leadership. First, leading a business organization, large or small, is the most modern and prevalent field of leadership. Second, developing a business corporation, a large public company, is the most economically and socially significant example of business leadership. Back in the 1940s Drucker declared that the business corporation 'has become America's representative social institution' and by the 2010s this was possibly true of not only America but the whole globalized world.[1] Third, developing a corporation is one of the areas of business where individual leaders clearly do 'make a difference'. Any business hall of fame, national or international, would be filled largely by founder developers of corporations, such as Ford, Bezos, and Dassault, and by the most notable postfounder developers of corporations, such as Sloan, Whitman, and Ohno. The proverbial 'man at the top' or the female equivalent plays a crucially important role when it comes to developing a corporation.

The corporation-developing version of rational leadership will therefore be viewed from a high-level perspective. The leadership is coming from a CEO-level leader, and the development is the establishing or enhancing of a corporation by

Rational Leadership. Paul Brooker and Margaret Hayward, Oxford University Press. © Paul Brooker & Margaret Hayward (2023). DOI: 10.1093/oso/9780198894643.003.0001

its founder or a later CEO. Establishing a corporation involves founding a firm and developing it into a large-scale public company. By comparison, enhancing a corporation occurs when a later CEO, not the founder, takes on the role of developing the firm into a corporation, as Meg Whitman did with eBay. Enhancing also occurs when an existing corporation is further developed by a founder or later CEO, as when Whitman further developed eBay by continuing to scale up the corporation and by giving it new features. Perhaps the most prominent example of enhancing development is how Amazon founder Jeff Bezos greatly enhanced Amazon after he had established the corporation. Whether establishing or enhancing, however, this is high-level leadership provided by a CEO or occasionally by a leadership team comprising the CEO and one or two other company directors or senior executives.

A high-level perspective will also be adopted when examining the rational means that a leader uses to establish or enhance a corporation. Instead of describing them as particular strategies, technologies, techniques, or procedures, they will be viewed in higher level, more general terms and, in fact, as generic rational methods, such as quantitative or strategic calculation. What is more, six of these generic rational methods—two adaptive, two calculative, and two deliberative—form a set of methods that is appropriate for any high-level leader developing any corporation in any circumstances.

The following eight chapters will provide some classic examples of a high-level leader using these methods to establish or enhance a corporation. In all of these examples, the leader was developing a corporation that became famous and indeed acquired iconic status. So they are 'best-practice case studies' in the sense of leaders inspiring their employee-followers with rational confidence by *very* capably using the appropriate rational methods. Furthermore, the seven main examples, and most supplementary examples, will feature the leader's autobiographical account of how he or she developed the corporation. This autobiographical material provides a 'leader's-eye' view of how the methods were used (corroborated and supplemented by historical and biographical sources).

The examples will cover a wide range of industries and landmark advances in business structure, techniques, and products. The industries range from high-tech to high fashion, from automobiles to microprocessors, and from fast food to e-commerce. The landmark advances include General Motors' creation of a decentralized divisional structure in the 1920s, Toyota's pioneering of a just-in-time production system in the 1930s and 1950s, McDonald's use of innovative franchising and joint-venture arrangements in the 1960s–70s, and Wal-Mart's introduction of advanced technology into retailing in the 1970s–80s. Later chapters cover landmark advances of the 1980s–2010s: the arrival of high-tech consumer products, notably personal computers and mobile 'smart' phones; the arrival of the Internet's e-commerce opportunities; and, less technologically, the extension of product pyramids in the fashion and luxury industries.

This wide-ranging collection of classic examples will confirm as well as illustrate. They confirm that the set of six generic rational methods are indeed the appropriate means of developing a corporation. The main examples indicate that a leader tends to use all six methods and that in fact the major variation is in the leaders' emphasizing of favourite or key methods. As this set of six methods is so important, the next section of the chapter will describe them in some depth and from a theoretical as well as practical perspective.

Corporation-Developing Rational Leadership

Rational leadership: capably using the appropriate rational means of achieving the objective

Capably Using

↓

Appropriate Rational Means

Select from set of six appropriate rational methods of developing corporations
(1) rapid adaptation
(2) innovative adaptation
(3) quantitative calculation
(4) strategic calculation
(5) diverse deliberation
(6) institutionalized deliberation

↓

Achieving Objective

Establish or enhance a corporation: a large-scale public company

---

Adapting, Calculating, and Deliberating

The set of six appropriate corporation-developing methods is a set of *three pairs* of methods: the adaptive, calculative, and deliberative. They are being listed alphabetically, not in terms of their relative importance or how frequently they are used. However, the two calculative methods, quantitative and strategic calculation, are the most obviously business methods. Indeed, more than a hundred years ago Weber pointed out that modern business enterprise 'rests primarily on calculation', which even included lawyers calculating how the enterprise would be affected by 'public administration and the administration of justice'.[2] He singled out the quantitative form of calculation as particularly important, declaring that 'the extent of quantitative calculation or accounting' is the characteristic feature of the modern, rational form of economic activity.[3]

The prevalence of numbers and number-crunching increased markedly during the next hundred years. By the 1960s, Chandler was noting that numbers provide 'a fairly precise and objective criterion' for assessing the performance of not only a firm but also its individual departments and operating divisions.[4] The quantitative assessment of a firm's performance was expanding from the classic profit and loss to include such numbers as net income, earnings per share, cash earnings, and EBITDA: earnings before interest, taxes, depreciation, and amortization.[5] Similarly, quantitative assessment of the performance of the firm's divisions and departments has expanded to include even such creative departments as marketing and advertising. For example, in the early 2000s the target of Samsung advertising campaigns was to overtake Sony in the international brand-value rankings, which meant assessing performance in terms of quantitative rankings and billion-dollar brand values.[6]

Of course there are some circumstances in which quantitative calculation does not seem appropriate, such as when making decisions under conditions of uncertainty. Back in the 1920s Knight highlighted the distinction between *risk* as any uncertainty that can be 'reduced to an objective, quantitatively determinate probability' and *true uncertainty* as those uncertainties that are 'not susceptible to measurement and hence to elimination'.[7] Many of the crucial decisions made by business leaders are made under conditions of true uncertainty in which relying upon quantitative calculation may be inappropriate. For example, Christensen points out that this method is not appropriate—and may even be damaging—when firms are deciding how to respond to disruptive technology:

> Companies whose investment processes demand quantification of market sizes and financial returns before they can enter a market get paralyzed or make serious mistakes when faced with disruptive technologies. They demand market data when none exists and make judgments based on financial projections when neither revenues nor costs can, in fact, be known.[8]

In these circumstances the appropriate method is not quantitative calculation but rapid adaptation. The key point, however, is that leaders cannot inspire rational confidence unless they are using a broad enough selection of rational methods and therefore can switch from one method to another when a change in circumstances makes another method more appropriate.

Furthermore, it may be appropriate to use two rational methods in combination, such as quantitative and strategic calculation. Although strategic calculation is now clearly associated with developing a business corporation, it originated as the distinctive rational method of high-level military leaders. In the 1830s, Clausewitz's treatise *On War* defined strategy in obviously rational terms, namely as furthering the object (ends) of the war through the use (means) of a planned, organized, and coordinated series of engagements with the enemy.[9] In fact he was so rational that he could identify and conceptualize the *limitations* of strategic calculation. Clausewitz's famous concept of 'friction' assumed that whenever some military action is undertaken, the unexpected difficulties 'combine to lower the general level of performance, so that one always falls far short of the intended goal', if only because of 'unique episodes' and effects 'due to chance'.[10] And he pointed out that the interaction between two enemies or competitors adds an element of unpredictability to strategic calculations. When 'calculating' the effect of a measure upon the enemy and what will be the enemy's reactions, a strategist is faced 'with the fact that the very nature of interaction is bound to make it unpredictable'.[11] Clausewitz concluded that a strategist's calculated plan would therefore have to be adjusted continuously to fit war's constantly changing circumstances.[12]

Strategic calculation has similar limitations when it is applied to business activities. Some modern business leaders have been well aware of these similarities and have even adopted a Clausewitzian perspective, as in the case of General Electric's long-time CEO, Jack Welch. Early in his 1981–2001 tenure he mentioned the Clausewitzian concept of friction when he espoused an adaptive conception of business strategy, namely 'the evolution of a central idea through continually changing circumstances'.[13] Near the end of his tenure, Welch mentioned Clausewitzian interactive changes when he argued that business strategy should not rely on data-crunched plans (combining the two calculative methods) because business success 'is less a function of grandiose predictions than it is a result of being able to respond rapidly to real changes as they occur'.[14] Clearly some modern business strategists have come to the same conclusion as Clausewitz about having to adapt strategic calculations to fit forever changing, unforeseeable circumstances. In this situation, strategic calculation has to be used in combination or conjunction with another rational method but that method is rapid adaptation rather than quantitative calculation.

The other adaptive method, innovative adaptation, is occasionally used in conjunction with a higher level and form of strategic calculation—devising what the military term 'grand' strategy.[15] Grand strategy is concerned with the 'big picture' and 'big issues' that may involve a change in priorities or approaches or even a restructuring of the organization. It has become increasingly prevalent in business and is now an important special case of leaders using strategic calculation to develop a corporation. Indeed, there has recently been an impressively researched study of the role of grand-strategic leadership in the development of an iconic corporation, Hewlett-Packard.[16] And this corporation's founding leaders used innovative adaptation in conjunction with grand-strategic calculation, as is described in Chapter 6.

The two adaptive methods, rapid and innovative adaptation, were identified in the 1930s-40s by Schumpeter: the pioneering theorist of economic innovation.[17] In his early writings he viewed innovation and adaptation as separate and indeed contrasting economic processes.[18] He noted that the normal form of economic change is the marginal or incremental, not innovative, adaptive response that a competitive market economy continually forces firms to make, such as making an adjustment to their pricing or production. In contrast, the unusual form of change is the innovative entrepreneurial initiative by an extraordinary individual who is driven by economically *non*-rational motives, such as seeking the pleasure of creating or wanting to prove themselves superior to their rivals. But later, in the 1940s, Schumpeter wrote about the eventual demise of such entrepreneurs. He argued that individuals with entrepreneurial 'personality and will power' and non-rational motivation are less required as societies become accustomed to economic change, and therefore entrepreneurial innovation would eventually become just another form of routine organizational behaviour in economies that had become accustomed to change.[19]

Schumpeter's vision of trends and tendencies was implicitly confirmed in the 1980s by a celebrated theorist of management. Drucker's *Innovation and Entrepreneurship* referred to a form of innovation that was the 'proper and profitable course', was 'systematic innovation', and was the result of a whole business organization developing the habits of entrepreneurship and innovation.[20] Indeed 'in a period of rapid change the best—and perhaps the only—way that a business can hope to prosper, if not to survive, is to innovate': not innovating 'is far more risky'.[21] However, it seems that such innovations are often adaptive responses to changes occurring in this period of rapid change. Successful innovations normally 'exploit change' and in fact systematic innovation involves a 'purposeful and organized search for change' plus a 'systematic analysis of the opportunities such changes might offer'.[22] This innovation will therefore typically be an adaptive innovation or, in other words, an innovative adaptation, which seems to be just routine and indeed what Schumpeter termed a 'forced' adaptive response.

But an innovative adaptation is better viewed as what Schumpeter termed a 'creative' response. In the 1940s he described it as going beyond a merely adaptive response because its creative response to change not only has a significant and lasting effect but also is so innovative that the content of the response could not have been predicted beforehand.[23] This perspective on innovative adaptation would view it as a rational, but not routine innovation, which has significant and lasting effects—including the effects it produces as a rational method of developing corporations.

Although it is usually less significant than innovative adaptation, rapid adaptation can be a crucially important method in some situations. Schumpeter raised the issue of rapid adaptation when he was writing about rigidity. He referred to rigidity as 'resistance to adaptation' that slowed or prevented such adaptive responses as a business adjusting its prices to reflect changes in supply or demand.[24] Resisting this merely incremental adaptation was economically irrational and would mean 'loss and reduced output'.[25] Resisting more serious kinds of adaptation will have more serious consequences and may undermine a firm's position or survival. Christensen's disruptive-technology 'innovator's dilemma' epitomizes this situation and is discussed at length in Appendix 1.

But rapid adaptation should not be viewed only from the perspective of rigidity and protecting a firm. In some situations, rapid adaptation will enhance a corporation by giving it a winning advantage over competitors that are slower to adapt. Furthermore, rapid adaptation may even help establish a corporation. For example, part of the disruptive-technology 'innovator's dilemma' is that a firm which adapts too slowly to disruptive technology may well be overtaken by *new* firms which have come from nowhere by exploiting the new market created by this new technology.

In some cases the new firms have grown into corporations and so here rapid adaptation has been an appropriate method of not just enhancing but actually establishing a corporation.

In these situations, too, the rapid adaptation has been exploiting a new opportunity—the new market created by the disruptive technology. In fact, their leaders have responded in the manner described by a military definition of adapting: 'identifying and taking full advantage of the opportunities offered'.[26] More generally, exploiting an opportunity is often the way in which rapid adaptation—and innovative adaptation—have been used to develop a corporation. The two adaptive methods of developing a corporation are the most opportunistic as well as the most creative.

In addition to the adaptive and calculative, there are the two deliberative rational methods of developing a corporation—diverse and institutionalized deliberation. Even 500 years ago diverse deliberation was seen as important and as being reduced by reticence. For Machiavelli noted that a prince 'should be very ready to seek information and opinions and to listen patiently to candid views about matters that he raises. Indeed, if he learns that anyone is reticent for any reason, he should be angry'.[27] Modern rulers, too, are plagued by this problem of reticence. For example, an analysis of President Kennedy's decision-making in the 1962 Cuban Missile Crisis discovered 'reticence' by the president's advisors and subordinates because they believed that their opinions would alienate him.[28]

Modern leaders also have to deal with a new, modern source of reticence and reduced diversity—bureaucratic politics. Thanks to bureaucratic politicking, policy issues and options 'may not rise to the presidential level, or when they do, they often take the form of concealed compromises that reflect the special interests at lower levels'.[29] But there are ways and means of counteracting this modern form of diversity-reducing reticence. A standard ploy was pioneered by President Franklin Roosevelt and was recounted a generation later by Neustadt, 'the most penetrating analyst of power since Machiavelli'.[30] Neustadt noted how Roosevelt mixed competing jurisdictions with competitive personalities: he would 'keep his organizations overlapping and divide authority among them' and would also tend 'to put men of clashing temperaments, outlooks, ideas, in charge of them'.[31] However, this ploy requires leaders to have a ready supply of diverse people to put in charge of their organizations. And the supply is unlikely to meet the demand, especially if the leader favours diversity to the same degree as Roosevelt or Ray Kroc, the founder of the McDonald's fast-food empire, who declared that 'if two executives think the same, one of them is superfluous'.[32]

The other deliberative method, institutionalized deliberation, was also recognized by Machiavelli. He saw the need for some institutionalization of deliberation, even if only through informal rules of behaviour. He warned that a ruler 'should discourage anyone from giving advice uninvited' and should allow only his chosen advisors to speak frankly to him—and only when he asked for their advice.[33] Some formal institutionalization of deliberation had already evolved by Machiavelli's time, if merely in the shape of consultative councils of notables and officials. Even medieval kings' formal policy-making had taken place in their consultative council, which comprised 'members of the royal family, royal favourites, heads of baronial factions and the chief officers of household and government departments'.[34] The rulers' councils would eventually evolve into parliamentary democracies' ministerial councils or cabinets, and their array of specialized committees.

The business equivalent is the corporation's board of directors, plus the array of specialized committees that was pioneered by Alfred Sloan at General Motors and is discussed in Chapter 2. Other business leaders have used more informal varieties of institutionalized deliberation when enhancing or establishing a corporation. Instead of formal committees and procedural rules, they have used informal rules about how managers should deliberate with their leader, such as when selling the leader a policy proposal.

Such deliberation involves a special, 'deliberative' form of leadership. It is very different from the authoritative form of leadership, which sets a direction by exercising some legitimate authority that followers feel obligated to obey. In contrast, deliberative leadership:

> sets a direction not by obedience but by choice and consent; it gives a lead that, if accepted, will have been considered on reflection or after debate to be the best option available ... Deliberative leadership is characteristic of any situation of collective choice or consultation in decision-making, whether by an electorate, assembly, committee or any combination of two or more people.[35]

This politics-oriented definition can be phrased in economic or business terms, too, with a lead being 'sold to a potential customer who has the choice of whether or not to "buy" it or indeed to prefer a different, competing lead from another seller'.[36]

The deliberative rational methods merge the deliberative and authoritative forms of leadership: in several different ways or contexts. Perhaps the simplest variant is when an authoritative leader allows one or more followers to 'sell' him or her policy proposals. For instance, even such an authoritative and opinionated leader as Winston Churchill was willing to be sold policy proposals in private deliberations with a trusted individual, as in the case of his wartime naval supremo, Admiral Pound, who 'knew the sure way to get something approved by Churchill was to sell him the idea verbally and then let him draft' it in writing 'as if it were his idea'.[37] Other leaders may prefer to be sold policy proposals in the highly institutionalized context of a committee meeting whose official purpose is to consider and assess policy options.

A rarer merging of deliberative and authoritative leadership is when a leader sells a policy proposal to one or more followers and allows them to choose whether to 'buy' this lead. Wal-Mart's founder Sam Walton claimed that he actually favoured the 'mavericks' who disagreed with him. 'I respected them, and, in the end, I listened to them a lot more closely than the pack who always agree with everything I said.'[38]

Example: Sandberg at Facebook and in Her *Lean In*

A relatively recent example of a leader using deliberative rational methods is Sheryl Sandberg, who used them to enhance Facebook's business practices and revenue. In 2008, Facebook's youthful founder and CEO, Mark Zuckerberg, recruited the 38-year-old Sandberg from Google to be his firm's chief operating officer (COO) and join him in a dual-leadership team.[39] Such leadership teams will be examined in more detail in the next section of this chapter. The key point here is that the two leaders may well focus on different aspects of their objective. In this case, Sandberg would focus on enhancing the business side of Facebook, making the firm more business-like and transforming its revenue potential by making the firm an online advertising giant. She was obviously better qualified than Facebook's CEO to take on these tasks as she had much more business experience and expertise, including a Harvard MBA. She was also willing and able to use the two deliberative methods—diverse and institutionalized deliberation.

Her use of deliberative methods to set a new, advertising-oriented direction in revenue earning is recounted in Kirkpatrick's *The Facebook Effect*. Soon after Sandberg arrived at Facebook she 'decided to host a series of meetings to get Facebook's management to focus on the ad opportunity'.[40] With Zuckerberg away on a month's leave, she was clearly in charge of these weekly or twice-weekly meetings.[41] However, she did not take charge of the discussions and obviously lead them in the direction of advertising revenues. She adopted a more subtle approach that encouraged diverse deliberation but also ensured that the discussions were moving on the right track, such as when she began the first meeting with the agenda-setting question:

> 'What business are we in?' These were bull sessions at first, giving everyone a chance to express their views ... Staffers researched various options and brought carefully compiled charts to the next meeting, showing the size of each market, its likely growth rate, the big players, and what Facebook could do uniquely well. After weeks of this, at the final meeting Sandberg went deliberately around the room and asked each person what percentage of Facebook's revenue would ultimately come from each category. Virtually everyone said 70 percent or more would be advertising.[42]

Sandberg's use of diverse and institutionalized deliberation had created the launch pad for an advertising-based take-off in revenues, which would nearly double in the following year and go on to surpass $1.3 billion in 2010.[43] Achieving this revenue take-off would involve other rational methods, such as strategic calculation, but the use of deliberative methods had played an important role. In particular, it had inspired employees with some rational confidence regarding the new revenue-earning direction and the newly arrived member of the dual CEO/COO leadership team.

However, Sandberg's enhancing of the business side of Facebook also involved her making the firm more business-like in its procedures and attitudes—a different task that required a different use of the deliberative methods. Several years later she referred to this task and its complexities in her partly autobiographical *Lean In: Women, Work, and the Will to Lead.*

> When I first joined Facebook, one of my biggest challenges was setting up the necessary business processes without harming the freewheeling culture. The company operated by moving quickly and tolerating mistakes, and lots of people were nervous that I would not just ruin the party, but squash innovation ... I faced a dilemma: I needed to bolster the business side of the company while respecting its unconventional culture.[44]

In other words, she had to find a way of making the firm more business-like in its procedures and attitudes without undermining the creative workplace culture that was a crucial factor in the firm's success.

In this context, the use of deliberative methods included her informally institutionalizing the nonconformist aspect of diverse deliberation. 'I also let them know that if they hear a bad idea, even one they believe is coming from me or Mark [Zuckerberg], they should either fight it or ignore it'.[45] However, she ran into the reticence problem that has so often hampered leaders' use of diverse deliberation. 'As often as I try to persuade people to share their honest views, it is still a challenge to elicit them'.[46] But it was a challenge worth undertaking, if only because, as she points out, 'reticence causes and perpetuates all kinds of problems'.[47] More immediately, her obvious commitment to diverse deliberation would have again inspired employees with some rational confidence regarding her and the direction in which she was leading them—towards becoming a business-like firm.

Lean In included an example of diverse deliberation that Sandberg experienced and learned from many years before she used such methods at Facebook. In 1996, she had been a new member of Secretary Rubin's Treasury department and had attended a policy meeting where Rubin asked for her opinion because 'you're new and not fully up to speed on how we do things. I thought you might see something that we were missing'.[48] He thereby 'sent a powerful message to all of us about the value of soliciting ideas from every corner'.[49] Sandberg, too, has sent a powerful message about the value of deliberative methods but in her case the message was sent through her deeds at Facebook and then her words in *Lean In.*

The conventional business wisdom, though, was that leadership is largely about 'charisma' rather than rationality. Khurana's *Searching for a Corporate Savior: The Irrational Quest for Charismatic CEOs* sceptically describes a conventional wisdom that favours charismatic leadership and, for example, believes that CEOs need charisma in order to carry out the key leadership roles of energizing people who are 'lethargic or sceptical' and 'increasing the self-confidence of employees when the company is collectively anxious'.[50] Yet charismatic leadership alone is unlikely to boost the confidence of rational, discerning employee-followers, as is discussed in Appendix 1.

A similar point can be made about the response to 'strong' leadership. In the 1990s, Grove argued that strong leadership is especially needed by a demoralized firm, whose employees have lost confidence in its management and in each other. 'This is exactly when you need to have a strong leader setting a direction', and the direction has to be 'a strong, clear one' because organizations 'are very sensitive to obscure or ambiguous signals from their management'.[51] But rational, discerning followers are also very sensitive to *irrational* signals from the leader; the direction set by the leader must be rational as well as clear if it is to restore these employees' confidence in management and in each other. Even more will be needed to inspire them with confidence about achieving such an ambitious objective as developing a corporation: their leader will have to be using the appropriate rational means of achieving this objective.

Using the Six Methods: Autobiographical Accounts

The appropriate rational means of developing a corporation are the six generic rational methods delineated in the second section of this chapter. It is worth reviewing here that earlier account before going on to discuss how leaders use these six methods when establishing or enhancing a corporation. The two adaptive methods, rapid and innovative adaptation, are the opportunistic and creative methods. Their key theorist was Schumpeter, especially in his 1940s writings, but some aspects of these two forms of adaptation have been explored by later theorists, such as Drucker in the 1980s and Christensen in the 1990s. The two calculative methods, quantitative and strategic calculation, are the obviously rational methods. Their key theorist was Weber in the early 1920s but strategic calculation's founding theorist was the military writer Clausewitz in the 1830s. The two deliberative methods, diverse and institutionalized deliberation, have the longest intellectual heritage, extending back to Machiavelli.

There are marked variations in how this set of six methods is used to establish or enhance a corporation. The leaders of iconic corporations have tended to use all six methods but usually emphasize at least one of the methods that they are using. And there is a marked variation in their choice of which method(s) to emphasize.

This variation in emphasis seems to be due to leaders' personal preferences rather than to differences in their circumstances. For example, Sam Walton's emphasis on quantitative calculation seems to have been due to personal preference rather than due to the method being appropriate for the circumstances. He noted that his 'appreciation for numbers' was one of his talents and strengths and that 'my style as an executive has been pretty much dictated by my talents. I've played to my strengths and relied on others to make up for my weaknesses'.[52] Walton did not rely on quantitative calculation, however, when he was making such key decisions as whether to make a major acquisition—he relied instead on a *non-rational* method. 'I try to play a "what if" game with the numbers—but it's generally my gut that makes the final decision. If it feels right, I tend to go for it, and if it doesn't, I back off'.[53]

Was this reliance on gut instinct due to a stronger personal preference or to the appropriateness of non-rational methods in such extraordinary circumstances? Walton went on to say that letting his gut make the decision was by no means a mistake-proof method. 'Sometimes, of course, that leads me into mistakes', as when 'I was mistaken in my vision of the potential the Hypermarket held in this country'.[54] Yet his non-rational methods of vision and gut instinct might be more successful than rational methods in such extraordinary circumstances as the 'true uncertainty' mentioned earlier in the chapter. Of course when leaders use non-rational methods, they are failing—by definition—to provide rational leadership, even if the non-rational methods are appropriate. In practice, however, the followers may still be inspired with rational confidence if the leader is *rationally selecting* the appropriate method, even if that method is as non-rational as vision or gut instinct.

The issues and insights provided by Walton's remarks also highlight the benefits of using examples that feature autobiographical material. It has similar advantages to interview material and it gives a leader's-eye view that personalizes and humanizes any example of developing a corporation. What is more, autobiographical material allows the distinctive 'voice' of each leader to be heard over the years or decades. It is therefore a constant reminder that although these leaders used the same set of rational methods, they were unique individuals who left behind distinctive corporations as monuments to their life's work.

The examples presented in the following chapters will feature autobiographical accounts of how the leaders established or enhanced their corporations. Of course featuring autobiographical material has its problems as well as its advantages. The obvious problem is that the leaders' autobiographical writings may contain biased and even erroneous recollections. However, these distortions can be countered by supplementing and corroborating the autobiographical writings with more objective biographical or historical accounts of what occurred. A less obvious but larger problem is that the available autobiographical material is often too limited. The leaders' autobiographical writings often give a too perfunctory account of how they used particular methods and/or describe too few of the methods that they are known to have used, and this is another reason why their writings have to be supplemented by biographical and historical sources. The most fundamental problem, however, is that many classic examples have had to be excluded because the corporation-developing leader has not produced an autobiography, memoir, or any other writings that include relevant autobiographical material.

Nonetheless, the following chapters present a wide range of classic examples of leaders establishing or enhancing an iconic corporation. The times range from the 1920s to the 2000s, the places include Japan, Italy, France, and Britain as well as America, and the industries include automobile assembly, aircraft construction, computer-chip production, discount retailing, high-fashion retailing, e-commerce auctioning and retailing, fast-food franchising, and cosmetics franchising. The seven main examples are Sloan enhancing General Motors, Ohno enhancing Toyota, Kroc establishing McDonald's, Walton establishing Wal-Mart, Grove enhancing Intel, Whitman enhancing eBay, and Bezos establishing Amazon. The supplementary examples include Dassault establishing Dassault Aviation, Roddick establishing The Body Shop, and Armani establishing his fashion empire. Plus, there is a chapter-like Addendum on Nordhoff's post-Nazi reconstructive development of Volkswagen.

Corporations, Industries, and Countries			
General Motors	Automobiles	US	Chapter 2
Toyota	Automobiles	Japan	Chapter 3
McDonald's	Fast Food	US	Chapter 4
Wal-Mart	Retailing	US	Chapter 5
Dassault Aviation	Aircraft	France	Chapter 5
Intel	Microchips	US	Chapter 6
eBay	Online Auctions	US	Chapter 7
Amazon	Online Retailing	US	Chapter 8
Giorgio Armani	Fashion	Italy	Chapter 9
The Body Shop	Cosmetics	Britain	Chapter 9
Volkswagen	Automobiles	Germany	Addendum

It is true that this selection of examples contains too many Americans and too few women but there are extenuating circumstances. Tedlow's biographical study of seven American business leaders, *Giants of Enterprise*, noted that 'founding and building new businesses' is 'what Americans do best' and he pointed out that these seven giants were individuals of 'extraordinary inner drive and competitiveness living in a country and culture which encouraged those traits and channelled them into business enterprise'.[55] He also acknowledged that even in America, however, the dice had been loaded against women achieving the same sort of business success. Women 'have not been given the opportunity to lead a large American corporation' and the 'rare, recent exceptions' amounted in the year 2000 to merely three women CEOs among the leaders of the largest 500 corporations.[56]

Another unrepresentative aspect of the selected examples is that they include only iconic, extraordinarily successful corporations. This is because such corporations are 'best-practice case studies' in the sense of leaders having inspired followers with rational confidence by *very* capably using the appropriate rational methods. Furthermore, the examples will show that this rational leadership was provided even in the early stages of the corporation's development, well *before* the extraordinary successes that made it iconic and made its leader a celebrated or legendary figure.[57] Indeed, the development of iconic corporations may include a period of high-level leadership by a *team* of rational leaders.

Such a high-level leadership team combines the CEO with one or two other board members. In the case of corporation-developing teams, however, it is usually dual, two-person leadership and seldom triple, three-person leadership.[58] Like management teams, their teamwork normally involves some division of labour, with each member of the leadership team having particular roles or tasks. In fact there are at least three distinct versions of the division of labour between two members of a dual-leadership team that is developing a corporation. The best known version combines a more business-oriented individual with a more creative or technically oriented individual, as in the case of the high-fashion Versace brothers or the high-tech Hewlett and Packard team. Another well-known version combines a semi-retired founder as chairman with a younger generation executive as the CEO. The third and most complex version combines the CEO with another prominent executive, such as the COO, who is introducing an enhancing innovation. All three versions are to be found among the classic examples of corporation-developing leadership presented in the following chapters and in fact the first two examples include leadership teams introducing an enhancing innovation: a new administrative system at General Motors and a new production system at Toyota.

2

General Motors

Sloan's *My Years with General Motors*

Alfred Sloan's leadership of the General Motors Corporation in the 1920s is one of the legendary feats in business history. He carried out an administrative rationalization of the corporation that dramatically improved its structure, processes, marketing, and policy-making. This multifaceted enhancement of the corporation would lead to him being 'hailed as the father of the modern corporation, the master of consumer mass marketing and the most effective chief executive officer ever'.[1] Sloan brilliantly reaped the rewards of his 1920s rationalization during his long tenure as leader of this iconic corporation. He was its president/CEO from 1923 to 1937, then CEO and chairman until 1946 and thereafter its chairman until his retirement ten years later. During this era, General Motors achieved a remarkable series of successes: defeating the legendary Henry Ford to become the leading firm in the automobile industry, trading profitably during the Great Depression, seeing its methods copied by competitors, and becoming the world's largest industrial corporation, with more than half a million employees.

In addition to these feats, Sloan was a pioneering exponent of rational business leadership. His biographer has pointed to the contrast with Machiavelli's view that rulers are either feared or loved; Sloan 'believed that he could run General Motors without fear or love: that reason alone would suffice'.[2] Rationality would inspire his employee-followers with confidence, while neither fear nor love would be needed to inspire them with commitment—this was produced by pay, promotions, and professionalism. His commitment to rationality was reflected in his use of appropriate rational methods of developing a corporation: he used all six of the methods discussed in Chapter 1. This was wholly appropriate in the dire circumstances he was facing in the 1920s when he became leader of the corporation. His wide-ranging administrative rationalization and restructuring was needed to rectify the deficiencies of an earlier era. And his enhancement of the corporation is characterized by the way in which he converted these weaknesses into strengths—through his use of rational methods.

For example, through innovative adaptation he converted an organizational weakness into an impressive new organizational structure, which became a standard type for manufacturing corporations. This type of organizational structure arranges a corporation into a headquarters and several operating divisions: firm-like, virtually self-contained units that are based on particular product lines, such as the Chevrolet

Rational Leadership. Paul Brooker and Margaret Hayward, Oxford University Press. © Paul Brooker & Margaret Hayward (2023). DOI: 10.1093/oso/9780198894643.003.0002

or Cadillac car. More importantly, decision-making is largely decentralized to these operating divisions, with most decisions being made at divisional level rather than centrally by the corporation's headquarters. Tedlow considers this 'an organizational innovation of exceptional value' and Sloan noted in the 1960s that it 'not only has worked well for us, but also has become standard practice in a large part of American industry'.[3] Even in the twenty-first century Sloan's organizational structure:

> remains a litmus test for all kinds of organizations today that are struggling to remain agile, efficient, and effective in a world of constant technological change and globalization. Despite the current emphasis on 'flat' and 'matrixed' organizations rather than the 'silos' of the Sloan organization chart, the key elements of Sloan's model are still followed across the globe: indeed, many companies have ended up either returning to it or borrowing from it.[4]

It has been described as 'a machine capable of adapting to any change in its environment' and Sloan noted in his memoirs that there needed to be such forms of organization that 'could adapt to great changes in the market. Any rigidity by an automobile manufacturer, no matter how large or how well established, is severely penalized'.[5]

Sloan's use of rational methods is recounted in his memoirs, which appeared in 1963 and became as legendary as his business success. He began working on *My Years with General Motors* before his retirement and employed a large team of professionals, including an accomplished writer, John McDonald, and an academic researcher, Alfred Chandler, who would later become a celebrated business historian.[6] Of all the autobiographical writings by business leaders, this is the one which is most like a management text rather than a memoir or autobiography. It is also the one that has best stood the test of time. It is still 'in print' in the twenty-first century, over a million copies have been sold, and the front cover displays a testimonial from Bill Gates: 'probably the best book to read if you want to read only one book about business'. Similarly, its 1990 introduction by Drucker was entitled 'Why *My Years with General Motors* Is Must Reading' and he declared that it was still 'the best management book'.[7]

Sloan's introduction to his memoirs expressed his strong commitment to rational management and methods. The book's approach would be 'to deal with business from the logical point of view' and it would be considering 'the logic of management in relation to the events of the automotive industry'.[8] Sloan's biographer suggests that the kind of person who appreciates *My Years with General Motors* is someone 'who wants to understand how to rationally manage men, money, markets, and machines'.[9] The book can also be appreciated, however, by anyone seeking a leader's-eye view of the way Sloan used rational methods to enhance the corporation. He used the whole set of six rational methods and emphasized three—innovative adaptation, strategic calculation, and institutionalized deliberation—largely because of the circumstances rather than any personal preference for these three methods.

The first section of this chapter will focus on his emphasizing of innovative adaptation, which restructured General Motors and produced a new, innovative organizational structure. This section will also assess his use of rapid adaptation and will show how he used quantitative calculation—quantitative controls and assessments—to strengthen his new organizational structure. The second section will describe his emphasizing of strategic calculation and particularly his strategically calculated marketing, which played an important role in reviving the firm's fortunes. The third section will describe his emphasizing of institutionalized deliberation and how his highly institutionalized, committee-based system of deliberation also involved the use of diverse deliberation. The final section will discuss the rivalry between his and Henry Ford's corporations and approaches which would result in Sloanism's administrative rationality defeating Fordism's focus on efficient production.

Adaptive Restructuring

Sloan's 1920s organizational restructuring of General Motors was an innovative adaptation which influenced many other corporations and became a standard organizational structure. As Chandler noted in his *Strategy and Structure*, the previous corporate standard had been a 'centralized, functionally departmentalized administrative structure' whose several departments each had a specialized function, such as the sales department or purchasing department; Sloan's innovative new structure, though, was a decentralized, multidivisional administrative structure whose several operating divisions each performed 'all the functions involved in the overall process of handling a line of products' in similar fashion to a self-contained, autonomous firm, such as the Chevrolet and Cadillac divisions of General Motors.[10] Even before Sloan's restructuring of the corporation it had a multidivisional structure, because its operating divisions had originally been independent firms acquired by General Motors when it was merely a holding company. Sloan created his innovative new structure by further *centralizing* the too-independent divisions, which had been behaving as if they were still independent firms. But he referred to his new structure, somewhat paradoxically, as a *de*centralized organization. In his memoirs, for example, he describes the new structure as a combination of decentralization with some centralization, and he terms it 'decentralization with co-ordinated control' or being 'co-ordinated in policy and decentralized in administration'.[11] In terms of what he had done to General Motors, however, the accent should have been on *central* control or 'coordination' of what had been a markedly *more* decentralized organization.

Sloan's organizational innovation had originated as his adaptive *conceptual* response to his corporation's organizational failings, which were largely a by-product of the way in which it had developed during the Durant era of 1908–20. William Durant established General Motors as a holding company of largely car-making and parts-making firms but he eventually converted it into an operating company, with the firms becoming operating divisions of the General Motors Corporation. Although Durant had therefore begun the process of centralization, he is depicted by Sloan as 'an extreme decentralizer' whose style of personal management led to a situation of 'almost total decentralization'; he was in fact 'a great man with a great weakness—he could create but not administer.'[12] In the later years of the Durant era, Sloan was an executive vice-president on the board of directors and was in a good position to see that corporate headquarters needed more control over the managers of the operating divisions. 'Without adequate control from the central office, the divisions got out of hand and failed to follow the policies set by the corporation management, to the great detriment of the corporation.'[13]

These organizational failings were highlighted and exacerbated by the corporation's rapid expansion in 1918–20. 'I became convinced that the corporation could not continue to grow and survive unless it was better organized.'[14] In late 1919 he began drafting a systematic plan, the Organization Study, aimed at centralizing and rationalizing the corporation's structure and processes.[15] In that year General Motors had begun a massive expansion programme aimed at doubling production capacity—through the operating divisions acquiring or constructing new factories—and based on the confident assumption that the booming demand for automobiles would continue unabated in the decade ahead.[16] Instead, however, demand began to decline in the summer of 1920 and the economy began an unexpected recession that would lead to 'a new awareness throughout the business world of how complex and unpredictable the economy and the consumer can be.'[17]

General Motors had been hit particularly hard.

> All of the elements of catastrophe abruptly came together: the cost of the 1919 expansion program, the accumulation of huge inventories in anticipation of more demand, the end of cash flow as dealers stopped ordering vehicles, the fall of the stock price, and the lack of an internal structure or mechanism to force the divisions to cut production and costs in a timely or orderly manner.[18]

By November 1920 both the share price and the production of vehicles had fallen to less than a third of what they had been in the spring of that year.[19] Not surprisingly, November also saw Durant's resignation as president of General Motors and his departure from the board of directors, who appointed their chairman, Pierre du Pont, to the additional post of president on a temporary, interim basis.

The corporation's directors followed this up with a farsighted response to the crisis. In December the board officially adopted Sloan's Organization Study as the basis for a rationalizing restructuring of the corporation: in his words, the board 'desired a highly rational and objective mode of operation.'[20] As the 44-year-old Sloan was the board's operations expert, the equivalent of a modern chief operating officer (COO), it also relied upon him to *introduce* his planned administrative innovation. In fact an innovation-introducing leadership team was formed between Sloan and Pierre du Pont; the latter would continue to be the corporation's temporary president as well as its chairman. The dual-leadership team of du Pont and Sloan would last until May 1923, when du Pont resigned from his temporary presidential position and Sloan became the new president of the corporation.[21] 'Sloan, at first under the gentlemanly but firm hand of Pierre du Pont, and then as chief executive, would use harsher instruments [than Durant's] to take General Motors from near extinction and lead it upward.'[22]

Sloan would convert his adaptive conceptual response, the Organization Study, into an innovative adaptation—a pioneering organizational restructuring of the corporation. He would be using and indeed emphasizing innovative adaptation as a method of enhancing a corporation. And his emphasizing of this method was not simply due to his personal preferences: it was largely because of the dire circumstances that his corporation was facing. Yet his innovative adaptation was by no means rapid, considering that there was a pre-existing blueprint—the Organization Study plan—which had the support of the chief executive and the board of directors. In fact the new organizational structure was still being developed in the 1930s, with new centralizing features being added or existing features evolving further in a centralizing direction. But much of the organizational restructuring was carried out in the first few years and seems slow only in comparison to his rapid rationalization of marketing strategy. Furthermore, Sloan's restructuring was a major 'political' change that markedly reduced the independence enjoyed by the operating divisions, and so it is not surprising that he took things relatively slowly.

The key to his organizational restructuring was creating a new relationship between central management and the operating divisions. For example, Sloan specified that divisional managers could not be members of the corporation's executive committee, because 'the top operating committee should be a policy group detached from the interests of the specific divisions'.[23] In Chandler's words, now central management would be responsible 'for strategic decisions and the divisions for tactical ones'.[24] This strategic/tactical distinction is particularly relevant because Sloan created an organizational structure similar to that of a modern army in the vertical terms of headquarters, corps, and divisional units and in the horizontal staff-and-line terms of staff officers advising 'line' officers on how to exercise their hierarchical command authority.

There was nothing new about business firms copying the military's practice of attaching staff units to senior 'line' commanders and headquarters. Large business firms had adopted a similar structure at their company headquarters, with staff units and staff executives providing information or advice about finance, law, and other specialized areas of expertise. General Motors in the Durant era, however, had more impressive staff resources at the divisional level than at corporate headquarters. Indeed even *after* Sloan's centralization, each divisional general manager was 'served by almost as complete a staff as if he were heading an independent business: production manager, chief engineer, sales manager, comptroller, personnel manager, etc.; in other words, each division is organized as an autonomous unit'.[25] But by then Sloan had shifted the balance in favour of the headquarters staff. His Organization Study had called for headquarters to have a much-expanded set of 'advisory staffs, which would be without line authority' and cover a wide range of specialized areas of expertise.[26] His implementation of this plan boosted headquarters staff and gave it new units for research, engineering, personnel, sales, purchasing, and even factory design.[27]

What is more, Sloan gave new, innovative roles to his headquarters staff. In addition to its standard role of providing central policy-makers with information and expert advice, it was given important *divisional* roles that involved monitoring as well assisting the divisions. Staff units were employed 'to keep a check on the divisions, to suggest ways to improve current methods, and to see how various policies were being followed'—eventually staff were even 'coordinating' divisions' activities.[28] In his memoirs Sloan acknowledged that the staff units and executives informally exerted some central authority over the divisions:

> In General Motors we do not follow the textbook definition of line and staff. *Our distinction* is between the central office (which includes staff) and divisions. Broadly speaking, the staff officers—being primarily specialists—do not have line authority, yet in certain matters of established policy, they may *communicate the application* of such policy directly to a division.[29]

In addition to these staff units, headquarters acquired a new type of corporate executive—the *group* vice-president.[30] This Sloan innovation was a follow-up to his Organization Study's plan for the corporation's divisions to be grouped 'according to like activities' while leaving each division as a self-contained unit that handled its own production, engineering, sales, and so forth.[31] The dozens of divisions and smaller units would be organized into four groups: car, accessory, parts, and a residual miscellaneous that included tractors, refrigerators, and the finance company GMAC.[32] In what was apparently an afterthought, Sloan suggested that an executive should be put in charge of each group, if only to take over the divisional managers' duties of reporting directly to the CEO.[33]

Several other duties, however, were eventually assigned to these group vice-presidents. In particular, they were given the extensive role of supervising, coordinating, and assessing their divisions and 'reflecting' central policies to them.[34] Officially this was still only an advisory role, like that of the staff executives, and officially the group vice-presidents likewise exercised 'only advisory and not line authority'.[35] But by the time of Drucker's 1940s study of General Motors, the group vice-presidents exercised 'informal but very real control' over their group's divisions: they possessed 'a very real power; but it is rarely, if ever, exercised in the form of orders'.[36]

According to Chandler, these group executives and the new headquarters staff 'made possible the transformation of the corporation from a federation into a consolidated enterprise'.[37] He also points out that the newly consolidated enterprise was flourishing under Sloan's centralizing leadership. Its share of the market had grown from less than 19 per cent in 1921 to more than 43 per cent in 1927, and it had taken over the number-one position in the industry: the new 'clearly and rationally defined' organizational structure had 'served General Motors well'.[38] There were other factors, however, involved in the corporation's success, and even the centralization factor had involved new *processes* as well as a new organizational structure.

These new centralizing processes typically involved quantitative calculation and the renowned 'numbers man', Donaldson Brown. Sloan used Brown's expertise to introduce a wide range of quantitative controls and assessments. Some of them were innovative but others were merely standard procedures that had been neglected in the Durant era. For example, Sloan had to enforce limits on divisional capital expenditure and establish a new capital-appropriation process to consider divisional requests for capital investment.[39] They were now considered from a corporation as well as divisional perspective and were evaluated objectively by applying the concept of rate of return on investment—in fact the corporation's financial staff had developed a new equation for calculating the return on investment.

Similarly, rectifying the corporation's lack of uniform accounting procedures also meant strengthening the authority of headquarters' financial staff over their divisional equivalents.[40] This ensured, too, that central management received adequate financial data from the divisions to make accurate assessments of their operations and how they could be improved. The assessments compared divisions with one another, analysed the sources of a division's strengths and weaknesses, and appraised the work of the divisional managers.[41]

These financial assessments of divisional activity were described by Sloan as 'the last necessary key to decentralization with coordinated control'.[42] Headquarters 'could safely leave' divisional operations in the hands of divisional managers because 'we had the means to review and judge the effectiveness of operations'.[43] The divisional managers were therefore left with some opportunity to show their capabilities as leaders and administrators. But although Sloan believed in giving executives such opportunities, he also believed that 'even good corporate men' sometimes forgot that General Motors existed not to make cars but to make money.[44] So it is not surprising that he introduced a range of structural, financial, and even *operating* controls which restricted divisional managers and ensured that they would make money as well as cars for General Motors.

Sloan had initially imposed operating controls as a response to the divisions' disastrously unprofitable tendencies in 1920 to over-produce and to over-stock inventory.[45] Their tendency to acquire overly large inventories of raw and semi-finished materials was countered by enforcing limits on their purchasing of materials and basing the limits on what was required to meet production schedules for a specified period of time.[46] Controlling the divisions' production was a more complicated problem. The new production controls involved more than just approving and enforcing the divisions' production schedules, the controls also ensured that these scheduled levels of production were based on accurate forecasts of demand and so would not lead to either over-production or unmet demand. Indeed Sloan established a sophisticated system of forecasting consumer demand, monitoring retail sales, and adjusting production schedules to meet unpredicted changes in the market.[47]

His various central controls proved of greatest benefit when General Motors had to respond to the economic crisis of the Great Depression. He thanked the corporation's 'financial and operating controls' for the fact that it 'did not approach disaster as it had in the 1920–21 slump. We made an orderly step-by-step retreat'.[48] It was the only car-making firm to operate profitably throughout the Depression, and Sloan claimed that 'the corporation was not demoralized' even in the trough year of 1932, when it operated at less than 30 per cent capacity and made a profit of merely $165,000.[49]

He claimed, too, that 'perhaps the greatest payoff' from his strengthening of controls was that 'we had simply learned how to react quickly.'[50] But the rapid adaptation to economic change in the early 1930s was virtually forced upon the corporation by the controls introduced in the 1920s, as these controls were now automatically and quickly reducing production and inventory in an autopilot-like manner.

In fact this was less impressive than the corporation's rapid adaptation in the early 1920s. Sloan and his dual-leadership teammate du Pont had rapidly adapted to the crisis conditions of those years. In particular, they had taken only months to institute a fundamental rationalization of marketing strategy. What is more, the rapid adaptation produced remarkable results. By the end of the decade there had been a remarkable recovery in the corporation's fortunes. In 1921, it made a *loss* of nearly $39 million on sales of about $300 million and with a workforce of some 80,000; by 1929 it was making a profit of more than $248 million on sales of about $1.5 billion and with a workforce of some 233,000: 'It was the largest turnaround and the most thorough transformation in business history.'[51]

It is, too, a remarkable case of using rapid adaptation as a method of enhancing a corporation. However, the 1920s saw an even more remarkable case of emphasizing the other adaptive method, innovative adaptation. Sloan's emphasizing of this method had underpinned his use of rapid adaptation and had ensured the longer term success of General Motors, for his innovative adaptation included both a new organizational structure and the innovative strengthening of this structure by quantitative controls and assessments. These were two crucial aspects of his overall administrative rationalization of General Motors, which was in turn the basis of its remarkable recovery. So although Sloan used both the adaptive methods, rapid and innovative, his emphasizing of the more creative form of adaptation had been the key to his enhancing of General Motors.

Calculated Strategy

As was shown in the previous section, Sloan used quantitative calculation very effectively as part of his innovative adaptation and his overall administrative rationalization of General Motors. He also used the other calculative rational method, strategic calculation, and indeed Sloan emphasized this method, most notably in the area of marketing. He calculated marketing strategies that would transform all four of what Tedlow terms the 'basic elements of the marketing mix—product policy, pricing, marketing communications, and distribution.'[52] Sloan's strategically calculated marketing was a very different aspect of his administrative rationalization than his introduction of quantitatively calculated controls and assessments. However, he was again rectifying a lack of rationality and converting a weakness into one of the strengths of his corporation.

Sloan's memoirs describe how he and du Pont quickly began rectifying the major marketing weakness and irrationality—the firm's product policy. In April 1921 a special committee, headed by Sloan, was set up to rationalize a product policy that was allowing the seven car divisions to produce ten different car brands or models, such as Chevrolet and Cadillac, and was allowing each division to make its own 'price and production policies, which landed some cars in identical price positions'.[53] Similarly, the reason why the corporation produced only high-price and middle-price cars was not because of a deliberate policy but simply because 'no one had figured out how to compete with Ford' in the low-price range.[54]

Sloan's committee soon produced a set of recommendations that became the corporation's official policy in June 1921.[55] There were three key recommendations that in combination created a new pricing and product policy.[56] First, General Motors should produce a line of cars and models that catered for each price range or grade, from the lowest price up to the highest grade of quantity-produced car. Second, the price grades or steps should not leave wide gaps or be too numerous. Third, there should not be any cases of General Motors cars or models competing against each other within the same price range. These policies were the basis of a new strategy that distinguished General Motors from other car manufacturers and would be maintained by Sloan throughout his many years as CEO. As his biographer notes, this idea of 'producing different cars with different qualities along a coherently formulated price spectrum' was a crucial marketing breakthrough; there would be more breakthroughs 'but this rational price spectrum was the paradigmatic first from which the others would spring'.[57]

The immediate implications of the new strategy were a drastic rationalization of car lines and an attempt to compete against Ford in the low-price range.[58] Now there would be only six standard cars/models in the list and there would be only four rather than *eight* cars/models in the middle-price ranges. Furthermore, the list would now extend into the low-price range and would compete against Ford's Model T. The 'strategy we devised was to take a bite from the top of his position' by offering a higher quality product at near enough to the same price to attract buyers from the top of the low-price range.[59]

This strategic move against Ford's Model T was an application of the new strategic principle: 'quality competition against cars below a given price tag, and price competition against cars above that price tag'.[60] Applying such principles would require an almost military-like strategic calculation, as when Sloan was identifying weaknesses in the product range.

From the strategic standpoint at that time, however, the most dangerous gap in the list was that between the Chevrolet and the Olds ... both offensively and defensively; offensively because there was a market demand to be satisfied there, and defensively because competitive cars could come in there and come down on Chevrolet as we planned for Chevrolet to come down on Ford.[61]

His calculations also involved another new strategic principle—variety—which had converted an irrational profusion of cars and models into the strategic principle of offering customers a wide range of variations to suit their budget, needs, and personal tastes.

The variety principle was communicated to the public through the new marketing slogan: 'a car for every purse and purpose'. Eventually the variety principle was taken so far that it seemed the objective had become a car for every purse, purpose, and *person*.[62] By the 1950s the corporation was producing no fewer than eighty-five different models of its five basic car lines and soon after would boast that its range of optional accessories and variations enabled it theoretically to 'go through a whole year's production without making two cars alike'.[63] What is more, the variety principle was developed in a new direction by constantly *changing* the cars or models, and in fact by the 1930s this had become the annual model change described in a later section of the chapter.

Sloan's marketing strategy also included a new concern for the styling of the firm's product. In the mid-1920s he began to highlight the potential of improved styling as a way of improving sales:

> His basis for this judgement was strategic: eye appeal would transform the car market. Consumers would purchase cars not just for utilitarian transportation but for personal pleasure and self-expression. General Motors had the production facilities and organizational know-how to take best advantage of car styling.[64]

He increased that organizational know-how in 1927 by giving headquarters staff an art and colour section, which was later renamed the styling section.[65] There was some resistance in the divisions to having their products' design determined by headquarters staff, but soon 'the market made it clear that appearance was selling cars' and that General Motors was enjoying a competitive advantage over other car-makers.[66]

Similarly, Sloan was a strong supporter of advertising. Within a year of him becoming its president, General Motors had become the largest buyer of advertising space in magazines.[67] Its 'massive spending' on advertising quickly exploited the corporation's competitive advantage in the styling of cars.[68] Such style-based advertising became controversial but Sloan was not interested in the moral issues raised about this form of advertising; 'He was interested in results'.[69] On the other hand, he was sufficiently concerned about public opinion to create a pioneering public-relations department. 'Sloan personally created the General Motors PR department in the 1930s' and in fact the corporation was 'the first company to have a full-time in-house public relations staff'.[70]

Sloan's focus on marketing strategy is somewhat surprising for an engineer who was known for his operational and organizational expertise. But the circumstances he was facing in the 1920s required him not only to use but to emphasize this marketing form of strategic calculation. It was crucially important to rectify the firm's weakness and lack of rationality in the area of marketing strategy. And Sloan's marketing strategy would play a key role in General Motors' remarkably successful competition against the dominant Ford Motor Company. Yet Sloan's personal preferences may have been an equally important reason for his later emphasis on marketing. After all, when he came to write his memoirs, he devoted five chapters to marketing topics: product policy, styling, the annual model change, the automobile market, and distribution through the retail car dealers. He included, too, a perceptive explanation of why any firm needs a marketing strategy. In 1921, General Motors needed a marketing strategy because 'it was necessary to know what one was *trying* to do, apart from the question of what might be imposed on one by the consumer, the competition, and a combination of technological and economic conditions.'[71]

Institutionalized Deliberation

Sloan's use of the two deliberative methods continued his tendency to emphasize one of each pair of rational methods, which in this case was institutionalized deliberation. Similarly, this section will again focus on the one that he emphasized but in this case because his version of institutionalized deliberation also involved the other deliberative method: diverse deliberation. Sloan created a highly institutionalized, committee-based system of deliberation that valued rational discussion and was certainly not dominated by the leader; in his committees, policy proposals were 'sold' and assessed without reticence, and policy decisions were made in a collective, collegial manner.

Sloan's creation of this highly institutionalized system was another aspect of his restructuring and administrative rationalization. It was another case, too, of rectifying a Durant-era weakness and administrative irrationality. Sloan's memoirs complained that during Durant's time as leader of General Motors many important corporate decisions 'had to wait until he was free, and were often made impulsively'.[72] Chandler confirms that decision-making processes left much to be desired, with major decisions being made 'by Durant and the heads of the operating divisions in occasional conferences or in individual talks. Sometimes they were made by Durant with no consultation, at other times by the division manager after only the most casual reference or contact with Durant's office'.[73]

In marked contrast to the Durant era, the Sloan era was characterized by institutionalized policy deliberation and decision-making. Sloan's book describes this institutionalized deliberation as safeguarding General Motors 'against [Durant-like] ill-considered decisions' as well as producing policies that were likely to have 'better-than-average results' because they had been successfully defended 'against well-informed and sympathetic criticism' at the policy-deliberation stage.[74] It is true that Sloan's institutionalization went further than was needed to rectify the Durant-era irrationality; his emphasizing of this deliberative method was more a matter of personal preference than of dealing with the circumstances. But a historian of the corporation's early years has suggested that Sloan's most crucial change and legacy was 'the concept of decision making based on facts and open discussion, as opposed to the Durant crew's more mercurial and spontaneous decisionmaking process'.[75]

Furthermore, Sloan's system of institutionalized deliberation is a revealing case study of a committee-based version of this deliberative method. Institutionalized deliberation occurs in a context created by one or more kinds of institution: (1) informal rules, (2) laws and other formal rules, (3) formal positions or offices, such as president or CEO, (4) formal small-group institutions, such as committees or boards, and (5) formal large-group institutions, such as assemblies or annual general meetings. In Sloan's case, the institutional context was created by formal and informal rules, small-group institutions, and the deliberative aspect of Sloan's position as president/CEO.

The rules were a mixture of informal conventions and formal rules. For example, Sloan was voicing a formal rule when he stated that divisional management 'must "sell" central management on any substantial changes in operating policies'.[76] But he was stating only an *in*formal rule, a convention, when he went on to say that likewise central management 'should in most cases sell its proposals' to divisional management: there was a 'tradition of selling ideas, rather than simply giving orders'. Other informal rules specified that any new policies should be deliberated and decided in formal small-group institutions: the committees. According to Sloan, 'it is doctrine in General Motors that, while policy might originate anywhere, it must be appraised and approved by committees before being administered by individuals'.[77] However, he implied that this informal rule might be difficult or irksome for some executives, for he acknowledged that there was a 'strong temptation for the leading officers to make decisions themselves without the sometimes onerous process of discussion, which involves selling your ideas to others'.[78]

Sloan personally was happy to make decisions through discussion and he publicly highlighted the deliberative aspect of his position as president/CEO. He famously declared in a 1924 interview that 'I never give orders' and explained that it was better 'to appeal to the intelligence of a man than to the military[-like] authority invested in you'.[79] Of course his intelligent subordinates were well aware that Sloan would use the authority invested in him if there was no other way of administering the corporation's policies or if he was facing an emergency that required immediate action.[80] But nonetheless he was presenting a new, more deliberative view of the position of president/CEO of a corporation like General Motors. When he became its president in 1923, he realized that his new position required him to become a public figure, if only to contribute to General Motors' public image, and he wanted to be seen as a professional corporate manager who was more deliberative than authoritative.[81] He depicted himself as 'a facilitator of correct judgements, reached through consensus, achieved after exhaustive consultation with all the relevant members of his corporate enterprise', and as someone who 'was useful because he had the ability to listen to others, to collate their insights and to parcel them together for appraisal and validation by the organization itself'.[82] In this sense he appeared the business equivalent of a British-style prime minister leading a collegial government of cabinet ministers rather than an American-style president heading the executive and administration.[83]

Sloan's strong personal preference for collective deliberation and decision-making best explains his emphasizing of institutionalized deliberation. 'With the pertinent facts before them, Sloan believed, rational men would and could come to agreement on the best available course of action and therefore devote themselves as a team to its implementation'.[84] Such agreement and teamwork was typically achieved in a committee. Sloan was often referred to as 'a committee man' and he agreed that 'in a sense I most certainly am'.[85] His conception of being a committee man included listening to others' opinions or information rather than espousing his own views and in fact he earned the epithet 'Silent Sloan' through 'the relative paucity of his replies' in conversation or discussion.[86]

The corporation's committees were therefore the most important element in Sloan's system of institutionalized deliberation. Legally, the key deliberations were those of the corporation's board of directors, composed of senior executives and outside directors. Yet although Sloan acknowledged that the board was the 'supreme body', he did not describe it as a deliberative and policy-making organ but instead as performing the *auditing* functions of continuously reviewing and appraising 'what is going on throughout the enterprise'.[87] At its monthly meetings, the board was given: (1) audio-visual presentations about the corporation's financial, operating, and competitive position, and about forecasted future developments; (2) monthly reports from the board's finance committee and executive committee; (3) periodic reports from its other standing committees; (4) oral reports from executives (on the board) regarding various areas of the corporation's business; (5) regular reports from staff and group vice-presidents on developments in their areas of responsibility; and, last but not least, (6) the opportunity to ask questions and seek explanations.[88]

However, the key deliberative and policy-making discussions occurred in the board's two governing committees: the finance committee and executive committee. The latter was composed of senior executives who were on the board and 'active in management', but the finance committee was largely composed of outside directors and dealt with the key issues of capital expenditure, raising capital, acquisitions, and setting the annual dividend.[89] These two governing committees' policy recommendations were apparently accepted by the board of directors in similar fashion to a cabinet government or congressional legislature accepting the recommendations of its specialized committees.

Another, lower tier of policy deliberation by committees had been added as part of Sloan's restructuring. In 1922, he began creating a layer of inter-divisional committees which each dealt with a specialized topic or area, such as purchasing, sales, advertising, and technical/engineering matters.[90] They 'included representatives from the comparable functional departments in each of the five car divisions' and their role was both to coordinate divisional activities and to make policy recommendations not only to the divisions' managers but also to the board's executive committee.[91] The inter-divisional committees were therefore providing a new tier of policy deliberation, which could consider new policies and recommend them to the executive committee for consideration and perhaps recommendation to the board of directors. Furthermore, by adding this lower tier of policy deliberation, Sloan had increased the *diversity* of deliberation, as the members of these committees were specialized experts who were also representing their particular car division.

In the 1930s, however, the inter-divisional committees were replaced by the policy groups. They, too, were functionally specialized committees, such as those dealing with engineering or personnel, but they were composed solely of headquarters' executives: no divisional representatives were included in the policy groups.[92] The change in membership reflected Sloan's principle that policy is made by central management and administered by divisional management, which in practice meant excluding the divisional managers from power at central level.[93] So the demise of the inter-divisional committees seems to have been simply a logical extension of the centralization that Sloan had begun and largely completed in the 1920s.

But the replacement of inter-divisional committees by policy groups was also reducing the diversity of deliberation. The removal of divisional representatives from this tier of policy deliberations had removed the divisions' close-to-the-coalface viewpoint and their knowledge of local conditions at a divisional level. Sloan and his centralizing allies, however, were more concerned about a divisional representative's biases and partiality. They believed that policy-making 'should be dealt with from an impartial understanding of the operating aspect' and that 'it is difficult for the individual to divorce himself from the departmental viewpoint'.[94] Yet they seem to have had no concerns about *central-level* departmentalism affecting the new policy groups' deliberations; apparently it was just the divisional, local-level viewpoints that posed a threat to the firm's policy deliberation.

The lack of local-level diversity was not the only weakness of Sloan's definitive version of policy deliberation by committees. The system produced 'a degree of corporate inertia—the many committees through which any one idea must pass did not make for speedy changes. This price Sloan was willing to pay'.[95] There was another price to pay, however, which Sloan acknowledged when describing how his system prevented policy-making by hunches:

> The manager who would like to operate on a hunch will usually find it hard to sell his ideas to others on this basis. But, in general, whatever *sacrifice* might be entailed in ruling out a possibly brilliant hunch is compensated for by the better-than-average results which can be expected from a policy that can be strongly defended against well-informed and sympathetic criticism. In short, General Motors is not the appropriate organization for purely *intuitive* executives, but it provides a favorable environment for capable and *rational* men.[96]

But did his corporation provide a favourable environment for rational and *innovative* executives or was there instead a sacrifice of innovation as well as intuition? It has been claimed that Sloan institutionalized a new, rational corporate culture that also 'fostered creativity, innovation and risk-taking'.[97] Yet the fostering of creativity, innovation, and risk-taking does not seem characteristic of General Motors after the 1920s era of change.

For example, the General Motors of the 1950s seems no different from the typical conformist corporation depicted in Whyte's 1950s cultural study *The Organization Man*. Whyte declared that 'corporation man' was the most conspicuous example of the rise of a conformist social ethic—'an organization ethic'—that included 'a belief in the group as the source of creativity' and therefore discouraged an individual from being the first to espouse a new idea.[98] Similarly, a 1955 speech by a senior executive at Ford, Robert McNamara, warned that conformist pressures were discouraging innovation and fresh thinking in society and business corporations. In the latter, there was 'a certain inertia, a tendency to discourage fresh thought and innovation' and it took 'a degree of moral courage to withstand that pressure', particularly 'when you are in competition from half-a-dozen eager beavers who eagerly spout the party line'.[99]

Such conformist pressure has serious implications for the diversity of deliberation. Here is the diversity-reducing reticence that Machiavelli identified long ago and was discussed in Chapter 1. Sloan, too, warned about the 'spirit of venture' being 'lost in the inertia of the mind against change', but he believed that this occurs when success has brought self-satisfaction and has dulled the 'urge for competitive survival'.[100] If he was correct, it must be assumed that in the 1950s, Sloan's General Motors was even more likely than McNamara's Ford to experience a conformist lack of diversity and innovation. For ever since the 1920s, Sloan's firm had been more successful than Henry Ford's and, more generally, Sloanism had been more successful than Fordism.

Sloanism versus Fordism

The difference and rivalry between Sloanism and Fordism was recognized by Sloan himself in the opening pages of his book. He pointed to the competition between General Motors and the Ford Motor Company as an example of how firms can compete with one another in their long-term way of doing business and in their type of organization, such as Ford's extreme centralization versus General Motors' decentralization.[101] Here and later in the book he also contrasted General Motors' variety of cars and continual model changes with Ford's belief in producing one static utility model at a constantly lower price—the famous Model T car.[102] He acknowledged that Ford had played the leading role in the industry throughout the 1908–27 lifespan of the Model T, but then what Sloan described as a different 'philosophy' had taken over: in the words of his biographer, 'Sloanism had defeated Fordism'.[103]

The key difference between Sloanism and Fordism was the different approach of Sloan and Henry Ford to the business of producing cars or other manufactured commodities. While Sloan focused on rationalizing his firm's administration, Ford focused on rationalizing *production* through his mechanized assembly-line production system. Fordism's efficient mass production enabled the price of the product to be reduced and the market for the product to be increased. Annual sales of Ford's cheap Model T car would increase from only 20,000 in 1910 to nearly 600,000 in 1916, largely because of price reductions created by the introduction of the assembly-line technique and its technology of 'conveyers, chutes and slides', which reduced the time to assemble a chassis from 12.5 human-hours to 1.5.[104] Ford was increasing productivity through new machinery and organization rather than adopting Taylorism's training of individual workers to do their job in a more efficient way: 'why worry about how a man could do a job better if a machine could do it more efficiently than he could?'[105] However, Ford certainly wanted his machines to do their job in an ever more efficient way and he sought continual increases in productivity regardless of how much it cost to replace outmoded machines and systems.[106]

Unlike Sloan, Ford was not interested in administrative rationalization and ran his company in a peculiarly personalist way. Sloan termed it extreme centralization but Tedlow's profile of Ford describes it more accurately as *dictating* company policy.[107] Drucker labelled it 'one-man tyranny' and 'personal misrule' when he presented Ford as a case study of an owner's attempt to run a corporation without sharing the management responsibilities with professional managers—or with managers who were allowed to be professional.[108]

A recent biographer has explained this personal rule as simply Ford's desire 'to run everything by himself'.[109] This preference for hands-on personal control would affect even production technology and product engineering. He frequently interfered in the company's engineering projects, delayed the shift from forged to cast and stamped parts, and even showed a strong commitment to particular types of brakes and springs.[110]

The peculiarities of his personal rule had particularly negative effects on the company's policy deliberations and organizational structure. 'By the late 1910s, Ford found it difficult to deal with men who did not kowtow to him' and any manager 'who risked telling him the truth risked dismissal'.[111] This of course prevented proper deliberation about his company's policy, as even if he had genuinely sought his managers' opinion, they would have been too reticent to provide truthful advice. Furthermore, the company's organizational structure and processes were undermined by his attempts to encourage conflict among his managers. Ford 'early began pitting his lieutenants against one another, giving them overlapping authority to see which turned out to be tougher in defending what he thought was his own territory'.[112] Not surprisingly, his company lacked an organizational chart and this seems symbolic of the difference between him and Sloan, the author of the Organization Study, who had created an organizational structure that Tedlow deems 'far superior' to the level of organization enjoyed by Ford's company.[113]

Ford's personal peculiarities affected several other aspects of administrative rationality. His 'quirky, eccentric management style' included a contempt for accounting, which he viewed as parasitical, and therefore the accounting-like departments were eliminated in his 1919 economy drive.[114] Advertising, too, was not held in high regard by Ford. He spent nothing on advertising in the period from 1917 to 1923, and considered style-based advertising to be a 'trick' that was aimed at 'fooling people into buying what they did not need for reasons that could not stand up to moral scrutiny'.[115]

A similar personal prejudice restricted his company's product development. Ford had come to view the Model T 'not only as a mechanical force but as a moral one. It was exactly as much automobile as people needed, and no more'.[116] So he was reluctant to change the Model T, let alone to consider that it was becoming outmoded. There was some gradual product development, such as replacing wood with sheet steel and adding an electric starter, but the basic shape and engineering was preserved.[117]

These personal prejudices and policies became wholly inappropriate as the times and circumstances changed. By the mid-1920s, American consumers were enjoying unprecedented prosperity and the hallmarks of the Model T—cheapness, durability, and utility—were now less important than style, colour, performance, and technical innovations.[118] For example, General Motors was pioneering 'several costly innovations that Ford resisted but which customers were eager to pay for', such as independent front-wheel suspension, electric turn signals, electric windshield wipers, and fully automatic transmissions.[119] As Sloan noted, not only prosperity but also the used-car trade-in and the introduction of instalment financing had encouraged middle-income buyers to demand something more than just basic transportation in their new car.[120] They sought 'comfort, convenience, power, and style. This was the actual trend of American life and those who adapted to it prospered'.[121] Even the low end of the market had been transformed, as the growth of the used-car market meant that low-income buyers now had cheaper and more up-to-date alternatives than a new but outmoded Model T.[122]

Ford's problems also arose, however, from his competitors' success in developing a flexible version of mass production that suited their marketing strategies. For example, Sloan's 1920s product-diversity strategy became less costly when he decided to use many standardized parts in the corporation's different products and annually changing models:

> Sloan's innovative thinking ... seemed to resolve the conflict between the need for standardization to cut manufacturing costs and the model diversity required by the huge range of consumer demand. He achieved both goals by standardizing many mechanical items, such as pumps and generators, across the company's entire product range and by producing these over many years with dedicated production tools.[123]

His brilliant production engineer, William Knudsen, also introduced more flexible machine tools to produce the parts that would have to be changed to fit different cars and models.

> He rejected Ford's reliance on 'single-purpose' machine tools. Instead, he installed 'new heavy type standard machines' that permitted flexible mass production. Knudsen was creating a manufacturing process to regularize consumer-appealing changes—by the mid-1930s, annual model changes—in the Chevrolet's appearance and its mechanical components.[124]

Sloan believed that the idea of annual model changes had been implicitly accepted in the 1920s. It had been 'inherent in the policy of creating a bigger and better package each year' and, more generally, in the awareness that the industry had 'entered a new period' that would mean 'continuous, eternal change'.[125]

Not surprisingly, the 1920s were a watershed for Ford's company as well as for the car market and industry. At the beginning of the decade, the company had been the number-one seller, with more than half the market, but in 1927 General Motors took over the number-one position.[126] Ford had attempted to restore the Model T's competitive position by improving its styling and equipment, resuming large-scale advertising, speeding up production, cutting prices, and even reducing production.[127] When these various responses failed the test of the market, he was forced to make the large-scale product adaptation that he had been resisting: in 1927 he ended production of the Model T and replaced it with the newly developed Model A.

With the Model A, Ford seemed to have adapted successfully to the new era in car design and marketing. The new model had up-to-date styling, performance, equipment, interior, and variety—more than a dozen different body styles and a range of colour combinations—plus the significant price advantage created by Ford's still superior production efficiency.[128] The Model A 'offered good looks and impressive mechanical sophistication for almost the same price as its predecessor.'[129] By 1929, it had captured more than a third of the market but the impressive sales figures were partly due to catching up with unmet demand—there had been serious problems in changing production over to the new model—and Sloan argued that Henry Ford never fully adapted to the idea of annual model changes.[130]

What is more, the Great Depression was about to hit the car market. The 1930s Depression decade would reduce Ford's share of the market to less than 19 per cent, compared to General Motors' market share of over 47 per cent, which was nearly a reversal of the firms' market shares some twenty years earlier.[131] Ford responded in 1932 by replacing the Model A with a dramatically new and effective design: an eight-cylinder model known as the V-8. Again Ford had opted 'to reinvent his main product' rather than upgrading it, and once again this brought a false dawn, with Ford briefly returning to the number-two position in the market but being relegated to the number-three position in 1936, where it would remain until 1950.[132]

The revival of the firm's fortunes occurred only after Henry Ford retired in 1945 and his grandson, Henry Ford II, instituted a Sloanist rationalization of the company. He not only introduced modern marketing but also hired former General Motors executives to help restructure the company along Sloanist lines.[133] Ford even introduced the Sloan-pioneered quantitative controls and assessments, which were installed for him by a number-crunching newcomer to the industry—Robert McNamara. He rectified the various accounting deficiencies, introduced inventory controls, monitored retail sales to detect changes in demand, and instituted performance targets for divisional managers.[134] Such Sloanism now seemed to be the American and indeed global way of making cars and money.

3

Toyota

Ohno's *Toyota Production System*

The previous chapter showed how Ford and Sloan had created the modern car industry and indeed the modern system of production. Ford had pioneered the assembly-line techniques of mass production and Sloan had given the system sufficient flexibility to meet modern marketing needs for different product lines and frequent changes in product styling or features. By the late 1930s, however, the source of production innovation was no longer America but Japan, thanks to the founding of the Toyota Motor Company and the origins of the famous 'Toyota production system'.

Founding leader Kiichiro Toyoda envisioned a new way of manufacturing automobiles and called it 'just-in-time' production. But for various reasons, including the outbreak of war, he was unable to introduce this innovative production system. In fact it would not be introduced until some years after he left the Toyota Motor Company in 1950. By then the idea of just-in-time production had been further developed in practice by a second pioneering innovator, Taiichi Ohno, who was adding other innovative features to what would now be called 'the Toyota' production system. His introduction of the new system in the 1950s–60s significantly enhanced Toyota and helped develop the firm into a global automobile giant and an iconic corporation.

Yet Taiichi Ohno was never a CEO-level leader of the corporation. He was part of a dual-leadership team whose other member was the CEO-equivalent president of Toyota. It was the same version of dual leadership—an innovation-introducing team—that Sloan and du Pont created in the early 1920s at General Motors, as was mentioned in Chapter 2. Unlike Sloan, however, Ohno would remain part of a leadership team and would not go on to become the corporation's president and sole leader. When his 1954–61 teammate retired, Ohno formed a new innovation-introducing team with the next president of Toyota. In fact Ohno was still only an executive vice-president when he retired from the corporation in 1978.

Although Ohno never became a CEO-level leader, his production innovations made a notable contribution to the corporation's rapid development in the 1960s. There was a five-fold increase in annual production during the decade, production surpassed a million vehicles a year, and Toyota became the third largest producer in the world, behind only Ford and the still dominant General Motors.[1] Furthermore, Ohno's production innovations enhanced the global competitiveness of Toyota and indeed the whole Japanese car industry. By the time Ohno retired in 1978 Toyota was

Rational Leadership. Paul Brooker and Margaret Hayward, Oxford University Press. © Paul Brooker & Margaret Hayward (2023). DOI: 10.1093/oso/9780198894643.003.0003

exporting half a million cars a year to the United States and soon, only two years later, Japanese vehicle exports reached an annual worldwide total of some six million.[2]

In addition, Ohno had made a significant contribution to global manufacturing. By the time he retired, the 'Toyota production system' was becoming internationally famous and would eventually be imitated in many countries, industries, and organizations. In the 1990s his system received a major boost internationally when it was depicted as the pioneering version of 'lean' production, which uses 'less of everything', in the 1990 Womack, Jones, and Roos bestseller *The Machine that Changed the World: The Story of Lean Production*.[3] In the twenty-first century 'the Toyota Production System has become increasingly a part of how hospitals, governments, universities, banks, mining operations, and retailers are choosing to improve performance and develop their people.'[4]

In 1978, Ohno published a partly autobiographical work about his production system and how it had been developed.[5] An English-language edition of the book appeared several years later under the title *Toyota Production System*. It provides a leader's-eye view of how Ohno used three of the six appropriate corporation-developing rational methods. In addition to using strategic and quantitative calculation, Ohno emphasized innovative adaptation and largely as a matter of personal preference—he was personally determined to develop and introduce an innovative production system. Through a series of innovative adaptations he succeeded in developing this system, the renowned Toyota production system, and introducing it throughout the firm's factories and even throughout its supplier network—the many small firms supplying car parts to Toyota's assembly lines. This series of innovations were largely opportunistic adaptations that took full advantage of the opportunities offered by Japan's distinctive market and factory conditions.

But Ohno's book does not describe him using the other adaptive method, rapid adaptation, nor the two deliberative methods, diverse and institutionalized deliberation. His selection of methods was appropriate, though, for the circumstances he was facing. He was a production expert seeking to develop and introduce a new production system; he was not a business executive seeking to introduce something like Sloan's administrative rationalization of General Motors. The Toyota presidents who formed innovation-introducing leadership teams with Ohno would be much more likely to use the two deliberative methods, and these chief executives may well have used a few other appropriate rational methods. Certainly Ohno and his leadership teammates were using rational methods capably enough to inspire their employee-followers with rational confidence.

The first section of the chapter will outline not only Ohno's production innovations but also the innovation-introducing leadership teams that he formed with two successive Toyota presidents, Ishida and then Nakagawa. They have faded into the background compared to their now world-famous teammate and in fact his main rival for fame is the visionary Kiichiro Toyoda, who was the 1930s pioneer of just-in-time production. Ohno was exposed to the just-in-time idea in 1943 when he joined the Toyota Motor Company as a young production manager.[6] His book describes how impressed he was by Kiichiro Toyoda's idea that in 'automobile manufacturing, the best way to work would be to have all the parts for assembly at the side of the line *just in time* for their use' in the assembly-line process:

> The words 'just-in-time' pronounced by Toyoda Kiichiro were a revelation ... The idea of needed parts arriving at each process on the production line when and in the quantity needed was wonderful. Although it seemed to contain an element of fantasy, something made us think it would be difficult but not impossible to accomplish.[7]

Kiichiro Toyoda had been unable to accomplish just-in-time production but his pioneering was so important that it will be discussed in the first section of the chapter, as a prelude to its account of how Ohno developed and introduced just-in-time production in the 1950s.

The second section goes a step further by showing how he was innovatively adapting to Japan's local conditions. It argues that Ohno was exploiting the opportunities offered by Japan's distinctive factory environment as well as adapting to the requirements of the Japanese car-market environment. Such opportunities enabled him to add continuous-flow production and other features to the innovative production system that he was developing and introducing. The third section explores other features of this just-in-time production system: the *kanban* information system, the problems of production levelling, and how parts suppliers were included in the system. Furthermore, the second half of the section shows how Ohno used the calculative rational methods, quantitative and strategic calculation, when developing this 'lean' form of production.

The final section, on Toyotaism versus Fordism, is in a sense a continuation of the final section of Chapter 2. In this case, however, it will be highlighting a rivalry between two different *production* systems. Ohno downplayed this rivalry in his overly generous assessment of Henry Ford but perhaps it was the most appropriate way for him to view his greatest predecessor—as a production innovator and a maker of modern manufacturing.

Pioneering Production Innovations

Toyota has long been an innovative firm and not only in the area of production. For example, its leaders' most obvious innovation has been the Toyoda family's long-term leadership of a corporation that the family does not own. The family founded the Toyota Motor Company in 1937 as a *public* company and soon owned only a minor shareholding but despite this lack of ownership control, it has provided the firm with a series of six presidents. In the eighty years since the firm was founded there have been only two periods when its president was not a member of the Toyoda family: 1950–67 and 1995–2006.[8] So it is not surprising that Togo and Wartman's 1993 history of the corporation was subtitled *The Story of the Toyota Motor Corporation and the Family that Created It*.[9]

The firm's innovative tendencies were evident from its inception in 1937. Japan was then decades behind the West in developing a modern economy but this new automobile firm was founded in a way that would have appeared 'advanced' in any economy of that era. For several years earlier the Toyoda Automatic Loom Works had experimentally diversified into automobiles and was now spinning off this new product department as an independent public company largely in order to fund its move towards mass production of these automobiles.[10] There was even a public competition to design the new company's car logo, which led to the word 'Toyoda' being changed to 'Toyota' when the new company was officially named the Toyota Motor Company.[11] Another innovative or at least unusual feature was that the firm's founding 'leader' was actually a dual-leadership team formed by two brothers: company president, Risaburo Toyoda, and executive vice-president, Kiichiro Toyoda. They were the sons of the parent company's deceased founder, who 'had recognized their potential as a team. Kiichiro was bursting with ideas and spunk, while Risaburo possessed the wisdom to keep him on track'.[12] In fact the leadership team of business-oriented Risaburo and visionary engineer Kiichiro almost became an innovation-introducing version of dual leadership. But they were unable to introduce the innovative way of manufacturing automobiles that Kiichiro had envisioned and labelled 'just-in-time' production.

Some forty years later Taiichi Ohno described this vision of just-in-time production as the original idea behind Toyota's famous production system. According to his book *Toyota Production System*, 'Toyoda Kiichiro, father of Japanese car manufacturing, originally conceived this [just-in-time] idea which his successors developed into a production system'.[13] Furthermore, the book depicts Toyoda's idea as having been an innovative adaptation to local, Japanese conditions.

> In 1933, Toyoda Kiichiro announced the goal to develop domestically produced cars for the general public: 'We shall learn production techniques from the American method of mass production. But we will not copy it as is. We shall use our own research and creativity to develop a production method that suits our own country's situation'. I believe this was the origin of Toyoda Kiichiro's idea of just-in-time.[14]

The idea of 'just in time' may well have originated as an adaptation of mass-production techniques to suit Japanese conditions. But the more immediate, short-term conditions prevailing in the 1930s were not conducive to introducing visionary production ideas. Fujimoto's history of Toyota production systems considers Kiichiro's 'vision' of just-in-time production to have been 'unrealistic at that time'.[15] Japan's economy and industrial sector was not sufficiently advanced, and the country was facing political and national-security problems that would soon lead to disastrous wars. According to Togo and Wartman, 'Kiichiro knew his master plan would take decades to enact, if it could be done, but in the meantime he carried forward the first parts of it' by keeping inventory warehouses as small as possible and ensuring that no more than one day's supply of components would 'sit idle beside the assembly line'.[16]

However, Kiichiro's opportunity to innovate was being continually reduced by Japan's wartime situation. A recent biography *Courage and Change* shows how he was hampered in the late 1930s by two factors—the supply problem and government pressure—that were intensified by Japan's growing war with China.[17] The government pressured Toyota to prioritize production of trucks and buses over cars and to bring the new Koromo plant into production as soon as possible, which meant that 'the move from the experimental production stage to the mass production stage took place more rapidly than Kiichiro had planned for' and obviously left no time for experimenting with a new production system.[18] The expedited move to mass production was also a cause of the quality-control problems that plagued the new plant, but another cause was the increasing supply problem, in terms of both quantity and quality, which in 1939 led Toyota to begin building its own steel mill.[19] The wartime situation became even worse after the 1941 outbreak of war with America and the British empire. The spiralling supply problem led to a manufacturing environment in which 'the availability of materials was determining the flow of production' and so any move towards just-in-time production 'ceased to exist'.[20]

In 1941, Kiichiro Toyoda had succeeded his brother as president of Toyota and therefore presided over the firm's wartime decline into makeshift manufacturing— and making trucks rather than cars.[21] But in these demoralizing circumstances he completed an innovative adaptation that was a landmark in the firm's development and would greatly assist the firm's later innovators. As Togo and Wartman point out, the wartime supply problems offered Toyota an opportunity to develop the supply network that later became a distinctive, crucial aspect of the firm's manufacturing process. 'Toyota was able to develop a more complete and competent network of suppliers. The Japanese automobile parts industry was disorganized and unsophisticated before the war, and Kiichiro had thus put only limited effort into developing suppliers'.[22] Kiichiro's biographers depict the new, wartime effort as a two-way process that included a major organizational effort by the parts suppliers. In 1939, Toyota's suppliers formed a Cooperation Association that developed into the 1943 Cooperation-with-Toyota Association, which was 'still going strong' in the 2000s.[23] Creating these cooperative relationships also required a major contribution from Toyota, including an innovative commitment that

> this company will consider those businesses it has chosen to be its suppliers as *branch factories* of this company, it will make it a general principle not to change to other businesses for no good reason, and it will make all possible efforts to *raise* the achievements of these factories.[24]

Establishing this network of suppliers was a remarkable example of innovative adaptation. In addition, it was a classic example of identifying and exploiting an opportunity even in disastrous circumstances. But it has been overshadowed by the great 'might have been' of what might have happened if Toyoda had been given the opportunity to develop his idea of just-in-time production. Instead he had seen his car firm sidetracked by 1937–45 wartime conditions into becoming a producer of trucks, and finding it difficult to produce even these kinds of automobile.

Kiichiro Toyoda's post-1945 leadership of the firm was plagued by new, post-war problems, and he was unable to convert the firm into a producer of primarily cars rather than trucks.[25] In 1950 the firm faced a recession-induced financial crisis that resulted in lay-offs, a lengthy labour-union strike and the resignation of the firm's president.[26] Toyoda had taken personal responsibility for the labour-relations disaster, which psychologically devastated him, and his premature retirement ended two years later with his death at the early age of 57. In Ohno's words, this 'was indeed a great loss. I believe just-in-time was Toyoda Kiichiro's dying wish.'[27]

The firm's new president, Taizo Ishida, was not a member of the Toyoda family and was not familiar with automobile manufacturing but had been an effective president of Toyoda Automatic Loom Works.[28] He would prove to be a very effective president of the Toyota Motor Company, which would develop into a corporation, a *large* public company, during his 1950–61 tenure. During the Ishida era, however, the most notable achievement was Taiichi Ohno's introduction of a production system that attained Kiichiro Toyoda's vision of just-in-time production. Unlike Toyoda, Ohno was in a favourable situation to make an innovative adaptation to Japan's local conditions. And Ohno's innovative production system significantly enhanced Toyota, perhaps to the same degree as Sloan's 1920s innovative adaptation had enhanced General Motors. In the Toyota case, however, the enhancing innovation was related to production, not administration, and was introduced in a much more piecemeal way. General Motors had been restructured by implementing Sloan's comprehensive and detailed plan, the Organization Study, which he had drawn up years earlier. But Toyota's new production system was based on an idea or vision, and was introduced largely by experimentation, trial and error and 'making things up as we go along'.

In other words, Toyota was *developing* as well as introducing a new system. As Fujimoto points out, the 'diffusion' of the new system was therefore 'rather slow, starting as Ohno's informal experiment as opposed to a company-wide movement. Initial experiments were made only where Ohno directly supervised'.[29] Furthermore, this reliance on Taiichi Ohno was typical of a firm that is relying on a brilliant individual or team to develop an innovative new system. 'While Ohno did not reorganize Toyota's system of production by himself, the extension of his techniques corresponded to his movements, between 1948 and the mid-1960s, from one shop or factory to another and up the ladder into top management'.[30] Ohno developed continuous-flow techniques when he was a machine-shop manager in 1948–52, as is discussed later in the chapter. In 1953, he became the plant's manager of manufacturing and began developing techniques inspired by Kiichiro's Toyoda's idea of just-in-time production. But Togo and Wartman point out that 'transforming the vehicle assembly line was far more difficult than transforming a machine shop. Engines and transmissions and other components poured into the assembly building from various locations, and orchestrating everything to arrive just in time was a monumental task'.[31] Ohno's book briefly refers to the long process of trial and error through which he accomplished this task.

Step by step, I solved the problems related to the system of withdrawal by the later process. There was no manual and we could find out what would happen only by trying. Tension increased daily as we tried and corrected and then tried and corrected again. Repeating this, I expanded the process of pickup by the later process within the company.[32]

His expanding of the process 'within the company' was moving these just-in-time innovations from the development stage to the introduction stage. The continuous-flow innovations he had developed as a machine-shop manager had already reached the introduction stage, and by 1955 had been extended, by other managers, to other manufacturing workshops in the plant.[33] But the clearest indication of the shift from development to introduction came at the end of the 1950s. Ohno was appointed general manager of the newly constructed Motomachi plant and now was able to supervise a plant-wide introduction of the new production system.[34] A few years later he returned to the main plant as its general manager, where he completed the company-wide introduction of the system and began extending it to the firm's suppliers.[35]

In the midst of his long pioneering journey, in 1954, the 42-year-old Ohno was made a director of the company.[36] Giving him a seat on the board was both recognizing what he had already achieved and encouraging him to continue with his difficult task, which was at the critical juncture of introducing innovations in the workshops and developing an innovative just-in-time process on the assembly line. Ohno's book mentions how he admires the attitude taken by 'top management' during this period, when there was the inevitable 'psychological resistance' to the innovative just-in-time approach, and, he admits, when 'the ideas that I boldly put into practice ... might have looked high-handed'.[37] The attitude of top management was made clear to all concerned by not only keeping Ohno on the job but also making him a director of the company. In addition to giving him symbolic support, it was forming an innovation-introducing leadership team that comprised this new member of the board and the president of Toyota, Taizo Ishida.

Ishida's role was particularly important because Ohno was such a junior member of the board and held such a low-ranking managerial position. He was not the equivalent of a chief operating officer (COO), as Sloan had been when he and du Pont had formed an innovation-introducing leadership team in the early 1920s. In fact Kiichiro's cousin, Eiji, was the nearest equivalent of a COO and some might say that Eiji Toyoda formed a triple-leadership team with Ishida and Ohno.[38] However, it is simpler to view the team as a dual leadership, with Ishida playing the role of 'sponsoring' the innovating member of the team. As well as sponsoring Ohno, president Ishida had the role of providing Toyota with CEO-level leadership. In doing so, he used rational methods that were also used by Ohno, such as the quantitative and strategic calculation described in the third section of this chapter. But Ishida used these methods in a financial and business context rather than a production and factory-floor context.[39]

More importantly, Ishida used rational methods that apparently were *not* used by Ohno, namely the two deliberative methods. Togo and Wartman provide several examples of Ishida engaging in diverse or institutionalized deliberation, such as allowing a colleague to win a policy argument with him, or 'buying' policy proposals that were not such a 'hard sell' as might have been expected.[40] A key example of the latter was his acceptance of Eiji Toyoda's proposal for massive investment in new equipment, specifically 'a five-year plan for modernization of production equipment (1951–5). The goal was to replace old equipment with new, to introduce conveyors and automation, and to expand production'.[41] Considering Ishida's reputation for prudent expenditure, Toyoda should have had a hard time selling this plan to him. But 'Ishida, who would not let a pencil be wasted, told Eiji he would obtain whatever money he needed for machinery'.[42]

Another key example of Ishida accepting policy proposals occurred near the end of his tenure, when he was in his 70s. This time it enabled Eiji Toyoda and Kiichiro's son Shoichiro Toyoda to introduce an ambitious Total Quality Control (TQC) programme like the TQC programmes already being introduced by other Japanese firms.[43] During the 1950s, Toyota had applied statistical quality-control methods to its production of military trucks; now these methods and other quality-control measures would be applied on a company-wide basis.[44] From June 1961 onwards all worksites sought to reduce 'defects in the processing of materials, claims from customers, and the need for touching-up after painting, welding and other processes'.[45]

Ishida retired from the post of president later in 1961 and became chairman of the corporation. During his time as president he had developed Toyota from a crisis-ridden company into a successful automobile corporation. In particular, Ishida and Ohno (and Eiji Toyoda) had achieved a near ten-fold increase in productivity as well as boosting production from fewer than 15,000 vehicles in 1951 to more than 200,000 in 1961.[46]

The new president of Toyota was Fukio Nakagawa. Like Ishida, he was neither a member of the Toyoda family nor an 'automobile man'. He had been in banking before joining Toyota and had been the executive vice-president for business affairs, not production, in the years before he was appointed president.[47] However, he formed a dual-leadership team with Toyota's production guru, Taiichi Ohno, and sponsored his next innovation-introducing task: extending the new production system to include Toyota's parts suppliers. Ohno's continuing contribution was given some formal recognition in 1964, when he was promoted to a more senior position on the board as now a 'managing' director of the company.[48]

Little has been written about Nakagawa's contribution to the corporation's development.[49] Yet in addition to sponsoring Ohno's supplier innovations, Nakagawa presided over a growth period in which Toyota became a car producer that also made trucks rather than vice versa. During the 1950s more than 70 per cent of its annual production had still been trucks rather than cars, but now its new Corona and Corolla car models would lead a surge in car sales and production.[50] For example, in 1965 it expanded its exports to the US by including Corona cars as well as the usual Land Cruiser jeeps, and five years later Toyota was second only to Volkswa-gen for export sales in the US market.[51] In 1966, the corporation at last achieved Kiichiro Toyoda's goal of being primarily a car-maker: it produced 316,000 passen-ger cars versus 271,000 trucks and buses.[52] Furthermore, in the following year the advent of Toyota's popular Corolla car helped stimulate a huge increase in Japanese car-buying, which increased by a third to a total of well over a million passenger cars.[53] Toyota's annual production of passenger cars therefore continued to surge and in 1968 reached 659,000, enabling the corporation to pass the milestone of annually producing more than a million motor vehicles: cars, trucks, and buses.[54]

Nakagawa had not lived to see this milestone, however, as he had died in 1967 and been succeeded by Eiji Toyoda as the new president of Toyota.[55] Although Naka-gawa's achievements seem to have been largely overlooked, this may be because they were very much a team effort by the corporation's management. For example, the innovation-introducing team that he had formed with Ohno had made good progress in its difficult task of extending Toyota's new production system to include its network of parts suppliers.

Furthermore, it was the previous innovation-introducing team that had provided the foundation for the achievements of the 1960s. Ishida and Ohno's innova-tive production system had given Toyota crucial productivity and therefore pric-ing/profitability advantages over its competitors. Cusumano's classic *The Japanese Automobile Industry* pointed out twenty years later that in 1965 'each Toyota worker was producing 70 percent more vehicles per year than employees at General Motors, Ford, Chrysler or Nissan [the other major Japanese producer]'.[56] In addition, Toy-ota's innovative production system was already showing that it could be 'scaled up' to ever higher levels of production without losing its productivity advantages. It had already been applied to levels of production that were far higher than those of the era when it was being developed: in 1954, for example, vehicle produc-tion was less than 23,000 and car production less than 5,000.[57] By the mid-1960s it was delivering productivity advantages at levels of production that were twenty times higher. In fact the system would deliver dramatically *greater* productivity advantages as levels of production rose still further in the 1970s, when Toyota was annually producing millions of cars. Cusumano noted that as Toyota's production volumes rose five-fold 'between 1965 and the early 1980s, productivity tripled'.[58] The renowned flexibility of Toyota's production system includes its ability to deliver pro-ductivity advantages whether it is producing thousands or *millions* of things each year.

However, its flexibility was best seen when producing large numbers of things in small batches of different varieties. This is why Ohno subtitled his book *Beyond Large-Scale Production*. He was not suggesting that the Toyota system was appropri-ate for a small level or volume of production; he was pointing to the system's capacity for efficiently producing small-scale batches of different products. Togo and Wart-man describe Toyota's production system as having 'the ability to "mass produce" cars by making numerous small lots of different vehicles'—an 'easily adaptable' pro-duction process.[59] And the next section shows that this adaptable, flexible system was developed through an 'adaptable' rational method: innovative adaptation, even if the method was by no means 'easily' applied in these circumstances.

Adapting to Japanese Conditions

The Toyota production system was developed through Ohno's innovative adaptations and in fact this may be the most extraordinary case of innovative adaptation in the history of manufacturing or any other kind of business. For example, the system developed into a complex combination that included several distinctive, innovative systems or processes 'in their own right', notably the just-in-time process, the continuous-flow process, and the *kanban* information system. Furthermore, Ohno's new production system took decades to develop and to introduce throughout the manufacturing process. So a key factor was Ohno's persistence and his willingness to keep emphasizing innovation as a matter of personal preference, not as something that was forced upon him by the circumstances. 'It took 15 years or more to perfect the process techniques that made O[h]no and Toyota famous. Many engineers might have given up long before'.[60]

The Toyota case is extraordinary, too, because it is a landmark example of adapting to local conditions—in this case, the conditions of Japan's market and factory environment. Kiichiro Toyoda's pioneering production adaptation to Japanese conditions had been virtually foredoomed by the unfavourable economic and political circumstances of the late 1930s. Ohno was in a more favourable situation and made the most of it, even if it took him more than fifteen years to do so!

Ohno's adapting to local conditions is mentioned by Fujimoto in his evolutionary analysis of Toyota's production systems. He notes that Ohno had 'integrated elements of the Ford system in a domestic environment quite different from that of the United States'.[61] In fact Japan's domestic *market* environment was so different that when Toyota and other producers integrated Fordist elements, these had to be adapted to fit the local market environment. Cusumano pointed out that Japanese automobile producers 'had to modify American mass production techniques' as an evolutionary adaptation to a small market with very low volume but an increasing number of variations.

> [T]o a large degree, the changes Toyota made were 'evolutionary' adaptations to the circumstances surrounding the company and the domestic market ... Volume requirements were extremely low in Japan in the 1950s, yet the domestic market called for an increasing number of different car and truck models.[62]

The producers' modification of American Fordist techniques therefore seems to have been a forced adaptive response to Japan's market environment. Toyota, however, adapted more innovatively than other Japanese producers, thanks to Ohno's ingenuity and perseverance.

In his book, Ohno points to the connection between market requirements and the development of Toyota's innovative production system. The 'unsurpassed flexibility' of this production system—which he describes as the source of its strength—had arisen because the system had been 'conceived to produce small quantities of many types for the Japanese [market] environment'.[63] This flexibility may have been a forced adaptive response but it was such an innovative adaptation that it became a source of strength and in fact later gave Toyota a competitive advantage in the American and global car markets. As Fujimoto notes, when the new system 'was implemented in the 1940s and '50s, managers did not regard this emergent system as a way to outperform their Western rivals, but rather as an imperative for surviving in their small and fragmented market'.[64] However, the 'flexibility factors' in the new system 'became a source of its competitive advantage in subsequent years, when the market size and Toyota's productivity both grew rapidly and major automobile markets worldwide began to emphasize product variety'.[65]

Yet Ohno's adaptive response to market requirements was only a part of his innovative adaptation to local conditions. The other, less obvious part was his adaptive response to the domestic *factory* environment. This was an opportunistic rather than forced adaptive response and therefore, as Chapter 1 noted, was exploiting the environment's opportunities rather than meeting its requirements. In Ohno's case he was innovatively exploiting opportunities offered by features—distinctive features—of Japan's factory environment: (1) the work group and its teamwork, (2) the availability (potentially) of multiskilled workers, (3) the cooperative, company-oriented labour unions, and (4) the firm's enterprise-family solidarity.

Ohno was by no means the only Japanese manager who innovatively exploited these opportunities. For example, some managers in other firms created the famous quality-control 'circles' as an innovative adaptation to the work-group feature of Japan's factory environment. As Cole pointed out, a distinctive feature of Japanese factories was that tasks were assigned:

> to the group, not its individual members, and that the responsibility for performing these tasks is shared by the entire group … Japanese foremen are not only first-line supervisors who regulate job assignments, they are also the senior members of the work group. Members of the work group share a common career ultimately, and this serves to produce a highly integrated and solidary work group.[66]

In the 1950s–60s this feature offered managers the opportunity to develop an innovative method of quality control. Initially, Japanese industry had imported American quality-control concepts and techniques, as in the well-known case of Deming's lectures from 1950 onwards teaching Japanese firms such basic statistical quality-control methods as sampling inspection and control charts.[67] However, some Japanese managers began to develop a new method by requiring foremen and their work groups to learn and implement quality control and indeed to form quality-control study groups.[68] In the early 1960s, the study groups developed into workshop quality-control 'circles' that would be widely adopted in Japanese industry and would be imitated in America and other parts of the world.[69]

Toyota's production system, too, exploited the opportunities offered by the work-group feature of Japan's factory environment. For example, Ohno's book has a section headed 'Teamwork is Everything' and stressing the need for harmony and teamwork in a work group, as 'at work things do not necessarily run smoothly just because areas of responsibility have been assigned. Teamwork is essential'.[70] Similarly, Western exponents of his 'lean' production system included its use of '*teams* of multiskilled workers' as part of their definition of the system.[71]

Another distinctive feature of the factory environment was the fact that these were 'teams of *multiskilled* workers' who epitomized what Western experts term 'job diffuseness'. This is a workplace situation in which job descriptions 'tend to be extremely brief and general', workers are 'less conscious of job changes', and a worker may be carrying out 'a whole range of jobs'.[72] By the 1970s, job diffuseness had been identified by Western experts as one of the distinctive and advantageous features of the Japanese factory environment.[73]

Multiskilled workers and job diffuseness were also a key element of the continuous-flow process that Ohno had developed in the 1940s–50s as part of his new production system. A continuous production flow already existed on Toyota's final-assembly line and Ohno's innovation was to develop a similarly continuous flow in other areas, such as machine-shop production, and eventually create a continuous flow throughout the whole car-manufacturing process. His book's example of continuous flow describes it as 'putting a flow into the manufacturing process. In the past, lathes were located in the lathe area, and milling machines in the milling area. Now, we place a lathe, a milling machine, and a drilling machine in the actual sequence of the manufacturing processing' and so for workers 'this means shifting from being *singleskilled* to becoming *multi-skilled*'.[74] The workers must be multiskilled because one of the productivity advantages of this continuous flow is that it 'directly reduces the number of workers' by reducing specialization: 'instead of having one worker per machine, one worker oversees many machines or, more accurately, one worker operates many processes'.[75]

But clearly in this case, his first production innovation, Ohno was exploiting the opportunity to *shift* from single-skilled to multiskilled workers. In other words, a distinctive feature of Japan's factory environment in these pioneering years was that managers could *potentially* use multiskilled rather than single-skilled workers. Exploiting the opportunity offered by this feature was not easy, though, as Ohno discovered when he tried to introduce the continuous-flow innovation. Furthermore, he succeeded largely because he exploited the opportunities offered by another distinctive feature, namely Japan's company-based labour unions, which was certainly the most significant feature of Japan's factory environment.

Ohno developed his continuous-flow innovation in the late 1940s as an extension of his duties as a machine-shop manager at Toyota's main plant. When he moved from experimental stage to implementation stage, however, he ran into resistance from the machine shop's skilled craftsmen, who had always operated a single lathe or other specialized machine. 'Our craftsmen did not like the new arrangement requiring them to function as multiskilled operators' overseeing 'many machines in different processes'.[76] His book goes on to describe the situation in positive terms or as a case of all's well that ends well. Apparently, 'the transition from the single- to the multi-skilled operator went relatively smoothly although there was initial resistance from the crafts-men'.[77] But Cusumano presents a rather different picture of events, based partly on his interview with an elderly Ohno:

> The [continuous-flow] reforms in the machine shop were one of the main issues in the 1950 strike. 'Had I faced the Japan National Railways union or an American union', Ohno mused, 'I might have been murdered'. As it turned out, he was able to control the Toyota union, partly because management threatened to fire dissident workers, which it did in 1950, and partly because he was personally close to the union leaders.[78]

Indeed Ohno 'considered his success in controlling the union to have been the most important advantage Toyota gained over its domestic and foreign competitors' and he claimed that its main domestic competitor, Nissan, had been hindered in its 'attempt to match Toyota in productivity' because the union had 'challenged management policies'.[79]

Ohno's book does not make such sweeping claims but it acknowledges that the labour-union factor was crucial in this case and in the overall development of Toyota's production system. His machine shop's transition to continuous flow had gone relatively smoothly 'because we lacked function-oriented unions like those in Europe and the United States'; in the United States 'this system could not be implemented easily' because 'there is a union for each job function with many unions in each company'.[80]

In contrast, Japan's labour unions were company oriented, not function oriented or even industry oriented. In fact, each labour union was based on the company which employed its members, such as Toyota or Nissan, and included the company's white-collar employees as well as its blue-collar workers.[81] For example, Ohno had served as a full-time union official in 1947 even though he was a production engineer with management experience and had just been promoted to the position of machine-shop manager.[82] Probably no other well-known business leader has ever served as an elected union official! Probably, too, this was why in later years he was personally close to Toyota's union leaders and was so successful in winning the union's cooperation with his production innovations. When Cusumano noted how Japanese unions cooperated with management to increase productivity, he pointed to Toyota as 'the best example of what managers were able to achieve' with such a cooperative workforce.[83]

Ohno clearly took full advantage of the opportunities offered by this distinctive feature of Japan's factory environment. But in his book he was careful to say that the cooperativeness of Japanese unions did not mean that they were 'weaker than their American and European counterparts. Much of the difference lies in history and culture.'[84] Certainly, there were historical and cultural differences as well as the basic difference in orientation and membership. In the 1920s–30s, Japan's emerging labour-union movement had been channelled into an 'enterprise union' mould 'where a union represented the workers of only a single factory or company'.[85] In addition, the unions had been mostly confined to small and medium-sized firms, as the large firms had established new cultural and institutional barriers to unionization.

These large companies had pioneered a version of employer paternalism that incorporated the familial aspects of Japan's traditional culture. The new version was similar to Japan's prevailing paternalist ideal of industrial relations, with its reciprocal obligations of manager-employer's affectionate care and worker-employee's deference and self-sacrifice. Now, however, these reciprocal obligations were based upon the principle that managers and workers were members of the same business-enterprise 'family'. The new ideal of *jigyo ¯ ikka* (enterprise family) and 'familial harmony in the firm' was also supported by material benefits, such as free or low-cost nurseries, health clinics, and recreational facilities.[86] The key benefits, however, were the permanent employment (no lay-offs or redundancies) for regular male workers and the *nenkō* (length of service) system for determining individuals' wages and promotions within the enterprise family.[87] These benefits created a compelling institutional context for the enterprise-family culture, which was much more credible and appealing in a context of job and promotion security.

This whole cultural and institutional package was revived by large firms after the Second World War as part of their strategy for dealing with the labour movement. The post-war rebirth of the union movement was so successful that even large firms had to accept unionization, but this was channelled into the pre-war mould of company-based unions, thanks largely to the revival of the pre-war package of cultural themes and institutional supports.[88]

The permanent-employment and *nenkō* systems became a standard feature of large firms, who also provided their workers with a variety of other benefits, such as leisure activities and housing assistance.[89] Similarly, there was a revival of familial paternalism and the notion of enterprise-family solidarity. Some of its trappings, such as company songs and badges, were soon recognized internationally as characteristic of Japanese industry.[90] Like other large firms, Toyota had adopted this institutional-cultural package and indeed Cusumano argued that Ohno's impact confirmed that individuals could 'make an enormous contribution even in a large Japanese firm that prided itself on maintaining a "family" atmosphere'.[91]

Ohno made such an enormous contribution, however, because he exploited the opportunities offered by this familial atmosphere—and any other thing that produced a cooperative workforce. That was the pre-condition for developing and introducing an innovative new production system. The pioneering Toyota founder Kiichiro Toyoda had been well aware that changing 'the automobile production process' would require a factory atmosphere 'of mutual trust and cooperation. Without this milieu, the just-in-time production process would never be realized'.[92] When

Ohno went on to realize Kiichiro Toyoda's vision of just-in-time production, it was by exploiting the opportunities offered by this atmosphere of cooperation—which was perhaps the most important feature of the local, Japanese conditions.

Just-in-Time, 'Lean' Production

To realize this vision of just-in-time production Ohno also had to develop it into a more comprehensive system of production. He had already created a continuous flow in machine-shop production, but much more would be required in the years ahead. He had to create a new information system and to extend processes 'backward' to include the firm's network of parts suppliers.

More fundamentally, he had to adopt a new perspective on production. His book sums up just-in-time production as having 'the *right* parts needed in assembly reach the assembly line at [just] the *time* they are needed and only in the *amount* needed' and therefore, in conjunction with continuous-flow production, enabling a firm to 'approach zero inventory'.[93] But it also involved a new perspective on production. It meant looking at the production flow 'in *reverse*: a later process goes to an earlier process to pick up only the right part in the quantity needed at the exact time needed'.[94] In fact Ohno's working model of this production flow was the American-style supermarket. 'The later process (customer) goes to the earlier process (supermarket) to acquire the required parts (commodities) at the time and in the quantity needed. The earlier process immediately produces the quantity just taken (restocking the shelves)'.[95]

However, Ohno's most obvious innovation was the new information system that he created for just-in-time production. Indeed, his creation became so famous that Toyota's whole production system was often described by outsiders as 'the *kanban* system'.[96] The *kanban* (signboard) was a means of communicating information about what parts and production were required to fulfil just-in-time requirements. Each *kanban* was simply a rectangular piece of paper in a vinyl envelope that carried information about the pickup, transfer, and production of parts: it specified what part was required, how many were required, and when they would be required.[97] The relatively simple individual *kanban* were part of a complex system in which, for example, the number of required *kanban* was calculated by using an algebraic formula $D(Tw + Tp)(1 + N)$: the D was demand (units per period), Tw the waiting time for *kanban*, Tp process time, and N a policy variable.[98] The *kanban* system 'pulled' parts and work in progress through the assembly line, while comparable computer-controlled systems tended to 'push' them through.[99] Even when improved computer systems became available in the 1970s, Ohno preferred to stick with the *kanban* not only because the high-tech alternative was expensive but also because 'the real world doesn't always go according to plan' and the *kanban* could more readily adjust to unplanned events.[100]

The *kanban* system had been introduced in a similar way to the introduction of just-in-time production processes. In the mid-1950s Ohno had introduced *kanban* on particular production lines, in 1959 at the new Motomachi plant, and in 1962 at a company-wide level.[101] The next step would be to extend the *kanban* system to Toyota's parts suppliers as part of the wider move to include them within the firm's new production system.

Including its parts suppliers within the new production system was essential because they contributed so much to the firm's manufacturing process. As with any other modern automobile producer, the final-assembly lines that assembled components into automobiles were only a small part of the total manufacturing process. 'The bulk of the process involves engineering and fabricating more than 10,000 discrete parts and assembling these into perhaps 100 major components'—such as engines and suspensions—which are in effect the raw material of the final-assembly lines.[102] Like any other modern automobile producer, Toyota could either produce these components in-house, through divisions or subsidiaries of the company, or have them manufactured by independent supplier firms that specialize in particular parts. The usual approach to parts procurement has been a mixture of in-house and out-sourced manufacturing. For example, Sloan's General Motors made about 70 per cent of its parts in-house and procured the other 30 per cent from independent supplier firms.[103]

Instead of a mixture of in-house and out-sourced, Toyota preferred outsourcing to suppliers who were a mixture of independent firm and Toyota subsidiary. As noted earlier, this approach was adopted at the end of the 1930s as an innovative adaptation to wartime conditions. It was developed further in the 1950s–60s, though, when Toyota integrated its supplier firms into a two-tiered cooperative alliance that avoided both (1) the bureaucratic tendencies of in-house manufacturing; and (2) the market problems of out-sourcing to independent suppliers.[104] The first tier of suppliers developed and made major component parts for Toyota automobiles. In addition, it created the second tier of suppliers, which were a multitude of small firms that supplied the first tier with parts for their Toyota components. These second-tier suppliers were organized into cooperative, information-sharing associations. The first-tier supplier firms, however, were integrated with one another and with Toyota through cross-holding of shares as well as through cooperation in technical matters and other areas. Toyota would even lend money or personnel to first-tier suppliers who were installing new machinery or experiencing workload surges.

The strong ties between Toyota and its suppliers reduced the risks involved in being so dependent on their contribution to the production process. They did much of the value-adding work and employed much of the workforce required to manufacture a Toyota automobile. Even when Toyota became the world's third-largest car producer, its assembly plants were responsible for less than a third of the value-adding work and were employing a workforce of fewer than 40,000.[105]

However, this dependence upon parts-supplying firms meant of course that they had to be included within Ohno's just-in-time production process. They would have to deliver their parts 'just in time' so that Toyota's assembly plants experienced neither a build-up of unused parts nor a shortage of the parts needed to keep production flowing. Although Ohno realized that the suppliers would play a big role in the new production system, he waited until after it had been fully developed and introduced company-wide before he began including suppliers within the system's just-in-time processes and *kanban* information system.[106]

> Experiments were always carried out at a plant within the company that did not deal with parts ordered from the outside. The idea was to exhaust the new system's problems within the company first. In 1963, we started handling the delivery of the parts ordered from outside. It took nearly 20 years.[107]

One of the reasons why it took so long was simply the suppliers' problems with the new system. For example, Ohno acknowledges that 'the cooperating firms' initially viewed the *kanban* system as 'troublesome'.[108] But there were also structural reasons, such as the sheer number of supplier firms. By the end of the twenty-year introduction period there were some 200 firms in the first tier of suppliers and some 5,000 in the second tier.[109] Furthermore, throughout this period Toyota was expanding production at a rapid rate and therefore asking its suppliers to boost production at the same time as they were introducing just in time and *kanban*. Indeed when Ohno began extending the system to suppliers in the mid-1960s, Toyota was beginning a surge in car production that would quadruple annual production from less than 75,000 in 1962 to more than 316,000 in 1966.[110]

In the midst of this surge in production, suppliers were depending on Toyota to reduce *fluctuations* in its assembly lines' flow of production. As Ohno's book explains, if a final-assembly stage uses parts 'unevenly', its fluctuating requests for parts will force the parts-producing stages to carry 'extra manpower and equipment' to accommodate these fluctuations, and the 'greater the fluctuation in quantity picked up [by final assembly], the more excess capacity is required by the earlier [parts-producing] process'.[111] His book acknowledges, too, that fluctuations in Toyota's production flow affected 'the cooperating firms *outside* Toyota *using kanban*' because their parts production was tied to and synchronized with the corporation's assembly lines.[112] As these suppliers were providing Toyota with the earliest stages in its production system, they fully deserved the effort Ohno made to reduce fluctuations in the assembly plants' flow of production.

Ohno's goal was 'production levelling' that would ideally result in 'zero fluctuation' at the final-assembly stage of production.[113] He levelled out production by such rational means as minimizing the size of each batch lot. For example, an assembly line producing three different models of a car design might assemble only one car per model batch lot: 'one sedan, one hardtop, then a sedan, then a wagon, and so on. This way, the lot size and fluctuation in production can be minimized'.[114] However, such small batch lots required a drastic reduction in the time required to change over and set up the machinery required for each particular batch lot. These reductions were accomplished by replacing large stamping presses with smaller, easier-to-change machines, 'using rollers or carts to move dies or other fixtures', adopting simple die-change techniques and of course mobilizing the workforce.[115] Ohno's book describes how workers were trained to reduce changeover and set-up times and how their 'desire to achieve the new system intensified' so much that set-up times were reduced to just fifteen minutes in the 1950s and to merely three minutes in the 1960s.[116]

Their achievements had beneficial effects in other areas, too, such as reducing the need to invest in new equipment and plant. Cusumano noted that their rapid changes 'made it economical to produce different models on one assembly line and saved Toyota from having to invest in additional facilities'.[117] This is just one of many examples of the cost saving that led Womack and others to say that 'lean' production was pioneered by Toyota's production system. He and other exponents of 'leanness' described Toyota's system as lean production because 'it *uses less of everything* compared with mass production', notably its use of 'half the human effort in the factory' and its ability to keep 'far less than half the needed inventory on site'.[118]

When Toyota's system is viewed from a lean-production perspective, it is clear that Ohno used other rational methods in addition to emphasizing innovative adaptation. He used the calculative methods, quantitative and strategic calculation, and even employed a cost-reducing *grand* strategy. Indeed his production innovations can be seen as at least partly an extension of this grand strategy and particularly its aim of eliminating all forms of waste in the production process.

Ohno's cost-reducing strategy focused on production costs and aimed to reduce them by eliminating waste in production processes. According to his book, he was committed to the 'absolute' elimination of waste, which he defined as eliminating anything that only increases cost without adding value, such as 'excess people, inventory, and equipment'.[119] His more complete list of forms of waste included: over-production, time on hand (waiting), inventory (stock on hand), waste in transportation, waste in processing, waste in movement, and, last but not least, making defective products.[120] Cusumano confirms that Ohno 'and his assistants, beginning in 1948, subjected every process, machine, and worker to rigorous analyses to eliminate "waste"—which they defined as anything that did not contribute to "value added"'.[121]

As for *how to* eliminate this waste, Ohno's many production innovations obviously helped eliminate excess inventory and 'excess people'. For instance, the previous section showed how his machine-shop experiment with continuous flow had replaced single-skilled machinists with a smaller number of multiskilled operators. Ohno had continued to take a calculated approach to labour efficiency, as when his book argues that the term 'using fewer workers' is more accurate than 'labour saving' because saving the labour of 0.9 of a worker will still leave the labour cost of paying wages to a worker to contribute the remaining 0.1.[122]

Clearly Ohno used quantitative as well as strategic calculation to enhance Toyota. Whether reducing labour costs, levelling production, or operating the *kanban* system, he was constantly using quantitative calculation. For example, his book contains a humorous anecdote about calculating how many extra workers would be needed to double production of engines for the Corolla car.[123]

As for rapid adaptation, his book does not describe him using this rational method but it advocates adaptive responses that are so rapid that they are analogous to reflexes. They are fine-tuning adaptive responses that are virtually instantaneous and do not involve the firm's leader or managers: firms 'should have reflexes that can respond instantly and smoothly to small changes' and indeed the larger the business, 'the better reflexes it needs'.[124] This seems similar to the autopilot-like controls that Sloan instilled in General Motors and that were discussed in Chapter 2. But those controls were based on quantitative information, not on human judgement. Ohno describes reflex-like adaptive responses as 'making judgements autonomously' and he advocates that they be decentralized to the lowest possible level.[125]

Toyotaism versus Fordism

Unlike the Chapter 2 section on Sloanism versus Fordism, this section's contrast of Toyotaism and Fordism is focused on production—on the assembly line and the factory floor. It is a contrast between the greatest *technical* innovation and the greatest innovative *adaptation to local conditions*, specifically to Japanese conditions. As discussed earlier, Toyotaism arose through a series of innovative adaptations to the requirements and opportunities presented by Japanese market and factory conditions. Ohno's book refers to a 'uniquely Japanese production system' and to Toyotaism originating in the 1930s in the thinking of Kiichiro Toyoda.[126] But Toyotaism as a large-scale form of car production did not emerge until the 1950s–60s and has always been an alternative to Fordism, not its opposite or antithesis. 'It is a myth that the Toyota system is a unique antithesis of the Ford system' asserts Fujimoto and he argues instead that Toyota's leaders 'adopted various elements of the Ford system selectively and in unbundled forms and hybridized them with their indigenous system and original ideas'.[127]

This may explain why Ohno's book has such a positive attitude towards Henry Ford and protectively disassociates him from the failings of 'the Ford system' of production. For example, Ford's system apparently was 'never intended to cause workers to work harder and harder, to feel driven by their machines and alienated from their work'.[128] But of course whatever Ford may have intended, he certainly did not abandon or modify his assembly-line system when he discovered how much his workers hated their jobs. His response was instead to offer increased incentives that would reduce the assembly line's high labour turnover—he offered workers in 1914 the unprecedented wage of $5 a day.[129]

It is true that Ford was ahead of his time in his employment policies, even if for typically Fordist reasons. A recent biographer notes that Ford not only sought a 'clean, light and airy' workplace but also had 'highly enlightened employment policies concerning the handicapped, blacks, ethnic groups, women, and even ex-criminals'.[130] For example, the range of opportunities offered to African-American workers seems a generation ahead of its time. By 1917 Ford had become 'the industry's leading employer of African Americans, many of them on the highly paid assembly lines, and some in supervising positions with the authority—nearly unique in that place and time—to fire white workers'.[131] However, Ford's employment policies were motivated by a rational concern for profit-making productivity. He would characterize them as 'just good business' because through these policies 'he got good, productive, and motivated workers'.[132]

So it is not surprising that Ford did not abandon or modify his productive assembly-line system and its tedious work of 'endless repetition of one single task'.[133] More than fifty years after he created it, Ford's assembly line was still being seen as a symbol of the modern world's combination of efficiency and tedium. According to Beynon, Ford had created 'one of the most powerful images of the twentieth century. An image that combined "efficiency" with "tedium": the twin pillars of modern life'.[134]

In contrast, Toyota's assembly line was both more efficient and *less tedious* than Ford's creation. In particular, Toyota workers were multiskilled generalists, not specialists confined to a single narrow task, and they were members of small work groups that operated as socially interacting teams. Even Toyota's use of small batch lots, with its rapid changeovers and set-ups, reduced the tedium of working on the assembly line. Cusumano pointed out that as smaller batch lots 'lessened the monotony of assembly work', they also 'improved quality control'.[135] Reciprocally, quality-control roles introduced in the 1960s lessened the monotony by giving workers an additional, less repetitive task and responsibility. In addition to the quality-control circles, there was the rule that any worker had the right and obligation to stop the assembly line if a quality problem emerged. Line-stopping quality control was described by Cole as a policy partly designed 'to encourage workers to believe they drove the conveyor belt, as opposed to being driven by it'.[136] But Ohno described line-stopping in purely quality-control terms, as allowing a quality problem to be investigated at the assembly-line stage, forcing everyone to be aware of the problem and ensuring that countermeasures were taken to prevent the problem recurring.[137]

Similarly, his book's contrast between the large Fordist and small Toyota batch lots does not refer to workers' experiences and instead focuses on the market and economic implications. The Japanese market's demands for many types of cars in small quantities is contrasted with the American market's demand for a few types in large quantities.[138] And Ohno even makes some claim for the superiority of the Toyota system: it 'is better suited to periods of low growth' or, in other words, is better suited than Fordism to the low-growth economies of the 1970s.[139] Yet he then claims that if Henry Ford 'were still alive, he would be headed in the same direction as Toyota', because 'I believe Ford was a born rationalist'.[140] Presumably Ohno believed that Ford, like any rational business leader, would be adapting to the 1970s low-growth economic environment.

Again, however, Ohno was too generous in his assessment of Henry Ford's motives and actions. For the Ford Motor Company responded to the negative and low growth of the Great Depression by simply reducing the labour costs of its existing system of production. As late as 1938, the company was employing only 11,000 of its workforce of nearly 90,000 and was enforcing a notorious speed-up: production quotas were being ratcheted upwards and workers were being closely monitored for 'even the slightest infraction of work rules'.[141]

Furthermore, Ford's lack of adaptability had been a key factor in his 1920s defeat by Sloan's General Motors. Ohno's book acknowledges that Sloanism represented a new era in the American car industry. He refers to *My Years with General Motors*, cites its analysis of the market changes that occurred in the 1920s, and notes that Sloan exploited these changes in the marketplace by offering an increasing number of different models.[142] Yet Ohno has little to say about the more flexible production methods that enabled General Motors to offer a diverse range of five car lines and eighty-five models and to establish the annual model change as another new feature of the American automobile market. In his view the Fordist production system 'was not modified to any great extent' by Sloanism and 'became deeply rooted' in the American automobile industry.[143]

So when Toyota began exporting cars to America, it was entering a market that had been based on Fordism for more than a generation. What is more, Toyotaism had not yet defeated Fordist remnants in its own domestic car market. According to Cusumano, 'not until after the 1973 oil shock did Nissan and other firms in the Japanese automobile industry attempt to match Toyota in lowering inventories' and as late as 1980 'Honda and Isuzu had yet to impose effective controls on inventory and production'.[144] Toyota was therefore still the standard-bearer of just-in-time production when Japanese car producers began to make inroads in the American market in the 1970s.

However, this export aspect of Toyotaism versus Fordism was not discussed in Ohno's 1978 book. This is probably because the expansion of Japanese exports had not involved direct, head-to-head competition between the two systems. Although Japan-to-US vehicle exports grew from some 500,000 to over two million in the 1970s, Fujimoto notes that there was still

a fairly clear division of market territories between U.S. makers, who were producing and selling large American cars, and Japanese makers, who were exporting small cars. The small-car segment grew typically as a second car for American households and partly as a growing preference by young baby boomers for small economical cars.[145]

The watershed came at the end of the 1970s and was largely due to the international oil crisis. The problems with petrol supplies and prices led to more US consumers buying smaller, more economical cars, which boosted sales by Toyota and other Japanese car exporters.[146] More importantly, the crisis led to US car producers focusing on small and medium-sized cars and therefore beginning direct, head-to-head competition with Japanese imports.

'Many of the new American models had to compete directly with the Japanese small cars' and Fujimoto also points out that 'the Japanese advantages in productivity was first recognized at this time by some American researchers and practitioners'.[147] These productivity advantages would later be seen as not simply 'Japanese' but as specifically Toyotaist advantages developed and introduced by Taiichi Ohno. By the end of the 1980s, Womack and his co-authors were writing their book on Toyota's 'lean' production, which would be described in the book's subtitling as a 'secret weapon in the global auto wars'.

In 1983, Toyotaism finally established a production beachhead in Fordist America. Toyota entered a joint-venture arrangement with General Motors to build Toyota cars at the latter's recently closed plant in Fremont, California.[148] As Togo and Wartman relate, Toyota successfully reorganized its American auto workers into Toyotaist teams:

> Instead of having rigid job classifications, workers would be organized into five- to ten-man teams. Each team member would be trained in every job the team performed and would rotate among them. In addition to installing parts, they would perform their own maintenance, quality inspections, and machine 149 set ups.[149]

Ohno's book had predicted that the Toyota system would be applied successfully in America and would have a competitive advantage over 'the American system' of mass production and quantity sales, which 'generates unnecessary losses in pursuit of quantity and speed'.[150] However, Toyota would not have a complete, parts-to-final-assembly system in place until the 1990s and so there was plenty of time for American competitors to imitate Toyotaism's advantages.[151] In fact by 1989, the Ford Motor Company had imitated them so successfully that American exponents of lean production considered Ford's plants to be 'now practically as lean' as the average Japanese assembly plant in America.[152]

This might be viewed as the ultimate victory of Toyotaism over Fordism, which Ohno lived to see before his death in 1990. Through innovative adaptation to Japanese conditions he had both enhanced the Toyota Motor Corporation and created a Toyotaism whose global influence upon the car industry and many other industries has been comparable to the influence of Fordism and Sloanism. Since then no new 'ism' has been as influential as these three landmark breakthroughs.

4
McDonald's

Kroc's *Grinding It Out*

Ray Kroc's autobiographical *Grinding It Out: The Making of McDonald's* was published in 1977, the year that he became the semi-retired senior, founding chairman of the McDonald's corporation. Unlike Sloan and Ohno, Kroc had *established*, not merely enhanced, a corporation that would become nationally and globally iconic. He had founded the firm more than twenty years earlier and had developed it into the largest and most famous fast-food chain in America. McDonald's was so well known that a year before Kroc's death in 1984 a sociologist used the term McDonaldization to characterize 'the rationalization process' that was 'sweeping through society'.[1] What is more, Kroc had instituted a global expansion that would make McDonald's a symbol of globalization. For example, in the 1990s a political scientist applied the label McWorld to the cultural effect of globalized commerce and consumer products.[2] McDonald's was clearly becoming a globally as well as nationally iconic corporation.

But Kroc's personal fame had declined and would not be restored until the 2010s. The vintage year of the Kroc revival was 2016. Cinematically, there was the film *The Founder*, with Michael Keaton starring as Ray Kroc. Biographically, there was the publication of Napoli's portrait of Ray and his remarkably philanthropic widow, Joan: *Ray & Joan: The Man Who Made the McDonald's Fortune and the Woman Who Gave It All Away*.[3] Autobiographically, there was a third, reissued edition of Kroc's *Grinding It Out*. His book, like Sloan's and Ohno's autobiographical writings, is still in print more than thirty years after it was written.[4]

Although Kroc's book is more personally autobiographical than Sloan's or Ohno's, it provides a compelling leader's-eye view of how he established a now globally iconic corporation. Like Sloan, he used all six of the set of appropriate corporation-developing rational methods. And again like Sloan, he emphasized innovative adaptation, strategic (marketing) calculation, and a deliberative method, which in this case was diverse rather than institutionalized deliberation. Kroc emphasized diverse deliberation as a matter of personal preference but his use or emphasizing of the other five methods was due to the circumstances he faced in developing his start-up venture into a business corporation.

He was also facing difficult personal circumstances. Something other than rationality was required for a small-business seller of milk-shake machines to start a fast-food venture late in his business career and not in good health. When the McDonald's venture began in 1954:

Rational Leadership. Paul Brooker and Margaret Hayward, Oxford University Press. © Paul Brooker & Margaret Hayward (2023). DOI: 10.1093/oso/9780198894643.003.0004

> I was a battle-scarred veteran of the business wars, but I was still eager to go into action. I was 52 years old. I had diabetes and incipient arthritis. I had lost my gall bladder and part of my thyroid gland in earlier operations. But I was convinced that the best was ahead of me.[5]

His almost irrational confidence would prove to be justified when his new venture developed into a firm that led and modernized the fast-food industry.

For instance, McDonald's would pioneer the mass production of fast-food items and particularly hamburgers. Watson labelled this a Fordist method of food production, with hamburgers 'produced in assembly-line fashion', and Kroc himself described it in a Fordist or indeed Ohno-like manner: the smoking griddle 'was the vital passage in our assembly line and the product had to flow through it smoothly or the whole plant would falter'.[6] As Watson noted, McDonald's went on to pioneer the automation of fast-food production, as when it installed computers that automatically adjusted the cooking time and temperatures.[7]

Kroc's success was largely due, however, to his *administrative* pioneering and in that sense he is a fast-food version of Sloan rather than Ford or Ohno. The franchising system developed by Kroc was a particularly important administrative innovation. Anderson noted in the posthumous second edition of *Grinding It Out* that Kroc's greatest contribution was 'creating the McDonald's franchising system', which 'brought entrepreneurs into a structure that both forced them to conform to high standards of quality and service and freed them to operate as independent business people'.[8]

However, his franchising system was 'selling' a fast-food operation that was *not* a Kroc innovation. As his book acknowledges, the McDonald brothers had developed this innovative operation several years before Kroc began to franchise it. He notes how Mac (Maurice) and Dick (Richard) McDonald had pioneered a new kind of drive-in fast-food operation, which sold only hamburgers, french fries, and beverages, and, more importantly, prepared them 'on an assembly line basis'.[9] Kroc acquired this innovation through his 1954 licensing agreement with the McDonald brothers, which also included their McDonald's brand name, their golden-arches marketing symbol and their marketing strategy of offering a low-price, 15-cent hamburger.[10] The brothers licensed Kroc to franchise this whole 'package' in return for them receiving a share of the service-fee royalties paid to Kroc's firm by his franchisees. But although he had acquired a brilliant fast-food operation, Kroc still faced the problem of selling the operation to potential franchisees and simply earning enough money to keep his new firm afloat.

His innovative franchising system would be the key to his success and enabled him to develop this start-up venture into a business corporation. The first section of the chapter will show how Kroc created his franchising system by emphasizing innovative adaptation and combining it with rapid adaptation. The second section of the chapter will describe how he emphasized strategic calculation in his marketing and how he used quantitative calculation, especially in relation to the revenue-earning expertise of his 'numbers man Harry Sonneborn'. The third section will describe

Kroc's use of often informally institutionalized deliberation and will highlight his distinctive, personally preferred emphasis on diverse deliberation.

The final section of the chapter will explore the international joint-venture system that he pioneered in the last stages of his leadership of McDonald's. This joint-venture system enabled his corporation's formula to be adapted to different cultures and markets around the globe. McDonald's had already expanded into more than twenty countries by the time his book appeared; by the end of the century McDonald's could be found in more than a hundred countries and was a truly global fast-food empire.

Kroc has been called an 'instinctive' leader but he is better described as a rational leader.[11] For he used the appropriate rational methods of developing a corporation and used them capably enough to inspire his employee-followers with rational confidence. It is true, however, that he also used a non-rational method—his visionary imagination. Kroc proudly acknowledged: 'I've been dreaming all my life'.[12] This was not a method that Sloan or Ohno included among their means of enhancing a corporation but it may be one of the appropriate methods of *establishing* an iconic corporation.

Adaptively Building a Fast-Food Empire

Although this section will focus on Kroc's emphasizing of innovative adaptation, he also used the other adaptive method—rapid adaptation. For example, his book mentions the rapid adaptive response to early indications in the 1960s that the market for drive-in eating was declining. His response was 'to experiment with larger buildings and inside seating' and then introduce a sit-down form of McDonald's restaurant.[13] But Kroc's most significant use of rapid adaptation was when he developed his franchising system through a *combination* of rapid and innovative adaptation.

Kroc developed his franchising system by emphasizing innovative adaptation, like Sloan and Ohno, but he *rapidly* as well as innovatively developed this system in the second half of the 1950s. The rapidity of Kroc's adaptation is in marked contrast to Ohno's fifteen years of dogged persistence or to the time that it took for Sloan to implement his preconceived Organization Study plan. Kroc rapidly developed his complex new franchising system through a series of innovative adaptations that were not preplanned and often followed on from one another or developed in unforeseen ways.

This rapid series of innovations was opportunistically adapting to the fast-food franchising environment of 1950s America. Kroc took full advantage of the opportunities that it offered but, unlike Ohno, he was not adapting to local conditions; he was adapting to a historical interlude in the 1950s that had great potential for developing fast-food franchises. Napoli points out that by then franchising was an idea whose time had come. She notes that the 'franchise model was deployed to distribute all manner of goods and services', from ice cream to motel accommodation, and it had advantages for consumers as well as potential franchisees:

Franchise ownership was a compelling conceit for the would-be businessman (and it was, more often than not, a man) industrious enough to want more than to punch a clock, but not necessarily confident enough or inventive enough (or wealthy enough) to launch a business entirely from scratch. Consumers were attracted to them for different reasons. As trains, then roads, broke down geographic barriers and allowed for seamless flow from one community to another, the public began to put stock in the cachet of a recognizable brand, trumping the unreliable unknown of a local merchant.[14]

But the franchising of fast-food products was still in its early stages. Kroc notes in his book that 'in the late fifties we didn't have the proliferation of franchise operations and the fierce competition for commercial fringe property that developed in the course of the next twenty years'.[15]

There was room for Kroc to innovate in many different ways and in fact during these years he developed a franchising system with as many innovative aspects as Ohno's production system.[16] For example, he decided not to become a parts supplier (of beef, buns, potatoes, and so forth) to his franchisees but instead would help them deal with suppliers and would help the *suppliers* raise their quality standards, lower their costs, and reduce the prices they charged his franchisees. Another early decision of Kroc's was that his firm would build the restaurants that it franchised: it would offer franchisees not just the rights to a McDonald's operation but also a ready-to-go McDonald's restaurant. Several years later Kroc went a step further by deciding to create a network of company-owned restaurants and indeed eventually almost a third of the McDonald's chain of restaurants were owned and operated by the company rather than franchisees. Kroc could afford to develop these company-owned restaurants because his franchising system also included innovative financial arrangements, the leasing arrangements discussed later in this chapter, which provided his firm with mortgage financing and with much-needed additional franchising revenue.

However, the most well-known aspects of Kroc's franchising system were associated with his early marketing strategy of pioneering a quality-oriented fast-food chain. As Napoli notes, this meant creating 'a consistent dining experience', which was based on what Kroc viewed as high-quality food:

> We wanted to build a restaurant system that would be known for food of *consistently high quality* and methods of preparation. Our aim, of course, was to ensure repeat business based on *the system's reputation* rather than on the quality of a single store or operator. This would require a continuing program of educating and assisting operators and a constant review of their performance.[17]

It would also require a degree of centralization that had never been seen before in any fast-food franchising system.

For example, the constant review of operators' performance would require the corporation to supervise the franchisees' operation of their restaurants. Love's

McDonald's: Behind the Arches notes that Kroc 'introduced a level of supervision that was unknown in the fast-food industry'.[18] In the late 1950s, McDonald's began to develop a corps of inspectors who would ensure that the restaurants were meeting the chain's quality standards for service and cleanliness as well as for food and methods of preparation. The inspectorate comprised dozens and eventually hundreds of field representatives, the field consultants, each of whom visited a group of twenty or more restaurants several times a year. Although initially intended to be advisors, the field consultants evolved into 'inspectors of system quality' who reviewed franchisees' performance in terms of their compliance with the corporation's operating standards.[19]

There was also a more positive form of reviewing performance—learning from the franchisees' experience. McDonald's sought to document 'all the knowledge that it was gaining from the collective operating experience of its franchisees. While other chains virtually ignored franchisees once their stores were opened, McDonald's studied everything they did, trying to learn what worked and what did not'.[20] This knowledge was then circulated throughout the chain and passed on to new franchisees through the corporation's impressive programme of educating franchisees and helping to train their staff.

Indeed Kroc's education and training programme was yet another innovative aspect of his franchising system. Love points out that no other fast-food chain 'had even thought of opening a full-time training center' until Kroc opened a Hamburger University (HU) that awarded a Bachelor of Hamburgerology (BH), with a minor in french fries.[21] Hamburger University started life in 1961 as merely a basement lecture room but even the inaugural class was awarded a BH degree, and by the 1970s Kroc could boast that HU had 'a handsome campus with classrooms equipped with the latest teaching aids' and offering an advanced operations course that every new franchisee attended.[22]

In addition, franchisees were provided with an impressive operations manual as a reference work and to help them train their restaurant staff. As early as 1958 there was a seventy-five-page manual and, not long afterwards, a much larger version seemed aimed at converting restaurant operations into a management science.[23] By the post-Kroc era, it had become a 600-page *Operations and Training Manual* that claimed to be the fruit of much experience and research and was updated by regular bulletins from the corporation to its franchisees.[24]

Kroc's franchising system therefore involved unprecedented regimentation as well as centralization. Leidner points out that it regimented much more than the restaurants' assembly-line production processes: it 'standardized procedures for bookkeeping, purchasing, dealing with workers and customers, and virtually every other aspect of the business'.[25] It had developed an overall operating system that included administration as well as the production system and was as standardized and uniform as any bureaucracy or assembly line.

But this centralized, uniform operating system was counterbalanced by a decentralization of product development and marketing.

The rules could provide only a framework, and that alone could not unleash the real potential of any franchising system—the human ingenuity of hundreds of independent businessmen. In essence, the secret to McDonald's success was that its nearly fanatical operations specialists, *led by Kroc himself*, recognized that the chain's operating system—easily the strongest in the fast-food business—was not enough.[26]

Kroc and his operations specialist recognized that an element of decentralization was needed to unleash this 'human ingenuity' and therefore his franchisees were given a limited but important sphere of independence: the equivalent of Sloan allowing his operating divisions to engage in product development and marketing.[27] Kroc's franchisees responded to this 'unleashing' decentralization by duly displaying an impressive amount of ingenuity. He acknowledged their ingenuity when he pointed out that many new items had been added to McDonald's product menu: 'the Filet-O-Fish, the Big Mac, Hot Apple Pie, and Egg McMuffin. The most interesting thing to me about these items is that each evolved from an idea of one of our operators'.[28] In contrast, the corporation's managers and specialists had been unable to come up with a similarly successful product innovation until the 1972 Quarter Pounder and 1980 Chicken McNuggets. 'All other major new products', Love points out, 'can be traced to the experimentation of local franchisees'.[29]

Marketing was another area in which Kroc's firm had benefited from its franchisees' ingenuity. The most dramatic example is the invention of the clown, Ronald McDonald. Love provides a detailed account of how franchisees in Washington had created this clown, named him Ronald McDonald, and featured him in television advertisements as early as 1963, two years before McDonald's included Ronald in its first venture into nationwide television advertising.[30] He was just one of many examples of how 'Kroc's franchisees put McDonald's on the road to becoming the food service industry's most creative marketer'.[31]

Kroc had therefore *de*centralized marketing and product development to nearly the same degree as he had centralized the franchisees' operating system. His book notes that the reason for this decentralization was simply that the corporation depended upon its franchisees for its vitality.[32] This was also a reason for ensuring that a large majority, about 70 per cent, of the McDonald's restaurants were operated by franchisees, not by the extensive network of company-owned restaurants.[33]

However, Kroc recognized that the creativity of his franchisees was almost a forced adaptive response to competition in their local market. Competition had been the 'catalyst' for each of the new items that his franchisees had added to the McDonald's product menu, as when a franchisee 'came up with Filet-O-Fish to help in his battle with the Big Boy chain in the Catholic parishes of Cincinnati'.[34] In other words, this competition had almost forced the franchisee to come up with an innovative adaptation: a fish product for his local market's predominantly Catholic consumers.

Franchisees' marketing innovations, too, were almost forced upon them by local competition, as in the notable case of Ronald MacDonald. His inventors had originally been sponsors of a local television show for children that featured a clown called Bozo. When the show was cancelled, the franchisees tried to preserve the competitive advantage Bozo had given them, but their substitutes for Bozo failed and finally they had to create a new clown, Ronald McDonald, to be the frontman for children-oriented advertising spots on local television—and the rest is history.[35]

Kroc's decentralization had therefore given McDonald's the capacity to make continual innovative adaptations. As Chapter 2 described, Sloan had long ago instilled an adaptive capacity in General Motors. But it was a capacity for automatic autopilot-like *rapid* adaptation and it had been instilled by imposing operating and financial controls. In contrast, Kroc instilled a capacity for *creative* adaptation by giving franchisees the freedom to innovate and by relying on local competition to motivate them to innovate.

Calculating Strategy and Revenues

Kroc's use of the two calculative methods is comparable to Sloan's, as both leaders used quantitative calculation and emphasized strategic calculation in the area of marketing. Another similarity is that both Kroc and Sloan used a 'numbers man', respectively Harry Sonneborn and Donaldson Brown. However, Sonneborn's quantitative calculation was focused on revenue and financial affairs rather than controls and assessments. For his firm's leader was establishing the McDonald's corporation rather than enhancing General Motors through an administrative rationalization. His use of the calculative methods was building for the future, not rectifying the past, especially in the case of his emphasis upon strategic (marketing) calculation.

Two of Kroc's early marketing strategies led to McDonald's pioneering both the quality fast-food market and the family fast-food market. His *quality*-oriented strategy was a central theme of his franchising system, as was noted earlier. His *family*-oriented strategy was less central but was strongly supported by McDonald's operating system. As Napoli notes, 'ensuring that the stores remained as family-friendly as possible continued to be a top priority' in the 1960s and it would continue to be a priority throughout Kroc's time as leader of the corporation.[36] In his book he points out that 'the family image we wanted to create' had been developed in the early years of McDonald's, when it was still a drive-in operation and when other drive-in 'restaurants' were typically, in Love's words, a 'high school hangout' frequented by teenagers.[37] Kroc's strategy therefore seems to have been calculated to distinguish McDonald's from other drive-in chains as well as to exploit the potential 'family' market. The implementation of the strategy required further calculation, such as forbidding McDonald's restaurants to install jukeboxes, cigarette dispensers, and vending machines because they might attract teenagers or detract from the family-oriented image.[38]

In the 1960s Kroc's family-oriented strategy was supported by an increasing amount of television advertising and children-centred marketing.[39] Yet, while this proved very successful, it was preventing or hindering the corporation from targeting other, non-family markets. Furthermore, his strategy was likely to be imitated and perhaps surpassed by one or more of his competitors: the increasing number of other fast-food chains.

So it was farsighted strategic calculation by Kroc to strengthen his marketing by reinvigorating the quality-oriented image—which would now highlight McDonald's remarkable operating standards. As Watson notes, 'clean toilets are universally appreciated' and so are high standards of customer service and food preparation.[40] What is more, no competitors would be able to equal, let alone surpass, the operating standards that McDonald's had instilled in its restaurants and had encapsulated in its slogan QSC&V (Quality, Service, Cleanliness, and Value). According to Love, as early as 1957 the field consultants' assessment of a restaurant's standards included the subject categories of service, quality, and cleanliness, which were abbreviated to SQC, and two years later Kroc 'put quality first in the grading system, and QSC—the universal symbol of performance in the fast-food trade—was born'.[41] Kroc added a Value component to the formula in the mid-1960s, although franchisees were free to choose how they priced products and were not graded on value.[42] The resulting QSC&V formula would later become a performance-based marketing slogan that highlighted his firm's unequalled operating standards.

Kroc viewed QSC&V as more than a marketing slogan and it seems to have been his equivalent of a corporate culture. By the 1960s Hamburger University was sending out a stream of trained franchisees and managers who, in Kroc's words, 'spread the gospel of Quality, Service, Cleanliness and Value'.[43] Leidner, too, refers to the formula in religious terms. She confirms that McDonald's wanted 'both managers and workers to dedicate themselves to the values summed up in its three-letter corporate credo, "QSC". Quality, service and cleanliness' was also the ultimate goal of 'the company's thousands of rules and specifications'.[44]

The corporation's advertising, however, tended to focus on individual components of the QSC&V formula. For example, the cleanliness component was the focus of a television advertisement which featured a song-and-dance routine about staff giving the restaurant its daily clean.[45] In the early years, before the firm could afford such advertising, the quality component of QSC&V was almost inadvertently advertised by media coverage of Hamburger University trainees marching to class in their white uniforms or being presented with their Bachelor of Hamburger diplomas.[46] In later years the firm was paying for an impressive advertising campaign that could make the most of the formula's components and was driving the internal campaign to maintain high operating standards. By the post-Kroc era, 'the strict quality-control standards applied to every aspect of running a McDonald's outlet' were applied mainly 'to help franchise owners keep the promises made in the company's advertising'.[47]

By the 1990s, too, QSC&V was becoming known globally as well as nationally. For instance, when McDonald's restaurants opened in Beijing, the local media publicized 'McDonald's corporate philosophy of QSC & V' in order to reinforce the government's policy of modernizing the city's business environment.[48] McDonald's attention to hygiene was constantly mentioned by the Beijing media and, if Kroc had still been alive, he would probably have been gratified to see his corporation setting the standard for food hygiene even in communist China.[49]

Cleanliness was the component of QSC&V that was the most identified with Kroc. He gave McDonald's its 'passion for cleanliness', such as its operations manual having 'five pages alone on how to clean stainless steel'.[50] The service component of QSC&V was no less important, however, and its accent on friendliness made 'smiling service' an integral part of what Watson calls the 'total experience' of eating at McDonald's.[51] But quality was the first and fundamental component of QSC&V. Kroc's book dwelt upon the high quality of his hamburger patties and, especially, his french fries: 'the quality of our french fries was a large part of McDonald's success'.[52] High-quality french fries may well have been important but no more so than Kroc's distinctive and brilliantly calculated marketing strategies.

Although Kroc did not emphasize the other calculative method, quantitative calculation, he used it in several different contexts. His book mentions how it influenced a crucial pricing decision in 1967. Apparently Kroc decided that an increase in the price of the 15-cent hamburger should be limited to just 3 cents, instead of the proposed 5 cents, partly because his accountant's price/demand graph had predicted the 'diminishing demand for our product for every cent of increase in price'.[53] Furthermore, Napoli mentions that in the mid-1960s Kroc still 'religiously' monitored the sales figures of his restaurants, and even in the 1970s he was monitoring the sales reports from newly established restaurants.[54]

The most important way, however, in which he used quantitative calculation was in relation to the revenue and financing arising from the firm's leasing arrangements. In 1957 Kroc's new 'numbers man', Harry Sonneborn, devised these leasing arrangements to solve the pressing problems of how to finance the development of new restaurants and extract more revenue from their franchised operators.[55] Thanks to his leasing arrangements with owners of sites for new restaurants, the banks were willing to finance the building of these new restaurants by McDonald's development team and its contractors. In addition, he created a new source of revenue by applying a leasing formula to the franchisee operators of the new restaurants. McDonald's would lease the restaurants to franchisees in return for a percentage of their sales revenue. A franchisee of one or more restaurants would pay a 5 per cent rental, which was calculated on the same sales-percentage basis as the almost 2 per cent service-fee royalties that a franchisee paid Kroc's firm and was shared with the McDonald brothers. The addition of the 5 per cent lease rents to the almost 2 per cent franchising royalties was a huge revenue boost for Kroc's firm and in his book he refers to this as 'the beginning of real income'.[56]

Sonneborn's innovative leasing arrangements were therefore a crucial factor in the development of the corporation. Indeed Love argued that without them, 'McDonald's would never have become a viable competitor in fast food'.[57] But at this early stage in the corporation's development, Sonneborn's position and role were similar to Brown's at General Motors when he devised the quantitative assessments and controls that Sloan introduced in the 1920s.[58] 'Brown and his financial team created the means by which Sloan's goal could be met' and indeed these Brown-led number crunchers were the *human* means through which Sloan met his goal and through which he used quantitative calculation as a rational method of developing the corporation.[59] Similarly, Sonneborn was the human means through which Kroc used quantitative calculation to develop McDonald's. It was not until the end of the 1950s that Sonneborn became something more than Kroc's 'numbers man': he became part of a dual-leadership team with Kroc and in fact several years later began to pursue his own corporate goals, as will be discussed in the next section.

Diverse Deliberation

Kroc seems to have had an ambivalent attitude towards using deliberative methods. He distinctively emphasized diverse deliberation but seems to have shown little interest in the institutionalized form of deliberation, especially the committee-based version epitomized by Sloan's system at General Motors. On closer examination, however, Kroc appears a very capable user of institutionalized deliberation, even if often it was only *informally* institutionalized.

In contrast, Kroc's emphasis on diverse deliberation is very evident and was a well-known feature of his leadership. His public commitment to diverse deliberation was summed up in two remarks: 'if two executives think the same, one of them is superfluous' and 'I like people who level with me and speak their minds'.[60] In other words, he wanted not just diversity in thinking but also the open expression of this thinking, without any reticence. Furthermore, Love confirms that Kroc's desire for diversity was evident in his deeds as well as words. 'From the beginning, his management team consisted of extremely diverse individuals, not the type of managers who typically survive in corporate bureaucracies. These were not organization persons'.[61] They were not the type of corporate managers portrayed by Whyte in *The Organization Man* and discussed in Chapter 2.

For example, Kroc's book describes the remarkable case of McDonald's manager, Luigi Salvaneschi. He arrived in America with a PhD in canon law but found himself working in a McDonald's restaurant and, by the mid-1960s, managing the corporation's real estate: 'Luigi was always after me to improve the architecture of our [restaurant] buildings' and 'I would usually wind up getting mad and throwing him out of my office when he started carrying on about aesthetics and Michelangelo'.[62] Yet Kroc recognized that Salvaneschi was right, though financially unrealistic, and eventually the restaurants' architecture was indeed redesigned. Similarly, Kroc mentions that he and his construction manager 'started butting heads' when the latter was still only an area supervisor and 'I have always considered our conflicts creative'.[63]

Although Kroc may have benefited from such diverse 'deliberation' with his managers, his emphasis upon diversity seems to have been a matter of personal preference. He was not facing circumstances that required him to emphasize diverse deliberation as a key method of establishing his corporation. The mere use rather than emphasizing of this method would have been sufficient to provide him with the diversity he needed, such as two key executives he recruited in the 1950s: his 'numbers man' financial expert, Sonneborn, and his operations expert, Fred Turner. Kroc refers to the benefits he gained from this complementary diversity. 'We were different, Harry [Sonneborn] and I, but for a long time we were able to splice our efforts so that the differences made us stronger. Fred Turner added [in 1957] another dimension to the combination.'[64] Turner was more concerned with operational procedures and institution building, which led to such important contributions as his field-consultants inspectorate and his drafting of a comprehensive operations manual. However, it was Sonneborn who made the crucial revenue-enhancing and financing contributions. In addition to the leasing arrangements discussed earlier, he put together the loans which financed the network of company-operated restaurants and, in 1961, the buy-out of the licensing agreement with the McDonald brothers. Kroc's book describes these two loans in some detail and gives due credit to Sonneborn for his expertise and enterprise.[65]

By the end of the 1950s Kroc had actually formed a dual-leadership team with Sonneborn. In 1959 Kroc gave him the positions of president and CEO: 'I continued as chairman, and we worked substantially as equals.'[66] Such equality is typical of a different version of dual leadership than the innovation-introducing version that arose at General Motors in 1921–2 and Toyota in the 1950s–60s. As Chapter 1 pointed out, there are at least three different versions of a dual-leadership team, and the Kroc–Sonneborn team is an example of not the innovation-introducing version but a more widely known and less complex version. It combines two leaders with different roles but holding similarly high official positions and often similarly high ownership stakes in the firm. The division of labour between the two leaders normally involves one of them performing a more business-oriented role and the other a more creative or technically oriented role. Furthermore, a distinctive feature of the two-role version of dual leadership is its longevity and cohesion.[67] There have been a number of cohesive and enduring two-role leadership teams, such as the remarkable Hewlett and Packard team that will be a focus of Chapter 6. A more recent example is the Larry Page and Sergey Brin pairing that founded Google and was sometimes referred to within Google 'as the single unit LarryandSergey.'[68]

Kroc and Sonneborn, however, were an unusual example of this two-role version of dual leadership. Their division of labour was particularly unusual because it involved two different business and geographical roles. Sonneborn had a finance-administration business role and the geographical role of running the company headquarters in Chicago; Kroc had an operations-suppliers business role and the geographical role of expanding and experimenting in California.[69] More importantly, their dual leadership lacked the typical cohesion and longevity of a two-role leadership team.

By the mid-1960s their differences and conflicts had become irreconcilable. During this period McDonald's was enjoying notable successes: it had become a public company, listed on Wall Street, and was on the way to becoming a 1,000-restaurant chain. However, the two leaders were now communicating through an intermediary and were even taking their policy disputes to the board of directors.[70] In particular, Kroc and Sonneborn were increasingly disagreeing about the goals of the corporation, not just about ways and means of achieving its goals. Kroc's faith in expansion had 'run headlong into Sonneborn's numbers. Kroc saw the sky as the limit; Sonneborn saw it as the excess' and 'began exercising much stricter financial discipline'.[71]

The situation was resolved by Sonneborn's resignation in 1967 and his replacement by Turner in a new and far more cohesive dual-leadership pairing with Kroc. It lasted beyond the changeover in 1977 that saw Turner shift from being president/CEO to chairman and Kroc shift to the new position of semi-retired senior chairman, which he held until his death in 1984. At Kroc's memorial service, Turner gave a eulogy that referred to their close relationship:

> Ray was the best boss, his best friend—a second father, said Turner. 'He gave us an example—to be generous, to be thoughtful to others, to be fair-minded, to have balance, to do nothing to excess. We loved his sense of humour. And we accepted his shortcomings'.[72]

Among these shortcomings was perhaps Kroc's lack of interest in institutionalized deliberation. But it is easy to underestimate his use of this method if comparisons are made with Sloan's highly structured, committee-based system of centralized deliberation. Kroc's approach to institutionalization is more difficult to discern and analyse than Sloan's formal and systematic approach. The difference in their approaches is reflected in their different deliberative styles. Kroc acknowledged that 'I always say exactly what I think' and that he would 'jump into the fray in administrative sessions and yell and pound on the table'.[73] He differed from Sloan, too, in having a policy of decentralizing decision-making, from headquarters to lower level managers, and in having a 'less is more' view of management structure: 'for its size, McDonald's today is the most unstructured corporation I know'.[74]

The lack of structure included the absence of a Sloanist committee-based system of deliberation.[75] Some years later Love pointed out that McDonald's was (still) a relatively unstructured corporation and that 'Ideas are never homogenized by committees'.[76] In contrast, Sloan had given General Motors the rule that policy ideas and proposals must be appraised and approved by committees so as to safeguard the corporation against ill-considered decisions or managers following their hunches.[77] This rule would have cramped Kroc's style of policy-making. He acknowledged in his book that he had always been 'willing to take big risks' and therefore was 'bound to blow one once in a while'.[78] More generally, 'the key ingredient in Kroc's management formula is a willingness to risk failure and to admit mistakes'.[79] These risk-taking and trial-and-error aspects of Kroc's policy-making would not have been compatible with Sloanist committees and their protective policy deliberations. So it is hardly surprising that he was not interested in developing or adopting a committee-based system of deliberation.

He used institutionalized deliberation in less obvious ways than Sloan but with similarly beneficial effects on the firm's policy-making. It seems that Kroc's board of directors discussed key policy decisions as well as dealing with policy disputes between Kroc and Sonneborn. For instance, his book mentions that the board resisted management's 1968 plan for a redesign of the restaurants' architecture: he 'had to fight like hell to push it through the board of directors'.[80]

Furthermore, Kroc and his senior managers engaged in some *informally* institutionalized policy deliberations. These were typically one-to-one, off-the-record discussions institutionalized by informal rules. Napoli mentions two instances of such informal policy deliberation.[81] In the early 1960s, Kroc persuaded Sonneborn to make the deal through which Ronald McDonald was acquired from his franchisee inventors. Later in the decade Kroc was himself persuaded to back a new way of improving the firm's image but in this case it was through boosting his own public image as a benevolent, philanthropic business tycoon.

What were the informal rules that institutionalized Kroc's informal policy deliberations? Looking again at the Salvaneschi case, it appears that the informal rules allowed a manager to lobby Kroc about policy and to *keep* lobbying him even after having been thrown out of the office. There seem to have been informal rules, too, about the most effective way to lobby Kroc, according to his description of how he was sold the proposal to begin advertising on television. In 1963 he was sold this policy by a manager who presented him with a logical, well-researched, and financially attractive argument: 'the logic of his one page memo was irrefutable. It demonstrated precisely how an ad campaign would repay its cost many times over, while failing to spend the money would cost us much more in the long run'.[82] It has been suggested that Kroc 'had a habit of picking up new ideas from anyone who offered them. What counted was not where the idea came from but whether it worked'.[83] However, when he bought ideas from his managers, the deliberations seem to have been institutionalized by an informal rule that the idea was *likely* to work according to the logic, research, and financial projections of the seller's argument.

Certainly Kroc had made good use of institutionalized deliberation as one of the appropriate rational methods of establishing his corporation. More generally, he had used all six of these appropriate rational methods and had emphasized one of each pair: innovative adaptation, strategic calculation, and (from personal preference) diverse deliberation. But Kroc's selection of appropriate methods also included *non*-rational methods, notably the visionary imagination of a dreamer.

His use of this non-rational method is memorably described in a passage near the end of his book. Here Kroc notes that he was looking forward to McDonald's restaurants more than doubling in number, from the present 4,000 to a future 10,000. 'A lot of people would say I'm dreaming. Well they'd be right. I've been dreaming all my life, and I'm as sure as hell not going to stop now'.[84] By the end of the century, the number of McDonald's restaurants had increased to more than 27,000 and, what is more, they could be found in no fewer than 119 countries.[85]

This globalization had been another of Kroc's dreams. 'I'm dreaming about new things for McDonald's International operations' because 'people everywhere—from Japan to Sweden—are welcoming the Golden Arches'.[86] From these people's perspective, the arrival of McDonald's meant a transfer of American business know-how as well as the opportunity to eat a better hamburger and french fries.[87] From the corporation's perspective, this global expansion meant that by the mid-1990s, McDonald's was earning more than half of its revenue from its international operations.[88]

Globalized Adaptability

The first stage of the global expansion had been achieved under Kroc's leadership. By the time he semi-retired in 1977, McDonald's was already established in twenty-one countries outside the US: its global presence extended from the Americas to Europe, Asia, and Australasia.[89] By then, too, McDonald's had developed a highly successful joint-venture system that took Kroc's franchising system a step further by treating the corporation's foreign subsidiaries as superfranchisees.

According to Love, the model for this approach was the 1971 entry of McDonald's into Japan. It involved a pioneering joint-venture arrangement with a Japanese entrepreneur that gave him the same sort of autonomy and adaptive potential that Kroc franchisees had long been given.[90]

> Japan proved that the key to success in the international market was the same as it was at home: *local control* by local owner/operators. The policy resulted in such a diverse range of local joint-venture partners that McDonald's—now the most international of all retailing organizations—is anything but a typical multinational corporation. Rather it is a loose *federation* of independent local retailers who happen to market the same thing ... but tailor their marketing approach to their country's different cultures.[91]

Watson, too, depicted global McDonald's as resembling a 'federation of semi-autonomous enterprises' and he viewed it as a worldwide system adapted to local circumstances.[92] He attributed McDonald's global success to its 'localization strategy' and its 'multilocal' mode of operation.[93] Furthermore, he pointed out that the foreign joint-venture partners were operating in local environments that differed significantly from the American environment in which McDonald's had evolved. In the Japanese and Hong Kong cases, the joint-venture partners 'are credited with turning what appeared to be impossible tasks ("Selling hamburgers in Tokyo or Hong Kong? You must be joking!") into dramatic success stories.'[94]

The joint-venture partners' adaptations to local conditions therefore often included more than just tailoring their marketing approach to fit their country's culture. Love argued that although they 'made major changes in marketing to sell the American system', they did not change the American system's menu or restaurant design.[95] But some foreign partners have in fact made changes or additions to the menu. Watson points out that the Israeli operation serves Big Macs without cheese in several outlets, as required by kosher restaurants. 'McDonald's restaurants in India serve Vegetable McNuggets and a muttonbased Maharaja Mac, innovations that are necessary in a country where Hindus do not eat beef, Muslims do not eat pork, and Jains (among others) do not eat meat of any type'.[96]

Other menu innovations have included: cold pasta in Italy; teriyaki burgers in Japan, Taiwan, and Hong Kong; grilled salmon sandwiches in Norway; and chilled yoghurt drinks in Turkey.[97] What is more, there have also been changes to the restaurants' design. For example, British operators distinguished themselves from other fast-food operations by developing large-scale and relatively plush restaurants, with lavish interiors and exteriors.[98]

The two most interesting examples of localization and adaptation are Japan in the 1970s and China in the 1990s. The pioneering Japanese case has been studied by an anthropologist, who points to several innovations carried out by this local joint-venture partner. He added new items to the menu, including Chinese-style fried rice, curried rice with chicken or beef, a shrimp burger, and a teriyaki burger with soy sauce.[99] He innovatively used central-city locations in fashionable shopping areas as the best way for McDonald's to enter a new country, but he also used locations near train stations in order to compete against the stand-up noodle shops that catered for people wanting a quick bowl of noodles before catching a train.[100] Similarly, his marketing promoted McDonald's as an eating place for young people seeking either a fashionable cultural experience of Americana or a practical alternative to traditional fast-food options.[101]

The image of McDonald's as a young people's place had to accommodate a new development introduced by these young customers. They tended to use the McDonald's restaurant as a place to relax and socialize rather than to eat fast food quickly and then depart. In Japan and other parts of Asia 'McDonald's restaurants are treated as leisure centers, where people can retreat from the stresses of urban life'.[102] In Japan, restaurants in favourable locations spontaneously became meeting places for young people, with high-school and even elementary-school students spending hours relaxing and socializing.[103] This might well be viewed as a revival of the 'high-school hangout' and teenager-oriented approach of the drive-in restaurants that Kroc had competed against so many years earlier—in a different era and society.

In the 1990s, McDonald's arrived in communist China. Its arrival in Beijing has been studied by another anthropologist, who mentions several localization and adaptive features that are reminiscent of what occurred earlier in Japan. For example, the McDonald's restaurants successfully attracted 'yuppies' seeking an Americana cultural experience, and the local customers spontaneously used the restaurants as a place to relax and socialize.[104] However, the differences from the Japanese case are just as significant. There were no experiments with local food items and there was no attempt to compete with local forms of fast food, such as the small boxes of rice sold at street stalls.[105] Furthermore, the young people attracted to McDonald's were from an older age group and used the restaurants for a different purpose. Young couples considered the McDonald's environment to be 'romantic and comfortable', especially for those with limited budgets, and the restaurants responded by creating 'a relatively remote, private service area with tables for two only' that in some restaurants was nicknamed 'the lovers' corner'.[106]

The key difference, however, was that in China 'localization strategies have centered on children as primary customers' and exploited the effect of China's one-child policy upon family life:

> children are the object of attention and affection from up to half a dozen adults: their parents and their paternal and maternal grandparents. The demands of such children are always met by one or all of these relatives, earning them the title of 'Little Emperors' or 'Empresses'. When a Little Emperor says 'I want to eat at McDonald's', this means that the entire family must go along.[107]

This child-based marketing strategy included 'Aunt McDonald' receptionists to support the Ronald McDonald clown figure imported from America and known as 'Uncle McDonald' in China. A restaurant would employ five to ten of these female receptionists to care for children and talk with their parents, to host children's birthday parties, and 'to establish long-term friendships with children and other customers'.[108]

Although this strategy may seem to be re-emphasizing Kroc's children-centred advertising of the 1960s, it was more of an adaptive response—an innovative adaptation—to local Chinese conditions. Like the previous examples described in this section, it shows that the joint-venture system had instilled a capacity for innovative adaptation in *global* McDonald's, just as Kroc's franchising system had instilled a similar adaptive capacity in the American McDonald's of the 1960s–70s. In fact the need to adapt to local conditions and competition was more evident in the case of the international joint-venture system and so it is not surprising that joint-venture partners seem to have been more innovative than Kroc's franchisees in adding to the menu, modifying the design, marketing in different ways, and even developing new markets, such as the teenager-oriented marketing that is reminiscent of Kroc's competitors in the 1950s.

McDonald's had 'come a long way' geographically and commercially since Kroc started up his fast-food venture in 1954. He had taken it from a start-up to a globalized corporation that would soon be part of the global culture. Considering the personal circumstances that he faced, Kroc seems to epitomize the values that he highlighted in the final chapter of his book. 'The only way we can advance is by going forward, individually and collectively, in the spirit of the pioneer' and taking 'the risks involved in our free enterprise system'.[109]

5

Wal-Mart

Walton's *Made in America*

Sam Walton's autobiographical *Made in America: My Story* appeared the year he died, 1992, at age 74.[1] He was still chairman of the massive retailing corporation, Wal-Mart Stores, which he had founded and which had made him the wealthiest man in America.[2] Tedlow's *Giants of Enterprise* describes Walton as arguably 'the most successful retailer in American history. More than that, he was arguably the nation's most successful executive.'[3] Although Walton's book is largely an autobiography, it is less personal than Kroc's and gives a better leader's-eye view of how the appropriate rational methods were used to establish a corporation.

Walton used these methods very capably to establish an iconic corporation that is now almost as internationally famous as McDonald's. Unlike Kroc, Walton did not preside over the early stages of his firm's globalization. In 1992, the year that he died, Wal-Mart was an almost entirely US operation, with nearly 2,000 stores and nearly 400,000 employees.[4] Only twelve years later, Wal-Mart (now known as Walmart) was operating in eleven countries and had become the world's largest corporation, with some 5,000 stores and over 1.5 million employees.[5] By 2012, the majority of its stores were located outside America and indeed its international branch Walmart International had become the world's second-largest retailer—second only to the corporation's retail operations in America.[6]

Like Kroc and Sloan, Walton used the whole set of six appropriate corporation-developing methods. More importantly, Walton was also using and indeed emphasizing a *seventh* rational method—learning—that has not been mentioned in earlier chapters. Chapter 1 did not include it among the set of six appropriate corporation-developing methods, but the Walton example shows that it must be included as an additional, seventh appropriate method of establishing or enhancing a corporation. Furthermore, like Sloan, Walton seems to epitomize the leader who inspires employee-followers with rational confidence because he or she is very capably using the appropriate rational methods. It is true that Walton also used the non-rational methods of vision and gut instinct but, as was argued in Chapter 1, he seems to have used these non-rational methods only when they were rationally appropriate in the circumstances he was facing. Otherwise he would use one of the appropriate rational methods, as when he was using and indeed emphasizing learning.

Walton's emphasis on learning was not the only way in which he differed from Sloan and Kroc in selecting methods to emphasize. Instead of selecting one adaptive

Rational Leadership. Paul Brooker and Margaret Hayward, Oxford University Press. © Paul Brooker & Margaret Hayward (2023). DOI: 10.1093/oso/9780198894643.003.0005

and one deliberative method, he selected *both* calculative methods—quantitative as well as strategic calculation. Unlike Sloan and Kroc, he chose, as a matter of personal preference, to emphasize quantitative calculation: he was his own 'numbers man' and could do without someone like Brown or Sonneborn.

Where Walton was particularly unusual, however, was in the way he 'founded' a corporation. For his Wal-Mart corporation was founded by enhancing an existing firm so successfully that this enhancement, the introduction of 'Wal-Mart' stores, became the driving force behind the firm's development into a corporation and even gave the new corporation its name: Wal-Mart Stores. When he opened his first Wal-Mart store in 1962, the 44-year-old Walton was already the founder and owner of a regional retailing empire in the southwest of the country, primarily in the state of Arkansas. His firm already operated more than fifteen large or sizeable variety stores in a regional chain that Tedlow terms a 'variety store empire':

> By the early 1960s, Walton had achieved an altogether remarkable record: 'That whole period—which scarcely gets any attention from people studying us—was really very successful. In fifteen years' time, we had become the largest independent variety store operator in the United States'. In his early forties, Sam Walton was already a rich man.[7]

His 1962 venture into discount retailing was aimed apparently at protecting his firm from the threat of discount stores challenging his variety stores. Although these challengers had not yet arrived, Walton would pre-empt and perhaps deter them by opening his own discount store, the first Wal-Mart.

The first section of the chapter will describe how he then used rapid and innovative adaptation to develop a superb expansion system, which soon spread these discount stores throughout the region. The second section will describe his emphasizing of both quantitative and strategic calculation and will examine distinctive aspects of his strategic calculation. Unlike Sloan and Kroc, he did not focus on marketing and was instead mainly concerned with an Ohno-like cost-reduction grand strategy and with the more specialized strategies that it drove or influenced, such as his labour-relations and political strategies.

The third section of the chapter will explore his use of diverse and institutionalized deliberation. It will highlight the way in which his use of these methods involved the technocrats and new technology that enabled his firm to expand so rapidly into a retailing empire. The fourth section, however, will explore his use and indeed emphasizing of a method—learning—that has not been mentioned in earlier chapters. Obviously this section has a wider significance than the others and therefore it is followed up by a special, fifth section that presents a supplementary example of another leader, Marcel Dassault, emphasizing learning as a rational method of establishing a corporation—the French aircraft corporation Dassault Aviation.

Adaptively Expanding Wal-Mart

Walton's most significant use of the adaptive methods was when he developed an expansion system for spreading his new Wal-Mart stores throughout the southwest. The expansion system was a major innovation, but, as in the cases of Kroc's franchising system and Ohno's production system, it was developed through a series of smaller innovative adaptations, which Walton made during the 1960s. These innovations, the key components of his new expansion system, included (1) a small-town strategy, (2) a policy of rapid-as-possible expansion, (3) a superb distribution system, and (4) a saturation growth strategy. Like Kroc's franchising system, this was also a case of *rapid* adaptation being used in combination with innovative to produce a rapidly developed innovative system. Walton's system was developed largely in the late 1960s, just as Kroc's had been developed largely in the late 1950s, and in both cases the rapidity was crucial because it enabled the system to take advantage of opportunities before they evaporated or were exploited by the firm's competitors.

However, Walton's system was less innovative than Kroc's and Ohno's because it had not been developed by creatively taking full advantage of opportunities. Walton's innovations had instead usually been forced adaptive responses or, in his words, were taking opportunities that had been 'created out of necessity'.[8] The earliest example of this was his small-town strategy, which was also the most obvious component of the expansion system. In a sense it was nothing new but merely the continuation of Walton's existing strategy, as he acknowledges in his book when recounting the 1940s origin of the 'small-town strategy that got Wal-Mart going almost two decades later'.[9]

His small-town strategy had been a feature of how in the 1940s–50s he had created a chain of variety stores located in small towns in the southwest—and with the firm's headquarters located in the small town of Bentonville, Arkansas.[10] When the history of Wal-Mart was written many years later, the historians noted that 'Walton's strategy of using small-town locations would be an undeniable outgrowth of the variety-store years'.[11] They also noted how his variety-store empire was endangered by the rise of discount retailing in the 1950s. Discount retailing was nothing new, and was based on high sales volume through rapid turnover produced by low (discount) prices, which were in turn produced by low profit margins, low costs, and, particularly, having merchandise supplied not through a wholesaler but directly from the manufacturer. Discounting had evolved in the 1950s, however, into a more sophisticated form of discount store, with a supermarket's self-service techniques and a department store's lay-out and wide range of merchandise.[12] This modern form of discount store could be expected to spread, as had other retailing innovations, even to Arkansas and the small towns in which Walton had established his chain of variety stores. 'Like other merchants before him who had been *forced to adapt* when their businesses had been threatened by new forms of retailing, Sam Walton would be compelled to come to terms with this latest innovation in the history of American retailing'.[13]

Walton's response was to open his own version of a modern discount store. In his book's words, 'I wasn't about to sit there and become a target' and so in 1962 he opened a modern discount store and called it a 'Wal-Mart' store.[14] He was apparently seeking just to pre-empt and perhaps deter a discount-retailing challenge to his small-town variety stores, but his forced adaptive response had 'invented' the innovative retailing strategy of locating modern discount stores in small towns. The first Wal-Mart store was the first of many that would be located in small towns: the first fifty would be located in towns with 'a median population of just under nine thousand people'.[15]

Furthermore, the Wal-Mart stores were soon being opened at a very rapid rate, thanks to the new policy of rapid-as-possible expansion. According to Walton, the small towns were showing much greater demand for discount retailing than he had foreseen, but this also meant it was more likely that other firms would soon copy his strategy of locating discount stores in small towns.[16] 'We figured we'd better [therefore] roll the stores out as quickly as we could' through a new policy of rapid-as-possible expansion.[17] Although it was another forced adaptive response, the new policy was aimed at pre-empting or deterring competition with his new *discount* stores rather than his chain of variety stores. By opening new Wal-Mart stores 'as rapidly as earnings and credit would permit', Walton increased the rate of openings to five stores a year in 1968–9.[18] By converting his firm into a public company in 1970, he was able to finance a more rapid rate of expansion and in fact his Wal-Mart Stores Incorporated added some 200 new stores during the 1970s by 'stretching our people and our talents to the absolute maximum'.[19]

This rapid rate of expansion was also partly due to another component of his expansion system—the superb distribution system. It, too, was a forced adaptive response but in this case the problem was not potential competitors but the lack of distribution services to supply the firm's small-town discount stores in the rural southwest. Walton notes in his book that being 'out in the sticks with nobody to distribute to our stores', the firm had to supply its Wal-Mart discount stores through its own warehouse distribution centres and in fact was 'forced to be ahead of our time in distribution'.[20] Wal-Mart's historians agree that this forced adaptive response proved very beneficial in the longer term. 'Wal-Mart's rural locations had compelled the firm to invest in its own inventory-replenishing system, which had evolved into an intricate network of distribution centers, an extensive fleet of trucks, and state of the art computer and communications systems that enabled the firm to function with great efficiency'.[21] For example, the new Bentonville distribution centre built in 1969 included one of the first computerized warehouses in the country, and the distribution centre built in Searcy in 1978 had an automated warehouse that pioneered mechanized distribution.[22] According to Ortega, Wal-Mart developed 'perhaps the leanest and fastest distribution system in the country', enabling the firm to supply 'merchandise to its stores faster and at less expense than its rivals'.[23]

In the 1960s, however, the system's limitations forced Wal-Mart to adopt a growth strategy that Ortega terms 'the saturation strategy'.[24] It was markedly different from the growth strategies of Wal-Mart's rivals and it became the fourth component of the expansion system. Although this was another forced adaptive response, Walton made the best of the situation through some innovative strategic calculation. He was adapting to the logistical fact of life that Wal-Mart's distribution system was a hub-and-spoke system that required each new Wal-Mart store to be located within a day's truck drive (spoke) of a distribution centre (hub).[25] Walton's book points out that other, larger discount-retailing firms were expanding 'by sticking stores all over the country' but Wal-Mart 'couldn't support something like that' with its regional hub-and-spoke distribution system.[26] He acknowledges that therefore Wal-Mart's 'growth strategy was born out of necessity, but at least we recognized it as a strategy early on' and devised a new saturation technique: open a store 'as far as we could from a warehouse' and then 'fill in the map of that territory' by opening new stores until the area and market had been saturated.[27]

By the 1970s this growth strategy was being applied in not only Arkansas but also several other states in the surrounding region, such as Missouri and Texas. Later in the decade, new distribution centres were being built some distance from Bentonville. Now Wal-Mart was able 'to overcome the logistical problem that prevented it from expanding beyond the 350-mile [a day's truck drive] ring around Bentonville' and its nation-wide expansion would lead to many more distribution centres 'placed strategically in our trade areas across the country—still mostly within a day's drive, or about 350 miles, of the stores they serve'.[28]

The nation-wide expansion in the 1980s was a remarkable triumph for the expansion system, as is related in Vance and Scott's history of Wal-Mart.[29] By 1981, Wal-Mart was the country's second-largest discount chain, even though these some 400 stores were confined to a thirteen-state area stretching from Texas in the south to Illinois in the north. By 1985 there were more than 700 stores, now in twenty states, and by 1987 there were nearly *1,000* Wal-Mart stores in America. Only three more states had been added to the empire but it was becoming one of the country's largest retail, not just *discount*-retail, corporations, and in 1989 it 'became the nation's third largest retailer, despite the fact that it operated in only half the states'.[30] The remarkable rate of expansion continued into the early 1990s. Wal-Mart now moved into the west coast and northeast regions and was operating in two-thirds of the states when it became the nation's *largest* retailer in 1991.[31] This was the ultimate triumph for an expansion system that had originated in Arkansas nearly thirty years earlier and was based on four innovative but forced adaptive responses.

However, Walton's expansion system had abandoned its small-town and saturation strategies when Wal-Mart entered the cities in the 1980s. In his book, Walton notes that he had 'never planned on going into the cities. What we did instead was build our stores in a ring around a city—pretty far out—and wait for the growth to come to us'.[32] Ortega described this strategy more clearly as waiting 'for the growth of suburbs to bring out the shoppers. Eventually, Wal-Marts would ring the outskirts of dozens of cities'.[33] But this long-term strategy was superseded or at least supplemented by a more direct approach. For by the 1980s, Wal-Mart was actually going into the cities. Now there would be such combinations as having four stores *in* a city of 150,000 as well as five or more 'within 30 miles'.[34] The urban trend increased during the decade as the corporation expanded into a nation-wide retail empire. Wal-Mart's historians note that this 1980s expansion led to 'a growing interest in more densely populated areas' and the firm 'accelerated its expansion into larger cities'.[35] As Walton acknowledges in his book, 'we've moved into some cities outright'.[36]

In addition to moving into the cities, Wal-Mart had moved into several new regions in the 1980s and into the west coast and northeast regions in the early 1990s. So it had to adapt to new *regional* environments as well as the new urban environment of the cities that it was moving into 'outright'. Furthermore, it had to adapt very rapidly during this period of only twelve years. In fact the corporation's most impressive feature in this stage of its development is how rapidly and successfully it adapted to 'local' urban and regional conditions.

Yet Walton's book has little to say, implicitly or explicitly, about rapid adaptation. The only account of Wal-Mart adapting rapidly is the description of how he personally took charge of the firm's response to a competitive challenge in the early 1980s. The challenge came from a new form of discount retailing that was labelled 'subdiscounting' because it undercut discount retailers by selling (1) a wide range of goods at wholesale prices, (2) in warehouse-like stores, and (3) to customers who belonged to the stores' subdiscounting 'club' and therefore were entitled to buy these goods at wholesale rather than retail prices.[37] Walton's adaptive response appeared as early as 1983. He created a subdiscounting form of Wal-Mart store, called a Sam's Club store, which supplemented the standard Wal-Mart stores and competed for the newly discovered subdiscounting market. By the end of the 1980s there were nearly a hundred of these warehouse-like Sam's Club stores, and they had taken Wal-Mart further into big-city retailing.[38]

A more important example of rapid adaptation occurred in the 1990s and was foreshadowed in Walton's book. He mentions that Wal-Mart was preparing to 'push on' into the grocery market, 'where we feel the customers are ready for our way of doing business'.[39] The push into the grocery market would be led by a new form of Wal-Mart store—the Supercenter—which had developed out of Walton's failed experiment with 'hypermarkets'.[40] The Supercenter combined a grocery supermarket with a standard Wal-Mart store and therefore gave the corporation a means of competing for the huge grocery market.[41] By 2001 there were more than 1,000 Supercenters and they had made Wal-Mart the largest food retailer in America—a remarkably rapid adaptation to this massive market and difficult line of business.[42]

This post-Walton success confirmed that a capacity for rapid adaptation had been instilled in the corporation by Walton in the 1980s. He had instilled it on a much larger scale than Sloan's autopilot-like quantitative controls at General Motors, and Walton seems to have instilled it through a non-rational method—his corporation's culture.[43] In his book he declares that 'I've made it my own personal mission to ensure that constant change is a vital part of the Wal-Mart culture' and, furthermore, he claimed that 'one of the greatest strengths of Wal-Mart's ingrained culture is its ability to drop everything and turn on a dime'.[44] Clearly this was not far from the truth as regards Wal-Mart's capacity for constantly and rapidly adapting to new conditions. And it would be reconfirmed in the 2000s by Wal-Mart's rapid adaptation to being a globalized corporation and operating in global conditions.

Looking back at the corporation's development, the instilled capacity for rapid adaptation therefore seems no less important than the innovative expansion system of the 1960s–70s. This is one reason why the chapter has not suggested that Walton *emphasized* innovative adaptation; the other reason is that the expansion system was obviously not as creative and permanent a contribution as the innovative systems described in the previous two chapters.[45] There are no doubts, however, about his emphasizing of the two calculative methods.

Calculating Numbers and Strategy

This section will examine Walton's use and indeed emphasizing of the two calculative rational methods: quantitative and strategic calculation. Chapter 1 referred to Walton's liking for quantitative calculation as a typical example of a leader emphasizing a particular rational method as a matter of personal preference. In the case of strategic calculation the circumstances were more important than personal preferences. Like Sloan and Kroc, Walton relied on strategic calculation for key elements in his success, but in Walton's case it was not his marketing strategy but his cost-reduction strategy that was so important—it gave his firm a crucial advantage over his competitors. As this section will show, cost reduction was a fundamental and wide-ranging 'grand' strategy that influenced Walton's strategic calculation in other areas, such as his distinctive labour-relations strategy.

Quantitative calculation, however, was Walton's personally preferred method of developing a corporation. As Fishman notes, Walton was known as a 'numbers man' who expected his managers, too, to have the numbers at their fingertips and on their mind.[46] It is evident in his book that Walton liked being his own 'numbers man' and emphasizing quantitative calculation. When he described his managerial style as playing to his strengths, the only ones he mentions are an appreciation for numbers and a talent for remembering numbers.[47] An appreciation for numbers had 'kept me close to our operational statements and to all our other information that we have pouring in'.[48] For example, each week Walton checked each and every store's numbers for that week's sales, wage costs, and so forth. 'It usually takes about three hours, but when I'm done I have as good a feel for what's going on in the company as anybody here'.[49] This was an incredible feat of analysis and memory, considering that Wal-Mart had hundreds of stores and that Walton would cite their numbers, from memory, in his weekly management meetings. Soderquist quotes a Wal-Mart manager reminiscing about Walton's 'uncanny ability to retain and remember performances. He also expected everyone, from the CFO [chief financial officer] down to the department managers in the stores, to "know your numbers"' and of course to know what they meant.[50]

Walton's appreciation for numbers was focused on interpreting what the numbers meant. He believed that the numbers told him when and where there was mismanagement and also when a concept was 'getting out of control' or where 'the next trouble spot' would appear.[51] This was why he liked the corporation's computerization—'all those numbers'—and its satellite-based communication system: 'I like my numbers as quickly as I can get them'.[52] Such concern with his personal quantitative monitoring of the corporation was one of the most distinctive features of his leadership.

But being his own 'numbers man' was less important to the corporation than his emphasis on *strategic* calculation. Walton was clearly a believer in adapting his calculated strategic plans to fit changing circumstances.

> 'Dad always said you've got to stay flexible', reported his son Jim. 'We never went on a family trip nor have we ever heard of a business trip in which the schedule wasn't changed at least once after the trip was under way. Later we all snickered at some writers who viewed Dad as a grand strategist who intuitively developed complex plans and implemented them with precision'.[53]

Walton was a truly 'grand' strategist, however, in the sense of devising a *grand* strategy. Chapter 1 pointed out that grand strategy is concerned with 'the big picture' and 'the big issues' and in Walton's case he devised a cost-reduction grand strategy that was fundamental and wide-ranging, influencing his strategic calculations about many other things, areas, and issues.

What is more, Walton's cost-reduction grand strategy helped produce a revolution in retailing. Lichtenstein's *The Retail Revolution* notes that in the early 1960s it appeared that (1) consumers were paying too much for distribution and retailing, when compared with what they paid for manufacturing; and (2) there was a huge contrast between manufacturers' scrutiny of production costs and the absence of such cost-reduction scrutiny when the products were distributed and retailed.[54] But the times were beginning to change. Soon many retailers would be scrutinizing their costs as closely as any manufacturer scrutinized production costs. One of the reasons for this change was Walton's reorientation of discounting's price-competing formula. He developed a 'frugal' version of discount retailing that reduced his discounted prices still further by frugal cost savings—and a cost-reduction grand strategy.

Walton's book mentions how in the 1960s Wal-Mart developed this new, frugal version of discount retailing. 'What we were obsessed with was keeping our prices below everybody else's. Our dedication to that was total. Everybody worked like crazy to keep the expenses down'.[55] This frugality was epitomized at the end of the 1960s by Walton's new headquarters building:

> The firm's general headquarters in Bentonville, with its inexpensive décor throughout, was symbolic of Walton's devotion to frugality. Subsequent to its construction, the installation of conveniences such as an elevator and carpeting in some areas provoked complaints from Walton ... And he considered the carpeting an outright waste of money.[56]

Achieving a competitive advantage by frugally keeping the expenses down became a well-recognized feature of the Walton way of discounting. Wal-Mart's historians refer to his 'zeal for cost-cutting' and to economy of operation being 'almost a fetish', while Trimble refers to 'frugality in the extreme' being a principal element in Wal-Mart's success.[57] This frugal version of discounting was institutionalized as a cost-reduction grand strategy that Wal-Mart would continue to stress in the 1970s–80s and when it expanded into a global empire in the 1990s.[58]

Walton's grand strategy seems very similar to Ohno's cost-reducing grand strategy. For example, Walton notes in his book that Wal-Mart had 'always operated lean. We have operated with fewer people. We have had our people do more than in other companies'.[59] But Walton was more concerned than Ohno with the competitive aspect of reducing or minimizing costs. Wal-Mart's 'heritage' and 'obsession' was to be 'more productive and more efficient than our competition'.[60] The competitive aspect was also evident when Walton pointed to cost control as one of his rules for running a successful company. 'Control your expenses better than your competition. This is where you can always find the competitive edge'.[61] Furthermore, his book shows that he practised what he preached. It points out that for twenty-five years Wal-Mart 'ranked number one in our industry for the lowest ratio of expenses to sales'.[62] He had increased this competitive edge during the 1980s when the corporation was rapidly expanding into a nation-wide retail empire. Wal-Mart's historians note that its operating expenses as a percentage of sales would decline from about 20 per cent early in the decade to only 15 per cent in 1990.[63] Office expenses were an obvious example of Walton seeking a competitive edge through controlling costs. From the outset he sought to keep office expenses at 2 per cent of sales in an era 'when most companies charged 5 per cent of their sales to run their offices'.[64]

His cost-reduction grand strategy was wide-ranging as well as competitive. Unlike Ohno's, Walton's was not confined to a retailing equivalent of production and indeed it influenced or drove other, more specialized strategies. For example, Walton's reduction of labour costs was supported by an impressively calculated labour-relations strategy. He needed an effective labour-relations strategy to help reduce not only labour costs but also the prospect of unionization or other serious labour 'problems'. In fact his tight control of labour costs was potentially a very problematic part of his cost-reduction grand strategy. Critics indicted him on several counts, notably the heavy reliance on part-time and temporary workers, and the reliance on near-minimum-wage workers, who were still being paid 'below the retail industry's average wage' even after Wal-Mart became the country's largest and most successful retail corporation.[65]

His book, not surprisingly, highlights the many positive aspects of his labour-relations strategy, notably the brilliant profit-sharing plan. In 1971, Walton had extended his managers' profit-sharing plan to include store workers who had been employed by Wal-Mart for two years or more.[66] This decision to give store workers 'more equitable treatment in the company', was without a doubt the single smartest move we ever made at Wal-Mart': they would be included in the profit-sharing plan and would be the target of new share-buying and bonus programmes.[67] The shrinkage and sales bonus programme would also lead to more equitable treatment in the sharing of information. Ortega notes that Wal-Mart employees 'would be told such things as the sales figures at their stores, and the losses from shrinkage, figures that, at other companies, were for management's eyes only'.[68]

Walton's labour-relations strategy was developing in the 1970s into a complex mixture of new features and long-standing policies.[69] The new features included (1) profit sharing, share buying, bonuses, and information sharing; (2) the decision to call workers 'associates' rather than employees; (3) the description of managers as 'servant-leaders' of teams of workers; (4) the 'open-door' policy, which allowed workers to take their problems directly to Walton; and (5) a Wal-Mart company cheer led by Walton himself. The longstanding policies included strongly opposing unionization and, more positively, promoting an egalitarian informality, such as by using first names throughout the corporation—from 'Mr Sam' on down.

His strategic calculations were therefore directed not towards a complex plan of action but towards creating and managing a complex package of interrelated features and policies. This complex, impressively calculated strategy helped prevent unionization and any serious labour problems. But something more was required to deal with the prospect of *political* intervention in the area of labour relations. In 1978, Walton was one of the business leaders who lobbied against proposed new labour legislation, which he believed would favour unionization.[70] Although the proposed legislation did not become law, 'Walton castigated himself for ignoring the political arena too long, until this threat was upon the company, and he warned employees that from now on both he and they would be called upon to address specific issues'.[71]

In fact the prospect of political intervention was a 'wild card' that could threaten the corporation in other ways and in relation to a wide range of issues. The calculating of political strategy therefore often required him to tailor his means to achieve particular ends. For instance, dealing with pro-unionization bills in Congress required different means than defending the corporation against calls to save small-town businesses from having to compete against Wal-Mart. In the latter case, the strategy included a different ideological means to the end. Tedlow points out that Walton's political strategy here was to use the typical 1980s language of 'consumer democracy', which provided a ready justification for small-town stores succumbing to price competition from Wal-Mart.

> He didn't put that Ben Franklin [store] out of business. The customers shut the old store down: 'They voted with their feet'. Walton was a fervent believer in consumer democracy. Consumers have choices in a free country. They 'vote' for us by patronizing our stores.[72]

Furthermore, Wal-Mart did not indulge in predatory or monopolistic pricing. As a 2000s critic acknowledged, it had never engaged in the predatory practice of going into a small town, putting the local merchants out of business with its lower prices and then, some months or a year later, reaping the benefits by increasing its prices: 'Wal-Mart is brutally competitive, but it is not technically predatory. It's not "low prices until the competitors are strangled"—it's *always* low prices'.[73]

These 'brutally competitive' low prices were largely due to Walton's cost-reduction grand strategy. It had played a key role in developing the corporation ever since his 1960s invention of a frugal version of discount retailing. He had long been emphasizing strategic calculation as a key method and in relation not just to his grand strategy but also to other, more specialized strategies. Unlike in the case of quantitative calculation, this was not due to his personal preferences but to the requirements of establishing a discount-retailing corporation during a revolutionary era in retailing.

Deliberation and Technology

Walton used both diverse and institutionalized deliberation as methods of establishing his corporation but, unlike Sloan and Kroc, did not emphasize either of them. Yet there were some noteworthy and distinctive features about Walton's use of the deliberative methods. The distinctive structural feature is that he used Kroc-like informally institutionalized deliberation as well as Sloan-like formally institutionalized deliberation by committees and other groups. Another distinctive feature was that technocrats and technology issues played a prominent role in his informally institutionalized deliberations and in his use of diverse deliberation. This was very unusual, indeed unprecedented, for a retailing firm and so, too, was the amount of deliberative time and effort spent discussing when and how to introduce new technology.

The most important aspect of Walton's diverse deliberation was that it provided him with high-tech options and viewpoints. Although Chapter 1 pointed to the liking for 'mavericks' that he displayed in his book, *technocrats* were much more important to him and his policy deliberations. In the 1960s–70s. 'Walton had scoured the country for techno-whizzes and experts in distribution, logistics, communication, and any other discipline he felt he knew nothing about'.[74] In his book he acknowledges that this diverse range of technocrats had played an important role in his firm's remarkable growth.[75] In particular, he notes that 'one of the main reasons we've been able to roll this company out nationally was all the pressure put on me by guys like David Glass and earlier, Jack Shewmaker and Ron Mayer, to invest so heavily in technology. Yes, I argued and resisted, but I eventually signed the checks'.[76]

His technocrats were certainly not reticent in lobbying him about new technology and selling him proposals for specific projects. For example, Glass began 'pushing' for investment in warehouse mechanization as soon as Walton recruited him in 1976, Glass and Shewmaker were also 'pushing hard for heavy investment in more and more, better and better computer systems', and in the 1980s Shewmaker 'worked really hard to get me to invest in bar coding'.[77] He also had to work really hard to get Walton to invest in a satellite-based communication system. According to Ortega, Shewmaker realized this would be 'a tough sell' because the satellite system was not only 'so untried' but also so expensive: possibly the equivalent of a quarter of the corporation's annual capital expenditure at a time when it was rapidly expanding into a nation-wide empire.[78] Although Shewmaker successfully sold the proposal to

Walton, the new system ran into technical problems as well as cost over-runs and for a time it seemed the project 'might turn into a fiasco'.[79] Yet Walton continued to allow his technocrats to pressure him—successfully—for more investment in new technology.

His technocratic executives participated, too, in deliberations about policies that were not related to technology. Walton has even been described as *goading* his executives to argue about important decisions, though apparently 'there's no shortage of people who can recall Walton, on the short end of some debate or another, shutting it off by booming out "I still own most of the stock in this company, and this is what we're going to do"'.[80]

Walton presumably did not goad his board of directors and shut off their debates in this peremptory manner. But his recruitment of the board's outside directors shows the same concern for diverse expertise that he showed when recruiting his technocratic executives. By the mid-1980s there were 'eight outside directors with particular areas of expertise Walton figured would be useful to his business', such as Charles Lazarus of Toys 'R' Us, who had pioneered the warehouse-size discount retailing of a single category of merchandise.[81] In 1986, Walton markedly increased the deliberative as well as gender diversity of the board by adding a woman lawyer with political expertise, Hillary Clinton, who would push Walton towards more environmentally friendly, 'green' policies in the late 1980s.[82]

His concern for diverse deliberation seems to have increased as his firm grew into a big corporation and a nation-wide retail empire. In his book, he warns about the stultifying effects of bigness and bureaucratization upon a firm's vitality and enterprise. In this situation 'there's absolutely no room for creativity, no place for the maverick merchant' or for 'the entrepreneur or the promoter' and, not surprisingly, he was 'worried about Wal-Mart becoming that way. I stay on these guys around here all the time about it'.[83] In the 1960s–70s, it had been more appropriate to recruit technocratic executives rather than mavericks, entrepreneurs, or promoters. By the 1980s, however, he was clearly making an effort to counter the effects of stultification.

One of the ways Walton countered stultification was 'his frequent practice of asking his managers to switch jobs'.[84] Both at the time and in his book, he explained this job swapping as simply a way of ensuring that managers had a wide knowledge of the corporation's various parts and activities.[85] But job swapping was not just a means of preventing parochial narrow-mindedness; it was also a means of preventing routinized thinking and expectations. Walton apparently had such a 'strong feeling for the necessity of constant change, for keeping people a little off balance', that he sometimes made a change 'for change's sake alone'.[86]

However, his most dramatic example of job swapping seems to have been motivated by his need to find a suitable successor. In 1984, president and chief operating officer (COO), Shewmaker, exchanged jobs with CFO Glass in what Walton depicted as just another case of job swapping.[87] In his book, though, he admits that he wanted to see how Glass would handle the job of president and COO, presumably because Walton viewed him as a potential successor and perhaps even the preferred successor.[88] In 1988, Walton ended the suspense about the succession by passing on his

CEO post to Glass but retaining the chairmanship and creating a dual-leadership team with Glass.

The Walton–Glass team was a different version of dual leadership than the two-role and innovation-introducing versions discussed in earlier chapters. Chapter 1 described this version as combining a semi-retired founder as chairman with a younger-generation executive as the CEO. Like the two-role version, it involves each member having their own, particular role to perform. But this is not an equal division of labour, as the older member is semi-retired, and another inequality is that the (in most cases male and elderly) founder-chairman usually retains such a large ownership stake that he has the power to replace his CEO 'teammate'. There is also likely to be a psychologically deferential relationship between the younger-generation CEO and the celebrated or legendary founder-chairman, who will have chosen his teammate and may well have mentored or tutored him or her in the earlier stages of their careers. Such a psychologically deferential relationship was particularly apparent in Kroc and Turner's dual leadership of McDonald's, and in fact they may have been the model for the 'two-generation' version of dual leadership that Walton adopted in the twilight of his career.

There was no model, though, for his distinctive version of *institutionalized deliberation*. It was a mixture of formally and informally institutionalized deliberation, of Sloan-like and Kroc-like features, but developed into a distinctive combination that included its own unique features. In particular, the Saturday-morning management meetings were an innovative example of institutionalized deliberation and became a widely known feature of Wal-Mart. They were just one of many ways in which Walton used institutionalized deliberation to develop an iconic corporation.

Like both Kroc and Sloan, Walton espoused a deliberative conception of his position as CEO. As noted earlier, he encouraged diverse deliberation and participated in debates, with a deliberative style that seems less like Silent Sloan's and more like the exuberant Kroc's. Walton also used informally institutionalized deliberation in a similar way to Kroc at McDonald's. In both cases the leader allowed senior managers to sell him policy proposals according to informal rules about how, who, and when. Walton's informal rules, like Kroc's, allowed executives to lobby him and to sell him policy proposals and ideas, with the proviso that they were *likely to work* financially, technically, and in any other way.

Considering Walton's focus on his cost-reduction strategy, it is not surprising that he was particularly concerned about costly projects—and particularly if there were doubts about their technical effectiveness. Walton was therefore especially concerned about proposals that involved costly investment in new, untried technology, such as the satellite-based communication system that was mentioned earlier in this section. 'I want them to think hard how they are going to justify the expense before they even come to me with it'.[89] Berg and Roberts point out that he had an ambivalent attitude towards the new technology. While he 'almost certainly' appreciated its potential benefits, 'it is equally certain that he resented the large initial capital outlay on what was then relatively unproven technology'.[90]

So he vigorously enforced the informal rule that any proposed policy should be likely to work as effectively as its seller promised. Walton notes in his book that he 'always questioned everything' because it was important to make a lobbyer or seller think that 'maybe the technology wasn't as good as they thought it was, or that maybe it really wasn't the end-all they promised it would be. It seems to me they try just a little harder and check into things a little bit closer'.[91] Even then, the technology often failed, at least temporarily, to deliver the promised benefits, as in the case of the satellite-based communication system that Shewmaker had sold to Walton. Similarly, there were problems in the 1970s–80s with the introduction of electric cash registers, the mechanization of the Searcy distribution centre, and the introduction of barcode scanning.[92] Without Walton's wariness there would have been even more problems with new technology as well as more difficulty controlling the spending on these expensive items.

Yet he seems well aware that new technology was needed to maintain Wal-Mart's competitiveness as well as its remarkable rate of expansion. Ortega noted that 'Walton's willingness (once convinced) to spring for such technology' gave Wal-Mart an important advantage over its leading competitor, whose tardiness in upgrading technology contrasts with Walton's pioneering approach, however wary and thrifty.[93] From a broader perspective, the contrast highlights the effectiveness of Walton's use of informally institutionalized deliberation, which enabled an innovative executive to sell a new idea to his or her cautious leader.

However, Walton also used Sloan-like *formally* institutionalized deliberation by committees or other formal groups. To begin at the top, his board of directors was a deliberative as well as auditing institution. For example, a 1980 decision about acquiring Kuhn's Big K stores was debated by the board for over a year before being decided by Walton's tie-breaking vote as chair of the board's executive committee.

> Finally, the Executive Committee sat down to vote on it one morning and it came out split right down the middle, fifty-fifty. It was just as well because it gave me the opportunity to take the ultimate responsibility for the decision. The whole thing had been really cloudy all along, with a lot of arguing.[94]

The seven members of the executive committee included Walton's brother Bud and son Rob, which reflected the important role played by the Walton family in the corporation's ownership, policy-making, and even management: Rob Walton was company secretary and general counsel, while Bud Walton headed and later supervised the real-estate and construction division.[95] The four non-Walton members of the committee were the COO, CFO, and two other senior executives, which included the CEO after the 1988 shift to Walton–Glass dual leadership.

There were other, lower level committees and, as mentioned earlier, the unique Saturday-morning management meetings.[96] By the 1980s this weekly meeting was attended by (1) Walton and his senior executives; (2) his regional managers, who were all based in Bentonville; (3) any of his other managers who worked in Bentonville or were visiting headquarters; and (4) often some invited Wal-Mart store workers—which meant that several hundred people might be attending one of these 'management' meetings.[97] Walton presided over the meetings, dominated their agenda, and focused their deliberations on quickly solving relatively low-level problems.[98] 'I like to see a problem come up and then hear suggestions as to how it can be corrected', so that when 'the solution is obvious, we can order changes right then and carry them out over the weekend'.[99] Problems might be raised when the meeting dealt with merchandising issues, discussed competitors' activities, or reviewed 'computer information charting the performance of every store for the week'.[100] These problems and the meeting's solutions were rapidly communicated to all levels of management either by relayed telephone messages or, once the satellite system was operating, by a live television broadcast of the meeting to all the corporation's stores.[101]

Learning—A Seventh Rational Method

The Saturday-morning management meetings were a learning experience as well as a deliberative institution. Those who attended the meeting were sharing and learning about new ideas and information as well as problems and solutions.[102] Walton notes that the Saturday-morning meeting was a focal point 'where we share ideas we've picked up from various places' and therefore even store workers 'who have thought up something' were invited 'to come share those ideas'.[103] Similarly, there was a sharing of new information, such as competitors' activities or merely the stores' weekly performances.

Among the many learners was of course the meeting's and corporation's leader, Chairman/CEO Walton. Ortega argues that learning was actually the distinctive feature of Walton's greatness as a business leader.

> Hailed as the greatest entrepreneur of his age, Walton disclaimed having any genius or unique ability and freely admitted he borrowed ideas from anywhere he could. If he did have a genius, it was in his ability to know what he didn't know, to recognize his own shortcomings as a businessman and to assume, even after his enormous success, that he still could learn something from almost anybody.[104]

Likewise, Tedlow's profile of Walton in *Giants of Enterprise* noted that 'one of the key characteristics of his career was that he kept learning until the day he died' and indeed 'he spent his life in the quest for more knowledge about retailing'.[105]

This entrepreneur's learning fixation highlights the fact that learning is an additional, seventh rational method of developing a corporation. It should be included in the set of rational methods described in Chapter 1 as the appropriate set for establishing or enhancing a corporation. This set of six methods should be expanded to include learning as a separate and no less appropriate rational method, comparable to any of the other six.[106]

Walton is not the only leader who has used learning as a rational method of establishing or enhancing a corporation.[107] But his use and indeed emphasizing of learning is a classic example of how this rational method is just as appropriate—and can be just as important—as any of the other six corporate developing methods. Learning is mentioned, explicitly or implicitly, more than fifty times in his book, although in some cases the learning occurred before he founded Wal-Mart and began to use learning as a corporation-developing method. Clearly it was a favourite method, which he would have emphasized as a matter of personal preference, as in the case of quantitative calculation. But it was also a *key* method, which was needed to deal with the circumstances he faced when establishing his corporation. His emphasis on learning was therefore 'doubly determined' and this may explain why it is mentioned so often in his book—in various forms and in various contexts.

There were four particularly important contexts and forms of learning. First, he learnt through reading and research, including what might be termed 'field' research. Walton read 'every retail publication I get my hands on' and became an 'avid student of management theory'.[108] His research into new developments in the retail industry was particularly important in the period leading up to the opening of his first Wal-Mart store. He had spent 'years and years of studying the discount business' by 'visiting every store and company headquarters I could find' and asking questions about pricing and anything else that seemed relevant: 'I learned a lot that way'.[109]

A second form of learning was what he learnt from his mistakes, experience, and experimenting.[110] Even near the end of his career, he was still making mistakes and learning from them, such as the very profitable lesson learnt from his failed venture into 'hypermarkets' in the late 1980s. It 'taught us what our next step should be in combining grocery and general merchandising—a smaller concept called the Supercenter'.[111] The great success of the Supercenter stores is a dramatic example of making the most of mistakes. As Ray Kroc said, 'when you strike out, you should learn as much as you can from it'.[112]

When it comes to learning from more positive experiences, a crucial example was his pre-Wal-Mart experience of establishing a large retail firm. Years before the 1962 opening of his first Wal-Mart store, he had already established a chain of fifteen variety stores, which Tedlow termed a 'variety store empire'.[113] As Tedlow notes, Walton had already 'learned a lot of lessons which were to stand him in good stead in the future'.[114] In particular, he had learnt how to establish a retail empire in this southwest region of the country. In a sense his 1960s–70s creation of a regional Wal-Mart empire was merely applying what he had learnt to a *different type* of retailing—to discount retailing rather than variety-store retailing. It was only when Wal-Mart spread from the southwest to other regions that Walton entered unfamiliar territory in his empire-building.

Walton learnt, too, from experimenting with his pre-Wal-Mart retail empire and small-town strategy. Tedlow points out that he was experimenting with larger-scale variety stores in the same year as he was moving into discount retailing with his first Wal-Mart store. For in 1962 he opened a very large variety store in a very small town and, later in the year, opened another of these Family Center stores in a similarly small town of only 2,000 people.[115] According to Walton, he 'learned that by building larger stores, which we called family centers, we could do unheard of amounts of business for variety stores' in small towns.[116] In fact the opening of the first Wal-Mart store may have been a similar experiment, not just a forced adaptive response to the rise of discount retailing.

Certainly the early Wal-Mart stores benefited from Walton's willingness to experiment with large stores in small towns. An early Wal-Mart store was located in a town of 6,000 people to find out if customers in such a small town would buy merchandise from this kind of store 'strictly because of price. The answer was yes'.[117] And a larger Wal-Mart store was located in a larger town 'to learn something else: would a really big, nice store work in a larger town?'[118] Once again, the answer was yes and once again Walton had learnt from experimenting.

Perhaps the most memorable example of learning from mistakes, experience, and experimenting was what Walton learnt from an experience on a tourist trip. His book mentions how in 1975 he was visiting Japan and South Korea and came across the idea of a company cheer.[119] He was so impressed that he introduced a similar cheer at Wal-Mart and would lead store workers in this company cheer when he visited their stores. 'During these visits it was Walton's practice, on arrival, to gather his employees around him and lead them in a rousing corporate cheer'.[120]

The company cheer was also an example of a *third* form of learning: what he learnt and copied from other businesses. But this form of learning was largely about copying from his competitors. Walton acknowledged that 'most everything I've done I've copied from somebody else'—who was often one of his competitors.[121] This might be viewed as merely an extension of his research into new developments in the retail industry but Walton was very open about how much he had copied from his competitors and on occasion even described this as stealing ideas.[122] Kmart in particular was a competitor who provided Walton with a lot of ideas in the early years of Wal-Mart. He wandered through their stores 'talking to their people and trying to figure out how they did things'.[123] Trimble refers to him as 'haunting' his competitors' stores, 'on the lookout for methods and means, finesse and fault, the winning and losing tricks of mass merchandisers'.[124]

A fourth form of learning involved visiting his *own* stores, to learn from his store workers. Walton maintained that visiting his stores and listening to store workers was one of the most valuable uses of his time.[125] Ortega describes store-visiting Walton as 'attentive and avuncular, getting hourly workers away from their managers to get their feedback'.[126] They gave him, too, new ideas for marketing and customer-relations improvements. According to Walton, 'our best ideas usually come from our people in the stores' and especially from 'the people who are actually on the firing line, those who deal with the customers'.[127] Furthermore, the store workers provided him with the sort of information about a store that did not show up in its performance figures for sales, payroll, and so forth. Walton learnt much from his computerized monitoring of these figures, but he also believed that monitoring store performance by computer could never be 'a substitute for getting out in your stores and learning what's going on'.[128] One of his senior executives later made a similar point in more dramatic fashion. Soderquist suggested that 'nothing will demoralize those who work for you more quickly than when you no longer have an active knowledge of what's going on in the business.'[129]

Dassault's *Talisman* Aviation Learning

The final section will leave Wal-Mart and retailing for a very different industry in a different country: the aviation corporation established in France by Marcel Dassault. For Walton was not the first leader to use learning as an appropriate rational method of developing a corporation: some years earlier, Dassault had used and indeed emphasized learning as a rational method of establishing a corporation. So this section will be confirming, through the Dassault example, that learning is an additional, seventh rational method of developing a corporation and can be just as effective as the adaptive, calculative, and deliberative methods.

In the 1940s–60s, Dassault established the iconic aircraft-construction corporation Dassault Aviation.[130] And he became France's wealthiest businessman by developing it into an aviation-based high-tech empire that even in the post-Dassault era was Europe's most successful producer of military and civil aircraft.[131] Furthermore, he provided an autobiographical, leader's-eye view of his use and indeed emphasizing of learning as a method of establishing a corporation.

His autobiography *The Talisman* was first published in France in 1969, with an English edition appearing two years later.[132] However, it dealt very briefly—only about a dozen pages—with his establishing of Dassault Aviation. Many more pages were spent describing his two earlier aircraft-construction firms and his life outside aviation, which included political and media pursuits and being sent to a Nazi concentration camp. When the book does discuss Dassault Aviation, though, it often mentions Dassault's use of learning and in fact this seems to be the only corporation-developing method that is mentioned anywhere in the book. But Dassault, like Walton, emphasized learning as a key method as well as a favourite method: because of his circumstances as well as his personal preferences.

The autobiography's account of even his first aircraft-construction firm displays his emphasis on learning. A chapter entitled 'How to Be an Airplane Manufacturer' begins by methodically explaining how he had acquired the expertise which enabled him to establish a successful firm in 1917. He had studied at an aeronautical engineering school, then learnt about design and manufacturing when employed to work on the Caudron G-3 and, finally, learnt about flight testing when in 1916 he became a major supplier of propellers to aircraft manufacturers.[133] They had allowed him to follow the development of their new airplanes and that was how he 'learned the techniques of flight testing and final preparation of a new airplane. Having learned which new models succeeded and which ones failed, I was able to acquire a great deal of experience in deciding what should and should not be done to make a good airplane'.[134]

He became confident enough to start up his own aircraft-construction firm, which designed and manufactured a new, two-seater fighter plane.[135] This new learning experience included working with a business partner who was 'a very good engineer, an excellent businessman and a discerning financier. He taught me a lot of things during that period which stood me in good stead in later years'.[136]

When the war ended in 1918, Dassault did not try to keep his firm alive with airplane-related work but instead began a new career as a real-estate developer. The venture was financially successful and taught him many useful business lessons. It 'taught me a great many things which many people who have the luck (or bad luck) to succeed too early and too fast never are able to learn'.[137] And by 1930 he was prepared to start up a new aircraft-construction firm to take advantage of the new opportunities that were emerging.

When Dassault began his second career in aircraft construction, he had much to learn about new technology in this field and industry. As wood-and-fabric construction was becoming outmoded in 1930, he decided that his first aircraft—a postal-courier plane—would be an advanced, all-metal-construction design and therefore he hired several engineers to help him with the design and production.[138] Although the plane failed to win a production order, he used 'the techniques learned' to produce other all-metal-construction aircraft that were more commercially successful.[139]

He went on to become one of France's leading aircraft manufacturers.[140] In addition to building a twin-engine passenger plane for Air France, he built a series of military aircraft—a single-seat fighter, a twin-engine bomber, and a fast reconnaissance plane—as France modernized its air force to meet the threat from Fascist Italy and Nazi Germany. By the end of the 1930s he was building the prototype of a large four-engine transport plane that was impressive enough to be ordered into production by Nazi Germany's armed forces after they conquered France in 1940. Unlike his aircraft, however, Dassault was not well treated and was eventually sent to Buchenwald concentration camp.

After the Second World War, this 53-year-old survivor of a concentration camp began his third career in aircraft construction—and once again had to learn about a dramatic change in aviation technology. Now jet propulsion was making propeller engines outmoded for high-performance aircraft. But Dassault initially focused on simply producing his pre-war design for a large transport plane and developing a new propeller-driven twin-engine transport, which received a 300-plane production order in 1947.[141] By then he had begun developing a jet fighter airplane that would emerge two years later as the Ouragan, followed soon after by the Mystere and the supersonic Super-Mystere. In 1956, this line of jet fighters culminated in the Mirage prototype, which could fly at twice the speed of sound. All four fighter designs were ordered by the French air force and, furthermore, they won substantial export orders. Dassault Aviation also produced a shipboard fighter for the navy's aircraft carriers, a strategic bomber for the air force, and in the 1960s a business/executive jet—a very successful entry into the civil-aircraft market.

The success of Dassault Aviation was a vindication of the start-up strategy Dassault had learnt from the experience of his previous two careers in aircraft construction. His start-up strategy was noted by the French authors of a book on business heroes,

From Predators to Icons. They summed up the start of Dassault's third career in aircraft construction by pointing to the similarities with his two previous start-up ventures in this line of business.

> The relaunching of Marcel Dassault's business followed the same pattern as in 1917 [and 1930?]: manufacture of propellers, hiring of engineers, design of an aircraft that was *not* very innovative but responded perfectly to a precise need of the colonial administration, reconstruction of an industrial manufacturing apparatus, and finally the design of a more ambitious and *innovative* airplane: the Ouragan jet fighter in 1949.[142]

Yet his second, 1930s, career in aircraft construction had in fact *begun* with an innovative, all-metal-construction design. He had not stuck with the familiar but increasingly outmoded wood-and-fabric construction or, more appropriately, opted for the compromise of metal-and-fabric construction. This compromise was adopted several years later by the British Hawker Hurricane fighter, which was still numerically the RAF's main fighter plane when it defeated the Nazi aerial onslaught on Britain in 1940. The Hurricane has been described by a military historian as a 'derivative' design, in the sense of 'building upon a proven technology', and especially in the case of its braced-frame fuselage of metal frame and fabric covering.[143] It is surprising that Dassault did not choose a similar compromise when he returned to aircraft construction in 1930 and instead had preferred a more advanced, all-metal-construction design.

As the design initially failed to win any orders, he may well have considered in hindsight that this strategy was a mistake—and that he had been taught a lesson for future reference. So his start-up strategy in 1945–7 may well have been based on a lesson he had learnt from the 1930 start-up, namely not to begin too innovatively. Indeed, Dassault Aviation's official history notes that as late as 1947 Dassault felt that military jets were an opportunity to be exploited 'on condition that one avoided falling into the trap of trying to produce unduly ambitious aircraft'.[144]

This lesson from the 1930s may even have been the basis of the distinctive Dassault Aviation product-development strategy. It had been evident ever since his military-jet programme began in 1947 and it led to a series of very successful designs. The strategy

> seeks to draw maximal advantage from the technical experience acquired from working on successive aircraft, and to avoid disruptive changes, leading—one step at a time—to progress on new models and to innovations limited to the intended objective, wherever possible using tried and tested solutions at a minimum of risk.[145]

Dassault's personal contribution to this product development was an area in which his emphasis on learning was very evident. In his autobiography he recounts presiding at Saturday-afternoon deliberative and learning meetings to 'talk about the final preparation of our planes and new projects to be developed'.[146] Unlike Walton's Saturday-morning meetings, there were not many participants and most were technical specialists, such as his firm's technical director, testing-centre engineers, and test pilots.[147] Dassault's willingness to learn from his test pilots was evident, too, at flight-testing stage and helped him to make improvements during this late stage in the development of his airplanes. 'I analyse the impressions of the test pilots in order to improve the plane's stability and also to make it more responsive to the controls and easier to handle'.[148]

Such willingness to learn about what needs improving was not characteristic of all aircraft manufacturers in this era of aviation. For example, it seems to have been comparatively uncommon in the British aircraft industry during the pioneering 1944–54 decade of the jet age. Waterton's book on test-flying during this decade has argued that British firms tended to be influenced too much by airplane designers, who did not like a test pilot criticizing 'their baby' and, 'like doting parents, blinded themselves to its faults'.[149] The contrast with Dassault Aviation is highlighted by the French firm's test-engineering maxims: (1) the pilot is always right; (2) the engineer can never be too careful; (3) there is no such thing as 'normal'; and (4) optimism is the worst enemy.[150] Waterton claimed that British firms actually ignored test pilots' criticisms and warnings, even though the pilots were representing what customers and potential customers were going to say about the airplane.[151] In contrast, Dassault's autobiography depicts him as keen to learn from his test pilots so that he could improve the plane *before* it was assessed by outsiders and potential customers. His test pilots would therefore never experience the situation which Waterton had in mind when he noted that nothing is 'more infuriating and humiliating than to attempt to put over one's points to someone who just doesn't want to know—especially when he is the person who makes decisions'.[152] At Dassault Aviation, the person who made the decisions certainly did want to know about his airplanes.

Dassault's readiness to learn was evident, too, in his increasingly export-oriented marketing strategy.[153] It involved learning how to deal with foreign governments and companies that were very different from France's but could see the advantages of buying Dassault's excellent aircraft. He notes in his autobiography that the two planes of which he was especially proud had both been great export successes: more than 900 of the Mirage fighters had been sold to foreign air forces and more than 400 Falcon business/executive jets had been sold around the world.[154] The Mirage had become internationally famous as Israel's key fighter plane in its victorious 1967 war with Egypt, Syria, and Jordan. The Falcon had become well known in America, where the majority of Falcons had been sold, but it was not known so much as a Dassault, French product because Pan American Airways had acquired an exclusive agency and set up a Business-Jet Corporation to market the plane.[155]

By the time Dassault was writing about these export successes, he had long since relinquished managerial control of his corporation. In the 1950s, he resigned as managing director—though remaining in charge of 'technical and industrial management'—and seems to have formed a dual-leadership team with Vallières, his managing director.[156] Vallières also became company chairman when Dassault

Aviation became a public company in 1968, and he would continue as joint-leader until the founder's death in 1986, when Dassault's son Serge took over as chairman and CEO.[157] By then it was a classic example of a leader using learning to establish a corporation in an internationally competitive industry, which had undergone dramatic changes since he first began designing wooden propellers for airplanes that were little different from the Wright brothers' plane.

6
Intel

Grove's *Only the Paranoid Survive*

Some five years after Walton died, Andy Grove became *Time* magazine's 1997 'man of the year' and by then he was 'arguably, the most admired business leader of his era'.[1] He was leader of a brilliantly successful high-tech corporation, Intel, which manufactured silicon semiconductor microchips and specialized in the most sophisticated microchips: the microprocessor CPU (central processing unit) chips which were the heart and brain of desktop personal computers. Intel had been founded by Robert Noyce and Gordon Moore in 1968 but during the early 1970s their dual-leadership team developed into triple leadership, with their key manager, Andy Grove, joining them as the third member of the team. By the end of the 1970s, Noyce was taking a less active role in Intel's affairs, leaving CEO Moore and Grove to develop a two-role version of dual leadership.

In 1987, Grove became CEO and the sole leader of the corporation. He held the position until 1998 and then served as Intel's chairman until his retirement in 2005. During his eleven years as CEO, Grove presided over Intel's golden age. Sales increased from nearly $2 billion in 1987 to more than $26 billion in 1998 and there was a spectacular increase in profitability.[2] Intel's ranking on the Fortune 500 list of America's largest corporations rocketed up from 200 to 38, and it became the world's largest manufacturer of semiconductor microchips, with a near-monopoly in the production of personal-computer microprocessors.[3]

Another reason, however, why Grove was such an admired business leader is that he had written a highly acclaimed management text *Only the Paranoid Survive*. This partly autobiographical work was published in 1996 and when the paperback edition appeared a few years later, it had several impressive testimonials on its back cover. Reviewers had ranked it with Sloan's *My Years with General Motors* and there was a perceptive testimonial from Steve Jobs: 'This book is about one super-important concept. You must learn about Strategic Inflection Points, because sooner or later you are going to live through one'. The book was indeed largely about inflection-point crises but it also taught the reader how to survive or even exploit these adaptive crises and, furthermore, the lessons were based on what the author had learnt from personal experience.

Grove's book therefore provides a leader's-eye view of learning—the seventh rational method—being used to enhance a corporation. Indeed, Grove emphasized learning as a method of developing his corporation and so this chapter is in a sense

Rational Leadership. Paul Brooker and Margaret Hayward, Oxford University Press. © Paul Brooker & Margaret Hayward (2023). DOI: 10.1093/oso/9780198894643.003.0006

extending the previous chapter's account of how Walton and Dassault emphasized learning. Like them, Grove seems to have emphasized learning as both a favourite and a key method: this seems to be due to both personal preference and the circumstances he was facing. Unlike Walton and Dassault, however, he was enhancing rather than establishing a corporation and in fact he enhanced Intel in two different ways. First, through learning from experience Grove enhanced Intel's crisis management in the crucially important area of responding to adaptive crises.[4] Second, by basing a book upon this learning Grove enhanced Intel's reputation in the business world. The corporation was now seen to be led by an executive who was willing and able to teach the whole business world how to deal with these crises.

In addition to these enhancements, Grove was inspiring his employee-followers with rational confidence. He was using and indeed emphasizing an appropriate rational method, learning, and he had very capably learnt (acquiring broad and in-depth knowledge) how to deal with adaptive crises. The evidence was there for all to see in his book's theoretical as well as practical account of these crises. Grove's book included not just personal experiences but also (1) examples of how other firms and industries had suffered similar adaptive crises, (2) a crisis-management framework for dealing with these crises, and (3) new concepts—'inflection point' and '10x' change—with which to analyse and discuss such extraordinary crises.[5]

What is more, Grove's book and its crisis-management framework showed how to use the appropriate rational methods when dealing with an adaptive crisis. The most important method was rapid adaptation, even if Grove seemed to emphasize it more in theory than practice and as a lesson to be learnt rather than a method that he had used effectively in the past. In fact, the crisis-management framework is best termed the 'adaptive' framework because it is both dealing with adaptive crises and using rapid adaptation as the most important method of dealing with these crises. His framework also mentions, however, all the other rational methods of developing a corporation, even if they are not always mentioned clearly or favourably.

Grove's enhancement of Intel will therefore be viewed through the 'prism' of his book. The first section of the chapter will discuss his book's account of Intel's adaptive crises in 1985 and 1994. The second section will examine the three-stage adaptive framework that he presents as an aid to dealing with adaptive crises. The third section of the chapter will focus on a part of Grove's framework that is especially relevant to high-tech industries and firms: the *pre*-deliberation process of *experimentation*. This process provides alternatives, such as new products, to choose from when senior management is deliberating about how to respond to an adaptive crisis. Furthermore, the process is crucially important even when a firm is not facing an adaptive crisis but instead the more 'ordinary' problem of ensuring that it is producing a constant stream of innovations and even some diversification.

So this third section will look at how Intel encouraged the invention of the microprocessor and then will move on to David Packard's 1995 memoirs *The HP Way: How Bill Hewlett and I Built Our Company*. Packard's book tells how he and the co-founder of Hewlett-Packard (HP) encouraged experimentation and diversification. They even developed an innovative experimentation system that was based on

HP's version of the decentralized organizational structure which Sloan had pioneered at General Motors. However, HP's remarkable experimentation system eventually ran out of steam, and the chapter will end with a section that explores a different approach. This is Steve Jobs's relatively top-down and hands-on approach to experimentation and diversification, which gave Apple a series of brilliantly successful new products in the 2000s: the iPod, iPhone, and iPad.

Learning to Adapt Intel

Grove's book is subtitled *How to Exploit the Crisis Points that Challenge Every Company* and indeed his key concept is the adaptive 'crisis point' that he terms a 'strategic inflection point'. Grove coined this term to describe points in time, in the history of a business or industry, when 'the old strategic picture dissolves and gives way to the new'.[6] The old ways of doing business are giving way to the new and, after the inflection point, business is more like the new ways than the old ways. But these 'full-scale changes in the way business is conducted' are often difficult to identify and understand:

> All businesses operate by some set of unstated rules and sometimes these rules change—often in very significant ways. Yet there is no flashing sign that heralds these rule changes. They creep up on you ... You know only that something has changed, something big, something significant, even if it's not entirely clear what that something is.[7]

It is not surprising that 'companies struggle to adapt' to such changes in the rules of business but it is more surprising that Grove wanted 'to share the lessons I've learned' about these adaptive crises—to share the thinking about them that 'has helped our business survive in an increasingly competitive environment'.[8]

His key lesson was the need to emphasize *rapid adaptation* to overcome the tendency towards rigidity—resistance to adaptation—that often occurs in these adaptive crises. The tendency towards rigidity is evident in the two Intel cases that Grove presents as illustrations of a strategic inflection point. The earlier of the two occurred in the mid-1980s, when Intel was led by the dual-leadership team of CEO Moore and chief operating officer (COO) Grove. The origins of the crisis can be traced back to the founding of Intel in 1968 as a manufacturer of memory microchips—the silicon semiconductor chips that were used to store memory in computers and other electronic devices. The new firm was very successful, becoming a public company as early as 1971, and by the 1980s Intel was one of the leading firms in the now greatly expanded memory-chip business. But by then, too, Japanese firms had become increasingly competitive players in the American semiconductor industry. Grove acknowledges that 'the Japanese started beating us in the memory [chip] business in the early eighties'.[9] In fact their mass production of low-priced high-quality memory chips was changing the rules of business in the industry.

Fortunately for Intel, however, its other microchip product—the microprocessor—was becoming increasingly popular and was not so vulnerable to competition. Intel had developed this data-processing, calculating microchip in the 1970s but it seemed to have limited commercial potential until in 1981 IBM included an Intel microprocessor in the design of its first desktop personal computer. This 'IBM PC' was so successful that most later versions and brands of personal computer were called 'PCs'. Furthermore, Intel's microprocessor was also included in the 'cloned' versions of this IBM PC, which were developed and manufactured by new firms entering the rapidly expanding personal-computer market. This growing microprocessor business could therefore offset the losses produced by the change of rules in the memory-chip business.

But in 1984 the market for microprocessors suffered a cyclical downturn and so Intel's microprocessor sales and profits could no longer offset the losses in the memory-chip business.[10] Intel's forced adaptive response to this crisis was to get out of the memory-chip business and focus its efforts on microprocessor chips and markets. However, it took until mid-1985 to make the adaptive decision and took until 1987 to complete the adaptive change. Jackson's *Inside Intel* argues that the trends which provoked the 1985 decision 'had been at work for at least five years, and possibly more. Had Intel taken steps to respond to them early, it might never have been forced to abandon one of its two core businesses'.[11] What is more, Jackson criticizes the tardy way in which Intel implemented its long-delayed decision to make the appropriate adaptive response. After it was finally decided in mid-1985 to get out of the memory-chip business, 'it took a full further year before Intel had implemented the decision to pull out—and another full year before the company could return to profitability'.[12] So Intel's policy-making and policy-implementing response to the adaptive crisis seems a classic example of rigid resistance to adaptation.

Intel's second adaptive crisis occurred in 1994, when Grove was CEO and sole leader of the corporation. Its latest-generation microprocessor, the Pentium microchip, suffered from a slight design flaw that on extremely rare occasions—some once every nine billion times—produced a small error in the chip's long-division calculations. Near the end of 1994, Internet and media reports about the 'Pentium Bug' led to Intel coming under intense public scrutiny and criticism as well as having to handle thousands of inquiries and complaints from users of computers containing the Pentium microprocessor. Initially, Intel's response was to provide only *some* users with an error-free replacement Pentium, namely those who were making a lot of calculations and therefore much more likely to experience the error. It was not until weeks after the crisis began that the corporation changed its response and offered a replacement to *any* user who asked for one. This change in policy ended the crisis but, as in the 1985 case, the correct decision was too long delayed.

In the Pentium case, however, the delay and rigidity seems to have had both short-term and longer term aspects. For Jackson argues that the delay of weeks in responding with the appropriate policy was due to a preceding delay of *years* in adopting a more marketing-oriented perspective.

[Grove] and his colleagues still looked at the world from an engineering rather than a marketing point of view. Branding, image, consumer psychology—all the factors that argued for taking a short-term cost in order to maintain the value of the Intel name in customers' minds were just beginning to appear on the Intel horizon.[13]

If Intel's leadership had adopted a more marketing-oriented perspective in the early 1990s, it would not have been so slow in 1994 to respond in the appropriately apologetic and generous, full-replacement fashion.

Grove explains Intel's rigidity in 1985 and 1994 as largely due to its leaders' failure to perceive that the times or circumstances had changed. In the Pentium case, he acknowledges that the delay was due to his failure to perceive that the rules of business had changed. 'It took a barrage of relentless criticism to make me realize that something had changed' in Intel's marketing environment and that 'we needed to adapt to the new environment'.[14] In hindsight Grove ascribes the change to his firm's early 1990s 'Intel Inside' marketing strategy, because it had led owners of PCs emblazoned with the 'Intel Inside' label to consider themselves customers of Intel and to view its microprocessor in the same light as any other household goods they had bought—and would want replaced if the product was faulty.[15] But as Grove was not a marketing expert, it is hardly surprising that he had been slow to perceive this change in the marketing environment and had not seen the risks involved in the new marketing strategy when it had been proposed a few years earlier.

In the 1985 crisis, however, the problem and perceptions had been more complex. In this case, there had been a change in the competitive environment, not the marketing environment, and it had been created by the challenge from highly competitive Japanese firms. In this case, too, the resistance to adaptation had involved more than simply a failure of perception; it had also involved intellectual prejudices and an emotional attachment to memory chips—the product on which Intel had been based. 'Intel equalled memories in all our minds. How could we give up our identity?'[16] Grove notes that these are the sorts of situation in which CEOs who have been brought in from outside their firms have the advantage, being 'unencumbered by such emotional involvement and therefore are capable of applying an impersonal logic to the situation'.[17] Such impersonal logic would also be applied by any leader capably using the appropriate rational method—rapid adaptation.

At times it might also be appropriate to use the other adaptive method, innovative adaptation.[18] There seems to have been nothing innovative about Intel's adaptive responses in 1985 and 1994. The latter was merely adopting the standard crisis-management approach of any consumer-oriented corporation; the other was merely a 'strategic exit' downsizing, namely getting out of the memory-chip business. As Grove points out, downsizing is a low-risk as well as unimaginative response: 'after all, how can you go wrong by shuttering factories and laying people off if the benefits of such actions are going to show up in tomorrow's bottom line and will be applauded by the financial commu- nity?'[19] In Intel's case, the post-1985 downsizing involved closing factories, cutting more than 7,000 jobs, and laying off more than a quarter of the firm's employment base.[20]

But there may have also been an *innovative* aspect to Intel's adaptive response. For CEO Moore's biographers imply that Intel's innovative shift to sole-source production of its new 386 microprocessor was part of the response to the crisis: it was part of how 'Gordon Moore turned Intel around' and of 'Gordon's plan to reinvigorate Intel'.[21] According to Grove's biographer, becoming 'the sole source for the new microprocessor it introduced in October of 1985' was a 'vital part of Intel's strategy'.[22] By shifting to sole-sourcing, Intel was rejecting the standard practice of providing manufacturer customers with a second source of supply. Such second-sourcing 'was a long established practice in the semiconductor industry' as manufacturers 'demanded that semiconductor suppliers license their technologies to fellow chip companies to guarantee a continuous supply' and of course as protection against sole-source monopolistic pricing and practices.[23]

Intel could now, however, risk disregarding its customers' preferences and shifting to sole-source production of its 386 microprocessor. After all, its major customers were manufacturing IBM and IBM/clone PCs that had been designed to use not only Intel microprocessors but also Microsoft software, which was now being designed to run on Intel microprocessors. This monopolistic combination of Microsoft's Windows operating system and Intel's microprocessor—the 'Wintel' combination—gave Intel what Moore judged to be 'enough of a lock' on its computer-manufacturing customers to have them 'buy the processor from us anyhow, even if we were the sole source' and the customers preferred a less monopolistic situation.[24] As IBM/clone PCs were dominating the growing personal-computer market, Intel's decision to sole-source production led to its microprocessors being included in two-thirds of the nine million personal computers sold in 1987.[25]

This innovative, monopolistic aspect of Intel's adaptive response made a huge contribution to the firm's spectacular revival. 'Monopoly-based profits gave Intel an astounding recovery to revenue of $2 billion and a record $250 million profit' only a year after the corporation had made its first ever loss.[26] The leadership team's rigidity had been offset and overshadowed by the success and brilliance of its eventual response. Indeed Grove's biographer declares that the 'decision to sole-source the 386 [microprocessor] proved a masterstroke' and was 'among the most important strategic moves in the history of the computer industry'.[27] The lesson to be learnt from this case was that the rapidity of an adaptive response was less important than its *quality* and, furthermore, a high-quality response required some innovation.

When Grove became CEO in 1987, he inherited a crisis-management approach that he and Moore had oriented towards high-quality, innovative adaptations rather than rapid adaptive responses. But Grove significantly reoriented it towards an aspect of adaptation that is normally associated with a non-threatening situation, namely the opportunistic aspect of 'identifying and taking full advantage of the opportunities offered' that was mentioned in Chapters 1 and 3. Taking advantage of an opportunity is mentioned, too, in Grove's book and indeed he points out that an inflection-point change can be an opportunity rather than a threat. 'When the way business is being conducted changes, it creates opportunities for players who are adept at operating in the new way. This can apply to newcomers or to incumbents' who find that the change brings 'an opportunity for a new period of growth'.[28] Grove reoriented Intel's crisis-management approach towards this opportunity-for-growth perspective in the late 1980s and in fact he oriented it towards taking full advantage of this opportunity for growth. During his tenure as CEO, Intel took full advantage of its new position as a monopolistic supplier to the constantly expanding personal-computer market. By 1996, some *seventy* million personal computers were being sold worldwide, more than 80 per cent had an Intel microprocessor inside, and the corporation was enjoying gratifyingly high profit margins on these products: a few years earlier, its more than 25 per cent return on sales had led to Intel being described as the world's most profitable firm of that size.[29]

Taking full advantage of this opportunity had involved Intel's use of the fearsome 'treadmill' strategy. It had been devised by Moore and learnt by Grove in the 1970s and was employed against firms that were manufacturing their own versions of the microprocessor. The treadmill strategy was based on an idea that became known as Moore's Law of semiconductor development: the most famous generalization produced by the high-tech industries.[30] In 1975, Moore had explicitly formulated this 'Law' as a prediction that the capability of semiconductor microchips would continue to double every year for another decade and then would slow to a doubling of capability every *two* years.[31] With microchip capability growing at this rapid and predictable rate, he would aim to put his competitors on the 'treadmill' by continually producing new generations of ever more capable microchips—thereby staying ahead of his competitors and forcing them into perpetually running to catch up. In Moore's words:

> You must keep moving to stay with or ahead of the competition. Anyone who wants to compete has to make a huge investment. If we have 80-plus percent market share and our competitor has 20 percent, we spend fast enough that he has a really tough time keeping up. 'Get'em on the treadmill'.[32]

His Japanese competitors in the memory-chip business had eventually defeated the treadmill strategy, but when it was applied to the microprocessor business, the treadmill would continue to be an effective monopolistic strategy throughout the 1980s–90s.

Grove used the treadmill particularly effectively when Intel was threatened by a surge of competition in the early 1990s. This 'formidable competition' included rival microprocessors, rival technology, and some new competitors, especially a consortium of Apple, IBM, and Motorola that sought 'to break Intel's stranglehold on the personal computer CPU [microprocessor] industry'.[33] In typical treadmill fashion, however, Grove announced in 1993 the arrival of Intel's latest-generation microprocessor, the Pentium, which was *five times* more capable than its predecessor, the 486, and was better than anything the competition could offer.[34]

But the Pentium proved to be a mixed blessing for Grove, as was discussed earlier. The 1994 Pentium-bug adaptive crisis highlighted his failure to perceive an inflection-point change in the marketing environment. This may explain why his book, written the following year, tends to view inflection-point changes as a threat rather than an opportunity. For example, when he examines the causes of these strategic inflection points, his analysis is more concerned with threat than opportunity. He identifies six forces that 'determine the competitive well-being of a business': the power, vigour, and competence of (1) existing competitors, (2) potential competitors, (3) suppliers, (4) customers, (5) complementors, from whom customers buy complementary products, and (6) the 'substitution' factor, which is the 'possibility that your product or service can be built or delivered in a different way'—and is the 'most deadly' of these six forces.[35] A very large change in one of these six forces is called a '10x' change, 'suggesting that the force has become ten times what it was just recently'.[36] Among his examples were two which have been mentioned in earlier chapters. His example of a 10x change in competition was the change experienced by general stores in small towns affected by the arrival of Wal-Mart, and his example of a 10x change in customers was the 1920s change in people's taste in cars, which caused the inflection point that threatened Ford and was an opportunity exploited by Sloan's General Motors.[37]

Grove viewed the Internet as an inflection point that represented more of an opportunity than a threat for Intel.[38] Exploiting this opportunity, though, would require Intel to make a major adaptive response to the new environment: 'we won't harness the opportunity by simply letting things happen to us'.[39] Intel was, however, already enjoying an Internet-propelled boom that was in fact simply happening to it without the need for a high-quality, innovative adaptive response. Malone points out that its consumer customers were upgrading their PCs (and the microprocessors inside them) in order to access the new features becoming available on the Internet: 'images, then audio, then video'.[40] Intel's revenue was therefore increasing 'at a pace that seemed almost impossible for a company of its size': from nearly $6 billion in 1992 to $16 billion in 1996 and over $33 billion in 2000.[41] This now iconic corporation was once again taking full advantage of its opportunities and seemed to be a great advertisement for the lessons taught by Grove's book, especially its recommended framework for overcoming adaptive crises.

The Three-Stage Adaptive Framework

Grove's book both described strategic inflection points and sought 'to provide a framework in which to deal with them'.[42] The later chapters of his book explain and explore this three-stage adaptive framework. In addition to adaptation, it involves other rational methods of developing a corporation—the deliberative methods and learning—which in this case are enhancing a corporation or any other firm by reducing the threat and/or exploiting the opportunity created by an adaptive crisis.

In effect Grove provides a framework for using rapid adaptation as a rational method of developing a corporation in these specific circumstances—dealing with an adaptive crisis. However, the adaptive framework is not 'all about' rapid adaptation; there is room for other rational methods to play a role in one or more of its

three stages. The first stage is basically about *learning* that an adaptive crisis is coming, the second stage is about *deliberating* on how to respond to this inflection point,
and the third stage also includes a deliberative element because the implementation
of the response will involve discussions with employees about why and how the firm
is going to implement this new direction.

In the first stage of the framework, learning is crucial because it provides some
warning—as early as possible—that a crisis is coming. Learning that a crisis is coming
will involve listening to the firm's Cassandra-like 'prophets of doom', because they are
'quick to recognize impending change and cry out an early warning' that the change
may well create a crisis.[43] Cassandras are typically middle-management people who
have a different perspective from senior management and have a tendency to 'take
the warning signs more seriously' because they are serving in the front lines of the
firm.[44] Listening to them is 'an investment in learning what goes on at the distant
periphery of your business' and of course 'the flow of bad news from the periphery'
should never be discouraged by a leader if he or she wants some early warning of an
impending inflection-point crisis.[45]

In contrast, Grove is dubious about using quantitative calculation in this first,
learning stage. In fact 'when dealing with emerging trends, you may very well have to
go against rational extrapolation of data and rely instead on anecdotal observations
and your instincts'.[46] Furthermore, relying upon quantitative calculation may cause a
delay in moving on to the next stage and making some response to the crisis. 'Timing
is everything' but 'that means acting when not everything is known, when the data
aren't yet in. Even those who believe in a scientific approach to management will
have to rely on instinct and personal judgement'.[47]

It should be noted that Grove was happy to use and indeed emphasize quantitative calculation in *other circumstances*, when dealing with other problems and policy
decisions. He 'believed that everything should be measured, quantitatively if at all
possible', and had developed an Intel culture that valued not only quantification
but problem-solving based on quantitative data.[48] Yet when the circumstances—an
adaptive crisis—demanded it, he downplayed the role of quantitative calculation.

The other calculative method, strategic calculation, has an ambivalent role in his
adaptive framework. Grove mentions strategic calculation only by implication—by
referring to strategy—and his remarks indicate that not much calculation is required.
He expresses a preference for strategic actions rather than plans and for pursuing
an 'early-mover' strategy: only through 'such a strategy can you hope to compete
for the future' of an industry, even if being early leads to mistakes that require the
firm to 'course-correct'.[49] So Grove can hardly be said to advocate using strategic
calculation in these inflection-point circumstances, even if in other circumstances
he clearly favoured its use.[50]

Unlike strategic and quantitative calculation, the two deliberative methods play a
crucial role in his adaptive framework. In the first stage, there may be some deliberation about whether a particular development is indeed an inflection point and
then, more importantly, in the second stage there is always deliberation about how
to respond to the crisis: a 'powerful adaptive organization' therefore 'tolerates and

even encourages debate. These debates are vigorous, devoted to exploring issues, indifferent to rank and include individuals of varied backgrounds.'[51] Such debates are an excellent example of diverse deliberation, but Grove does not provide any comparable examples of the institutionalized form of deliberation. In fact his memorable example of this form of deliberation occurs in the following, final stage of the adaptive framework.

The final, third stage is focused on *implementing* the firm's *response* to the inflection-point crisis—implementing the firm's new strategic direction. Grove's account of this stage is largely concerned with how firms' leaders communicate the response, the new direction, to their firms' employees. He stresses that this communication must involve an interactive element, which enables employees to ask the leader for clarification, explanations, and solutions.[52] So there will be some discussion about why and how the firm is taking this new direction and the discussion will include some deliberation, even if only about finding solutions to problems that may arise when implementing the new direction.

Furthermore, the interactive communication will involve some *institutionalized* deliberation, such as the leader having workplace discussions with employees. Grove argues that the best method of communicating a new direction to employees is to 'go to their workplaces, get them together and explain over and over what you're trying to achieve' by speaking to them and answering their questions.[53] However, this kind of institutionalized deliberation is not very appropriate in a corporation or any large firm because its leader is 'often distanced from direct contact with many managers and employees'.[54] How can a leader communicate with all of a corporation's many employees and still retain an interactive element in the communication?

Email was Grove's solution to the problem of combining interaction with mass communication. He saw email as a way of not only reaching large numbers of employees but also answering their questions: 'the electronic equivalent of answering a question at an employee forum'.[55] Email had begun to be adopted by some firms in the early 1980s, and so by the time Grove's book appeared in 1996 email was a well-established way of communicating with employees.[56] However, two shortcomings had already emerged.

Email was an emotionally 'distant' form of communication that lacked the personal, facial, and voice aspect of leaders' workplace visits or even a Walton-like television broadcast.[57] In addition, there was the practical problem that emails from the leader might produce too many replies for personal interaction and discussion to be feasible. For example, there were nearly 6,000 replies when General Electric's CEO Jack Welch sent out his first company-wide email.[58]

But there seemed to be no alternative for a corporation as large and global as Intel. Grove argued that in these cases, '"managing by walking around" has to a large extent been supplanted by letting your fingers do the walking on your computer'.[59] Managing by walking around (MBWA) was a Hewlett-Packard invention that Packard described as a technique 'for helping managers and supervisors to know their people and understand the work their people are doing, while at the same time making themselves more visible and accessible to their people'.[60] Now the computer had to provide an electronic equivalent of MBWA and of the workplace employee forum's questions, answers, and discussion.

Anyway, communicating the new direction was only part of this final, implementation stage in Grove's framework. Implementing the new direction would involve other processes, problems, and perhaps even further stages towards a 'resolution' of the adaptive crisis. Similarly, the second, deliberative stage had both included and been preceded by a process of experimentation. Grove describes this experimentation process as the *pre*-deliberation aspect of the debates about how to respond to the adaptive crisis. He points out that 'in order to explore your alternatives' there have to be alternatives *available*, such as new products that are worth considering.[61] They are products that the firm has been experimenting with and now considers sufficiently credible alternatives to be worth exploring in a debate about how to respond to the adaptive crisis. And it is too late to *begin* experimenting at this stage of the adaptive process. As Grove stresses, 'you can't suddenly start experimenting when you're in trouble' and wondering how to respond:

> It's too late to do it once things have changed in your core business. Ideally you should have experimented with new products, technologies, channels, promotions and new customers all along ... Intel experimented with microprocessors for over ten years before the opportunity and the imperative arose to make them the centrepiece of our corporate strategy.[62]

His depiction of the 1985 crisis as 'the opportunity and the imperative' is much more accurate than his remark about Intel having 'experimented' with microprocessors for over ten years beforehand. Intel had been selling this 'new' product for several years and indeed came to depend upon it in the early 1980s as sales of the firm's memory-chip product were increasingly affected by Japanese competition.

In fact, Intel seems to have reduced its experimentation in the ten years before the 1985 crisis. It had publicly announced the invention of the microprocessor as early as 1971 and was producing its third-generation microprocessor by 1975, when co-founder Noyce was Intel's president/CEO, co-founder Moore its executive vice-president, and Grove its operations manager.[63] Noyce's biographer suggests that 'the microprocessor would not have happened at Intel if it had not been for Bob' and certainly Noyce seems to have been the leading advocate of the microprocessor's technological and commercial potential.[64] When in 1975 he announced his retirement as president/CEO, he noted that Intel's 'entrepreneurial phase is not entirely over but the emphasis is shifting'.[65] And in the mid-1970s Grove was announcing that Intel would be copying McDonald's standardization of product and production.[66]

Intel's lack of an experimentation process can readily explain the corporation's poor record of diversification in the 1980s–2000s. In 2005, Grove presented a blunt, revealing assessment of his corporation's track record of experimentation and diversification:

Intel had been 'shitty' at diversifying no matter whether through acquisition or internal venturing [within the firm]. The reason was a combined lack of 'strategic recognition' and 'strategic will'. Whatever Intel tried did not, after a year or two, look as good as the microprocessor. The result was that the company consistently gave up too soon.[67]

If Intel 'gave up too soon' on innovations because they did not 'look as good as the microprocessor', this may have been largely because Grove had reoriented the corporation towards taking full advantage of opportunities—as it had with the microprocessor—instead of coming up with high-quality, innovative adaptations. The post-Grove leadership seems to have been unable to re-reorient and, furthermore, it seems to have been unable to create an effective experimentation process that would supply new products when they were needed.

In the 2000s, Intel was in need of new products to consider in its deliberations about how to deal with a new technological change. Mobile high-tech and IT products, especially mobile phones, were becoming more prominent than personal computers, and the change was being exploited not by Intel but by such firms as ARM. Malone notes that this British chip-designing firm had 'spotted the opportunity in mobile early and created superb designs specifically for use in laptop computers, palmtops, and the new generation of cell phones'.[68] As Apple was one of its founding investors, ARM also had 'an inside track to be maker of the processor of choice for the greatest run of innovation in tech history': the iPod, iPhone, and iPad.[69] Although Intel missed out on this run of innovation, its former leader had at least provided an analysis of how to deal with the problem of being an innovative firm and diversifying into new products. His analysis of experimentation and deliberation was arguably his book's most significant and widely applicable lesson, as it applied not only to adaptive crises but also to a firm's 'ordinary' problems of innovation and diversification.

Experimentation and *The HP Way*

As Grove described, deliberating about new products and having a pre-deliberative experimentation process are vital aspects of high-tech firms' deliberative and adaptive processes. For example, Intel's successful 1985 adaptation can be traced back to its invention of the microprocessor in the far-off days when the firm still had an effective experimentation process. This invention crucially had been encouraged by Intel's CEO, who at that time was the co-founder, Robert Noyce. His biographer relates how Noyce encouraged the microprocessor's inventor, Ted Hoff, when he first broached the idea to him in 1969.

> Noyce, who never would have claimed to know anything about computers, kept pushing Hoff, asking question after question, all of them so basic that Noyce was almost apologizing for his lack of knowledge. 'Um, can you tell me the functions of a computer operating system?' ... It was the same Socratic method of forcing people

to 'argue ourselves into some smart things', as Vadasz put it, that had worked so well in the lab. At the end of the conversation, Noyce told Hoff, 'Why don't you go ahead and pursue those ideas?'[70]

This Socratic method was similar to Noyce's style in deliberative policy-making meetings, where he was 'seemingly more interested in understanding his colleagues' ideas than in expressing his own'.[71]

Arguably his encouragement of Hoff was a deliberative meeting, too, even though it was just two people discussing whether and how to develop a new idea. In this case it was deliberation about new products rather than policies, but it took the same form of something being 'sold' to the leader: a new product idea that should be selected for more experiments, more development, or even putting into production. Such *product* deliberation was brilliantly institutionalized by another high-tech firm, the iconic Hewlett-Packard.

HP's deliberation about new products is described in David Packard's 1995 memoirs *The HP Way: How Bill Hewlett and I Built Our Company*. His book provides a leader's-eye view of how a two-man firm established in 1939 in a San Francisco garage was developed into one of the world's iconic high-tech corporations. It is included here only as a supplementary example, like the Dassault example, and in this case to show leaders establishing a corporation partly through the use of both product deliberation and an innovative adaptation—an impressive experimentation system—outlined later in the section. Both factors helped to create the firm's remarkable track record for developing new products, such as hand-held calculators and desktop printers, which in turn explains the firm's development into an iconic corporation. Indeed Packard declares that this 'constant flow of good new products is the life-blood of Hewlett-Packard and essential to our growth'.[72]

The flow of good new products was the result of not just having new ideas but also product deliberation about which ideas to put into production. As Packard points out, 'there is no shortage of ideas. The problem is to select those that are likely to fill a real need in the marketplace' and, furthermore, 'an invention must not only fill a need, it must be an economical and efficient solution to that need'.[73] The problem of selection also involved the problem of turning down creative, innovative ideas while still giving the ideas' inventors some encouragement and helping them 'retain enthusiasm in the face of such disappointment'.[74] He therefore paid special tribute and attention to how Hewlett had brilliantly solved both problems by institutionalizing product deliberation about whether or not to select a new product idea for further development.

Like Packard, Hewlett was an electrical engineer and was the more technically oriented member of their dual-leadership team. When selecting product ideas for further development, he followed a three-stage deliberative process which was based on a series of informal procedural rules. When first approached by the inventor, Hewlett would receive the new idea with enthusiasm. 'He would listen, express excitement where appropriate and appreciation in general, while asking a few gentle and not too pointed questions'.[75] A few days later, there would be an inquisitorial stage.

He would go back to the inventor and begin a 'thorough probing of the idea, [with] lots of give-and- take' and 'very pointed questions' but without any final decision.[76] Not long after the inquisitorial stage, there would be a final-decision meeting with the inventor. 'With appropriate logic and sensitivity, judgment was rendered' and even if the decision went against this new idea, the institutionalized deliberative process would have given the inventor some sense of satisfaction: 'a vitally important outcome for engendering continued enthusiasm and creativity'.[77]

This institutionalized deliberation was not the only innovative way in which Hewlett and Packard encouraged the flow of new products. They also developed an experimentation system, involving various parts and levels of the firm, which encouraged the invention and development of new product ideas. It was an institutional and indeed organizational means of ensuring that the inventors and developers were creating a flow of product ideas for the leaders' product deliberations.

Their innovative experimentation system was an adaptive response to a growth crisis that the firm experienced some twenty years after it was founded. By the time HP became a public company in 1957, it was selling over a hundred different products and was adding more each year.[78] These products, however, were specialized high-tech tools and instruments with specialized, narrow markets lacking much growth potential. As Packard's memoirs describe, HP was 'becoming the largest supplier in most of the major segments of the electronic-instrumentation business. But these segments, in total, were growing at only 6 percent per year, whereas we had been growing, out of our profits, at 22 percent. Obviously, that kind of growth could not continue without diversification' into other kinds of high-tech product, perhaps even into new product categories.[79]

So 'the need for diversification was clear' by the late 1950s, when he and Hewlett began to develop their experimentation system by instituting what he terms a 'divisionalizing' restructuring of the firm.[80] HP adopted a version of the organizational structure that had been pioneered by Sloan at General Motors in the 1920s. By introducing Sloanist 'operating divisions', Hewlett and Packard were hoping to encourage the initiative and creativity required for experimentation and diversification. Packard notes that a key goal of this divisionalizing was 'creating an environment that fostered individual motivation, initiative and creativity'.[81] As Malone's biography of Hewlett and Packard argues, their Sloanist restructuring was not motivated by the same concerns as many other firms' move in this direction, which usually 'was done for product line or marketing reasons'.[82] In the HP case, however, the leaders seem to have been mainly concerned with encouraging experimentation and diversification.[83]

This may explain why they took divisionalizing to the level of what Packard termed 'local' decentralization. As he relates, any division which grew to the 'substantial' size of 'producing many different products and employing as many as 1,500 people' was required 'to split off part of the division, giving it responsibility for an established, profitable product line and usually moving it to a new but nearby location'.[84] The key implication of this policy was that each division would produce only a small range of specialized products and therefore would focus on a relatively small, specialized, and 'local' market.

HP's local decentralization produced similar results to McDonald's local-control structure, namely adaptation to the local market. *The HP Phenomenon: Innovation and Business Transformation* notes that HP's small, 'atomized' divisions were able 'to invent their way to success in adaptive fashion, following dictates and whims of markets they had already served'.[85] In addition, the divisions were able to employ treadmill-like strategies against their competitors in these markets and, more importantly, to help HP enter or create *new* markets—divisional experimentation with new products would help diversify and transform HP.[86] The firm would be transformed from a maker of scientific instruments into a maker of scientific computers, then business computers and, eventually, desktop printers. Indeed 'HP's experience with product line renewal and company transformation' is 'among the most dramatic and effective of any corporation in history'.[87]

But the small-divisions structure created a major coordination problem. As the firm continued to grow, the number of divisions would also grow and become increasingly anomalous. By the mid-1960s, there were already more than a dozen divisions and during the next thirty years they would spawn more than *fifty* new product-manufacturing divisions.[88] As early as 1968, however, HP dealt with this problem by adopting the Sloan-pioneered measure of organizing divisions into groups headed by group managers. Packard describes HP's shift to a group structure as 'combining, organizationally, divisions with related product lines and markets into a group headed by a group manager with a small staff'.[89] By 1980, there were already ten groups or subgroups and eventually there would be *thirteen* product groups, each headed by a group vice-president.[90] Unlike Sloan's group managers, they were a separate, intermediate layer of management and leadership which was responsible for the groups' planning, finances, operations, and experimentation.[91]

Another coordinating factor was the influence of the two leaders and their informal rules about experimentation with new products. The most basic rule was the tacit understanding that about 10 per cent of a division's revenues were to be allocated to its research and development department.[92] The key rule relating to coordination was Hewlett's ban on needless duplication. He allowed 'overlaps and cross-divisional competition to flourish, with but one clear rule—if a team had an inferior solution they were expected to abdicate the field'.[93]

The most obvious central contribution to the experimentation system was the assistance provided by headquarters' HP Laboratories. According to Packard, HP Labs was established in 1966 'to help lead the company into new technologies and product diversification'.[94] For example, it transferred new technologies to the divisions through strategy groups that reported to a group vice-president and involved all three levels of the experimentation system, central, group, and divisional, in a combined effort to develop new products.[95] These new products renewed existing product lines and also led to continual diversification into new lines or even a new product category.

Some twenty years later the experimentation system was still 'delivering' such triumphs. In the 1980s, local divisions and the vice-president of the Peripherals Group played important roles in the experimentation stage and development of HP's inkjet desktop printer—perhaps the most lucrative product that the corporation ever developed.[96] The experimentation system had clearly been a very successful as well as innovative adaptation to the growth crisis of the late 1950s.

Furthermore, the system's creation of new product categories had led to diversifications that transformed the corporation not once or twice but several times. Looking back from the early twenty-first century, *The HP Phenomenon* pointed out that by 'changing its leading products each decade', HP 'morphed its main product line six times in six decades—unheard of in American industry at this level'.[97] The first transformation occurred in 1949–59 and was a shift from audio-video to microwave products within the wide category of 'frequency-domain tools'; the second transformation had occurred by 1968, as acquisitions and internal diversification led to the category 'scientific instruments' becoming the leading source of revenue.[98] But by 1976, it had been overtaken by 'scientific computing', thanks to such pioneering new products as a desktop calculator, a hand-held calculator, and a small computer that would be adopted by businesses as well as scientists.[99] Indeed 'business computing' would become the leading product category by 1986—this was HP's fourth transformation—and by then nearly half of the firm's revenue was derived from the two product categories of business computing and scientific computing.[100]

The HP-type of transformation was not created by making a 'strategic exit' from a major product category, as Intel did in 1985. An HP transformation was instead created by a successful expansion into a new product category, which became so successful that the older product categories were soon overshadowed by this latest triumph of HP's experimentation system. It had been the driving force behind decades of consistent expansion into new product categories and, furthermore, expansion into a large and iconic high-tech corporation.

The experimentation system was therefore the greatest product of Hewlett and Packard's dual leadership, which ended in 1978 when Hewlett retired from the post of CEO. By then the corporation had begun its transformation from scientific computing to business computing. Similarly, the rise of the desktop printer—the fifth transformation—was well underway when Packard retired in 1993 from the post of chairman of HP.[101]

But only a few years later the experimentation system was clearly in decline or already defunct. Its decline seems largely due to longer term tendencies identified in Burgelman, McKinney, and Meza's recent history of HP's strategic leadership *Becoming Hewlett-Packard*. These longer term tendencies can be traced back to the 1980s and to the leadership of Packard and John Young, who became CEO after Hewlett retired. In the 1980s, Young focused on developing the new 'business-computing' product category and its associated technology, systems, and product lines.[102] He also refashioned HP's organizational structure by integrating and centralizing the various groups and divisions associated with the business-computing product category. However, HP's *other* groups and divisions remained decentralized and continued to contribute to the experimentation system. In fact the long-established system 'delivered' again during these years, as noted earlier, and the 1980s saw the dramatic rise of the desktop-printer product category, specifically the LaserJet and the InkJet printers.

Yet chairman Packard was unhappy and attempted to reduce HP's organizational complexity by restoring the traditional degree of decentralization.[103] The resulting 1990 reorganization, however, saw a new approach to 'decentralization' that weakened central control but was no longer a 'local' decentralization; instead of strengthening the divisions at the periphery, it strengthened the group-level *intermediate* layer of management. Ten years earlier there had been ten groups or subgroups but now there would be just three huge groups entitled 'organizations'.[104] Such powerful and broad intermediate-level entities would prove to be less willing and able than their group predecessors to facilitate divisional-level innovation. And so this inadvertent weakening of the divisions-based experimentation system became the unintended trade-off for Young's success in developing business computing as a new product category.[105]

In 1992 he retired and was replaced as CEO by Lew Platt. Unlike Young, Platt did not focus on creating a new product category but instead promoted an existing product category, PCs, which had been under-emphasized by his predecessors. Although he achieved his goal of making HP a leader in the personal-computer industry, he did not develop any new product categories: 'No major new businesses emerged during Platt's time as CEO'.[106] This did not seem to be a problem in his first four years, as annual revenue more than doubled in this period, from $16 billion to $38 billion, and HP was judged by *Forbes* magazine to be the outstanding corporate performer of 1995.[107] However, soon after this triumph HP ran into problems and by the late 1990s the corporation was in a crisis situation. In fact it was a Grove-like adaptive crisis that had been caused largely by the success of Grove's firm, Intel. For HP's business-computing products were threatened by Intel's increasingly powerful microprocessors, by cheaper Intel-based computers, and by 'the rise of Wintel-based industry standards'.[108] HP therefore desperately needed its experimentation system to deliver an innovative new product category like the lucrative desktop printers. But the next transforming diversification would not begin until 2006 and would take the form of 'services' rather than a distinctive and lucrative product category.[109]

The experimentation system failed to deliver in the late 1990s because the longer term debilitating tendencies had increased during the Platt era.[110] He continued to follow HP's new, intermediate-level approach to decentralization, which strengthened the intermediate level rather than the 'local' or 'grassroots' elements.[111] The 'effect on HP's fabled capacity to innovate' was disabling, as is explained by Burgelman, McKinney, and Meza: senior executives 'were not motivated to take on the hard and risky work of activating what we have called the strategic context determination—really discovery processes—necessary to evaluate truly radically new innovative ideas and decide whether to create entirely new businesses based on them'.[112] The authors then point out again that Platt, unlike any previous HP CEO, 'did not launch at least one major new business that generated the profit needed to keep the company outperforming the market'.[113]

This failure of innovation and diversification highlighted the decline of HP's brilliant experimentation system. HP's divisions did not act as the equivalent of start-ups in the late 1990s era of dot.com and e-commerce start-ups, such as Omidyar's eBay, Bezos's Amazon, or Page and Brin's Google. Then in the 2000s, HP saw the start-up attitude of Steve Jobs produce three HP-type transformational diversifications, including Apple's mobile phone. The next section, however, will show that his HP-type diversifications arose in a very different way from the innovations that had once been produced by HP's decentralized system.

The Steve Jobs Way at Apple

Steve Jobs left no autobiographical writings and so there is no leader's-eye view of his enhancing of Apple in the 2000s. But he has been added to this chapter as a crucial comparison with HP's leadership and legacy in the area of technological innovation and diversification. His biographer describes Jobs as 'the ultimate icon of inventiveness, imagination and sustained innovation'.[114] These qualities were best displayed in the 2000s, when his diversifying innovations transformed Apple into a mobile-tech empire rather than a desktop-computer firm fighting for survival against the dominance of the IBM/clone PCs and their Wintel allies. It was a triumphant vindication or redemption for the co-founder of Apple, who had been ousted from the firm in 1985. Twenty years later in a speech at Stanford University he recalled feeling 'that I had let the previous generation of entrepreneurs down—that I had dropped the baton as it was being passed to me. I met with Dave Packard and Bob Noyce and tried to apologize for screwing up so badly'.[115] But in 1997, Jobs returned to Apple as its new CEO and would carry on from the Packard and Noyce generation by opening up a new field of high-tech entrepreneurship.

Jobs achieved these diversifying innovations with a much more centralized organization than the HP of the 1960s–90s. As his biographer notes, 'Jobs did not organize Apple into semiautonomous divisions; he closely controlled all of his teams and pushed them to work as one cohesive and flexible company, with one profit-and-loss bottom line'.[116] At his regular Monday-morning meetings with senior executives, he instilled 'a sense of shared mission' and discussed Apple's products with them in a 'freewheeling discourse' that focused on the future: 'What should each product do next? What new things should be developed?'[117]

This institutionalized product deliberation clearly included some selection of envisioned products for *top-down* experimentation. In top-down cases, the firm's leadership envisions a product and then asks the firm's researchers to experiment with ways of making that vision a reality. Top-down experimentation therefore typically occurs *after* rather than before the product-deliberation stage of selecting a product for development or production. Jobs's use of top-down experimentation was very evident in Apple's 2001 development of the iPod—the first of his diversifying innovations. According to Young and Simon's account of its development, the iPod began life as Jobs's vision of a pocket-size portable music-player whose music had been downloaded from the Internet by a personal computer and then on-loaded to the portable music-player. 'He saw the new frontier, recognized the market potential, and seized it'.[118] In this case of top-down experimentation, the leader gave his research and development team some exacting specifications about timing as well as design. The envisioned product would have to be not only 'distinctive enough and intuitive enough to use' but also ready 'in time for the Christmas buying season, less than twelve months away'.[119]

What is more, this leader had a hands-on approach to experimentation. He 'stayed close to the project all the way, his brilliance as a marketer and his flawless taste in design shining through in his rigorous-as-ever demands for the highest standards' and in his constant demands for improvements, such as easier use or higher sound volume.[120] The results of his hands-on approach speak for themselves. 'How many companies could tackle a project in a brand-new category, create a groundbreaking widget that looked great and worked better than anyone else's—and do it all in under a year?'[121] Perhaps the nearest recent equivalent of this achievement is Amazon's development of a portable device for reading e-books, the Kindle, which appeared in 2007. And Amazon's Kindle is another example of a leader, in this case Jeff Bezos, adopting a top-down and hands-on approach to experimentation.[122] The Kindle's development was more protracted than the iPod's but of course Jobs and Apple had benefited from their decades of experience designing high-tech widgets— the computers that had made them famous. This high-tech design heritage helped them diversify rapidly and brilliantly into a new category with greater growth potential. By the end of 2002, the iPod was 'vastly outselling' Apple's Macintosh computer and was transforming Apple into a music corporation.[123]

Jobs's other diversifying innovations, the iPhone and iPad, followed the same pattern of top-down, hands-on experimentation, as is described in Isaacson's biography. The 2005 origins of the iPhone can be traced back to Jobs's Grove-influenced paranoia about protecting Apple from a threat, namely the threat that mobile phones would pose to the iPod if they were given a music-playing capability.[124] Later in the year, though, he began to see the mobile phone as more of an opportunity than a threat, as now it seemed to him that the various mobile phones available on the market 'all stank'.[125] He therefore began top-down experimentation with what would become the iPhone. This was also another case of his hands-on experimentation. 'In session after session, with Jobs immersed in every detail, the team members figured out ways to simplify what other phones made complicated'.[126] He made such key decisions as opting for the multitouch interface, changing from a plastic to a glass screen and demanding a redesign some nine months into the project.[127] The result, the iPhone, would be a landmark in the development of the mobile 'smartphone' and its apps. The iPhone was eventually unveiled in early 2007 and by the end of 2010 Apple had sold *ninety* million of its new product: 'it reaped more than half of the total profits generated in the global cell phone market'.[128]

The iPad had a more protracted development than the iPhone. As early as 2002, Jobs had envisioned producing a tablet without a stylus or keyboard, but the project was put on hold during development of the iPhone and was not 'revved up' until a 'brainstorming' Monday-morning meeting in 2007.[129] Again, this involved hands-on as well as top-down experimentation. At 'every step' in the iPad's revived development, 'Jobs pushed to remove and simplify'.[130] The new product was unveiled in early 2010, and within little more than a year Apple had sold fifteen million iPads: this was, by some measures, 'the most successful consumer product launch in history'.[131] Jobs lived long enough to witness his final triumph before dying in 2011 at the age of 56.

During the 2000s, he had pushed through the most successful series of diversifying innovations in high-tech history and perhaps in business history. But his top-down and hands-on approach to experimentation may have been appropriate only for a genius—a special case governed by special rules. Even Sloan's *My Years with General Motors* acknowledged that there were such special cases. 'In some organizations, in order to tap the potentialities of a genius, it is necessary to build around him and tailor the organization to his temperament'.[132]

Genius is in such short supply, however, that most corporations have to rely on some form of organizational substitute. The HP example indicates that a decentralized experimentation system can produce or at least encourage innovation and diversification. A more recent and extreme example of this decentralized approach is Google's 'innovation machine', which was 'designed to create hundreds or thousands of research projects' as part-time and small-scale supplements to the firm's official research projects.[133] Decentralization had been taken down to the level of the individual scientist or engineer by allowing them to spend 20 per cent of their work time—typically one day a week—on their own projects.[134]

Google also decentralized product deliberation down to the level of individual researchers. As Brandt notes, researchers could deliberate in cyberspace about each other's product ideas at the early stages of envisioning or experimentation:

> The [innovation] process goes beyond giving researchers the ability to take time off from their regular jobs. Ideas are shared, discussed, analyzed and criticized. To make that happen, Google has created a database of information about every project every engineer is working on. All the engineers in the company have access to the database and can find out what anyone else is doing.[135]

In addition, there was high-level product deliberation about whether to select a particular project for further development into a commercial product. This deliberation seems to be the equivalent of Hewlett's three-stage deliberative process at HP, as any Google project, official or unofficial, has 'to withstand the scrutiny of Larry [Page] and Sergey [Brin] if they think it has commercial potential. The founders decide where the company will go next. And they are ruthless judges of product designs'.[136]

Google appears to be very like HP in being a high-tech corporation established by a dual-leadership team. But Chapter 14 will suggest that from 2001 until at least 2011 Google was being led by a *triple*-leadership team that included CEO Eric Schmidt as well as the two founders, Larry Page and Sergey Brin. During these years, Google's leadership team was therefore less like HP's and more like Intel's in the 1970s, when Noyce, Moore, and Grove formed a brilliant team. The Intel team was based upon a three-role division of labour that was described by Grove in the 1970s. He was referring to a chapter in a favourite management book where:

> Drucker takes on the question of what makes an ideal chief executive officer. He says that such an individual is really a tripartite character or, as Andy read it, applying its message to Intel, *three* people: 'an outside man, a man of thought, and a man of action.' To Andy, who sent copies of this chapter to his two partners, Bob Noyce was Mr. Outside, Gordon Moore was Mr. Thought, and Andy was Mr. Action.[137]

By the 1990s, Grove was the sole leader and had to take on all three parts. In doing so, however, he was playing to 'what was his greatest strength: his ability to learn'.[138] Even one of Grove's critics noted that he quickly learnt Noyce's role of Mr Outside. 'Grove was clearly learning, just as he always had. It wouldn't take him too long to pick up the skills needed for his new role' as a 'media star and high-tech visionary'.[139] But it had been his ability to learn Moore's role of Mr Thought—to become a man of thought—that gave him a more lasting fame as the author of *Only the Paranoid Survive*.

7
eBay

Whitman's *The Power of Many*

Meg Whitman's 2010 autobiographical work, *The Power of Many: Values for Success in Business and in Life*, was written after she had retired as CEO of eBay and was seeking a political career. It provides a leader's-eye view of how she used all seven appropriate rational methods to develop the corporation during her 1998–2008 tenure as CEO. In this sense she is similar to Walton, especially as she too emphasized the calculative methods and learning. In fact Whitman and Walton are perhaps the best examples of leaders inspiring rational confidence through their very capable use of the appropriate rational methods.

However, Whitman enhanced rather than established a corporation and she is similar to Grove in the sense of enhancing a high-tech firm that was based on a recent technological revolution. Just as the computer chip was the basis of Grove's Intel, the Internet was the basis of Whitman's eBay and its rapid development from start-up to iconic corporation. As an Internet-based firm it is an example of the most modern type of business—e-commerce—and is a modern-day 'classic' example of how corporation-developing rational methods are used and emphasized by a rational leader.

eBay exemplifies firms that were products of the Internet revolution. Founded in 1995 as a free online-auction site, eBay soon became an e-commerce enterprise and in fact the Internet's standout performer. Cohen's 2003 *The Perfect Store: Inside eBay* described it as the most successful e-commerce firm 'to emerge in the early years of the Internet' and as the one that 'more than any other company, fully harnessed the potential of the Internet'.[1] By the 2010s, another early Internet-based firm, Amazon, was overshadowing eBay but the latter was still the leading example of a firm fully harnessing the Internet's potential. Since its inception, eBay has exemplified the advantages of being a 'virtual' goods-trading enterprise that operates in cyberspace and does not need land-based sites and facilities. It was an online-auction site where other people sold their own goods, not eBay's, and paid it fees for the use of its site. So it was an early version of an Internet 'platform' used by other firms or applications and was pioneering a form of goods trading that is 'completely "virtual": it does not own inventory or warehouses; it does not ship items or take returns. It is an amazingly efficient model', which enabled eBay to expand rapidly and 'to achieve gross profit margins of more than 80 per cent'.[2]

Rational Leadership. Paul Brooker and Margaret Hayward, Oxford University Press. © Paul Brooker & Margaret Hayward (2023). DOI: 10.1093/oso/9780198894643.003.0007

Another example of eBay harnessing the Internet's potential was the late 1990s creation of an online community of eBay users. The thousands of sellers and buyers who used its auction site were transformed into an online community of eBay users, serviced by community-building online institutions. Whitman's book points out that this pioneering approach was being widely adopted by the 2010s: 'across the business landscape, more and more companies are talking about the importance of using the Internet to build a community, not just customer base, whether they are selling hybrid automobiles, pharmaceuticals, gardening tools or even diapers'.[3] Through its online user community, eBay also successfully bridged the gap between the Internet's commercial and social spheres, between e-commerce's online selling and e-socializing's online messages, conversations, and social networking. Conversely, by the 2010s Facebook and Twitter had successfully bridged the gap between commercial and social spheres by moving in the opposite direction: from e-socializing to e-commerce and from online meeting place to online marketplace. Van Dijck's history of social media notes that such firms are a *mixture* of 'meeting places (places to make contacts and socialize) and marketplaces (places to exchange, trade or sell goods)'.[4] eBay had pioneered this mixing of social and commercial spheres when, in 1996, its auction marketplace also became a meeting place, thanks to online institutions that allowed and indeed encouraged its growing user community to engage in e-socializing as well as e-commerce.

Whitman's experience of eBay's impressive user community inspired her concept of 'the Power of Many' type of company or organization. It 'utilizes the communication and networking powers of modern technology ... not only to save costs and improve efficiencies but also as a way to engage the energy, ideas and goodness of people, their desire to team up with others who share their interests and work together'.[5] The Power of Many company had been pioneered by eBay many years earlier, when it was harnessing the Internet's potential by creating an online user community as well as a completely virtual goods-trading enterprise.

Whitman had inherited the benefits of eBay's pioneering when she became CEO in 1998 and began her enhancement of the firm. It was a markedly different form of enhancement than (1) Grove's improvement of Intel's crisis management, (2) Sloan's administrative rationalization of General Motors, and (3) Ohno's development of the Toyota production system. Whitman enhanced eBay by *expanding* the firm into a large corporation. When she became CEO, eBay was 'a $4 million company with thirty employees'; when she retired ten years later, it was 'a nearly $8 billion company with 15000 employees around the world'.[6]

As she points out, expanding or 'scaling up' a company in this fashion is a 'harder act to manage' than it might appear:

> [I]t is not common for an executive who is good at running a $4 million business to be good at running a $400 million business, and then be good at running a $4 billion business, and then an $8 billion one. Each of those steps demands that you focus on different things, withdraw from certain functions while embracing others. Those transitions are hard ... That is the reason why boards tend to recruit individuals

from outside a company as it grows, individuals who have experience at that next level.[7]

She, too, had been recruited from outside eBay to be its CEO and in this sense she differs markedly from Grove and from the other two enhancers described in earlier chapters: Sloan at General Motors and Ohno at Toyota. Whitman had been 'head-hunted' from not only a different firm but a different industry and business culture in a different region of the country. She was then the manager of the Playskool toy division of Hasbro, located in Massachusetts rather than California. But the 40-year-old Whitman clearly had the expertise to scale-up eBay into a major corporation. She was a Princeton economics graduate, with a Harvard MBA, and a wide range of practical experience. She had served her postgraduate apprenticeship with Proctor & Gamble and then begun a 1981–9 stint with a large firm of management consultants. This was followed in the 1990s by a series of senior appointments with Disney, Stride Rite, Florist Transworld, and then Hasbro's Playskool. Becoming CEO of eBay in 1998 was a great chance to take her career to new heights and she made the most of the opportunity.

This chapter will show how she used all seven appropriate rational methods of enhancing eBay. The first section of the chapter, however, will look at the early years in eBay's development, before the arrival of Whitman. During its early years, this Internet start-up was developing its distinctive online-auction system and was becoming a Power of Many company as its user community benefited from its pioneering mixture of e-commerce and e-socializing. The second section of the chapter will describe how Whitman used the two adaptive and two deliberative rational methods in her scaling-up enhancement. The third section will show how she not only used but emphasized the other three methods, namely learning and the two calculative methods: quantitative and strategic calculation. Finally, the fourth section will broaden the chapter's perspective on e-commerce by comparing her scaling-up opportunities with those offered to Amazon's founding leader, Jeff Bezos. It will be seen that Whitman made the most of what was a comparatively short-term opportunity to scale-up eBay into one of the iconic corporations of global e-commerce.

The Internet and eBay

In 1994–5, the number of Americans with access to the Internet increased explosively from some six million to some thirty-seven million.[8] And in 1995 a young IT expert living in San Francisco, Pierre Omidyar, set up a free online-auction website, Auction Web, linked to the address 'www.eBay.com'. Auction Web soon became a commercial enterprise and thus one of the many examples of a start-up based on the Internet's e-commerce. However, Omidyar's start-up operated in a distinctive field of e-commerce: it was auctioning and, more specifically, hosting other people's auctions; the goods that they auctioned were typically 'used' rather than new; and these sellers were engaged in consumer-to-consumer transactions, not business-to-consumer or business-to-business transactions.[9]

However, increasingly large numbers of small businesses, new and old, part-time and full-time, would also sell goods on Auction Web. Bunnell's *The eBay Phenomenon* noted that by 2000 Omidyar's vision of a consumer-to-consumer channel of exchange had been 'overshadowed by small-business-to-consumer trans-actions', as some 80 per cent of eBay's revenue was being generated by only 20 per cent of its registered users: 'mostly small businesses that use the site and competing portals as their public storefronts'.[10] By 2005 some half a million people were making most or all their living by selling on the auction website that Omidyar had established ten years earlier.[11]

From the outset, his auction site had let anybody sell anything, from computers to collectibles. This inadvertently gave Auction Web a crucial competitive advantage over more specialized auction sites, not only the existing computer-equipment sites but also the many later sites that auctioned such specialized items as guitars and antique photographs.[12] His auction system was a site-only, single-item, and fixed-duration system. In other words, he did not store or ship the items being sold, each item that a seller listed for sale on the site was individually auctioned, and each auction was of a fixed duration of 'three, five, seven or ten days'—it ended on the final minute or indeed second of that set period, 'even if someone desperately want[ed] to place a higher bid'.[13]

Revenue was derived from the fees that sellers paid Auction Web for using its site. In 1996, Omidyar introduced a small listing fee, charged on a graduated scale, to deter sellers from listing 'junk' on the site, but the main revenue earner was the 'final sales price' fee that he had introduced earlier in the year.[14] It charged sellers a percentage of the sales price paid to them by buyers who had 'won' the auction by bidding the highest amount: the fee was set at 2.5 per cent for a final sales price of more than $25 but 5 per cent for prices below that amount. Although he was collecting fees from the sellers, his site-only auction system meant that he did not have to deal with the payments between buyers and sellers or with any other aspects of the transactions. As noted earlier, it was a very efficient and profitable model of e-commerce, especially when compared to those e-commerce start-ups that had to sell, ship, and store their goods.

By the end of 1996, Auction Web had more than 40,000 registered users and, fur-thermore, these users had created their 'own ever-expanding community' that 'took care of itself' through its own online institutions: the Bulletin Board and the Feed-back Forum.[15] This greatly reduced the administrative burden on Omidyar and his few employees, enabling his start-up to achieve higher levels of growth and profitabil-ity than could otherwise have been expected. However, Whitman's book depicts the user community as having more than a self-administering, cost-reducing role. 'We trusted our users to figure out the best way to use our services' and 'I have always said that we did not build eBay; our community of users did'.[16] eBay therefore seems to epitomize what she terms a 'Power of Many' company.

The development of a Power of Many company and self-administering user com-munity began in early 1996 when Omidyar added a Bulletin Board and a Feedback Forum to his website. According to Cohen, these online institutions were 'designed to limit his role and place more of the Auction Web's administration in the hands of the community'.[17] The Feedback Forum was an online public forum where users could post positive and negative feedback—as comments and numerical grades—regarding their dealings with a particular seller or buyer, such as a seller's description or shipping of goods or a buyer's bidding or payment practices. This has been compared to the role that reputation plays in small towns and has also been depicted as self-policing by the user community.[18] The Bulletin Board was a different type of communal online institution, where users could post their questions or problems in the hope that at least one of the users monitoring the Bulletin Board would post a workable answer.

Later in 1996, Auction Web was given another communal online institution: the e-socializing eBay Café. The Bulletin Board was renamed the Q&A Board and was joined by a new, more social bulletin board that was called 'the eBay Café'.[19] The Café was clearly an e-socializing type of online institution and was described a few years later as the 'chat room', where 'people stop to relax, catch up on news and hearsay, and exchange information. For example, eBay's Café posts a daily mix of remarks, user tips, sociable banter, and even advice for the lovelorn'—an online version of social chatter that 'served the same need for social connectivity'.[20]

Auction Web was here bridging the gap between e-commerce and online social connectivity, between the commercial and social spheres of the Internet. And it was being more successful than attempts to bridge the gap in the opposite direction, from the social sphere to the commercial sphere. Ever since e-socializing appeared in the 1980s, its promoters had been less successful in making a buck than in making social connections through these online messages, conversations, and communities.[21] When 'modern social networking finally began in early 1997' with the launching of sixdegrees.com, this new form of e-socializing gained millions of registered users but so little revenue that the firm went out of business three years later.[22] Internet social networking was revived in the mid-2000s by Myspace and then Facebook, but again they were much more successful in attracting users than earning revenue: by the end of 2005, Zuckerberg's Facebook had five million users and revenue of little more than $1 million a month.[23] In 2006, Twitter's 'tweeting' message-sending created a new form of social connectivity and yet again social success did not bring similarly impressive revenues—indeed two years later Twitter was still earning zero revenue.[24] By the 2010s, though, e-socializing was earning billions and in fact Chapter 1 mentioned how Sandberg's arrival at Facebook in 2008 led to its transformation into an online advertising giant. More than a decade earlier, however, Auction Web had bridged the gap between online social connectivity and e-commerce by moving in the opposite direction. Although Auction Web was renamed eBay in 1997, it deserves a permanent place in the history of the Internet.

In addition to being renamed eBay, the site continued to experience huge growth in the number of registered users and of items listed for sale. During 1997, registered users increased to nearly 350,000 and listings to more than 100,000 a day, helping the firm dramatically increase its annual revenue to more than $4 million.[25] The growth in users and listings was partly due to the continued expansion of Internet access and usage, as now more than fifty million Americans were using the Internet; but it was also partly due to eBay's dominance over its competitors, as it now had 'more than 80 per cent of the consumer-to-consumer online auction market'.[26]

Although the firm still had fewer than thirty employees, there was a growing need for more high-powered business expertise. Omidyar had in fact recruited the young Jeff Stoll as co-founder in 1996 to provide his start-up with the business orientation and MBA-graduate training that he lacked.[27] In 1997, the co-founders' recruiting of new staff included three more MBA graduates to help with marketing and business development, but something more was required to transform eBay into a public company and major business corporation:

> Selling shares to the public meant that Omidyar and Skoll had to be more professional about the company's leadership. As Omidyar admitted, 'We were entrepreneurs and that was good up to a certain stage, but we didn't have the experience to take the company to the next level'. They brought in a headhunter, someone who helped them look for top-quality leaders.[28]

So in early 1998, Whitman arrived at eBay to take on the position and tasks of CEO. The former incumbent, Omidyar, became eBay's chairman, while its former president, Skoll, became vice-president of strategic planning and analysis—the co-founders would soon disengage from the firm and leave Whitman as the sole leader.[29]

Her situation was similar to what Sandberg experienced in 2008 after she was recruited by Zuckerberg to be Facebook's chief operating officer (COO). As Chapter 1 described, Sandberg had the task of professionalizing a typical IT start-up and its free-wheeling business culture. Similarly, Cohen depicts Whitman taking on the task of 'professionalizing a rather unruly start-up' and making professionalization the theme of her first year in the job.[30] She was in a stronger leadership position than Sandberg, however, and was joining a firm with impressive profitability and revenue as well as the prospect for continuing rapid growth. Not surprisingly, when eBay became a public company later in the year, its opening share price was just as impressive and gave it a market valuation of more than $2 billion.[31] It clearly had much potential for the scaling-up enhancement that Whitman had already begun: 'From day one, I could see that eBay had all the ingredients of a great company at a remarkably young age'.[32]

Adapting and Deliberating

Whitman's scaling-up enhancement used all seven rational methods, but this section will focus on her use of the two adaptive and two deliberative methods. In the case of the adaptive methods, her book has an almost Grove-like exposition of a 'bias for action'. It included a two-stage conception of rapid adaptation, with the first stage rapidly exploiting opportunities and the second stage fixing the mistakes that had been made during the first. A bias for action 'is about a leader moving an organization quickly to capture opportunities, knowing full well that mistakes will be made but that the organization can adjust and fix mistakes'.[33] The adjusting, mistake-fixing stage also has to be quick and avoid any rigidity:

> In a competitive environment you have to take risks … before you have all the information you might need to make the best possible decision. The trick is to be bold but not stubborn. *Don't put on blinkers or discourage realistic feedback* about what's happening, and if you've made a mistake, *fix it fast*.[34]

This is similar to points that Grove made about rapid adaptation, but Whitman has a different perspective on when this method will be used. Unlike Grove, Whitman is not preoccupied with the rare occasions when leaders have to deal with an inflection-point adaptive crisis; she is more concerned with leaders constantly having to make rapid decisions about seizing opportunities.

However, Whitman acknowledges that the leader of a high-tech firm has to be capable of adapting rapidly to crises.[35] And she experienced a technology-related crisis that was similar to the Pentium-chip crisis Grove had experienced in 1994. Whitman's crisis began on 9 July 1999 when eBay's website went down. It was by no means the first time its over-burdened, unstable system had crashed, but this time it seemed that the technical experts might be unable to get the site back up.

> Whitman had to tell her management team she feared the worst—that the engineers might never get the site up. It would, of course, be possible to reconstruct it and relaunch eBay. But if all the data were gone—user registrations, feedback, live auctions that had been underway at the time of the crash—it could be a loss from which eBay would never recover.[36]

She had quickly responded to the crisis by enlisting the aid of firms which supplied hardware or software to the eBay site, and by having a plane chartered to bring home eBay's senior systems engineer from his holiday in Venezuela.[37] Thanks to such measures and the technical experts' non-stop efforts, the site was up and running again twenty-two hours after it had crashed.

But this was not the end of the 'outage' crisis. The firm needed to rebuild its relationship with the eBay user community, especially the thousands of small businesses that depended upon this e-commerce and might be tempted to switch to a more reliable online-auction site. Whitman's response included telephoning 'the thousand or so top sellers' to apologize for the outage, each phone call coming from her personally or from a senior manager.[38]

This response is just one of several examples of innovative Whitman adaptations that are mentioned by her and other writers.[39] Another customer-related innovation was the Voice of the Customer programme, which she introduced in 1999. 'Every few months, a dozen regular customers are flown to company headquarters in San Jose to meet with Meg and eBay managers and express their ideas about what's working and what's not'.[40] This face-to-face interaction with customers was providing a valuable supplement to the feedback given on eBay's message boards and in the thousands of customer emails it received each day. Whitman notes that 'as important as e-mail and message boards were to us, I knew there was a special kind of value to looking real customers in the eye'.[41]

Like the two adaptive methods, the two deliberative methods—diverse and institutionalized deliberation—were used by Whitman and appear in her book. For example, it expresses her liking for diverse deliberation's variety of viewpoints and lack of reticence. 'I can't abide yes-people. I feel energized by other people with new and different perspectives from my own'.[42] And if 'you bite employees' heads off when they don't agree with you, well, you are training them to tell you only good news and conspire to hide problems'.[43] Another writer noted her tendency to elicit colleagues' opinions before giving her own, as when she was chairing a meeting of senior managers and asked each of them, one by one, to rank the options that the meeting was considering.[44] This Sloan-like tendency to elicit other managers' opinions before giving her own 'did not, however, mean that she had any hesitation in making a decision, even if it provoked opposition'.[45]

Furthermore, Whitman mentions two of the policy-making benefits of diverse deliberation. It helps policy-makers to take account of a plan's unintended impact in other areas and to take advantage of 'new opportunities that might emerge in unexpected places'.[46] Cohen described an example that occurred in 1999, when a middle-level manager identified the used-car market as an opportunity for eBay. In a typical case of a subordinate giving deliberative leads to his superiors, he sold them a policy proposal to introduce a used-car category on the eBay site and, later on, he sold them the idea of giving this category its own, separate site: eBay Motors.[47]

This example also illustrates Whitman's use of the other deliberative method, institutionalized deliberation. It seems that she, like Walton and Kroc, used an area of informally institutionalized deliberation, where managers could sell proposals for new policies. More importantly, she combined this with a deliberative conception of her position as CEO and with an almost Sloan-like appreciation for formal small-group deliberation. For example, soon after taking over as CEO 'she instituted weekly management team meetings, each lasting up to four hours'.[48] Even at board level she seems to have viewed the board of directors as another opportunity for group deliberation.[49] Apparently she presented board meetings with a 'parade of horribles'—an agenda of problems to solve—because 'I didn't need my board's input on the happy stuff—I needed their help on the hard stuff'.[50] And when the board was dealing with weighty matters, she would 'go around the table, asking every board member's opinion one by one' and withholding her own opinion until 'every board member had stated his or hers'.[51] This informal rule ensured not only diverse deliberation but also that every board member lived up to his or her responsibilities. It meant that 'we developed a tone of openness and *responsibility* on the board. Every person would be respected for what he or she had to say, but I also made it clear that opinions needed to be heard'.[52]

Years after she retired as CEO of eBay, Whitman herself would provide a prominent example of a board member living up to her responsibilities. She had joined the board of Hewlett-Packard (HP) after her unsuccessful attempt in 2010 to be elected governor of California. And in September 2011 she would meet her board-member responsibilities by accepting the post of CEO and the task of leading HP out of a crisis. The previous incumbent's strategizing had led to a falling share price as well as his early departure, and HP was in a similar situation to the late 1990s crisis described in Chapter 6.[53] Whitman's solution was to split Hewlett and Packard's creation into two separate companies. HP Inc would focus on personal computers and printers while Hewlett Packard Enterprise would focus on the business-computing legacy and later further narrowed its focus by spinning off its services operations as part of a new company.[54] So Whitman was associated with a strategy that might be considered 'scaling-down' but was calculated to reinvigorate the specialized components of a diversified corporation. In eBay's case, however, she had been using strategic calculation to scale-*up* a specialized company and in fact the calculative methods, plus learning, were her three key methods when she was scaling-up eBay.

Calculating and Learning

Like Walton, Whitman emphasized quantitative calculation and the 'numbers' or 'metrics'. Her book indicates that it was both personally preferred and required by the circumstances: both a favoured and a key method. She declares, 'I am very focused on what are called key metrics' and she points out that 'the focus on metrics that I believe is *so vital to success*' is particularly relevant in an Internet firm, 'where it is possible to measure many more things than in the land-based world'.[55] As soon as she arrived at eBay, Whitman asked for regular reports about how it was faring in terms of the standard quantitative measures of Internet performance.[56] Her book identifies a few metrics that she watched especially closely, such as the number of new users and listings, but she was also interested in a wide range of other measurements:

> She wanted to know how many people were visiting the site and how many of those then registered to become users. Breaking it down further, she wanted to know how long each user remained per visit and how long the pages on the site took to load ... which days were busiest ... and which days saw a drop-off in sales.[57]

By the mid-2000s the focus on metrics was a well-known feature of Whitman's eBay. She was quoted as saying, 'if it moves, measure it' and 'if you can't measure it, you can't control it', while eBay's managers were depicted as being 'practically obsessed' with measuring the behaviour of its customers.[58] However, Whitman's book warns of the limitations and dangers of number-crunching. She notes that 'when you are metric driven', there is the danger of 'not drawing the right conclusions from your numbers. Numbers alone never tell the whole story'.[59]

Whitman's book has less to say about *strategic* calculation but clearly it was emphasized by her as a key method of scaling-up eBay. Whatever her personal preferences, emphasizing strategic calculation was required by the circumstances. And two crucially important instances of strategic calculation are described in her book and by other writers.

The first was in 1998, when she made a key strategic decision about marketing. She calculated that eBay should focus on a relatively narrow market, collectibles, where its online auctions clearly had a competitive advantage. In fact its listings were already 'dominated' by collectibles—such as stamps, coins, magazines, or sports cards—and their collectors seemed to be eBay's most 'ardent' buyers and sellers.[60] 'Instead of spreading our advertising and marketing dollars across huge categories where we would have to compete with established and well-heeled retailers, I argued that we should focus on collectibles, which we could market more effectively and efficiently than anyone else could' and which still had much untapped potential as 'only a fraction of collectors were online'.[61]

Her collectibles-focused strategy was presented in similar terms by Cohen but from a different perspective. He refers to Whitman 'arguing that eBay's success at the moment depend[ed] more on keeping and expanding on the hard-core users than on reaching out to the "periodic buyers" who were stopping by other, more expensive categories'.[62] He also refers to the range of measures taken to implement the new strategy. Advertising was aimed at collectors' magazines and newsletters, such as *Postcard Collector* or *Elvis World*, the marketing department sent representatives to collectors' conventions or trade shows, such as the Doll & Teddy Bear Expo, and some categories of collectors were given their own eBay home pages, discussion boards, and specialized category managers.[63] In these ways eBay encouraged and exploited what was later labelled 'the collectibles boom' of the late 1990s.[64]

Whitman's collectibles-focused strategy therefore succeeded in maintaining eBay's very rapid growth and its dominance over its competitors. In 1999, the number of registered users increased from 2.2 million to more than ten million, sales figures quadrupled from some $700 million to $2.8 billion, and eBay was hosting more than 90 per cent of the online-auction sales by consumers and small businesses.[65] But a collectibles-focused strategy also had some inherent limitations and disadvantages. Cohen noted that collectibles had low average sales prices, which meant low final-sales fees for eBay, and that the more faddish collectibles, such as Beanie Babies toys, went through hard-to-predict cycles of popularity.[66] Another writer cited a Wall Street analyst's remark that there 'are only so many Beanie Babies and old records you can sell'.[67] In other words, collectibles were sold in vertical markets with limited supply and demand, low prices and final-sales fees, and limited long-term prospects for eBay. It is not surprising therefore that Whitman was soon recalculating her marketing strategy and overall strategic direction; something new and more ambitious would be needed for the next stage in her scaling-up enhancement of eBay.

So as early as 1999 there was another crucial instance of Whitman's emphasis on strategic calculation. There was 'a shift in strategic thinking', which she publicly confirmed in a September speech that declared eBay's intention to 'extend beyond the core business of United States collectibles'.[68] The new strategy included initiatives to diversify what was being sold on eBay, such as the earlier-mentioned move into the used-car market. Cohen describes 'initiatives like eBay Motors' as 'designed to push up the average sales price of items sold and, given eBay's fee structure, to increase revenues'.[69] Other diversifying initiatives would increase revenues by markedly increasing the *volume* of items sold, even if they were relatively low-priced items, such as books and CDs.

But the most important example of diversification was eBay's acquisition of Half.com. This was a strategic move into a new line of e-commerce business, in which a firm's site was a platform for fixed-price selling rather than auctioning. Half.com was offering sellers and buyers a fixed-price system for selling used items or indeed discount-price new items: the site's name 'Half' was derived from the rule that nothing was to be sold on the site for more than half its retail list price.[70]

Whitman's shift in strategic direction also included a move towards globalization. In 1999, eBay began to move into Britain, Germany, Japan, and Australia; in the early 2000s it would move into many other markets outside the US, including the huge new market emerging in China.[71] Although globalization and the other strategic initiatives were straining eBay's finances, shrewd observers could see the strategic calculation behind Whitman's willingness to squeeze eBay's margins:

> The cause of the big squeeze is clear: aggressive investment in Web infrastructure, sales and marketing, product development and acquisitions ... Like an aggressive army, eBay's strategy is to move quickly to capture territory and key positions in the new world of online auctions before opposing forces can do so, the costs be damned ... Competitors will find eBay deeply entrenched and difficult to dislodge, and margins will return to enviable levels.[72]

Whitman's shift in strategy enabled eBay to achieve the ambitious long-term growth target that she had announced in 1999 along with the new strategy. As a motivating 'stretch goal' she committed eBay to achieving $3 billion in annual revenue by 2005, which would require a 50 per cent growth in annual revenue each year.[73] By 2003, it was well on the way to reaching that goal, with some $2 billion in annual revenue being derived from the $32 billion of business that had been created by eBay customers—who would soon number more than a hundred million and be found in some thirty countries around the world.[74] Two years later eBay reached and easily surpassed Whitman's goal, with annual revenue of $4.5 billion, and by then, too, collectibles accounted for less than half of the items sold on eBay.[75]

After the 2005 triumph, however, eBay began to lose momentum, especially when compared to e-commerce's other leading firm. Stone's *The Everything Store: Jeff Bezos and the Age of Amazon* notes that in 2008 Amazon's share-market valuation 'surpassed eBay's for the first time in nearly a decade'.[76] He attributes eBay's loss of momentum to the fact that 'the appeal of online auctions had faded' because customers 'wanted the convenience and certainty of a quickly completed purchase' through a fixed-price system and they were also becoming increasingly 'disgruntled with the challenges of finding items on eBay and dealing with sellers who overcharged for shipping'.[77]

Another explanation, though, is that eBay was reaching the limits of the consumer market for online auctions, just as previously it had reached the limits of the more specialized, collectibles market. As early as 1999, analysts were pointing to the limits of the online-auction consumer market and were predicting that by the mid-2000s 'bargain hunting' shoppers would comprise less than a quarter of the online consumer market in the US.[78] Stone acknowledges that eBay, too, had foreseen the problem and was making an adaptive response, but he argues that its 2004 response was slow and half-hearted:

> It spent two years working on a separate destination for fixed-price retail, called eBay Express, which got no traffic when it debuted in 2006 and was quickly shut down. Only then did eBay finally commit to allowing fixed-price sales to share space alongside auctions on the site and in search results on eBay.com.[79]

But this criticism seems to overlook the fact that Whitman had responded to the fixed-price challenge several years earlier, in 2000, by acquiring the Half.com site that had ventured into what she terms the 'hybrid space between eBay and Amazon.'[80] After a build-or-buy analysis showed that creating an eBay fixed-price system would take too long, she began negotiations to buy Half.com and, furthermore, she gave sellers on eBay the option of offering a fixed-price alternative when they listed an item for auction.[81]

eBay's later moves in the fixed-price direction were riskier, however, because they were bringing it closer to head-on competition with Amazon and other big online retailers. Whitman notes that by about 2006 'we had seen growth in the auction business slow down' and in order to maintain eBay's high growth rate 'we had to embrace fixed-price retailing that involved formidable competitors, such as Amazon.'[82] Moving too far in this direction would have raised the risk and resources issues that she mentioned when explaining how her plan to move into the Japanese market in 1999 had been hobbled by the crisis created by the eBay system's instability. 'The system demanded my full attention and many of the resources we would have needed in Japan. To have moved forward would have put the entire company at risk. That was a failure due to limited resources, not inaction.'[83] Similarly, in the mid-2000s she would have put the corporation at risk by moving forward without the resources that would be needed to compete head-on against such formidable competitors as Amazon. Whitman may in fact have learnt from her 1999 experience that she was right to be cautious about over-stretching eBay's resources.

She certainly emphasized learning as a method of developing the corporation. Learning was one of her key methods and especially so when she first joined eBay as its new CEO in 1998. Whitman had to learn about a new firm, a new industry, and even a new business culture: an informal, non-hierarchical culture in which even the most senior executives would not have an office but instead 'would work in a cubicle, even Whitman.'[84]

Learning seems to have been a favourite as well as key method, considering how often it is discussed or mentioned in her book. Often it is mentioned as part of other processes, such as iteration and validation, or in the form of listening to what other people have to say.[85] For example, Whitman declares, 'I am a listener. I do not like to delegate my own education.'[86] Although she therefore seems similar to Silent Sloan, Whitman also makes the Kroc-like remark that she learnt more from the failures in her career than from successes.[87]

She presumably also favoured learning because she had a special aptitude for this rational method, like Walton's special aptitude for quantitative calculation. Whitman had shown an aptitude for learning during her earlier career, before arriving at eBay, and she would show it again in her later career, after leaving eBay. When she became CEO of Hewlett-Packard in 2011, 'Whitman had a reputation as a capable and principled leader, but ... some questioned whether she had the experience necessary to run a $100 billion computer hardware, services, and software company, particularly one facing many strategic challenges.'[88] She soon showed that her aptitude for learning on the job—and learning quickly—outweighed her lack of experience in leading such a huge corporation and dealing with so many strategic challenges.

In the case of eBay, her aptitude for *quickly* learning on the job had been essential. For she was not given as much time as Kroc and Walton to learn how to scale-up the company: the e-commerce world was more rapidly evolving than the fast-food world of the 1950s–60s or the discount-retailing world of the 1960s–70s.[89] The rapid evolution of e-commerce was reflected in the rapid development of eBay from start-up to globalizing corporation. Only three years after eBay was founded it had become a public company, with a market valuation in the billions, and only a year later it was shifting its strategy towards diversification and globalization.

Furthermore, eBay was under competitive pressure from other fast-growing Internet firms. As previously noted, its commitment to rapid global expansion was largely because 'eBay wanted to move into key markets before Yahoo, Amazon, or local companies locked them up.'[90] By the time Whitman retired, eBay was even feeling competitive pressure from Google. 'We had seen the rise of Google and its extraordinary search capabilities, which play a larger and larger role in directing consumers to products.'[91]

However, the key competition, comparisons, and contrasts were still provided by eBay's great e-commerce rival, Amazon. Both firms had been launched in 1995, but Amazon founder Jeff Bezos did not follow eBay's lead of bringing in an expert manager to develop the firm into a corporation. On the contrary, Bezos continued on as CEO, establishing Amazon as a notable corporation and then continually enhancing it—to iconic status and beyond—until he retired as CEO in 2021. Chapter 8 recounts his enhancing development of Amazon, which was a remarkable feat for a leader who lacked the business training and experience that Whitman possessed when she took charge of eBay.[92] Like her, though, he used all seven rational methods of developing a corporation.[93] And Bezos's firm was engaged in a form of e-commerce that offered great opportunities for long-term, continuous development. Whitman highlighted e-commerce's opportunities when she noted near the end of her book: 'I don't think there will be another eBay for me. What we accomplished was so novel, our success was so unprecedented, that other business opportunities pale in comparison'.[94] But eBay's form of e-commerce did not offer great opportunities for long-term, continuous development. Whitman was therefore facing different opportunity circumstances than those faced by Bezos during his development of Amazon. Indeed, the next section will compare—and contrast—these two leaders' opportunities for using rational methods to develop their firms into corporations and then continuously enhance them: developing them into iconic corporations.

When comparing the two leaders' opportunities, though, there is another factor to take into account. In the late 1990s, Bezos was establishing a corporation, Amazon.com, which he had founded years earlier as an online retailer that specialized (temporarily) in selling books and would 'offer an unprecedented number of books at the cheapest price possible and deliver them quickly'.[95] In Whitman's case, however, she was *enhancing* a start-up, eBay, that had been founded by someone else and whose direction had already been set—as an online-auction platform—before she arrived at the firm.

In addition, eBay was already very successful, as was described in the first section of the chapter. So when Whitman took charge in 1998, there was no need for a Sloan-like or Ohno-like enhancement, and in fact her options for enhancing eBay may have been limited to scaling-up the firm by taking it further in the direction already set by its founders and user community. Furthermore, her opportunity to carry out this scaling-up enhancement was limited by the form of goods trading that eBay epitomized. As the next section's comparison will show, Whitman was more limited, in the longer term, by eBayism than Bezos was by Amazonism.

Opportunity: eBayism Versus Amazonism

This section will look at opportunity from a different perspective than in other chapters, where it was viewed as the opportunity to use the adaptive methods, rapid and innovative adaptation, to develop a corporation. In this section, however, opportunity will be viewed in more general terms, as the opportunity to develop a corporation by any or all appropriate rational methods, not just the adaptive methods. In the case of Whitman and Bezos it was the opportunity to scale-up an e-commerce firm into a corporation, and the opportunity was provided by two different forms of Internet-based goods trading, which will be termed 'eBayism' and 'Amazonism'. eBayism offered an opportunity for rapid and profitable growth that reaches its limits in a decade or so; Amazonism offered a longer term opportunity for less rapid and profitable growth that continues for a longer period and creates a larger and more diverse corporation.

When Whitman joined eBay in 1998 as its new CEO, she was given an excellent short-term opportunity for a scaling-up enhancement. As her book states, 'eBay proved to be incredibly scalable' and 'at its core is a business model that we scaled up in a remarkably successful fashion, even exporting it to other countries and cultures'.[96] This scalability is highlighted by the contrast with Amazonism's much less 'virtual' form of goods trading, in which an online retailer is selling, shipping, and storing its own goods rather than simply providing a platform for other sellers. Whitman herself made this contrast when she returned from a 1998 visit to Amazon:

> Whitman was not impressed by Amazon's bricks-and-mortar assets. 'They have all these warehouses and inventory they're so proud of', she told her management team when she returned to Campbell. 'I'm glad that we don't have to deal with any of that'.[97]

But Amazon did have to deal with that and with the problem of expanding these land-based facilities to keep pace with the rapid growth in Amazon's sales and customer numbers. What is more, Amazon therefore had to spend a larger amount of money than eBay to maintain a rapid growth rate and so was under more financial strain, especially as its form of goods trading was inherently less profitable than eBayism. Becoming a public company in 1997 had eased the financial strain, but Amazon's share price reflected its rapid growth and great potential rather than its profitability or in fact *lack* of profits. In the years ahead it would make substantial losses as it acquired new facilities and firms as well as millions of new customers; in late 2001 it finally made a profit, but only after a long efficiency campaign and laying off hundreds of staff.[98]

Amazonism was also more difficult than eBayism to expand on an international scale—to globalize. As Whitman points out, the 'exporting' of eBayism to dozens of other countries is an illustration of its scalability. In contrast, Amazon was operating as an online retailer in only ten countries in the early 2010s, largely because so few countries had both a sizeable enough market and an acceptable 'shipping infrastructure' and 'credit card processing system'.[99] Unlike eBay, Amazon was a seller and shipper of goods, and did not have the advantages of being simply a platform that other firms and people used as an online means of selling their goods.

Whitman alludes to these platform advantages when she describes how eBay's scalability was partly due to its user community and the Power of Many. 'By tapping the Power of Many, we created a virtuous cycle where the better our sellers did and the happier our buyers were, the more successful eBay was as a facilitator of all those transactions'.[100] In contrast, Amazon was a retailer, selling goods to consumers, and so could not rely on other firms and people to make its buyers happier and Amazon more successful. The 'customer obsessed' Amazon devoted much money and effort to making consumers happier with its prices, inventory, shipping, and so forth—to making them not merely satisfied but actually happy customers.[101]

In addition, Amazon introduced an element of eBayism into its goods trading. It would allow other firms to use its online site as a platform, in return for a fee or commission, and would even allow these 'third-party' sellers to compete with Amazon for sales. As early as 1997, it was considering 'how to become a platform and augment the e-commerce efforts of other retailers. Amazon Auctions was the first such attempt, followed by zShops, the service that allowed small retailers to set up their own stores on Amazon.com'.[102] The Auctions initiative made little headway against eBay, but the 1999 zShops initiative was 'very attractive to many small merchants in that it gave them access to Amazon's growing legions of customers, which then numbered 11 million'.[103] These small-business retailers handled their own billing, shipping, and inventory, and paid Amazon both monthly listing fees and a commission on all sales where the customer made a credit-card purchase processed by Amazon. In 2000, its focus shifted from small to *big* retailers, such as Toys 'R' Us, as Amazon began to make online-partnership deals with them.[104] This was the year, too, that it launched the Marketplace initiative, which allowed sellers of used books to compete directly with Amazon.[105] During the 2000s, Marketplace was extended to many other categories of used or new goods and whether or not they were also sold by Amazon.[106]

Despite this move towards eBayism, Amazon continued to be in a less advantageous position than eBay. In fact as late as 2005 this was still the assessment being made on Wall Street. Analysts focused on Amazon's 'slender margins and the superior business models of other Internet companies' but eBay was 'still viewed as a perfect venue for commerce' and had a market capitalization 'three times larger than Amazon's'.[107] Whitman's strategy of diversification and globalization had produced huge increases in scale and revenue in the early 2000s and with markedly better profit margins than Amazon's.

Diversification had been an Amazon strategy too. This online bookstore was aiming to become an 'everything' store, which would provide customers with online access to a much wider range and choice of goods than any land-based store could provide. The range of goods available to Amazon customers had been increased by its introduction of platform selling by third-party sellers.[108] And Amazon itself was selling a much wider range of goods. In 1998, it had begun selling CDs and DVDs as well as books; in 1999 it added video games, consumer electronics, and home-improvement products; in 2000, kitchen products, health and beauty aids, and even outdoor furniture.[109] Bookselling still made up more than half of Amazon's business, but the title at the top of its website had changed from 'Earth's Largest Bookstore to Books, Music and More, and, soon after, to Earth's Biggest Selection—the everything store'.[110]

However, Amazon lacked two of eBay's advantages, namely 'network effects' and not having to compete with big retailers. Whitman's firm benefited greatly from these advantages, as is evident in her book and other writers' descriptions of eBay. The advantage of not having to compete with big retailers is evident when Whitman relates, as noted earlier, how her strategic calculations in 1998 had included a desire to avoid any form of competition with big retailers. But Amazon, in contrast, *had to* compete with big retailers, as it diversified from books into a wide range of retail items. Indeed it was facing an increasing amount of head-on competition from these giants of retailing, for this was the era in which the big retailers moved into e-commerce and set up Internet versions of their land-based stores. By the end of the 1990s long-established land-based companies were going online in what Bunnell termed at the time: 'the second stage of the Internet revolution'.[111] These e-commerce extensions of land-based companies were increasingly evident in online retailing. Most sold such specialized items as computer equipment, but a few of the newcomers sold a much wider range of products. For example, Wal-Mart set up an Internet operation in 1999 and headquartered this e-commerce extension in a town near Silicon Valley rather than in Bentonville, Arkansas.[112] The second stage of the Internet revolution therefore created an increasingly wide area of head-on competition between big retailers and the diversifying Amazon—but *not* between them and eBay's online auctions.

The other advantage enjoyed by eBay, network effects, had helped the firm expand its online user community and deal with its online competitors. Whitman's book describes network effects largely in terms of the expansion of the user community and as another example of the Power of Many. Network effects occur when the Internet accelerates growth created by word-of-mouth recruiting: users of a network like eBay's 'actively recruit other users' and 'the more people join the network, the faster even more people join the network'.[113] Whitman points out that the rapid growth of eBay's user community was an early example of the network effects that would later 'fuel the rapid growth of social sites such as Facebook and Twitter'.[114] Facebook acquired more than five million users in its first two years, and Twitter's growth was similarly rapid once Internet users became aware of what this new kind of social site had to offer: in its first six years it acquired some 500 million registered users worldwide.[115] This was much greater expansion than eBay could have achieved in its first six years, having been launched as an e-commerce site and during the first stage of the Internet revolution. But eBay, too, had benefited greatly from network effects, which had rapidly expanded its user community at so little cost to the firm.

Amazon, however, did not have the advantage of network effects. The rapid expansion of its customer base in its first six years therefore cost the firm a lot of money and effort. Although many customers were attracted by word-of-mouth recommendations, this was the result of Amazon's costly focus on customer happiness—and the firm had spent much money on advertising and other marketing efforts.[116] It did not have the benefit of network effects' cost-free attraction of new users and customers.

Similarly, Amazon did not have the benefit of the *anti-competitive* aspect of network effects. This aspect of network effects was highlighted by Cohen in his description of eBay-like networks and Metcalfe's Law, 'which holds that the utility of a network equals the number of users squared' because 'every new member added to a network like eBay represents not just a single networked relationship, but a relationship with all other eBay users. Those eBay relationships work in both directions: anyone in the network can buy from or sell to the new user'.[117] In contrast, 'one-to-many e-commerce sites' like Amazon add 'only one new relationship' when they add a new user—a new customer for the company's goods or services.[118] However, Cohen was mainly concerned with the contrast between large and small networks and particularly the competitive advantage enjoyed by *larger* networks. He pointed out that 'being the first to build up a large network gives a site a critical edge' over its smaller competitors; from then on, it 'made no sense for users to go to any other site. Buyers who did were less likely to find what they were looking for; sellers were less likely to get a good price'.[119] In fact this competitive edge has been described, in the case of Facebook, as a winner-takes-all effect.[120] The effect is just as strong in an e-commerce network and, in the case of eBay, helped it achieve a monopolistic position as early as 1996.

More importantly, the competitive advantage given by network effects would help eBay maintain its monopolistic position against old and new competitors. This was particularly important because the downside of eBayism for eBay was that competitors could so easily set up a new online-auction site to compete with it.[121] The other side of the coin, however, was that competitors found it 'considerably more difficult to build up a *network* that can compete with eBay'.[122]

For example, Amazon's 1999 failed attempt to create an auction enterprise was foredoomed by the network problem. Bunnell's analysis of the failure of Amazon Auctions pointed out that this venture had been well planned and seemed to offer an attractive alternative to eBay. Amazon's auction site was similar to eBay's, provided better customer services and buyer guarantees, and offered sellers a no-fee holiday period.[123] It made a good start and grew impressively for several months but then 'the number of listings stalled out' as eBayism's anti-competitive network effects protected eBay's monopolistic position.[124]

Amazon was in fact being hit with a double whammy. For in addition to suffering from anti-competitive network effects when challenging eBay, Amazon lacked the *benefits* of such effects when its retail operations established a monopolistic or winning position in an online retail market. Without these winner-takes-all and monopoly-protecting benefits, the diversifying Amazon lacked a significant advantage as it dealt with online retail competitors in an increasingly wide range of products.

Nonetheless, by 2007 Amazonism was beginning to overshadow eBayism. Amazon's growth in sales was far higher than 'the growth rate for the rest of e-commerce. That meant Amazon was stealing customers from other Internet players' in retailing and platform selling, for even Amazon's Marketplace 'third-party sellers were reporting a surge of activity on the site and a corresponding decrease on rival platforms like eBay'.[125] What is more, this was the year that Amazon launched its Kindle device for reading e-books. As Chapter 6 noted, the Kindle's development was relatively protracted when compared to the speed with which Apple developed the iPod. But the Kindle was a rapid adaptive response for an online retailer that had never before developed a piece of technology, let alone a portable device using advanced electronic-reading technology.[126] Development had begun in 2004 in response to the threat that Apple or some other high-tech firm might instigate a bookselling version of the iPod music-selling revolution: 'if Amazon was to continue to thrive as a bookseller in a new digital age, it must own the e-book business in the same way that Apple controlled the music business'.[127]

Another impressive Amazon adaptation had occurred in the mid-2000s, when the firm put its spare computer capacity to work by renting it out over the Internet. Through Amazon Web Services other firms could rent 'basic computer infrastructure like storage, databases, and raw computing power' and in fact would be able to rent exactly as much computing power as they needed through Amazon's Elastic Compute Cloud.[128] Renting these services from Web Services was an attractive proposition and especially for start-up entrepreneurs, who no longer had to invest in their own computing power and could instead 'run their operations over the Internet as if the high-powered servers were sitting in the backs of their own offices'.[129] From Amazon's perspective, too, Web Services was an attractive proposition and it would become an increasingly lucrative area of activity. By 2010, it was earning an estimated $500 million in annual revenue, with much higher profitability than online retailing, and was growing at an extraordinary rate.[130]

Amazonism was therefore harnessing the Internet's potential in an innovative way as well as developing technologically innovative products. The latter included not just the Kindle reader but also the development of a Kindle-based device that would compete against the Apple iPad. By 2010 Amazon was 'preparing to confront Apple in the high stakes tablet market' and would launch the Kindle Fire tablet in the following year.[131]

eBayism, however, had not provided Whitman with similar opportunities for diversification—whether through the Internet or in other areas of technology. When she retired, Whitman felt she 'had reinvented eBay several times in ten years'.[132] But eBayism offered only limited opportunities for reinvention when compared to what Amazonism offered Bezos. Whitman could only play the cards she had been dealt.

This inferiority was part of an overall lack of longer term opportunity that became evident in the late 2000s as Amazon began to overshadow eBay. By 2008, Amazon was considering what further improvements and initiatives would be required for it to become a $200-billion corporation like Wal-Mart.[133] Although Amazon was still seven years away from reaching even $100 billion in revenue, it was much closer than eBay to ever being comparable to the giant Wal-Mart corporation.[134]

When Whitman became leader of eBay in 1998, eBayism provided a better short-term opportunity than Amazonism for scaling-up an Internet-based firm—and she had made the most of that opportunity. But Amazonism provided Bezos with a better longer term opportunity than Whitman's, so long as he and Amazon could stay the distance and make the most of this opportunity. By the 2010s it was clear that he and his firm had succeeded and had made it big. 'Amazon was spoken of in the same breath as Google and Apple' and indeed it was already paying a political price for its success and fame: 'the rise of Amazon's visibility and market power' led to it facing a 'growing chorus of critics' as it 'now seemed to many like a remote and often arrogant giant'.[135] eBay, too, had suffered from the political factor, as in 2008 Whitman had retired from business in order to pursue a political career. From Whitman's perspective, an advantage of the shorter term kind of opportunity that she received in 1998 is that it left some room for her as a leader to move on to new things, such as entering the political arena and then returning to the business world as the saviour of an iconic corporation like Hewlett-Packard.

8

Amazon

Bezos's *Invent & Wander*

The Amazon case has already been introduced by the section in Chapter 7 that compared eBayism with Amazonism. The present chapter will focus on Amazon and show that the firm's rational leader developed it into an iconic corporation—and beyond—by using all seven of the appropriate rational methods. Founding leader Jeff Bezos had developed this 1995 Internet start-up into an iconic corporation by the end of the 2000s. In the 2010s he developed Amazon a step further. It eventually employed more than half a million people and was the global leader of online retailing. In addition, it invented high-tech devices, sold cloud-computing services to businesses, and provided consumers with video streaming and programmes: it competed against Netflix and Microsoft as well as Walmart. Amazon had in fact been developed into a uniquely 'multifaceted' high-tech corporation, thanks to brilliant rational leadership during technologically changing times.

In 2021, Bezos retired from his long-held post as Amazon's CEO, becoming instead its executive chairman. And he published *Invent & Wander: The Collected Writings of Jeff Bezos*. It is not an exact equivalent of the autobiographical accounts written by leaders featured in previous chapters, but it provides some leader's-eye view of his rational development of Amazon, including his need to get a good night's sleep!

> I need eight hours. I think better. I have more energy. My mood is better. And think about it: As a senior executive, what do you really get paid to do? You get paid to make a small number of high-quality decisions. Your job is not to make thousands of decisions every day ... When Amazon was a hundred people, it was a different story, but Amazon's not a start-up company ... If I make, like, three good decisions a day, that's enough, and they should be just as high quality as I can make them.[1]

This decision-making was improved not only by a good night's sleep but also by his use of the appropriate rational methods of developing his corporation. Bezos used all seven of these methods—and emphasized three—in his development of Amazon into an iconic corporation.

The chapter's first section examines his use of the two adaptive rational methods in the 2000s. His rapid adaptive responses and emphasizing of innovative adaptation led to such successes as Prime, the Kindle device, and the cloud computing of Amazon Web Services (AWS). The second section looks at Bezos's use of four

Rational Leadership. Paul Brooker and Margaret Hayward, Oxford University Press. © Paul Brooker & Margaret Hayward (2023). DOI: 10.1093/oso/9780198894643.003.0008

other appropriate rational methods of developing a corporation, namely quantitative and strategic calculation plus diverse and institutionalized deliberation. He indeed emphasized strategic calculation, particularly a customer-centric sales strategy and a 'big picture' grand strategy of rapid growth and diversification. Such strategic calculation, along with the other rational methods, helped him to develop Amazon into an iconic corporation by the end of the 2000s.

The third and fourth sections survey his use of rational methods in Amazon's 2010s–20s era of development. In this era he quickly developed Amazon into a multifaceted high-tech corporation, pioneering a new kind of development that will be labelled 'Bezist'. Amazon's leader had to combine the high-tech inventiveness of a Steve Jobs with the retailing acumen of a Sam Walton. Finally, the fifth section will show how Bezos emphasized learning as a key rational method of developing Amazon, from its inception as an Internet start-up to its maturity as a multifaceted high-tech corporation.

Bezos's leadership is arguably *the* best-practice case of rationally leading the development of a corporation. He has even been described as 'hyperrational'.[2] His rational approach was evident from the very beginning, when deciding to start up a firm based on the Internet. Bezos had graduated from Princeton in 1986, with a degree in computer science and electrical engineering, and then worked for financial-computing firms until in 1994:

> I came across the fact that the web—the World Wide Web—was growing at something like 2,300 percent a year. Anything growing that fast, even if its baseline usage today is tiny, is going to be big. I concluded that I should come up with a business idea based on the internet and then let the internet grow around it.[3]

His rational approach was evident, too, when he devised a business idea that would exploit the Internet opportunity. The idea was to be an online retailer and to sell a product that was well suited to this form of e-commerce. 'So I made a list of products I might sell online. I started ranking them, and I picked books'.[4] Selling books had several advantages, as is explained by Brandt in his *One-Click: Jeff Bezos and the Rise of Amazon.com*.[5] For example, the two main wholesale distributors had hundreds of thousands of titles stored in their warehouses, ready to be supplied to an online retailer. And Bezos mentions that he located his start-up in Seattle partly because 'the largest book warehouse in the world at that time was nearby in a town called Roseberg, Oregon'.[6]

He launched Amazon.com in 1995. According to its mission statement, it aimed to be the world's 'most customer-centric company' and, from the outset, customers were given an excellent delivery service and a website that expanded their online shopping experience.[7] But the new start-up needed time to build momentum as an online bookseller. Although Bezos mentions 'how excited we were in 1996 as we crossed $10 million in book sales', he was fortunate that the big chainstore booksellers did not begin competing for the online market until 1997.[8] By then Amazon had gained some momentum. During that year, sales grew from some $16 million to nearly $148 million, while the workforce grew fourfold to a total of more than 600.[9] And in mid-1997 Bezos converted his start-up into a public company. During 1998/9 he developed and diversified Amazon into an online retailer that sold more than just books, as was described in the Amazonism section of Chapter 7. By 2000, Bezos had established a notable corporation, with some 8,000 employees.[10]

Amazon then navigated a 2000/1 crisis created by external shocks. A stock-market crash of shares in Internet-based companies, the 'dot-com crash' in mid-2000, led on to a recession in the e-commerce economy. Amazon's future seemed in doubt, as Bezos noted later. 'At the pinnacle of the internet bubble our stock price peaked at $116, and then after the bubble burst our stock went down to $6. Experts and pundits thought we were going out of business'.[11] This was an externally, not internally, generated crisis. But Bezos took the necessary steps to restore confidence. In 2001, Amazon laid off about 15 per cent of its workforce and carried out other cost-cutting measures.[12] With the recession easing, the firm soon resumed its development into an iconic corporation—indeed the mid-2000s would be a pivotal period in Amazon's development.

Adaptive Successes in the 2000s

Bezos's highly successful use of adaptive methods in the mid-2000s had a crucial effect on Amazon's development. His emphasis on innovative adaptation led to the Kindle, Prime, and AWS successes. In all three cases, too, there was rapid adaptation. The Chapter 7 section on Amazonism has already described the Kindle device as a rapid adaptive response to the prospect of a digital revolution in bookselling. Although Amazon took from 2004 to 2007 to develop the Kindle, this was a 'rapid' adaptive response 'for an online retailer that had never before developed a piece of technology, let alone a portable device using advanced electronic-reading technology'. Furthermore, the Kindle project was quickly *initiated* by Bezos. The project was in fact a classic example of the rapid-initiation lengthy-development (RILD) pattern or problem that often occurred when his rapid adaptations led to new products.

His initiating of the Kindle project is recounted in Bryar and Carr's recent *Working Backwards: Insights, Stories, and Secrets from Inside Amazon*. Although their book is mainly about the working-backwards technique, the authors provide many other insights from their careers as Amazon executives.[13] They point out that 'in the early 2000s, the transformation from physical media to digital media posed an existential threat to Amazon's business. Roughly 75 per cent of Amazon's business at that time consisted of selling physical books, CDs, and DVDs to customers'.[14] Bezos's awareness of the digital threat can be traced back at least as far as a 2003 meeting with Steve Jobs at Apple headquarters. Here Jobs warned him that Amazon's selling of music CDs would be marginalized by the shift to digital music, which was being led by Apple's digital-music iPod and iTunes.[15] After this meeting Bezos created a Digital unit and worked with it to formulate a plan for digital media: a plan that focussed on books rather than music.[16] Books were still Amazon's largest sales category and also digital e-books was an area where, unlike in digital music, the firm would not be trailing behind Apple. Amazon's ambitious plan was both to sell digital books and to offer customers an excellent device for reading these e-books, even though 'we would need to invent the device ourselves, and the potential development time might take years'.[17] So by 2004, Amazon was developing the e-book reading device that would be revealed to the world in late 2007 as the Kindle.

The Kindle project also shows Bezos using *innovative* adaptation and indeed emphasizing this method of developing Amazon. With the Kindle, he was not only aiming for innovation but also making an innovative effort to accomplish it. As he points out, 'Amazon had never designed or built a hardware device, but rather than change the vision to accommodate our then-existing skills, we hired a number of talented ... hardware engineers and got started learning a new institutional skill'.[18] Bezos even created a special unit to carry out the project. And this secretive 'Lab126' unit was located in Silicon Valley, not in Seattle with the other parts of Amazon.[19]

Although Bezos was physically distant from the new unit, he 'stayed so deeply involved in the project that he was unofficially known as the chief product manager for Kindle'.[20] Through this hands-on control he ensured that the product included such innovative features as E-Ink and Whispernet.[21] The latter was the Kindle's connection to a wireless carrier network, which enabled a reader to download e-books directly rather than first downloading them to a personal computer and then 'sideloading' them to the portable Kindle device. The E-Ink feature was a black-and-white screen that was more reader-friendly than a computer screen and was much more economical in its use of battery power. Such innovations added to the time and money required to develop the Kindle. But its technological superiority enabled the Kindle and upgraded Kindle 2 to dominate the market for e-book reading devices in 2008/9.[22] A strong challenge was made by Jobs and Apple in 2010, when they launched the iPad tablet computer. It could be used to read e-books and soon made inroads into Amazon's dominant market share.[23] However, Amazon had by then developed such a strong hold on the market that there was no chance of Apple gaining the sort of hold that it had gained over digital music in the mid-2000s. Bezos's innovative adaptation had ensured that his corporation did not face such a daunting prospect; more positively, he had made a significant contribution to Amazon's development into an iconic corporation.

The Kindle was not the only innovative adaptation emphasized by Bezos in the mid-2000s. An innovative sales technique was introduced, too, as a rapid adaptive response to a dangerous trend in the firm's sales. In 2004, Amazon's online sales were still growing quickly but the *rate* of growth was decelerating, in contrast to the acceleration in the overall expansion of online commerce. So 'if Amazon's growth continued to decelerate, the company would become a smaller and smaller player in online commerce over time'.[24] This dangerous trend generated a rapid adaptive response. By October 2004, Bezos was pushing for a change that was soon developed into a major new sales technique, namely Amazon 'Prime', which was launched in February 2005.[25]

The innovative new sales technique was not conjured out of thin air. Amazon already knew that the most effective way of boosting online sales was to deliver the purchases to customers at minimum cost and maximum speed.[26] So now a budding special-delivery idea was promoted by Bezos and developed into a new sales technique.[27] It offered customers a special-delivery subscription service or club called 'Prime', whose members would receive fast and free delivery of goods they had purchased from Amazon. Specifically, an annual subscription of $79 gave a member an unlimited amount of *free* two-day shipping, plus upgrades to one-day delivery for $3.99.[28] But Bezos notes that while 'customers love free shipping', Prime was initially very expensive for Amazon:

> It cost us a lot of money because what happens when you offer a free all-you-can-eat buffet? Who shows up to the buffet first? The heavy eaters. It's scary. It's like, oh my god, did I really say as many prawns as you can eat? And so that is what happened, but we could see the trend lines. We could see all kinds of customers were coming, and they appreciated that service, so that's what led to the success of Prime.[29]

The Prime sales technique succeeded in both attracting new customers to Amazon and encouraging customers to be heavier eaters at this 'all-you-can-eat buffet'. Customer spending was boosted by the privilege of free shipping and also by two factors described in Stone's book on the rise of Amazon, *The Everything Store*. Customers who had joined Prime 'gorged on the almost instant gratification of having purchases reliably appear two days after they ordered them', and furthermore there was that 'faintly irrational human impulse to maximize the benefits of a membership club one has already joined'.[30] Hence the Prime innovation soon eased the sales-growth problem and a few years later was seen as 'a huge success': even its costs had markedly improved, thanks to increases in shipping efficiency and scale.[31]

Bezos's third innovative adaptation in the mid-2000s was a new kind of online services, sold by Amazon Web Services. The Chapter 7 section on Amazonism described this innovation but did not mention that it was an adaptation and that the term 'cloud computing' is a widely used label for this kind of online services. Cloud computing has recently been defined as 'on-demand delivery of IT resources such as computing power and data storage over the internet with pay-as-you-go pricing'.[32] Such cloud computing, specifically the infrastructure form of cloud computing, was pioneered by AWS in the mid-2000s.

Its cloud computing was a rapid and innovative adaptation to a new opportunity. Even before AWS was established, Amazon had been supplying online data and software to allied or associated firms, helping these firms' software experts to develop better websites and applications.[33] In 2002, such free online services were offered to all software developers by the newly launched Amazon Web Services. Bezos announced that Amazon was 'putting out a welcome mat for developers', and indeed over 25,000 software developers had enrolled with AWS by mid-2003—over 64,000 by mid-2004.[34] More importantly, Bezos and AWS's leader Andy Jassy were preparing to offer developers something new: such 'building blocks' of software development as computing power and data storage.[35] But creating these new online web services was another case of RILD adaptation. The Simple Storage Service and Elastic Compute Cloud services took years to develop.[36] In 2006, the new services were finally ready to be delivered, and AWS was relaunched as a supplier of the new kind of services to the old kind of recipients. Later that year Bezos noted that 240,000 developers were registered with AWS, which was 'targeting broad needs universally faced by software developers, such as storage and compute capacity—areas in which developers have asked for help.[37] Amazon had adapted to their needs and also to their potential as paying customers. The new kind of services were not free and had the pay-as-you-go feature that is typical of cloud computing.

During the late 2000s, AWS's new services began boosting their revenues by meeting the broad needs of firms as well as software developers. Start-up firms wanted access to large-scale computing power and data storage, while bigger companies wanted to shift from using their own IT equipment to using the equivalent online services provided by AWS's equipment. The bigger companies' shift to using online services was depicted by Bezos in 2009 as analogous to the long-ago shift to the electric-power grid.

> You go back in time a hundred years, if you wanted to have electricity, you had to build your own little electric power plant, and a lot of factories did this. As soon as the electric power grid came online, they dumped their electric power generator, and they started buying power off the grid … And that is what is starting to happen with infrastructure computing.[38]

As supplier of 'the grid' Amazon carried a heavy responsibility and had to invest heavily in its IT equipment. The pay-off, though, was cloud computing's huge revenue-earning potential, which would be fully exploited in the next decade of development. And AWS leader Jassy would eventually be Bezos's successor as CEO of Amazon. By then AWS's cloud computing was clearly the most successful way in which Bezos had emphasized innovative adaptation as a means of developing his corporation.

Calculating and Deliberating

In addition to the two adaptive methods, Bezos used the five other appropriate rational methods of developing a corporation: the calculative pair, the deliberative pair, and learning. This section looks at his use of the calculative and deliberative methods, which played a significant role in the development of Amazon. Bezos in fact emphasized the strategic-calculation method. For example, his customer-centric sales strategy played a vital role in Amazon's development during the 1995–9 period, as was noted earlier in the chapter and in Chapter 7. The customer-centric strategy continued into the 2000s. Prioritizing the customer's needs or likes 'continued to be a guiding beacon', and the firm's culture still catered 'obsessively to its customers' in these later years of development.[39]

Bezos's most important strategic calculation, though, was his 'big picture' grand strategy of rapid growth and diversification. This grand-strategic design emerged as early as 1996, when Amazon was still in its start-up period.[40] Bezos's decision to focus on rapid growth was explained to his employees as competing in a frontier-like race to capture territory. In this 'race to establish brands on the new digital frontier', the firm 'that got the lead now would likely keep it'.[41] There were other reasons, too, for adopting a strategy of rapid growth. As Bezos later pointed out, the online version of retailing was 'a scale business characterized by high fixed costs and relatively low variable costs'.[42] So this was another good reason to scale up his new business as rapidly as possible. Indeed he gave Amazon the new motto Get Big Fast.[43]

The strategy was broadened in 1998/9 to include rapid diversification as well as growth. Amazon diversified into selling CDs and DVDs and then began partnering in various ways with other online or offline retailers, so as to speed up its diversification into an 'everything store'.[44] The strategy was also partly defensive, as an increasing number of American retailers, even Walmart, were starting to take their business online.[45] Amazon had already fallen behind eBay in the online-platform race, and in fact Bezos's 1999 diversifications included an attempt to catch up with eBay, as described in Chapter 7. Although Amazon Auctions was a complete failure, the zShops for third-party sellers became a success after being reinvented and relaunched in 2000 as Marketplace.[46]

Bezos's grand strategy was constrained by the 2000/1 crisis, but the following years saw a return to rapid growth and diversification. In 2005, Marcus's memoir *Amazonia* described this revival as 'madcap expansion' and a return to 'wolfing down new partners like salted peanuts'.[47] Although the new partners were often simply acquisitions, even acquired firms were normally allowed to operate separately rather than being absorbed into Amazon. In addition to its 'drive to add new partners and product lines', Amazon was making some 'starry-eyed initiatives, with their mad scientist overtones', which also resulted in new product lines.[48] Such mad-scientist high-tech products were a new, internal form of diversification. It seems to be epitomized by the Kindle device and AWS cloud computing, initiated by 2004 and leading to new product lines in 2006/7. But they had originated as adaptations and in this sense are less typical than other, later examples of high-tech diversifying that will be described in the next section.

The new form of diversification by no means replaced the partnership form. Amazon continued to seek and add new partners, such as its acquisition of online retailers Zappos (shoes) and Quidsi (diapers) in 2009.[49] That year also saw a move to reinvigorate an old eBayist diversification: the third-party sellers' Marketplace described in Chapter 7. In 2009, there was an effort to improve its operations and boost the number of sellers using Marketplace.[50] This reinvigoration project benefited from a service for third-party sellers, 'Fulfillment by Amazon' (FBA), which had been launched two years earlier. The FBA service allowed third-party sellers, for a modest fee, to store their merchandise in Amazon's warehouses and have it delivered to their customers by Amazon.[51] Such services helped Marketplace increase its sales and attract more third-party sellers, so Bezos could tell his shareholders that in 2009:

> Sales of products by third-party sellers on our websites represented 30 percent of our unit sales ... Active seller accounts increased 24 percent to 1.9 million for the year. Globally, sellers using Fulfillment by Amazon stowed more than one million unique items in our fulfillment center network.[52]

Clearly the eBayist diversification had not been overshadowed by that year's two notable partnership acquisitions, nor by the launch of such an impressive high-tech device as the second-generation Kindle 2.

Bezos's diversifying was therefore advancing strongly on all three fronts: high-tech initiatives, new partnerships, and Marketplace. This impressive three-pronged diversification was also providing plenty of impetus to his grand strategy of rapid growth and diversification. For instance, in 2009 Amazon's net sales increased by 28 per cent and were fifteen times higher than in 1999.[53] During these ten years, his grand strategy had played a huge role in Amazon's development into an iconic corporation.

But Bezos had used quantitative as well strategic calculation to develop Amazon. In particular, this other form of calculation helped him make the less strategic, more quantitative decisions. Bezos himself has pointed to the difference between strategic decisions and the more quantifiable 'operating' decisions.[54] He has also noted that many important decisions can be made through quantitative calculation, as 'math tells us' the right or better answer.[55] His examples seem to be typical operating decisions: opening a new fulfilment-centre warehouse, gauging inventory purchases, and estimating replenishment times. An increasingly large number of these operating decisions arose as Amazon grew in size from start-up to big corporation. However, he could delegate many of the decisions, knowing that his employees were influenced by a metrics-oriented culture and would let 'math' tell them the answers. Imbuing Amazon with this metrics-oriented culture was therefore perhaps his most important use of quantitative calculation.

When Amazon was still only a start-up, Bezos had promised what he termed a Culture of Metrics.[56] By 2000, Amazon's 'famously data-driven culture was prevalent throughout the company', according to Bryar and Carr.[57] The data-driven, metrics-oriented culture was also having a marked influence on the company's activities. Amazon's website was an early and ready example. For 'a company like Amazon could (and did) record every move a [website] visitor made, every last click and switch of the mouse. As the data piled up', the firm 'could draw all sorts of conclusions about that chimerical creature: the Consumer'.[58] These data-based conclusions helped the website pursue the firm's customer-centric sales strategy. New features were added to the website, and others removed, according to what the metrics revealed about customers' needs and wants.[59]

The metrics culture was then extended to the logistical, supply side of the business. Amazon's warehouses were now called 'fulfilment centres' and their operations were based on quantitative data and calculations.[60] This logistics upgrade was led by Bezos's new 'numbers man', Jeff Wilke. Recruited in 1999, he in turn recruited a team of quantitative experts that helped him 'devise dozens of metrics' related to logistics.[61] As with the website, such quantification produced customer-centric benefits: customers' purchases were supplied to them more quickly and reliably.

In the early 2000s, too, the metric culture's influence on administration was boosted by the invention of a new form of weekly meeting. Stone has described them as 'metrics meetings' and in fact the metrics-related chapter in Bryar and Carr's book is largely about this Weekly Business Review (WBR) technique.[62] An administrative unit could closely monitor its situation and performance by reviewing its metrics at WBRs. Not surprisingly, the WBR was widely adopted throughout Amazon, with teams, departments, and business categories each having their own weekly meeting—even Bezos attended a WBR.[63]

In addition to using quantitative and strategic calculation, he also used the two deliberative rational methods, diverse and institutionalized deliberation. Although he did not emphasize either of them, he used these methods in distinctive ways. For instance, there was his theory and practice of varying the *amount* of deliberation to fit the type of decision. He described this as avoiding a 'one-size-fits-all' decision-making process.[64] More positively, it means 'customizing' the amount of deliberation to fit the type of decision. Crucial decisions 'must be made methodically, carefully, slowly, with great deliberation and consultation', and they are termed a 'one-way-door' decision because 'you can't get back to where you were before' if the results are disappointing.[65] But few decisions are really crucial; most decisions are of the reversible, *two*-way-door type. These are decisions that if suboptimal, 'you don't have to live with consequences for that long. You can reopen the door and go back through.'[66] In such cases therefore a firm can afford to reduce the amount of deliberation and thereby speed up the decision-making process. This can be done by limiting the number of groups or people involved in the deliberations and by adopting procedures or approaches that streamline deliberation.[67] For example, a firm can adopt a disagree-and-commit approach, whereby deliberators speed up the decision-making process by committing to support a decision even though they disagree with it. Bezos believes that even the firm's boss should adopt this approach: 'I disagree and commit all the time'.[68]

In contrast, however, he has often slowed down the other type of decision, the crucial and irreversible *one*-way-door decision.

> I often find myself at Amazon acting as the chief slowdown officer. 'Whoa, I want to see that decision analysed seventeen more ways because it's highly consequential and irreversible' ... You do not want to make one-way-door decisions quickly. You want to get consensus or at least drive a lot of thought and debate.[69]

Furthermore, Bezos was increasing the *diversity* as well as the amount of deliberation. He was slowing down the decision-making partly because he wanted more diverse deliberation, such as having the decision analysed in 'seventeen more ways'! Clearly when crucial decisions were being made, he wanted diverse deliberation and did not care if this slowed down the decision-making process.

His commitment to diversity had been expressed in the Leadership Principles developed in the mid-2000s by a human-resources team and Bezos.[70] Principle Four included the requirement that leaders 'seek diverse perspectives and seek to disconfirm their beliefs', which seems as sweeping a commitment to diversity as could be expected of any principle.[71] Another Principle forbade reticence, as leaders were 'obligated to respectfully challenge decisions when they disagree, even when doing so is uncomfortable or exhausting'.[72] Such challenges have been depicted in more adversarial terms. Stone noted that executives 'battled it out in arguments' and that Amazon's culture was 'confrontational'.[73] But if there was an adversarial aspect to Amazon's diversity, this at least had prevented reticence and had created some diversity in the firm's deliberations.

Bezos also used the vertical, bottom-up version of diverse deliberation. Here subordinates provide their leaders with policy proposals, product ideas, or other items for deliberation. Chapter 7 mentioned the eBay example of a subordinate proposing that a used-car category be added to eBay's online auction categories. In Amazon's case, the vertical version of diverse deliberation was successfully encouraged and institutionalized by Bezos. His success was partly due to his distinctive liking for discussion documents. His PR/FAQ (press release / frequently asked questions) type of discussion document will be explored in the next section; his other type—the narrative memo—will be explored when looking at his use of *institutionalized* deliberation.

Bezos was a user but not an exponent of institutionalized deliberation. His book certainly does not display any Sloan-like appreciation for formal small-group deliberation. For example, he does not even mention Amazon's board of directors.[74] And there is little mention of Amazon's senior leadership team. Known as the 'S-Team', it originated in 1999 and included the firm's senior vice-presidents and other senior executives.[75] Bezos attended a weekly four-hour S-Team meeting plus 'an informal Monday-morning S-Team breakfast' at a near-office location.[76] However, his writings contain just one, indirect reference to the team's deliberations: he mentions that it monitors the firm's progress towards achieving the most important of Amazon's annual goals. 'We review the status of each of these goals several times per year among our senior leadership team, and add, remove, and modify goals as we proceed'.[77] Doubtless some deliberation occurred when making these reviews and decisions. Similarly, some deliberation would have occurred when deciding *which* annual goals were important enough to be labelled 'S-Team goals' and hence given priority status within the firm as well as special attention by the S-Team.[78]

But Bezos's most prominent and distinctive use of institutionalized deliberation was his focus on discussion documents. This began in 2004, when he made Amazon renounce PowerPoint presentations and instead present types of discussion document.[79] The policy-proposing type is described by him as 'narratively structured six-page memos'—the narrative memos.[80] They were presented at meetings of managerial groups or leadership teams, notably Bezos's S-Team. The narrative memos encouraged vertical, bottom-up deliberation as well as aiding deliberation initiated within a managerial group or leadership team. A narrative memo 'can be used to explore any argument or idea you want to present to a group of people—an investment, a potential acquisition, a new product or feature, a monthly or quarterly business update, an operating plan, or even an idea on how to improve the food at the company cafeteria'.[81]

The narrative memo or 'six-pager' is described in some detail by Bryar and Carr.[82] They note that the standard length of six pages enabled presenters to make an informative proposal or appraisal, and the standard narrative structure raised the intellectual level of the memo. So the presentation of these memos seems to be the business equivalent of academic papers being presented at seminars. The main difference from a seminar is that the memo was not read aloud by a presenter. Instead a copy was given to each member of the audience and they spent some twenty minutes silently reading and digesting it, perhaps jotting down notes. Bezos aptly compares this stage of the meeting to a study hall.[83] Bryar and Carr note that Bezos 'was usually among the last to finish' reading and digesting a narrative memo, and he apparently had 'an uncanny ability' to arrive at insights not seen by the other readers.[84] These insights were offered at the next stage of a memo's presentation.

> [Now] the audience members ask questions of the presenting team. They seek clarification, probe intentions, offer insights, and suggest refinements or alternatives … The key goal of the meeting, after all, is to seek the truth about the proposed idea or topic. We want that idea to be the best it can possibly be as the result of any adjustments we can make along with the presenting team … You are not just commenting on a document, you're helping to shape an idea.[85]

The memos could therefore become the focus of important deliberation. Bezos notes that some memos 'set up the meeting for high-quality discussion', though some others 'come in at the other end of the spectrum'.[86] Overall, however, his discussion-document way of institutionalizing deliberation has proven to be very successful, helping him to develop Amazon from the mid-2000s onwards into the 2010s.

Amazon and Bezism in the 2010s–20s

By the beginning of the 2010s, Amazon was an iconic corporation, but there was still room for development. The corporation continued to grow rapidly in scale and value during the new decade. In 2018, its stock-market value reached $1 trillion, sales revenue was well over $200 billion, and its workforce numbered more than half a million.[87] From a development perspective, however, the most significant feature was that Amazon had developed into a 'multifaceted' high-tech corporation. In the 2000s, Bezos had added two important new high-tech facets: the Kindle and AWS's cloud computing. In the 2010s he added several other facets and indeed made Amazon 'uniquely' multifaceted, in the sense that no other high-tech firm had so many and such diverse facets. Furthermore, Bezos had carried out this multifaceted development remarkably quickly. It had taken him little more than a decade: from the mid-2000s to the late 2010s. Other high-tech firms had developed in a similarly multifaceted way in other times or places, as with the 1960s–80s Hewlett-Packard case studied in Chapter 6. But none had gone so far so quickly as Bezos-led Amazon. Bezos had led a historically unparalleled example of this kind of development.

From a rational-leadership perspective, the key point is that he had used rational means. Bezos in fact used the same seven rational methods that he had used to develop Amazon into an iconic corporation. These seven methods therefore are apparently *also* the appropriate rational means to use when developing a *multifaceted* high-tech corporation, even when not seeking to go so far and so quickly.

As confirmation, this section and the next will survey Bezos's use of these methods in Amazon's new era. Here he led a new *kind* of corporation development: it was new to his employee-followers and was also new to the world in going so far so quickly. 'Bezist' therefore seems an appropriate label for this kind of development. After all, the term 'Bezonomics' has been applied by Dumaine to the business model developed by Bezos.[88] And this leader seems just as entitled to have the term 'Bezist' applied to the kind of development that he personifies.

Dumaine's book *Bezonomics* was one of several important Amazon-related works published in 2020/1. Two others have already appeared in this chapter, namely Bezos's own writings and Bryar and Carr's book on the working-backwards techniques at Amazon. In addition, Stone published a sequel to his earlier book on Amazon, his impressive *The Everything Store*. Its sequel is entitled *Amazon Unbound: Jeff Bezos and the Invention of a Global Empire*. Stone's new book and Dumaine's *Bezonomics* provide broad and in-depth coverage of the new era. Dumaine also provides some insights into Amazon's likely Bezist development in the post-Bezos 2020s. As for Bezos's own book, it continues to provide a leader's-eye view as he led Amazon into the Bezist 2010s.

During the new era, he continued to use all seven rational methods of corporation development. But the two adaptive methods were not as important as they had been in the 2000s. Kindle-like technological innovations were being initiated not as adaptations but as part of Bezos's diversification strategy. However, two of the innovative adaptations from the earlier era became increasingly important in the 2010s. AWS's cloud computing became in fact the most important of Amazon's high-tech facets. By 2015, AWS had more than a million customers and annual sales of $10 billion.[89] Even government agencies, notably the CIA (Central Intelligence Agency), were buying infrastructure cloud computing from Amazon.[90] And it had an unassailable lead in this rapidly expanding cloud-computing area of business. Bezos has described AWS's lead as:

> the greatest piece of business luck in the history of business, so far as I know. We faced no like-minded competition for seven years … I think that the big, established enterprise software companies did not see Amazon as a credible enterprise software company, so we had this long runway to build this incredible, feature-rich product and service that is just so far ahead.[91]

By 2019, AWS had reached an annual revenue of $35 billion and an estimated stock-market value of more than $500 billion.[92]

'Prime' was the other mid-2000s innovative adaptation that became a pillar of 2010s Amazon. Dumaine even describes Prime as Bezos's 'crown jewel' and as the 'most powerful force' driving Amazon's growth.[93] Although Prime led to new high-tech facets being added, it was not a technological innovation but an innovative sales technique, as the first section explained. Prime boosted Amazon's online-retailing sales by offering customers a subscription service or club, Prime, whose members received free and fast shipping of their Amazon purchases in return for an annual subscription fee. The Prime programme had attracted a lucrative number of members during the later 2000s, and membership continued to increase impressively in the new era. By 2013, there were 'tens of millions' of members worldwide, by 2017, a hundred million members, and that year more than five billion items were shipped to Prime members.[94]

The sales-boosting Prime innovation also revolutionized Amazon's supply system of fulfilment-centre warehouses. As Bezos noted, the 'precise delivery-date promise of Prime required operating our fulfillment centers in a new way' to meet this new standard.[95] By the mid-2010s the number of centres had increased from just thirteen to more than a hundred and furthermore they displayed a new high-tech facet: they deployed 'more than fifteen thousand robots' in support of a software system that managed the 'receipt, stowing, picking and shipment' of the merchandise.[96] Thanks to Prime, Amazon had the retail sector's best supply system as well as an increasingly large set of high-spending customers. Bryar and Carr therefore credit Prime with having 'transformed Amazon from a fairly successful company in the e-commerce space to a top player in the retail space'.[97]

Furthermore, Prime led to the new era's key innovative adaptation, Prime Video. This video-streaming service was not technologically innovative, but it introduced a new sales technique that strengthened Prime and also preserved a high-tech facet that later proved markedly successful. The facet originated in the mid-2000s as Amazon's Unbox video-downloading service, which downloaded movies to its customers' computers. It can be counted as one of the high-tech initiatives that were a new part of Bezos's diversification strategy, as recounted in the previous section. But Unbox was perhaps the least successful of these high-tech initiatives, largely because its technology had serious limitations, even after being made television-compatible. Unbox was therefore superseded when video *streaming* to television and other devices was introduced by the Netflix corporation in 2007/8.[98] Amazon soon shifted its technology from downloading to streaming but then began lagging behind in other areas. Netflix was offering its subscribers a more impressive catalogue or 'library' of movies and television shows: thanks to heavy investment in licensing deals with the studios that owned these items.[99] And Amazon had stuck with a pay-per-item approach that later seemed inferior to Netflix's paid-subscription approach.[100] Bezos, however, made an innovative adaptive response to this disappointing situation. He decided in 2010 that Amazon's video-streaming service should be converted into a free add-on for members of Prime.[101]

In February 2011, Prime's members were offered a free video-streaming service, Prime Instant Video, later known simply as Prime Video. This innovative adaptation was introducing a new sales technique by offering free video streaming as an incentive for people to join and stay with the sales-boosting Prime programme. The new sales technique also proved to be a lasting success. As late as 2017, Amazon believed Prime Video was still 'a formidable and profitable way to attract new Prime members': it had attracted around a quarter of the new members who joined Prime in 2014–17.[102] As well as strengthening Prime, the new sales technique had preserved the high-tech facet that had originated in the mid-2000s with Unbox. Instead of being a disappointing venture, the downloading/streaming of video products had become a successful high-tech facet.[103] Furthermore, it was ready to take on new roles, where it would have a more direct effect on sales.

In 2016/17, Amazon took this next step and set up a worldwide subscription version of Prime Video. The new version was not free, was offered to people who were not members of Prime, and was aiming for worldwide coverage. As Stone notes, by aiming 'to introduce Prime Video in 242 countries', Amazon was entering 'many parts of the world where it didn't yet operate an online retail business'.[104] So Prime Video's sales of video streaming would create a fully 'globalized' Amazon. And Bezos's innovative adaptation had apparently created a *double-barrelled* sales technique, whose longer ranged barrel was now hitting its target with global effect.

His innovative adaptation had also led to a notable example of rapid adaptation. Bezos had rapidly started producing television programmes for his 2011-launched Prime Instant Video. As early as 2010 he began trying to produce shows and started up Amazon Studios.[105] This was not a response to Prime Instant Video being short of programmes: his new service's catalogue contained some 5,000 movies and television episodes.[106] But Amazon wanted Prime Instant Video to 'enjoy the benefits of having exclusive, first-run TV shows' on offer.[107] Here was an opportunity to increase the new service's appeal and its ability to compete with Netflix. However, the RILD problem emerged again, as the rapidly initiated adaptation was followed by years of development.[108] So Netflix, not Amazon, pioneered made-for-streaming shows. Its *House of Cards* series was aired in February 2013, two months before Amazon unveiled its first batch of home-grown programmes.[109] Amazon aired four series—two comedies and two children's series—and in later years produced several drama series, such as *The Man in the High Castle*.[110] Bezos's rapid adaptation was at last starting to pay off. By the 2020s, Amazon Studios was established 'at the forefront of the Hollywood vanguard, along with Netflix and rising competitors'.[111] Video streaming was still a highly competitive business, but Bezos had at least kept Amazon in the game.

He had also made video streaming one of Amazon's most influential high-tech facets. Prime Video and Amazon Studios had given the corporation a new way of entering the lives of many millions of people throughout the world. Amazon was even offering them its own version of the television set-top box that enabled video streaming. Launched in 2014, the Fire TV box was not an innovation but was an impressive development of existing technology. Fire TV was therefore a commercial success and was still 'one of the top-selling TV-connected video streaming devices in the world' in 2020.[112] Bezos had promoted the new product in his 2013 letter to shareholders. He pointed out that the device gave viewers access to non-Amazon streaming services as well as Prime Video, and enabled a television to be used as a games console.[113] He could also have pointed out that Amazon was now benefiting from three different aspects of video streaming, thanks to content-creator Amazon Studios, service provider Prime Video, and set-top box Fire TV.

Amazon's video streaming had likewise benefited from his use of three different rational methods. In addition to innovative and rapid adaptation, he had also used some strategic calculation. For Fire TV was one of several high-tech diversifications that arose from Bezos's 2010s grand strategy of rapid growth and diversification. This strategy had proved its worth in the 1990s–2000s and he continued to emphasize it during the new era.[114]

The rapid-growth aspect of his grand strategy was very evident in the 2010s. His company was the fastest ever to reach $100 billion in annual sales, achieved in 2015, and Bezos pointed out that the workforce had grown at a similarly rapid rate. 'We've grown from 30,000 employees in 2010 to more than 230,000 now [2015]. We're a bit like parents who look around one day and realize their kids have grown—you blink, and it happens.'[115] The rapid growth continued in the second half of the decade. Amazon's domestic retail sales had grown by an impressive 25 per cent in 2015 but reached a remarkable 33 per cent in 2017.[116] In 2018, annual sales reached more than $232 billion, while the workforce of full-time and part-time employees had grown to over 647,000.[117] Amazon's Marketplace third-party sellers, too, experienced rapid sales growth in the 2010s, even though most of these sellers, some two million, were only small or medium-sized businesses.[118] In addition to boosting its domestic sales, Amazon was continuing the global expansion mentioned in Chapter 7. Stone's book highlights Amazon's expansion into a 'global empire', such as its extension into India's huge economy.[119] The corporation was therefore being scaled-up globally as well as seeing an amazing increase in the scale of its sales revenue and workforce.

However, the rapid *diversification* aspect of his grand strategy, not the rapid-growth aspect, was adding such high-tech facets as Fire TV. During the 2010s, the diversification strategy added the new facets that completed Amazon's Bezist development. Without these additions, Amazon would still have had an unusually wide range of high-tech facets, such as cloud computing and Prime Video. But Amazon would not have been a *uniquely* multifaceted high-tech corporation. Strategic diversifying, as the next section shows, created the crucial additional facets.

From strategic balancing to VIT and AI

This section is an extension of the previous one and begins by highlighting Bezos's adept balancing of his diversification strategy with his customer-centric sales strategy. Specifically, he waited until the mid-2010s before diversifying into the high-tech advertising pioneered by Google over a decade earlier. Bezos's other high-tech diversifying was more strategically straightforward. The section surveys his three 'Fire' projects and describes in some detail his innovative Echo/Alexa device, with its impressive voice information technology (VIT). The second half of the section moves on from strategic to quantitative calculation and to the machine-learning techniques associated with artificial intelligence (AI). The focus then shifts to diverse and institutionalized deliberation, such as Amazon's product-proposing discussion documents. Finally, there is a look at where Amazon's Bezist development is likely to go in the post-Bezos 2020s.

Returning then to the theme of diversification, the most strategically interesting high-tech diversification was the delayed move into advertising. This was a classic example of strategic balancing: the strategic calculation that occurs when a balance is struck between the needs or benefits of two different strategies.[120] In Bezos's case he struck a balance between his diversification strategy and his customer-centric sales strategy, whose importance was highlighted earlier in the chapter. The needs of his vital sales strategy outweighed the potential benefits of diversifying into high-tech advertising, and so this diversification was delayed for a decade—until the mid-2010s.

The diversification had become technically feasible as early as 2004, when Amazon introduced its A9 search-engine software. The A9 was one of the new 'starry-eyed initiatives, with their mad scientist overtones', mentioned in Marcus's memoir *Amazonia*.[121] As he foresaw, the A9 did not threaten the dominant position won by Google's search engine, but Amazon's version was developed into a successful in-house search engine, used by customers to search for items on Amazon's websites.[122] So Amazon could have locally, on its own websites, diversified into Google-style search-based advertising. Google had pioneered this lucrative form of advertising in 2001/2, through the AdWords advertising system.[123] AdWords was based on the Google search engine's unrivalled ability to provide searchers with the desired results from a search through an index of *three billion* web documents.[124] Searchers would visit the Google site, enter their search keywords, be sent web pages with the results, see some small ads included on these results pages, click on the ads that interested them, and arrive at the clicked ads' websites. The advertisers paid Google for each click on their ads and competed, through an auction process, for the right to have their ads appear with a particular keyword. Google's technology had automated the whole system, even the auctioning of keywords to the advertisers.[125] The result was not only a new era in advertising but also a 'money gusher' or 'money machine' for Google, as Auletta noted in his *Googled: The End of the World as We Know It*.[126]

Yet Bezos did not add a similar high-tech advertising system to Amazon's websites. He delayed this diversification until the mid-2010s. Both Stone and Dumaine attribute this delay to Bezos's desire to please customers and not compromise the 'customer experience'.[127] In other words, the needs of his customer-centric sales strategy outweighed the potential benefits of a shift to Google-style advertising.

In the mid-2010s, though, Bezos shifted the balance towards advertising. He now allowed search-based advertising by Amazon's third-party sellers, and granted these ads an increasingly prominent position on search-results pages.[128] But Amazon 'had trouble developing the necessary technology fast enough. It had to build a search auction system to take bids from advertisers and a tool to track the effectiveness of the ads'.[129] Although the technology had been pioneered long ago by Google, this was still high-level tech and was giving Amazon another high-tech facet. Furthermore, it produced significant financial benefits. By 2018, advertising's annual revenue had reached about $10 billion and, a year later, was predicted to have reached $40 billion annually by the mid-2020s.[130] Bezos's shift towards advertising therefore seemed a well-calculated piece of strategic rebalancing.

His other high-tech diversifying was more strategically straightforward. During the 2010s he diversified into a range of 'Fire' devices that gave Amazon new high-tech facets as well as new product lines. The Fire TV products mentioned in the previous section might well be considered a new high-tech facet, like the Fire Tablet computer that Amazon launched in 2011. Although the Tablet was not a technological innovation, this was an attractive lower-price alternative to the pioneering Apple iPad tablet computer. The Amazon version of a tablet computer was initially called the 'Kindle' Fire Tablet, as if it was a follow-on to the successful Kindle e-book readers, but the Kindle part of the name was dropped a few years later. The new device had shown its worth by becoming 'the second-bestselling tablet after the iPad' and, thanks to continual improvements, the Tablet was still 'a staple of the Amazon device offering' in the early 2020s.[131]

However, not all of Bezos's high-tech diversifications were as successful as Fire TV and the Fire Tablet. Amazon's version of a mobile phone, the Fire Phone, was technologically innovative but a commercial failure. The Fire Phone was unveiled in 2014 as not just a mobile phone but a 'smartphone' mini-computer stacked with software. Smartphones were nothing new and were widely made by many companies. As Chapter 6 described, Apple's pioneering iPhone smartphone had appeared as long ago as 2007. But Amazon's Fire Phone offered an innovative feature, which had been proposed by Bezos: 'an advanced 3D display, responsive to gestures in the air, instead of only taps on a touchscreen' or pressing buttons on the phone.[132] The feature took years to develop, however, and did not prove very popular when the Fire Phone finally appeared. 'The phone never caught the public's imagination', partly due to its software shortcomings, and the product was abandoned not long after its launch.[133]

But later in 2014, Bezos launched a device that was more successful and innovative than any of the Fire projects. This Echo/Alexa device, initiated by him three years earlier, would change 'the way people thought about Amazon': they would think of it 'not only as an e-commerce giant, but as an inventive technology company that was pushing the very boundaries of computer science'.[134] Specifically, Amazon was pushing boundaries in the 'voice' area of computer science—in voice information technology. VIT has its own key concepts: 'voice-activated' devices can be used by giving them verbal commands; 'voice recognition' or 'speech recognition' is the devices' software recognizing verbal commands or cues; and 'voice interaction' is the devices' software responding verbally to these commands or cues—and perhaps even seeming to converse with their users. A famous interaction occurred in 2011 when Steve Jobs tested the iPhone's new Siri VIT during an Apple board meeting.

Then he turned existential, asking [Siri] 'Are you a man or are you a woman?' Responded Siri. 'I have not been assigned a gender, sir'. Laughter ensued, and with it some relief.[135]

Such voice interaction is one reason why VIT software is frequently personalized and given a human name, such as Alexa or the Norwegian name Siri. VIT-enabled devices were not widely used until Siri appeared in 2010, performing the personal-assistant role of providing information and secretarial skills. Apple had not invented Siri but quickly acquired it, making VIT a standard feature of the iPhone.[136]

By contrast, Amazon had to develop its VIT internally and was developing a more difficult version. Amazon's VIT device would perform a domestic-assistant as well as personal-assistant role. Its device was linked by wireless and Internet not only to data centres but also to devices or mechanisms, and so was able to carry out such domestic duties as operate the music system or control the heating system. This VIT device's microphone-speaker hardware, the Echo, was to be 'about the size of a Coke can' and sit on a table or elsewhere in the home.[137] So Echo's software, Alexa, had to be 'far-field' VIT: 'comprehending speech from up to thirty-two feet away', often with background noise, and with echoes from walls, ceilings, and furniture.[138] Furthermore, Alexa required years of machine learning, as discussed later in the section, before the Echo/Alexa device was finally launched in 2014.

Echo/Alexa was presented to the public as a device that offered homes a range of useful services. These included 'delivering the news and weather, setting timers, creating shopping lists, and playing music'.[139] Bezos later described Echo/Alexa in similar terms.

> It could sit in your bedroom or in your kitchen or in your living room and play music for you, answer questions, and ultimately even be the way you might control some of your home systems, like lighting and temperature control. Just saying, 'Alexa, please turn the temperature up two degrees' or 'Alexa, turn off all the lights' is a very natural way of interacting in that kind of environment.[140]

In 2016, however, Alexa began to face some serious competition, as Google unveiled its VIT Google Home device. But Amazon had not been sitting still. There was now a battery-powered portable version and a small-sized version, the Echo Dot.[141] Amazon kept its lead in domestic-assistant VIT devices, and by 2018 a hundred million Alexa-enabled devices had been sold.[142] From a wider perspective, this diversification had shown that Amazon was a truly innovative high-tech corporation. Dumaine declares that indeed Amazon 'has sparked nothing less than the biggest shift in personal computing and communications since Steve Jobs unveiled the iPhone'.[143]

The Echo-Alexa device had also reflected a change in Bezos's use of quantitative calculation. Alexa software's VIT abilities were based on its 'machine-learning models' and its 'deep' learning of human speech behaviour.[144] Such machine-learning software is usually considered a low-level version of AI or at least a first step towards it. And machine-learning software was adopted not just by Echo/Alexa but also by

Amazon's businesses. In Bezos's 2010 letter to shareholders he noted that 'advanced machine learning techniques' could help Amazon handle 'complex data processing and decision problems'.[145] In the years that followed, these problems were increasingly handled by machine-learning techniques. Dumaine presents a dramatic example that involves Jeff Wilke, the 'numbers man' who had led a metrics-based upgrade of logistics in the early 2000s.[146] In the late 2010s, Wilke was Amazon's head of e-commerce.

> Before machine learning came along, Wilke conducted weekly retail reviews with as many as sixty managers ... The company's computing systems provided lots of useful data about sales trends on which to make their decisions, but it was still human beings making the decisions. Amazon has now ... designed machines to make decisions based on those factors. 'We were able', says Wilke, 'to close the loop so humans no longer have to decide'.[147]

This decision-making software could be viewed as a new way of using quantitative calculation to develop Amazon. Certainly Bezos's *cultural* use of quantitative calculation—his metrics-oriented culture—was playing a reduced role. Although the culture still influenced Amazon's employees, these people were losing their influence on Amazon's decision-making.

However, humans still had to make the *less* quantifiable, non-operating decisions about such crucial matters as strategy, adaptation, and product development. Here the deliberative methods, diverse and institutionalized deliberation, continued to be used and were used seemingly without any major changes. These deliberations seem as diverse in the 2010s as in the earlier era. Dumaine describes a 'confrontational' culture, with 'confrontational' meetings, but a 'search for truth at all costs' through this uninhibited expression of opinions.[148] As in the earlier era, this confrontational diversity was not extended to meetings of the board of directors. Dissent was rare and kept within bounds, as Stone recounts in the case of Bezos's heavy spending on Prime Video in 2016/17. This made the 'usually agreeable board' so apprehensive that they asked 'pointed questions' and indeed there was 'continued debate' the following year, even if the objections were 'not quite as loud'.[149]

Amazon's other forums for institutionalized deliberation likewise continued to function as they had in the earlier era. In particular, meetings of the S-Team and its counterparts still focused on the same two types of discussion document.[150] The narrative-memo type was discussed in an earlier section, but the other type is best discussed here—in the context of Bezist development—because this other discussion document was the way that new high-tech products were proposed to Amazon's leaders. Bryar and Carr explain how the document 'became known as the PR/FAQ', with its first page written like a press release about the new product and the other pages written as answers to questions likely to be asked by the media or by Amazon's managers and technical experts.[151] The PR/FAQ proposals for high-tech or other products were mostly unsuccessful: most of the proposed products were never developed or never launched. But Bryar and Carr also point out that there was 'intense competition for resources and capital among the *hundreds* of PR/FAQs that are authored and presented each year within the company'.[152] So Amazon seems to have been supplied with a wide range of product ideas through this vertical, bottom-up version of diverse deliberation. As an earlier section recounted, such vertical deliberation had been institutionalized in the mid-2000s by Bezos's introduction of the narrative memo and PR/FAQ.[153] Now PR/FAQ documents were supplying the wide range of product ideas that Amazon needed in its new, Bezist era of development.

Learning was the seventh rational method used in the Bezist development of Amazon. But learning's contribution will be examined in the final section; the present section will instead finish by looking forward to Amazon's development in the mid- and late 2020s. Amazon has been in a *post*-Bezos era since 2021, when he retired from his long-held post of CEO. Bez*ism*, however, will likely continue for many years. For instance, space-satellite technology will probably be the next high-tech facet. Even before Bezos retired, he had 'helped to develop Project Kuiper, an ambitious plan to launch satellites that would provide high-speed internet connectivity to people around the world'.[154]

Other high-tech facets are likely to appear as Amazon pursues new initiatives. Some of these initiatives are foreshadowed by Dumaine's *Bezonomics*. His book covers a very wide field, as is indicated by its subtitle: *How Amazon is Changing Our Lives and What the World's Best Companies Are Learning from It.*[155] And he offers some insights into the future direction of Amazon's development. In particular, he envisages Amazon moving into industries where it can exploit its lead in machine-learning techniques and AI research. The potential targets are therefore industries:

> that to a greater or lesser extent are ripe for disruption through AI—for example, businesses where costly human labor (and thinking) can be replaced by smart machines. The industries that most closely match those characteristics are advertising, health care, banking, and insurance. Amazon has already made some very early moves into these sectors, suggesting that these industries are already in its sights.[156]

However, Dumaine also suggests that Amazon might well target physical-store retailing. Amazon might expand into a hybrid form of retailing that 'merges physical stores with cyberspace', offering customers a combination of 'the best of online shopping with the best of brick-and-mortar' shopping.[157] This retailing expansion may seem unlikely to create new high-tech facets. But Amazon has already shown that physical retailing can in fact be the scene of impressive high-tech innovation. In 2018, the corporation introduced a high-tech way of combining physical shopping with online payment. 'Ceiling cameras scan purchases and charge them directly to the shoppers' Amazon account'.[158] There is no need for human cashiers or a customer-operated checkout system. Although the new technology had its problems, it was successfully introduced through Amazon's Go stores: a string of physical convenience-store outlets that Amazon began establishing in 2018.[159]

Amazon's retailing indeed saw several new initiatives during Bezos's final years as CEO. In addition to the Go stores, there was the 2017 acquisition of a large chain of physical stores, the Whole Foods supermarkets. These hundreds of grocery supermarkets made up a distinctive chain, specializing in healthy 'organic' food, and Bezos declared that Amazon would be expanding the Whole Foods 'mission' of bringing 'organic, nourishing food to everybody'.[160] John Mackey, the founder-leader of Whole Foods, extolled its acquisition by Amazon when he published his *Conscious Leadership* in 2020. Whole Foods had kept its name, much of its autonomy, and even its founder CEO in this 'merger' with Amazon.[161] In 2017/18, Amazon's retailing was also strengthened by the expansion of its private-label sector, such as its Amazon Basics brand. The number of private-label or 'house' brands was increased from only about twenty in 2016 to more than 140 in 2018.[162] But the most important retailing initiative came in 2020: Amazon's response to the COVID pandemic. Amazon and Bezos rose to the occasion, expanding the retailing effort to meet the needs of a society now heavily dependent on the online retailing he had pioneered in 1995.[163]

Learning and High-Tech Adaptations

This final section looks at how Bezos used and indeed emphasized learning as a rational method of developing his firm—from start-up to Bezist maturity. Like his use of deliberation, his emphasis on learning had a distinctive aspect. Instead of customized deliberation and discussion documents, here the distinctive aspect is using forms of active learning and showing a positive attitude towards their accompanying failures. The section's description of this aspect of learning will lead on to a different kind of topic: a discussion of high-tech adaptations. They display tendencies and raise issues that will be discussed in relation to other chapters' cases as well as Bezos's development of Amazon.

Learning was a key method in his development of the corporation. By learning on the job, he was able to lead and develop it from start-up stage to globally influential giant. Twenty years after founding his online bookselling firm he was leading a corporation with hundreds of thousands of employees and a wide range of e-commerce businesses: retailing, advertising, video streaming, cloud computing, and such high-tech devices as Kindle and Echo. This learning achievement is highlighted, too, by the eBay comparisons and contrasts that were made in Chapter 7. The eBay founders did not attempt to develop their successful start-up into a corporation, preferring instead to headhunt Meg Whitman and hand the job over to this widely experienced business manager with a Harvard MBA. In contrast, Amazon's founder learnt on the job how to carry out this development, even though he lacked the benefit of either wide business experience or high-level business training, such as an MBA. Furthermore, in these years his firm faced a difficult competitive environment—more difficult than eBay's—and although Amazon later had wider opportunities, Bezos had to learn how to exploit these new and varied opportunities.

During his learning on the job, there were of course many instances of more specific forms of learning. Bezos's use of *active* learning processes, notably iteration, was particularly important. Indeed Brandt believed that iteration had played a crucial role in the development of Amazon. 'What really made the difference for the company was Bezos's dedication to iteration. He worked at things over and over again until he got it right'.[164] Such iterative learning is vividly described by Bezos. He notes that when facing difficult opportunities, 'success can come through iteration: invent, launch, reinvent, relaunch, start over, rinse, repeat, again and again' in a highly repetitive learning process.[165] Invention, too, is an active learning process, whether or not it is part of some iteration. And the chapter's previous sections have shown that invention played a crucial role in his development of Amazon in the 2000s–10s.

Invention and other active learning processes were a favourite as well as key method of development. Bezos even entitled his book *Invent & Wander*. Wandering around may seem a rather unfocused learning process but he explains that Bezos-style wandering is not random. It is guided 'by hunch, gut, intuition, curiosity, and powered by a deep conviction that the prize for customers is big enough that it's worth being a little messy and tangential to find our way there': the big 'nonlinear' discoveries in fact 'are highly likely to require wandering'.[166] He refers in other passages to the role of wandering in the creation of the Echo device and of an important AWS feature. The latter was the result of 'years of wandering—experimentation, iteration, and refinement, as well as valuable insights from our customers'.[167] However, inventing seems to have been his most favoured learning process, perhaps because he and his firm have a special aptitude for invention. He has been depicted as having 'enormous faith in his talent for invention', and certainly there was good reason for him to have faith in the inventiveness of Bezos-led Amazon.[168]

Yet he acknowledges that failure is an inherent part of the invention learning process. For example, he has pointed out that failing 'comes part and parcel with invention. It's not optional. We understand that and believe in failing early and iterating until we get it right'.[169] The 'failing early' is typically a failed experiment. Bezos points out that inventions involve experimenting and its accompanying failures: indeed inventions' huge returns can be worth experiments which fail 'nine times out of ten'.[170] His firm has long been oriented towards experiments as, for instance, when its engineers continued experimenting even after the onset of the 2000/1 crisis.[171] Amazon's experimenters became big spenders in the 2010s. 'By 2018, Amazon was spending $28.8 billion a year on R&D, more than any other company' anywhere in the world.[172] And when 'a company spends more than any other company in the world on R&D, it gets to do a lot of experimentation'.[173] More importantly, the firm has long had a positive attitude towards the failures that are an inherent part of experiments, inventing, and other active learning processes.[174] Bezos pithily expressed this positive attitude in his remarks to a congressional subcommittee in 2020. 'Failure inevitably comes along with invention and risk-taking, which is why we try to make Amazon the best place in the world to fail'.[175]

What did it mean in practice, though, to work in such a good place to fail? Bryar and Carr recount a case from 2006, namely the failed launch of Unbox Video. 'In any other company I would probably have been fired', but Amazon understood 'that when you innovate and build new things, you will frequently fail. If you fire the person, you lose the benefit of the learning that came along with that experience', as Bezos pointed out to executives who experienced Unbox-like failures.[176]

> Jeff would say something like this ... 'Why should I fire you now. I just made a million-dollar investment in you. Now you have an obligation to make that investment pay off. Figure out and document where you went wrong. Share what you have learned with other leaders throughout the company. Be sure you don't make the same mistake again and help others avoid making it the first time'. I learned a lot from what went wrong with the launch of Unbox, and I was able to share my knowledge with others at Amazon.[177]

This positive attitude to failure—and to active forms of learning—is the distinctively 'Bezist' aspect of how Bezos used learning to develop Amazon.

However, he is not the only leader to have used some form of active learning to develop a corporation. Chapter 5 described Marcel Dassault learning from test flights and pilots how to improve his aircraft designs, thereby helping him to develop Dassault Aviation into an iconic corporation. Another similarity is that both leaders' active learning occurred during eras of rapid and major technological advances.[178] Dassault Aviation was developed during aerospace's great era, the 1940s–60s. Amazon was developed during—and contributed to—the second half of IT's great 1980s–2000s era.

Like Amazon, many of the corporations discussed in this book were developed—wholly or partially—during the IT era. In eBay's case, the firm was developed from start-up to iconic corporation in the second half, 1995–2009, of the era. Other cases went through part of their development during the IT era and often contributed to its advances, as when Intel's 1980s 'treadmill' strategy constantly upgraded microprocessor chips.[179] Even if a firm was not contributing to the IT advances, it had to adapt to them and to adapt rapidly: the advances in knowledge or capability were being rapidly outdated by new advances.[180]

This rapid adaptation was indeed institutionalized and became a routine form of high-tech adaptation. Firms were regularly—and routinely—updating their software and hardware to conform to the latest standard or 'state of the art' in IT. Updating to the latest in IT might be cynically compared to keeping up with the latest fashion or keeping up with the neighbours. But a better cynical comparison is with consumers buying the latest model car. Although cars' annual model changes may be largely stylistic, there is usually some technical improvement, however marginal or dubious, which can rationally justify the expense of acquiring the latest model.

There were of course important exceptions to this pattern of routine high-tech adaptation. Occasionally a corporation was facing an adaptive crisis, or what Grove termed an 'inflection point', and the firm's survival depended on its rapid adaptation to the new technology.[181] In fact many retail corporations have had to adapt rapidly to the Internet or else fall victim to Amazon-like competition. Earlier, the invention of the personal computer led to some high-tech adaptations that were far from routine. A different kind of exception to the routine is that some adaptations are *not* technological and are not responding to IT advances. As Chapter 9 describes, they are responding to cultural or social changes, and the response is a high-*fashion* rather than high-tech adaptation.

9
Giorgio Armani

Armani's *Giorgio Armani*

The earlier chapters have described how leaders used rational methods in highly technological or technical industries. This final chapter, however, will be mainly concerned with a stylistic and indeed artistic industry—the high-fashion line of business. It will show how the fashion designer and business leader, Giorgio Armani, very capably used rational methods in these unusual business circumstances, where these corporation-developing methods were just as appropriate as in high-tech industries. Even in *artistic* industries like high-fashion a leader's employee-followers will be inspired with rational confidence by his or her capable use of the appropriate rational methods.

A leader's-eye view of Armani's use of rational methods has been provided by his 2015 *Giorgio Armani*. But it is a mainly photographical account of his fashion-designing career and there is only enough textual material to provide a leader's-eye view of him using the two *adaptive* methods: rapid and innovative adaptation. The Armani case will therefore be viewed, like the Dassault case, as one of the supplementary rather than main examples. It shows a leader using a particular pair of rational methods—rapid and innovative adaptation—in the unusual circumstances of the artistic high-fashion business. In fact Armani's designs have been the subject of an art-gallery exhibition.

> I have always said that fashion is not art, and yet I was the first and I think only fashion designer to be exhibited at the Solomon R. Guggenheim Museum in New York. In 2000, that contemporary art institution dedicated itself to a retrospective to my work, analysing it as one would that of a painter, architect or inventor.[1]

But Armani describes his role as a fashion designer as 'closer to that of a sociologist than to that of an artist.'[2] The sociological aspect is apparent in his book's account of how in the 1970s he became an independent fashion designer with his own company. 'I began to perceive the advance of a new kind of femininity' which was linked to the feminism that was 'so explosive in those years when I started'.[3] His stylistic adaptation to the new times resulted in a new high-fashion style and also the establishing of a very successful company that bore his name and derived its iconic status from his prestige—a rare example of a private company becoming as large and famous as an iconic business corporation. The Armani case of rapid and innovative

Rational Leadership. Paul Brooker and Margaret Hayward, Oxford University Press. © Paul Brooker & Margaret Hayward (2023). DOI: 10.1093/oso/9780198894643.003.0009

adaptation therefore confirms that these rational methods can be just as appropriate for an artistic, high-fashion firm as for a scientific, high-tech firm like Intel.

The first section of the chapter will show how Armani adapted fashion to the new times—to social change and the accompanying change in fashion preferences. It will also show that Armani, like Kroc and Walton, used the two adaptive rational methods in combination to establish his large and iconic company. For he adapted both rapidly and innovatively in the 1970s when he created a new high-fashion style and then in the 1980s used both adaptive methods when he created a new kind of leading high-fashion firm.

The second section will compare Armani's adaptations with those of another Italian fashion designer of that era, Gianni Versace. The comparison of Armanian and Versacian adaptations will focus largely on the different ways in which they adapted *stylistically* to the opportunity offered by fashion's new times. The two leaders used the same adaptive methods to exploit this opportunity but used them in different ways. While Armani targeted the new market created by fashion's new times, Versace instead targeted what remained of the old market. Although Versace's rapid and innovative adaptation was successful stylistically and commercially, it had a serious flaw that became very evident after his violently premature death in 1997.

The third section will therefore compare the two leaders' adaptive legacies and argue that Versace did not use adaptive rational methods *as capably* as Armani in the 1970s–80s. This difference in capability highlights an aspect of rational leadership that has not been discussed in earlier chapters, which looked for variation in leaders' selection and emphasizing of particular rational methods but ignored the variation in how capably they used these methods. This was largely because there have been no instances of two leaders' times and circumstances being so similar that it is fair to say something about their relative capability in using particular rational methods. In this final chapter, however, capability can be compared in a credible manner because both Armani and Versace used the adaptive rational methods in the same times and circumstances—the 1970s–80s change era in their high-fashion line of business.

But the chapter ends with a section devoted to a classic example of a leader *not* using the adaptive methods or any of the other appropriate rational methods. It is 'an exception that proves the rule' because it shows what occurs when a corporation-developing leader abandons the appropriate rational methods that he or she has used successfully in the past. This case arose in the beauty industry in the 1980s–90s when the British businesswoman Anita Roddick abandoned the adaptive methods she had used to establish her corporation, The Body Shop, and did not replace them with any other appropriate rational methods. Roddick's move away from rational business methods may have been due to her increasingly prominent charismatic role as a political activist and a publicist for new attitudes towards business and its social responsibilities, as is recounted in her partly autobiographical *Business as Unusual*.[4] However, her increased public profile was no substitute for a decline in business rationality that led to a decline in business success and to her employee-followers losing their jobs or career prospects—and their rational confidence in the future development of the corporation.

Adapting Fashion to New Times

Armani's success was a classic case of adapting to new times. In the 1970s–90s, the high-fashion business underwent such a dramatic change that Agins entitled her book *The End of Fashion*. She explained the change by pointing to three 'megatrends' in western societies' upper and middle classes: (1) 'women let go of fashion', as they became successful career women; (2) 'people stopped dressing up', as casual wear became more acceptable at the workplace as well as for social occasions; and (3) 'people's values changed with regard to fashion', as they became more concerned with value for money and with finding a bargain.[5] These megatrends brought an end to the traditional high-fashion world, which had been dominated by family firms or 'houses' located in Paris and focused on the *haute couture* (high dress-making) art of designing and tailoring handcrafted made-to-fit womenswear. But the megatrends also created the opportunity for a previously unknown Italian designer, Giorgio Armani, to gain a huge competitive advantage and establish a very successful firm.

The megatrend that most benefited Armani was the way in which affluent women 'let go of fashion' clothes as their socioeconomic situation changed. Agins refers to this trend as the end of the 'trickle-down' and 'planned obsolescence' fashion system in which 'Paris designers had set the standard' for high-fashion womenswear throughout the western world and had introduced a succession of new styles and modifications through their seasonal fashion shows.[6] This system ran into a new socioeconomic reality as the female members of the upper and middle classes became career women and lost interest in the high-fashion designs being displayed by models on the runways or catwalks of Parisian fashion shows.

> By the 1980s millions of baby-boomer career women were moving up in the workplace and the impact of their professional mobility was monumental. As bank vice-presidents, members of corporate boards, and partners at law firms, professional women became secure enough to ignore the foolish runway frippery that bore no connection to their lives. Women began to behave more *like men* in adopting *their own uniform*: skirts and blazers and pantsuits that gave them an *authoritative, polished, power look*.[7]

These new fashion preferences therefore both undermined the old fashion system and offered an opportunity for designers who could meet the new demand: career women's desire for 'their own uniform' of trouser suits, blazers, and skirts that gave them an authoritative and polished look.

Armani responded as early as the mid-*1970s*, when he was starting up his firm. As mentioned earlier, his book refers to him perceiving a new kind of femininity, which 'required a wardrobe that fully complemented the way men dressed' while 'preserving elegance and distinction and the idea that others should notice you for your mind and your self-esteem. I imagined women in new roles', such as women 'taking their place at the table for a business meeting'.[8] His response was a new fashion style that was an *innovative* as well as rapid adaptation to the new times.

Giorgio Armani SpA was founded in Milan in 1975, soon after Armani's 41st birthday and more than a decade after he became a full-time fashion designer.[9] Armani's biographer notes that the firm's first womenswear presentation featured his first jackets for women and that his 1976 runway presentation 'introduced tweed women's suits. The jacket had a decidedly mannish cut' and in fact he had 'invented a different kind of women's jacket' that 'conferred an unprecedented authority on the female figure'.[10] A similar point is made by White in her book on the Armani contribution to fashion. His redesign of the jacket offered career women a mixture of 'femininity and power-dressing' in a restrained, not over-exposed fashion, just as 'easy' trouser suits became signature garments of his style, included in each new collection of Armani womenswear.[11]

Armani's rapid adaptation to women's new fashion preferences may have been because he was primarily a *menswear* designer until he started up his own firm in 1975. In fact for the rest of his career he would design men's as well as women's high-fashion clothing and he would become famous for inventing a new style of men's jacket in the mid-1970s. His biographer describes this deconstructed or unstructured style of jacket as a blend of the 'hippie tradition' and the 'bourgeois uniform', but White views the blend in gender terms, as 'bringing the sexes closer together sartorially' and creating a design theme of 'languid androgyny'.[12] Armani, too, refers to his designs taking on 'a more androgynous image', but he also presents the gender issue in terms of his supportive response to social change and 'liberation, both female and male':

> I became convinced that those attitudes could be created out of the way people dressed. How was a women rising up the ranks of power going to be credible, in an environment that was still all-male, if she was dressed like a doll or restrained by excessively formal feminine clothing? How was a young, dynamic, and uninhibited man going to contrast with the old modes of thinking if he was constrained inside a suit that denied his individuality and oppressed his energy and physique?[13]

Men as well as women were expressing two of the new fashion preferences discussed by Agins: it was 'people', not just women, who 'stopped dressing up' and whose 'values changed in regard to fashion'. These two changes in fashion preferences therefore suited Armani's menswear as well as womenswear. He was still, however, having to adapt rapidly and innovatively to take full advantage of the opportunities offered by fashion's new times; he was not simply benefiting from the fact that they were moving in the same direction that he had chosen.

The change in values regarding fashion—this new concern with value for money—suited Armani because he was a designer of ready-to-wear rather than handcrafted, individually tailored, and therefore very expensive garments. Armani stuck with the ready-to-wear approach that he had learnt as a menswear designer and he outsourced the production of his designs to womenswear and menswear manufacturers in northern Italy's modern clothing industry.[14] Agins noted that 'setting himself apart from the rest of high fashion, Armani consistently manufactured high-quality tailored garments on an industrial scale. Nobody did it better, retailers agreed.[15] Any affluent customers who showed the new preference for value for money needed to look no further than Armani's garments.

The other change in men's and women's fashion preferences—the shift to casual wear rather than dressing up—suited Armani in a less obvious, almost indirect way. A 1973 article on fashionable elites' liking for blue-denim jeans pointed to the difference between the elite who had 'turned their backs on the idea of "fashionable" clothes' and the elite who were 'still in revolt against the old sartorial rules but continue to be concerned with the way they dress'.[16] The latter group of elite denim-wearers were therefore receptive to Armani's elegant styling. 'He understood back in the mid-1970s, that although consumers were rejecting formality in favour of more casual clothing, they did not want to give up elegance' and would be receptive to what became known as 'Armani' styling: 'refined yet relaxed modernity in clothing, in muted col- ours'.[17] Armani's book, too, refers to his pursuit of elegance in his menswear and womenswear designs of the 1970s. He was 'always seeking a sort of elegance that never turned into arrogance' in his menswear designs and he was 'offering women the unusual elegance of pantsuits' that were the elegant equivalent of denim jeans as well as women's equivalent of a business suit.[18]

Armani's rapid adaptive response to fashion's new times brought him early rewards and recognition. His firm had been founded in 1975 with capital of only some $10,000 but had a turnover of some $500,000 in 1976, some $2 million the following year and by 1982 had worldwide sales of some $140 million.[19] Armani also received dramatic international recognition in 1982 when he appeared on the cover of *Time* magazine. The cover bore the headline 'Giorgio's Gorgeous Style' and inside there was an eight-page story that included 'a confident judgment: Armani is the best'.[20] Buoyed by such recognition, his firm would achieve total worldwide sales of $300 million by 1985, with North America contributing some 25 per cent of these sales and another 25 per cent coming from parts of Europe outside Italy.[21] In the decade since its founding, Armani's firm had become a big-earning international fashion company that derived its earnings and iconic status from its leader's fashion-designing successes.

The rapid rise of Armani's firm seems similar to the way in which Kroc and Walton rapidly established their corporations. Armani's combination of rapid and innovative adaptation, however, was adapting to the kind of dramatic change that Grove categorized as a '10x' change. As Chapter 6 mentioned, Grove's book listed some examples of the '10x' kind of change and one of them was customers 'drifting away from their former buying habits', such as when Americans' taste in cars changed during the 1920s: 'style and leisure had become important considerations in people's lives'.[22] Clearly this is similar to the change in customers' fashion preferences in the 1970s–80s, and just as the car example was exploited by Sloan's General Motors, so the fashion example was exploited by Armani's Giorgio Armani SpA.

But in Armani's case the change was exploited by a *new* firm, not an established corporation like Sloan's General Motors. In this respect it is similar to cases where new firms have exploited the opportunity offered by disruptive technology.

As Appendix 1 describes, Christensen's theory of disruptive technology points out that new firms can win the leading position in an industry by adapting rapidly to disruptive technology and the new market that it creates. Similarly, Armani's new firm won a leading position by adapting rapidly as well as innovatively to the new market created by the change in fashion preferences.

What is more, Armani's new firm became a new *kind* of leading high-fashion firm—adapted to fit the fashion and business world of the 1980s–90s. This new kind of high-fashion firm would have an extensive, diverse range of products and a globalized retail network, with stores in many countries around the world. In fact this was a second case of Armani using innovative and rapid adaptation in combination to develop his firm and in this second case he was similar to Kroc and Walton. Like them, he was creating a new system or organization that would play a crucial role in expanding his firm into a large-scale, very successful operation.

If Armani had not created this new kind of high-fashion firm, he would not have reaped the full business reward for his rapid stylistic adaptation to customers' changing preferences. In particular, he would not have been able to establish a large company that was a modern business corporation in all respects except that it was not a public company. Even after it became an iconic billion-dollar company, Armani did not take this final step—going public—that would have created a high-fashion *corporation*. Nonetheless, developing Giorgio Armani SpA into a new kind of firm was a major achievement by Armani and his partner Sergio Galeotti, whose death in 1985 prematurely ended this two-role leadership team of creative designer and business-oriented partner. Even before his death, however, it was clear that the firm would reap great rewards from having followed up the 1970s adaptation with another rapid and innovative adaptation: the 1980s creation of a new kind of high-fashion firm.

It sold a much more extensive 'pyramid' of products than any previous leading firm in the high-fashion business. Armani's product pyramid extended downwards through several different price levels and extended horizontally across a wide range of clothing, accessories, and related products.[23] In pre-Armani times, the leading French haute couture firms had shown little tendency to diversify beyond crafting womenswear and perfumes and, more recently, selling their designs and licensed brand name to other firms. Then in 1966, Yves Saint Laurent 'changed the fashion paradigm' by supplementing his haute couture collections with a line of *ready-to-wear* clothing that was aimed at a younger market and was much more affordable.[24] 'Now there was a new pyramid model' that set a new standard for any leading firm in the high-fashion business.[25]

The new model was adopted and further developed by Armani in the 1970s–90s. Initially, the distinctive feature of his pyramid of products was that it *lacked* the traditional summit or peak—a haute couture collection of womenswear—and was instead crowned by ready-to-wear lines of womenswear *and* menswear.[26] However, the Armani pyramid became distinctive, too, for how far it extended downwards through different price levels and for how far it extended horizontally across a diverse range of products. By the end of the 1990s the Armani range of products included 'not only the main clothing ranges for men, women and children, but also jeans, skiwear, underwear, shoes, sunglasses, jewellery, hosiery, watches and perfume'.[27]

The vertical extension downwards into lower price levels came largely through the introduction of cheaper lines of clothing. As early as 1978, Armani 'started a more affordable line, which he named Le Collezioni', and a few years later he took the key step: starting Emporio Armani. The Emporio clothes were aimed at 'a younger market at around 60 per cent below the [prices of the] top Borgonuovo (or Black Label) line'.[28] In fact Armani's book observes that initially many experts thought that the Emporio Armani level of menswear and womenswear was a marketing mistake:

[They were] casual clothes, most made of denim, all at affordable prices. It was seen as being the wrong move in terms of marketing, an irreparable blow to my image. Was *the* fashion designer of the 'power woman' and the 'new man' really lowering himself to making things for the Average Joe?[29]

On the other hand, Emporio Armani met two of the new fashion preferences—casual wear and value for money—and might well be viewed as an adaptive response to these changes in customers' fashion preferences. Not surprisingly, the 'downmarket' Emporio soon vindicated Armani, proving to be very successful and playing an important role in the firm's expansion. Ten years later he was still moving in the same direction: 'the new A/X (Armani Exchange) line which was launched in the US in response to the economic recession' was 'considerably cheaper than the other clothing labels' sold by Armani.[30]

In 2005, he added the traditional summit to his pyramid of products by launching an Armani haute couture 'house' in Paris—some twenty or even thirty years 'late'.[31] Although this had removed some of his pyramid's distinctiveness, its vertical and horizontal extensiveness made it a still distinctive 'Armani' creation. The clothing lines now descended from the new haute couture Armani Prive to 'Giorgio Armani, then Armani Collezione, then Emperio Armani for the young, and then beneath these the very casual Armani Exchange or Armani Jeans'.[32] Each of these clothing lines and pricing levels also extended horizontally into a set of appropriate accessories, 'leather, shoes, watches', and then there were the stand-alone horizontal extensions into 'glasses, cosmetics, perfumes', and the furnishings and interior design of Armani Casa.[33] Although the Armani brand was being widely stretched by these extensions, the brand continued to be imbued with the personal charisma—the personal touch or vision—of the iconic designer. 'From jeans to underwear, from haute couture to handbags and watches, I offer a piece of my vision to everyone, making no distinctions, and always with the same creative rigor'.[34]

In addition to this pyramid of products, Armani's firm developed a globalized retail network, which he and his partner instigated several years after the firm was founded. In the 1970s 'there were virtually no single-brand boutiques, most shops sold an array of French and Italian brands. But that left a designer at the mercy of the boutique owner, who decided how much to buy and how to display the clothes'.[35] In the early 1980s, however, Armani established his Emporio Armani chain of stores, which sold only his brand and indeed was selling a new line of Armani clothes specially designed for these new retail outlets. The first store opened in 1981 and two years later 'there were ninety Emporio Armani shops scattered throughout Italy'.[36] Eventually, each of the Armani clothing lines and its accompanying accessories would be sold exclusively or specifically through its own particular chain of stores.[37] Furthermore, during the 1980s–90s, the firm's retail network expanded throughout Europe, Asia, and North America, becoming virtually a global network with stores in more than *thirty* countries. At the end of the century, Armani's 'billion-dollar empire' boasted a retail network that 'included 53 Giorgio Armani stores, 6 Le Collezioni stores, 129 Emporio Armani, 48 A/X Armani Exchange stores, 4 Armani jeans and 2 Armani junior stores in 33 countries'.[38] In the US, for example, there were nine Giorgio Armani boutiques and twelve Emporio Armani shops, plus the new A/X Armani Exchange stores.[39] By creating this far-flung retail network Armani was again, as with his product pyramid, adapting his firm to fit the new times—even if this meant creating a more complex firm that was more difficult to lead in the personal manner of the pre-Armani era.

Another structural complexity was that Giorgio Armani SpA became just one of a group of companies belonging to the Armani Group. However, Giorgio Armani SpA and the Group were still private companies wholly owned and controlled by Armani: the 'sole shareholder, president and managing director'.[40] In fact he had increased his control over the Armani empire through having his firm become more involved in the manufacturing of Armani clothes and accessories.[41] By the mid-2000s he was an industrialist as well as a retailer and designer. 'Gruppo Armani is now one of the largest manufacturing groups in the world of fashion, with forty-nine hundred employees and thirteen plants'.[42] As in many other ways, Armani's firm was now very different from a Parisian fashion house making handcrafted haute couture.

Armanian versus Versacian Adaptations

Any account of Armani's career, adaptations, and opportunity requires some comparison with those of the other great fashion designer of his time, Gianni Versace. Like Armani, he emerged from the ready-to-wear clothing industry of northern Italy in the 1970s and became an international figure in the 1980s. His career and life came to a violently premature end on 15 July 1997, when the 50-year-old Versace was murdered by a serial killer in Miami, but in his relatively short career he had made a remarkable impact on the fashion world: in 1999, White's *Versace* referred to the Versace fashion label as perhaps the world's best known.[43]

Furthermore, Versace's style had become famous despite being very different from Armani's and in fact being virtually a *contrasting* style. The contrast between the two styles is most apparent in their high-fashion womenswear collections. Versace's collections became famous for their 'blatantly sexy, body-revealing clothes, brash prints and the ostentatious use of gilt' and indeed 'the overt display of wealth and sexuality' were the two facets that seemed 'to encapsulate the essence of Versace's style'.[44] Versace's style was often analysed in terms of *glamour*, including glamour that was 'intrinsically linked to the creation of sexual fantasy. There has been considerable debate about whether Versace's clothes empower or subjugate women.'[45] If they did in any way empower women, it was not in the way that Armani's suits empowered career women. And the exuberant glamour of Versace's style was clearly very different from the Armani style's understated elegance. So it is hardly surprising that the high-fashion world had divided views about these two famous designers. Armani's biographer dramatically describes this conflict of opinion:

> Skirmishes over the relative merits of the two designers swept the small but prickly world of fashion. Fashion journalists coined unwieldy adjectives such as 'Armanian' and 'Versacian' and used them whenever possible ... [as] the rivalry between these two designers split the world of fashion into two armed camps.[46]

These terms, Armanian and Versacian, may seem similar to the terms Fordism and Sloanism but the fashion terms refer to differences in artistic style, not to differences in business approach or to the difference between production rationality and administrative rationality.

Yet the Armanian versus Versacian distinction can in fact be viewed from a 'rationalist' as well as stylistic perspective. The difference in style can be seen as the result of two leaders using the same rational methods to exploit the same opportunity but using them in *two different ways*. Both Armani and Versace were rapidly and innovatively adapting to fashion's new times, but their adaptive responses went in two different directions and produced contrasting artistic styles. While Armani targeted the new market, Versace instead targeted what remained of the old market, as the new times had given him the chance to 'catch a jump' on the firms which dominated this market: the French haute couture firms. They were too distracted or too much 'in denial'—thanks to the new fashion preferences, new market, and new styles—to be capable of fending off a modernizing challenge in what remained of their old market.

Versace's adaptive response came soon after his ready-to-wear firm was founded in Milan in 1977. So in a sense it was less rapid than Armani's response of some two years earlier and in a sense Versace's response was also less innovative. For he aimed to conquer the *old* market by *modernizing*, not reversing, the haute couture style. He would change femininity into sexuality, in contrast to Armani's androgynous jackets, and he would change dressed-up stylishness into extravagant glamour, in contrast to the elegant casualness of Armanian style. Furthermore, Versace would keep up-to-date with cultural trends, which in the 1980s became a combination of the sexual freedom of the 1960s and the ostentatious or frivolous display of the 1920s.

From an adaptive perspective therefore the dramatic differences between Versacian and Armanian styles seem to be simply different adaptive responses to fashion's new times. From a business perspective, too, this is simply two different ways in which new firms can replace the leading firms in an industry. Armani's firm replaced them by taking over a new market; Versace's firm replaced them by competing for the remains of the old market whose leading firms had been unable to respond effectively. In fact as late as the 1990s, the French haute couture firms had still not responded effectively to the Versace challenge, even when he competed head-on by adding a haute couture collection to his pyramid of ready-to-wear lines. Ball's *House of Versace* depicts the 'traditional Parisian couture houses' as relatively 'stodgy' when compared to how Versace projected the latest cultural trends onto his haute couture clothes: the French couturiers 'would struggle to compete with such bracing, exciting designs'.[47]

What is more, Versace developed his modernized haute couture market into such a rewarding niche that he rivalled Armani commercially as well as stylistically. Versace's start-up was no less successful than Armani's and by 1983 the Versace firm had sales of some $150 million.[48] Continuing success took its total sales to some $700 million by 1991 and its total retail sales to the $1 billion mark by 1997.[49] So Versace, like Armani, was eventually the leader of a 'billion-dollar empire' that derived its iconic status from the prestige of its designer-leader. The Versacian adaptation therefore seems comparable to the Armanian not only stylistically but also as a way of establishing a firm with a rewarding niche in the fashion environment of its times.

But this begs the question of how in fact did Versace glean such commercial rewards from the remains of an old market. Part of the explanation is that this was still a sizeable market, which also had potential for growth and development. Gastel's *The Versace Legacy* argues that 'Armani and Versace divided the territory' in the 1980s, as Armani 'created the perfect image for the professional, the career woman' and Versace became 'the great interpreter of the decade's drive for show, for appearances'.[50] As she implies, Versace was not being left with a small patch of territory in a far corner. After all, many affluent women did not have a career and some affluent career women would wear Versace designs, if only in their after-work social life. In Italy, Versace's 'core market was the so-called "Signora", the established woman who is perhaps not in the first flush of youth, but is keen to convey her sexuality and her wealth. Versace was also enviably successful in most other countries': they provided him with ample territory for a flourishing high-fashion firm.[51]

In some countries, too, notably the US, Versace's territory seems to have increased in later years. He had difficulty selling in the US in the early 1980s, but by 1995 North America was contributing nearly a fifth of his annual sales.[52] Ball refers to a 'new yen for fun, exuberant clothes' in the 1990s and she suggests that 'women who had flocked to safe designers such as Armani when they first entered the workforce wanted to cut loose'.[53] This new tendency was encouraged by the continuing economic boom, with its 'rampant consumerism', and by the American fashion media, which had adopted a more Versacian attitude.[54]

Another factor, however, was that Versace had moved into Armani's territory. There were now Versacian 'day suits, jackets, pants. His daywear was popular with women who wanted a more feminine uniform than Armani's androgynous suits'.[55] These Versacian uniforms not only were relatively feminine but also were manufactured in realistic sizes. Versace reminded the factories that not all women were runway fashion models.[56]

The new daywear was an example of how Versace extended his market by extending his *pyramid of products*. In the 1980s he added several new ready-to-wear lines, including the expensive Couture daywear and two more affordable lines, Update and Versus.[57] These two were aimed at the younger market and indeed Versus was launched with his 33-year-old sister, Donatella, as its youth-oriented designer.[58] Such lines were not simply offering lower pricing levels on the pyramid, they were also adjusting the *style* of the clothes to suit younger customers. Similarly, Versace adjusted the style of clothes to suit the many customers who did not want to wear the more outlandish or extreme examples of Versacian style. For Versace was the forerunner of a technique that was described by Agins in *The End of Fashion*:

> Even though the leading designers tart up their runways with outlandish, crowd-pleasing costumes, they are grounded in reality. The bulk of the actual merchandise that hits the sale floor is always palatable enough for millions of consumers around the world, thus generating the bottom line that Wall Street expects.[59]

Versace had been doing something similar when he marketed realistic or palatable versions of the Versacian style displayed on the runway. Ball refers to them as 'more-wearable versions' or 'toned-down variations' and an Italian boutique owner observed that Versace 'could take that striking item and dilute it, dissolve it into ten other versions that would sell like crazy because they had his fashion edge but not the extremism shown on the runway'.[60] This diluted extremism was sold through supplementary lines of clothing that are often termed 'diffusion' lines. In 1997, Turner noted that 'the Versace diffusion lines sell by the bucket load' and she listed no fewer than seven diffusion lines, which were 'a little cheaper' than the 'core lines' but were clearly contributing their fair share to the firm's billion-dollar sales revenue.[61]

The extension of Versace's product pyramid had therefore markedly extended his modernized haute couture market—and made it much more rewarding. In addition, the pyramid was extended horizontally into *non*-clothing products. Turner's figures show that by 1996, the year before Versace's death, his clothing items were earning little more than half of the firm's revenue: $560 million versus $250 million from accessories, $150 million from perfumes, and $40 million from homeware.[62] The accessories category included jewellery as well as 'bags, belts, shoes, ties, scarves, gloves, hats, sunglasses and, most recently, cosmetics'.[63] Like Armani's pyramid, each kind of item was sold at various price levels, with each variant linked to particular clothing lines. For example, a handbag linked to the Istante diffusion line would be different in design and less expensive than 'a Versace main line handbag'.[64] Clearly the modernized haute couture market had come a long way and been developed in many directions in the years since Versace started up his firm in the late 1970s!

However, this process was not part of his adaptation to change in the late 1970s but instead was part of a second rapid and innovative adaptation, which began in the early 1980s. As in the Armani case, establishing a high-fashion empire required the adaptive rational methods to be used in combination not once but twice: first stylistically in the 1970s and then organizationally in the 1980s. In Armani's case the organizational adaptation, as described earlier, produced a new kind of leading high-fashion firm that was well adapted to fit the new fashion and business world of the 1980s–90s. In Versace's case, too, the organizational adaptation produced a new kind of high-fashion firm but it was a *modernized haute couture* firm that had been adapted to fit the new fashion and business world.

Versace's new kind of firm was generally similar to Armani's but there were also some marked differences. The similarities included the modernizing of production and marketing, the extension of the product pyramid, the creation of a globalized retail network, and the anomaly of remaining a private company even though going public would have better adapted the firms to fit the new fashion and business world. The differences between the two kinds of firm were sometimes only differences of degree or emphasis, such as Versace's great concern with marketing. His marketing grand strategy included (1) massive magazine advertising, (2) dramatic fashion shows, (3) pioneering the use of celebrity 'supermodels', and (4) adopting the Armani-pioneered strategy of having celebrities wear his designs at media events.[65]

Marketing strategies aside, there were marked differences between the two firms' product pyramids. Perhaps the most obvious and characteristic was the 'dilution' of Versacian stylistic extremism. While Versace's extreme or outlandish designs were realistically toned down in his diffusion clothing lines, Armani's new-market designs were not extreme enough to need such dilution. Another characteristic structural difference was that Versace had added haute couture to his pyramid by 1990, only thirteen years after founding his firm, but Armani waited *thirty* years, until 2005, before adding a haute couture line.[66] A further characteristic difference was that menswear was less prominent in Versace's product pyramid than Armani's, as would be expected of a modernized haute couture firm when compared with a new-market fashion firm.[67]

There were also marked differences between the two firms' globalized retail networks. Both firms began developing these networks in the early 1980s but Versace focused on boutiques selling top-line products, not on downmarket stores like the Emporio Armani stores that were the backbone of Armani's new retail network. Another difference was that Versace's firm adopted a more 'modern' approach, namely franchising, which was so new to Italy that there was no business or legal term for such an arrangement.[68] The network of franchised retailers soon spread beyond Italy and Europe to New York, Los Angeles, and even far-off Sydney in Australia.[69] By the mid-1980s there were more than a hundred Versace boutiques around the world, and the network was further developed and globalized during the 1980s–90s: by 1997 there were 'over 300 boutiques [and] in every major capital in the world'.[70] But by then, too, the company had still not gone public and, as Versace's death revealed, this meant that his firm had no long-term solution to a problem that had originated twenty years earlier and in fact was a side-effect of Versace's 1970s stylistic adaptation to fashion's new times.

Adaptive Legacies and Capability

Gianni Versace's death in 1997 left his family firm in the hands of his sister Donatella and his older brother Santo, who had been its CEO and joint leader for some twenty years. The two Versace brothers' dual-leadership team, like Armani and Galeotti's, had been a two-role team in which the creative designer was supported and protected by a business-oriented teammate. However, Santo's business expertise was being challenged by a difficult business situation in the late 1990s, and his planned remedy evaporated when Gianni's unexpected death ended their plan to take the company public.[71] But Gianni's death left Donatella with an even worse predicament. She would have to take on his role as the firm's internationally famous designer, who had imbued Versace products with the personal charisma of an iconic designer.

She was also facing the negative consequences, the side-effects, of a crucial difference between Versace's and Armani's stylistic adaptations to fashion's new times. By seeking to modernize haute couture Versace had placed great artistic demands on himself and on his successor as the firm's chief designer. Not only was there a need to dilute stylistic extremism to fit the diffusion lines of clothing but also there was a need to create a succession of *new* designs, seasonal collection after seasonal collection, to maintain the designer's reputation for novelty. For Versace's modernization of haute couture had retained the traditional high-fashion accent on what Agins described as 'planned obsolescence': the seasonal changes in what is fashionable and what is out of fashion.[72] His modernized version of this planned obsolescence had become more intensive as he attracted an increasing amount of media attention. Versace noted not long before he died that 'the media exhaust the new quickly' and therefore he would be adding another two more collections to the four he was already presenting each year.[73] Here again, as with his diluted extremism, he was the forerunner of a later tendency. In the 2000s the high-fashion business, 'with its bottomless hunger for something new', had become a treadmill for designers who must churn out frequent flash collections between their semiannual runway shows'.[74]

This treadmill of constantly having to create 'something new' puts great pressure on the designer and the firm. It is much greater than the pressure produced by the microprocessor-manufacturing treadmill discussed in Chapter 6. As Turner noted, are any manufacturing industries 'required to produce a totally new product line, with all its attendant production and marketing problems, every six months'?[75]

In contrast, Armani's stylistic adaptation to new times had been directed towards a new high-fashion market that did not require a dramatically new product line each and every fashion season. Armani could instead adopt the standard manufacturing approach of continually making incremental modifications or marginal variations but only occasionally producing a dramatically *new* product line. Agins described Armani as producing something 'new and original in 1975' and then 'only a few modifications each season' but pointed out that 'variations of his look continued to remain in style for two decades'.[76] More importantly, she explained why he retained his customers despite his lack of novelty. 'Armani epitomized the end of fashion', partly because his customers 'no longer cared if fashion moved forward or backward; they just wanted fashion to provide them with attractive clothes suited for modern living'.[77] In other words, customers' preferences in this new high-fashion market allowed him to avoid the novelty treadmill and its pressure for new products—this was a key advantage of the direction his stylistic adaptation had taken in the mid-1970s.

Another key advantage was that if Armani had died in the 1990s, his firm would have been left a manageable stylistic legacy. For his successor as chief designer would have needed only to continue in the Armanian style and with Armani's approach to stylistic innovation. This approach has been characterized by his biographer as 'triggering a great initial revolution and then introducing many small advances, all clustered around the central core of what constitutes his style'.[78] However, White pointed out that 'Armani's style has in fact seen several revolutions' as he moved from the unconstructed jacket to the power-suit shape, to the roomier 'sack suit', and, in the mid-1990s, to a more feminine, occasionally Versacian style of womenswear.[79] Yet she also acknowledged that Armani was 'not dominated by a need for novelty in every collection'.[80] Armani puts it more colourfully in his book. He describes himself as 'allergic to the fireworks of fake revolutions that fizzle out in the time it takes to see the fashion show' and he is 'not particularly interested in the idea that radical renewal every six months is of value'.[81]

Unlike Armani, Versace *was* seeking radical renewal in each collection—he had climbed on the novelty treadmill. Gartel depicts Armani as an 'extremist' of consistency compared to Versace, who 'took a different route every time', and indeed his 'creative turnover was so fevered that his style never settled into a definite mould'.[82] So if he did create a distinctively Versacian style, he was certainly not a consistently Versacian designer—the pursuit of novelty required him to explore other possibilities. For example, in 1992 his sadomasochistic collection was followed by a collection in an almost hippie-like 'country' style, in 1995 his haute couture collection displayed 'demure women' wearing long skirts and high necklines, and this so-called 'conservative chic glamour' was followed by a relatively Armanian ready-to-wear collection aimed apparently at 'busy women, women who work hard in their careers'.[83] In fact Versace showed amazing artistic creativity in his search for a new theme for each of his collections, as is evident from even a partial analysis of the 1987–97 period. In addition to varying the 'Versacian' style, he also presented at least *thirteen* major changes in style, beginning with a collection showing mini-skirted models wearing 'jackets perfect for high-powered women executives' and ending with a collection inspired by the Ravenna church mosaics and using 'metal mesh fabric woven with Byzantine crosses'.[84]

Without such creativity and novelty, Versace's famous marketing 'sizzle' would have been unable to transform him into an iconic designer. He might still have gained the attention of the fashion and mass media through his marketing efforts but the media attention would have soon led to cynical media comments about too much sizzle and not enough steak. So whatever the Versacian style may have been, the Versace *image* and *charisma* were based on creativity and on mastery of the novelty treadmill.

This was a daunting legacy to leave to Donatella or anyone else who succeeded Versace as the firm's lead designer. Ball notes that Versace 'had dipped into so many different themes and references over twenty years that Donatella was left without a single clear path to follow'.[85] But the crucial point is that Donatella would have to follow her brother onto the treadmill and, like him, dip into many different themes and references. This would also provide the extremist designs that were required, no matter how diluted, by the firm's array of diffusion lines. Only then, too, would the Versace brand retain the charisma that was so important in selling the non-clothing items on the product pyramid.

Furthermore, the late 1990s were a period of intensified competition in high-fashion design. For luxury leatherwear companies had entered the field in order to gain more publicity and prestige for their brand of handbags and other luxury products.[86] They were producing notable high-fashion collections through Gucci's Tom Ford, Prada's Miuccia Prada, and the designers associated with Arnault's LVMH (Louis Vuitton). In addition, they were producing increased competition in the *non-*clothing items on the Versace product pyramid at a time when the firm's business problems made it difficult to respond.[87]

Not surprisingly, Versace's firm was unable to meet this huge challenge. For example, Donatella was a talented designer but at this stage in her career, according to Ball, 'she lacked the creativity and ingenuity to conjure up her own ideas from scratch' and so she inevitably fell far short of her brother's mastery of the novelty treadmill.[88] Similarly, she was unable to continue his practice of diluting extremist designs to suit the diffusion lines and in fact 'the various lines took off in different directions'.[89] The challenge also took a huge toll on her psychologically, and in 2004 she entered a rehab clinic to deal with her drug problem.[90] She would go on to rebuild her career as a designer and soon achieved international renown. But by then the firm had lost momentum in the highly competitive markets for high-fashion clothes and luxury goods. By 2003 sales had dropped to 'less than half' the level they had been in 1997, the firm 'fell from no. 2 among fashion companies in 1997 to no. 10 in 2004', and its sales were only one-fifth the size of Armani's by 2006.[91] Management consultants and outside CEOs were brought in and there were two rounds of lay-offs that led to hundreds of employees losing their jobs.[92] The firm was eventually put on a sound enough footing to face the 2010s with some confidence but it was no longer in any sense a rival of Armani's increasingly large company.

Versace's firm was going down a path that had been set decades earlier by the direction of his stylistic adaptive response in the late 1970s. And the path had been confirmed by his failure to include a key feature of the modern firm—becoming a public company—in his organizational adaptation in the 1980s. If his company had gone public as early as possible, it could have coped with the risks of Versace's attempt to modernize haute couture. For it would have had the salary and stock options available to hire a world-class designer or strategist to handle the post-Versace era, whether by climbing on the stylistic treadmill or by devising a strategy that put the firm on a new path.[93] However, Versace had not used the adaptive rational methods as capably as Armani, who had made a less risky stylistic adaptation in the 1970s and so, unlike Versace, could both keep his firm a private company and protect his employee-followers' career prospects.

Roddick's *Business as Unusual*

Like Armani and Versace, Anita Roddick used the two adaptive methods in the 1970s–80s to establish a large and iconic company—which in her case was the British cosmetics corporation, The Body Shop. It was smaller and less iconic than their high-fashion companies, but in 1984 it became a public company and therefore, unlike their firms, was truly a corporation. Furthermore, Roddick had used the two adaptive methods in a different manner from Armani and Versace; instead of combining them, she had used one after the other, with an innovative adaptation being followed by a separate rapid adaptation.

In addition to establishing The Body Shop, Roddick wrote, co-authored, or edited several books before she died in 2007, aged 64, and these writings included the partly autobiographical *Business as Unusual* published in 2000 and the earlier, largely auto-biographical *Body and Soul*. This relative abundance of autobiographical material provides a fascinating leader's-eye view but there is a scarcity of biographical or his-torical material describing how she established The Body Shop corporation.[94] In combination, however, there is sufficient material to cover the key feature of this example of rational leadership, namely the *abandoning* of adaptive rational methods in the latter half of the 1980s.

Roddick's abandoning of adaptive rational methods provides a crucial 'exception that proves the rule' example of what occurs when a leader fails to use the appropri-ate rational methods. For in this case the corporation lost momentum and was in a crisis situation by the late 1990s, which led to lay-offs and to employee-followers los-ing rational confidence in the future development of the corporation. In fact, there would have been a loss of rational confidence years earlier, when it was clear that the corporation had lost momentum and that its leader had abandoned the adaptive rational methods which she had used so successfully in the past.

Roddick began using adaptive methods even before she opened her first Body Shop in 1976 in Brighton. Her decision to open this new kind of store was an inno-vative adaptation to a drastic change in her personal situation. Her husband had decided to pursue his 'long-term ambition to undertake a horseback expedition from Buenos Aires to New York and while he made plans for that we decided that I would make ends meet [financially support herself and their two young children] with a small shop of some kind'.[95] And she decided that it would be a *new* kind of shop:

> When we started out, we invented a new concept—a shop where you could buy anything for the bath and the body and the hair. Nobody had done that before. The department stores couldn't really compete with us because they had 20,000 other products to sell.[96]

Another advantage was that specialized retail outlets for such items as skincare or haircare products could not compete with Roddick's wide range of products for the bath, the hair, the face, and various other parts of the body—her new shop was aptly named The Body Shop. Classifying The Body Shop as a cosmetics store and corporation is therefore a narrow approximation; it might be better described as belonging to the beauty industry, with its wide range of cosmetic and other personal products.[97]

Roddick's success in this industry, however, arose from her use of *rapid* as well as innovative adaptation. She saw the opportunity to ride a new, 'green' wave in consumer preferences—and she rapidly adapted to these new, greener times. Roddick would later acknowledge that the green market had not been part of her initial adaptive innovation: 'I make no claim to prescience, to any intuition about the rise of the green movement.'[98] But her shop's use of recycling and natural ingredients was both accidentally and ideally suited to meet the green movement's preference for natural and environmentally friendly products.

This happy coincidence was apparently due to several improvisations Roddick had made when she was preparing to open her new kind of shop. Her use of natural ingredients seems to have been largely because of her lack of chemical expertise and lack of laboratory and factory facilities. 'I'm not a cosmetics chemist or a pharmacist' and before opening the shop she had been 'doing a lot of research on do-it-yourself cosmetics in Worthing public library and mixing ingredients in the kitchen.'[99] She had also discovered that mainstream cosmetics manufacturers were not interested in producing the small quantities she needed and were even less interested in using the natural ingredients she wanted, such as cocoa butter and aloe vera.[100] However, she found a herbalist manufacturer who was willing to produce small quantities 'and we drew up a list of twenty-five possible products using those natural ingredients that were readily available.'[101] Another forced improvisation was her environmentally friendly use of packaging and containers.

> The cheapest containers I could find were plastic bottles used by hospitals to collect urine samples, but I couldn't afford to buy enough so I thought I would get round the problem by offering to refill empty containers or fill customers' own bottles. In this way we started recycling and reusing materials long before it became ecologically fashionable. *Every element of our success was really down to the fact that I had no money.*[102]

In fact, the firm's obvious lack of resources was itself one of the things that attracted customers to The Body Shop in the new, greener times of the 1970s–80s. 'It was clearly evident to everyone that The Body Shop was a hick little cottage industry, and therein, I think, lay a lot of its attraction.'[103]

But it was Roddick's rapid adaptation to the new, greener times that enabled her to scale up a small shop into a famous public company—and as early as 1984. She created a green public profile for her firm and exploited its competitive advantages in the green niche market. The Body Shop is described by Jones as one of the 'iconic "natural" firms of the era' and he also notes that its retail chain had '43 outlets in Britain and 83 abroad' by 1984.[104] This was largely because Roddick had created a sizeable demand for Body Shop franchises as well as products. Franchisees provided the financing for their new shops and 'we provided a license to use the Body Shop name and the products to sell'.[105] The result was comparable to the network of franchised stores established by Versace in these years as he, too, rapidly adapted to his market opportunity. However, Roddick went a step further by going public and providing her firm with the resources and status of a public company. She was therefore well positioned to go on and create a global empire within the beauty industry.

Instead of taking this step, however, Roddick abandoned the adaptive methods she had used to establish The Body Shop and that she needed to *continue* using if she was going to expand it into a global empire. Such expansion meant moving into the giant American market and, furthermore, making the move quickly, before US firms adapted to the opportunities offered by the new, greener times. Already 'many mass market firms had joined the "natural" bandwagon. During the late 1970s Clairol captured a large share of the US shampoo market with Herbal Essences, a green shampoo with a high fragrance content based on the essences of sixteen herbs and wildflowers'.[106] And by the late 1980s even Wal-Mart was launching a green campaign that displayed its environmentally friendly practices, as was mentioned in Chapter 5. The Body Shop, though, did not rapidly adapt to the mid-1980s window of 'green' opportunity in the American market—there would be years of delay before it belatedly went for the biggest prize in its industry.

Roddick's abandoning of rapid adaptation in the mid-1980s can be explained by two factors: the influence of her husband Gordon and the diversion into charismatic leadership. After his 2,000-mile ride around South America, Gordon became the 'numbers man' in his wife's start-up and later her teammate in their dual leadership of The Body Shop corporation.[107] According to Roddick's 1991 *Body and Soul*, she and Gordon initially had different views about expansion into the American market. 'Initially, I was much more enthusiastic than Gordon about going into America'; his view was that 'while the United States offered The Body Shop the greatest potential for growth, it also represented the greatest potential for disaster'.[108]

The other likely explanation for the delay is that she was diverted and distracted by her new role as a charismatic leader. It was not charismatic *business* leadership but instead the role of celebrity political activist publicizing new social issues and values. Roddick's activism was often an extension of her and The Body Shop's green public profile, such as their campaigning to save the whales and to support Greenpeace and Friends of the Earth pressure groups.[109] However, her personal political activism eventually covered a wide range of social issues and values: someone writing about Roddick declared that she had 'campaigned about everything, from stopping tests on animals to getting housing for homeless people'.[110] In particular, she campaigned for a new attitude towards business and its social responsibilities, which she sums up in her 2000 *Business as Unusual*:

> Businesses have become hypnotized by the bottom line and have forgotten their moral obligations to civil society. The message I have been repeating *in every speech I've made and every article I've written* on business in the last 15 years is that we must include in our measures of success enough to sustain communities, cultures and families.[111]

As her reference to the 'last 15 years' confirms, Roddick took on this time-consuming charismatic role in the mid-1980s, just when her corporation should have begun to move into the American market.

But instead this move would be delayed until the *late* 1980s. As Roddick acknowledges, 'we had more than two hundred stores in thirty-three countries around the world before the first Body Shop opened in the United States in the summer of 1988'.[112] By then the green movement and attitudes were so well established that there was no chance of The Body Shop becoming an iconic green corporation as it had in Britain; it was just one of many firms in the American market, including Wal-Mart, which were already or soon would be presenting themselves as green or greenish. Furthermore, The Body Shop would be facing competition from firms selling 'natural' beauty products and from at least one firm that would sell such products in a similar kind of store to her once innovative Body Shop format and range of products. What Jones describes as her 'retail model' was 'later used by other companies selling green brands, such as the [American] clothing retailer Limited Brands, which founded a natural-toiletries store chain called Bath & Body Works in 1988'.[113] So an American equivalent of The Body Shop was founded in the same year that Roddick's corporation arrived in the country. By 1990, The Body Shop had twenty-two stores in the US but the Bath & Body Works (B&BW) chain had opened nearly five times as many stores.[114]

Roddick acknowledges in *Business as Unusual* that she had not anticipated 'how incredibly fast the competition would come in'.[115] She refers to B&BW as 'a copycat of The Body Shop' and seems to view anyone selling natural beauty products as an imitator as well as competitor: 'there were around 30 different lookalikes of The Body Shop' and such competitors as 'H2O Plus, Goodbodies, Origins and Garden Botanika jumped on the natural products bandwagon, developed their own lines of fruity potions and sold them for less'.[116] She also mentions several other features of the retail and business culture that had not been anticipated or that involved a more difficult adjustment than she had anticipated.[117] Furthermore, she explains that initially The Body Shop opened only company-owned stores—waiting until 1990 to begin franchising—in order 'to give us time to adjust to the new market'.[118]

As in the mid-1980s, however, Roddick needed to adapt more rapidly. The alternative was to use innovative adaptation, such as seeking a joint-venture arrangement with an American entrepreneur, like the international joint ventures that McDonald's had pioneered in the 1970s. This would have markedly increased The Body Shop's chances of becoming an iconic green corporation in America as well as other regions of the world.

Not surprisingly, the failure to use either of the adaptive methods led to the eventual failure of the American expansion. Roddick describes a 'golden age' of growth in the early 1990s as more than a hundred franchised stores were opened, but the growth slowed in 1993 and by the following year it was in reverse: The Body Shop actually began to lose customers.[119] This disappointing end to high expectations was reflected in the corporation's share price. 'The share market decided we were no longer their darling and hacked our share price to pieces' to such an extent that at one point the corporation had 'lost more than half its value'.[120] The share price would never return to its early-1990s peak. Looking back at this turning point, Roddick commented that hopefully The Body Shop would 'always be the leader—if not in profits, then in ideas and principles. In those areas, I don't believe anybody can offer us any competition'.[121]

Roddick's move away from rational leadership was confirmed by the lack of rapid or innovative adaptive response to the loss of momentum. For example, there was no business-oriented equivalent of Roddick's innovative social auditing of the corporation's activities.[122] A management consultant was employed in the mid-1990s but his reorganization ended when the firm's leaders realized that they 'had made a mistake trying to fit a business with a distinct social agenda into the straitjacket of the standard disciplines of management, marketing, finance and operations'.[123] Not surprisingly, the adaptive methods had not been replaced by other appropriate rational methods, such as strategic calculation. Eventually a new situation developed and in 1998 an outside CEO was brought in, with Anita and Gordon now becoming co-chairs of the corporation.[124] The new CEO pruned the firm's administration, closed its manufacturing plant, and laid off some 300 employees.[125] By then, 'Roddick's focus was really more on social causes than on the company itself', and three years later she and Gordon resigned as co-chairs.[126] In 2006, The Body Shop was acquired by the French corporation L'Oréal for more than $1 billion—thirty years after Roddick had opened her first shop.[127]

PART II
REDEVELOPING CORPORATIONS

10
Leaders Rationally Redeveloping Corporations

This chapter begins Part II, which will look at the *re*development of corporations. The Part I chapters have looked at the development of corporations (large-scale public companies) and have focused on especially successful cases of development, those creating iconic corporations. Now the book's focus will shift to a special *form* of development: the remedial renewal of a corporation. This *re*development is more than just a 'redoing' of the development that established or enhanced the corporation. A successful redevelopment solves the problems of a troubled, stagnating, or declining corporation and gives it a bright new future. The corporation is propelled forward—even perhaps to iconic status, as when Steve Jobs redeveloped Apple in the 2000s.

Redevelopment's objective, remedial renewal, is achieved through specialized means. The leader of a rational redevelopment uses a specialized set of appropriate rational means, different from those used for the corporation development discussed in Part I. The rational *re*developer uses a 'tool kit' that contains five tools. They are change-making organizational processes, such as a structural transformation. Each of the five tools is—potentially—an appropriate rational means of redeveloping. A rational leader selects the tools that are appropriate for the redevelopment that he or she is carrying out. If the appropriate tools are capably used by the leader, he or she will inspire employee-followers with confidence, in typical rational-leadership fashion, and confidence will also be felt by other people or institutions with a stake in the redevelopment.

Part I's seven cases of iconic development included two instances of redeveloping. In the General Motors case, a redeveloping structural transformation triggered the 1920s–30s enhancing development of the corporation. Similarly, the enhancing development of Intel in the 1980s–90s was begun by a redeveloping reorientation towards microprocessor products. The GM and Intel instances of redeveloping will not, however, be revisited in Part II. Rather, its chapters will start afresh and present a series of classic cases of redevelopment from the 1980s–2010s.

These are five cases of high-quality rational leaders using appropriate tools to redevelop well-known corporations. Only the Nike and Apple redevelopments led to the corporation becoming iconic. In the other three cases, an already iconic or renowned corporation was being rescued from disaster or stagnation. The cases even

Rational Leadership. Paul Brooker and Margaret Hayward, Oxford University Press. © Paul Brooker & Margaret Hayward (2023). DOI: 10.1093/oso/9780198894643.003.0010

include a classic example of failure, as one of the leaders was insufficiently rational to overcome the difficulties of redeveloping his corporation. Much can be learnt from the five cases, but their key lesson is that redeveloping a corporation is a special form of corporation development and requires a distinctive version of rational leadership.

Using Rational Means—Transform, Reorient, Hybridize?

The distinctive set of appropriate rational means for redevelopment is a tool kit that contains five tools. They are cultural or structural transformation, a diversifying or prioritizing reorientation of the range of products, and hybridization through a merger with another company. All five tools in the repair kit are change-making organizational processes, some internal and others external. Hybridizing is an external process that makes changes by combining organizations, usually through the merger of two different companies. Cultural and structural transformations, however, are internal change-making processes that occur within an organization. Diversifying and prioritizing reorientations are more flexible, as reorienting can be internal, external, or a mixture of the two. When the reorienting is external, it adds or removes organizations, usually through acquisition or divestment.

These organizational processes—transforming, reorienting, and hybridizing—are an effective set of tools. Later in the chapter they will be described in action, with the redevelopment of three corporations in the 2000s–10s. The other chapters in Part II will present more extensive, classic case studies that show why the five tools are appropriate and confirming that each of the five is a potentially appropriate—depending upon the circumstances—rational means of redeveloping a corporation.

Normally, however, only two or three of the tools are used by a rational leader of redevelopment, as some of the five are less or not at all appropriate in dealing with a particular corporation's problems or circumstances. Plus, there is the danger of overloading. A redeveloping leader must be careful not to overload the firm with too many change-making organizational processes. Hence if three or more are used, they are best used in a sequence that allows the corporation to focus on just one or two at a time. Sequencing incorrectly or simply overloading the corporation may be almost as damaging as selecting the 'wrong' tools from the repair kit. The leader of a redevelopment therefore must be discerning when selecting and applying these organizational processes. Discernment has indeed been viewed by political scientists as the 'pre-eminent' or 'master' skill of presidents and prime ministers.[1] Similarly, discernment might be viewed as the master skill of the rational redeveloper.

Corporation-Redevelopment Version of Rational Leadership

Redevelopment: remedial (problem-solving) renewal of a corporation
Rational leadership: capably using the appropriate rational means of achieving the objective
Capably Using

Appropriate
Discerned to be appropriate for the corporation's problems and other circumstances

Rational means
Select two/three appropriate tools from 'tool kit' of change-making organizational processes
(1) cultural transformation
(2) structural transformation
(3) diversifying reorientation of product range
(4) prioritizing reorientation of product range
(5) hybridization through merger with another company

Achieving objective
End troubles, stagnation, or decline, and give the corporation a bright new future

One or more of these five organizational processes may also be used by the developer of a corporation. The developer is not, however, engaged in a remedial renewal: he or she is using the organizational process to implement a developmental decision. And his or her distinctive means of achieving development is a set of rational methods, such as strategic calculation, that shape decisions about development.

Diversification is the organizational process that is most likely to be used for development purposes. Many developers have reoriented their product range by diversification, often as the result of some strategic calculation. Bezos's strategy of diversification has already been discussed in some detail in Chapter 8. And Chapter 14 will look at Google's strategically calculated diversification into the Android software for 'smart' mobile phones.

The most significant similarity, though, between developing and redeveloping is that there is no guarantee of success. Sometimes the circumstances are too difficult and sometimes the luck is too bad. The failed redevelopment of Yahoo in 2012–16 was clearly a case of the problems and other circumstances being too difficult. Cases of bad luck are less straightforward. For instance, the luck factor has been mentioned in a memoir that describes the failed redevelopment of General Electric (GE) in

2014–17. But there was also insufficient use of rational means in this classic case of rational but failed redevelopment.

The following chapters present various cases of leaders rationally redeveloping a corporation. A series of four chapters examines four classic cases from the 1980s–2000s, beginning with sneaker firm Nike and automobile giant Chrysler. They are followed by a high-tech case, the redevelopment of computer colossus IBM (International Business Machines). Then there is the emblematic case of Jobs redeveloping Apple from a computer company into a mobile-tech corporation, known mainly for its iPhone smartphone. Three other redevelopments from the 1980s–2000s era are studied in chapter sections that illustrate important aspects of rational redevelopment. Some notable 2010s cases, too, are examined in various other chapter sections and in the final chapter. They study not only the classic GE failure but also the redevelopment of Microsoft, Nokia, and Yahoo.

Leaders, Corporations, Industries, and Chapters			
Nadella	Microsoft	Software/Cloud	Ch. 10
Siilasmaa	Nokia	Mobile-Network	Ch. 10
Fiorina	HP	Printers/Computers	Ch. 10/15
Knight	Nike	Sneakers	Ch. 11
Iacocca/Lutz	Chrysler	Automobiles	Ch. 12
Gerstner	IBM	Computers/Services	Ch. 13
Mayer	Yahoo	Internet Portal	Ch. 13
Jobs	Apple	Computers/Smartphones	Ch. 14
Page/Brin/Schmidt	Google	Online Search	Ch. 14
Ollila	Nokia	Mobile Phones	Ch. 15
Welch	GE	Industrial/Financial	Ch. 16
Immelt	GE	Industrial/Financial	Ch. 16

In addition, there is a separate chapter on charisma and rational redevelopment. A corporation redeveloper who combines charismatic and rational leadership will be strengthened by the combination. In other cases, however, rational redevelopment has been impeded by the routinized charisma of a corporation's founder or former leader.

Charismatic leadership typically relies upon such *non*-rational means as the leader's vision or gut instinct. These can be readily distinguished from *ir*rational means of redevelopment, such as relying on divine aid, resorting to violence, or diversifying into criminal activities. Using the leader's inspirational personality and speeches is an irrational means, too, if it is not combined with appropriate rational means. As IBM's redeveloper noted, passion is 'not a substitute for good thinking' and passion alone 'is simply a cheerleader doing flips on the sideline while the team gets crushed'.[2]

When a corporation is being 'crushed', there are remedial options that are less ambitious than a redevelopment. Corporate turnarounds or rectifications are problem-solving procedures that have less ambitious objectives than a redevelopment. The turnaround is aimed at turning around the firm from looming disaster, typically bankruptcy, and returning it to profitability. The rectification is aimed at rectifying particular mistakes or negative tendencies and undoing the damage that they have caused. In contrast, redevelopment brings radical change that not only solves problems but also aims to give the corporation a bright new future—a re*development*. Hence while turnarounds and rectifications can usually be completed in one or two years, redevelopment may take twice as long and there can be second or even third stages of redevelopment. Another significant difference is that turnarounds typically use cost-cutting techniques or measures, especially lay-offs. By contrast, redevelopment's organizational processes create change through the more positive means of transforming, reorienting, and hybridizing.

As in Part I, much attention will be paid to the leader's-eye view of events. This personal perspective on redevelopment is created by citing and quoting from these leaders' autobiographical writings. Most chapters include a leader's-eye view, corroborated and supplemented of course by historical and biographical sources. Even this opening chapter includes a leader's-eye view in its remaining sections. The second and third sections use the 2010s examples of Microsoft and Nokia to illustrate how transformation and reorientation are used to redevelop corporations. The final section uses the 2000s example of Hewlett-Packard (HP) to illustrate the use of hybridization and to show why it is the most problematic tool in the redeveloper's tool kit!

These examples show the redeveloper's tools being used in action and 'on the job'. But they also reveal another facet of the capability part of rational redevelopment: the leader's capable use of appropriate rational means. This of course includes capably carrying out the transformation, reorienting or hybridizing. However, it also includes choosing the right cultural or structural transformation, the right product to prioritize or diversify into, the right company to merge with when hybridizing. Making these choices is a different area of capability from the more practical task of carrying out the chosen transformation, reorienting or hybridizing. Making the choices is more a matter of judgement and indeed is part of the discernment shown by a rational redeveloper when he or she selects the appropriate tool for the circumstances. In addition to selecting the appropriate tool, the redeveloper will be choosing the right transformation, the right product, or the right company for a hybridizing merger. This is another reason why discernment is the 'master skill' of any rational leader whose objective is to redevelop a corporation.

Satya Nadella Transforms Microsoft in His *Hit Refresh*

Cultural transformation and structural transformation are an intriguing pair of tools, with marked similarities and differences. Obviously, they both make big, transformational changes. Less obviously, they are both internal change-making organizational processes: they make changes within an organization rather than by adding, removing, or combining organizations, such as through acquisitions, divestments, or mergers. However, the transformational tools make very different kinds of change. Structural transformations will change the way 'personnel are deployed' and include physical changes to workplaces, to meetings, and to units' written titles. This was apparent in the developmental case examined in Chapter 2: the Sloan restructuring of General Motors.

By contrast, a cultural transformation is aimed at the 'hearts and minds' of employees, such as their values or attitudes. Cultural transformations may well have physical elements and features. There is often a written creed or formula, which might be propagated with some of the enthusiasm and effort of a proselytizing sect or a totalitarian regime. But the end result is difficult to judge. Have the employees been convinced or are they just showing outward conformity? In practice, however, there is little difference: a cultural transformation has occurred if it has elicited the new, culturally required behaviour. Obviously, the best result is when the new cultural direction is genuinely accepted and followed. This has the added benefit, too, of reducing the need for incentives or enforcement. But the adage 'don't let the best be the enemy of the good' seems very applicable to cultural transformations.

Both the transformational tools need to be used capably and discerningly. While discernment is needed to choose the right changes, capability is needed to make the changes in the right way. Levels of discernment and capability vary: ranging from the merely adequate to the very good and even the exceptionally good. Hence changes might be very well chosen but only adequately carried out—or vice-versa. Some very good choices should be made by structural transformers, as so much has been written about structurally changing or transforming corporations. Cultural transformers have a more difficult choice, however, because the change must be tailored to fit a particular corporation's problems and other circumstances.

Furthermore, the new culture preferably will seem unique or distinctive, and will increase the firm's sense of identity. Three such distinctive cultures, the Nokia Way, the HP Way, and IBM's Basic Beliefs, are discussed in Chapter 15. The culture's distinctiveness need not be this prominent and intentional, but few firms will be happy to accept a new culture that is in no way distinctive and perhaps seems no different from a competitor's culture. In contrast, few firms will be averse to a new *structure* that is not distinctive and no different from a competitor's structure. This similarity may in fact be reassuring and seen as evidence that the leader is making the right structural change. Structural transformation is here, as in other areas, a less problematic tool than its cultural counterpart.

Yet the problematic cultural tool has achieved notable successes. A relatively recent instance is the cultural transformation of Microsoft in the 2010s, which is this section's example of the transformational tools in action. Microsoft's CEO Satya Nadella used the cultural tool during his mid-2010s redevelopment of the corporation. In his view, 'transforming the Microsoft culture' was the 'grandest endeavour, the highest hurdle' that he and the firm attempted during those years of redevelopment.[3] A leader's-eye view is provided by his partly autobiographical *Hit Refresh: The Quest to Rediscover Microsoft's Soul and Imagine a Better Future for Everyone*. The redevelopment is also covered by a recent book with a similarly long subtitle, namely Good's *The Microsoft Story: How the Tech Giant Rebooted Its Culture, Upgraded Its Strategy, and Found Success in the Cloud*.

Microsoft had initially found success, in the 1980s–90s, by supplying software for the personal-computer revolution. During that era there was a huge expansion in the use of desktop or laptop 'personal' computers. As Chapters 6 and 13 describe, the expansion was led numerically by designs based on a 1981 IBM desktop, which was labelled the IBM 'PC' and began the confusing tendency for the PC abbreviation to be applied both generally to any personal computer and specifically to any design derived from this archetypal IBM desktop. However, the archetype's software had not been developed by IBM; the operating-system software had been supplied by the Microsoft (microcomputer software) start-up. The firm thereafter supplied software to the many derivatives of the archetypal PC design, whether made by IBM or by companies 'cloning' that design.[4] So Microsoft became, in effect, the standard supplier of software to the personal-computer revolution.

Hence Microsoft benefited greatly from the huge increase in sales of personal computers. US sales of personal computers had topped nine million a year by 1990 and reached forty-six million a year in 2000.[5] In particular, some 90 per cent of these personal computers were PCs equipped with Microsoft's Windows and other software.[6] This adaptable firm had therefore developed into an iconic corporation, with a rapidly rising stock-market valuation. By 1993, the young corporation was more valuable than IBM; by 1998 Microsoft was the most valuable company in America.[7]

But in the 2000s, the personal-computer revolution moved into its consolidation phase, with troubling consequences for Microsoft. There was a severe downturn in the high-tech sector and later there were signs of a permanent decline in the demand for Microsoft's Windows and other PC software products. 'By 2008, storm clouds were gathering over Microsoft. PC shipments, the lifeblood of Microsoft, had leveled off'.[8] The storm arrived in the 2010s. Sales of PCs began to decline, leading to a dramatic 10 per cent fall in 2013.[9] In the following year, Satya Nadella was appointed CEO of this troubled corporation.

He had been preceded by two famous Microsoft CEOs. Founder-leader Bill Gates had retired in 2000 and been succeeded as CEO by his long-time lieutenant Steve Ballmer. Like them, Nadella was very much a Microsoft person. He had joined the company more than twenty years earlier, after immigrating from India and completing an MS in computer science at the University of Wisconsin. By 2011 he was leader of one of Microsoft's three main product groups, the Server and Tools Business (STB). Only three years later the 46-year-old Nadella had become leader of the whole corporation.

The new leader realized that his firm was suffering from more than just declining PC sales. Microsoft had also missed the opportunity to be a standard supplier of the new mobile-tech software. Nadella had seen years earlier that 'we'd been very publicly missing the mobile revolution'.[10] The mobile-tech revolution had started in the second half of the 1990s. Those years had seen an explosive growth in the use of mobile (cell) phones and the emergence of smartphones: mobile phones equipped with computer-like software.

However, Microsoft had not rapidly adapted to this new opportunity. The firm had not quickly diversified into smartphone software and begun supplying the emerging smartphone market. On the contrary, the first Microsoft version of software for smartphones, Windows Mobile, did not appear until 2002/3.[11] By then there were already other, well-established versions and suppliers of smartphone software. For instance, since 1998 Symbian software had been supplied to the smartphones made by the Nokia corporation, the leading maker of mobile phones.[12] Microsoft had therefore adapted too slowly to the emergence of smartphones and furthermore its adaptation was not sufficiently innovative. Although its Windows Mobile was successful, this software did not replace the Symbian systems or other well-established smartphone software.

Windows Mobile was also not innovative enough to survive the second wave of the mobile-tech revolution. This second wave began in the late 2000s with the arrival of Apple's brilliant iPhone and the arrival of Google's Android smartphone software, which was freely licensed to any suitable phone-maker. Windows Mobile 'couldn't match the iPhone or Android in aesthetics or ease of use', and was overwhelmed by them in 2009/10.[13] Microsoft was therefore unable to capitalize on the explosive growth in smartphone sales during the following years: the smartphone market was larger in value than the PC market by 2014.[14] By missing out on this smartphone boom, Microsoft CEO Ballmer had left his successor a difficult inheritance, as was noted by a business magazine:

> The Microsoft that Nadella inherited was regarded by both Wall Street and Silicon Valley as *fading towards irrelevance*. The tech industry had shifted from desktop computers to smartphones—from Microsoft's Windows to Apple's iPhone and Google's Android. (Windows' market share on phones was less than 4%.) ... Microsoft's stock price had stalled.[15]

Microsoft was clearly stagnating and in danger of decline; the firm needed a redevelopment that would solve its problems and give it a bright new future.

In 2010–13, Ballmer had tried a less ambitious form of remedial action. He had tried unsuccessfully to rectify Microsoft's mistake of missing the mobile-tech revolution. His rectifying measures included a vital software improvement, with Windows Mobile being replaced in late 2010 by the more advanced Windows Phone.[16] Less predictably, Microsoft then entered an alliance with leading phone-maker Nokia. The two firms were partners in developing a new smartphone that combined Windows Phone with Nokia's phone hardware. Although this joint-venture phone failed to make an impact, Ballmer was not deterred and in 2013 actually acquired Nokia's phone-making business.[17] Moving into the phone-making business, however, did not markedly improve Microsoft's position in the smartphone standings. As Nadella observes, there had been 'a smartphone explosion that we at Microsoft had failed to lead and barely managed to participate in'.[18] Instead of trying to rectify that mistake, Nadella wanted to redevelop Microsoft and thereby ensure that it never again missed such a crucial opportunity.

New CEO Nadella had discerned from the outset that Microsoft needed a culturally transforming redevelopment. His book recalls that on the 'February day in 2014 when Microsoft's board of directors announced that I would become CEO, I put the company's culture at the top of our agenda'.[19] Even before his appointment was officially announced, he had been thinking about how to transform the culture.

Rediscovering the soul of Microsoft, redefining our mission, and outlining the business ambitions that would help investors and customers grow our company—these had been my priorities with the first inkling that I would become CEO. Getting our strategy right had preoccupied me from the beginning. But as management guru Peter Drucker once said, 'Culture eats strategy for breakfast'.[20]

In Microsoft's case, a cultural defect had indeed been 'eating' strategy and had also been eating adaptability. The firm's cultural defect was in fact the fundamental, underlying problem that needed to be solved by Nadella's redevelopment.

This cultural problem is highlighted by Good in his book on Microsoft. He argues that the firm's size and success had slowed its response to the mobile-tech revolution in the 1990s–2000s. 'When you have more than fifty thousand employees and a market cap of $300 billion, it's difficult to recognize the right time to shift, to abandon the central strengths that have been successful to your company in favor of something new. Microsoft wasn't nimble' anymore.[21] In other words, the firm had developed bureaucratic traits: an unintended cultural change that was apparently a side-effect of growth and success. This bureaucratic aspect of the firm's culture had reduced its 'nimbleness' and adaptability, as is illustrated by an incident that Nadella recalls. When he took charge of the STB product group in 2011, his new team resisted his prioritization of cloud computing. 'Their attitude was one of frustration—they were making all this money [with the existing products] and now this little squeaky thing called the cloud came along and they didn't want to bother with it'.[22] Although he overcame their resistance, it illustrates how a bureaucratized culture had led to more rigidity and less adaptability.

An anti-bureaucratic cultural transformation was therefore a very appropriate means of redevelopment. And Nadella had discerned that the right cultural change was to counter bureaucratic culture by introducing an attractive alternative. He introduced a modern and distinctive cultural formula that was based on the idea of a 'growth mindset', an idea that he had borrowed from psychologists. A growth mindset is the opposite of a 'fixed' mindset, which merely continues doing something that has been done many times before.[23] A growth mindset therefore would be an effective alternative to the rigidity created by a bureaucratic culture. Similarly, the three ways of 'exercising a growth mindset' were attractive alternatives to particular attitudes and perspectives that are typical of a bureaucratic culture.[24]

Three Ways of Exercising a Growth Mindset
(Alternatives to Bureaucratic Attitudes/Perspectives)

1. Obsess about our customers—meeting their unarticulated and unmet needs
(not complacency and indifference)

2. Actively seek diversity and inclusion—in the workforce and decision-making
(not conformity and bias)

3. One company: one Microsoft—a family of individuals working together
(not subgroup parochialism and rivalry)

Nadella knew from the outset that this cultural tool was a problematic means of redeveloping. 'Cultural transformation would be slow and trying before it became rewarding'.[25] But he was willing to make a big effort to propagate his new cultural formula. 'I talked about these ideas every chance I got. And I looked for opportunities to change our practices and behaviors to make the growth mindset vivid and real'.[26] By changing such practices and behaviour he was also ensuring that his new formula elicited the culturally required behaviour from employees. Even if they were not truly believers, their outward conformity to his cultural formula would be sufficient—the transformation would be an effective as well as appropriate means of redeveloping Microsoft.

As the previous section pointed out, however, rational redevelopers typically use two or three appropriate tools. Nadella was no exception. In addition to the cultural tool, he reoriented the product range by prioritizing cloud-computing services. He had already been prioritizing cloud services during his 2011–13 leadership of STB. Although there had been no prospect of catching up with Amazon, Nadella had made sure that Microsoft did not 'miss' the cloud-computing opportunity.[27] After being appointed CEO, he reoriented the firm's whole product range towards cloud computing. Nadella declared that Microsoft's mission was to 'deliver the best cloud-connected experience on every device', and furthermore he set the target of building a $20 billion cloud business.[28] In the subsequent year this prioritizating was confirmed by his acquisition of the cloud-security firm Adallom.[29]

Prioritizing cloud services also meant reorienting *away* from other products. As Good observes, Windows was 'deemphasized': it 'was not the company's marquee focus anymore', though it continued to be 'the dominant operating system on PCs'.[30] Unsuccessful products, notably the mobile phones, suffered a worse fate than being de-emphasized. Here 'hard choices were necessary in order to refocus. What the company was doing wasn't working anymore'.[31] Such products were cut back, as were their workforces.

In July 2014, Microsoft laid off 18,000 employees—about 14 percent of its workforce—and the biggest layoffs in the company's history. Most of the employees had been part of the Nokia [mobile-phone] acquisition. Nadella, in an email to employees, stressed that the changes would keep the company agile ... Additional layoffs were announced in July 2015 and May 2016.[32]

The lay-offs seem similar to the divestments that might accompany a prioritization. But instead of seeing their businesses sold off, these 'surplus' employees were being laid off by their redeveloping corporation.

The final round of lay-offs, in 2016, seems a symbolic endpoint for the redevelopment—the end of its drastic prioritizing. As for the cultural transformation, Nadella's book notes that the cultural change was 'making great progress, but we should never be done. It's not a program with a start and end date. It's a way of being'.[33] After all, 'transformed' employees will seldom have a wholly genuine commitment to the new culture, and even a genuine commitment will need to be reinvigorated.

Furthermore, cultural transformations can also succeed, as noted earlier, by merely eliciting the culturally required behaviour through obedient compliance and outward conformity.

What about the success of the overall 2014–16 redevelopment? The stock market certainly thought that Nadella had given the firm a bright new future. By 2018, Microsoft was the most valuable company listed on Wall Street. 'Eighteen years after Microsoft last stood as America's most valuable corporation, our employees, partners, and shareholders once again achieved that moniker in the days following Thanksgiving 2018'.[34] The remarkable revival was partly due to the prioritizing of cloud services, which had solved the problem of Window's declining importance.[35] For Microsoft's Azure cloud business had prospered in the race to meet a soaring demand for cloud services, and the business was securely established in cloud services' number-two position: second only to the long-dominant Amazon Web Services. But Nadella would be the first to say that his redevelopment's success was also due to Microsoft's cultural transformation. Although the cultural tool is problematic, it had helped him remedially renew this iconic corporation.

Risto Siilasmaa Reorients in His *Transforming Nokia*

The other pair of tools in the redeveloper's tool kit are the diversifying and prioritizing reorientation of the product range. Diversifying reorients the product range by adding a new type or category of product. Prioritizing reorients by focusing on a type or category of product that is already in the range, as with the cloud services mentioned in the previous section. Choosing the right product for a diversification or prioritization is as important as choosing the right changes for a cultural or structural transformation. The right choice of product is part of the discernment shown by rational redevelopers when they select prioritization or diversification as the appropriate tool for the circumstances.

However, prioritizing redevelopers have a very limited range of product choice. They are choosing from their firm's existing range of products and may have no realistic alternative to their chosen product. For instance, cloud services appears to have been the only choice available to Microsoft's prioritizing CEO Nadella. By contrast, diversifying redevelopers seem to have an almost limitless choice, as they can choose from any type or category of product that is not already produced by their firm. Of course realistically the choice is far more limited, but usually there is at least one realistic alternative to the chosen diversification. The diversifier is therefore showing some degree of discernment when choosing between the alternatives or when simply choosing one of them and ignoring the others. This situation is comparable to a redeveloper choosing cultural or structural changes: there is a range of capability that extends from the merely adequate to the exceptionally good. Redevelopers made exceptionally or very good diversification choices in three of the cases studied in later chapters, and the final chapter points to some instances of relatively mediocre diversification choices.

Whether diversifying or prioritizing, this pair of tools is very flexible—able to reorient internally and/or externally. They reorient internally by diversifying or prioritizing within an organization; they reorient externally by adding or removing organizations, usually through acquisition or divestment. In contrast, the transformational tools operate only internally, within an organization. The ability to operate externally as well as internally is a major advantage of the reorienting tools, making them more effective as well as more flexible. Their diversifying can be improved or sped up by adding organizations through acquisitions, which supplement the internal diversifying and may even be a substitute for internal diversification. Prioritizing, too, can be improved or sped up by adding organizations, through acquisitions that supplement the internal prioritizing. Furthermore, prioritization can also be strengthened by removing organizations, divesting businesses, that are not linked to the prioritized product. This removal will intensify the firm's focus on the prioritized product, can end a misuse of resources, and can provide extra funding for the prioritized product.

Reorienting externally, though, requires an extra capability and occasionally some extra discernment. Externally reorienting leaders need to be capable of ably making apt acquisitions and/or divestments. For instance, the previous section mentioned Nadella aptly acquiring Adallom as an external supplement to his prioritizing of cloud services. Occasionally, some discernment may also be required. In these instances, a leader has discerned that a diversification should be made through acquisition, not by internal diversifying: this acquisition will therefore be a substitute for internally diversifying.

Externally supplemented or substituted reorienting is not unusual. Reorienting acquisitions or divestments appear in six of the eleven cases of redevelopment studied in Part II. However, the emblematic example of reorienting is Apple's wholly internal diversifying into the iPod and iPhone. The Apple example has been described already in Chapter 6 and will be studied in more detail in Chapter 14. To counterbalance this case's prominence, the present chapter will look at a very different—almost contrasting—example of reorienting. Here there was no internal diversifying but instead a largely external prioritizing, with a necessary acquisition as well as a massive divestment.

This example of reorienting in action occurred during the redevelopment of the Finnish Nokia corporation in 2013–15. Risto Siilasmaa has provided a leader's-eye view of the redevelopment in his memoir *Transforming Nokia* (though his redevelopment was not based on a cultural or structural transformation but on a reorienting of the product range). The key source of scholarly information and analysis is Doz and Wilson's impressive study of Nokia, *Ringtone*. The company was founded in the nineteenth century as a timber-processing firm, located near the town of Nokia in the north European country of Finland. The Nokia company grew into a large conglomerate but ran into serious problems in the late 1980s. In the mid-1990s new CEO Jorma Ollila brilliantly redeveloped Nokia by prioritizing mobile phones, as is recounted in Chapter 15. Ollila was so successful that Finland, with a population of only five million, became home to the world's leading mobile-phone company.

Nokia led the first wave of the mobile-tech revolution and pioneered the smartphone. By 1999, this corporation was ranked the world's eighth most valuable company and 'in 2003 Nokia was the world's sixth most valuable brand, behind Coca Cola, Microsoft, IBM, General Electric, and Intel.'[36] Nokia could also claim to be Europe's only world-renowned technology company.

In 2008, Risto Siilasmaa was invited to join Nokia's board of directors. *Ringtone* describes the 41-year-old Siilasmaa as 'a tech entrepreneur, co-founder of cyber-security firm F-secure and one of Finland's few dotcom billionaires.'[37] He was also an admirer of Nokia's long-standing and celebrated leader. 'Jorma Ollila was one of the primary reasons that I was so thrilled to be on the board of directors', he recalls in *Transforming Nokia*.[38] Although Ollila had retired as CEO two years earlier, he had retained his position as chairman and continued to be Nokia's leader.

From 2008 onwards, however, Ollila and Nokia were facing increasingly difficult circumstances. In particular, the corporation's position was being undermined by the brilliant iPhone and by the increasingly prevalent Android software.[39] Nokia's smartphones could not match the iPhone, and neither could the firm's software match the Android operating system that was being widely adopted by Nokia's competitors.

By 2012, Nokia was clearly in decline. The corporation was falling behind the Korean firm Samsung, which had taken over Nokia's leading position as the world's largest producer of mobile phones.[40] More importantly, Nokia was in financial decline. In 2011/12, it was making operating losses rather than profits.[41] The corporation was also laying off many of its employees. Twelve per cent of its workforce, some 7,000 employees, were laid-off in 2011; in 2012 Nokia announced that a further 10,000 were to be laid off.[42] In that year, too, the corporation lost its celebrated leader, with the long-expected retirement of Ollila.

In May 2012, he was succeeded by Siilasmaa as the new chairman and leader of Nokia.[43] Although he was taking over a declining corporation, he had also inherited some hope of a revival: the alliance formed with Microsoft in 2011. The alliance partners hoped to develop a new smartphone that could compete against the iPhone and the Android software. The alliance's new phone, the Lumia, combined Nokia's phone hardware with Microsoft's Windows Phone software. But the Lumia phone's first few models, appearing in 2011/12, were not very successful commercially.[44] So Nokia's new leader, Siilaasma, was pinning his hopes on the 920 model of the Lumia, which appeared in the latter half of 2012. 'Everything we knew was packed into the 920. If it sold well, our marriage with Microsoft might be saved.'[45] His hopes were dashed however. As *Ringtone* records, 'the expected sales volumes didn't materialize', and indeed sales growth had stalled by 2013.[46] Nokia and Siilasmaa therefore seemed to be facing a bleak future. 'We had bet the company on Lumia. We had failed.'[47]

However, a redevelopment opportunity was emerging in 2013. There was an opportunity to reorient the product range away from mobile phones and towards the *infrastructure* products associated with mobile phones. Mobile-phone wireless networks were based on an infrastructure of cell towers and other equipment that was supplied by network-infrastructure businesses. Nokia's long-established network business had been overshadowed in the 1990s by the huge expansion in Nokia's production of mobile phones.[48] In 2006, the network business was removed from the corporation and became part of a joint venture, Nokia Siemens Networks (NSN). 'The new company brought together the bulk of Nokia's and Siemens's network operations. Nokia and Siemens each owned half the company', but with the CEO coming from Nokia.[49] The new venture struggled to be profitable and could not make much headway against the industry leaders: the Swedish firm Ericsson and the rising Chinese firm Huawei.[50] But NSN's fortunes improved dramatically in 2011/12. The company was restructured, given new investment, and benefited from the global wave of upgrading to 4G networks.[51]

By 2013, NSN was a prospect for prioritization, as a replacement for the declining mobile-phone business. As Siilasmaa recalls, NSN was 'perhaps not quite yet the heir apparent but certainly something that looked increasingly and intriguingly attractive'.[52] In other words, he had already discerned that prioritizing network infrastructure might well be the appropriate means of redeveloping Nokia. By mid-year this prospect was attractive enough for him to put money on it. In July, Nokia bought out Siemens's half of NSN, for over $2 billion, and renamed the venture Nokia Solutions and Networks.[53] Siilasmaa was now taking his opportunity to reorient the product range towards network infrastructure.

In mid-2013 he was also taking his opportunity to reorient away from mobile phones—by divesting the mobile-phone business. Fortunately, Nokia's alliance partner Microsoft wanted to buy these mobile-phone assets. In April, Microsoft made its first offer to buy them and eventually, in September, the two firms announced that the mobile-phone assets had been sold to Microsoft for $7 billion: a price that was 'a dream come true' for Siilasmaa.[54]

He is in fact an example of the redeveloper who is lucky as well as rational. He acknowledges that he had been 'hugely lucky' with the divestment and NSN buyout.[55] Looking further back, he had been lucky to inherit in 2012 not only a stronger NSN but also the Microsoft alliance, which had given Nokia some hope and then later the opportunity for a key divestment. From a rational-redevelopment perspective, he was lucky that a likely successful way of using the reorienting tool had appeared at the right time.

But Siilasmaa was a capable as well as lucky redeveloper. In particular, he ably made apt acquisitions and divestments. There is no doubt about the aptness of buying out Siemens's half of NSN and selling off Nokia's mobile-phone business. The NSN buy-out was not just apt but essential, as the network-infrastructure activities had to be brought back in-house. Selling off the mobile-phone business was essential too. Although that business had propelled Nokia to greatness, Siilasmaa could not afford to be sentimental or complacent. The mobile-phone business was now a misuse of Nokia's resources - and had to be ended before it jeopardized the whole corporation. In addition, the sale of the mobile-phone business would provide extra money to invest in the network-infrastructure business. As Siilasmaa confirms, the divestment to Microsoft was a boost to Nokia's finances that 'enabled Nokia to be a stronger player in the infrastructure industry'.[56]

He had not only aptly but also *ably* made the NSN buy-out and mobile-phone divestment. In the NSN case, he overcame Nokia's financial constraints by negotiating a low price and resorting to 'short-term, expensive' loans.[57] Then he improved the buy-out's financing by having the loans refinanced by Microsoft. As part of the divestment negotiations with Microsoft, he elicited a relatively cheap and long-term loan that helped 'us out of the financial hole we were in from the NSN purchase'.[58] This beneficial side deal was typical of his able negotiating with Microsoft as he sold off the mobile-phone business. He was Nokia's lead negotiator for the several months that it took to gain the excellent sales price, some 70 per cent higher than Microsoft's initial offer for the mobile-phone assets.[59]

Siilasmaa's capability was displayed again when he began the second stage of Nokia's redevelopment. The first stage was not completed until 2014, as the divestment to Microsoft was delayed by government regulatory issues.[60] Only a year later, however, the redevelopment's second stage was underway. Nokia announced in April 2015 'the acquisition of Alcatel-Lucent through a share purchase worth 15.6 billion euros to create the world's second-largest infrastructure firm, just behind Ericsson'.[61] Redevelopment had given Nokia a bright new future, and this remedial renewal was mainly due to Siilasmaa's capable use of the appropriate tool—a prioritizing reorientation. Furthermore, the prioritizing had not been an internal organizational process but instead largely a matter of adding/removing organizations through acquisition/divestment. Siilaasma had shown how flexible the reorienting tool can be as a rational means of redeveloping corporations.

Carly Fiorina Hybridizes HP in Her *Tough Choices*

The fifth tool in the redeveloper's tool kit is hybridization. Like the other four tools, it is a change-making organizational process. In this case, though, change is made by combining two different organizations. The hybridizing tool therefore has its distinctive complications and problems. For instance, a rational redeveloper who uses hybridization has to discern which particular company is the right target for this hybridizing merger. And choosing the right company is more complicated than choosing the right change or product for a transformation or reorientation. The right company not only must have the features sought by the hybridizer but also must be free of problems that could impede the redevelopment.

A further complication is that hybridizing redevelopers seem to need a special capability. A hybridizer faces enough difficulties 'merely' combining the two companies into a working unit; having the desired effect on redevelopment is almost a bonus in these circumstances. The technical difficulties of mergers therefore may have discouraged redevelopers from using the hybridizing tool, for the tool is rarely used and indeed there is only one widely studied case of hybridization being used to redevelop a corporation.

This case of hybridization occurred in 2002, during the redevelopment of Hewlett-Packard. HP was being rationally redeveloped by CEO Carly Fiorina, who had already used structural and cultural transformations in 2000/1. They had failed to make much progress, though, and she moved on to a third rational means: hybridizing HP through a merger-like acquisition of Compaq Computer Corporation. Her hybridizing of HP with Compaq was the first successful merger of high-tech corporations: 'conventional wisdom before the HP-Compaq deal was that large mergers of technology companies do not work'.[62] Yet although Fiorina's merger was a technical success, her redevelopment failed to solve HP's problems and give it a bright new future. Her redeveloping of HP is in fact an excellent illustration of why rational leaders cannot guarantee a successful redevelopment. This case of redevelopment therefore illustrates not just hybridization but also why redevelopment is subject to factors that are beyond the leader's and rationality's control.

Fiorina's *Tough Choices: A Memoir* provides a leader's-eye view of HP's redevelopment. Furthermore, her redeveloping of HP has been extensively studied, such as by Anders's *Perfect Enough: Carly Fiorina and the Reinvention of Hewlett-Packard* and by Burrows's *Backfire: Carly Fiorina and the High-Stakes Battle for the Soul of Hewlett-Packard*. Both these works were published in 2003, while the hybridizing was being completed, and they are another indication that Fiorina's redevelopment of HP was a notable enterprise. As well as these sources, there are more general studies or histories of HP, such as the 1939–2016 overview, *Becoming Hewlett Packard*, by Burgelman, McKinney, and Metz. Long-lived HP has been the subject of many books and seems to be almost the totemic American corporation.

However, Chapter 6 pointed out that HP had lost its momentum by the late 1990s. During the 1990s this great multifaceted high-tech corporation was no longer diversifying and adding new facets to its business. Towards the end of the decade, HP had indeed started to stagnate and seemed likely to decline. As Fiorina observes, 'innovation had stalled' and there was 'flagging growth and profitability'.[63] By 1999, HP's board of directors was ready to take drastic action. 'All the stagnation issues that had bothered them a year earlier had grown worse', and the 'company's stock-market performance had gone from troubling to pathetic'.[64] The board's first response was to spin off HP's scientific-instruments business as a separate company, eventually named Agilent Technologies, which took away 40,000 of HP's 125,000 employees.[65] And HP now had a two-part product range: half computers and half desktop printers.

The board's second response was to hire a new CEO, Fiorina, who was recruited from outside HP and had never been a CEO. The 44-year-old Fiorina was a Stanford medieval-history graduate, with a Maryland MBA, who had joined AT&T and risen to a vice-president position before moving sideways when her branch of the company was spun off as Lucent Technologies.[66] She was a sales-and-marketing expert, had not worked in the computer or printer industries, and seems surprised that the HP board had chosen her for the job: 'that the Board was looking outside the company was revolutionary enough. To consider someone from outside the industry, a nonengineer, not to mention a woman, would indeed be controversial'.[67] HP's board clearly was looking for a high-potential outsider who would take a new approach to solving the corporation's problems.

Fiorina was named CEO in July 1999 and by early 2000 had begun redeveloping HP. She started with a structural transformation that aimed to improve HP's sales-and-marketing competitiveness. As an expert in this area, she had quickly realized that HP was being seriously out-marketed and out-sold by its competitors.[68] Her remedy was an unusual kind of structural transformation. Chapter 6 described how 1990s HP had emphasized the intermediate 'group' layer of management, operating between the central level and the divisional level. By the time Fiorina arrived at HP, there were four huge group-level organizations: two computer groups and two printer groups. She rearranged their functions and had two of the four groups focus on sales and marketing, with one catering for business customers and the other catering for consumer customers.[69] These two groups set prices, forecast sales figures, and were 'responsible for making the quarterly numbers'.[70]

Her structural transformation was a short-lived success. Initially, there was an impressive growth in sales revenue.[71] Later in 2000, however, HP was hit by the onset of a recession in the high-tech sector. As Chapter 8 mentioned, a stock-market crash ended the 'dot-com' boom in shares of Internet firms and this led on to a 2000/1 recession. It hit not just e-commerce but the whole high-tech sector. In *Tough Choices*, Fiorina recalls that corporations' spending on technology 'came to a halt': the 'downturn and bear market made every aspect of my job more difficult'.[72] Another setback to her redevelopment was having to abandon her attempt at reorienting HP's product range. She had wanted to prioritize HP's consultancy services relating to computers and information technology (IT). But in late 2000, she had to forego the acquisition of a large firm of computer-services consultants.[73] Furthermore, she was having difficulty carrying out her cultural transformation of HP. As Chapter 15 discusses, this cultural change was part of her attempt to boost HP's competitiveness but there were strong impediments to change.

In 2001, though, she discerned that HP's redevelopment could be revived by a hybridizing merger.[74] And she had discerned that the right company to target for a hybridizing merger was the Compaq Computer Corporation. This Texan firm was to be absorbed by and into HP through a takeover merger that would add Compaq's 65,000 employees to HP's 90,000.[75] Compaq had risen to prominence in the 1980s as a maker of IBM-clone PCs, but in recent years its leadership of the PC market had been lost to Dell Computer. Although Compaq had diversified into more sophisticated areas of computing, it was still very much a computer firm.[76] A merger would therefore reorient HP's product range towards computers and change HP into a primarily computer corporation. This reorientation was towards the less profitable half of HP's product range: computers were less profitable than laser and inkjet printers. But merging with Compaq would make HP the world's number-one maker of PCs and the number-three in computer consultancy services.[77] Plus HP's range of computer products would be broadened to include items that HP did not sell but that complemented its existing product range. Her memoir eloquently depicts the 'scale and scope' advantages. 'I knew a broader and more complete product portfolio, favourable economies of scale, leadership market share positions and the size to both serve our largest customers better and negotiate as equals with our largest

partners, particularly Microsoft and Intel, all combined to create a persuasive strategic case' for acquiring Compaq.[78] Merging the two firms' product ranges therefore
seemed an appropriate way of improving HP's competitiveness.

Merging the firms' *cultures* was another appropriate way of improving competitiveness. The cultural merging was also more like a biological hybridization, which
combines genetic material from two different species or varieties.[79] The cultural difference between HP and Compaq was more marked than the difference between
product ranges. Culturally, HP was more 'genteel' and Compaq 'much scrappier': a
'brasher' company, whose personnel were more aggressive.[80] The Compaq culture
was therefore more like the culture that Fiorina wanted for HP, as a more aggressive
culture would improve HP's competitiveness. So merging Compaq's culture with
HP's was a key reason for the acquisition. It has been said that HP sought a generous
'merger of equals' with Compaq because it wanted 'to ensure that Compaq's executives and other employees stuck around to change its [HP's] ways'.[81] In Fiorina's
words, the goal of the acquisition was not a takeover but instead:

> to use the best of both companies to build something stronger and better. We
> would use the best of both product lines, both management teams, and both
> *cultures* ... We needed the fighting spirit, the speed and the can-do attitude of
> Compaq. We needed the HP focus on quality and integrity.[82]

Here Compaq's cultural contributions seem to be more prominent than HP's and to
be almost military-like: a shock-troop ethos that could defeat HP's competitors.

When the merger went ahead in 2002, Compaq personnel did indeed introduce a
new ethos into the ranks of HP. Experts on HP have observed that 'the merger with
Compaq brought in a vast number of senior Compaq executives used to working in
a regime with widely different core values, which unavoidably and fundamentally
changed the soft part of the HP culture'.[83] The cultural change was in the direction sought by Fiorina. The new HP 'showed serious competitive spirit', according
to House and Price's *The HP Phenomenon*, and this competitive spirit was particularly evident in the PC markets.[84] In these markets, the merger with Compaq seems
to have met her expectations. By 2006/7, HP clearly had the edge over its main rival
in the PC markets, Dell Computer.[85] But by then Fiorina was no longer CEO, and
in fact she had been pushed out of HP. What had gone wrong?

The underlying problem was that computer markets had not fully recovered from
the 2000/1 recession. These computer markets 'grew much more slowly after 2001
than HP had assumed', according to a standard scholarly account, and this slower
growth led to the merger having 'less-than-hoped-for short-term results'.[86] HP was
not the only firm to be affected by the slow growth: there were industry-wide reper-
cussions that lasted for years after the recession. The '2001 malaise stopped Intel,
Sun Microsystems, IBM, and Agilent Technologies for years thereafter; even growth
at Cisco, Dell, and Microsoft was severely stunted'.[87] How could hybridizing HP have
done any better than these firms?

The HP case is indeed a useful reminder that rational leadership cannot guarantee a successful outcome. Fiorina's hybridizing of HP had been capably carried

out and was certainly a technical success. Even books that were sceptical about the merger acknowledged that HP and Compaq had been successfully merged into a huge new HP, now ranked number thirteen on the Fortune 500 list.[88] Many years later, the merger still looked technically impressive: 'technology mergers in particular are notoriously hard to pull off. Yet just two years after HP announced its intention to acquire Compaq, the company met or exceeded its ambitious integration targets'.[89] Despite its technical achievements, however, the merger was not so successful commercially or financially. Although the new HP was more competitive, it was competing in difficult and slow-growth markets.

Fiorina's redevelopment therefore had little chance of success. In particular, she had been unable to solve the stock-market performance problem that had emerged in the late 1990s. Her new HP 'often' missed its projected quarterly results, and by 2004 the share price was falling further behind those of its main computer-product rivals, Dell and IBM.[90] This continuing share-price problem in turn weakened Fiorina's standing with the board of directors, who pushed her out of HP in February 2005.[91]

She was replaced by Mark Hurd, another high-potential outsider. He has been depicted as almost a follow-on to Fiorina: 'building on what she had started and completing the job' of redevelopment.[92] He initially had more success. The new CEO boosted the share price, by 65 per cent within a year, thanks partly to cost-cutting that involved laying off some 15,000 employees.[93] The share price benefited, too, from the fact that 'the economy fully recovered' in 2005, helping Hurd but coming too late for Fiorina.[94] In 2006/7, HP had the edge on its computer rivals, as mentioned earlier, and the redevelopment therefore seems to have been on the verge of success. The computer industry, though, was not seeing a return to the good old days; mobile-tech was emerging as a new rival by the late 2000s. Smartphones and tablet computers 'posed a potential strategic threat to desktop and laptop computer products developed and sold by the original equipment manufacturers, such as HP and Dell'.[95] By 2008, Hurd had begun a new redevelopment, aiming to prioritize computer services. He quickly reoriented the product range in this direction by acquiring a major IT-services company. But this redevelopment also quickly ran into difficulties with the 2008/9 recession: 'a major stroke of bad luck' that badly hit the new acquisition's business.[96]

Hurd was replaced in 2010 by yet another outsider, this time from Europe. The new CEO lasted less than a year. Stable leadership returned when Meg Whitman, a member of HP's board, agreed to take on the job of CEO. She did not attempt any new redevelopment, and in 2014 split HP into two separate companies: HP Inc. for personal computers and printers; Hewlett Packard Enterprise for business computing.

So Fiorina's and Hurd's redevelopment of HP had been unsuccessful. They had not solved HP's problems and given it a bright new future. However, they had faced a difficult task that had been made more difficult by bad luck—the recessions. In contrast, good luck aided the redevelopment of Nokia in 2013–15 by Siilasmaa, as he acknowledges: 'I also learned about luck. We were hugely lucky and should always remember that'.[97] The importance of luck has long been recognized by theorists of leadership. Some 500 years ago, in *The Prince*, Machiavelli proposed that 'fortune' was 'the arbiter of half our actions, but that it lets us control roughly the other half'.[98] In modern times, however, rational leadership can perhaps do better than 50/50. There is good reason for modern people to be inspired with confidence by a rational leader.

The following chapters will present cases of rational leaders using appropriate rational means to redevelop their corporations. Chapter 11, however, will be building on Part I as well as beginning Part II, for the chapter will be presenting the hybrid Nike case of redeveloping being combined with development. The Nike case is a fascinating example of early-stage HDR (hybridized development-redevelopment), which expanded 1980s Nike into a corporation: a large-scale public company. HDR usually occurs at a later stage, after the corporation has been established. Indeed, later-stage HDR appeared in two of the Part I cases, General Motors and Intel, as some redevelopment occurred at the start of their enhancing development. By contrast, the Nike case will show HDR occurring while the corporation was still being established, when few could have foreseen that Nike would soon be a globally iconic corporation.

11

Nike

Knight's *Shoe Dog*

The Nike corporation is the world's leading sports-and-fitness shoe company. Its shoes have long led their market and have also long doubled as popular-fashion items. Popular fashion is a less celebrated business than the high fashion discussed in Chapter 9. However, Nike's redeveloping diversification into popular fashion in the 1980s was very successful. This American firm became a globally iconic corporation, whose name, symbols, and slogans are known throughout the world. More prosaically, by the early 2020s Nike employed nearly 80,000 people, generated over $40 billion in annual revenue, and earned some $6 billion in annual income.[1]

The redeveloping of Nike in the 1980s is the classic hybrid case of redevelopment being combined with the development that establishes a corporation. As Chapter 10 noted, Nike is a rare example of HDR (hybridized development-redevelopment) occurring before, not after, a corporation has been established. Nike had become a public company in 1980 but was not yet a large-scale public company, a corporation, when a crisis arose in the mid-1980s. This development crisis was partly due to a decline in rational leadership, but there was soon a revival of rationality. A redevelopment was begun, using the tool of diversification as the appropriate rational means. In addition, the development process was revived through a return to adaptive rational methods. Both these new measures were successful and in combination led to Nike recovering from its crisis, completing its growth into a corporation, and furthermore quickly becoming an iconic American corporation. The combination of redevelopment and revived development was so effective that Nike's leadership had needed to use only one of the five tools from the redeveloper's tool kit described in Chapter 10. That tool had helped Nike recover from the crisis and had propelled this emerging corporation forward to a very bright future—as an iconic corporation. The Nike case is therefore a classic hybrid combination of rational development and *re*development: remedial renewal.

Both parts of Nike's hybrid combination will be covered in this chapter. A leader's-eye view of Nike's development from start-up to public company is provided by Phil Knight's *Shoe Dog: A Memoir by the Creator of Nike*. But Knight's memoir only goes as far as 1980, though he continued to be Nike's leader until 2004 and his book was published some ten years after he retired. Fortunately, there is something like a leader's-eye view of the crucial mid-1980s period, when Nike was redeveloped and saw a revival in its development into a corporation. The 1991 *Swoosh: The Unauthorized Story of Nike and the Men Who Played There* was written by the wife and the

Rational Leadership. Paul Brooker and Margaret Hayward, Oxford University Press. © Paul Brooker & Margaret Hayward (2023). DOI: 10.1093/oso/9780198894643.003.0011

sister-in-law of Rob Strasser, who shared the leadership of Nike with Knight in the mid-1980s. This Strasser-phile book provides something close to a Strasser leader's-eye view of these crucial years and also covers the earlier development of Nike.[2] A few years after *Swoosh* appeared, Katz published *Just Do It* (the Nike slogan), which presented another perspective on the firm's development and redevelopment.

Nike's main product, sports-and-fitness shoes, went by several different names in the 1960s–80s. The most general and technical term was 'athletic' shoes. The most widely used popular term was 'sneakers' but this referred only to basketball, tennis, and trainer shoes plus any running shoes without cleats, spikes, or sprigs. Many books about sneakers and the sneaker industry have appeared. For instance, Vanderbilt's *The Sneaker Book* presented a wide-ranging analysis of how Nike and its rivals operated in the 1980s–90s. A more recent example is Smith's 2018 *Kicks: The Great American Story of Sneakers*, which gave Nike a prominent place in its history of the American sneaker and sneaker industry. In total, much has been written about Nike and its sneakers.

This chapter's four sections will add a new perspective on Nike, as a developing and redeveloping corporation. The first section shows how a 'crazy idea' was developed into a public company, Nike Inc., by co-founders Knight and Bill Bowerman. In the 1960s–70s they used all seven of the appropriate rational means of establishing a corporation. By 1980, Nike was being converted into a public company and was growing towards corporation size. But the second section shows that this emerging corporation was hit by a development crisis in the mid-1980s, after the firm's leadership had abandoned its key rational means of development: rapid and innovative adaptation. A return to these adaptive methods, however, led to a revival of development and a remarkable recovery from the development crisis. The success of new adaptive products, the Air Max and Air Trainer sneakers, pulled the firm out of its crisis and ensured that Nike developed into a full-sized corporation.

The third section argues that the revival of development had been preceded, a year earlier, by the start of a redevelopment. Instituted largely by Strasser, this redevelopment helped solve the crisis problems and gave Nike a very bright new future. The redeveloping tool was a diversifying reorientation of the product range. Nike diversified into a new type of product, popular-fashion items, by giving basketball sneakers a new, additional function as popular-fashion items for young males. The diversification included an external supplement, but not by adding an organization through acquisition—the process discussed in Chapter 10. Rather, there was an innovative joint-venture arrangement with an emerging sports hero, Michael Jordan. He promoted Nike's basketball sneakers so effectively that the firm was able to sell them as popular-fashion items as well as sports products. And the fashion diversification also contributed to the success of Nike's new adaptive products, the Air Max and Air Trainer sneakers. This contribution was only one aspect, however, of the hybrid relationship between redeveloping and development. A more important aspect was that the redeveloping propelled Nike forward to iconic status in the 1990s.

The short final section looks at this 1990s phase in Nike's diversification into popular fashion. During this phase, a product's fashion appeal often depended on it being seen as a 'cool' item, not just a product associated with a sports hero. So Nike had to stay in touch with the latest trends in 'coolness' as well as maintain its products' sports-and-fitness reputation. The section also points out, however, that Jordan and the sports function of Nike's products played an important role in extending the firm's global impact in the 1990s. By the time founder-leader Knight retired in 2004, Nike had become an iconic corporation globally as well as in America.

Developing His 'Crazy Idea' into Nike Inc.

Knight used all seven appropriate rational means to develop Nike into a corporation. As Part I described, these seven are generic rational methods: rapid or innovative adaptation, quantitative or strategic calculation, diverse or institutionalized deliberation, and learning. The learning method was how Knight developed the idea for starting up Nike. His *Shoe Dog* memoir recounts that this 'Crazy Idea' first came to him while studying for an MBA at Stanford University in the early 1960s. He had been a star athlete, a runner, at the University of Oregon before he went to Stanford. And his Crazy Idea was to import Japanese running shoes, as a way of undercutting German firms'—especially Adidas's—dominance of the running-shoe market in America.[3] Knight's idea was expressed in an MBA research paper that involved a lot of learning. He 'spent weeks and weeks on that paper. I'd moved into the library, devoured everything I could find about exporting and importing, about starting a company'.[4] Nike may therefore have been the first iconic corporation to have originated as a student's research paper. During the rest of Knight's time at Stanford he 'pondered going to Japan, finding a shoe company, pitching them my Crazy Idea', and seeing if 'they would want to partner with a shy, pale, rail-thin kid from Oregon'.[5] After graduating, he carried out his plan and ended up as the US distributor for running shoes made by the Japanese firm Onitsuka. Hence in 1964, the Blue Ribbon Sports firm was started up by Knight, in partnership with his former running coach, Bill Bowerman.[6]

Their Blue Ribbon start-up merely distributed Onitsuka's running shoes and indeed was only a part-time venture. Knight's main job was working as an accountant for an Oregon accounting firm and then for the Portland branch of Price Waterhouse.[7] Although his start-up was doubling its sales year after year, he did not want to risk being its full-time manager. Rather, he looked for a new job that would allow him more time for managing his growing firm: in 1967, he became an assistant professor, teaching accounting classes at Portland State University.[8] He left academia in 1969 and finally became the full-time business manager of Blue Ribbon. He and co-founder Bowerman continued to operate as a dual-leadership team, with Knight as the business manager and Bowerman the product developer.

The two leaders also continued to use appropriate rational methods of developing Blue Ribbon into a corporation. Bowerman used the two adaptive methods to create new products from the shoes that the firm's supplier Onitsuka made in Japan for sale in the US. Bowerman had begun by rapidly adapting the design of Onitsuka's running shoes so that they would suit American feet.[9] Then in 1966 he had innovatively adapted by combining two different Onitsuka designs and creating the very success-ful Cortez running sneaker.[10] His mid-1970s 'waffle' shoe sole was another successful adaptive innovation. The waffle sole was initially just his adaptive response to the new surface being applied to running tracks, but this innovative shoe sole also proved to be well suited to other running surfaces.[11] His most impressive adaptive feat, how-ever, was when he responded to a new fitness idea—jogging—that expanded the market for running shoes. He quickly became jogging's most important promoter: his 1967 bestseller *Jogging* 'sparked a movement'.[12] And it sparked a big increase in the demand for running shoes, including those of Blue Ribbon. By 1973 an esti-mated 'six and a half million Americans were jogging, many in footwear designed by Bowerman'.[13]

Knight, too, was capably using appropriate rational methods, as a business man-ager rather than a product developer. For instance, in 1971 his adaptive response to the firm's financial needs was an innovative funding deal with a huge Japanese trading company, Nissho Iwai.[14] In the following year, he adapted rapidly to a supply crisis. When his long-time supplier Onitsuka ended their association, Knight quickly found new suppliers for Blue Ribbon.[15]

His most significant adaptation, however, was the 1971 creation of a new logo and name for his company. It had begun importing Mexican soccer shoes to sell in the US as American-football shoes, but Knight believed that this 'new soccer-qua-football shoe would need something to set it apart' from the logos of other sports-shoe firms.[16] He responded with an innovative adaptation. A young artist and advertising designer was asked to create a distinctive logo. She came up with the brilliant 'swoosh' logo: 'we gave Carolyn our deepest thanks and a check for thirty-five dollars'.[17] Knight wanted the new logo to be accompanied by a new brand name. His associates and employees disliked his suggested brand name, 'Dimen-sion Six', and one of them suggested 'Nike' as an alternative.[18] The 'Nike' advocate pointed out that iconic brands tended to have short names with a strong, memorable sound. 'Also, I [Knight] liked that Nike was the [ancient Greek] goddess of victory. What's more important, I thought, than victory'.[19] The firm therefore acquired a new brand name, 'Nike', and soon the company's name became Nike Inc. rather than Blue Ribbon.

Knight was using not only adaptive methods but also the calculative pair of ratio-nal methods. Accountant Knight put quantitative calculation to good use, as when he asked Nike's advertisers: 'Can you say definitively that people are buying Nikes because of your ad? Can you show it to me in black-and-white numbers?'[20] His most important use of strategic calculation was his 1978 decision to diversify into sports apparel. He believed Nike's main competitor, Adidas, enjoyed 'a psychologi-cal edge' through selling sports apparel as well as shoes and he surmised that 'if we ever wanted to go public, Wall Street wouldn't give us the respect we deserved if we were just a shoe company'.[21] As he calculated, the diversification into apparel led to Nike being seen as a sports-and-fitness company, not just a shoe company, and eventually—more than a decade later—sports apparel produced about a quarter of Nike's revenue.[22]

The deliberative pair of rational methods were distinctively used by Knight in his biannual 'Buttface' meetings. He and around a half-dozen of his long-time managers gathered at an Oregon resort for a management 'retreat'. Their policy deliberations were institutionalized, if only informally, and were remarkably diverse, especially in their lack of reticence.

> no idea was too sacred to be mocked, and no person was too important to be ridiculed ... While floating ideas, and shooting down ideas, and hashing out threats to the company, the last thing we took into account was someone's feelings. Including mine. Especially mine. My fellow Buttfaces, my employees, called me Bucky the Bookkeeper, constantly.[23]

The Buttface meetings discussed some important issues, however, such as the decision to convert Nike into a public company in 1980.[24] Becoming a public company was a big step in Nike's development into a corporation, but the firm had only a few thousand employees and was not yet a corporation-size business. Furthermore, the emerging corporation would actually be downsized in the 1980s: turbulent times lay ahead in Nike's development.

Dealing with a 1980s Development Crisis

The turbulence arose partly from a decline in rational leadership. By the early 1980s, Nike's leadership was no longer using two rational methods, rapid and innovative adaptation, that had played a key role in the 1960s–70s. Abandoning these adaptive methods led on to a demoralizing development crisis. It is a stark warning of the dangers of insufficiently rational leadership.

Nike's move away from the adaptive methods was already evident by the late 1970s, when it failed to adapt to a new running boom. Unlike the jogging boom, this new running fad was about individuals running for fitness on their own, not in a group, and the runners were often preparing themselves for competitive races, particularly the marathon.[25] The new fad was promoted not by Bowerman but by such sources as Jim Fixx and his 1977 bestseller *The Complete Book of Running*. Having already developed impressive running shoes and commercial kudos, Nike had met the requirements of the new fad. For instance, Fixx's running book advocated good quality running shoes, made by the leading companies, and specifically mentioned Bowerman's waffle-sole trainer as a shoe with good traction.[26]

Nike missed an opportunity, though, to adapt innovatively to the running boom. For the firm was offered a revolutionary technological innovation in 1977. An inventor had inserted gas bags in a shoe's sole and heel to cushion impact, thereby creating 'air shoes'.[27] Nike did adopt this sole/heel cushioning technology, known as 'Air', and introduced it commercially in 1978 through a new shoe called the Tailwind. But the vaunted Tailwind had a design flaw that led to a recall and the offer of a full refund.[28] The design flaw was not related to the shoe's innovative Air cushioning; the flaw was in the innovative silver paint applied to the shoe. As Knight noted in *Shoe Dog*, Nike 'learned a valuable lesson. Don't put twelve innovations into one shoe. It asks too much of the shoe, to say nothing of the design team.'[29] That was not the only valuable lesson to be learnt. Another was, 'don't pay too much attention to innovation rather than adaptation.'[30]

Yet Nike's leadership continued to move away from the adaptive rational methods. Hence Nike failed to adapt to the rise of aerobics fitness in the early 1980s. Aerobics had advantages over jogging or running as a fitness routine. First, 'for many people looking to get into shape, cardio work, especially when done in public, only held so much appeal'; the workout routine introduced by aerobics was more concerned with getting into shape and 'was more intimate—just an instructor leading a small group in a series of stretching, stepping, and reaching routines.'[31] A second advantage was that aerobics could be done alone at home, thanks to the 1982 release of the video *Jane Fonda's Workout*. Those too shy to work out in a group 'could now do so in the privacy of their living rooms, while overscheduled stay-at-home moms and career women could avoid the hassle of attending fixed-time classes.'[32] As this implies, aerobics was the first fitness trend to be favoured by women and was creating a multitude of new fitness consumers in the early 1980s.

Nike might have adapted to the change by exploiting its innovative 'Air' gas-cushioned shoe sole. Shoes with Air cushioning would have helped millions of aerobics-fitness consumers who 'subjected their aging joints and tortured ligament encapsulations to high impact jumping up and down' in aerobic work outs.[33] Nike missed the opportunity, however, for a winning Air aerobics sneaker. One explanation for the miss is that Air was an innovation that had already 'failed to take on a more graspable public meaning.'[34] Nike's designers had attempted to solve this problem by making the Air visible to consumers.

> Because consumers seemed to have a hard time comprehending the cushioning Air provided, R&D had tried to figure out how to make see-through soles. At first, they tried 'Air weenies', little Air bags shaped like Vienna sausages that were stuffed under the heel. But on trial runs the weenies kept popping out.[35]

So the idea of visible Air was not pursued further until 1985/6, when the idea was brilliantly resurrected as part of the return to adaptive methods. In the meantime, though, there was no rapid adaptive response to the aerobics boom: there was no new product marketed as an 'aerobics' shoe. Adaptive methods therefore seem to have been abandoned.

Nike's missed opportunity was lucratively exploited by a more adaptable firm. Reebok introduced a specialized aerobics shoe that lacked Air cushioning but was attractive and highly popular. Until the aerobics trend emerged, Reebok had been a small company that made running shoes. Then one of its salesmen came up with the idea of 'aerobic shoes' and his CEO was eventually convinced that such a shoe was worth producing.[36] Reebok's Freestyle shoe appeared in 1982 as an attractive wrinkled-leather design that has been described as a mixture of sneaker and dancing shoe.[37] The Freestyle 'took off' and so did Reebok. The company's sales grew from merely $1.5 million in 1981 to $65 million in 1984, $307 million in 1985, and $1.4 billion in 1987.[38] In 1986, Reebok had overtaken Nike as the leading seller of athletic shoes, ending the year with 30 per cent of the market compared to second-place Nike's 21 per cent.[39] Nike had been overtaken by a firm that had come from nowhere by rapidly and innovatively adapting to the aerobics boom. Reebok's success therefore highlighted Nike's move away from these two adaptive methods, which had previously played a key role in the firm's development.

Furthermore, Nike had needed to adapt to the aerobics boom to offset a decline in the running fad. 'The running boom, it turned out, had peaked at exactly the time Phil Knight had taken his company public', and by 1981 there had been a marked fall in Nike's running-related sales.[40] By the middle of the decade, Nike had clearly lost momentum and indeed was going backwards. Its share price fell from $23 to $16 in 1983 and plummeted in 1984 to an ultimate low of less than $7.[41] It was 'somewhat cash-strapped' and made a loss in two quarters of 1984/5.[42]

The emerging corporation was suffering a severe development crisis, which led to substantial downsizing rather than development. There were 400 lay-offs from Nike's workforce of only a few thousand.[43] In *Shoe Dog*, Knight writes of his regret that he had not been 'a good enough manager to avoid layoffs'.[44] The lay-offs were indeed partly a result of insufficiently rational leadership, but it is difficult to assign responsibility for this move away from adaptive rational methods.

The decline had been most obvious in the areas of product development and bringing products to market. So Bowerman—the product leader—might appear to be responsible for the dual-leadership team's declining rationality. However, he had ceased being an equal financial partner in 1975, when he had sold 44 per cent of the company's stock to Knight.[45] Bowerman remained on the board of directors and held a major design position, but he gradually lost influence even over design matters. By 1982, his design team was working on twenty-three projects, including an aerobics shoe, but most of his projects either 'had little mass-market appeal' or 'rarely made it into production in the shape or with the alacrity Bill wanted'.[46] He may have been responsible for the move away from adaptive methods in the late 1970s and early 1980s. During this period, however, Knight seems to have been Nike's sole leader and therefore ultimately responsible for the decline in rationality. On the other hand, Knight gave 'his top people plenty of freedom. You could make some big things happen with that freedom, but you could also make some big mistakes'.[47] Perhaps he had allowed his top people too much freedom in areas—product areas—where he had little expertise or experience.

Knight's hands-off leadership style peaked in 1983/4. He handed over his CEO-like post of president to a long-time associate, Bob Woodell, who was one of the founding members of the Buttface coterie. Woodell took over Knight's post 'from June 1983 through September 1984' while the founder-leader went into sabbatical-like semi-retirement as the company's chairman.[48] An additional complexity was that in 1983 Knight assigned the firm's top marketing role to another founding member of the Buttface coterie, lawyer Rob Strasser. So in 1983/4 there seems to have been a triple-leadership team of Woodell, Strasser, and Knight. Woodell introduced administrative changes aimed at making Nike more big-business-like and he tried, unsuccessfully, to increase apparel sales to offset the falling sales of running shoes.[49] His tenure as president lasted little more than a year. By October 1984, chairman Knight had reassumed the position of president.[50]

From then on, Knight and Strasser operated as a dual-leadership team. Two years later, however, the leadership situation changed yet again. In October 1986, Strasser took three months' sabbatical-like leave and on his return became so dissatisfied that he left Nike late in 1987.[51] The Strasser-phile *Swoosh* book quotes Knight telling someone that Strasser had run the company for 'two years', which presumably refers to the period from October 1984 to October 1986.[52] If so, Strasser held the day-to-day leadership role when there was a move back to the adaptive methods of rapid and innovative adaptation. This revival of rational leadership in turn produced a revival of Nike's development into a corporation.

Nike Dual/Triple Leadership Teams
1960s–70s Knight and Bowerman
1983–4 Woodell, Strasser, and Knight
1984–6 Strasser and Knight
1986–7 Knight and Strasser
1987–2004 Knight

The move back to adaptive methods began with the innovative Air sole described earlier in this section. The Air sole had become a standard feature of Nike sneakers and was included in their names, such as the 'Air' Jordan and later the 'Air' Trainer. However, this technical innovation had not achieved its full marketing potential as a way of attracting consumers who were looking for something extra in their sneaker soles. Now, in 1985/6, there were brilliant redesigns of Air that made it more likely to attract these consumers. 'In 1985, when Nike was searching for new ideas, the visible Air project resurfaced'; this time 'as a shoe with a window cut in the midsole where you could see an Air bag'.[53] In 1986, visible Air was combined with a beefed-up Air sole to create the Air Max running sneaker, whose small window in the side of the heel made some Air visible.[54] Here at last was the innovative adaptation in design that allowed Nike to make the most out of marketing its technological innovation.

There was also a move back to rapid adaptation. Nike adapted rapidly in 1986 to a new fitness concept called 'cross-training': training that involved a variety of sports or fitness routines.[55] Nike had designed a suitable sneaker, with sufficient Air cushioning for a few miles' running plus the structural support needed for tennis or basketball.[56] The new design was also well suited to cross-training in a gym through a combination of running on a treadmill for cardiac fitness and using weights or exercise machines to keep in shape.[57] Nike presented this new sneaker to fitness consumers in 1986. It was presented as a cross-trainer fitness shoe, the Air Trainer, aimed at an emerging mass market.[58] In fact the market had hardly begun to emerge. Until Nike's cross-trainer shoe appeared in stores, 'it is unlikely more than a few people in America would have known what cross-training was, and fewer still would actually have done some of it'.[59] Nike had adapted so rapidly that the company was having to promote the new trend, just as in the 1960s it had promoted the new trend of jogging for fitness. When the new Air Trainer shoe was launched in 1987, it quickly secured 80 per cent of the rapidly growing cross-trainer market.[60] By the mid-1990s cross-trainers had overtaken and partially replaced aerobic shoes: cross-trainers were now the predominant fitness shoes in America. They comprised some 20 per cent of the athletic shoes sold each year, compared to aerobic shoes' 6 per cent and running/jogging's 8 per cent.[61] Nike had achieved as much success with the cross-trainer as with the innovative visible Air of the Air Max sneaker.

The products' success created a remarkable recovery from its mid-1980s development crisis. Nike's sales had doubled by 1989 and would double again by 1993, reaching some $4 billion a year.[62] During this 'wild growth-spurt' in 1987–93 Nike's work force grew 'by close to 40 percent each year, to a force of almost ten thousand'.[63] The growth spurt had therefore completed Nike's development into a full-fledged corporation, and indeed this new corporation was on track to achieving iconic status. Nike had overtaken market leader Reebok in 1991 and would dominate the US athletic-shoe market by 1996, with 42 per cent of the market compared to Reebok's mere 16 per cent.[64]

Redevelopment and Michael Jordan

The firm's remarkable recovery, however, was partly due to redeveloping that had started a year earlier than the revival of development. More importantly, the redeveloping was propelling Nike forward into becoming an iconic corporation in the 1990s, for the redeveloping had diversified Nike into young-male popular fashion, a lucrative and huge new market. Although Nike continued to be a producer of sports-and-fitness shoes, the products now often had an additional function and market, as popular-fashion items. The diversification into this new type of product was the only redeveloping tool needed to give Nike a very bright new future.

The redeveloping diversification originated in 1984, when Nike was suffering badly from its development crisis. As the previous section pointed out, the emerging corporation was laying-off many of its employees and had shifted to a triple-leadership team of Woodell, Strasser, and Knight. Strasser was the firm's marketing director and believed that Nike's brand should be promoted in a new way. As *Swoosh* explains, Strasser wanted to promote Nike through superstar sports heroes.

> The public had gotten smarter and they knew that athletes were paid to wear products. No longer was it necessary or even desirable to have a lot of athletes in Nike shoes. 'Individual athletes, even more than teams, will be the heroes; symbols

more and more of what real people can't do anymore—risk and win', Strasser wrote in a 1983 memo. Strasser was determined to take individual athletes and make them superstars.[65]

His initial attempt at hero-based promotion had focused on four runners at the 1984 Los Angeles Olympics, but later he envisaged a much more ambitious project: 'one big marketing package—tie the brand, the product, the advertising, and the athlete into one [superstar] personality'.[66]

Furthermore, Strasser decided that the hero-athlete superstar would be a basketball player. The new project would prioritize basketball sneakers, instead of the running shoes that had historically been the firm's main product.[67] In addition, the promotion and prioritizing of basketball sneakers was not aimed simply at the basketball *sports* market. 'Since most basketball shoe consumers did not play basketball, the shoes clearly had an appeal beyond their functional [sporting] attributes'.[68] The consumers had in effect given the product other functions, even if the sneakers were used for nothing more than just 'walking around'.[69] However, these other functions—and markets—had not been exploited by the companies that produced basketball sneakers. The companies 'were slow to pick up on' basketball sneakers' broader appeal to consumers.[70] In particular, the companies had not exploited the sneakers' appeal as popular-fashion items. Converse-brand sneakers, for instance, 'were a popular fashion item as far back as the 1950s, worn by cool students at California universities and workers at General Motors'.[71] These were only niche markets, comparable in size to the select markets of high fashion. But clearly basketball sneakers had potential as popular-fashion items—a potential that was not being exploited. Another missed opportunity was the hip-hop niche market that had emerged in the 1970s–80s. Adidas and Puma designs had become popular-fashion items within the hip-hop music scene, as is discussed in the next section. Yet Adidas and Puma had failed to exploit the unintended fashion appeal of their products.

By contrast, Nike was intending in 1984 to give its basketball sneakers some fashion appeal—and create a huge popular-fashion market. Nike was aiming at a potential popular-fashion market among young males who watched televised basketball. In other words, there was to be a major diversification of Nike's product range, as its basketball sneakers were to be popular-fashion as well as sports products. This diversification was intentionally making the sneakers multifunctional products. And their new function as fashion items was to be commercially more important than their basic function as sports shoes.

The diversification was due to marketing-leader Strasser's discerning that it was the appropriate tool for remedially renewing crisis-hit Nike. However, this diversification and redevelopment was relying on an external factor, the hero athlete, to supply the required marketing power. The hero athlete was to be the external supplement to diversification, as described in Chapter 10. It observed that capable rational leaders 'ably make apt' acquisitions of companies that will help a diversification or prioritization. However, Nike's external supplement was not an acquired company but rather a hero athlete, who would have to be treated as a partner in this diversification venture.

In other words, there was to be a joint-venture arrangement between the hero and Nike. Strasser's 'ably make apt' capability would therefore be aptly choosing the right person to be Nike's hero-athlete superstar—and ably making the right deal with that person.

His apt choice of basketball hero was the young Michael Jordan. Nike's college-basketball representative had spotted the extraordinary potential of Jordan, who was about to begin his professional career.[72] Strasser aptly accepted this recommendation and then very ably made a deal with Jordan. The young basketball genius was reluctant to link up with Nike and was initially looking for a deal with Adidas.[73] However, Strasser offered him an extraordinarily attractive deal, especially when compared with other basketball players' deals—whether with Nike or other sneaker companies. Many of the sneaker endorsement contracts paid less than $10,000 a year and only one player 'was thought to be making even $100,000 a year from his shoe deal'; by contrast, the relatively unknown Jordan was being offered a five-year $2.5 million package.[74]

Furthermore, the deal had joint-venture features never before offered to a basketball player. Jordan was to have a personal brand of 'Air Jordan' sneakers and other basketball products. The sneaker was to be designed especially for him and have a distinctive logo and colour scheme.[75] He would also be given a sizeable financial stake in the new venture.

> Jordan was to receive money for each pair of Air Jordan basketball shoes sold, and another royalty on all Nike Air basketball shoes sold—not just Air Jordan—exceeding the 400,000 pairs sold by Nike the prior year. He was also to get a percentage of the net sales of all Jordan apparel and accessories, and some shares of Nike B stock.[76]

Jordan's contribution to the venture would include being 'the new face of Nike's advertising, fitting in with Strasser's vision of marketing individual athletes as heroes'.[77]

The venture was arranged and agreed in August–September 1984. Strasser was then part of a triple-leadership team, along with Nike's president Woodell and chairman Knight. Although founder-leader Knight seemed semi-retired, he was still a key figure. 'Knight allowed extroverts like Rob Strasser to conduct much of the day-to-day operations of Nike. The big decisions and strategies, however, still required his blessing'.[78] He 'dropped in' at the deal-offering meeting with Jordan, and Knight at least tacitly approved the momentous arrangement with the new hero-to-be.[79]

Jordan became a fully-fledged hero in his first season of professional basketball. He was the only first-year player ever to have led his team in points, assists, rebounds, and steals, and he helped the team reach the play-offs for the first time in four years: 'a fresh face seemingly turning a failing team around by himself'.[80] Thanks to his heroic deeds and Nike's advertising, his Air Jordan sneakers and apparel were an immediate success. 'Little kids and big ones lined up in stores to get the shoes worn by America's latest hero'.[81]

He went on to be a superstar hero, who dominated games in a way no player had ever done before. By the time Jordan's long career ended in 1998, he was acknowledged to be the best-ever player of basketball. Plus, he had a charismatic personality, which was highlighted by the media cult of 'Michael'. Jordan has been called 'the first black athlete ... to become an icon of popular culture'.[82]

Jordan's status as an icon of popular culture helped his Air Jordan sneakers become items of popular fashion. His 'on-court shoe choice became an off-court fashion choice for millions, from die-hard fans to casual onlookers'.[83] Kawamura's *Sneakers: Fashion, Gender, and Subculture* sees the launch of Air Jordan in 1985 as a watershed for the sneaker industry. A new era 'started with the launch of Nike Air Jordan sneakers', as 'the fashion and the adornment aspects of sneakers became increasingly important'.[84] Kawamura highlights, too, the sneakers' function as young *male* fashion items. They were 'definitely a male fashion phenomenon', and this gender factor was evident in young males' regard for Jordan and his sneakers:

> Jordan became a role model to many boys and young men who needed someone to look up to. Jordan was strong, powerful, rich, and charismatic. He personified all the qualities that anyone would aspire to attain. He personified *masculinity* and success. They also vicariously enjoyed their status by wearing the sneakers endorsed by Jordan.[85]

The Air Jordan venture had therefore succeeded in creating a major popular-fashion market for its basketball sneakers. It had found a huge and affluent market among the young males of America.[86]

The venture's success was due partly to Jordan but also partly to Nike's support for Air Jordan. This diversification into popular-fashion items was an internal process within Nike as well as an external joint venture with Jordan. The diversification was aided by changes in Nike's marketing and in its product design, which was now aiming for a fashionable as well as sports-functional product. Their first Air Jordan sneaker had a distinctive and innovative red-and-black colour scheme. Their second-generation design, launched in late 1986, was an expensive Italian-made sneaker that has been described as 'high flyer meets high fashion'.[87] The fashionable Air Jordan II (AJ II) sneaker had disappointing sales, however. The fashion aspect of the shoe was apparently too similar to high fashion rather than more popular styles. *Swoosh* describes the fashionable AJ II as 'a shoe ahead of its time. When Nike introduced a similar product in 1990, it sold'.[88] But the design could not afford to be ahead of its market. The 'high-fashion misfire' was replaced in 1988 by the Air Jordan III model, which was more modestly priced and based on Jordan's thinking about the best structural design for a new basketball shoe.[89] From then on the annual design changes seem to have been well attuned to popular fashion in taste and trends. By 1991 the latest design, the Air Jordan VI Infrared, had a black colour scheme that made it perhaps the most distinctive sneaker yet produced by Nike.[90]

Nike's design support for the Air Jordan products was matched by its marketing support for Jordan and Air Jordan. The marketing effort seems particularly impressive because it involved a complete turnabout in Nike's traditional attitude towards advertising. Knight's *Shoe Dog* acknowledges that his 1960s–70s view of advertising had been sceptical and rather negative. He had believed a product 'speaks for itself, or it doesn't. In the end, it's only quality that counts. I couldn't imagine that any ad campaign would ever prove me wrong or change my mind'.[91] Nike's traditional attitude to advertising began to change in the late 1970s. The firm's marketing team was starting to take advertising more seriously.[92] In 1984, Strasser pushed Nike into television advertising, with the Olympics' running-star commercials mentioned earlier in the section. He went a big step further, however, with the large advertising campaign that promoted the Air Jordan brand and helped Jordan 'emerge as a national icon'.[93] The campaign included in 1985 the remarkable 'Jordan Flight' television commercial. It showed a slow-motion shot of Jordan suspended in the air, while he slam-dunks, and the ad asks: 'Who said a man was not meant to fly?'[94] This brilliant commercial epitomized Nike's shift towards more innovative forms of advertising. And the firm's spending on advertising increased from $20 million in 1985 to $150 million in 1992.[95]

The new attitude towards advertising benefited not just Air Jordan but also other Nike products. For instance, the Air Max and Air Trainer sneakers benefited from Nike's shift to more innovative forms of television advertising. The Air Max running sneakers were supported by a 1987 commercial that used the Beatles song 'Revolution' as background music: 'the first time the original recording of a rock classic was used in a major advertisement'.[96] The Air Max commercial's visual aspect was innovative too. The version 'that attracted attention was a very jerky black-and-white, hand-held camera film', which showed sports heroes and ordinary people 'clowning around while participating in a variety of sports'.[97] Two years later, the Air Trainer cross-training sneakers were supported by an innovative commercial that was more ironic than artistic. It 'celebrated' the sports hero 'Bo' Jackson, who played both football and baseball at the highest level. 'Inside a sixty-second commercial, the cross-training implications projected by Bo really "knowing" football and baseball could be overtly ironized through testimonials to his limitless powers from other Nike stars', such as Jordan intoning that 'Bo knows basketball'.[98]

The new products were benefiting, too, from Nike's reputation as a venturesome brand and firm. Its Air Jordan diversification in the mid-1980s had shown that Nike was still able to come up with successful new ideas. When Air Max and Air Trainer appeared in 1986/7, they were coming 'from the firm that brought you' Air Jordan. There was nothing surprising or dubious about Nike innovatively introducing a visible-air sneaker and a cross-training sneaker. The Air Jordan diversification had therefore prepared the way for them as well as boosting Nike's ability to advertise these new products.

Here the Air Jordan diversification was having a hybridizing effect on Nike's revived development. This revival of development was discussed in the previous section, which showed how the return to adaptive rational methods in 1985/6 led on to the Air Max and Air Trainer. The introduction of these new adaptive products was now being aided by the redevelopment that had begun in 1984 and led on to Air

Jordan. Furthermore, there were also hybridizing effects in the opposite direction, as the revived development of Nike helped the redevelopment to solve the firm's problems. The most obvious example is how the new adaptive products, Air Max and Air Trainer, helped propel Nike out if its development crisis.

Strasser had always believed that Air Jordan alone could not rescue Nike from its development crisis.[99] His cautious assessment was confirmed when the Air Jordan venture lost momentum in 1986, partly because a foot injury had severely limited Jordan's appearances on the basketball court.[100] Nike was left mired in uncertainty and seemingly permanent crisis. The situation was so bad that a new round of layoffs was announced in December 1986.[101] Some confidence was restored, though, by the success of Air Max and Air Trainer, and these new products made a big contribution to Nike's strong recovery in 1988/9. Their sales' contribution was actually much greater than Air Jordan's, even after it regained momentum.[102]

The Air Jordan diversification had, however, played the crucial role in the recovery. As noted earlier, the new adaptive products benefited from the Air Jordans preparing the way for them and increasing their impact. More importantly, Nike might not have survived in the mid-1980s without the Air Jordan diversification. This redeveloping had not solved all Nike's problems but at least it had given the firm some hope, credibility, and prospect of recovery.

The redevelopment's longer term influence was similarly important. The Air Jordan diversification had converted Nike into a popular-fashion as well as sports-and-fitness company. In the 1990s, some experts even viewed Nike as essentially a fashion company. 'Many Wall-Streeters who "covered" the company regarded Nike's distinctive corporate ways and products as part of the fashion industry, and thus as the most successful company growing out of an athletic-goods [sports-and-fitness] explosion that could be a passing fad'.[103] Indeed the shift towards popular fashion had given the firm a very bright new future. Nike became not just a full-sized corporation but also an outstanding one and soon in fact iconic. As Knight observes, 'Air Jordan changed Nike, took us to the next level, and the next'.[104]

The redevelopment initiated by Strasser in 1984 had therefore been very successful. But he did not reap the rewards of his rational leadership, as he left Nike in late 1987.[105] The firm had gone on to achieve great success by the time Strasser died in 1993, aged only 46. By then he was working for Adidas and was a foe rather than friend of Knight. In *Shoe Dog*, Knight notes that 'I wish Strasser and I had patched things up before he died, but I don't know that it was possible. We were both born to compete, and we were both bad at forgiving'.[106]

Reoriented Popular-Fashion Nike

In the 1990s, Nike's diversification into popular fashion moved to a new level. Here a Nike product might have young male fashion appeal because it was a 'cool' item, whether or not it was associated with a sports hero. Even Air Jordan highlighted the fashion 'coolness' of its sneakers as well as the heroic stature of Jordan. In this post-Strasser era, the hero might be viewed as a cool celebrity rather than a doer of great deeds. The diversification had therefore in effect moved into a second phase which had begun as early as a 1988–90 series of Air Jordan television commercials.

These watershed commercials starred Jordan and actor-director, Spike Lee. The latter reprised the role of Mars Blackmon that he had played in his innovative movie *She's Gotta Have It*.[107] From the outset, the Mars and Michael series displayed a cool, not-an-ad attitude.

'This is something you can buy', said 'Mars' in the first execution. His face was filmed in extreme close-up, as he cradled a pair of shoes to his cheeks and overtly invited the viewer into the commercial. The spot jump-cut to Jordan executing his 'patented, vicious, high-flying 360' slam dunk. 'This is something you cannot do' informed Mars, impishly denying the ad's implicit, transubstantiating promise. Subsequent commercials in the series employed other elements of the not-ad ad, including … yelling out the window at noisy neighbors, 'Shut up! I'm doing a Nike commercial here'.[108]

The most memorable of the commercials had a great punchline. 'It's gotta be the shoes', says Mars when asking himself why Jordan was the best player in the universe and was so liked by starlet Nola Darling.[109] These commercials seem almost self-parodying or self-ridiculing when compared to the superhero Jordan Flight commercial of 1985. But Nike's new advertising was associating its products with 'a cool lifestyle attitude'—and a 'special Nike strain' of coolness—rather than associating them with the deeds of a sporting hero.[110]

Associating basketball sneakers with 'coolness' was nothing new. In the 1970s–80s two distinctive models of basketball sneaker had been deemed 'cool' by music and dance performers. The Clyde sneaker model, made by Puma, had been adopted by break-dancers and many hip-hop musicians.[111] Similarly, the Superstar sneaker model, made by Adidas, became 'an icon of the hip-hop scene' and a 'carrier of cool'.[112] However, Puma and Adidas failed to exploit the fashion potential of these cool sneakers. For example, Adidas's endorsement deal with a hip-hop group came too late, in 1986, when 'Nike was growing like crazy' and already winning the young male popular-fashion market.[113] Nike eventually took over the hip-hop market, too, but not through Air Jordan basketball sneakers. Rather, the Air Max running sneaker was the 'cool' model 'adopted by the hip-hop youth of the 1990s and 2000s'.[114] Coolness was therefore not necessarily associated with a sports hero, a particular brand, or even the basketball form of sneaker.

Popular fashion's young male 'coolness' can in fact be a very fickle kind of fashion. For 'today's cool can be tomorrow's totally uncool'.[115] Nike and other sneaker companies therefore had to stay in tune with the latest trends in coolness. Sneaker designs tried to 'incorporate the colors, styles, and influences bubbling amid youth culture', and new designs were often tried out on target groups, particularly 'ghetto kids'.[116] Sneaker companies also had to comply with two of the standard concerns of young male coolness: being technologically up to date and being authentic rather than phony. The need for even sneakers to be technologically up to date was typical of the changing high-tech times of the 1990s–2000s. Vanderbilt's *The Sneaker Book* observed that sneakers had often become more like 'personal technology products than shoes'.[117] Cutting-edge sneaker technology was therefore as 'cool' as cutting-edge phone or personal-computer technology. And ever since Nike had adopted the Air sole, the firm had enjoyed an unbeatable lead in sneaker 'tech'. This technology also sustained Nike's reputation as an authentic sports-and-fitness company, whose products were authentically sport or fitness shoes and not just fashion items.[118]

The sneaker-tech factor, however, intensified the sneaker-design treadmill. If designs 'do not go out of style first, the technology will be eclipsed by the next-generation pad or pod, cell or gel'.[119] Nike kept rolling out new lines of sneakers, which were soon replaced by new models or the revival of classic models. In the 1990s, multiple new lines appeared each year, 'each batch loaded with new colors, styles and technology features'.[120] There is a striking similarity here with the high-fashion treadmill described in Chapter 9. Another similarity is that the high-fashion price and product pyramid had a sneaker counterpart. Nike's technological or other design innovations would first appear in the high-price shoes and then spread to the mid-price levels.[121] These levels were the equivalent of high-fashion companies' clothing diffusion lines, where the avant-garde designs are toned down and sold at more economical prices. In Nike's case, only 10 per cent of its sneakers retailed at the high-price level; the huge majority of its sneakers were sold in the 'middle price points', the 'lucrative center of the market' in the 1990s.[122]

The Nike pyramid and treadmill reflect an increasing fashion orientation. In the second phase of the diversification, Nike was clearly moving further towards being a popular-fashion as well as sports-and-fitness firm. And these internal changes were accompanied by a further contribution from the external, joint-venture aspect of the diversification.

The Jordan joint venture was boosting the global expansion of Nike. An increasingly large proportion of Nike's revenue was coming from international sources, so that by 1996 some $2.5 billion, over a third of its annual revenue, was coming from outside the US.[123] Jordan's contribution to this expansion was highlighted in 1999 by LaFeber's *Michael Jordan and the New Global Capitalism*. His book pointed out that Jordan's heroic presence was brought to global markets not only by advertising but also by the spread of televised American basketball. The number of countries viewing these basketball games increased from thirty-five to more than 175 in the period 1986–96.[124] Jordan had therefore 'helped make Nike a great transnational', thanks to the 'ability of basketball, U.S. advertising techniques, and American-dominated media to penetrate other cultures'.[125]

Significantly, even this critic of Nike viewed it as a 'great transnational' corporation. By the end of the 1990s, Nike was also 'one of the world's most recognized brands', according to Vanderbilt.[126] The firm was therefore perhaps already a globally iconic corporation. Nike was certainly iconic in America. As Vanderbilt observed, 'in the 1990s it has been Nike that changed the very meaning of what an athletic shoe represents, in terms of reach, sales, profit margins, and cultural impact. One marketing company even found Nike to have the highest logo recognition among children it had ever recorded'.[127]

Nike's globally iconic status was consolidated in the 2000s as the corporation's influence spread around the world. By the end of the decade, the firm was being ranked alongside Toyota and Apple as 'corporations that changed the world'.[128] When Knight retired from his post of CEO in 2004, he could look back at a 'crazy idea' that had been 'insanely' successful. From his perspective, an important indicator of Nike's success was its victory over Adidas. This was perhaps the ultimate triumph for someone who had been provoked in his student and start-up years to challenge the mighty Adidas. 'That one German company had dominated the shoe market for a couple of decades, and they possessed all the arrogance of unchallenged dominance. Of course it's possible that they weren't arrogant at all, that to motivate myself I needed to see them as a monster'.[129] Adidas had proven to be a redoubtable rival. It had fallen far behind Nike by the early 1990s but then made a remarkable comeback and in 2005 took over Reebok.[130] Yet the Reebok-enlarged Adidas remained a clear second to Nike. The new entity had some 25 per cent of the global athletic-shoe market, compared to Nike's nearly 38 per cent.[131] So, in Knight's post-2004 semi-retirement as chairman of Nike, he had good reason to feel triumphant. His firm has continued to stay in the lead, some sixty years after he had the Crazy Idea.

12
Chrysler

Lee's *Iacocca* and Lutz's *Guts*

Chrysler corporation is 'no longer with us', having been merged into Fiat-Chrysler in 2014 and then into Stellantis in 2021. But Chrysler was second only to General Motors (GM) among American automakers from the early 1930s to the early 1950s, and thereafter it held the number-three position. More importantly, it gave the automobile industry two new product categories. In the 1980s–90s Chrysler not only invented the minivan but also popularized the SUV (sport utility vehicle).

Furthermore, Chrysler holds a special place in American corporate history for having carried out the twentieth-century's 'comeback of the century'.[1] The comeback occurred in the early 1980s and brilliantly combined a turnaround and a redevelopment. A remarkable cost-cutting turnaround was accompanied by the first stage of a classic case of rational redevelopment. In this first stage of redevelopment, both diversification and prioritization were used as appropriate rational means. The second stage of the redevelopment occurred several years later and here hybridization was the appropriate rational means. Hybridization is one of the more rarely used tools in the redeveloper's tool kit but proved to be a very successful means of redevelopment.[2] The hybridization and the first stage of redevelopment produced a remedial renewal that gave Chrysler a bright new future—until it was side-tracked by later generations of leadership.

The CEO who led Chrysler's redevelopment, Lee Iacocca, became the most famous business leader of his time. One of the reasons for this fame was his 1984 *Iacocca: An Autobiography*. The book was a bestseller, with millions of copies sold to an admiring public.[3] A large part of the book covers his long career at the Ford Motor Company, before the 54-year-old Iacocca was recruited by Chrysler.[4] But later chapters of his book provide a leader's-eye view of his 1979–92 tenure as CEO of Chrysler. There have been several other books about or covering the Iacocca era. For instance, in his time there was Moritz and Seaman's *Going for Broke: Lee Iacocca's Battle to Save Chrysler* and Levin's *Behind the Wheel at Chrysler: The Iacocca Legacy*. In recent times there has been Hyde's magisterial history of the Chrysler Corporation, *Riding the Rollercoaster*. Like Iacocca's book, these sources tell an epic story of survival and revival that has much to teach later generations of business leadership.

This chapter will therefore begin by looking at how Iacocca's remarkable turnaround saved Chrysler from disaster in the early 1980s. The second section of the chapter examines the redevelopment—a first stage—that accompanied his great turnaround. His first-stage redevelopment used both a prioritization and a

Rational Leadership. Paul Brooker and Margaret Hayward, Oxford University Press. © Paul Brooker & Margaret Hayward (2023). DOI: 10.1093/oso/9780198894643.003.0012

diversifying reorientation of the product range. These changes were made internally rather than through acquisitions or divestments.[5] Iacocca internally diversified into a new semi-car category, the minivan, and internally prioritized front-wheel drive cars. However, the third section argues that the redevelopment was left unfinished: the firm's product-development activities had not been properly reoriented towards front-wheel drive cars. The product range of cars therefore became increasingly outdated in styling and engineering.

The fourth section, though, will show Iacocca finishing the job of redevelopment in the late 1980s. He carried out a second stage of redevelopment, using hybridization as the appropriate rational means. Chrysler was hybridized with American Motors Corporation (AMC). It had long been the small and struggling number four in the American car industry. But AMC's famous Jeep brand had pioneered the SUV. So the Chrysler takeover merger with AMC reinforced Iacocca's earlier diversification into minivans: they were now joined by another semi-car, the Jeep SUV. In addition, hybridizing with AMC led to Chrysler's product-development activities being restructured into what were called 'platform' teams. This structural hybridization markedly improved Chrysler's ability to develop a new generation of more advanced front-wheel drive cars. Hence the late 1980s' structural hybridization completed the early 1980s' redevelopment and was the key feature of Iacocca's second stage of redevelopment.

The hybridization was led, however, by Robert Lutz as well as Iacocca. They formed a dual-leadership team, and a leader's-eye view of these years is provided by Lutz's partly autobiographical *Guts: The Seven Laws of Business that Made Chrysler the World's Hottest Car Company*. Lutz also provides a pithy assessment of Iacocca's leadership.

> Mercurial, inconsistent, controversial, a little insecure, given to posturing and bluster, Iacocca nevertheless was the incarnation of the successful leader ... The job got done! He has been called 'the greatest American industrial CEO of all time'. I'm not one to argue![6]

Iacocca may not have been the greatest, but he was certainly the most change-making CEO. His tenure as CEO was full of change, as he found new missions and responded to new crises.

Lee Iacocca Saves Chrysler from Disaster

Chrysler Corporation was heading towards a crisis when Iacocca was recruited in 1978 as an outsider who could stem its decline. Chrysler was the mediocre number three in the American automobile industry and was falling yet further behind General Motors and Ford.[7] Iacocca was initially given the secondary post of president, with the understanding that he would soon take full charge, and he duly took over as chairman and CEO in September 1979.[8] By then Chrysler was in a crisis that threatened its survival, for a severe economic recession had intensified the firm's problems. Chrysler 'had to sell 2.3 million cars and trucks just to break even. Unfortunately, we were only selling around 1 million'.[9] After becoming CEO, Iacocca almost immediately asked Congress for government-guaranteed loans that would save Chrysler from bankruptcy and give it some chance of longer term survival. He therefore had to testify to congressional committees about the need for the loans and also how the loan money would be used by Chrysler. His strong performance in these televised hearings helped secure the loan guarantees, for more than $1 billion, and made Iacocca a nationally known figure.[10]

Although he had secured some funding, he still had to carry out a massive cost-cutting turnaround. Employment fell by more than 50 per cent, with job losses of nearly 76,000.[11] These job losses were among the highest ever experienced by an American corporation. Iacocca's book acknowledges the 'great many casualties' among employees and other people associated with the corporation.[12] 'A lot of people—blue-collar, white-collar, and dealers—who had been with us in 1979 were no longer around to enjoy the fruits of victory' a few years later.[13] Other casualties were collateral victims of the cost-cutting. In particular, the 'closing of dozens of plants' in Detroit and other cities hit many businesses and jobs that were indirectly dependent upon Chrysler.[14]

However, Iacocca was able to win an impressive amount of support for his cost-cutting. He co-opted the leader of the United Auto Workers labour union, Doug Fraser, who joined Chrysler's board of directors. According to Iacocca, Fraser 'found out first-hand what was going on at Chrysler from the perspective of management' and indeed 'learned and understood so much that some of the workers began to see him as a turncoat, because he told them the truth when we were too weak to take a strike'.[15] Iacocca also won support from a wide assortment of other stakeholders. Hyde's history of Chrysler refers to 'the willingness of all of the members of the Chrysler "family" to make painful sacrifices' during this crisis.[16] The corporation's extensive 'family' included: organized labour, who made crucial wage and work concessions; the suppliers of parts and services; 'the stockholders, who saw their dividends disappear while the value of their stock plummeted; Chrysler's lenders, primarily its banks; and the many provincial, state, and local governments who granted loans or forgave taxes'.[17]

Thanks to these sacrifices and the congressional loan guarantees, Iacocca's cost-cutting could go far beyond just downsizing Chrysler. Inventory systems and financial controls were improved and there was a large reduction in the number of different parts that Chrysler's plants were assembling into automobiles.[18] Iacocca also increased the amount of parts-making that was outsourced to parts suppliers, who were more economic than Chrysler. Its Japanese-like use of outsourcing became a distinctive feature of the firm. Chrysler eventually 'made only 30 per cent of its parts in-house, versus 55 percent for Ford and 70 per cent for General Motors'.[19] Furthermore, Iacocca spent money to save money, such as investing in a Japanese-like emphasis on quality control. These 'areas where Iacocca's management poured in new funds—quality control being the most important one—repaid the effort with interest', as when the improved quality control led to a sharp drop in warranty payments.[20] Similarly, Chrysler's large capital investment in modernizing and robotizing its plants led to more quality-control benefits as well as lower labour costs.[21]

What were the overall results of this massive, wide-ranging, and at times imaginative cost-cutting? Hyde sums up the results as a 'stunning turnaround' and the creation of a 'much smaller, leaner, and more efficient' Chrysler.[22] The new Chrysler was in much better shape to compete with the two leading automakers, General Motors and Ford. Although Chrysler had lost some size, the new leanness and efficiency had increased its competitiveness.[23] The turnaround's most important benefit, though, was removing the threat of bankruptcy: the firm had survived. The $1.7 billion loss in 1980 had turned into a profit of $170 million in 1982.[24] Not surprisingly, this led to a spectacular rise in the firm's share price. Chrysler's share price soared in 1982 from about $4 to nearly $18: the firm was 'the darling of Wall Street'.[25] Most notably, these turnaround results were achieved despite the recession of the early 1980s. US car sales in 1982 were at the lowest level they had been for more than twenty years.[26]

The rapid recovery from this recession created a boom year in 1983. All the automakers benefited but especially the lean and efficient Chrysler: 'we made an honest operating profit of $925 million—the best by far in Chrysler's history'.[27] Another key statistic was that its share of the market had increased from 10 per cent in 1982 to nearly 13 per cent in 1983.[28] The firm's profitability and competitiveness was reflected by two other signs of revival. Its new share offering was highly successful and later in the year it paid back all the government-guaranteed loans, making the repayment seven years earlier than required.[29] This was perhaps the ultimate sign of success for Iacocca as well as Chrysler. According to Hyde, Iacocca had emerged 'as the most easily recognized and admired corporate executive in the United States, a mythological figure in many respects'.[30]

The First Stage of 1980s Redevelopment

From a rational-leadership perspective Iacocca seems so admirable because his cost-cutting turnaround was accompanied by a rational redevelopment. Such redevelopment was an essential accompaniment or follow-on to the turnaround, which was just a short-term solution to Chrysler's competitiveness problem. Only a redevelopment could solve the problem of how to compete with GM and Ford in the longer term—in the second half of the 1980s. Without that longer term competitiveness, Chrysler's new future would be short-lived and a disappointment.

Iacocca had committed Chrysler to a redevelopment in his 1979 congressional loan-guarantee testimony. Among the promises that Iacocca had made to Congress there was a commitment to be a leader in fuel economy, at a time of global oil shortages and price hikes, and therefore 'to convert our entire fleet of cars to front-wheel drive technology'.[31]

Using front-wheel drive design was the fastest and most cost-effective way to meet federal gas mileage standards. Front-wheel drive let the designer eliminate the drive shaft and the center hump on the floor and make the car 'bigger on the inside and smaller on the outside'. Downsizing and eliminating the drive shaft also brought weight savings. Lower weights and more efficient drive trains meant in turn that smaller engines could power the vehicle.[32]

But Chrysler, like other US automakers, had predominantly produced *rear*-wheel drive vehicles. Less than 20 per cent of Chrysler's production capacity was for front-wheel drive automobiles, such as the then recently launched Omni and Horizon cars.[33] Iacocca had therefore committed Chrysler to a sweeping reorientation of its product range: a huge prioritizing shift towards front-wheel drive cars. He clearly would be leading a redevelopment as well as a cost-cutting turnaround.

His prioritizing reorientation did not convert the whole product range to front-wheel drive. Three rear-wheel drive car models, minor product lines, survived for another decade.[34] But Chrysler had quickly reoriented the product range towards front-wheel drive and a complementary size of engine: the four-cylinder rather than six-cylinder engine.[35] The four-cylinder engine was more economical and suited the relatively small cars that were leading Chrysler's shift to front-wheel drive. By 1981 cars with this combination of drive and engine made up a large majority of Chrysler's production.[36] An extensive and rapid reorientation had been capably accomplished, even though the firm was in the midst of a cost-cutting turnaround.

The reorientation was centred on the new 'K-car' design. This compact-size car had front-wheel drive, a four-cylinder engine, and more room than the firm's subcompact-size Omni/Horizon cars.[37] The K-car had been designed before Iacocca arrived at Chrysler in 1978, but he soon became a strong supporter of its development.[38] The K-car design played a crucial role in 1979–80, during the congressional hearings on loan guarantees and then in negotiations with the banks. As Iacocca observes, the K-car was 'just about all we had to offer' and was 'what got us through' those dark days.[39] The letter K was merely the code letter, for internal use, which Chrysler's stylists had assigned to the design in its early stages of development. But the public had taken notice of the K-car design, thanks to the publicity associated with Chrysler's loan guarantees, and so the firm's marketers exploited this design-name recognition.[40] Chrysler had announced that the 'the K-cars are coming' and, even after they had arrived on the market, continued to call them K-cars instead of using their official names: Dodge Aries and Plymouth Reliant.

When they hit the market in late 1980, Chrysler had high hopes and expectations. Iacocca trumpeted that this 'is K-Day for Chrysler, it's D-day for Detroit and it's a new day for America.'[41] He admits, however, that he and the marketers bungled the K-car launch. They had loaded up many of the cars with expensive options—to increase the cars' profit margins—and thereby had lost many potential customers who had wanted a car that was economical to buy as well as economical to run.[42] Although the mistake was soon corrected, the K-cars did not make an Iacocca-style comeback. 'Sales eventually revived, but amounted to only 307000 units for the 1981 model year, only half of the volume predicted'.[43] This disappointing level of sales became the pattern for the years ahead. K-car sales averaged only about 260,000 a year in 1982–5.[44]

The K-car had also suffered from factors outside Chrysler's control. The economic recession had continued into 1981/2 and, more importantly, there was a glut in global oil that 'made a mockery of all the dire predictions of 1979–80. Gasoline became not only plentiful but cheap'.[45] The fuel-economic K-car had therefore lost some of its distinctive appeal. The wider problem was that Chrysler had reoriented its whole product range towards fuel-economical front-wheel drive only to find that there was no longer any need for consumers to be concerned about fuel economy. Hence Iacocca's prioritizing reorientation no longer appeared to be the appropriate rational means of redeveloping Chrysler. It had been appropriate and discerning in the circumstances of 1979, when he had been dealing with Congress as well as an oil crisis. But times had changed and had left Chrysler with a product range that lacked much appeal in an era of now glutted oil markets. How could Chrysler compete with GM and Ford without a product range that appealed to customers?

However, Iacocca's redevelopment was also using a second appropriate rational means—diversification—that proved to be more successful. His reorientation of the product range had included a diversification as well as prioritization: the product range had been diversified into something new and indeed pioneering. Hyde describes it as 'a breakthrough product that redefined the automotive market'.[46] The new product was an automobile with Chrysler's usual front-wheel drive and four-cylinder engine but also a pioneering, breakthrough feature: three rows of seating, with room for seven passengers. Called a 'minivan', this semi-car was a mixture of 'the station wagon and a small van'.[47] It had the wagon's low step-up passenger entry, plus a van's spaciousness and sliding side entry door, yet was no lengthier than a K-car.[48] The new product or product category was aimed at a sizeable niche market. Iacocca categorizes the minivan as something that suited people who wanted something more spacious than a station wagon yet small enough to fit into a normal size garage.[49]

Pioneering this semi-car automobile had been risky. Looking back, Levin noted that 'as a new *category* of vehicle, the odds against the minivan were far greater than for a typical new model'.[50] Chrysler had not even been sure how to categorize this new semi-car: initially, it was sometimes labelled a T-wagon, T-van, or mini-wagon.[51] But pioneering such niche products can have huge advantages, as Iacocca argues: 'if you're not number one, then you've *got* to innovate' and 'find market niches that they haven't even thought of. You can't go head to head with them—they're just too big. You've got to outflank them'.[52] In Chrysler's case, this would help it solve the problem of how to compete with GM and Ford in the longer term—in the second half of the 1980s. Iacocca's diversification into the minivan had therefore been very discerning.

However, the diversification had been a heavy cost burden for Chrysler to bear during its cost-cutting turnaround. There had been a big investment in tooling-up for production of the minivan. The assembly plant was expensively modernized and automated, with over a hundred robots being added to the assembly line.[53] Funding problems had in fact delayed the launch of the minivan. Planned for introduction in 1982, the minivans only started rolling off the assembly line in late 1983.[54] Yet this was still a notably capable effort in the circumstances. Iacocca modestly presents the accomplishment, and his risky diversification, as simply a matter of necessity.

> Whenever I speak to students in our nation's business schools, someone always asks me how we managed to bring out the minivan so quickly after our prolonged crisis. 'How could you as a businessman put seven hundred million dollars on the line three years in advance while you were going broke?' It's a good question. But really, I had no choice. I knew we couldn't eat the seed corn. There would be no point to our struggle if there was nothing to sell when we were back on our feet again.[55]

In other words, only an appealing product could give Chrysler the bright new future that comes with successful redevelopment. And the minivan diversification proved to be a very discerning choice of the appropriate means of redeveloping Chrysler.

The first minivans, the Plymouth Voyager and Dodge Caravan, 'enabled the corporation to prosper'.[56] Even though the minivan was a niche product, its sales compared favourably with K-car sales. During the minivan's first three years, 1984–6, Chrysler was selling an average of more than 212,000 a year, compared to the K-car's 260,000 a year, and minivan production was having difficulty keeping up with the demand.[57] More importantly, the minivans were much more profitable than the K-cars. Minivans were 'very profitable', according to Iacocca, and this is something of an understatement.[58] They must have been one of the most profitable automobiles ever mass produced. For Levin estimated that they 'were yielding as much as $5,000 in gross profit per unit, an astonishing margin'.[59] He also observed that Chrysler's American and Japanese competitors were slow to respond—effectively— to the minivan. 'Chrysler had the burgeoning minivan market mostly to itself' for 'five delicious years'.[60] Its diversification into the semi-car minivan had therefore been hugely successful. But Chrysler was facing a very different situation in its K-car markets, largely because the prioritizing aspect of its reorientation had been left unfinished by Iacocca.

The Unfinished Reorientation of Chrysler

The redevelopment of Chrysler had apparently been completed in 1983, with the minivan in production and soon to be launched. However, Iacocca had not finished his prioritizing reorientation: it had not been properly extended to product development. The product-development activities—design and engineering—had not been reoriented towards creating new generations of front-wheel drive cars. This part of the reorientation eventually occurred in 1988/9, but the delay had harmed Chrysler. The firm had needed a new generation of cars to replace the increasingly outdated K-car design.

Why had Iacocca failed to finish off his redevelopment? One likely reason for this lack of discernment is that he had a big-issue personality. 'Lee Iacocca was at his finest when energized, when there was a crisis, when he had a sense of mission'.[61] And Chrysler's crisis, his key mission, had ended with the successful turnaround and the minivan diversification underway. By comparison, finishing off the prioritization was a burdensome anti-climax, not a crisis or something that could give him a sense of mission.

Iacocca was also distracted by new missions that had appeared by 1983. For instance, he was a public critic of the Japanese government's trade practices, and his 1984 autobiography included a chapter on 'The Japanese Challenge'. There are chapters, too, about 'How to Save Lives on the Road', 'The High Cost of Labor', and even 'Making America Great Again'. Plus, there is a chapter on Iacocca's emergence as a public figure and on the calls for him to run for the public office of president. This chapter is entitled 'Public Man, Public Office' where he rejects any idea of him seeking public office. Among his reasons was simply tiredness. 'I'm exhausted. I've grown old during my years at Chrysler'.[62] He confirmed this view in an interview several years later. 'I might have been so tired that I laid back on the oars a bit'.[63] Doubtless this tiredness made him even less interested in finishing off his redevelopment.

Yet by 1985 he was not too tired to take on a huge new business mission— diversifying Chrysler into non-automotive businesses. This further distracted him from finishing his redevelopment and also led to a marked decline in his rational leadership.[64] Years later he acknowledged that his biggest misjudgement:

> was trying to diversify [outside the automotive field]. He saw GM and Ford moving into defense, aerospace, and financial services, and figured that was the wave of the future. 'If I made a mistake, it was following those other companies, and maybe those were grandiose schemes'.[65]

As he pointed out, those 'grandiose schemes' were not merely a personal whim. All the American automakers, not only Chrysler, had begun to diversify into non-automotive businesses.[66] And Iacocca was indeed just following GM's and Ford's example. In 1984/5 they bought companies in the aerospace, technology, car-rental, and finance businesses.[67] Iacocca adopted a similar approach. In 1985 he bought Gulfstream Aerospace and financial-services companies; in later years he bought more finance companies, the high-tech Electrospace Systems and a flock of car-rental firms.[68] But Chrysler was not big enough or successful enough to afford grandiose diversions into non-automotive businesses. These diversifying acquisitions indeed weakened rather than strengthened the corporation.[69]

Chrysler was therefore experiencing a marked decline in rational leadership. Iacocca's new business mission in fact seems wholly lacking in discernment.[70] Furthermore, the new mission had distracted him from rationally finishing the redevelopment by properly reorienting product development. As noted earlier, this delay in finishing the redevelopment was harming the corporation, because Chrysler lacked new-generation cars to replace the aging K-car design.[71]

The replacement problem was aggravated by Chrysler's overdependence on the K-car design. The 'K-car platform, including the drive train and other components, served as the basis for most new Chrysler products'.[72] In effect, product development was focused on propagating the K-car design. Iacocca's book acknowledges that the K-car design 'serves as the foundation for almost everything we do. Virtually all our other cars have been derived from its platform, including the LeBaron, Chrysler E-class, Dodge 600, the New Yorker and to a lesser degree our sports cars, Dodge Daytona and Chrysler Laser'.[73] Iacocca was able to widen the range of K-car products by making some versions more luxurious and/or lengthy than the basic design. The long 'stretched' models looked odd, however, because they 'couldn't get proportionately wider'.[74] The luxury models looked odd, too, because they were adorned with an outdated conception of luxury styling. Like all the K-car derived models, they were suffering from Iacocca's increasingly outdated styling preferences.[75]

By the late 1980s Chrysler's car products obviously needed an update. Even its supposedly new models 'were stylistic and mechanical throwbacks to the 1981 K-cars', and increasingly its 'potential customers recognized reskinned K-cars for what they were'.[76] Not only the styling but also the underlying engineering was from an earlier era. Chrysler's car-making was therefore becoming increasingly vulnerable to competition or an economic recession.

In 1990, Chrysler's vulnerability was exposed by a downturn in the car market. The firm's profits 'plunged to a piddling $68 million in an increasingly soft automobile market', and in 1991 'Chrysler's losses soared disastrously, to $795 million'.[77] Iacocca therefore introduced cost-cutting measures. Two assembly plants were closed in 1990 and severe administrative cost-cutting led to some 11,000 layoffs, close to a third of the white-collar workforce.[78] One positive feature, though, was the end of Iacocca's irrational business mission: his non-automotive acquisitions had to be sold off as part of the attempt to save Chrysler. Despite the sell-offs and cost-cutting, the corporation's future was in doubt. 'Conventional wisdom among business scribes (and their related species, financial analysts) was not just that the Japanese soon would dominate the auto industry, but that Chrysler, as the weakest and most uninspired of the [American] Big Three, would—*this* time—surely die'.[79]

Chrysler did not die this time, however, thanks partly to the effects of a revival in rational leadership in the later 1980s. From 1986 onwards there had been a steady reversal of the earlier decline in Iacocca's rational leadership. The return to rationality was evident in his 1987 takeover merger with AMC. This had been a very discerning choice and was a personal decision by Iacocca, not one suggested or supported by his senior executives.[80] After all, AMC had long been the small number-four of the American automobile industry and seemed to be forever struggling to survive. In recent years it had been kept afloat largely by the French car-maker, Renault, as its alliance partner and main shareholder. What would Chrysler gain by taking over and merging with AMC?

Chrysler gained a hybridizing second stage of redevelopment. The longer term benefits came through a structural hybridization that is examined in the next section. The more immediate benefit of hybridizing with AMC was the expansion of

Chrysler's product range. It gained a new product category, the SUV, which had been pioneered by AMC's Jeep brand and had a sizeable niche market. The SUV semi-car was closer in appearance to a car than to a van or a truck but differed markedly from Chrysler's cars. SUVs had four-wheel drive rather than front-wheel drive, a powerful engine of six cylinders rather than four, and a high ground clearance to improve their off-road travel. Despite their off-road capability, they have been 'designed primarily for urban consumers and marketed primarily to them', according to Bradsher's study of SUVs.[81] He also cites research about a key part of the niche market enjoyed by the Jeep SUVs.

> [These] buyers liked four-wheel-drive because it offered the promise of unfettered freedom to drive anywhere during their vacations. These customers might have given up their childhood dreams of becoming firefighters, police officers or super-heroes, and instead had become parents with desk jobs and oversized mortgages. But they told Ford researchers that SUVs made them feel like they were still carefree adventurous spirits who could drop everything and head for the great outdoors at a moment's notice if they really wanted to do so.[82]

This SUV market had been a boon for the small and struggling automaker AMC. In 1986 it had sold some 221,000 Jeep SUVs.[83] But in the following year AMC had been acquired by Iacocca and Jeep became a Chrysler brand. From then on, the Jeep SUV bestowed its benefits on Iacocca's firm, thanks to his eminently rational decision to acquire AMC.

Iacocca had shown a similar rationality when he expanded production of the mini-van. He had already been promoting a product-development improvement of the minivan: in marked contrast with his K-cars' lack of development. By 1987 he had introduced a larger model of the minivan, with either an improved four-cylinder engine or a more powerful six-cylinder engine.[84] More importantly, that year he also expanded production by opening a second minivan plant. In 1988/9 minivan production increased to 393,000/468,000, sales were doubling, and half were sales of the new model.[85] This doubling of production was a personal decision by Iacocca and had not been supported by many of his senior executives. 'Iacocca would have none of the handwringing caution: he made the decision to go for it, told the timid to deal with it, and was amply vindicated'.[86] He realized that the minivan diversification still had plenty of potential, especially as a new model was available. The minivan was later considered to be the most successful vehicle produced by any American automaker in the 1980s.[87]

In the 1990s the minivan and the SUV continued to flourish. A crucial reason for their success was that Chrysler kept introducing new models or versions, which pushed minivan sales to 565,000 in 1992.[88] Competition from other automakers was still not very effective, even though this seems too lucrative a niche market to pass up or mishandle. Chrysler was able to dominate the minivan market until the late 1990s, capturing at least half the sales.[89] Similarly, the Jeep SUV sales benefited from its new models and kept its hold on the market. A new-generation Jeep appeared in

1992 and was a notable success, with annual production starting at 200,000 units and climbing to over 300,000 within a few years.[90] Although its market was more competitive than the minivan market, its niche was expanding more rapidly and had more growth potential. By the end of the 1990s SUVs comprised nearly 17 per cent of all new vehicles being sold each year in America.[91]

The SUV and minivan were therefore verifying the Iacocca outflanking formula quoted in the previous section: smaller firms should outflank big firms by finding 'market niches that they haven't even thought of. You can't go head to head with them—they're just too big. You've got to outflank them'. Iacocca had begun outflanking competitors by diversifying into minivans; another niche market had been added by acquiring the Jeep SUVs.

Yet the SUV and the minivan were only a partial solution to Chrysler's problems. In the early 1990s, the corporation was deep in a cost-cutting turnaround and seemed to be facing a bleak rather than bright future. The SUV and minivan had at least ensured Chrysler's survival, but something more was needed: the standard-car sector of Chrysler needed to make a comeback. As the next section shows, this comeback occurred in 1992/3, thanks to the hybridizing merger with AMC. For the hybridizing changed Chrysler's product-development structure and completed Iacocca's unfinished redevelopment. Thanks to the second stage of redevelopment, the product-development reorientation left undone in 1983 was carried out in 1989. Although the sales and financial benefits were not seen until 1992/3, hybridization proved to be a very successful as well as appropriate means of redevelopment.

The hybridization also had a marked effect on the corporation's leadership. The senior executive who led the structural hybridizing, Bob Lutz, became a leader of Chrysler. He and Iacocca formed a dual-leadership team, which lasted until Iacocca's retirement in 1992. And Lutz later provided a leader's-eye view of the hybridization through a book titled *Guts: The Seven Laws of Business that Made Chrysler the World's Hottest Car Company.*

Bob Lutz, *Guts*, and Hybridizing with AMC

The combining of Chrysler and AMC was an unlikely case of hybridization. When AMC was taken over by Chrysler in 1987, the 'merger' was most likely to result in merely an acquisition-like diversification: adding the Jeep SUVs to Chrysler's product range. AMC was a relatively small corporation and its product range was focused on these Jeep SUVs. The firm had only about 20,000 employees and some three-quarters of the 288,000 cars that it had sold in 1986 were Jeeps.[92] Yet, while AMC's name disappeared, the firm had contributed more than just Jeeps to the merger. There was a wider hybridization, thanks to the continuing revival of Iacocca's rational leadership. He discerned that AMC had more to offer than just its Jeeps. For instance, he realized that he could draft in some AMC executives to 'improve the breed' of Chrysler management.

> Instead of pink-slipping all the AMC people, as many CEOs would have done with the acquired executives, he used them to improve the breed. To the astonishment and dismay of many Chrysler executives, it was *they* who were let go, replaced by hard-charging, bright, untraditional AMC people.[93]

This 'improving of the breed' is similar to the cultural hybridizing described in Chapter 10: the hybridizing of Compaq with Hewlett-Packard. But Iacocca went further: he carried out some structural hybridizing. He discerned that AMC was superior to Chrysler in product development and he capably assigned one of his senior executives to lead a structural hybridization.

The task was assigned to Bob Lutz. In 1988 Iacocca put him in charge of 'automotive design, development, and manufacturing' and gave him a mandate to reform product development.[94] In practice, this was a mandate to adopt AMC's distinctive system of product development: here there was to be a hybridizing mix of the two companies' structures. According to Lutz's book *Guts*, this hybridization occurred because AMC's product development was so obviously superior. After the acquisition, 'what we soon found is that, far from being a bunch of brain-dead losers', AMC's designers and engineers 'had in recent years rolled out an impressive succession of new products'.[95] In contrast, Chrysler had waited until 1986 to begin designing a K-car replacement and was still years away from producing a new design. Another contrast was that AMC had achieved its impressive results with fewer than 700 engineering staff, compared to the some 6,000 employed by Chrysler.[96] Iacocca therefore 'agreed to keep the former AMC engineering unit intact ... in order to get a closer look at how they were able to get so much done with so little'.[97] He also agreed to Lutz's key personnel move. The former AMC vice-president for product and quality, Francois Castaing, was appointed Chrysler's vice-president for vehicle engineering.[98] This ex-AMC engineer would play a key role in the product-development hybridization. Lutz describes him as the lynchpin of the firm's new, AMC-like 'teamwork-based product development', based on project teams that were later known as 'platform' teams.[99]

The platform-team system was first adopted as a means of speeding up development of the LH-car. This project was the result of the 1986 move to develop a replacement for the K-car. Two years later, the LH-car's design was still not finalized, but during 1988 Lutz managed to finish the project by applying a platform-team approach.[100] The LH-car had been designed as a highly affordable front-wheel drive family sedan, with an innovative cab-forward design feature.[101] The cab-forward feature had major advantages. 'By moving the wheels to the outer edges of the chassis and shifting the entire passenger compartment toward the front, a large cavity for people and luggage was created, along with an aggressive, low-snouted shape that was a dramatic departure from the competition'.[102] By adding a platform-team approach, the designing process was speeded up and took impressive shape. The finalized LH-car design was officially approved by Iacocca in January 1989.[103] More importantly, he had been shown beyond doubt the advantages of AMC's team-based product development: it had been worth hybridizing with Chrysler's product-development activities.

Later in 1989 the platform-team system was officially adopted by Chrysler.[104] Product-development engineering was to be restructured into platform teams. Previously, a prototype vehicle had been developed by engineering groups that were each responsible for a specific component and employed people specializing in that component. But now the restructuring into platform teams 'completely dismantled each of these entrenched component-specific engineering groups. In their place we formed units that were responsible not just for components, but for a *whole vehicle* (or "platform" in industry jargon)'.[105]

The new structure also changed the process of product development. Previously, each specialized department had added its contribution in a sequence that also involved 're-do loops', whereby something was sent back to be redone by a prior contributor to this sequential process.[106] But now the process was one of interactive teamwork within a multidisciplinary, cross-functional team of engineers—plus designers, parts procurers and manufacturing advisors.[107] Such a broad cross-functional team could make decisions that were more simultaneous than sequential. The team was constantly interacting, redoing, and problem-solving as it tried to meet its project's schedule, budget, and other goals.

The new system of product development met Lutz's expectations and Iacocca's requirements. Only a platform-team system could have achieved Iacocca's goal of launching the LH-car just forty-two months after he had officially approved the design.[108] This mid-1992 target was met by the platform team and with an additional achievement. The team of initially 850 members had not gone over budget; on the contrary, the project had been completed well under budget.[109] And by the end of the year Iacocca knew that the team had produced a winner. The stylish cab-forward LH-car 'had buyers pouring into Chrysler showrooms' by the end of 1992.[110] Clearly the firm had a more than adequate replacement for its outmoded K-cars. The new LH-cars were initially produced at the rate of hardly more than 160,000 a year, but by 1994 annual production had jumped to some 270,000.[111] In addition, the new cars were markedly more profitable than the compact K-car. The LH models were a more up-market product, not a compact but a full-size car.

A new, compact-size design—the Neon car—emerged soon after the LH-cars. This new, smaller car was a further triumph for the platform teams. Designing began in 1990 and within a year the preliminary team had created a concept car that won Iacocca's approval.[112] The following stages of product development were similarly successful. The project was finished in 1993, met the severe cost requirements, and produced a front-wheel drive compact that could compete with its Japanese equivalents.[113] Part of the Neon's attraction was that, like the LH-cars, it had a cab-forward design and appealing styling. Lutz describes it as 'a great little car' that 'made even the Japanese sit up and take notice'.[114] Just as importantly, the Neon had shown that the platform teams could repeat the success they had achieved earlier with the LH-cars. The platform-team hybridization had obviously been very fruitful.

From a leadership perspective, there had obviously been a return to a high level of rational leadership. Iacocca had been very discerning in choosing to hybridize with AMC as the appropriate rational means of achieving a second-stage redevelopment.

With this second stage, he had finally completed his early 1980s redevelopment: his firm had been given the benefits of a proper reorientation of product development. The sales and financial benefits did not appear until 1992/3, though, and by then they were needed to revive Chrysler from another decline in its fortunes.

In 1990/1, a downturn in the car market had forced Chrysler to start a cost-cutting turnaround, as described in the previous section. Despite the cost-cutting, the firm had made a large loss in 1991 and had been written off by the media. 'In the media's eyes we remained laggards, a technologically (and stylistically) benighted company riding a tired, one-trick, K-car pony'.[115] This negative media assessment did not include the semi-car minivans and SUVs. They were acknowledged to be exceptions to Chrysler's apparent backwardness.[116] But the firm still needed to produce impressive new cars, not semi-cars, or else the early 1980s' redevelopment would be no more than a flash in the pan. The arrival of the LH-cars and Neon in 1992/3 were therefore the key factors in transforming Chrysler's media reputation, ensuring a healthy financial recovery, and leading to the firm's share price rising from under $10 in 1991 to $57 in 1993.[117] These 'better late than never' benefits of redeveloping highlight the rationality of launching a second stage of redevelopment.

Furthermore, the second-stage redevelopment had apparently created a more than temporary revival. Chrysler's product-development system was 'something beyond the reach of most other car companies: an efficient and repeatable system for turning out hits'.[118] With this boost to its longer term competitiveness, the corporation seemed set for a bright future. By 1994, Chrysler was achieving record-level profits and thereafter it produced healthy financial results as well as an impressive range of products.[119]

The second-stage redevelopment, however, had been a complex process. In particular, the structural hybridization had required some accompanying and unexpected cultural changes. Although Lutz argues that 'the real value' of the new platform teams lay 'in the freeing up of individual initiative', there first had to be an unexpected cultural change.[120] He describes how management had to change attitudes in the new Viper-roadster platform team:

> Alas, we forgot that over many years we had trained these employees to behave entirely differently ... Employees must be *led* to empowerment; they must be taught and coached. They cannot be declared 'empowered' by executive fiat. As Team Viper learned from our coaching that error-free *in*action would be frowned upon more than action risking error, its autonomy grew. As the team gained self-confidence, more and more program milestones were met successfully and on time.[121]

There also had to be a change in attitude at the top of the corporation. Chrysler's 'top management kept its promise not to meddle', even though 'men like Iacocca and Lutz had got used to waltzing through a design studio and, with a little wave of the hand, ordering a slight change'.[122] Iacocca now showed a different attitude. When he saw a problem with a headlight design, he allowed the platform team to make up its own mind about the issue.[123]

Iacocca's 1990s leadership has indeed been characterized as creative non-interference. 'In the early 1980s Iacocca had caused Chrysler's comeback to happen. But in the early 1990s he had stepped back and allowed it to happen'.[124] By then, he and Lutz were clearly operating as a dual-leadership team, with Lutz the more active partner. In *Guts* he modestly downplays his role but acknowledges that others saw it differently. 'A lot of people give me the credit for instituting teamwork-based product development at Chrysler'.[125] His importance was officially recognized in 1991 when he was promoted from co-president to sole president. Yet he did not succeed Iacocca as chairman/CEO in 1992; the board of directors instead chose Robert Eaton, a former GM executive, to be Iacocca's successor.

Iacocca, too, did not receive his just rewards. Early in 1992, the 67-year-old leader was persuaded or pressured to retire. He therefore failed to reap the rewards of his second-stage redevelopment. He missed out on Chrysler's 1993/4 financial rebound and the good years that followed, which would have enhanced his reputation as a business leader. The plaudits were instead bestowed on his successor, chairman/CEO Eaton. The 'accolades came cascading onto Eaton', and he was included in the *Business Week* selection of the world's twenty-five best managers.[126] Indeed, his record spoke for itself. By 1997, his firm's annual sales revenue was double that of a decade earlier, and Chrysler was named 'Company of the Year' by *Forbes* magazine.[127]

However, by 1997 Eaton had some serious concerns about his corporation. Among these worries were three strategic problems: increasing competition, especially from Japanese firms; Chrysler's inability to create a significant international presence; and the long-term replacement of the internal combustion engine with a cleaner means of propulsion.[128] Such problems and other factors led to Eaton supporting a merger proposal by German automaker Daimler-Benz, as recounted by Vlasic and Stertz in *Taken for a Ride: How Daimler-Benz Drove off with Chrysler*.

The 1998 'merger of equals' with Daimler-Benz created the DaimlerChrysler corporation. This was not a hybridizing merger and did not result in any problem-solving redevelopment. Instead, it led to what Lutz describes as 'chaotic misjudgement, misdirection, and mismanagement' by 'the powerful but cumbersome DaimlerChrysler'.[129] Furthermore, Hyde argues that the merger had in fact been a takeover by Daimler-Benz. 'Daimler stockholders owned 57 percent of the shares in the new company', and 'a majority of its management board came from the Daimler-Benz side' of the new corporation.[130] The Chrysler side of the corporation was sold in 2007 to investment firm Cerberus Capital Management. The onset of recession in 2008 sent the restored Chrysler into yet another crisis. However, help and investment was provided by Italian automaker Fiat. The two firms merged in 2014 to create Fiat-Chrysler Automobiles, headquartered in Europe. In 2021 Fiat-Chrysler merged with a French automaker, PSA Group, creating a new corporation called Stellantis.

So Iacocca's redevelopment had ultimately failed to give his corporation a bright new future. He could well argue, though, that the failure was due to events that began several years after he had left Chrysler. In the late 1990s he was no longer its leader and therefore could no longer provide the corporation with the benefits of his rational leadership.

13

IBM

Gerstner's *Who Says Elephants Can't Dance?*

Lou Gerstner's 1990s redevelopment is a legendary feat of business leadership, through which he rescued the twentieth century's most iconic computer company. International Business Machines (IBM) was an American firm that had been founded in pre-computer times, had pioneered punch-card devices in the 1930s, and had introduced its big mainframe computers to businesses all over the world in the 1950s–70s. When Gerstner became CEO in 1993, IBM operated in more than a hundred countries and employed more than 300,000 people.[1]

The corporation's size was reflected in the title he chose for his memoir, the 2002 *Who Says Elephants Can't Dance? Inside IBM's Historic Turnaround.* The subtitle reflected the corporation's need for a turnaround when he took over as CEO in 1993. His book's second edition, however, had the more accurate subtitle *Leading a Great Enterprise through Dramatic Change.* For IBM needed not just a turnaround but also a remedial renewal—a redevelopment—and some high-quality leadership. Specifically, it needed the rational type of high-quality leadership. As Gerstner observes, this was 'a company of 300,000-plus professionals', who were 'bright, inquisitive, and (alas) opinionated'.[2] Only the rational type of leadership could inspire them with confidence in the leader's attempt at redevelopment: at solving the declining corporation's problems and giving it a bright new future.

IBM had been in decline since the late 1980s, and Gerstner was brought in to rescue it in 1993. The situation was not as disastrous as that faced by Iacocca at Chrysler fourteen years earlier, as described in Chapter 12.[3] But Gerstner had to carry out a cost-cutting turnaround before beginning his redevelopment. He therefore made some soon-to-be-famous remarks at a press conference held a few months after he took charge of IBM. 'There's been a lot of speculation about when I'm going to deliver a vision of IBM, and what I'd like to say to all of you is that the last thing IBM needs right now is a vision ... the number-one priority is to restore the company to profitability'.[4] His 1993/4 cost-cutting turnaround achieved this goal and then he quickly used three of the tools in the redeveloper's tool kit. Cultural and structural transformations were followed in 1996 by a reorientation of the product range, prioritizing IT (information-technology) services.

His successful redeveloping of IBM is recounted in his memoir, with its leader's-eye view, and in several other books. Notably, Slater's *Saving Big Blue* and Garr's *IBM Redux* appeared in 1999/2000. More recently, the redevelopment is an important part

Rational Leadership. Paul Brooker and Margaret Hayward, Oxford University Press. © Paul Brooker & Margaret Hayward (2023). DOI: 10.1093/oso/9780198894643.003.0013

of Cortada's notable history of the firm, *IBM: The Rise and Fall and Reinvention of a Global Icon.*

This chapter will take a similarly long view of IBM's redevelopment. The first section looks back to the 1980s, tracing the effects of disruptive technology, high-tech revolution, strategic mistakes, and attempts at rectification. The first high-tech revolution of the modern era, the personal-computer revolution, was initially a lucrative boon for IBM. By the mid-1980s the corporation was the world's most valuable company as well as its leading high-tech company. Yet only a few years later, this corporation was in decline and needing remedial leadership. IBM's new leader, John Akers, had attempted to rectify the firm's mistakes, but more ambitious remedial action was needed—a redevelopment. The second section moves on to Gerstner taking over in 1993 and adopting a different approach to IBM's problems. After a cost-cutting turnaround, he launched a redevelopment that initially used both transformational tools, cultural and structural, as appropriate rational means.

The third section shows how his mid-1990s redeveloping then used a reorienting tool as a third appropriate rational means. It reoriented the product range by internally prioritizing IT services (and eventually an acquisition supplemented the internal prioritization). IT services were expanded into a major source of new revenue as, for instance, increasing numbers of companies outsourced IT activities to IBM. By the time Gerstner retired in 2002, IBM was enjoying a bright new future. By then, however, the challenge of cloud-computing services was appearing on the distant horizon, as is also discussed in the lengthy Appendix 2 on cloud services.

The fourth section leaves the IBM case and looks at the attempt to redevelop a much younger high-tech corporation, namely Yahoo. (To prevent ambiguities, the corporation's name will be used without the exclamation mark: the firm's full and official name was 'Yahoo!') Redeveloping this relatively new and small high-tech corporation might be viewed as an easier task than Gerstner's redevelopment of the venerable and mammoth IBM. In Yahoo's case, though, the circumstances were very unfavourable. This corporation had been founded in the 1990s as one of the Internet's pioneering e-access firms, but it had been overtaken by new Internet firms in the 2000s. In 2012, a brilliant product developer, Marissa Mayer, was brought in to redevelop the declining Yahoo. Yet despite Mayer's abilities and best efforts, she could not succeed: the circumstances were just too unfavourable.

Disruption, PCs, and Rectification

The background to IBM's redevelopment is discussed in the most influential book of the high-tech era, Christensen's 1997 *The Innovator's Dilemma: When New Technologies Cause Great Firms to Fail.* He included IBM, as an example, in his model of how an industry is changed by 'disruptive' new technology. The model's key features are that disruptive technology is not introduced by leading firms but instead by new firms, who exploit the new market opened up by this new technology. Even great firms may fail 'to stay atop their industries' when confronted with disruptive technological change and markets.[5] In the IBM case, the disruptive 'minicomputer' technology of the 1960s–70s was not introduced by computer-industry leader IBM. Instead, 'Digital Equipment Corporation created the minicomputer market and was joined by a set of other aggressively managed [new] companies'.[6] IBM had missed this opportunity and therefore saw its leadership of the computer industry challenged by a set of new companies.

As Christensen pointed out, however, these new companies in turn missed the next wave of disruptive technology and markets. For 'each of these [minicomputer] companies in turn missed the desktop personal computer market' that appeared in the 1970s–80s.[7] A new wave of disruptive technology had created the desktop *micro*computer, the first personal computer. Each office worker now could have his or her 'own' personal computer rather than sharing the use of an office or company computer. Furthermore, the desktop could be owned and used by individuals or families in their home. So the personal computer had opened up a wholly new consumer market as well as a new business market that supplemented the existing business markets for computers.

The new markets were successfully exploited by new firms, notably Apple Computer. However, the personal-computer markets were also successfully exploited by IBM.[8] Here was an exception to the Christensen model of industry leaders being left behind by disruptive new technology. As Christensen acknowledged, 'IBM's success in the first five years of the personal computing industry stands in stark contrast to the failure of the other leading mainframe and minicomputer makers to catch the disruptive desktop computing wave'.[9] However, he also presented a convincing explanation for why IBM was the exception. 'It created an autonomous organization in Florida, far away from its New York state headquarters, that was free to procure components from any source, to sell through its own channels, and to forge a cost structure appropriate to the technological and competitive requirements of the personal computer market'.[10] In effect IBM had spun-off a start-up that was required and empowered—'free to procure components from any source'—to create a desktop that could compete in the new personal-computer markets. A competitive desktop was quickly created in 1980/1 by procuring hardware and software components.[11] As Chapter 10 noted, this component outsourcing included Microsoft supplying the IBM desktop with a licensed operating system. Such outsourcing gave IBM a shortcut that enabled it to get ahead of Apple Computer and other new personal-computer firms. Even if IBM's desktop was not as good as their designs, the big corporation's advantages in marketing and distribution would enable its new computer to take the lead. IBM was about to reap the rewards of leading the first of the modern era's high-tech revolutions.

In 1981, IBM launched its desktop as the IBM Personal Computer. The IBM PC desktop soon led and expanded the market, creating a boom time for IBM. Revenue increased from $29 billion in 1981 to $46 billion in 1984 and its share price more than doubled, making it the world's most valuable company as well as the world's leading high-tech company.[12] Disruptive technology had therefore apparently boosted, not undermined, the position of the venerable IBM. Nine years later, though, this world-leading corporation would need to be rescued by an outside CEO. What had gone wrong?

The shortcut's gate had been left open. As IBM did not acquire exclusive rights to its outsourced components, new entrants to the personal-computer market could use the same shortcut. Soon these firms were producing 'cloned' versions of IBM's PC desktop. Their versions were known as IBM-clone PCs or simply 'PC-clones', and the term 'PC' was applied to the clones as well as to IBM's product. Apple's personal-computer designs were not described as PCs, but Apple's personal computers were almost marginalized by the intense competition from PC producers. There was also intense competition among the PC-producing firms. And IBM was overtaken by its PC rivals, who were quicker to make performance improvements, price reductions, and marketing deals.[13] IBM's share of the personal-computer market declined dramatically in the second half of the 1980s, and was down to just 20 per cent by 1992/3.[14]

By the late 1980s, IBM was also experiencing the disruptive negative effects of the desktop personal-computer technology.[15] IBM's very successful version of a desktop personal computer had inadvertently accelerated and intensified the threat that the desktop presented to the big mainframe computer—the firm's long-standing core product.

> IBM's essential contribution was to position the [desktop] technology as suitable for wide use ... IBM contributed a technology standard—a format or model—that made sense to users and rivals. It also lent its eminence to this form of computing. If IBM had not participated in PC technology, these machines would eventually have spread, only more slowly.[16]

The rapid spread of the desktop PC was accompanied by improvements in performance and reductions in price. IBM's business customers were therefore seeing their mainframe computers undercut by the increasingly more economical PC: 'the cost of performing a calculation on a PC dropped so much that it was often a 100 times cheaper to do work using a little machine than on a mainframe computer'.[17] Such cost calculations were pushing IBM's customers from the mainframe to the PC. By 1987, IBM's 'mainframe business had entered a long, slow decline'.[18]

The venerable corporation was therefore feeling the effects of a sharp pair of market scissors. There was now a continuing decline in its mainframe-computer market as well as the continuing decline in its share of the PC market. Hence the firm's share of the overall computer market had been cut almost in half by 1991: 'IBM's overall market share worldwide had slipped to about twenty-three percent'.[19]

Furthermore, the corporation's problems had been exacerbated by two strategic mistakes. IBM had adopted 'a flawed strategy' in the early 1980s: a strategy which 'called for the company to expand massively' to meet the assumed growth in demand for mainframe computers.[20] A second strategic mistake had occurred soon after, when revenues from the booming PC sales were used to boost the mainframe-oriented growth strategy. There was 'lavish' spending on new factories and facilities, plus the hiring of thousands of new employees throughout IBM.[21] So the late-1980s decline in demand for mainframe computers had left the corporation with serious over-capacity and over-employment issues.

The growth-strategy mistakes led to a major rectification programme by the 1985–93 CEO, John Akers. He 'cut IBM's workforce by a quarter, closing ten plants and trimming manufacturing capacity by forty percent'.[22] His rectification of the growth-strategy mistakes began in the late 1980s and continued for several years. He 'began slowly and then took increasingly more drastic measures'.[23] In particular, there were more drastic cuts in the number of employees. During the early 1990s, the workforce was reduced by tens of thousands each year.[24]

The Akers rectification programme also decentralized IBM, so the firm could never again over-emphasize its mainframe business. In 1991/2, IBM was decentralized into nine product-based organizations that operated like separate companies, as with the Personal Systems organization based on PC products and called the 'PC Company'.[25] After this restructuring of IBM, the corporation was unlikely ever again to pursue an overall strategy that would favour mainframes or any other product category. The downside, however, was that the corporation was 'evolving into a holding company' for the new organizations and indeed eventually 'it was widely believed that Akers had latched onto a strategy for breaking up the company'.[26]

The idea of breaking up IBM was an admission that the rectification programme had not solved the firm's problems. In fact, the 1990s rectification of the growth strategy had itself created new problems. For the one-off costs of closing down the growth strategy had led to multi-billion-dollar losses each year.[27] And the firm's share price, not surprisingly, had fallen dramatically: from $175 in 1987 to $135 in 1991, and to below $50 by 1993.[28] Wall Street might have tolerated IBM's massive losses if Akers had succeeded in remedying the declining market appeal of his mainframes and PCs. But these negative market tendencies had not been rectified. Mainframe sales had continued to fall, with a 50 per cent decline in 1991–3.[29] Although PC sales still generated substantial revenue, the firm 'incredibly was making no profit' on the sales.[30] So Akers was facing a huge and complex profitability problem. His move towards the idea of breaking up IBM has been described as that of 'a desperate man' seeing a break up as 'the most prudent course of action'.[31]

Lou Gerstner's Redevelopment of 1990s IBM

The break-up tendency ended in 1993, though, after Akers was persuaded to retire.[32] By 1993, IBM's massive losses were due to not only one-off costs but also a calamitous fall in operating earnings.[33] Akers was therefore replaced in April by an experienced crisis-management CEO, the 51-year-old Lou Gerstner. He came from outside IBM and indeed from outside the computer industry. Gerstner was a Dartmouth engineering graduate, with a Harvard MBA, who had been a management consultant at McKinsey, then an American Express executive, and recently the turnaround CEO of foodstuffs giant RJR Nabisco. After becoming IBM's CEO he soon decided not to break up the corporation. For 'IBM's scale and broad-based capabilities' was a 'unique competitive advantage' that would be lost if the corporation was broken up.[34] His book admits that in 1993 he 'didn't know then exactly how we were going to deliver on the potential' of a unified IBM, but he was sure that if the corporation 'could serve as the foremost integrator of [information] technologies, we'd be delivering extraordinary value'.[35]

Keeping IBM intact, however, meant taking emergency measures to save the unprofitable firm from disaster. Gerstner observes that in 1993 IBM came close to running out of cash and perhaps even having to file for bankruptcy.[36] A major cost-cutting turnaround was required. The 'only way to save the company, at least in the short term, was to slash uncompetitive levels of expenses', specifically through a nearly $9 billion 'program of expense reduction'.[37] In particular, there was a further downsizing of the workforce. Gerstner describes this as 'reducing our employment by 35,000 people, in addition to the 45,000 people whom John Akers had already laid off in 1992. That meant additional pain for everyone, but this was a matter of survival, not choice'.[38]

The cost-cutting turnaround was a marked success. The firm went from a loss of $8 billion in 1993 to earnings of $3 billion in 1994, and the share price had risen to $75 by October 1994, compared to its all-time low of $40 in July 1993.[39] The 1993/4 turnaround, however, was only a prelude to the redevelopment of the corporation. As Gerstner points out, the post-turnaround second half of the 1990s would determine whether or not IBM was going to be 'a company that mattered'.[40] He could not hope to return IBM to the iconic status and dominant position that it had enjoyed a decade earlier. He could, however, give the declining firm a brighter future than that of being merely a living relic of IT's pioneering epoch. IBM could be redeveloped into a major player in the computer industry, and perhaps even contribute to the future evolution of the IT sector.

Gerstner's first step in the redevelopment of IBM was his use of the cultural tool. He had discerned that a cultural transformation was appropriate and indeed essential. As Chapter 15 will recount, IBM had evolved a commercially dysfunctional culture, which had led to what Gerstner claims was 'a general disinterest in customer needs, accompanied by a preoccupation with internal politics. There was general permission to stop projects dead in their tracks, a bureaucratic infrastructure that defended turf instead of promoting collaboration, and a management class that presided rather than acted'.[41] These values, attitudes, and perspectives had impeded IBM's ability to deal with changes in its markets. And its rectifying leader, Akers, has been described as 'a prisoner of IBM's culture'.[42] Gerstner, by contrast, intended to transform the culture into one that would assist, not impede, his remedial renewal.

In 1994, he began his cultural transformation by issuing a list of required behavioural changes and a list of required leadership competencies.[43] He eventually realized, however, that his cultural tool was not having much effect. In his words, 'the cultural transformation was stalling', as 'it all remained a predominantly intellectual exercise' that was not changing the way that people worked.[44] This was largely because changes to the official culture of a corporation were not affecting the 'everyday' informal culture, which shapes:

> how people actually go about their work, how they interact with one another, what motivates them ... [As] with national cultures, most of the really important rules aren't written down anywhere. Still, you can quickly figure out, sometimes within hours of being in a place, what the culture encourages and discourages, rewards and punishes.[45]

As Gerstner is implying, such informal culture is much more difficult to change than an official culture, which can be changed by simply promulgating a list of new company values or principles.

By 1995 he had adopted a new approach to culturally transform the corporation. He recast the new culture as a three-word formula—win, execute, and team.[46] This formula may seem an over-simplification that lacks discernment, but each word had a more specific meaning: the 'win' meant focusing on the market and competitors; the 'execute' meant getting things done quickly and effectively; the 'team' meant acting as a united IBM. Furthermore, the new cultural formula was capably supported by incentives and enforcement.

> 'Win, Execute, Team' began as a mantra—spread throughout the company through multiple media—and eventually took the form of a new performance management system. Every year, as part of our annual planning, all IBMers made these three 'Personal Business Commitments' (PBCs), then listed the actions they were going to take in the upcoming year that would fulfil the commitments ... And the PBC program had teeth. Performance against those commitments was a key determinant of merit pay and variable pay.[47]

Such measures helped his new cultural formula become part of IBM's informal culture. Yet the cultural transformation took 'at least five years', and 'I had to commit to thousands of hours of personal activity to pull off the change'.[48]

In 1995, Gerstner also began a structural transformation. He had discerned that the structural tool was appropriate and should be applied to IBM's global administrative structure. Specifically, the existing form of global decentralization—to country-level management—should be replaced with a new form of decentralization. Gerstner metaphorically depicts such a change as taking power from the existing 'barons' and bestowing it on new barons.[49]

IBM's existing barons drew their power from its traditional country-level decentralization. In the early stages of the firm's global expansion IBM was decentralized into what has been called 'a loose confederation of self-standing international subsidiaries. This confederation worked well for many decades' and indeed by the mid-1990s about half of IBM's revenue came from outside the US.[50] By then, however, the global decentralization had become problematic. 'Gerstner made the courageous decision to centralize what was about to become a splintered corporation. He decided to instil tighter controls—more rigid' than those of any earlier CEO of IBM.[51] His own book again uses a feudal metaphor. 'I declared war on the geographic fiefdoms' of the existing barons, who were so powerful that IBM staff 'practically had to ask permission to enter the territory of a country manager'.[52] Yet Gerstner's account of his war on these geographic fiefdoms does not mention tighter controls. He instead describes how he began a global restructuring of IBM in mid-1995. The firm created twelve worldwide group-level units, each focused on a particular category of customer, such as manufacturers or governments.[53] The managers of these new customer-based groups were presumably to be the new 'barons' of global IBM. Certainly the existing barons were opposed to the restructuring. 'The response from the country managers was swift and predictable', as they quickly warned Gerstner that the change would fail or even endanger the firm, and later he had to remind some country managers that 'you no longer manage a business. You now serve as a critical support function to our integrated worldwide customer organization'.[54]

The structural transformation was a long and hard-won struggle that tested Gerstner's capability as a rational leader. He admits that the new structure was not fully accepted 'until at least three years later', and that it 'took three years of hard work' to implement the restructuring properly.[55] His structural transformation therefore required more time and effort than some cultural transformations have required—in favourable circumstances.

Reorienting to IT Services in the 1990s–2000s

By 1996, Gerstner was ready to use a third redevelopment tool, a reorienting of the product range. This risked overloading IBM with too much change, as both the cultural and structural transformations were still unfinished 'works in progress'. However, his reorientation tool was prioritizing, not diversifying, and involved relatively little change when compared to the Chrysler minivan diversification mentioned in Chapter 12. So his rapid sequence of redeveloping changes, two transformations and then a reorientation, did not overload the corporation.[56] Gerstner had rightly discerned that the risk of overloading was low, and that he should quickly begin an appropriate reorienting of the product range.

The appropriate reorientation was his prioritizing of the 'IT services' product category. It was a broad category, stretching from routine maintenance services to consultancy services that showed firms how to improve their IT systems. The services category also included firms outsourcing their IT activities to IBM, such as outsourcing the operation of their mainframes to services supplier IBM. Supplying services could be a 'big earner', as would be shown by Gerstner's redevelopment of IBM. His prioritized IT services generated more than $20 billion of the $25 billion growth in revenue during his tenure as CEO.[57]

As early as 1993, he had started eyeing up IT services as an appropriate prioritization.[58] Services had been one of the few bright spots in the firm's recent history. 'Hardware maintenance, long a core service business', was joined by 'computer outsourcing deals' in the mid-1980s and then, in 1991, by a new Consulting Group of 1,500 consultants.[59] When Gerstner arrived at IBM, IT services were jointly providing more than 20 per cent of the firm's revenue.[60] Furthermore, he was soon presented with an interesting new idea by the head of a high-level services unit. The idea was to create an independent and comprehensive IT services unit, which could 'take over and act on behalf of the customers in all aspects of information technology—from building systems to defining architecture to actually managing the computers and running them'.[61]

Yet such a comprehensive and independent unit did not appear until years later. This prioritizing of IT services had to wait until after the turnaround and until after the transformations were underway.[62] In the meantime, Gerstner was making sure that the services prioritization was indeed the appropriate third tool for redeveloping IBM. Analyses and projections, by his staff and by other firms, confirmed that IT services would be a huge growth area: pursuing this opportunity 'seemed rational and straightforward'.[63] It was not straightforward, however, in organizational terms. Creating an independent and comprehensive IT-services unit was a difficult and sizeable project. Gerstner even had his services staff create a prototype unit: a not yet independent but fully integrated global services organization. As he recounts, creating the prototype 'was a Herculean task—common problem solving, methodologies, nomenclatures, skill definitions, capturing and disseminating knowledge on a global basis, and hiring and training thousands of new people' to operate the unit.[64] Gerstner's prioritization had therefore been well prepared when he put it to work in 1996.

'By 1996 I was ready to break the services unit out as a separate business. We formed IBM Global Services'.[65] This global IT-services unit operated in more than a hundred countries and was a huge organization. Its workforce of 90,000 had grown to 140,000 by the end of the decade.[66] The organization's two main services were outsourcing arrangements and consultancy services. A full outsourcing arrangement was sketched by Slater's book on IBM, when discussing the firm's relationship with the Monsanto corporation. In 1997, the two firms signed a ten-year outsourcing contract. 'IBM would run Monsanto's mainframe computer system, install and maintain its 20,000 personal computers, operate the network that connected Monsanto's facilities, and write new application programs for Monsanto'.[67] In effect, IBM was to supply the firm with a whole IT department and take responsibility for this department's effectiveness, personnel, and further development.

Consultancy was a higher level IT service than outsourcing and typically selected software for a customer's IT department. IBM's expert consultants selected the best software applications—regardless of who produced them—in each of the software categories required by the customer's business. Such 'best of breed' selection might lead to something like the 1996 deal between the Kellogg's corporation and the business-software corporation Oracle, a consultancy rival of IBM. Oracle provided Kellogg's with only the financial component of the proposed suite of software. 'The rest would come from other software firms: order management would come from IMI, logistics from Manugistics, maintenance management from TSW, manufacturing from Datalogix ... and warehouse management from McHugh Free-man'.[68] Oracle's main role was 'system integrator': its consultants created a cohesive software system out of these six specialized applications, each developed by a different software firm. System integration was much more difficult than the selection part of a consultancy contract. The integration often required a middleware form of software that could 'glue together' the various applications.[69]

Another kind of IT consultancy service was customizing a company's software. Its software would be made to conform to its 'peculiar business processes' and so the company would end up with an 'essentially unique' computer system, with the accompanying advantages and disadvantages.[70] The most important kind of consultancy service, however, was the longer term IT service contract that guaranteed consultants would be available to help the customer company solve any problems with its IT system. Often consultancy began with a selection-integration deal and led on to customization and then a longer term service contract or even an outsourcing arrangement.[71]

From Gerstner's perspective, however, the key feature of Global Services was its growing revenue and contribution to IBM's finances. By 2001, services were contributing $35 billion to IBM's $82 billion annual revenue, while computer hardware was contributing less than $26 billion.[72] Furthermore, services contracts had a higher profit margin than that of computer hardware, so in 2000 the services business was generating pre-tax income of $4.5 billion, compared to hardware's $2.7 billion.[73] The prioritizing of IT services had clearly been a discerningly selected and very capably used tool for redeveloping IBM. Cortada's history of IBM acknowledges that the firm's 'transformation into a services business was a remarkable achievement', though 'one hardly discussed by observers of IBM's history of the 1990s and the early part of the following decade'.[74] Gerstner had been left to blow his own trumpet. For instance, his book pointed out in 2002 that IBM's IT services had more than tripled in size in less than a decade, becoming a $30 billion business that 'accounted for roughly half of our workforce. I would guess there are few companies that have ever grown a multibillion-dollar business at this pace'.[75]

Fortunately, the services market had grown as rapidly as had been predicted back in the mid-1990s. The explosion in information technology that had first hit the US and Europe had spread around the world and created a global market for IT services. By 2000, the global market was estimated to be worth over $600 billion, and though IBM was the global leader in IT services, the firm had captured only a small fraction of this huge market.[76] There were still great growth opportunities for IBM's Global Services. Another reason for optimism was that existing customers kept coming back for more, as they were unable to find the staff and the time to keep up with the continuing changes in the world of IT.[77] Gerstner notes that a distinctive advantage of the services business was its 'astounding capacity for self-renewal. Every time the industry moves in a new direction, the IT services opportunity is reinvented'.[78]

His last major contribution to IBM was an apt acquisition that supplemented his prioritizing of IT services. Although Gerstner retired from his post of CEO in March 2002, he retained his post of chairman until the end of the year, while his successor settled in as the new CEO. They formed a transitional dual-leadership team, which later acquired the IT consultancy arm of PricewaterhouseCoopers (PwC).[79] This IT-services consultancy business was an attractive target for acquisition. It had been targeted by Hewlett-Packard (HP) in 2000, but the deal had collapsed due to price issues and other problems.[80] So PwC's IT-services business was still available in 2002 when IBM was looking to supplement its Global Services offerings. IBM ably acquired the PwC business at a bargain price.[81] More importantly, this IT-services business was a very apt acquisition, which strongly supplemented IBM's internal prioritizing of services. In particular, the 30,000 PwC IT consultants had industry-specialized expertise that filled a gap in IBM's IT-services offerings: 'customers increasingly wanted *industry-specific* consultancy and IT services, while much of what IBM was offering was still IT-centric'.[82] The gap had been filled by IBM's leaders making a supplementary acquisition, which had also supported the corporation's position as the world's leading supplier of IT services.

Gerstner was therefore leaving IBM in good shape when he retired in December 2002. By this time, IBM had become the leading supplier of IT services and therefore a major player in the IT industry. He had given the firm a much brighter future than seemed likely in post-turnaround 1995.

Another Gerstner legacy was that IBM had been left in a good position to continue exploiting its lead in IT services. There is a striking contrast with its 1980s loss of its lead in the PC market. IBM finally sold off its PC business in 2005 to the Chinese firm Lenovo.[83] The deal epitomized the reorientation from hardware to services carried out by Gerstner in the second half of the 1990s. And the prioritization's effects continued during the 2000s, as services revenue nearly doubled to reach $60 billion in 2010.[84] The only threat to its lead in IT services came in 2008, when Hewlett-Packard acquired the Electronic Data Systems corporation. The acquisition more than doubled HP's services revenue and made it second only to IBM as a supplier of IT services.[85]

However, HP's challenge to IBM was overshadowed by a new challenge to both firms' position in IT services. With the global 'financial crisis that started in 2008 clients began to seek cheaper service options, like on-demand cloud-based services'.[86] The rise of these cloud-based services is examined in Appendix 2 'From IT Services to Cloud Services'. By 2009/10, sellers of IT services were faced 'with the challenges and opportunities of the rapidly growing cloud computing paradigm'.[87]

Appendix 2 points out that Gerstner could have diversified into cloud services before he retired in 2002. If so, IBM might have made a major contribution to the future evolution of the IT sector. But the Appendix acknowledges that Gerstner was not in a good position to diversify into the emerging cloud-services technology at that stage. What excuses can be made, though, for the lack of cloud diversification by post-Gerstner IBM? This mistaken delay would have to be rectified by the CEO appointed in 2011, namely Virginia 'Ginni' Rometty. She had been a leader of IBM's IT-services businesses and therefore was a most appropriate inheritor of Gerstner's legacy, as is also evident in her 2023 memoir *Good Power: Leading Positive Change in Our Lives, Work and the World.*[88]

Internet Comparison: Marissa Mayer's 2010s Yahoo

Redeveloping a relatively new and small high-tech corporation was not necessarily any easier than redeveloping the venerable and mammoth IBM. Similarly, redeveloping a corporation in the 2010s was not necessarily any easier than redeveloping one in the 1990s. Both these points are illustrated by Marissa Mayer's 2010s attempt to redevelop Yahoo corporation. This was a small high-tech corporation that employed only 15,000 people rather than the 300,000 employed by IBM.[88] And Yahoo was also much younger than IBM. Yahoo was a product of the Internet high-tech revolution that began in the mid-1990s. In 1994, two engineering graduate students at Stanford University, Jerry Yang and David Filo, had created an online directory of the thousands of websites that were available on the newly emerging Internet. They named their directory site 'Yahoo!' (with an exclamation mark) because of the word's meaning and as an acronym for Yet Another Hierarchical Officious Oracle.[89] By 1996, Yahoo was a public company and would soon become a lucrative, globally used 'portal' to the Internet and the Web. However, the corporation was overtaken by new forms of e-access in the 2000s. And in 2012, a brilliant product developer, the 37-year-old Mayer, was brought in to revive Yahoo's fortunes. Her attempt to redevelop the firm aroused mixed feelings in many outside observers. Although 'many of Yahoo's investors, analysts, and advertisers have little faith in the ability of the legacy Internet company to regain its momentum', these observers were nostalgically and optimistically 'rooting for Mayer to execute a turnaround the likes of which the corporate world hasn't seen since Lou Gerstner saved IBM'.[90] Their pessimism was more rational than their optimism, though, as the circumstances were so difficult that Mayer's attempt to redevelop Yahoo could be seen as foredoomed. Nonetheless, although the attempt had indeed failed by 2016/17, much can be learnt from her courageous and capable effort. This final section of the chapter will therefore discuss why the circumstances were so difficult and, more importantly, how Mayer tried to beat the odds.

In hindsight, the odds against success might appear too great to be worth the effort of a redevelopment. For instance, Ring's *We Were Yahoo!* argued in 2017 that the redevelopment had been foredoomed. He pointed out that there had been no successful corporate turnarounds in the industry where Yahoo operated: the 'consumer internet industry'. Unlike in other high-tech industries, here there seemed to be no opportunity for a successful turnaround.[91] He also contrasted Yahoo's situation with the opportunities and capabilities of IBM under Gerstner and Apple under Steve Jobs. Yahoo clearly had no chance of emulating their 'turnaround' successes of, respectively, offering 'consultancy services to businesses' in the 1990s and inventing 'the next great thing' in technology in the 2000s.[92] Ring believes that Yahoo's decline could not have been reversed by Mayer or any other leader. 'I'm convinced that had Steve Jobs, Jack Welch, Lou Gerstner, Bill Gates, George Washington or Abraham Lincoln become CEO of Yahoo on July 16, 2012, none of them could have reversed the fortunes of Yahoo.'[93]

Ring's was not the only book to view Yahoo's redevelopment as foredoomed. Carlson's *Marissa Mayer and the Fight to Save Yahoo!* had appeared two years earlier, in 2015, but was almost as pessimistic. 'Maybe no person, no matter how talented, can save Yahoo', he concluded.[94] Carlson explains both why Yahoo needed redevelopment and why this was unlikely to succeed. He highlighted the lasting effect of Yahoo's mid-1990s creation and the particular line of Internet business, e-access, that it had pioneered. 'The early Internet was hard to use, and Yahoo made it easier', but then 'the need for Yahoo faded. The company hasn't found its purpose since—the thing it can do that no one else can'.[95]

Yahoo was the most notable e-access pioneer, along with America Online (AOL). In the mid-1990s each dominated a particular form of access to the Internet and its rapidly growing World Wide Web. AOL provided technical access through consumers' telephone lines; Yahoo provided an online directory and a search facility, thereby showing consumers the websites that were available and enabling them to search for what they wanted.[96] By the late 1990s, Yahoo and AOL had developed into Internet portals. They supplied consumers with a range of services, such as email, and generated huge revenue as platforms for advertising, especially advertisements by the flood of start-up Internet businesses.[97] The Yahoo portal had a home page and a network of websites. Users were offered such media-like services as news, weather, sports, music, and entertainment, plus 'chat groups and chat rooms, bulletin boards, maps and directions, help-wanted and for-sale ads, ads for homes and cars', and even some online shopping.[98]

Yahoo's development continued into the first half of the 2000s. The new decade began badly with the 'dot-com' stock-market crash, mentioned in several other chapters. The crash put an end to many Internet start-ups and therefore to their advertising on the Yahoo platform. However, Yahoo quickly recovered from this setback and continued its development. From 2001 to 2005 the firm went from a loss to healthy profits, expanded its workforce from 4,000 to nearly 10,000, and increased its annual revenue from $717 million to over $5 billion.[99] On the other hand, a major threat was emerging during these years. As Chapter 8 described, Google was emerging as a new competitor in the e-access business. Although Yahoo had adopted a licensed version of Google's search engine, in 2003 it brought out an alternative (Yahoo! Search) and ended its alliance with Google: 'the two companies were now bitter rivals'.[100]

In the latter half of the 2000s, Yahoo was defeated by its new rival. Google clearly won their competition for the US search-advertising market. In November 2004, the two firms 'were essentially tied', with Google holding over 34 per cent of the market and Yahoo 32 per cent, but then Google 'started to widen its lead in search market share', leaving Yahoo with only 21 per cent in 2009.[101] How could Yahoo rectify this negative tendency? Even co-founder Yang could not solve the problem when he served as CEO in 2007/8.[102] His successor Carol Bartz at least adopted an innovative approach. She leased Yahoo's search business to Microsoft through a 2009 licensing deal.[103] That year, however, another problem emerged. Yahoo was being 'rapidly overtaken by Facebook in the business of selling the Internet's other kind of ads: display ads, also known as brand advertising and sometimes called banner advertising'.[104]

The 2010s saw yet more problems for Yahoo, as it felt the effects of more Internet and high-tech innovations. As Chapter 14 recounts, the innovative iPhone and Android smartphones were proving very successful, and their success had dire results for Yahoo's email business.

> Yahoo's most important product, Yahoo Mail, began to show signs of weakness … The problem was, the entire web-based email market began to decline in 2010. The reason was the rise of the iPhone and Android-powered smartphones. Adults stopped checking their email on their computers because they had already seen it on their phones in the default apps provided by Google and Apple. Teenagers weren't emailing at all; they preferred to text or send messages through Facebook … Between 2011 and 2012 Yahoo email usage declined 25 percent.[105]

So Yahoo was now experiencing a decline in its email market as well as a declining position in the Facebook-affected market for display advertising. The firm was suffering from an equivalent of the market scissors that had hurt IBM in the early 1990s, when it had experienced declines in both its mainframe and PC markets. Like IBM's Akers, Yahoo's CEO Bartz was unable to rectify the negative market tendencies and she, too, would become a scapegoat for the firm's problems. In Bartz's case, she was in the especially vulnerable position of being an outsider CEO who had been expected to revive the firm.[106] In 2011, Yahoo badly missed its earnings expectations, the share price fell from $17.70 in April to $11 in August, and Bartz was fired in September.[107]

The corporation's problems increased in the first half of 2012. The new outside CEO resigned only months after he had arrived, and the firm's quarterly revenues shrank to below 2005 levels.[108] Yahoo was now clearly in decline and was something of an anachronism. Like IBM in the first half of the 1990s, Yahoo was apparently an outdated relic of an earlier, pioneering era. Yet there was some hope for the future. 'Over one billion individuals still used Yahoo! products and services. The Finance, Sports, News, and Email properties were still ingrained into the daily habits of people worldwide', and Yahoo's website was still 'one of the top five most visited websites in the world'.[109] Perhaps there some future for Yahoo, if the firm could be remedially renewed through a successful redevelopment.

In July 2012, the firm hired Marissa Mayer to carry out this remedial renewal of Yahoo. She was faced with the same kind of task that Gerstner had faced after his cost-cutting turnaround of IBM in 1993/4. Both leaders had to redevelop a famous high-tech corporation that had fallen into decline. Like Gerstner, Mayer was an outside CEO, but she had a very different and very high-tech background. She was an MSc computer-science graduate from Stanford University who had become a renowned product-development executive at Google.[110] So she had a far better high-tech and product background than Gerstner. On the other hand, she had much less management training and experience than Gerstner, who had even been a corporate CEO before he arrived at IBM. Another marked difference was Mayer's relatively young age, only 37, which was unusually young for anyone to be hired as CEO of a corporation, let alone such a problematic firm as Yahoo.

The new leader had some breathing space, however, thanks to Yahoo's financial windfall from a deal made back in 2005. Yahoo had bought a large stake in the Chinese firm Alibaba, a growing e-commerce firm on the Chinese Internet.[111] Alibaba had gone on to achieve huge growth in sales and in its value as an investment, thereby indirectly supporting Yahoo's share price. In May 2012, Alibaba had bought back half of Yahoo's stake, paying more than $7 billion and 'netting Yahoo some badly needed cash' during a time of falling revenues.[112] The remaining part of Yahoo's stake was so valuable that it boosted Yahoo's share price in 2012/3. And 'the soaring stock price meant that Yahoo's core business could be fixed without the normal scrutiny of the public markets' and the pressure of a declining share price.[113] In particular, the new leader did not have to bolster the share price with a cost-cutting turnaround. Soon after her arrival at Yahoo, 'Mayer announced to the staff that there would be no company-wide layoffs. All of Yahoo! cheered.'[114]

She also quickly used the reorienting redevelopment tool, specifically a prioritization. Unlike Gerstner at IBM, Mayer had no need to use the transformational tools, but she did need to reorient the product range quickly to take account of the increasingly prevalent mobile-tech devices. The 'mobile' revolution had entered a new phase by 2012, as the swarms of smartphones were joined by the iPad, Kindle Fire, and other tablet computers. Mayer ensured that her firm was responding appropriately: Yahoo expanded its mobile audience to 430 million, a growth of more than 250 per cent, in her first two years as CEO.[115] More specifically, she prioritized her firm's mobile-apps product category. 'Mayer believed that the best way for Yahoo to reinvent itself was to ride the shift from PC to mobile—to become a really great apps company.'[116]

Her prioritizing of mobile apps was a discerning selection of the appropriate rational means of redeveloping Yahoo. Mobile apps was a booming product category. Since 2008 there had been explosive growth in the number and revenues of mobile apps, as is recounted in Chapter 14. Mayer not only prioritized this product category but also prioritized *within* the category. She focused her apps developers on designing the best-available mobile apps for the consumer's 'daily habits' needs, such as email, news reports, and weather forecasts.[117] Her product-development expertise was clearly very useful and is evident, too, in her capable support for the mobile-apps prioritization. In particular, she vastly increased the firm's team of mobile-apps developers: there were only fifty when she arrived but more than 500 by mid-2015.[118] The increase was partly due to her extensive acqui-hiring. She cheaply acquired many start-ups whose apps had 'not really taken off': their developers now had the chance to do better as part of the mobile apps team at Yahoo.[119]

By 2014, Yahoo's mobile apps were flourishing. The firm was now the number-three in mobile advertising, behind only Facebook and the dominant Google; and Yahoo's mobile apps were generating $1.2 billion in annual revenue.[120] Yet this revenue boost was merely offsetting the continuing decline in revenue from other sources. In 2014/15, Yahoo was still 'a company that struggles to achieve annual sales of $5 billion.'[121]

Mayer had tried to boost revenues through a diversifying acquisition in 2013. Unlike Gerstner, she had begun using both the reorienting tools, diversification as well as prioritization. For she had discerned that Yahoo should diversify into the social-network area of advertising. Despite Facebook's dominance of e-socializing, there were still some advertising opportunities available if a firm focused on other kinds of e-socializing. Mayer therefore acquired in 2013 a blogging social network called Tumblr. She paid over $1 billion for a network with more than a hundred million users but without much revenue, so presumably she believed Yahoo could boost Tumblr's advertising revenues.[122] However, this was not a capable, apt social-network acquisition.

Marissa Mayer was intent on aggressively marketing Tumblr to advertisers, yet there were huge inherent obstacles that proved impossible to overcome. The first was that much [or some] of Tumblr's content was adult (i.e. porn) which is classified as 'NSFW' (not safe for work). It's also safe to assume that Proctor & Gamble was not rushing to spend its ad dollars on the Tumblr platform.[123]

Although Tumblr's user numbers eventually reached 500 million, it added too little revenue to be viewed as a successful diversification.[124] It would not contribute significantly to the reorientation of Yahoo's product range.

Yahoo's leader kept trying, however, and by 2015 was deploying a multipronged reorientation tool. She called it MaVeNS: an acronym for Mobile apps, Video, Native advertising, and Social networks.[125] The mobile-apps and social-networks prongs have already been described; the two additional prongs were prioritizing reorientations.[126] 'Video' referred to Yahoo Screen's video streaming and to the new emphasis on original programmes as well as television-repeat series (though all the material was being streamed to computers or mobile devices rather than televisions). 'Native advertising' referred to the prioritizing of a new way of presenting display advertisements on a web page. Rather than displaying them at the top or side of the page, the new approach was to insert less obtrusive, more relevant advertisements in the page's textual content. Yet even this multipronged MaVeNS tool did not have a significant effect on revenues, let alone lead to a bright new future for Yahoo.

The underlying problem was that Yahoo was not number-one in any important product area. For instance, although Mayer had strongly developed the mobile-apps product category, Yahoo was still only number-three in mobile advertising in 2015, with no prospect of overtaking Facebook or Google. By contrast, when Gerstner had taken charge of IBM in 1993, he had inherited a thriving IT-services product category, with the potential to be the world leader in the IT-services industry.

Yahoo therefore needed to develop a world-beating product; only this could give the firm a bright new future. Mayer told a board meeting in 2013 that Yahoo had not yet identified a 'breakthrough' product, but she 'reminded the board that Steve Jobs didn't come up with the iPod until five years into his return at Apple'.[127] She was setting a high standard, however, by pointing to the iPod-iTunes product. This had been a truly breakthrough product, opening up new opportunities for rapid and large-scale growth. Furthermore, did Yahoo have the capability to come up with such an innovative product? The firm certainly lacked the brilliant designers and software developers that had enabled Apple to create the iPod-iTunes breakthrough. And people with these exceptional abilities could not be easily recruited or acqui-hired by a small and, by this stage, mediocre corporation.

Similarly, Yahoo could not easily acquire a breakthrough product. The only affordable way of acquiring a potentially great product was by buying promising high-tech start-ups. However, they were not as prevalent and available in the 2010s as they had been in the 1990s–2000s. In that era Yahoo had 'botched' opportunities to acquire such firms as Google, Facebook, eBay, and YouTube.[128] By the 2010s, there were fewer promising high-tech start-ups and, if acquirable, they were being quickly snapped up by wealthier corporations than Yahoo.

So it is hardly surprising that in 2015 Mayer's firm had not yet launched a 'truly transformative product'.[129] In Yahoo's difficult circumstances, how could it have developed or acquired such a product? The corporation was not in financial difficulties, though, and its share price was still supported by the lucrative Alibaba investment.[130] Yahoo's problems lay elsewhere. Although Mayer had rescued it from decline, she could not prevent the corporation from stagnating. 'After years of honest attempts, it had become clear there was no magic wand that Yahoo! could wave to grow new areas of value for shareholders' or anyone else.[131]

The end came slowly. In January 2016, Yahoo announced that its core business would be sold, and in July it announced that the business was being bought by Verizon Communications.[132] Yahoo was dying a slow death, in what seems an anticlimactic ending to Mayer's attempt at redevelopment. She resigned in June 2017 when the firm was officially acquired by Verizon, which then merged Yahoo with AOL to form a subsidiary called 'Oath'.[133] A new Yahoo re-emerged in 2021 but without Marissa Mayer at the helm.

14

Apple

Redeveloped by Steve Jobs

Steve Jobs and his brilliant leadership of Apple have already been discussed in Chapter 6. Its final section highlighted his top-down hands-on approach to product development, as in the case of the iPod and iPhone. The present chapter has a much wider perspective and looks at how Jobs led the redevelopment of Apple from the late 1990s to the late 2000s. It is a long chapter, partly because this was a long redevelopment that had three different stages. Another reason, however, for studying this case at some length is that Jobs's redevelopment of Apple is the greatest ever example of a redevelopment.

Jobs left no autobiography or memoir when he died in 2011 at the age of 56, but he has had more written about him than perhaps any other business leader. The books include Isaacson's magisterial biography *Steve Jobs* and, from a different perspective, Mickle's 2022 *After Steve: How Apple Became a Trillion-Dollar Company and Lost Its Soul*. The almost legendary status of Jobs is due to his brilliant leadership and incredible success, especially his diversifying redevelopment of Apple in the 2000s. Yet the human drama of Jobs's career is that he and Apple were parted for many years before getting back together again and doing great deeds of creative diversification. Apple Computer was founded in 1976 by Jobs and Steve Wozniak. By 1980, it had become a public company and had produced two pioneering examples of the desktop personal computer, namely Apple I and Apple II. However, they were soon overshadowed by the IBM Personal Computer, the original 'PC' desktop, as described in Chapter 13. Jobs challenged the PCs with his Apple Macintosh desktop in 1984/5. But then he left the firm and sold his shareholding after falling out with the CEO he had recruited.[1] Apple Computer corporation continued successfully without its co-founder until the 1990s. Then the firm entered a downward spiral of decline and went through three CEOs. Although Jobs was now the renowned leader of the Pixar computer-animation company, he agreed to return to Apple as a part-time advisor and then, in 1997, as its new CEO.

The chapter's first two sections focus on how Jobs redeveloped Apple in the late 1990s. As well as completing a cost-cutting turnaround, he began a remedial renewal by using the transforming pair of tools in the redeveloper's tool kit. He had discerned that cultural and structural transformations were the two appropriate rational means of redeveloping the corporation. Apple's culture was transformed by adding a 'high-fashion' perspective: there was a new focus on aesthetic and distinctive design

Rational Leadership. Paul Brooker and Margaret Hayward, Oxford University Press. © Paul Brooker & Margaret Hayward (2023). DOI: 10.1093/oso/9780198894643.003.0014

as well as a new emphasis on innovation and perfectionism. Apple's structure was transformed through a strong centralization that personalized and 'quasi-privatized' the corporation. It became the corporate counterpart of a private company run by an owner-manager with micromanaging tendencies. This analogy sums up notable features of the Jobs-led Apple that have often been recounted. For instance, Jobs led a corporation that met his 'requirement that things be done his way'.[2] And he 'micromanaged to a shockingly high degree', particularly in such areas as product development—where he was 'maniacally focused on technical and design issues'.[3] His micromanaging tendencies were encouraged by the harsh fact that Apple's decline had reduced its workforce to fewer than 7,000 employees. Apple was therefore the corporate counterpart of a *medium-scale* private company run by a micromanaging owner-manager who exercised pervasive personal control.

The chapter's third section looks at how Apple went through more upheavals and a redevelopment a few years later. The 2000/1 recession pushed Apple back into decline, but this was followed by a new stage of redevelopment in 2001–3. This second stage of redevelopment was achieved by using a different tool from the tool kit. Jobs had discerned that a diversifying reorientation of the product range was the appropriate rational means. Apple diversified into making a portable music-player, the iPod, which was later linked to an online iTunes Music Store. Thanks to the iPod-iTunes combination, the second stage of redevelopment had reoriented Apple into a music and mobile-tech company as well as a computer corporation. After this second remedial renewal, the firm seemed to have regained its prospects for a bright future.

Yet there would be still another stage of redeveloping just a few years later, in 2005–7. The chapter's fourth and fifth sections examine this further stage, where again Jobs used the diversification tool. He had envisioned that Apple's iPod would soon be outmoded by the creation of music-playing mobile phones. And he solved the problem by proactively diversifying into mobile phones, unveiling the iPhone in 2007. He had carried out a third stage of redevelopment, which reoriented Apple into a mobile-tech rather than computer corporation. In addition, the diversifying reorientation had included the cyberspace dimension, as the iTunes platform added an App Store that sold software apps on behalf of third-party app developers. So the third stage of redevelopment had been very successful and given the firm a very bright future. When Jobs died in 2011, Apple had over 50,000 employees and the highest share-market value of any corporation in the high-tech sector of the economy. By 2021, Apple's value had gone beyond $2 trillion and was the highest in the world.

The final section shifts the focus to a different corporation, Google, and to diversifying that emerged from development rather than from *re*developing. Here the diversification was a developmental decision shaped by the rational method of strategic calculation. It led to Google diversifying into mobile-phone software in 2005, by acquiring the Android start-up, and then launching a mobile phone in 2008. Although the latter was not successful, the diversification into Android software has proved to be a huge success for the corporation and for the mobile-phone industry. Furthermore, a leader's-eye view of the diversification has been provided by Eric Schmidt's co-authored *How Google Works*.

The present chapter is dominated, however, by Steve Jobs. He belonged to a dying breed that was eulogized in his 'Think Different' advertising campaign.

Here's to the crazy ones. The misfits. The rebels. The troublemakers. The round pegs in the square holes. The ones who see things differently. They're not fond of rules. And they have no respect for the status quo. You can quote them, disagree with them, glorify or vilify them. About the only thing you can't do is ignore them. Because they change things. They invent. They imagine. They heal. They explore. They create. They inspire. They push the human race forward. Maybe they have to be crazy … We make tools for these kinds of people. While some see them as the crazy ones, we see genius. Because the people who are crazy enough to think they can change the world, are the ones who do.[4]

Jobs commissioned this campaign and message in 1997, when he had been crazy enough to take on the leadership of Apple and attempt to redevelop the corporation that he had left in 1985.

Jobs Redevelops Apple in the Late 1990s

During the dozen years since Jobs's departure, Apple had been challenged by new competition from PCs and Microsoft software. New companies were efficiently making 'cloned' versions of the IBM PC, as described in Chapter 13. These PC clones were equipped with powerful Intel microprocessors and with Microsoft's new Windows software, which had user-friendly features similar to those pioneered by the OS (operating-system) software in Apple's Macintosh 'Mac' computer. By the 1990s, Apple had to 'compete with dozens of vendors selling Intel-based PC clones running variations of Microsoft's Windows, each more Mac-like than ever'.[5]

The corporation's market share, revenue, profitability, and share price were therefore spiralling downwards. Market share, for instance, had declined from 20 per cent to 8 per cent in the ten years to 1993, and three years later was down to only 4 per cent.[6] The CEO who had pushed Jobs out was himself replaced in 1993, and his successor was in turn replaced in 1996. With Apple now in some danger of bankruptcy, a well-known member of its board of directors, Gil Amelio, was appointed as turnaround CEO. He did not last long, however, and in September 1997 Jobs was 'crazy' enough to take on the role of CEO and the task of redeveloping Apple.

However, Jobs had three major advantages that helped him redevelop this corporation. The most interesting advantage is that he had the extra authority of a truly charismatic leader, as is discussed in detail in Chapter 15.[7] His charismatic status arose from having been a co-founder of Apple and from having re-established himself as a successful business leader after he had left Apple in 1985. (His NeXT software company had recently been acquired for a gratifying amount and he continued to be the renowned leader of the computer-animation firm Pixar.) A second major advantage was that Apple had been reduced in size to little more than a medium-scale American firm. Even before Jobs took charge, the corporation was going through a downsizing that reduced the workforce to fewer than 7,000, which was far smaller than the 300,000 employees at Lou Gerstner's IBM in Chapter 13.[8] The company's smaller scale made it easier for Jobs to carry out cultural and structural transformations, especially a restructuring that helped him micromanage the firm.

Jobs had the third major advantage of inheriting a cost-cutting turnaround programme that was well underway. He was not taking over a firm close to bankruptcy that needed its new leader to start a drastic turnaround, as when Lee Iacocca took over Chrysler (Chapter 12). Jobs's predecessor as CEO, Amelio, had staved off the threat of bankruptcy and was already pursuing an extensive cost-cutting turnaround.[9] The main part of this turnaround was a massive reduction in Apple's labour costs. The workforce had already been cut back from over 15,000 employees to fewer than 11,000 in 1993–5.[10] More reductions were needed, though, to match Apple's spiralling decline in market share, revenue, and profitability. Amelio's CFO (chief financial officer) Fred Anderson therefore aimed 'to eventually eliminate fully half of its eleven thousand full-time employees' through lay-offs that 'would come in three waves over the next two years'.[11] Similarly, there were dramatic cuts in inventory, and the product range was simplified.[12] However, Amelio realized that money had to be spent on such crucial projects as upgrading the OS software and in fact he spent over $400 million to acquire Jobs's software company NeXT.[13] This was how Jobs returned to Apple. Amelio asked in the late 1996 NeXT negotiations that he return to Apple as an advisor; Jobs agreed to take on a part-time advisory role that would leave him free to continue leading his Pixar company.[14]

By mid-1997 Apple's board had decided to remove Amelio from the post of CEO. After his resignation in July, Apple was run by CFO Anderson and by Jobs as an advisor with a seat on the board. In August, Jobs showed that he was the *de facto* leader of Apple. He reorganized the board, deciding who stayed, who departed, and who would be the replacements.[15] In the following month, he agreed to the board's request that he become CEO. But he insisted that he still be unpaid and part-time, and that his title be 'interim-CEO'.[16]

The new CEO continued his predecessor's turnaround programme. For Apple had just posted an annual loss of more than $800 million and was only halfway through what Amelio had envisaged as a three-year turnaround.[17] Hence Jobs completed the planned cutbacks in the workforce. In early 1998, the third wave of planned lay-offs took the firm down to some 6,700 full-time employees.[18] Jobs also continued the simplification of Apple's product range. He shut down the product division that had been making desktop printers.[19] And he drastically simplified Apple's multitudinous range of computer products. Despite earlier simplifications, this product range still included many different lines and models of desktops and laptops, aimed at professional use by businesses or home use by consumers.[20] In September 1997, Jobs refocused this range on just four products: a (1) desktop and (2) laptop for professional business use, plus a (3) desktop and (4) laptop for home use by consumers.[21] Furthermore, these four products would be upgraded replacements for earlier models and indeed all four products were still under development. The new professional desktop and laptop models were in fact projects that had been backed by Amelio and his technology lieutenant, Ellen Hancock, one of the first women to be a corporation's CTO (chief technology officer), who had left Apple when Amelio resigned.[22] The two Amelio-Hancock computers were unveiled by Apple in November 1997. Aimed at business customers, the desktop Power Mac and laptop PowerBook proved to be lucrative as well as popular. Their high price and large profit margin ensured that Apple was back in the black by April 1998.[23]

Apple's turnaround was completed, and its redevelopment had begun. Jobs began redeveloping even while engaged in the turnaround phase, as Iacocca had done at Chrysler. Unlike Iacocca, though, Jobs used the transformational rather than reorienting pair of tools in the redeveloper's tool kit. Like Gerstner at IBM, Jobs discerned that cultural and structural transformations were the appropriate rational means in the circumstances that he was facing.

His cultural transformation was displayed by the iMac consumer desktop unveiled in May 1998. The iMac's technology had come largely from the Amelio-Hancock Power Mac computer, but the industrial design of the iMac was radically new and reflected the shift to a Jobs-era culture. For instance, the new computer had a translucent blue plastic exterior that let the consumer see the inner workings of the machine. The design was 'a cosmetic standout that, for the first time in years, gave the personal computer some personality'.[24]

The iMac therefore displayed a cultural transformation that emphasized innovation and distinctive design. The new desktop computer's design served to 'differentiate Apple from the "box" crowd—the Dells and Compaqs and HPs and IBMs' who made the blandly uniform PCs.[25] Such uniformity had led to the PCs being commoditized, and pushed down to the lowest price and profit margin by the competition among PC-makers. Apple, though, could set a higher price than the PC-makers, and reap a higher profit, because its new computer had a distinctive personality. So the Jobs cultural transformation would have a directly beneficial effect on Apple's bottom line. 'Apple was able to maintain a huge profit margin [on its iMacs] while other computer makers were commoditized'.[26]

Furthermore, the iMac's success was partly due to the *structural* transformation carried out by Jobs. He had discerned that Apple needed to centralize its administrative structure in order to make the most of its unique asset and competitive advantage—the genius of Steve Jobs. A highly centralized and personalized structure would give CEO Jobs the opportunity to use his gifts in any area. In particular, he would be able to dominate the product and marketing areas that were his special fields of expertise and were vital to the success of Apple. Hence the structural transformation enabled Jobs to exercise a pervasive personal control over the firm and to micromanage the key activities of marketing and product development.

His micromanaging of the iMac's product development was very evident. He set the direction, pressured for results, approved/rejected ideas, and added some ideas of his own.[27] For instance, he ordered that the iMac technology be upgraded with 'a bigger hard drive and an optical drive', and he agreed to the upgraded hardware being 'based on the [Power Mac] G3 desktop, a machine for professionals that had been in the pipeline before Jobs took over and had just been released'.[28] The iMac therefore went forward as a mixture of Amelio-Hancock technology and Jobs-era industrial design.

The new leader's micromanagement of marketing involved more than just the iMac. In July 1997, he had persuaded a gifted advertising agency to compete for Apple's account and furthermore he had arranged for the agency to propose an advertising campaign aimed at reminding people what was distinctive about the Apple brand.[29] The advertising would celebrate 'not what the computers could do, but what creative people could do with the computers'.[30] This was the origin of Apple's 1997 'Think Different' campaign, highlighting the contributions made by such famous innovators as Einstein and Picasso. The campaign helped Apple to sell its new Power Macs, which were targeted at the sorts of businesses 'that could tolerate and even celebrate "Think Different"'.[31]

In turn, the message Think Different provided a very apt background to Apple's launch of the distinctively designed iMac in mid-1998. And Jobs had already given the iMac its distinctive name, whose letter 'i' signified Internet-friendliness as well as an I/me aspect that chimed with the Think Different message.[32] Finally, Jobs gave the iMac one of his carefully stage-managed product presentations. This was 'a new kind of theatre' in which he unveiled and displayed a new product to an auditorium of employees, technology media, and Apple aficionados.[33] Such product debuts were the most public examples of him micromanaging—and showing his genius.

Jobs had therefore carried out a structural transformation that had similarly beneficial effects to his cultural transformation. The next section will look at the two 1997/8 transformations in more detail and show how they intermeshed in a high-fashion style of management. More importantly, it will point to their success in remedially renewing a corporation that had been in decline.

Culturally and Structurally Transforming

The cultural transformation carried out by Jobs had two prominent features that increased its chances of having a major and lasting impact. One of these features was the role played by 'routinized charisma', and the other was the role given to a particular unit of the firm, namely the industrial-design unit. By giving it a leading role, Jobs showed his capability in using the cultural tool in the redeveloper's tool kit. However, the role played by routinized charisma in this case seems more like a by-product of his charismatic status as the extraordinary leader of Apple.

The concept of routinized charisma can readily be applied to his leadership of Apple. For instance, Kahney referred to the way in which Jobs had turned:

his personality traits into Apple's business processes. This process is known as the 'routinization of charisma', a phrase coined by the German sociologist Max Weber in a classic study of the sociology of religion. Weber was interested in what happens to religious movements after the passing of their charismatic founders … their charisma and message must be 'routinized' if the movement is to survive. Their teachings and methods must be institutionalized, becoming the basis of new traditions. In business, the routinization of charisma is the process of turning a charismatic business leader's personality traits into a business method.[34]

Kahney identified Jobs's personality traits as being his passion for innovation and his 'perfectionism and attention to detail'.[35] These traits were institutionalized in Apple's culture. There was a new emphasis on the value of innovation and on taking a perfectionist attitude to products and marketing. In addition, Jobs gave the culture his focus on aesthetic and distinctive design, which was soon institutionalized in the values and attitudes of Apple's product-development process.[36]

The key instance of his focus on design was his exalting of Apple's industrial-design unit and its leader, Jony Ive. The young British designer led a relatively small unit, which had recruited a gifted group of industrial designers from around the world. Jobs shifted the unit into the main headquarters complex, classified the unit off-limits to other employees, and constantly visited the designers to look at how their work was progressing.[37] He and Ives developed a strong working relationship that was expressed, for instance, in their competitive perfectionism. 'Each wanted to beat the other in catching minor flaws that would make an Apple product fall short of the greatness to which they both aspired' as product perfectionists.[38] Ive became indeed Jobs's key lieutenant and confidante as the new CEO pursued his self-proclaimed objective: 'to make great products'.[39]

The personal was becoming the structural though, as Ive and his unit were given an increasingly important role within Apple. His unit of some twenty industrial designers was the main source of the iMac computer's distinctive features.[40] Organizationally, too, the designers had the leading role in Apple's product development. Their unit 'led product development and engineers worked to fulfil its demands' about hardware.[41] Similarly, Jobs overruled engineers who objected to an innovative iMac design feature that would increase the costs of manufacturing. 'There was a new way of doing things: Design came first'.[42]

A new and high-fashion cultural perspective was being implanted into Apple. Comparing the corporation to a high-fashion firm may seem far-fetched, but the comparison highlights Apple's new emphases on innovation and perfectionism, and on aesthetic and distinctive design. The comparison highlights, too, the *intermeshing* of cultural and structural transformations, as when Jobs gave Ive's design unit such an influential role in the corporation. The intermeshing is most evident if Jobs is compared to a high-fashion maestro who is owner-manager of his fashion house. Such a maestro would be expected to implant and enforce a high-fashion cultural perspective, even if this meant micromanaging and leading in an autocratic manner. Indeed, the cultural perspective would *legitimate* him managing and leading in this manner—another aspect of the intermeshing of cultural and structural transformations.

This legitimation is also an example of Jobs's capability in using the structural tool: in structurally transforming Apple. And it sheds a new light on some of the apparently negative characteristics of his leadership. He has been described as 'a different breed of CEO', who could exhibit 'narcissism, whimsy, disregard for the feelings of others', and could 'hog all the credit for a team's job well done'.[43] Yet this behaviour was almost to be expected of any CEO who was comparable to the maestro of a high-fashion house.[44]

Another example of his capability in using the structural tool is his centralization of Apple. As the previous section argued, his structural transformation was aimed at reaping the most benefit from his firm's unique asset—Steve Jobs. Apple would certainly have reaped fewer benefits from this asset if the firm had not been strongly centralized. For in the Amelio era, the CEO's orders had been viewed as 'mere suggestions that would often go unheeded' at the divisional level of the firm or by its array of committees and bureaucracies.[45] This weakness was the target of a sweeping centralization by Jobs. The divisional fiefdoms lost their accounting independence and lost other functions to new, specialized departments or groups that operated across the whole firm.[46] Bureaucracy and committees were outlawed; no longer could they ignore, modify, or delay central directives from the CEO.[47] Apple was indeed structurally transformed. The firm became a very top-down organization, lacking organizational checks and controls, and with a board of directors that 'doted' on its CEO.[48] After this centralizing transformation, Apple's administrative structure would be unable to impede the genius leader's pervasive personal control.

There was of course some institutionalization of his personal control and micromanagement. His two main concerns—products and marketing—were each handled in weekly three-hour meetings. The brainstorming meetings about products were held on Monday mornings, as is described in Chapter 6. The marketing equivalent was a Wednesday-afternoon 'freewheeling meeting' of Jobs and 'his top agency, marketing, and communications people to kick around messaging strategy' for the firm.[49] The meeting also gave Jobs an opportunity for some perfectionist micromanaging, as here he checked any and all Apple advertisements before they appeared in public.[50] His new structure's institutionalizing did not include administrative hierarchy, though, and he would communicate directly with talented employees instead of following bureaucratic procedures.[51] Similarly, he favoured 'rivalries between executives, encouraging people with egos to advance ideas that he could pick from to make great products. He could keep those duelling personalities in check' and connect 'all the different areas of their businesses'.[52]

> The CEO wasn't preoccupied with Harvard Business School concepts of organizational behavior. The company ... operated like a starfish. He sat at the intersection of legs that focused on excellence in marketing, design, engineering, and supply-chain management. He would crawl out to the end of a leg when he wished to and get personally involved.[53]

Hence the overall effect of his structural transformation was to personalize and 'quasi-privatize' the Apple Computer corporation. The firm was transformed into the corporate equivalent of a medium-scale private company run by an owner-manager who micromanaged any activities that stirred his interest.

The structural transformation was vindicated, though, by its success. In 1998/9, Apple's profitability jumped back to pre-decline levels, with annual profits of first $308 million and then over $600 million.[54] More significantly, Apple Computer doubled its overall market share from 3 to 6 per cent in the first year and then doubled its share of the consumer desktop market, reaching more than 11 per cent.[55] The latter success was due to the continuing success of the iMac. Over two million iMacs were sold in 1998/9 and indeed it was the top-selling desktop in the world.[56]

The iMac's success was due to a new model that appeared in early 1999 and epitomized Apple's cultural and structural transformations. This new model was innovative not so much in its technology as in its aesthetic and distinctive design: it had a plastic exterior that came in a range of different colours. And the design innovation was due not just to Ive's design unit but also to the micromanaging CEO. Jobs had not responded well—'you suck'—to the initial colour options presented by the design unit's colour expert, but a reconsidered presentation met with the leader's favour: 'I really like these colours, they remind me of Life Savers'.[57] Computer consumers were therefore given a choice of five fruity colours, namely blueberry, tangerine, lime, grape, or strawberry. This multicoloured model of the iMac 'introduced the concept of fashion' to the computer industry.[58]

The multicoloured iMac was just one of several Apple design successes in 1999. Existing models were redesigned or replaced—and exciting new models appeared.[59] The Power Mac G3 professional desktop was redesigned, with blue and white colouring, and was later replaced by the graphite-coloured G4. The PowerBook G3 professional laptop was redesigned and soon after was joined by a new consumer laptop, the clamshell-shaped iBook. With Apple also enjoying a financial and market revival, the firm seemed set for a bright new future. Its leader had clearly succeeded in remedially renewing the corporation.

The redevelopment had not met all of the leader's goals, though. His emphasis on innovation had not yet brought forth a new type of product.

'When we returned to Apple', Steve told me around this time, 'our industry was in a coma. There was not a lot of innovation. At Apple we're working hard to get that innovation kickstarted again. The rest of the PC industry reminds me of Detroit in the seventies. Their cars were boats on wheels. Since then Chrysler innovated by inventing the mini-van and popularizing the Jeep [SUV] ... Near-death experiences can help one see more clearly sometimes'.[60]

Yet Apple's near-death experience in 1996/7 had not led to innovation, certainly not to anything like the minivan innovation that emerged from Chrysler's near-death experience in 1979. Apple would suffer another of these traumatic experiences—unexpected and undeserved—before the firm went on to diversify into a new type of product and to achieve a second stage of redevelopment.

Jobs Reorients in the 2000s by Diversifying

The second stage of Apple's redeveloping arose after an unexpected external event pushed the corporation back into decline. This unlucky event was the recession triggered in 2000 by the dot-com crash on the stock market, mentioned in several other chapters. 'One thousand new Internet companies died, and even the most established companies in the [Silicon] Valley were temporarily crippled', as 'purchases of computer equipment fell off a cliff'.[61]

Yet 2000 had begun well for Jobs and Apple. In January, Jobs announced that he was no longer just an 'interim' CEO. He was therefore granted ten million stock options by the board of directors, but his CEO salary would continue to be merely a dollar a year.[62] In January, too, Jobs unveiled Apple's advanced OS X (OS 10) operating system, the software breakthrough the firm had been seeking as far back as the pre-Jobs, Amelio-Hancock era. A fully debugged version of OS X was still more than a year away, but the 'radical new operating system' would be the superb software basis for new-generation iMacs—and diversifications that were yet to be imagined.[63]

After his good start to the year, though, maestro Jobs seems to have become over-confident. He was certainly self-indulgent about a favourite design project, namely the 'Cube' G4 professional desktop computer that was unveiled in July.[64] The cube-like design was aesthetically stunning. The Cube computer indeed 'wound up in the Museum of Modern Art. Unfortunately, it didn't wind up in many homes or offices': the computer achieved only a third of its projected sales.[65] Its lack of market success was due not only to expense-versus-performance issues but also to the Cube's trade-off between aesthetics and engineering convenience.[66] Jobs had let his high-fashion perspective dominate, rather than supplement, the high-tech and business perspectives of Apple's culture.

This was a bad time for Apple to suffer a decline in rational leadership. In the second half of 2000, the recession arrived and started to push Apple back into decline. The recession's biggest effect on Apple was the downturn in businesses' demand for computers. Business sales were financially very important to Apple, and its Power Mac professional computer was still the firm's most important product.[67] Jobs's shrewd marketing had 'targeted the Power Macs at the new, more entrepreneurial class of small businesses emerging with the rise of the Internet economy: engineers, architects, publishers, advertising agencies, website designers, and so on'.[68] However, this class of small businesses was particularly badly hit by the dot-com crash and the recession in the high-tech sector. Apple therefore made a loss of $195 million in the final quarter of the year, while quarterly sales were lower than when Jobs had arrived at Apple.[69] Not surprisingly, the stock market was unimpressed. The firm's share price fell to below $15 by December, compared to the $60 it had been earlier in the year.[70] Apple was a corporation in decline—again.

Another bout of redeveloping was required. And Apple was fortunate that its leader's rationality had soon revived after his Cube-computer debacle. He quickly initiated a second stage of rational redevelopment. Indeed, his redeveloping was underway as early as 2001, even though the recession was worsening and was reducing Apple's revenue to less than half its pre-recession level. In May the annual-revenue figure hit bottom at $5 billion, and by September it had risen only marginally to $5.4 billion.[71] The firm was losing not just business customers—now it was losing some of its share of the consumer market.[72]

Jobs was reorienting Apple's product range, though, by diversifying into a new type of product. He had discerned that the appropriate rational means of redevelopment was a diversification into portable music-playing devices. This would reduce Apple's reliance on business customers and would give Apple a new type of product—music—to offer the consumers who bought its Macintosh computers. Jobs 'started pushing for a portable music player in the fall of 2000', perhaps as early as September, and he later admitted to feeling like 'a dope' because he had been so slow in responding to the rise of digital-music technology.[73] Since July, however, Apple had been making some digital-music progress. Some music-management software had been acquired and during the next several months was developed into iTunes software, which would play a crucial role in the music-player diversification.[74]

Jobs was not pioneering an innovative new product. The digital-music sector was laden with portable music-playing devices, though Jobs intended Apple's version to be superior to any other on the market.[75] His new device's speedy development was described in Chapter 6. During 2001, Apple's product-development team created a mobile digital-music player that was more portable and user-friendly than any of its rivals. The iPod's pocket-sized console was equipped with small headphones and a long list of digitally stored songs, as many as 1,000 which were selected by each user to suit his or her musical preferences. Consumers selected their iPod's list of songs by downloading each song from the Internet through their iMac desktop and its iTunes software. The connection between the iMac and this new device was underlined by calling the latter an 'iPod', as the technological term 'pod' meant a detachable, functionally specialized part, such as a spacecraft's landing or escape pod.[76]

The iPod was aesthetically as well as technically superior to its rivals. When the device was first released in October 2001, there were some fifty rival designs available on the market.[77] The iPod, however, was stylistically distinctive and aesthetically superior, thanks to the innovations by Ives and his industrial-design team. They had faced opposition within Apple to some innovations, such as having 'white rather than the more commonplace black headphones. Despite these competing views, Jobs supported the proposals' coming from Ive's design team.[78] Maestro Jobs added his own design 'proposals' too. In particular, he vetoed the idea of having a separate on-off switch.[79]

Jobs best showed his capability as a diversifier, though, when he made the iPod compatible with PCs' Windows software. 'Initially, the iPod was conceived as Mac-only. Jobs wanted to use it as bait to snare Windows users. He hoped it would be an incentive to switch to the [i]Mac'.[80] Eventually he changed his mind, after a long debate within Apple. 'Jobs introduced the first Windows-compatible iPod in July 2002', but the 'real change occurred nearly a year later', in May 2003, when the third-generation iPod appeared with a plug-in connection that was compatible with standard Windows PCs.[81] Like any capable diversifier, Jobs had been willing to listen to debate and change his mind about how to make the most of the new product.[82]

The new approach led to an explosive acceleration in sales of the iPod. Only a million were sold in the second part of 2003, but sales increased to eight million in 2004, and then to over twenty-five million in 2005.[83] The sales had been boosted partly by Jobs capably creating a product 'pyramid', comparable to those created by high-fashion houses and described in Chapter 9. He extended the pyramid in 2004 through the launch of a 'Mini' iPod. The Mini version was suitable for jogging or the gym, came in a range of colours, and was: 'the first iPod that people started wearing on their bodies, outside their pockets, with a strap or a clip. Some treated it like an [apparel or garment] accessory, a piece of fashion jewellery'.[84] A new mini version, the Nano, appeared in 2005 and was very popular, becoming Apple's best-selling product.[85] That year, too, the product pyramid was extended downwards by introducing a much cheaper iPod, called the Shuffle. Eventually there were 'more than half a dozen different models, from the bare-bones Shuffle to the high-end video iPod', and 'priced at every $50 price point between $100 and $350'.[86] The product-pyramid approach is therefore very evident with the iPod, as maestro Jobs extended the new product category in a typically high-fashion manner.

Jobs's key initiative, however, was extending the product pyramid into a new dimension—cyberspace. His new product category included online selling of music downloads and furthermore a cyberspace platform for third-party sellers of this music. By the mid-2000s, iPod users were buying songs online from third-party sellers—the big music companies—who were selling the songs through the iTunes Music Store. Apple took a commission from each sale and passed on the rest of the proceeds to the music company that owned the song. The new venture was described by a writer on Apple as 'revolutionary':

> [It] lets customers quickly find, purchase, and download music for 99 cents per song. Other competitive online music services ... failed to gain popularity because they required paying subscription fees, had unsophisticated user interfaces, placed severe limits on what you could do with your downloaded music, and offered only a limited number of songs ... Since Apple was able to obtain the cooperation of 'The Big Five' music companies—BMG, EMI, Sony Music, Universal, and Warner—the iTunes Music Store featured over 200,000 songs.[87]

The Big Five music companies, however, had not wanted to be third-party sellers through the iTunes Music Store, and so had to be persuaded by Jobs to cooperate with the new venture.[88]

By making these music deals, Jobs had personally carried out some brilliant product development. The iPod had been developed into a more innovative and effective digital-music player, whose users now had online access to a vast array of songs for selection, purchase, downloading, storage, and unlimited playing. Jobs had also gone beyond the e-commerce models of eBayism and Amazonism, as he had created a wholly cyberspace business. The iTunes Music Store was selling digital, not physical, goods and they were being sent online to consumers, not physically delivered to them.

The iPod and its iTunes extension was also a breakthrough product, opening up opportunities for rapid and large-scale growth. By mid-2004, Apple's revenue was already back to pre-recession levels, and the next quarter's revenue was the best since Jobs had returned to Apple.[89] The firm then went on to years of rapid growth in 2005/6. Annual revenue increased by 68 per cent to reach $14 billion in 2005, and annual sales revenue reached $19 billion in fiscal year 2006.[90] More significantly, the iPod-iTunes product was a breakthrough into the mobile-tech world and the e-commerce world of cyberspace platforms: new worlds that would be conquered in the next stage of Apple's redevelopment.

However, the second stage of redevelopment had already been successful enough to rescue Apple from the recessionary decline of 2000/1. Apple was enjoying a bright new future as a music as well as computer corporation. Thanks to the 'skyrocket-ing' sales of the iPod in 2005, the iPod-iTunes product 'accounted for 45 per cent of that year's revenue'.[91] A brilliantly capable diversification by Jobs had led to a very successful remedial renewal of his corporation.

Apple's Third Stage: From iPod to iPhone

Apple entered a third stage of redevelopment soon after the 2001–3 stage. The new stage took from 2005 to 2007, and once again Jobs used the diversification tool in the redeveloper's tool kit. Apple internally diversified into a new product category and again did so by developing a new mobile device. This time the product cate-gory was mobile phones, and the new device was called the 'iPhone'. The unveiling of the iPhone in 2007 was accompanied by a change in the firm's name, from Apple Computer to simply Apple.[92] The name change indicated that the computer aspect of the corporation was no longer dominant. Apple is best described in the late 2000s as primarily a *mobile-tech* corporation, with mobile-phone products as well as mobile music-playing products.[93] In the third stage of his redevelopment, Jobs had 'gone mobile', like a fashion maestro 'going luxury' by extending a product pyramid so broadly that the haute-couture fashion house has become a luxury-goods company.[94]

Yet the third stage of Apple's redevelopment begs the question of why bother. The second stage had been successful: solving Apple's problems after its 2000/1 decline and giving the firm a bright new future. Why risk diversifying again, so soon after a remedial renewal and major diversification into music?

The most likely answer is that Jobs had a vision of doom. He had envisioned that the second phase in the mobile-tech revolution would endanger the iPod. The first phase of the 'mobile revolution' had begun in the mid-1990s with the rise of the basic mobile phone, often called a 'cell' phone, which was merely a wireless phone that was a fully mobile device. This basic mobile phone was very rapidly and widely adopted by consumers in the late 1990s, as is described in Chapter 15. In the 2000s, though, a new phase of the mobile revolution emerged. An increasing number of phones were also miniature computers, stacked with software, and known as 'smartphones'. Their rise to prominence is recounted in Woyke's *The Smartphone: Anatomy of an Industry*. Her classic account appeared in 2014, when the smartphone was defeating the basic mobile phone and pushing it towards extinction: soon any mobile phone would be expected to have 'smart' software and a wide range of apps. Back in the 2000s, however, the smartphone-led second phase of the mobile revolution was still just emerging.

Yet by the mid-2000s Jobs had foreseen that the smartphone posed a grave threat to the iPod. Even before iPod sales skyrocketed in 2005, he had envisioned the danger ahead.

> The conclusion that he had come to: 'The device that can eat our lunch is the cell [mobile] phone'. As he explained to the board, the digital camera market was being decimated now that [mobile] phones were equipped with cameras. The same could happen to the iPod, if phone manufacturers started to build music players into them. 'Everyone carries a phone, so that could render the iPod unnecessary'.[95]

In 2005, his worries led to a joint-venture project by Apple and phone-maker Motorola. An iPod was built into a smartphone developed by Motorola. Although the resulting ROKR phone was unappealing, Jobs did not reassess the phone threat; instead he became convinced that an in-house effort was needed to defeat the threat.[96] Apple started developing its own version of a smartphone, which it later described as 'the best iPod we've ever created'.[97]

This diversification into mobile phones was therefore aimed at an envisioned threat to an earlier diversification, into mobile music-playing products. Hence the mobile-phone diversification was a *proactive* redevelopment—a third stage—aimed at a threat that had not yet appeared. Another unusual feature of the redevelopment is that it arose from the leader's non-rational, charismatic vision of doom or, less dramatically, his visionary sense of foreboding. However, this had become a vision of opportunity, too. Some 800 million mobile phones were sold each year, and the quality of the smartphones did not impress Jobs: he thought they 'stank'.[98] Apple's superb product-development people could surely develop a smartphone that was better than these mediocre products.

Consequently, Jobs was again using the diversification tool, but for charismatic rather than discerning reasons. Later events proved that he had rightly envisioned the need for this diversifying, proactive third stage of redevelopment. It was a charismatic vision, however, rather than a discerning selection of the appropriate rational means of achieving a rational redevelopment. Jobs's rational leadership would instead be displayed by his *capable use* of the diversification tool: he used the tool as capably as when he had diversified into the iPod-iTunes product category.

As with the iPod diversification, Jobs was leapfrogging rather than pioneering. He was not inventing an innovative new product but instead developing a superior version of an existing product: a superior version that was above and beyond anything that other firms were producing. Isaacson has argued that 'the mark of an innovative company is not only that it comes up with new ideas first, but also that it knows how to leapfrog when it finds itself behind'.[99] In the 2000s, though, some observers suggested that Apple's innovativeness had 'less to do with inventing brand-new technologies than taking existing technologies and making them easy to use'.[100] If so, then perhaps Apple's leader was rationally making the best of his firm's abilities, especially when Apple was diversifying into new product areas. Furthermore, Apple was markedly inventive when it came to industrial-design innovations, such as the innovatively designed versions of the iPod.

Design was also an area where Jobs prominently displayed his capability as a diversifier. During the design of the phone diversification the maestro played his usual hands-on role of appraising and being creative. Apple's design team came up with two competing prototypes, but one was dropped after a perfectionist appraisal by Jobs. He noticed that this prototype's 'metal bezel detracted from the screen. The design didn't "defer" to the screen' in the way that had been intended by the designers.[101] The other prototype, too, proved unsatisfactory and so the designers went back to an earlier model that was seen to have hidden or overlooked qualities.[102] This third prospect met requirements. It became the basis for a new design with an innovative dual-purpose display screen and touchscreen, which filled the whole face of the phone.[103] On the way to that final design, maestro Jobs played an important creative role. He wanted the phone's display-touchscreen to be made of a material that could not be scratched: a superstrong variety of glass was the answer—and the glass manufacturer was persuaded by Jobs to meet Apple's requirements.[104] At the last stage of the phone's development, Jobs made an appraisal that epitomized his capability as a diversifier. Late in 2006 he calmly reminded his product developers that the prototype phone was suffering from too many teething problems to be a viable product.[105] He elicited a huge effort that had the phone working properly weeks before its scheduled unveiling to the public in January 2007.

Jobs took on yet another role when he publicly unveiled the phone as the 'iPhone'. He displayed the phone's features in a brilliant presentation to a conference audience. 'Jobs was the ultimate showman', who had 'turned corporate presentations into product theatre', and never more so than with his great display of the iPhone product.[106] He told his audience:

> we're introducing three revolutionary products ... The first one is a wide-screen iPod with touch controls. The second is a revolutionary mobile phone. And the third is a breakthrough Internet communications device. An iPod, a phone, and an Internet communicator ... Are you getting it? These are not three separate devices; this is one device and we are calling it the iPhone.[107]

Here on two occasions he refers to the iPhone as primarily an (advanced) iPod: he still seems focused on protecting his earlier diversification into mobile music-playing products.

In 2007/8, however, the iPhone became more than just a remedy for the threat to his music success. The iPhone became a new breakthrough product that opened up new opportunities for rapid and large-scale growth. Apple therefore experienced another remedial renewal—a third stage of redevelopment—and the firm was given a yet brighter future.

Reorienting a Platform in Cyberspace

The iPhone's success was partly due to Job's reappraisal of the device's potential. He realized that this mobile device's most significant role was to act as a miniaturized personal computer: a more significant role than being just a mobile phone or even an advanced iPod. So Jobs innovatively equipped the iPhone with an apps-selling store in cyberspace, the App Store. The new store was a diversification by the iTunes Music Store platform. And this diversifying reorientation of a platform in cyberspace may have been Jobs's most capable use of the diversification tool.

The iPhone was of course not the first computer-like mobile phone. As noted in the previous section, the software-stacked smartphone was nothing new. The first mobile phone to be advertised as a 'smartphone' had appeared as early as 2000, and a few years later Microsoft had launched a mobile-phone form of Windows software.[108] When Apple's iPhone was unveiled in 2007, though, the device was clearly superior to all other firms' smartphones. Apple had leapfrogged them through software advances as well as such design innovations as the display/touchscreen.[109]

Apple's software experts had endowed the iPhone with a superb operating system. Later called iOS, the software had been developed by miniaturizing the iMac's OS X operating system.[110] So the software experts—whether developers, engineers, or programmers—had been no less important than Apple's industrial-design innovators. Indeed the firm had been fortunate to have not only innovative designers but also high-quality software experts: the highest level of software expertise and creativity is just as rare as its industrial-design counterpart.[111] And the software aspects of a high-tech project can be more of a problem or constraint than the hardware aspects. As Apple had exceptional capability in both hardware and software, the firm could quickly diversify into a new high-tech product category—and leapfrog other firms' versions of this computer-like phone.

Another Apple advantage was its e-commerce cyberspace platform: the iTunes Music Store. As iTunes was already being used for third-party selling of music, why not diversify the platform into third-party selling of software apps? So the iTunes cyberspace platform was reoriented by the diversifying addition of an App Store, catering for iPhone users who wanted to acquire some new apps for their phone.

> [Apple] not only built the App Store tightly into iTunes but also built the store directly into the iPhone, enabling users to quickly discover and enjoy iPhone apps. People simply purchased them with a click—or selected them in the case of free apps—and downloaded them wirelessly over cellular networks or Wi-Fi.[112]

This was a new kind of apps-selling operation, as the nearest equivalent had been phone-maker partnerships with independent app-selling companies. The latter were allowed to operate an app-selling 'storefront' on their partners' smartphones. 'These on-device storefronts let consumers browse and download apps over the air like the App Store, but the latter soon passed them in quality and diversity' of apps for sale.[113] Apple's iTunes diversification had therefore given the iPhone a third area of superiority over existing versions of the smartphone.

Yet the iTunes diversification into apps had been problematic for Jobs. When the iPhone first appeared in 2007, its users had access to three of Google's apps, namely Search, Maps, and YouTube.[114] Other third-party apps, however, had been vetoed by Jobs. 'He didn't want outsiders to create applications for the iPhone that could mess it up, infect it with viruses, or pollute its integrity'.[115] Neither would he listen to board members and senior executives who favoured opening up the iPhone to third-party apps sellers:

> But as soon as the iPhone was launched, he was willing to hear the debate … There were freewheeling discussions at four board meetings. Jobs soon figured out that there was a way to have the best of both worlds. He would permit outsiders to write apps, but they would have to meet strict standards, be tested and approved by Apple, and be sold only through the iTunes store.[116]

So the App Store originated as a compromise solution that met all requirements. By October 2007, Jobs was publicly predicting that hundreds of third-party apps would be available to iPhone users.[117] And in 2008 the iTunes platform opened its App Store for iPhone users.

The App Store quickly expanded its range of merchandise. Initially, it stocked fewer than 600 different apps, but the range had increased to more than ten thousand by the end of 2008.[118] Two years later, the facility was bursting with goods and activity. The Store stocked 300,000 apps, with some 500 million downloads being made each month by the army of iPhone users.[119] And of course an army of apps-developers was using the Store to sell their apps. The iTunes platform had therefore seen a major diversification in its suppliers, when compared to the five big companies who supplied the platform's Music Store. Many thousands of small firms and freelancers were selling their apps through the App Store, and paying Apple a commission or fee of 30 per cent of the proceeds from each sale.[120]

Hence the iTunes diversification into third-party apps had been a great success and shows Jobs at his most capable. He had listened to the opposing arguments and had come up with a compromise that added a cyberspace dimension to his new product category. This was not the first time he had shown such objectivity. As an earlier section recounted, he had changed his mind about making the iPod compatible with Windows.

In the iPhone apps case, his objectivity had ensured that the iPhone was leading the second phase of the mobile revolution. For thanks to its apps and great iOS operating system, the iPhone was showing the world that a phone could be 'a true handheld computer' and indeed the most mobile, personal, and intimate of computers.[121] Consequently, the phone form of personal computer posed a serious threat to the older form: the desktop and laptop PCs. As Chapter 10 noted, shipments of PCs had levelled off by 2008 and would start to decline in the 2010s.

Not all phone-makers, however, had seen that the times were changing. For instance, Nokia was still viewing smartphones as primarily phones rather than computers. Nokia experts therefore underestimated the iPhone, dismissing the initial iPhone model as 'a pocket computer with poor phone features' and without an up-to-date 3G (third-generation) wireless network.[122] But the iPhone's communication features were quickly upgraded in later models, while Nokia was unable to upgrade its smartphones' software to match the 'pocket computer' iPhone. By 2010, 'Nokia's sales in the highly profitable smartphone market were struggling, while Apple, with an improved product and increased distribution, had seen sales of its iPhone soar'.[123]

The iPhone's success showed that the third stage of redevelopment had been worth the effort. Apple had been given a yet brighter future as a mobile-tech firm, as was evidenced by its launch of the mobile iPad tablet computer in early 2010. Equipped with iOS software and iPhone-like hardware, the iPad tablet had immediate success, with first-year sales of over twenty million.[124] The iPad's success increased the shift towards a predominantly mobile-tech product range. By 2011, Apple's annual sales included some seventy-two million iPhones, forty-two million iPod music-players, and thirty-two million iPad tablets, but only seventeen million desktop or laptop computers.[125] Furthermore, the iPad started another phase of the mobile revolution, the tablet phase, and was soon joined by other tablet computers, such as Amazon's Kindle Fire tablet. The iPad's impact therefore confirmed that Apple was leading the way in the high-tech sector and that the firm was a globally iconic corporation.

More prosaically, the third stage of redevelopment had boosted Apple's growth and financial position. In particular, the iPhone helped Apple cope with the unexpected 2008/9 recession. In 2008, Apple's sales revenue increased markedly to $37.5 billion and profits increased to $6 billion.[126] Sales and profits were up again in 2009, and then in 2010 the soaring iPhone sales boosted the firm's sales revenue to over $65 billion, with profits reaching $14 billion.[127] So Apple was growing into a sizeable corporation. By the time Jobs retired as CEO in 2011, Apple had some 50,000 employees, compared to the fewer than 7,000 when he took over as 'interim' CEO.[128] The growth in revenue and stock-market value had been even more remarkable. By 2011, Apple had annual sales of $108 billion and a stock-market value of over $300 billion, much higher than that of any other high-tech corporation.[129] Apple was now a leading stock on Wall Street, despite Jobs having treated investors 'with something between ambivalence and contempt'.[130]

The corporation's growth in size and complexity had been an extra burden for Jobs during his third-stage redevelopment in 2005–7. Apple had been 'split into separate iPod and Macintosh divisions in 2004'.[131] And the firm was developing an extensive administrative hierarchy. Eventually, there would be some ninety vice-president-level executives as well as the group of senior vice-presidents who formed the executive team.[132] Yet Jobs was such a capable diversifier that he was still able to lead Apple in his characteristic manner, similar to that of a micromanaging owner-manager of a medium-scale private company.[133] He continued to lead the brainstorming Monday-morning meetings described in Chapter 6. And his hands-on appraising and creative role in designing the iPhone has been recounted not only in the previous section but also in a recent book about Apple.

> Jobs had had a designer's eye. He had once walked past the prototype of a forthcoming iPhone and barked, 'What is this shit?' The curvature and polish of the prototype had been changed only slightly during manufacturing, but he had caught the difference with a glance and been repulsed. He had demanded that it be fixed.[134]

Jobs was therefore still comparable to the maestro owner-manager of a high-fashion house, which was the comparison made in earlier sections' accounts of how he led the firm during its first and second stages of redevelopment.

When the 56-year-old Jobs died of cancer in 2011, he was one of the few leaders who had taken a corporation through three stages of redevelopment. The declining Apple Computer had been redeveloped into a dominant and iconic mobile-tech corporation. During this redevelopment, Jobs had shown exceptional capability in using the tools of redevelopment, and indeed he must rank as the greatest ever leader of the redevelopment, the remedial renewal, of a corporation or any other kind of organization.

Compared with Developing: *How Google Works*

Apple was not the only firm that diversified into smartphone technology in the mid-2000s. Google made a similar diversification, though from a very different background. Google was not a mobile-tech or computer corporation but rather an e-commerce firm that made its money from search-related online advertising. And Google was not a twenty-year-old corporation that had already been through two stages of redevelopment.

Google was instead a young firm that was developing into a corporation. As Chapters 8 and 13 recounted, the firm's rapid development had been based on advertising revenue derived from its search-engine software for searching the Internet. The search engine's inventors, Larry Page and Sergey Brin, had co-founded Google in 1998 and a few years later had created a triple-leadership team by hiring Eric Schmidt as CEO.[135] Their firm became a public company in 2004 and rapidly grew into a corporation, which by 2007 had over 16,000 employees and annual revenue of $16 billion.[136]

During this period of rapid growth, the emerging corporation diversified into smartphones. Unlike Apple's smartphone diversification, this was not solely an internal process. The acquisition of a smartphone software firm was the first step that led on to the internal process of creating and producing Google's equivalent of the iPhone. Unlike the iPhone, Google's smartphone was not commercially successful. However, the phone's Android software became a great success and the rival of the iPhone in the 2010s–20s. So Google's acquisition of the Android software firm is the most prominent example of diversifying through acquisition, whether the corporation is being developed or redeveloped.

As the Android acquisition shows, there were great opportunities to make diversifying acquisitions in the 1990s–2000s. In contrast to later decades, a corporation could readily acquire a firm with such potential as Android. Established in 2003/4, this start-up's eight software experts soon developed the prototype of a new operating system for smartphones.[137] During 2004/5, the software was pitched to smartphone manufacturers, who were told they 'didn't need to spend money on their own proprietary software' because Android could provide something much better.

> Frustrated consumers would flock to phones that worked better. Software developers would rush to write software [apps] for a platform in such demand. A self-reinforcing software ecosystem would be born.[138]

This was not, though, the reason Google acquired the Android start-up in 2005. Rather, Google was aiming to boost its search-advertising revenue and forestall a competitor. From this perspective, the opportunity to acquire Android—and for only $50 million—was one of the best things that ever happened to Google.[139]

Although Google was lucky to have this opportunity, the diversification was a rational development decision shaped by strategic calculation. The firm's leaders were strategically securing a new source of revenue from the mobile revolution and its smartphone apps. By the mid-2000s smartphones had some access to the Internet through browsers and the display of web pages on a phone screen. But 'the browsers were designed to show only the bare bones of a web page's content' and therefore something 'that wouldn't work in these crippled browsers were Google search ads.'[140] Hence Google needed an improvement in smartphone software, so that search ads would 'work' and revenue could be earned from firms who wanted to place these search ads. How could Google ensure that these events occurred? A sound strategy for ensuring that they would occur—and quickly—was to diversify into smartphone technology through an apt acquisition, such as buying the Android start-up and its operating-system software.

This strategy also protected Google from the danger of Microsoft dominating mobile-phone software. Microsoft had been slow to respond to the mobile revolution but Windows Mobile software for phones had appeared by the mid-2000s.[141] The software giant's new interest in mobile phones would likely lead to an improvement in smartphone software and furthermore to some degree of standardization. 'There was no standardization in the industry' and so 'software written for a Samsung phone often wouldn't run on a Motorola phone, which wouldn't run on a Nokia.'[142] Windows Mobile, though, might well become a standard operating system for smartphones. And any degree of standardization posed a threat to Google's prospects for phone search-ad revenue. 'Google executives were convinced that if Windows on mobile devices caught on, Microsoft would interfere with users' access to Google search on those devices in favor of its own search engine.'[143] Then Google would be unable to earn search-ad revenue from these mobile phones and would lose some opportunity to develop a new, mobile-phone source of revenue. So Google had good developmental reasons to be worried about Microsoft, whose Windows Mobile software did indeed become increasingly prominent in 2006/7.[144]

Google's diversification strategy, however, protected the firm against Microsoft domination. By acquiring Android, Google could quickly create software that rivalled Windows Mobile and also forestalled a Microsoft standardization of mobile-phone software. In fact the Android operating system might itself become standard software, which would be the ultimate vindication of the diversification strategy.

A leader's-eye view of the strategy is provided by *How Google Works*, a memoir co-authored by Google CEO Schmidt. 'Our hope was that Android could become the software guts for phones built by companies like Motorola, Nokia, or Samsung.'[145] Preferably, Android would become the 'software guts' of all the phones built by all the leading companies. To speed up this standardization, Google adopted the 'strategic tactic' of making Android an open system: freely available to all phone-makers to use and modify as they wanted and without paying fees or royalties.[146] Google co-founder Brin had been the first to suggest:

Why not make it [Android] open? Keeping Android open would help us scale quickly in the highly fragmented mobile operating system space. So that's what we did ... Android stayed open, grew extraordinarily, and helped Google smoothly navigate the platform shift from PC to mobile by giving us a platform that was highly complementary to search (more people online with smartphones means more people searching more often).[147]

Google's leaders had therefore rightly calculated that Android would quickly become a standard system if offered to phone-makers as an open as well as superior operating system. And Android's success had ensured that Google's search ads were as prevalent on smartphones as on personal computers.

However, this success came only after Google had backed the Android-using G1 phone, launched in 2008. The new phone proved that Android software was superior to the Windows Mobile operating system. Backing the G1, though, brought Google into head-on competition—phone versus phone—with the 2007-launched Apple iPhone. The Apple phone's software included three licensed Google apps: Search, Maps, and YouTube. But Google was 'worried about being overly dependent on Apple for mobile traffic', and anyway G1 versus iPhone competition was moderated by the two firms' 'different business priorities for their smartphones'.[148] Apple's priority was selling its phones; Google's priority was selling phone search ads and other apps ads. Hence the three Google apps continued to be part of iPhone software even after the G1 was launched. For Apple still wanted its phone to have the most popular apps, while Google still wanted its ads to be shown on the most popular phone.

Furthermore, Google was probably aware that its G1 had no chance of overtaking the iPhone. By launching its phone so late, in September 2008, Google had given the iPhone a crucial twenty-month head start. The delay was largely due to Google's shift to a more up-to-date phone prototype that included a touchscreen as well as a keyboard.[149] But in the first half of 2008, Apple had made improvements to the iPhone, upgrading its communication features and adding the App Store as a platform for selling approved third-party apps. The iPhone was also picking up the marketing momentum that led to its soaring sales in 2010. To overtake it, the G1's hardware and Android software would have to be markedly superior.

They failed to reach that very high standard. The G1 hardware fell well short of the iPhone's brilliant and beautiful design. 'Virtually no one preferred the G1's bulky design unless they were big fans of built-in keyboards' rather than large touchscreens.[150] The Android software was competitive with the iPhone's iOS, but the apps-selling 'Android Market' debuted with too few apps, only about fifty, to compete with the App Store.[151] So the Android factor could not save the G1 phone from seeming mediocre when compared to its superb Apple counterpart. Not surprisingly, Google's G1 phone had disappointing sales and has even been labelled a 'flop'.[152]

Yet Google's diversification into smartphones had been a big success in other ways. In particular, its Android software was widely adopted by phone-makers. By 2010, 'nearly two hundred Android phone models were available in fifty countries', Windows Mobile had been buried, and Android had overtaken the iPhone's iOS as the world's largest selling operating system for mobile phones.[153] With the success of Android came success for its accompanying apps: the operating system's business role was to be 'a Trojan horse for Google's consumer apps, chief among them mobile search'.[154] With the apps came the advertising. Android was 'a gateway drug' to Google's ads as well as apps.[155] And with the ads came the revenue from selling these advertising opportunities to other firms. In 2010, Google 'still made most of its money' from search ads accessed through personal computers rather than mobile phones.[156] However, its diversification strategy had helped Google 'smoothly navigate the platform shift from PC to mobile', in the earlier quoted words of *How Google Works*. Mobile-accessed ads would become the main source of Google's revenue later in the 2010s, thanks to the well-calculated strategizing in an earlier period of its development.

Other triumphs lay ahead for Google and Android in the 2010s. Firms competing against Apple's iOS-based tablet computer, the iPad, would use versions of Android, as in the case of Amazon's Kindle Fire tablet. The most important victory, though, was Android's success in becoming a standard smartphone system. Every phone-maker that adopted Android was another ally in the campaign to make it a standard system. When Android overtook iOS in 2010, this was largely because Android was carried by 200 phone models but iOS by only one. And Android had spread around the world. The South Korean corporation Samsung was in fact soon 'the leading maker of Android-based phones'.[157]

Samsung was therefore the main target of Jobs's anti-Android litigation in 2011. Suing Google was not feasible because it received so little direct financial benefit from Android, but Jobs could target Android-using device manufacturers. He 'accused them of copying outright many of the key user-interface features of Apple's iOS'.[158] His litigation eventually led to a legal victory for Apple over Samsung in 2014, but with little practical result, and meanwhile Samsung's 'super-successful Galaxy phones' were strongly challenging the iPhone.[159]

The Galaxy smartphones were so successful because they matched the iPhone's design as well as using Android to match its software. Galaxy phones could also undercut the iPhone's high price, as Apple's phone remained a high-end product that was not offered in a range of cheaper versions.[160] In product-pyramid terms, Jobs had not extended the iPhone downwards through diffusion lines; there were not yet any equivalents of the iPod Mini, Nano, and Shuffle models. In contrast, Samsung offered a wide range of cheaper smartphones than the high-end Galaxy, with dozens of different models at mid- and low-range prices.[161] The iPhone later matched this product pyramid, however, as Apple's new CEO Tim Cook added diffusion lines that offered a wide range of models and price points.

The iPhone was a great legacy from Jobs. Two years after his death the phone was still accounting for more than half of Apple's annual revenue and in fact the iPhone would continue making this huge contribution throughout the 2010s and into the 2020s.[162] The iPhone's success gave Jobs enormous prestige within the high-tech business world. *How Google Works* describes him as 'one of the greatest business divas the world has ever known', and meant this as a compliment: divas are 'unusual and difficult' but are capable of 'doing interesting things'.[163] Comparing Jobs to a high-fashion maestro seems a better way, though, to describe this creative leader of a design-oriented firm. Google's leaders seem very different from him and are perhaps best compared to the gifted strategists of a revolutionary army. They had certainly left a great legacy to Google—and the mobile-tech sector—through their diversifying acquisition of Android software.

15
Charisma and Rational Redevelopment

In this chapter, rational redevelopment is joined by a non-rational type of leadership—charismatic leadership. It does not mean that the leader has a 'charismatic' personality: an extroverted personality with a magnetic charm and the ability to sway an audience. Some charismatic leaders have such a personality; others have not, and yet have attained charismatic status. What then is charismatic leadership? The most famous analysis of charismatic leadership views it as a rare type that requires a leader to have exceptional attributes and success. Charisma is 'a certain quality of an individual personality by virtue of which he is considered *extraordinary* and treated as endowed with supernatural, superhuman, or at least specifically *exceptional* powers or qualities'.[1] This is the basis for the charismatic type of leadership, which inspires people with confidence and furthermore gives the leader some informal authority over his or her followers. Charismatic leadership sets a high standard, requiring that a leader be exceptional and extraordinary, so it has always been much rarer than the more 'ordinary' types of leadership.

Another reason for its rarity is that charisma is an inherently unstable basis for leadership. The charismatic leader's authority is derived 'solely by proving his [exceptional] powers in practice' and especially 'by bringing wellbeing to his faithful followers'.[2] If therefore a lack of success produces a loss of authority, this is clearly an unstable type of leadership. How many leaders have been consistently successful for any great length of time? But charisma is often supplementing a more formal authority, typically the legal or traditional authority of someone holding a formal leadership position. Here the loss of charisma reduces but does not end the leader's authority: there is still some underlying formal basis for his or her authority as leader.

Business leaders were not included in this famous analysis of charisma by Max Weber. Extraordinary business leaders were perhaps *too* rare at that time, more than a century ago.[3] In more recent times, however, the business version of charismatic leadership has been the most prevalent version. It is epitomized by the founder-leader who develops a start-up into a famous corporation. But redeveloping leaders, too, have been known to be charismatic: the case of Steve Jobs has already been mentioned in Chapter 14. Charismatic status gives a rational redeveloper the extra advantages of inspiring employees with more confidence and supplementing the leader's legal authority as CEO.

In the Jobs case, there was also an example of charismatic powers. As Chapter 14 observed, Jobs displayed a charismatic visionary awareness that his iPod might be made redundant by music-capable mobile phones. And this visionary awareness had led to Apple diversifying into mobile phones, specifically the iPhone. Its huge success

Rational Leadership. Paul Brooker and Margaret Hayward, Oxford University Press. © Paul Brooker & Margaret Hayward (2023). DOI: 10.1093/oso/9780198894643.003.0015

'proved' Jobs's charismatic visionary power, as in Weber's definition of charisma. However, there is another charismatic interpretation, with wider implications. Usually charismatic powers and qualities are non-rational, such as the power of vision or the quality of outstanding courage. Sometimes, however, the charismatic power is an exceptional *rational* capability, such as when using a rational technique or means. For instance, Jobs was exceptionally capable of using diversification—a rational means of redeveloping—and his charismatic capability was 'proved' by the huge success of his phone diversification, the iPhone. Furthermore, this proven charismatic power was part of his charismatic status: his status as a leader who is 'considered extraordinary', as in Weber's definition of charisma. For Jobs's lasting reputation as an extraordinary leader is based largely on the capability and success of his mobile-phone diversification. He is a classic example of a rational business leader who becomes charismatic through brilliant and successful use of rationality—the Einstein or Rutherford of business redevelopment!

Another classic but less famous example is Jorma Ollila, who redeveloped the Finnish corporation Nokia in the 1990s. Ollila's charismatic status was based on his exceptionally capable use of prioritization as a rational means of redeveloping. His discerning prioritization very capably reoriented the product range by focusing on the high-potential products and rigorously discarding the other product lines. Specifically, he focused on mobile-phone products and divested the corporation's various other businesses. His masterly use of redevelopment's prioritization tool led to a highly successful redeveloping of his troubled corporation. The firm was given a very bright new future as world leader of the burgeoning mobile-phone industry. In the 2010s, Nokia experienced another successful redevelopment, as recounted in Chapter 10. But its 1990s redeveloping is more significant from a charismatic perspective, as this case is the best illustration of the fascinating relationship between charisma and rational redevelopment. In Ollila's case, the relationship was created early in his leadership of Nokia and would continue until he retired some twenty years later.

This chapter is therefore largely concerned with Ollila's leadership of Nokia. The first section examines his prioritizing of Nokia's mobile-phone business and then shows how Ollila maintained his charismatic status in the 2000s through his charismatic quality of exceptional resilience. A leader's-eye view is provided by Ollila's co-authored memoir *Against All Odds: Leading Nokia from Near Catastrophe to Global Success*, which will be supplemented mainly by Doz and Wilson's *Ringtone: Exploring the Rise and Fall of Nokia in Mobile Phones*. These books are also sources for the second section's analysis of Ollila's leadership of Nokia in the problematic 2010s. Although the corporation needed another redevelopment, Ollila realized that even a charismatic rational leader had no realistic chance of redeveloping Nokia in these very adverse circumstances. Instead, he used his charisma and rationality to pursue a rectification programme in 2010/11, which created an opportunity for the later, Siilasmaa-led, redeveloping described in Chapter 10. The Ollila case therefore confirms that charisma does not give rational leaders enough extra advantage for them to be willing to risk redeveloping in very adverse circumstances. But charisma clearly can help them pursue an alternative, such as a rectification programme, that creates some new opportunity for their corporation.

The third section shifts the focus to how *routinized* charisma affects the rational redevelopment of corporations. Routinized charisma and its influence on Apple's redevelopment were discussed in Chapter 14. The present chapter looks at how Nokia's redevelopment was influenced by the routinized charisma of 'Nokia Way' values imparted by the charismatic Ollila. The Nokia Way also became a useful cultural legacy that helped Risto Siilasmaa's mid-2010s redeveloping of Nokia. Yet routinized-charisma cultural legacies may instead impede the redeveloping of a corporation. Lou Gerstner's redeveloping of IBM, for instance, might have been impeded by a routinized-charisma cultural legacy that dated back to the founders of IBM. Gerstner's charismatic status helped him to overcome this cultural impediment, but a leader with less charismatic status would have faced a serious problem. So the fourth section looks at the routinized-charisma problem faced by Carly Fiorina in her redeveloping of Hewlett-Packard (HP). Her redeveloping of the corporation was seriously impeded by its founders' routinized charisma, codified in their 'HP Way' cultural legacy. And she did not fully overcome this impediment until she hybridized HP with Compaq. Her situation therefore makes a striking contrast with the relationship between charisma and rational redevelopment in the case of Ollila and Nokia.

From Redevelopment to Charisma: *Against All Odds*

The Nokia case has many unusual features. The Chapter 10 account of Nokia's 2010s redeveloping has already highlighted the fact that this large high-tech corporation originated in a small nation of only five million people, the north European country of Finland. Another unusual feature is that Nokia did not originate as a high-tech start-up, whether in recent or past times. It is not the equivalent of modern Apple, old Hewlett-Packard, or ancient General Electric. The Nokia mobile-tech firm grew out of a comparatively low-tech conglomerate, created in 1967:

> from the merger of forestry, paper, and pulp group Nokia AB (established in 1865 and named after the town in which it was founded), Finnish Rubber Works (established 1889), and Finnish Cable Works (FCW, established 1912). By far the biggest constituent in the newly merged entity, FCW can also be viewed as the real forerunner of the modern Nokia due to a ... shift from producing telegraph cables to radio communications and electronics.[4]

The Nokia conglomerate soon shifted further in this direction, as it responded to the Finnish government's 1968 decision to create a mobile telephone network. There was good geographical reason for this decision, as *Ringtone* observes. 'With almost 75 percent of the country being dense forest, over 180,000 lakes, and a similar number of small islands, Finland has a particularly challenging topography which, combined with low population density', gave the government good reason to opt in 1968 for a mobile telephone network rather than a nationwide fixed-line system.[5] The newly created Nokia conglomerate was therefore an early starter in the mobile-tech businesses.

However, the conglomerate's future was in danger by the late 1980s, due to its leader's attempt to develop Nokia into a European-level corporation. His risky acquisition of a lacklustre part of Europe's television-making industry was a huge burden for Nokia.[6] The overextended corporation was in a crisis situation by the late 1980s, and a new leader 'began to rationalize Nokia, cutting the workforce in half (to 22000) over the next two years'.[7] But a redevelopment of the corporation did not occur until he was replaced by a new CEO in 1992.

The new CEO was the 41-year-old Jorma Ollila. He had joined Nokia several years earlier, had then headed its mobile-phone business in 1990/1, and was now taking charge of a Nokia that 'was still in trouble', according to *Ringtone*.[8] Ollila very quickly prepared a plan for redevelopment based on a prioritizing reorientation of the product range. He later also led a cultural transformation, as is recounted in the chapter's third section. However, this cultural tool was not the appropriate key rational means of redeveloping Nokia. Ollila had discerned that the key tool for a remedial renewal was a prioritization of Nokia's mobile-tech products: 'mobile phone networks would be the investment of the future'.[9] Mobile phones and mobile infrastructure networks were the only fields in which Nokia was a global player. Although its mobile-phone business contributed only a tenth of Nokia's revenues, it had a tenth share of the global market and indeed had become the world number-two in 1991 by acquiring a British mobile-phone firm.[10] Ollila's 1990/1 years as head of the mobile-phone business had given him a first-hand insight into its potential. He had seen Nokia's product-development ability and had seen the potential for growth in the global market for mobile phones, though he acknowledges that 'no one could have predicted that global growth would be as impressive as it was by the end of the decade'.[11]

Ollila's prioritization plan was presented to the workforce later in 1992, as he describes in *Against All Odds*. He 'communicated the decision at workplace meetings, typically to about a hundred people at a time. Of these perhaps twenty would find a place at the Nokia of the future that I believed in; the other eighty belonged to the parts of the company we had decided to sacrifice'.[12] The sacrifice would take the form of divesting Nokia of all but its mobile-tech businesses: mobile phones and mobile-network infrastructure. Nokia had already withdrawn from its traditional paper business in 1989–92; and had sold off its relatively new computer business.[13] However, Ollila was not leading a desperate turnaround aimed at staving off collapse; he was leading a redevelopment aimed at giving Nokia a bright new future in the decades ahead. He in fact delayed the major divestitures until 1995/6, when the businesses were in better shape to flourish under their new owners. Only then did he divest the company of its profitable rubber and cables businesses and, at last, manage to sell off the burdensome television-making business.[14]

By the mid-1990s the focus on mobile phones was proving very successful. They were still only basic mobile phones, often called 'cell' phones, and had none of the computer-like capabilities of the 'smart' phones described in Chapter 14. Nokia's product developers, though, had given the firm superb 'basic' mobile-phone products.[15] This had helped Nokia achieve explosive growth in mobile-phone sales during the first half of the decade: 'between 1990 and 1994 the firm's mobile phone output grew from 500,000 units per annum to five million.'[16]

In the second half of the 1990s, the market for mobile phones continued to grow at an explosive rate. By 1998, Nokia was selling more than forty million phones a year, about a quarter share of the global market.[17] To keep up with this increase in demand, the firm had to increase production at a similarly staggering rate. *Ringtone* observes that from 1995 to 2000 Nokia's production of mobile phones grew at an 'unprecedented pace for an industrial manufacturer', and the firm's mobile-phone workforce expanded by some 150 per cent, reaching a total of over 27,000.[18]

Ollila's employee-followers were therefore being given plenty of proof that he had used prioritization with exceptional, charismatic capability. Another 'proving' success was that their firm was now world number-one in mobile phones. In 1998, Nokia had overtaken American firm Motorola globally and Nokia's share of the US market had grown to 36 per cent, leaving Motorola with 26 per cent.[19] An underlying reason for Nokia's victory was that by 1991 the firm was adopting new, digital technology and was adopting it markedly earlier than industry leader Motorola.

> At Nokia we started to believe the future was digital much earlier than our competitors did … From our point of view, it was well worth investing all our efforts in something that could transform the entire market. While Nokia was pushing digital phones, Motorola was living in the analog era. Nokia passed Motorola partly because we were early adopters of digital technology.[20]

This technology's potential fully justified Ollila's 1992 assertion that 'mobile phone networks would be the investment of the future', and indeed Nokia's lead in this new technology was another excellent reason for him to prioritize mobile phones.

The new, digital technology had wide implications for the future of mobile phones. Digital technology enabled the cost and size of phones to be reduced. In addition, there was a major improvement in performance, largely because there had been a shift in wireless technology from analogue first-generation (1G) to digital second-generation (2G).[21] The analogue 1G networks had been designed 'to support only voice communications' and suffered from interference and coverage problems; the digital 2G networks enabled the operators or carriers 'to serve more subscribers' and give them better service in terms of emails as well as voice messages.[22] The shift to 2G therefore led to better basic phones and later to 'smart' phones that had the capabilities of a personal computer. A smartphone, the Communicator, was pioneered by Nokia as early as 1996.[23] However, the smartphones' time had not yet come. As Chapter 14 described, they did not rise to prominence until the late 2000s. And they did not numerically surpass the basic mobile phone until 2013.[24]

The basic mobile phone began the 'mobile revolution' in high-tech products. By the late 1990s digitalization had opened up a vast new, mass-consumer market for mobile phones. Previously, the market for mobile phones had just been an assortment of specialized users, such as emergency services, business executives, and busy socialites.[25] Now the mobile revolution had arrived. A much wider range of consumers were being offered ever cheaper and better digital mobile phones.[26] The consumers responded with alacrity. The mobile phone was 'more and more a universal means of personal communication' and 'would surpass every previous consumer or electronic product in the speed at which it was adopted' in the late 1990s.[27] The revolutionary expansion of the mobile market was also highly lucrative. A quarter share of this market enabled Nokia to make huge profits and become the eighth most valuable company in the world by 1999.[28]

Ollila's 1992–5 redevelopment of Nokia had therefore given the corporation a bright—very bright—new future. His exceptionally capable use of prioritization had been proven beyond a doubt and is comparable to Jobs's use of diversification with the iPhone. Not surprisingly, Ollila attained charismatic status, not just within Nokia and Finland but also in Europe. He 'became an iconic corporate leader in Europe', while internationally 'a number of articles in leading business papers lauded CEO Ollila'.[29]

During the 2000s decade, his charismatic status was maintained by proof of his exceptional resilience. This charismatic quality enabled him to deal with major challenges to Nokia's success. Internally, he had to deal with the one-by-one loss of the brilliant team of four executives that had helped him operate and integrate Nokia.[30] Externally, he was faced with the 2000/1 tech-sector recession discussed in Chapters 8, 10 and 14. Another external crisis was Nokia's dispute with dissatisfied network-operating companies, such as Vodaphone, who had been buying many Nokia phones for on-selling to consumers of their network services.[31] A constant high-tech challenge was the need to keep up with phone software improvements and with such innovations as the camera-equipped phone.[32] More generally, there was the constant challenge of responding to price and design competition from Nokia's old rival, Motorola, and from new competitors, notably Samsung, emerging in Korea and China.[33]

In dealing with these various challenges, Ollila's charismatic resilience had been proven by its success. In 2007, Nokia produced its best ever results, and having won some 40 per cent of the mobile-phone market, the firm and its 50,000 employees seemed to have a secure future.[34] This success met the charismatic criterion of a leader bringing well-being to his faithful employee-followers. So there was little decline in Ollila's authority when he retired as CEO in 2006 (handing the post to Olli-Pekka Kallasvuo) and thereafter led Nokia from his position as chairman of the board. When Risto Siilasmaa joined Nokia's board in 2008, Ollila seemed to be 'a ruler on his throne':

> he was an almost mythic character—equal parts revered and feared. Jorma cultivated a serious demeanour, usually wearing a conservative dark suit, a stylish but unremarkable tie, and professorial tortoiseshell glasses. He didn't laugh much and rarely joked. In the boardroom, he sat at the head of the polished wood table ... an unquestioned ruler on his throne.[35]

Although there were no signs of a charismatic personality, he had achieved truly charismatic status through his exceptionally capable prioritization in the 1990s and exceptional resilience in the 2000s.

Jorma Ollila's Charisma and a 2010s Redevelopment

However, 2008 was the turning point for Ollila as the charismatically successful leader of Nokia. Harbingers of Nokia's decline appeared, foreshadowing a difficult ending to his tenure as leader. In fact the decline of Nokia's mobile-phone business seems inevitable. As *Ringtone* concludes, 'Nokia's core problem was that it simply kept doing what it excelled at for too long before exiting'.[36] This begs the question, though: what could Nokia have exited to? After all, Ollila had begun looking for a diversification in the late 1990s, without success. The search was gradually abandoned in the 2000s and has been described as unrealistic.[37] Chapter 10 described how Nokia finally managed to exit the mobile-phone business, in 2013, by prioritizing its network-technology subsidiary, Nokia Siemens Networks (NSN). But in 2008–12, NSN was a problematic project that had not yet started to show results, so even exceptionally capable prioritizing could not have been successful.[38] Throughout this period therefore Ollila could not have used prioritization or diversification as an appropriate rational means of redeveloping Nokia.

Yet he might well have been tempted to risk a redevelopment. Although the circumstances were less favourable than in the 1990s, he now had the extra advantages of being an established charismatic as well as rational leader. Charismatic status gave him extra authority and inspired his employee-followers with the extra confidence that came from being led by a person with exceptional powers and qualities. Ollila had lacked these advantages when he had taken over at Nokia in 1992 and began to redevelop it.

That he did *not* try to redevelop again is further proof that he was a rational leader. His rationality told him that the circumstances were too adverse: there was no realistic opportunity for prioritizing or diversifying. Neither do the other three rational means of redeveloping appear appropriate in the circumstances. There was either no opportunity for them or they did not provide a solution to the corporation's problems. Hence there could be no repeat of his successful rational redevelopment in the 1990s. His charismatic status and resilience would have to keep Nokia going until circumstances changed, and there was an opportunity to solve its problems through redevelopment.

So what exactly were these problems: what had started to go wrong in the late 2000s? The most obvious problem was the 2007/8 arrival of the iPhone and its App Store, as was described in Chapter 14. Ollila acknowledges that 'Apple had created something really new: a wonderful experience for the phone user where the phone was the key to an entire ecosystem of services and applications'.[39] This iPhone 'ecosystem' included not only the iOS software but also Google's Search, Maps, and YouTube apps, plus a platform for third-party sellers: the iTunes Music Store and

App Store. Furthermore, the iPhone was strong where Nokia was weak. *Ringtone* notes that the 'culture and understanding within Nokia were based on a hardware-first approach' and there was a 'reluctance to recognize the value and importance of platforms and software'.[40] This cultural lag was reflected in its increasing lag in software development. Nokia and other phone-makers had in 1998 joined a new venture, called Symbian, that would supply them with software for the 'smart' versions of their mobile phones.[41] But from the mid-2000s onwards, the Symbian software was increasingly unable to keep up with smartphone users' expectations. Siilasmaa points out that 'Symbian devices were notoriously cumbersome to use, with confusing menus, numerous options and settings, and a multitude of confirmations required by the user whenever something new was done with the device. Users were buying Nokia devices, but they were also complaining'.[42]

Nokia's software weakness was highlighted by another late 2000s problem—the arrival of Android. In 2008, Google introduced their superb Android operating system for mobile phones, as described in Chapter 14. Android was being offered, too, in combination with Google's apps and a platform for third-party apps, Android Market. This ecosystem was less impressive than iPhone's, but it was better than anything else on the market. Hence from 2008 onwards Nokia's phones were facing competition from two software ecosystems, the Android and the iPhone, which were each superior to anything that Nokia could offer.

What could Nokia do in response to these software-based challenges? The firm had discovered years earlier that 'it simply wasn't possible to develop a strong team of software experts in a short time' by looking to America, and 'there didn't seem to be such people anywhere in Europe'.[43] Recruiting such people was no easier in the late 2000s period of software competition. Nokia therefore, according to Ollila, adopted an attitude of rational fatalism and emotional denial.

> Nokia had been forced into a contest that would be decided by the competitiveness of the operating system, the users' experience (which was based on our software expertise), and the apps. Nokia's software capability was inadequate ... We understood the problem, but at some deep level we couldn't accept what was happening.[44]

This emotional denial may well have been due to the confidence that charismatic leaders inspire in their followers. Ollila's charismatic status had been well 'proven' by a record of success that extended back to 1992. Surely Nokia could rely on its extraordinary leader to deal with this latest challenge? Why should Nokia be concerned about a problem that was perhaps nothing worse than the others that Ollila had solved or weathered?

Ollila did eventually try to solve the software problem but, as noted earlier, he did not attempt another redevelopment. He discerned that the circumstances were too unfavourable, despite his charismatic advantages of extra authority and unusually confident employee-followers. With or without these advantages, he had no real chance of achieving a redevelopment. His problem solving instead took the form of a rectification programme aimed at Nokia's software deficiencies. By 2010, Nokia had formed a software alliance with Intel corporation to help develop a new operating system, MeeGo, which was seen as Nokia's 'software saviour'.[45] And CEO Kallasvuo was replaced by a Canadian, Stephen Elop, who had been recruited from software giant Microsoft. New CEO Elop formed a dual-leadership team with Ollila to continue Nokia's rectification programme.[46]

The corporation was starting to be hit hard, though, by the competition from the iPhone and the Android software. The iPhone was hitting Nokia at the high end of the smartphone market, while the Android software was doing even more damage at the lower end of the market. This part of the smartphone market was being reshaped by Korean and Chinese phone-makers' shift to the freely available Android software, which was leading to the commodification of the market.[47] Some years earlier, the market for basic mobile phones had been commodified by new phone-makers, including a dozen Chinese firms, who had entered the market with phones that competed with Nokia's on price and squeezed its profit margins.[48] Now commodification was also occurring in the lower end *smart*phone market, thanks to the arrival of Android-equipped phones. Nokia was once again facing stiff price competition and seeing its profit margins squeezed. It needed to offer better software than Android or at least software that was comparable in quality and would differentiate Nokia's phones from their commodified competitors. Although the projected MeeGo operating system might meet requirements, Nokia also had to offer a competitive ecosystem of supplementary apps and third-party selling.[49] How could Nokia hope to catch up—and catch up quickly?

Its leaders' answer was to expand the rectification programme into a partnership with Microsoft and its Windows Phone software ecosystem. The result was a 'strategic alliance' between Nokia and Microsoft that was extensively discussed in Chapter 10. The idea of this alliance had been a daunting prospect for many Nokia employees and supporters. Although the idea was deftly presented to employees and the Finnish public, they were not very supportive when the alliance was announced in early 2011.[50] Siilasmaa notes that Nokia's shares fell 12 per cent and that to 'many of the Nokia faithful, the news of the Windows Phone partnership was like the announcement of a funeral', as Nokia's Symbian software was being replaced and the firm's emerging MeeGo software was being side-lined.[51] At least, however, Ollila would remain Nokia's co-leader. And his charismatic status must have helped to legitimate the new alliance.[52]

The Microsoft alliance became the key part of the rectification programme. For although the alliance was a commercial failure, it created the opportunity for a successful redevelopment: a year after Ollila retired in May 2012. His successor, Siilasmaa, sold Nokia's mobile-phone business to Microsoft in 2013 and then successfully prioritized the Nokia network-technology subsidiary NSN, as described in Chapter 10. Nokia is one of the few corporations to have undergone two successful redevelopments, with Siilasmaa's redevelopment following on—some twenty years later—from Ollila's success in the 1990s. This success had given Ollila a charismatic status that was maintained in the 2000s by his charismatic resilience and then helped produce crucial benefits in the early 2010s, namely a rectification programme that created new opportunities for a successful redevelopment.

Redeveloping versus Routinized Charisma

The relationship between rational redevelopment and charisma is more complicated in the case of 'routinized' charisma. It is an institutionalized form of charismatic leadership and was identified by Weber's classic analysis of charisma. A standard historical instance is when a charismatic leader's powers or qualities are viewed as a model to be imitated and are then institutionalized, creating a cultural legacy that influences future generations.[53] Another historical instance is when the charismatic leader brings a message, as in the case of a prophet, and the message is imbued with the leader's charisma—with this again being institutionalized into a cultural legacy that influences future generations.[54]

In modern times, routinized charisma is sometimes to be found in business corporations, including corporations that are being redeveloped. For instance, when Apple was redeveloped by charismatic Steve Jobs, there was an imitate-the-leader version of routinized charisma. Chapter 14 mentioned how his personality traits were routinized and how this had helped him culturally transform Apple.[55] Another instance is Ollila's use of routinized charisma as a way of culturally transforming Nokia. He used the other version of routinized charisma, the leader's-message version, with the message embodied in what was called 'the Nokia Way'. But the message was not simply a personal revelation passed on to his followers; it was a collaborative leader-and-followers message, comparable to the HP Way that had emerged during the development of Hewlett-Packard.

The Nokia Way emerged early in Nokia's redevelopment. Soon after Ollila became CEO, he discerned that a cultural transformation was appropriate and should be based on a collaborative 'Nokia Way' message. Through discussions within the company, he brought forth a Nokia Way based on four core values: Customer Orientation, Achievement, Continuous Learning, and Respecting the Individual.[56] The leader then personally helped spread the Nokia Way throughout the corporation. 'I had thrown myself behind the new values' and 'spoke about values in hundreds of meetings', thereby imbuing the Way with the charisma that he was acquiring from his extraordinarily successful redevelopment.[57] And the leader capably ensured, through his personnel department, 'that *The Nokia Way* was the crucial principle in recruitment, managerial appointments, and team-building'.[58] Hence the Way was widely and strongly instilled in Nokia's culture. In the 2010s, the values of the Way were re-emphasized by Siilasmaa during his leadership of Nokia's second redevelopment. In his view, these values had 'created the Nokia we all loved. We had faith they would steer us through our reinvention and propel our revival'.[59]

Such cultural legacies are more likely, though, to hinder rather than help redevelopment, especially if they date back to a charismatic founder of the corporation. IBM was one of those 'companies that successfully routinized their charismatic founder's way of doing things'.[60] However, the founder's cultural legacy later hindered the redevelopment of IBM. The mid-1990s redevelopment of IBM by Lou Gerstner was examined in Chapter 13. Although he does not discuss routinized charisma in his book, Gerstner argues that the culture of a large company may well impede change, especially when the company 'is the creation of a visionary leader. A company's initial culture is usually determined by its founder's mindset—that person's values, beliefs, preferences, and also idiosyncrasies'.[61] As Gerstner discovered, this situation had arisen at IBM.

The corporation's founder, Thomas Watson, had been CEO of IBM until 1956. He had created a paternalistic corporation that boasted company songs, public rituals, and ubiquitous signs displaying the founder's or firm's unique set of principles.[62] His son and successor, Thomas Watson Jr, summarized the founder's principles as three Basic Beliefs: excellence in everything we do; superior customer service; and respect for the individual. These principles seem so beneficial that it is hard to imagine how they could be an impediment. But the principles had been distorted by the informal interpretations they had been given during the many years since the founder had departed.[63] Gerstner stresses that by 1993 the beliefs had come to mean something markedly different from the founder's intended meaning. For instance, the belief in 'excellence in everything we do' had led to a 'stultifying' culture of obsessive perfectionism, with a 'spider's web of checks, approvals, and validation'.[64] A similar kind of misinterpretation had occurred with the belief in 'respect for the individual'. It had been distorted into an attitude of entitlement that let individuals ignore orders and excuse poor performance.[65]

A highly visible part of the founder's cultural legacy had been distorted by stultification. The founder's 'dress code' had never been updated and still specified that formal 1950s-style business attire had to be worn inside the office and when visiting customers or other companies.[66] Retaining the founder's dress code had created a symbol of cultural continuity that also diverted attention from how other—much more important—elements of his cultural legacy had been misinterpreted and distorted. Abolishing this outdated dress code was the easiest change that Gerstner made in his difficult, five-year-long cultural transformation of IBM.

The Chapter 13 account of this transformation did not mention the routinized-charisma problem. Neither, though, did it mention how Gerstner's personal charismatic status had helped him capably carry out his transformation of IBM's culture. He had acquired his personal charismatic status by leading a successful cost-cutting turnaround and then beginning a successful redevelopment. Even a critic of Gerstner acknowledges that he 'was a great leader' who saved IBM through his emergency measures; the 'alternative was oblivion, and everyone knew that'.[67] Gerstner was therefore in a sense the refounder of IBM. He had delivered the extraordinary success required of charismatic leaders, proving his exceptional powers through a success that had brought well-being to his employee-followers.[68]

Gerstner's personal charismatic status had then helped him to transform IBM's routinized-charismatic culture. As a refounder, he was charismatically entitled to replace the founder's 'message' with a newer, more relevant message. Gerstner's charisma therefore aided his capable transformation of the culture, and ensured that his redevelopment was not seriously impeded by the cultural legacy of routinized charisma.

There are similarities and differences with the case of Carly Fiorina and Hewlett-Packard discussed in the next section. Chapter 10 has already given a brief account of her redevelopment of HP, with a leader's-eye view provided by her memoir *Tough Choices*. Like Gerstner, she was an outside CEO faced with a cultural legacy of routinized charisma, but her situation was yet more problematic than that he had faced several years earlier at IBM. HP's cultural legacy came from the charismatic co-founders, Bill Hewlett and David Packard, who had started up the company in the 1930s and led it until the 1980s. The founders' routinized charisma had been codified in an 'HP Way' that was stronger than Watson's cultural legacy at IBM.

The HP Way's strength was partly due to its breadth and depth. It had been formally expressed in a list of *seven* corporate objectives, which served as the constitution-like core of the Way.[69] The list was finalized by the founders in 1966, after input from employees, and the objectives received wide publicity outside HP through their inclusion in Packard's memoir, *The HP Way*.[70] His book listed the Way's seven objectives as Profit, Customers, Field of Interest, Growth, Employees, Organization, and Citizenship. Each one of the seven had an accompanying clarification or explanation of its meaning. Citizenship, for example, was defined as 'making contributions to the community and to the institutions in our society which generate the environment in which we operate'. Profit, though, was the list's first objective: profit was 'the best single measure of our contribution to society' and so the objective was 'to achieve the maximum possible profit consistent with our other objectives'.

There were many other HP Way doctrines and practices. For instance, the 'full texts' of the seven core objectives supplied additional values or principles.[71] The corporation therefore had a very comprehensive cultural legacy, which any redeveloping leader would have difficulty replacing. Wisely, Fiorina did not attempt to replace it through what Gerstner describes as 'revolution' and tackling the culture 'head-on'.[72] Such a head-on clash might not have succeeded, and even a successful revolution would have absorbed too much of her time and energy. She instead adopted a more gradual, reformist approach to overcoming this impediment to her cultural transformation.

Carly Fiorina versus the HP Way in *Tough Choices*

If culturally transforming HP was so difficult, why did Fiorina bother making the attempt? The answer is 'simply' she discerned that a cultural transformation was an appropriate and indeed necessary means of redeveloping HP. As Chapters 6 and 10 have described, HP was a multifaceted high-tech corporation that had run out of innovation. During HP's long history, the firm had benefited from a number of innovation-based business transformations, which have been chronicled by House and Price's *The HP Phenomenon: Innovation and Business Transformation*.

The transformations had been based on new, innovative product lines that gave HP new markets to exploit.[73] But these innovative high-tech diversifications had died out years before Fiorina became HP's CEO in 1999.

Her remedy for the dearth of innovation was to redevelop HP into a competition-based firm. Such a firm would be competitive in existing markets instead of creating new markets through innovation. Experts on HP have suggested that 'it is questionable' whether Fiorina 'really understood and appreciated the nature of the HP innovation process, which was deeply rooted in serendipity and some redundancy'.[74] She doubtless understood, however, that HP's innovation process no longer delivered breakthrough products. Rather than trying to revive that innovation, she chose to focus on boosting HP's competitiveness, such as its efficiency and its marketing. There was plenty of room for improvement in these areas and, as a sales-and-marketing expert, she was well suited to leading a drive for greater competitiveness. A competition-based HP, however, would be 'fighting for supremacy in some of the world's most competitive industries, where the winners ran ruthless businesses'.[75] To reach that level of competitiveness, HP would need a more competition-oriented culture. Its new leader would therefore have to initiate a cultural transformation.

Fiorina was also expected to make some cultural changes: she had been hired by the HP board as a charismatic outsider who would and could change the culture. The board 'wanted someone to shake up the traditional culture', according to Khurana's *Searching for a Corporate Savior: The Irrational Quest for Charismatic CEOs.*[76] Fiorina had a charismatic personality and her success as an executive at Lucent Technologies had led to *Fortune* magazine ranking her 'The Most Powerful Woman in American Business'.[77] She therefore seemed fully capable of shaking up HP's culture. And her memoir *Tough Choices* recalls that the HP board apparently wanted a 'change agent', specifically a 'transformational CEO'.[78]

HP employees probably had little idea of what changes to expect from this new and apparently charismatic CEO. Fiorina initially described her changes as a 'reinvention', because 'invention was a key virtue of Bill and Dave's, and I needed to find a word for change that captured their pioneering spirit'.[79] In this way, she was invoking the charismatic founders' heritage, as might a reformist leader seeking to modernize the doctrine of a religion or a political party. She needed to do a lot of modernizing, though, otherwise the HP Way could severely impede her attempt to boost HP's competitiveness.

The HP Way posed such a threat partly because its core objectives had long been interpreted in unintended ways. For instance, the 'Employees' objective' included 'job security based on performance', which had long been interpreted as a guarantee of permanent employment.[80] The proviso that job security was 'based upon performance' had been nullified by such practices as managers performance-rating everyone as above average. According to Fiorina, 'employees who really weren't performing up to standard (and despite the ratings, everyone in an organization always knows who these people are) were moved from one organization to another, if possible, or were otherwise simply tolerated'.[81] This tolerance of substandard performance was contrary to the tough-minded attitude—or ruthlessness—required by a successful competition-based corporation. Fiorina would have to return the HP Way to a stricter, narrower interpretation of the 'Employees' objective'.

Misinterpretations had also distorted the values or principles derived from the fuller texts of the core objectives. Two of these distortions are described in Fiorina's memoir:

> Respect for the Individual had come to mean being courteous and noncombative even when candid, serious disagreement and debate was what the business really required. Highest Standards of Integrity applied to sins of commission—you didn't lie. It didn't apply to sins of omission—you could be silent instead of speaking up; you didn't need to say what you really thought.[82]

In other words, these distortions had encouraged a damaging reticence in policy deliberations and in other meetings of HP's managers or experts.

Even the undistorted meaning of an HP Way objective could hinder the firm's competitiveness. A crucial example was the objective entitled 'Customers', which highlighted products and services, but said nothing about sales and marketing.[83] Here, the objective had been strictly and narrowly interpreted. Fiorina's book contains a long, forceful complaint about the sales-and-marketing weaknesses she found on her arrival at HP.[84] She would have to instil a broader interpretation of the objective: customers had to seen not just as recipients of products and services but also as targets of sales and marketing.

However, her reform of the HP Way was derailed by her attempt at structurally transforming HP's sales-and-marketing performance. As Chapter 10 mentioned, the new structure was hit by the 2000/1 recession in the high-tech sector of the economy. HP's earnings result for the August–October quarter fell markedly below expectations: 'the biggest, most damaging miss of Fiorina's career', according to Burrows's book on her redeveloping of HP.[85] Her handling of the recession was 'better than some—she slashed her growth target for the year [2001] to just 5 percent in January, long before many other executives had given in to the sombre reality—but her credibility seemed damaged beyond repair'.[86]

In charismatic terms, she had lost whatever charismatic status she had in 1999 when taking over as CEO. Weber warned that a charismatic leader's exceptional powers had to be proved in practice. If success eludes the leader, 'above all, if his leadership fails to benefit his followers, it is likely that his charismatic authority will disappear'.[87] HP's new leader had failed to prove in practice that she was indeed exceptional. Success had eluded her and, in particular, her structural transformation had failed to meet expectations. She was therefore without charismatic status and would be unable to perform a Gerstner-like role: there was no chance now of being a charismatic refounder who replaces a legacy of routinized charisma with something more appropriate for the times and circumstances.

Yet Fiorina did manage to have some effect on the HP Way, thanks largely to the recession. As she observes, the recession 'made the requirement to cut costs more obvious' and furthermore this cost-cutting meant having 'to lay off a lot of

people.[88] Such lay-offs were informally prohibited by the HP Way's objective entitled 'Employees'. The objective had long been interpreted as forbidding not just
performance-related terminations but also mass lay-offs in response to a recession.
Fiorina acknowledges that HP's culturally 'acceptable way of dealing with soften-
ing economic conditions was for everyone to agree to an across-the-board pay cut
or fewer hours in the factory'.[89] The practice dated back to CEO Hewlett's response
to the boom-to-downturn crisis that struck the high-tech sector in the early 1970s.
He asked employees for a temporary reduction in their time at work so that labour
costs could be reduced by 10 per cent without lay-offs and with everyone sharing
in the pain.[90] So this interpretation of the objective' had been started by one of
the charismatic founders and been assimilated into the routinized-charisma cultural
legacy.

Fiorina, however, responded to the 2000/1 recession by seeking a more permanent
reduction in labour costs—and hence improvement in competitiveness. 'From the
day she arrived, she believed HP's payroll was bloated, to the point that judicious
cutbacks would make the company more competitive and more productive', but she
had made little headway with lay-offs, even after the structural transformation had
led to thousands of employees becoming surplus to requirements.[91] After all, she
was facing a key element of the HP Way, its Employees objective. She waited until
late 2000—when the firm was hit by recession-affected earnings problems—before
she reinterpreted this element of the HP Way. Initally, too, she sought only to return
HP to its original performance-rating system.

In late 2000 we'd begun the tough work of asking managers to actually use the
performance evaluation as it had been *originally* designed. We would force a bell-
shaped distribution curve so that we identified, and dealt with, those employees
who'd been rated as Unsatisfactory or Needs Improvement. We would reward
Superior employees appropriately ... we would learn to become, *once again*, a
meritocracy.[92]

By the end of 2000, Fiorina was ready to go a stage further in her reinterpretation of
the HP Way. Now she began cutting labour costs, but in a manner that would not
too blatantly contravene the routinized-charismatic practice of avoiding recession-
related lay-offs.[93] In December 2000 therefore, labour costs were cut by asking all
employees to take five days' unpaid leave. Although in the month that followed 1,700
were laid off, these were staff made superfluous by the structural transformation of
nearly a year earlier. Recession-related lay-offs did not occur until April 2001, when
3,000 were announced. By June more cuts in labour costs were said to be needed, but
the workforce was offered a typically HP way of making those cuts, and most employees volunteered for either a 10 per cent pay cut lasting for four months or alternatively
an equivalent amount of unpaid leave. They had been warned, though, that this vol-
untary sacrifice was unlikely to be a sufficient response to the cost-cutting pressures.
In the event, the following month HP announced their largest ever lay-off of 6,000 out

of a workforce of some 90,000. Fiorina acknowledges that many employees blamed her for the lay-offs, even nicknaming her Chainsaw Carly.[94]

Her cultural transformation was still not having much effect, such as making managers more toughminded. By mid-2001, Fiorina was still not satisfied with progress in this area. The management team 'had to learn how to manage performance and productivity. We had to build new skills, and among the most important was the ability to look people in the eye and tell them they weren't performing, or that they were being terminated.'[95]

The recession, however, helped Fiorina introduce a third rational means of redeveloping—hybridization—which had marked cultural effects. As Chapter 10 recounted, her hybridizing was based on a takeover merger with Compaq Computer Corporation. The merger was announced in September 2001, while HP was still in the depths of recession, and so the merger's supporters could argue that 'it's this or the abyss' for HP.[96] Anders's book on HP's redevelopment agreed with this view, but presented the argument in milder terms. As the 'high-tech sector was mired in the worst slump in decades', the merger with Compaq 'beat the alternative of sitting still and doing nothing as HP's own computer businesses eroded'.[97]

Yet a corporate proxy fight broke out after the HP board announced the merger deal. When the board sought the required approval from HP's shareholders, a battle emerged between the Fiorina-led HP board and an opposing alliance composed of founders' offspring and charitable foundations plus many of the past and present employees who owned HP stock. In addition to being worried about the merger's riskiness, they wished to protect the HP Way and were concerned about 'announced plans' to lay off some 10 per cent of the merged firm's workforce.[98] The HP board had sufficient support from institutional investors to win the March 2002 merger vote, but the five-month battle was continued in a law court, with Fiorina having to fight off a last-ditch lawsuit by the merger's opponents.[99] During the whole proxy fight, her greatest advantage was the opposition's lack of any credible alternative to the merger, especially as a make-or-break response to the recession. Its alternative has been sympathetically summed up as 'restore the Hewlett-Packard culture of trust, get out of commoditized products [PCs], focus on high-margin goods [printers and servers], and reassert HP's talent for invention to innovate the company out of its present doldrums'.[100] Innovating HP out of its problems was at best a long-term option however, and the company now seemed not just in the 'doldrums', but in a desperate situation.

Many HP employees, however, did not support Fiorina's decision to merge with Compaq. The proxy fight's voting figures indicate that a majority of HP's American employees opposed the merger.[101] From Fiorina's perspective therefore the fundamental advantage of the Compaq merger would be acquiring over 60,000 new employees who had a positive view of her leadership and what she was trying to accomplish. In a sense, she had become their charismatic leader, for the merger with HP would save Compaq employees from the effects of a defeat at the hands of the Dell corporation. 'Dell trounced Compaq between 1998 and 2000' in what was 'a shocking comeuppance for the one-time PC leader; no computer company had ever squandered a lead so quickly'.[102] After that experience, HP's ex-Compaq employees had good reason to view Fiorina not only as their charismatic leader but also as a rational leader who understood that computer firms had to be highly competitive to survive and succeed. The attitude of ex-Compaq employees is evident in their positive view of Fiorina's leadership, as House and Price discovered when they interviewed HP employees a few years after she had left the firm. The interviews 'revealed surprisingly significant support for her approach and achievements' among employees in the computing businesses but not among those in the printer businesses nor among 'HP old-timers'.[103] By then, HP was largely a computer firm and 70 per cent of its employees had joined 'via or since the 2002 Compaq merger'.[104] Fiorina therefore by then probably enjoyed majority support among employees, as a charismatic and/or rational redeveloping leader.

However, HP's board of directors did not think so highly of her: they replaced Fiorina with a new CEO in early 2005. The board had brought in Fiorina in 1999 to be a 'transformational' leader and indeed she had soon made transformational changes. But she had not been a charismatic leader—she had not succeeded. As Chapter 10 observed, the technical success of the hybridization had not led to similar commercial and stock-market success. As a rational redeveloper Fiorina could at least point to her success in making HP more competitive. In particular, the hybridization had removed the influence of the HP Way and had sped up her cultural transformation. As *Tough Choices* recounts, HP 'would toughen and mature. By 2002, managers knew that achieving best-in-class cost structures was an ongoing part of their jobs, and so there were more job cuts in 2002, 2003, 2004, and planned (and later executed) for 2005'.[105] Chapter 10 observed that Fiorina had produced the first stage of a redevelopment that new CEO Mark Hurd was unable to build on successfully: his second stage ran into problems and bad luck. Realistically, it is unlikely that HP could have been redeveloped successfully, regardless of the luck factor. Could even the rational capability and charismatic powers of Steve Jobs have done the business in this case?

16
General Electric

Immelt's *Hot Seat*

This final chapter looks at a classic case of failed rational redevelopment. Here a leader was insufficiently rational to overcome the difficulties of redeveloping his corporation. He used two appropriate tools from the redeveloper's tool kit. But he also needed to use a third, the cultural tool. Without this tool, there was no real chance of the redevelopment succeeding: solving the corporation's problems and giving it a bright new future.

The leader was Jeff Immelt and his corporation was General Electric (GE), which he tried to redevelop in the mid-2010s. GE was a large, venerable, and iconic corporation with some 300,000 employees. Cohan's recent history of GE, *Power Failure: The Rise and Fall of an American Icon*, shows that the firm was perhaps America's most important twentieth-century corporation.[1] Founded in the 1890s, GE was one of the earliest high-tech companies. It initially focused on electrical product lines, ranging from huge power plants to small light bulbs. Then GE pioneered the multifaceted high-tech approach that was later adopted by Hewlett-Packard and Bezist Amazon.[2] The GE of the 1920s was the multifaceted high-tech company of its era, thanks to such products as radios, refrigerators, X-ray machines, and diesel-electric locomotives. These products lost their high-tech status as time and technology moved on, but new facets were added in later decades. The 1930s saw the addition of plastics, the 1940s televisions and jet engines, the 1950s nuclear power plants, the 1960s laser equipment, and the 1970s medical scanners. By the 1980s, GE was a huge corporation that was being redeveloped into a financial as well as industrial conglomerate: the world's most valuable company in 2000, with a stock-market value of some $600 billion.

Yet the corporation had underlying problems that were inherited by Immelt when he became CEO in 2001. He eventually, in the mid-2010s, attempted to redevelop GE. His rational redevelopment was unsuccessful, however, and the corporation seemed in decline by the time Immelt retired in 2017. GE was indeed in decline and announced in 2021 that it would be split into three separate companies. That year also saw the publication of Immelt's memoir, *Hot Seat: What I Learned Leading a Great American Company*, so there is a leader's-eye view of his failed attempt to redevelop GE. Furthermore, the GE case is highlighted by Gelles's 2022 *The Man Who Broke Capitalism: How Jack Welch Gutted the Heartland and Crushed the Soul of Corporate America*. The Jack Welch whom Gelles accuses of doing such damage had

Rational Leadership. Paul Brooker and Margaret Hayward, Oxford University Press. © Paul Brooker & Margaret Hayward (2023). DOI: 10.1093/oso/9780198894643.003.0016

been Immelt's predecessor as leader of GE, from 1981 to 2001. Welch was the most celebrated CEO of the 1980s–90s and had promoted a new business approach and 'worldview' that Gelles terms 'Welchism'. In the GE and Immelt case, Gelles's book highlights the problematic legacy that Welch left to his chosen successor, Immelt.

The problematic inheritance was not some obvious crisis, requiring drastic turnaround measures. Immelt had inherited a corporation that seemed in excellent condition but had underlying problems that needed to be solved. He therefore did not have the benefit of facing an obvious crisis and being expected to take drastic remedial measures. On the contrary, Immelt was expected to continue delivering the superb earnings and shareholder returns that his predecessor, Welch, had delivered during his twenty-year 1981–2001 tenure. If Immelt had highlighted the problems that he had inherited in 2001, he would have seemed to be ungratefully criticizing his former leader, Welch, who had handpicked him to be the new leader of GE. Such criticism would also have meant challenging the reputation of the most celebrated CEO of the era, the great Jack Welch.

This predicament helps explain why Immelt waited until the 2010s to redevelop GE. But what explains the failure of his 2010s redevelopment? Immelt's book declares that 'as CEO, I'd been about as brilliant as I was lucky, by which I mean: too often I was neither'.[3] He was indeed unlucky, but lapses in 'brilliance' are also evident and provide useful insights into where rational leadership can fail to deliver its potential. For though Immelt was a rational leader, he was not rational enough—not fully rational—in his redeveloping of GE. He used appropriate rational means but too few of them. This is the opposite problem to overloading a firm by using too many of these means: a problem discussed in Chapter 10. In the present chapter, a rational leader instead shows a lack of discernment by using too few appropriate means for the difficult circumstances of this redevelopment. Immelt used two appropriate rational means but should have included a third, namely a cultural transformation. By using these three means, in a one-then-two sequence, he would have had some chance of achieving a successful redevelopment.

The chapter's first and second sections look back to GE's redevelopment by Welch in the second half of the 1980s. His highly profitable redevelopment made Welch a celebrity CEO but led to long-term problems that plagued his successor Immelt. A leader's-eye view of Welch's redevelopment of GE is provided by his memoir *Jack: Straight from the Gut*. Welch's redevelopment success was largely due to his prioritizing of GE's financial arm, GE Capital. But this approach was running into problems by the time Welch retired in 2001 and was succeeded by Immelt. The third section looks at how Immelt coped with Welch's problematic legacy. The new CEO did not launch a rectification programme, let alone a redevelopment; instead he tried to reduce the firm's dependence on the financial services of GE Capital. After the 2008/9 global financial crisis, however, a redevelopment was required to enable GE's industrial businesses to take on the 'growth engine' role once played by the now restricted GE Capital. The fourth section looks at the cultural problems affecting GE before and during this redevelopment. A lieutenant's-eye view is provided by Beth Comstock and her partly autobiographical *Imagine It Forward*. Her book confirms that innovation was inhibited by GE's Welch-legacy culture and therefore that a cultural transformation needed to be included in the redevelopment.

The fifth section examines the failure of Immelt's mid-2010s redevelopment of GE. He did not discern the need for a cultural transformation and used just the reorienting tools in the redeveloper's tool kit. He prioritized industrial products and diversified into software associated with the Industrial Internet. However, his redevelopment had badly needed a preliminary cultural transformation to help the firm create innovative, breakthrough products. His diversification's effects were too little and too late, while the prioritization was focusing on businesses that lacked the potential to be growth engines for GE. By the time Immelt retired in 2017, GE was facing worse rather than better times.

Prelude: Jack Welch's Famous Redevelopment

Welch's redevelopment of GE is a newly famous case, thanks to Gelles's recent *The Man Who Broke Capitalism*. His book depicts Welch as a pivotal figure, who led or at least personified a huge change in the worldview of American corporations. Until then their worldview was that of 'the Golden Age of Capitalism' in the third quarter of the twentieth century.[4] But a new worldview, 'Welchism', took over in the 1980s and 'continues to shape much of corporate America to this day'.[5] The most significant features of Welchism are apparently that it prioritizes shareholders' profits and 'thrives' on downsizing, deal-making, and financialization.[6] The downsizing is largely through lay-offs, the deal-making largely acquisitions, and the financialization is a shift towards the financial-services area of business.

However, this new worldview would not have been so influential if Welch had *failed* to redevelop GE. Without his successful 1980s redevelopment, the new worldview would have lacked a leader or at least would have lacked a personification of success, providing living proof that this was a winning worldview. And Welch used appropriate rational means to redevelop GE, so he must be classed as a rational redeveloper. He used both the reorienting tools, and he used them in an interesting manner, as seldom have acquisitions played such a large role in both prioritizing and diversifying. There is also a leader's-eye view, provided by his memoir *Jack: Straight from the Gut*. So why not devote a whole chapter to the famous and historically influential Welch's case of rational redevelopment?

The simple answer is that the Welch case is not a classic. For instance, he had not rescued a corporation that was obviously troubled, stagnating, or declining. His redevelopment was proactive in responding just to the prospect of stagnation. Furthermore, Welch's redevelopment did not lead to a breakthrough product or to any new high-tech facets being added to GE. Its development as a multifaceted high-tech corporation had ended in the 1970s and had not been revived by Welch. Instead, his 1980s redevelopment expanded GE's financial services and pushed up the stock-market value of this already big and valuable corporation. In 1993, GE overtook Exxon to become number one on Wall Street, with a value of nearly $100 billion, and GE's value had reached some $600 billion the year before Welch retired in 2001.[7] This rise in share value was not due to innovations or pioneering. Welch had delivered these shareholder gains through consistent and sizeable quarterly increases in earnings per share.[8] But serious problems surfaced during the tenure of his successor, Immelt. During Immelt's 2001–17 tenure as CEO, 'GE was the worst-performing stock in the Dow Jones Industrial Average. A half trillion dollars in shareholder value had been wiped out.'[9] So Welch's proactive redeveloping had not created a long-term basis for GE's prosperity.

Another reason why Welch's redevelopment is not a classic case is that his diversifications were not very discerning. Although he saw that GE should diversify through acquisitions, he did not discern that it should acquire firms with new high-tech products.[10] Hence in the second half of the 1980s, GE missed the chance to acquire firms linked with the emerging personal-computer revolution. Similarly, the Internet and mobile-tech revolutions were underway in the second half of the 1990s, but again GE missed the chance to acquire firms with revolutionary high-tech products. Welch had not taken the opportunity to launch a second stage of proactive redevelopment, which would have prepared GE for the mobile-tech and Internet 2000s–10s. Overall, he had missed the opportunity to continue GE's development as a multifaceted high-tech corporation: the 1920s–70s' diversification into new facets was not continued through the 1980s–90s' acquisitions. From his personal perspective, he had missed the opportunity to leave a valuable high-tech legacy to his employees, shareholders, and successor.

Welch's business world, however, viewed GE's redevelopment with admiration— as something to be emulated. By the early 1990s, business writers were hailing Welch's achievement, as in *The New GE* by Slater or in Tichy and Sherman's *Control Your Destiny or Someone Else Will*. At the end of the 1990s, Welch was 'the talk of corporate America' and *Fortune* magazine entitled him 'manager of the century'.[11] His management approach had come in for some criticism though, notably from O'Boyle's *At Any Cost: Jack Welch, General Electric, and the Pursuit of Profit*. But Welch was being criticized for other faults than a lack of high-tech acquisitions. O'Boyle's perspective was an earlier version of Gelles's anti-Welchism and so, too, was Kuykendall's more recent *Rebuilding the GE House That Jack Blew Down*. Her and O'Boyle's perspectives on GE have now been applied more widely by Gelles's theory of Welchism in *The Man Who Broke Capitalism*. But Welch's redevelopment weaknesses were not criticized by corporate America, even after he retired from his long-held post of CEO.

Welch was appointed GE's CEO in 1981 at the age of 45. He had started out with GE as a chemical engineer, equipped with a PhD, and made his name leading GE Plastics.[12] In 1981 he took charge of a corporation that was 'the ninth most profitable company in the Fortune 500 and the tenth largest'.[13] But there was a looming threat from foreign competitors, especially from Japanese firms. They were 'tearing apart the cost structure in industry after industry', according to Welch's memoir.[14] New CEO Welch therefore believed that he had to boost the competitiveness of his firm's industries. With foreign competitors presenting 'the gravest of threats', the new leader took heed of the 'storm signals' and decided:

to reshape a corporation that outwardly exhibited no sign of needing repair. ... But he felt he had no choice. He did not want to wait until General Electric was in trouble. He did not want to act with a gun pointed at his head. ... Welch knew that he [now] had to push the company to become more competitive.[15]

Rather than waiting until his firm was in trouble, he took proactive remedial action. In his words, the 'costs of fixing a troubled company after the fact are enormous—and even more painful'.[16]

He launched a major rectification programme aimed at improving the firm's competitiveness. GE's workforce of 400,000 was severely reduced by lay-offs and sell-offs. There were 80,000 lay-offs and a further 37,000 employees departed because their businesses had been sold: more than seventy businesses were sold, mostly smaller enterprises and with poor growth or profit prospects.[17] However, the rectification programme included more than just lay-offs and downsizing. There was also an attempt to improve management efficiency by focusing on numbers-based performance standards.[18] The new focus was largely a return to the 1960s era, when 'meeting the numbers' was the cultural and career standard of success. Senior managers had to achieve specified numerical rates of return on sales and investment: managers 'who "made the numbers" kept their jobs; those who did not were sent into the wilderness'.[19] Welch revived this numbers-based performance standard and added a more positive dimension, rewarding success as well as punishing failure. He was, in effect, shifting the firm's culture towards performance-numbers values and attitudes. Clearly he believed that the new cultural slant would improve the firm's efficiency. And evidently he was not concerned that the performance-numbers culture might discourage innovation.[20] He either believed this downside was unlikely or thought that efficiency should have a higher priority than innovation.

Another important aspect of his rectification programme was the physical upgrading of GE's industries. Welch invested heavily in new plant, equipment, technology, and product development.[21] But the new level of investment was not sustained for long. Kuykendall has argued that indeed within two years Welch 'did a 180' and thereafter made 'no more major investments in plant and equipment, product development labs or basic research unless the government paid for it'.[22] O'Boyle's assessment was similar to hers and also argued that Welch had been disheartened by unsuccessful product development. New CEO Welch had initially hoped 'to grow new technologies into blockbuster businesses', but the firm's product development failed to meet his high expectations.[23]

So GE had apparently lost its long-standing ability to diversify into new high-tech products. From the 1920s to the 1970s, GE had added new high-tech products and facets, developing into an iconic example of a multifaceted high-tech corporation. If GE had lost that ability to diversify, the corporation was facing the prospect of eventual stagnation.[24] In addition, the corporation would not have a long-term solution to the problem of foreign competition. The short-term solution had been the rectification programme's creation of a leaner, more efficient, and better equipped GE. But Welch realized that the best solution in the long term was to avoid head-on competition with the foreign companies: specifically, by diversifying into new high-tech product categories where GE would have an unassailable lead over the foreign competition. That solution failed to materialize, though, in 1982/3 and indeed he had been left with a new and broader problem. GE was now facing the prospect of eventual stagnation, even if its foreign competitors disappeared overnight. Their continued presence, however, made the threat of stagnation more obvious and pressing. Stagnation might occur in just a few years and certainly by the end of the 1980s.

However, Welch solved the problem by launching a proactive redevelopment. In 1985/6 he diversified by making a $6.3 billion acquisition that added a new type of product—television broadcasting—to GE's range of products. 'At the time, it was the biggest non-oil deal in history. We bought RCA primarily to get NBC', its television broadcasting network, which 'gave us pizzazz and great cash flow—and the hideaway I wanted from foreign competition.'[25] Adding this type of product was therefore a way of expanding GE while avoiding head-on competition with foreign companies. As Gelles observes, the RCA acquisition was also 'pivotal' in Welch's move away from the 'in-house innovation' that leads to new businesses: in fact, he would later declare that his firm was 'not interested in incubating new businesses'.[26] This policy probably stems from GE's failure to diversify internally in 1982/3. After that disappointment, Welch likely discerned that the firm should diversify through acquisitions, such as buying RCA.[27] As in that case, acquisition could create almost immediate large-scale expansion rather than having to wait for a new business to be (or not be) developed successfully.

Yet the RCA diversification had an important weakness. The RCA/NBC television broadcasting had not been a very discerning choice of product type for diversification. Television broadcasting had been an adequate enough choice: discerning enough for the diversification to be viewed as appropriate. But this type of product had little potential for further growth and might even add to GE's long-term stagnation problem.[28]

Welch therefore would have shown more discernment if he had instead acquired companies with new high-tech products. In 1985 there were companies linked with the personal-computer revolution that were small enough to be buyable, had tremendous growth potential, and enjoyed an unassailable lead over any foreign competition. Microsoft, Apple, and Intel (microprocessors) are a few possibilities that come to mind and that have been the subject of earlier chapters.[29] GE could surely have acquired one of these companies for the same huge price that it paid for RCA. At a much smaller price, GE could have bought one or more of the start-ups, such as Compaq, that were beginning to make IBM-clone PCs.[30] These companies, too, had an unassailable lead over the foreign competition and would have given GE a new high-tech facet with impressive growth potential.

Although Welch did not explore these high-tech options, he at least realized that his redevelopment needed something more than RCA. He discerned that a prioritization, too, was appropriate in the circumstances. Specifically, GE's financial services should be prioritized.

Reorienting towards Financial Services

Welch used both the reorienting tools to achieve his proactive redevelopment of GE. In addition to diversifying into television broadcasting, he prioritized GE's financial-services type of product. Reorienting the product range towards financial services may seem a strange move for a firm that made such products as electrical appliances and medical scanners. A financial type of product, however, was not threatened by foreign competitors, such as Japanese manufacturers. And financial services had some growth potential, unlike the television broadcasting that GE would acquire as a diversification.

Welch had long been aware of financial-services growth potential. In the late 1970s, he had supervised a GE subsidiary, GE Credit, that provided finance for the corporation's business and consumer customers. GE Credit was a relatively small subsidiary, with some 7,000 employees, and it earned less than 8 per cent of GE's total annual earnings.[31] But Welch's non-rational gut instinct told him that this financial-services business had great potential.

> My gut told me that compared to the industrial operations I did know, this business seemed an easy way to make money. You didn't have to invest heavily in R&D, build factories, and bend metal day after day. You didn't have to build scale to be competitive. The business was all about intellectual capital—finding smart and creative people ... This thing looked like a 'gold mine' to me. Leveraging brainpower is easier than grinding out products.[32]

And there was no foreign competition either. Here then was a huge opportunity for GE. 'All we had to do was take the business from the back of the boat to the front'.[33]

In other words, these financial services should be prioritized. The product range should be reoriented by giving priority to a type of product that hitherto had been just an add-on or auxiliary rather than a major product. Yet Welch did not prioritize financial services when he became CEO in 1981. After GE's 1982/3 failure to develop new high-tech businesses, though, Welch looked to financial services as 'the one field that to him seemed a sure way to make money'.[34] GE Credit, renamed GE Capital, would become the focus of his attention. As he recalls, however, GE Capital did not 'aggressively' expand its business until 'the second half of the 1980s'.[35]

This expansion was the prioritizing part of his redevelopment of GE in 1985–9. The prioritizing was the crucial part of his redevelopment, as reorienting the product range towards financial services gave GE some potential for long-term growth. Welch's prioritizing of GE Capital's financial products was his long-term solution to the problem of stagnation.

GE Capital certainly met his expectations, and is described in his memoir as 'the growth engine' of GE.[36] The unit propelled GE to ever-growing prosperity in the late 1980s and the 1990s. GE Capital was the main factor that 'allowed Welch to deliver' consistently high growth in earnings.[37] But why was GE Capital so successful? Its success was partly due to the unit's special advantages over its competitors.

For instance, it had a very high credit rating because it belonged to a huge corporation that included major industrial businesses. So GE Capital could borrow 'more cheaply in the capital markets while also bearing a heavier debt burden than many of its rivals' in financial-services business.[38] Another special advantage was the flexibility that GE Capital enjoyed. 'It issued consumer credit cards' for other companies, 'gobbled up portfolios of loans, lent out fortunes to developers, and got into arcane lending markets with razor-thin margins, but enormous volumes'.[39]

In addition, the unit developed a lucrative non-lending role as an acquirer of companies. Welch refers to this acquiring as 'deal making' and he recounts how GE Capital was given deal-making skills as part of its prioritization in the second half of the 1980s. 'We used talent from our industrial businesses to turn GE Capital from a pure financial house into a business with deal making as well as operational skills': the business had become 'an acquisition machine' by the end of the 1980s.[40] In the 1990s, this acquisition machine buzzed along nicely. GE Capital 'closed more than 400 deals involving over $200 billion in assets', according to Welch.[41] Many companies were acquired with an eye to reselling them profitably. After an acquisition had been restructured, it might be profitably sold off as a whole or by selling off its parts.[42] Many other companies, however, were acquired as a permanent addition to GE Capital or some other part of GE. During Welch's tenure, the corporation made nearly 1,000 acquisitions but only about 408 divestments, so there were clearly hundreds of permanent acquisitions and additions.[43] GE Capital's additions were often supplementing its financial services in some way, as when the globalizing of these services in the mid-1990s led to the acquisition of several banks in eastern Europe.[44] However, GE Capital's additions were in other cases helping it to diversify into less financial types of product. For instance, a diversification into transport leasing resulted in the unit leasing out some 900 aircraft, 100,000 trucks, and 200,000 rail cars.[45]

Yet neither GE Capital nor GE corporation diversified into the new high-tech products that were appearing in the second half of the 1990s. In particular, there was no diversification into the Internet revolution that was being led by such firms as Yahoo, eBay, and Amazon. Although GE Capital was running some twenty different businesses in 2000, it apparently had not added any Internet-based business.[46] It had been buying up insurance businesses rather the Internet start-ups. According to Immelt's *Hot Seat*: 'In the late nineties, GE Capital had loaded up on primary-care insurance, reinsurance (property and casualty) assets, and long-term care insurance. Insurance had become our largest business within GE Capital'.[47]

The lack of high-tech acquisitions may have been a reflection of CEO Welch's attitudes and perspective. Immelt observes that Welch was not very interested in technological innovation and 'focused more on management techniques such as Six Sigma'.[48] He belonged to a pre-tech era that was fascinated by managerial and financial ingenuity rather than technological progress. When Chapter 6 referred to Welch's company-wide emails, it failed to mention that his first such email was sent in June 1999. 'I know I was late', his memoir admits, and it also confesses that he did not take the Internet seriously until late 1998.[49] In the following years he launched various Internet-related initiatives within GE. As they show, he was aware that GE's businesses might be both threatened and improved by the Internet.[50] But his initiatives did not include any expansion into Internet-based businesses; there was nothing similar to GE Capital's recent expansion into insurance businesses.

When he retired in 2001, Welch was probably well satisfied with the redevelopment that he had launched sixteen years earlier.[51] Prioritizing GE Capital's financial services had apparently solved the long-term problem of stagnation. And GE Capital was still hard at work. In recent years it had not just expanded into insurance but also emphasized consumer finance and globally extended its financial activities. By 2001, GE Capital was present in nearly fifty countries, owned $370 billion in assets, employed almost 90,000 people, and was producing more than 40 per cent of GE's annual earnings.[52]

But the reorienting towards GE Capital had come at a price. Unlike in the 1920s–70s, GE was no longer a multifaceted high-tech corporation. For GE's numerous acquisitions had missed all three of the high-tech revolutions that occurred in the 1980s–90s: personal-computer, mobile-tech, and Internet. By failing to buy into these high-tech revolutions, GE had degenerated into just a conglomerate, with a variety of industries and a huge financial arm. Furthermore, GE was becoming a financial-industrial conglomerate, dominated by the financial activities and perspective of GE Capital. The conglomerate might even be headed towards an identity crisis. Was GE still an industrial firm, based on such products as plastics, jet engines, and electrical equipment? Or was GE now a major financial institution, multifaceted and global, that should have its headquarters on Wall Street?

GE's industrial businesses were certainly lagging behind growth engine GE Capital. This was partly due, however, to the prioritizing of GE Capital and its perspective on growth. For instance, the lack of diversification into new high-tech products meant that the industrial businesses were missing out on intra-GE technological stimulation and interaction. The industrial businesses were also suffering from a lack of attention and investment. They had never again received the level of investment and attention that Welch had given them in 1982/3 as part of his rectification programme. After that short period, they were relatively neglected and overshadowed by the prioritization of GE Capital in the second half of the 1980s. In the 1990s, GE Capital's success and perspective had relegated the industrial businesses to the status of second-class citizens, which led to cases of serious neglect.[53] The plastics case is described by Immelt. GE 'failed to invest in the future' of GE Plastics during the business's pivotal years in the late 1990s.[54] In those years, attention and investment were focused on GE Capital's expansion into insurance businesses.

Yet GE Capital, too, had its problems. Its expansion into insurance was not successful and would require remedial action in the years ahead. There were also prudential issues arising from GE Capital's bank-like feature. The issues would be raised publicly in 2002, when an investment analyst 'identified a crucial vulnerability at the heart of GE Capital': in a crisis, 'GE would be dangerously exposed'.[55]

With the benefit of hindsight, the corporation therefore seems to have been set for a bleak future. On the other hand, if Welch had been a more discerning diversifier, GE's prospects might have been much brighter. As noted earlier, a diversification into new high-tech products had been needed in the 1980s and/or the 1990s. This would have been diversification by acquisition, as an alternative to choosing to acquire RCA in the mid-1980s and/or as a second-stage redevelopment during GE's acquisition-inclined 1990s. If Welch had made these very discerning diversifications, he might have achieved a classic redevelopment, with a bright future for GE and a truly long-term solution to the problem of stagnation. He instead became the standard bearer of 'Welchism' and was hailed as the greatest of CEOs. GE's next leader would not be so fortunate: he had to deal with Welch's problematic legacy.

GE in the 2000s: Jeff Immelt's *Hot Seat*

Jeff Immelt was Welch's personally chosen successor, after a long selection process within GE's senior management. The 45-year-old Immelt had a Dartmouth degree in applied mathematics, a Harvard MBA, and a strong track record at GE. In the 1990s he had moved up from sales to general-manager positions at GE Plastics and then the healthcare GE Medical Systems.[56] In September 2001, he took charge of GE and so inherited the underlying problems left by Welch. Immelt's memoir is aptly titled *Hot Seat*. He did not complain about this problematic legacy though, not until a phone conversation in 2008 that is described in Immelt's memoir:

> [Welch] called me, and for the first time ever, I addressed his less-than-perfect legacy head-on. 'Following you has been no fun', I said. 'I've kept my mouth shut about the problems you left me. I bolstered your legacy, when I could easily have shot it full of holes. And because I've done so, you are still "Jack Welch, CEO of the Century"'.[57]

If Immelt had not bolstered Welch's legacy and instead had 'shot if full of holes', the prestige of Welchism might have been sorely diminished. But Immelt would have suffered, too, and his tenure as CEO might have been yet more difficult. The key point is that he was not prepared to launch a rectification programme, let alone a redevelopment, aimed at the problems inherited from Welch. Immelt would have to find other means of handling the problematic Welch legacy.

The most awkward problem of the Welch legacy was the growth engine, GE Capital. New CEO Immelt was concerned about GE's dependence on its financial arm, but 'while I wanted to operate differently, in the short-term, GE Capital was our strategy. We had *no other engines of growth*'.[58] GE Capital therefore would not be downsized or limited, except to remove its problematic insurance businesses. The rest of GE Capital would be allowed to grow, 'so that we could keep earnings on a steady path, while the industrial businesses could catch up'—after an investment in technology that would 'rejuvenate' these businesses.[59]

Circumstances were less favourable, however, in the 2000s than in Welch's golden-age 1990s. As several earlier chapters have described, the economy and stock market were less buoyant, with recessions and crashes occurring in the early and late 2000s. The corporate environment had changed too. GE, like other corporations, faced greater scrutiny from regulators and greater scepticism from investors, as Gryta and Mann note in their recent *Lights Out: Pride, Delusion, and the Fall of General Electric*.[60]

In these circumstances, should Immelt have been more ambitious and at least initiated a rectification programme? Gelles argues that Immelt had 'a unique opportunity to reset GE' after the 9/11 terrorist attacks in September 2001:

> He could have reined in GE Capital, offloading some of its riskier financial bets, and reinvesting in manufacturing. He could have taken a onetime charge and acknowledged that GE Capital had serious flaws that needed to be fixed. … If GE had a rough quarter after 9/11, no one would have been surprised. The stock would have likely fallen, and analysts might have fretted. But after the initial hardship, GE may well have been in better shape, less dependent on the magic of GE Capital.[61]

This rectification programme could also have been blamed on the post-9/11 situation: there was no need for any criticism of Welch and his legacy.

Immelt did not take the opportunity, however. He held to the long-successful 'Welchism' and 'thanks to the magic of GE Capital he was able to sustain that success': delivering Welch-like earnings growth after 9/11 and until the 2008/9 recession.[62] Immelt was not able, though, to achieve Welch-like success on Wall Street. Times had changed since the 1990s. Investors were no longer so attracted to the GE business model of a financial-industrial conglomerate that relied on financial services as well as industrial businesses. There was now more scepticism about GE Capital, and indeed some public criticism of its bank-like feature. As mentioned earlier, an investment analyst publicly raised prudential issues that affected GE as well as GE Capital. The famous analyst claimed that GE Capital's short-term borrowing was not 'sufficiently backed by lines of credit', and therefore 'there was a dangerous mismatch between what GE owed and what it could pay back should a crisis hit': the corporation might then be 'out of business'.[63] Although this dire view was not widely accepted, it signified a less positive attitude by analysts and investors towards GE's financial services. Immelt therefore had no chance of achieving the stock market success enjoyed by Welch. For instance, 2006 was a good year for stocks, but 'GE's stock rose 5.2 per cent while the S&P 500 rose 15.6 per cent'.[64]

The stock market was also not giving Immelt much credit for his attempts to rejuvenate GE's industrial businesses. The rejuvenation effort included a new emphasis on research and development (R&D), which had been underfunded in the Welch era.[65] Immelt provided more funding, promoted GE's central research centre, and created specialized research centres in other parts of the world.[66] But this was a long-term investment in technology. In the meantime, he had to find other ways of rejuvenating businesses that were not technological pioneers or leaders in their field. As the previous section noted, part of Welch's legacy was a lack of new high-tech businesses. Immelt points out, too, that none of GE's industrial businesses were 'truly world class, by which I mean none of them demonstrated consistent technical, global, or cost leadership'.[67]

He therefore also tried to rejuvenate his businesses through acquisitions and divestments. GE Healthcare was boosted by a large high-tech acquisition. The Amersham med-tech and bio-tech firm was acquired through a $10-billion share deal in 2003.[68] As for divestments, the most notable was GE Plastics. The increasingly uncompetitive Plastics was sold in 2007 for more than $11 billion.[69] The NBC television network might have been sold off, too, but 'doing so would have shrunk our industrial base, making financial services an even bigger gorilla within GE'.[70]

Yet the GE Capital 'gorilla' might itself have been shrunk in the mid-2000s. The opportunity arose when Immelt was addressing the insurance problem that he had inherited from Welch. As the previous section mentioned, GE Capital had expanded into various insurance businesses in the late 1990s. Insurance eventually accounted for some 40 per cent of GE Capital's earnings, but its insurance businesses were an 'over-levered mess': they were being poorly run 'in a highly regulated industry with low returns. It was clear to me that we had to get out'.[71] By 2003, Immelt was ready to start divesting these businesses. Although the process took years, he removed its various insurance ventures from GE Capital.[72] The slimmed-down GE Capital continued, however, to be flexible and voracious. For instance, the unit accelerated its expansion into commercial real estate. A huge investment portfolio was built up through 'acquisitions of real estate investment trusts and then loads of smaller deals' by the skilled deal-makers of GE Capital.[73] Its assets had grown to $564 billion by the end of 2006, and had reached some $700 billion by mid-2008.[74] The financial services 'gorilla' was therefore actually bigger than before: how could this growth engine be matched, let alone surpassed, by GE's industrial businesses?

Their growth prospects were the major concern of a 2007 academic appraisal of Immelt's leadership. *Judgment: How Winning Leaders Make Great Calls* devoted a chapter to Immelt and his strategy judgements about boosting GE's industrial businesses. But the book's authors issued a warning. 'He has spent five years repositioning GE for future [industrial] growth; now he needs to demonstrate that his strategic judgments will yield the promised results'.[75] Two years later, another book showed that these results had still not been achieved. Magee's 2009 *Jeff Immelt and the GE Way* mentioned that GE Capital was generating 'almost half of the company's earnings' in 2008.[76]

Immelt had clearly been unable to boost the industrial businesses to high enough growth rates. He acknowledges that GE Capital's 'dominance within GE had stayed about the same', six years into his tenure, and 'over half of GE's overall profits' were contributed by GE Capital.[77] However, he does not seem disappointed in his industrial businesses. He notes that the three years from 2006 to 2008 'had been a record for GE's industrial businesses, whose performance had been through the roof'.[78] Yet this was not enough. Something more radical was needed to produce new growth engines: businesses that could rival the growth rate of GE Capital.[79] The alternative was simply to restrict or reduce GE Capital. And by 2008, Immelt was apparently moving towards this simpler approach.[80] In that year, though, the main problem was how to keep GE Capital alive in the midst of a global financial crisis.

In 2008, the world entered a recession and financial crisis that made the Welch legacy yet more problematic. The financial crisis in fact hit GE Capital so badly that

GE itself was endangered. The first obvious sign of trouble for GE was its failure to hit its first-quarter earnings target. As the emerging financial crisis had affected GE Capital, the finance arm could not make its usual contribution to the corporation's quarterly earnings—they were markedly below expectations when the figures were announced in April.[81] This ended GE's long Welchist tradition of meeting expectations, and an indignant Welch rebuked Immelt on national television, saying that 'Jeff has a credibility issue. He's getting his ass kicked' and must focus on delivering the earnings.[82] On the following day, the two men had the phone conversation quoted earlier, during which Immelt complained about Welch's legacy. More importantly, the following months seemed to confirm the prophecy of doom made by an analyst six years earlier: that GE might be in danger if GE Capital's short-term borrowing was hit by a financial crisis.[83] This short-term borrowing was indeed badly hit by the growing crisis and was endangering the whole corporation. 'Like the banks, we were facing an existential threat', according to Immelt.[84] The threat had eased, however, by November, as GE was allowed to join the federal government's new bank-guarantee programme.[85] Yet GE's share price kept falling. In February 2009, the share price went below $10, compared to $28 in September 2008 and to $35 in September 2001.[86] Immelt's more than seven years as CEO therefore appeared a disaster from the Welchist perspective of shareholder profits.

After the 2008/9 crisis, Immelt seemed ready to make a fresh start. He had come to the conclusion that this financial crisis presaged 'the destruction of our [GE's] business model. GE Capital was a large, debt-funded finance company whose need for a cash buffer was a serious drag on Big GE. More and more I realised that we needed to unwind GE Capital, which might take a decade'.[87] The immediate problem, however, was that the unit could no longer be the engine of growth. In 2010, GE Capital entered a new era, epitomized by the Dodd-Frank 'Wall Street Reform' legislation. From now on GE Capital would be restricted by tighter government regulations and closer scrutiny by government regulators.[88] While this meant that GE Capital could no longer pose any financial threat to GE, neither could the unit ever again be GE's growth engine. So the corporation was facing a new form of the stagnation problem that had arisen in the mid-1980s, before GE Capital had been prioritized by Welch's redevelopment. Now a second redevelopment was required: to deal with the stagnation threat, create a new business model, and give GE a bright future in the 2010s.

Furthermore, the financial crisis had given Immelt all the justification he needed for launching a redevelopment. He had a much better opportunity for remedial action now than in 2001. GE was no longer the seemingly outstanding corporation that he had inherited from Welch. And there was no need to criticize the Welch legacy in order to justify remedial action. Like Immelt, analysts and investors had concluded that the financial crisis presaged 'the destruction of our [GE's] business model' of depending upon GE Capital.[89]

Yet Immelt did not launch a redevelopment until 2014, leaving GE almost in limbo during 2010–13. Although the share price recovered and growth returned, no new growth engine appeared to fill the gap left by the unshackled GE Capital of the 1990s–2000s. Immelt's reluctance to redevelop is understandable however, considering the risks involved in a redevelopment. If it failed, his firm might be left facing the threat of decline rather than stagnation. And failure was more likely than success, because the redevelopment solution to the stagnation problem would have to be based on GE's industrial businesses.

The limitations of these businesses have already been discussed in this section and in the previous two sections. How could these limited performers take on the growth-engine role that GE Capital had played in the 1990s–2000s? Clearly the industrial businesses' only hope of becoming growth engines in the 2010s was to create innovative new products, and these innovations had to be truly 'breakthrough' products—opening up new opportunities for large-scale and rapid growth.

It is true that breakthrough products might instead be obtained through acquisitions. But the 2010s offered little chance of acquiring firms with breakthrough products or potential. This problem was discussed in the Chapter 13 study of Yahoo's redevelopment: GE would be facing the same problem in the 2010s. By contrast, the 2000s had offered much better prospects of making breakthrough acquisitions, such as Google's acquisition of Android recounted in Chapter 14. GE, though, had not made any breakthrough acquisitions, nor bought into the mobile-tech and Internet revolutions that had revived Apple and created such firms as Google and Amazon. Indeed, a key similarity between Immelt and Welch is that both leaders showed little interest in diversifying GE into the new high-tech products that were appearing in the 1980s–2000s. The main exception was Immelt's acquisition of the Amersham med-tech and bio-tech company. As he points out, however, this acquisition 'was built on top of an already successful business', GE Healthcare.[90] In other words, Amersham was not a diversifying acquisition that would take GE into a new industry or area of business. Similarly, only some of the acquired Amersham products were diversifications; others were just supplementing the existing products of GE Healthcare.[91] Even a wholly supplementary acquisition can of course be very beneficial, and more high-tech supplements might have helped GE's industrial businesses not only boost their performance but also create breakthrough products.

However, the help most needed in this area was not technological but cultural. GE's culture did not encourage innovation and needed to be transformed into an innovation-encouraging culture. If this had occurred, the industrial businesses would have been more likely to create the breakthrough products that, in turn, were these businesses' only hope of becoming growth engines—in the 2000s or as part of a 2010s redevelopment. As the next section shows, though, Immelt never attempted this cultural transformation, and hence he lost his only chance of carrying out a successful redevelopment in the 2010s.

Culture: Beth Comstock's *Imagine It Forward*

A crucial missing feature of GE's mid-2010s redevelopment was the cultural transformation that was never attempted. GE's culture had long been oriented towards efficiency, competitiveness, and meeting quarterly-earnings targets. By the 2010s, however, the firm required not just competitive products but also one or more break-through products. Without them, the firm's industrial businesses had no hope of becoming growth engines and taking over the role that had been played by GE Capital in the 1990s–2000s. The required breakthrough products could not be obtained through acquisitions; the industrial businesses would have to create these products: whether as innovative diversifications or as innovative developments of existing products.[92] GE therefore badly needed an innovation-encouraging culture, very different from its present culture, but such a cultural transformation was not included in its 2010s redevelopment. Its leader did not use the cultural tool in the redeveloper's tool kit.

GE's culture in the 2010s was still largely an inheritance from the Welch era. The key aspect of this legacy had emerged as long ago as the 1980s. He had shifted GE's culture towards values and attitudes related to performance and numbers.[93] They became the main cultural feature of the Welch era. It was 'numbers-obsessed' and, from Welch's perspective, was 'all about performance', culminating of course in the crucial quarterly-earnings figures.[94]

The Welch-era culture had a negative effect on innovation, as Beth Comstock notes in her 2018 *Imagine It Forward: Courage, Creativity, and the Power of Change*. Her main topic is how marketers can boost innovation, but her partly autobiographical book also provides a lieutenant's-eye view of both Welch-era and Immelt-era GE. In the final years of the Welch era, she was GE's head of public relations.[95] Her book recalls how the firm's culture had a negative effect on innovation. Welch's 'command and control culture' valued 'predictability and exactitude, not exploration' of new areas.[96] Plus, the culture's performance-numbers aspect had the side effect of discouraging innovation. As Comstock notes, expectations of perfect performance, plus the glorification of numbers, left little room for 'risky new ideas' and in fact managers 'shunned innovation to avoid failure'.[97]

It is true that GE paid more attention to innovation after Immelt became CEO in 2001. For instance, he soon began 'measuring our leaders' on innovation, expecting each industrial business 'to find two or three technical breakthroughs' each year.[98] However, he also retained Welch's performance-numbers values and perspective. Immelt-led GE had a 'results-oriented culture where consequences typically met numbers misses', observed Magee, and there were few worse managerial fates than 'missing your numbers' at 'performance-driven' GE, according to *Lights Out*.[99] GE's culture in the 2000s was therefore not very different from that of the Welch era.

This cultural continuity was accompanied by a continuing lack of innovative, breakthrough products. During the 2000s, GE did not create anything remotely comparable to Amazon's cloud computing or Apple's iPhone. GE did not have the benefit of Amazon's active-learning culture or Apple's perfectionist-innovation culture.[100] A similarly innovation-encouraging culture would have helped GE to create break-through products. In any case, the firm's lack of innovation in the 2000s showed that Immelt's pro-innovation measures had been insufficient; something more was needed to help the firm create breakthrough products in the 2010s. But even during his redevelopment of GE in 2014–17, an innovation-encouraging cultural transformation was not included.

GE's need and lack of cultural transformation is evident in Comstock's *Imagine It Forward*. She was Immelt's innovation lieutenant in the 2010s, when she helped him give GE the public image of 'a producer of innovation', an image expressed in the firm's 'Imagination at Work' slogan.[101] But Comstock knew from her experience in the 2000s, as Immelt's head of marketing, that GE's Welch-legacy culture actually inhibited imagination and innovation.

> GE managers put their efforts into what I call 'kicking the can'—squeezing every penny they could out of it, putting all their efforts into cutting costs ... Clearly, the all-consuming mastery achieved at optimization came at a substantial cost: a diminishing ability to create and grow new assets.[102]

Managers' efforts and abilities followed a similar pattern in the 2010s, despite Comstock's attempts to make them more innovative. She was impeded by a cultural legacy that she was powerless to remove and that was more influential within GE than the firm's public image of pursuing innovation. By 2015, she was disillusioned and thinking of leaving GE. 'I was feeling I had reached the end of the road there, and frankly I was tired of pushing the change and innovation boulder up an ever steeper incline'.[103] She decided later in the year, though, to keep pushing for innovation at GE. Immelt had appointed her vice-chair of the corporation and had made a persuasive personal appeal for her help in speeding up cultural change in the digital-industrial and outcome-selling areas.[104] In the event, there seems to have been no marked cultural change during the final years of his tenure, in 2016/17. In particular, the performance-numbers aspect of the culture still seems very influential.[105] The overall impression is therefore one of marked continuity with the Welch-era culture of the 1980s–90s.

This continuity meant that GE's culture continued to inhibit innovation throughout the Immelt era—during the 2010s as well as the 2000s. In particular, the culture discouraged the 'disruptive' kinds of innovation that Christensen highlighted in *The Innovator's Dilemma*. His account of disruptive technological change was discussed in Chapter 13 on IBM, as the computer industry was one of his examples of an industry being disrupted by this kind of radical innovation. Initially, however, disruptive technologies generally 'underperform established products in mainstream markets'.[106] Such underperforming innovations were likely to be shunned by any GE manager, whether in the Welch era or the Immelt era.

Immelt's managers might not have shunned, though, the innovations of what Christensen called 'sustaining' technologies. Unlike disruptive technology, a sustaining technological innovation 'improves the performance of established products, along the dimensions of performance that mainstream customers in major markets have historically valued'.[107] These technological improvements were presumably attractive to any Immelt-era managers who had to find 'technical breakthroughs' in order to meet their performance-numbers targets. But Christensen noted that some sustaining-technology improvements are in fact radical and difficult.[108] They were presumably avoided by Immelt-era managers seeking technical improvements but wanting to avoid risk and failure. These managers would instead be attracted to the more incremental kinds of improvement. GE was already known in the 2000s as 'a maker of innovative incremental improvements in jet engines and MRI machines', so this level of innovation was the obvious goal for managers seeking technical improve-ments in the 2010s.[109] On the other hand, this level of innovation could not generate breakthrough products and certainly GE did not create any during the 2010s.

So why did Immelt not discern that a cultural transformation was appropriate in GE's circumstances? The simplest explanation is that he underrated the importance of creating innovative, breakthrough products. He acknowledges that since retiring from GE 'and becoming a venture capitalist, I have grown more aware of the link between innovation and value creation inside companies'.[110] Another explanation is that he was unaware that his firm's Welch-era culture was inhibiting innovation. The most 'rational' explanation, however, is that he knew an innovation-encouraging transformation was needed but believed such a change could not be carried out—or not without too high a cost in other areas.

There was indeed good reason to believe that the transformation would be too difficult or too costly. Its target would be cultural themes, notably the performance-numbers emphasis, that had been inherited from the celebrated Welch. Although not a founder or re-founder of GE, Welch had been successful enough to attain charis-matic status and imbue his cultural legacy with the routinized charisma discussed in Chapter 15. That chapter showed that transforming a routinized-charisma culture was a difficult task for Carly Fiorina and that it had been achieved by Lou Gerstner only because he was the charismatic re-founder of IBM. He had therefore been able to replace its routinized-charismatic culture with a newer, more relevant culture—a transformational change. By contrast, Immelt had not been successful enough to attain charismatic status, and he could hardly expect to accomplish anything more than supplementary or add-on modifications to the Welch cultural legacy. To have gone further and have attempted a cultural transformation would have meant chal-lenging and trying to replace Welch's performance-numbers cultural theme. This task was a daunting prospect: failure was likely, and even success would have been costly in other areas. Most significantly, there was bound to be a costly effect on GE's quar-terly earnings, perhaps for years to come and certainly in the short term. As Comstock observes, the GE case shows 'how hard it is to navigate the tension between short-term gains and long-term readiness. Investors have little patience and markets don't forgive'.[111]

Nonetheless, there was clearly some scope for culturally transforming GE in the early 2010s. Obviously, Immelt had an opportunity to make big changes in the aftermath of the 2008/9 financial crisis. He had an even better opportunity than in post-9/11 2001 to make remedial changes, as was argued at the end of the previous section. Comstock confirms that after surviving the financial crisis, the corporation was 'like a heart attack patient who had been stabilized with a jolt from a defibrillator: alive, yes, but not long for this world unless we seriously changed our plan, our story, our narrative'.[112] Yet Immelt still did not take the opportunity for an innovation-encouraging cultural transformation, even though he could now have proclaimed that clearly the Welch-era culture had failed to meet GE's needs in the new millennium. A discerning leader would have realized that this was a 'now or never' opportunity.

Immelt's Problematic 2010s Redevelopment

Immelt's redeveloping of GE in 2014–17 is a classic example of rational redevelopment failing because it is not sufficiently rational. His prioritizing and diversifying were appropriate rational means but were not sufficient in the circumstances he was facing. His prioritizing and diversifying tools could not solve GE's long-term stagnation problem and give the firm a bright new future. He needed to use not just these two tools but also the cultural tool in the redeveloper's tool kit. As earlier sections showed, the cultural-transformation tool should have been used, and before using other tools, because the firm's culture needed to be changed from innovation-inhibiting to innovation-encouraging. This change would have helped GE's industrial businesses to create the breakthrough products that were the business's only hope of taking over the growth-engine role previously played by GE Capital. Similarly, the two redevelopment tools' only hope of success was if breakthrough products were available for prioritization or diversification.

Why did Immelt not discern that his two tools were insufficient and had no real chance of achieving a successful redevelopment—a remedial renewal? An obvious reason has already been discussed: adding a cultural transformation was not considered or was considered too daunting. Another reason is that his two tools were succeeding in achieving other remedial objectives, not as important as redevelopment but still highly significant for Immelt and GE. The diversification tool was putting an end to GE's thirty-year failure to diversify into new high-tech products. The prioritization tool was putting an end to Welch's conversion of GE into a financial-industrial conglomerate: the firm was now being reshaped into a predominantly industrial corporation. Such successes may well have obscured the fact that these tools alone were inadequate for achieving the much harder objective of redeveloping the corporation.

If the redevelopment was so hard, why then did Immelt ever begin this difficult task? After all, it was risky and presumably he knew that he was neither lucky nor brilliant enough to be a great redeveloper.[113] By the mid-2010s, however, he was running out of time to 'do something' about his legacy. In 2013, he and the board of directors had decided that his successor would be named in 2017.[114] This meant he had only a few years left to shape his legacy and ensure that problems were not irresponsibly passed on to his successor. Immelt had already shown a broad sense of responsibility to his firm, as when he socially updated GE by making it more environmentally aware and by introducing more gender and racial diversity into its management ranks. 'Immelt won plaudits, even among those who thought him a less than brilliant businessman, for a genuine commitment to improving GE's mediocre track record on diversity in race and gender'.[115] Comstock's rise to prominence is an obvious example of this increased diversity and, not surprisingly, she has a high opinion of Immelt. She describes him as a courageous leader who 'had focused the company on industrial technology; pushed to new places; absorbed risks, setbacks, and fears of those around him'.[116] In particular, he was a leader willing to take risks in order to leave his firm in good shape for its post-Immelt future.

From the mid-2010s onwards, Immelt was clearly seeking to achieve redevelopment objectives: solving his firm's problems and giving it a bright new future. The beginning of this attempted redevelopment can be more precisely dated to 2014, when he made a huge prioritizing acquisition that will be examined later in the section. However, the origins of his key *diversification* can be traced back to the early 2010s. The project would take too long to have a marked diversifying effect: the benefits would be 'too little and too late'. With this project, though, the firm seemed to be returning to its great high-tech heritage of the 1920s–70s, and certainly it was modifying the Welch-era attitude towards new high-tech products.[117]

In the early 2010s, GE began the project by pioneering the 'industrial' Internet and its associated cutting-edge software. A new GE unit, later to become GE Digital, was started from scratch and located in Silicon Valley: an appropriate home for this innovative high-tech product.[118] Predictably, the product had not originated in GE's culturally innovation-inhibited businesses. Rather, Immelt and his corporate marketers had been the source of the new diversification. It had originated in 2010/11 through an Immelt-led 'digital initiative' and through the idea of an 'Industrial Internet', a term invented by one of his marketing executives.[119] The Industrial Internet meant in practice that customers received Internet-carried data about the performance and repair needs of their GE-supplied equipment, such as jet engines or medical-imaging devices. Digital data from this equipment would be carried by the Internet and processed by the Predix cloud-based software being developed by GE.[120] There were major implications for the customer and for GE, as Comstock observes. 'By embedding software, the machines could be upgraded remotely' and furthermore 'remote software could replace in-shop repairs in many cases. If we didn't offer this, someone else could', and thereby threaten GE's markets.[121] So GE's 'digital' software diversification was an appropriate defensive, proactive measure as well as being a means of dealing with the firm's stagnation problem.

The emerging digital diversification was part of the firm's public image by the mid-2010s. Immelt was publicly referring to 'the "industrial internet" that GE would build', and the term 'digital' was suffusing

the company's vast marketing operation, the adjective having swollen to crowd out all others in everything from Immelt's public speeches to the PR network of his top lieutenant Beth Comstock. The communications office revised the boiler plate attached to every press release, the corporation's description of itself, to pronounce GE the world's first 'digital-industrial' company. Immelt proclaimed in 2014 that GE would be a 'top 10 software company' by 2020, with $4 billion in annual revenue from its new Predix software alone.[122]

But Predix had not yet been launched on the market, and its predicted annual revenue in 2020 seems unimpressive when compared to the $100 billion coming from GE's industrial businesses in 2014.[123]

The Predix digital diversification was therefore not creating a breakthrough product. Predix was in fact 'too little and too late' to be of any real help in solving the stagnation problem. The anticipated revenue was too little when compared to the conglomerate's huge size and growth requirements. Plus, the new revenue was coming too late to affect the redevelopment's chances of success. This was partly because the diversification's expansion was delayed by problems with software, recruitment, and implementation.[124] The diversification needed to be speeded up—and expanded—by acquiring or partnering with a software company. Immelt admits that one of the diversification's flaws was 'failing to take on an established partner, like Microsoft'.[125] The flaw also showed a lack of rational leadership, as GE's leader had not shown much discernment by relying on internal diversification rather than diversifying through acquisition or partnership.[126] GE had been left with a huge high-tech task. As *Lights Out* notes, GE's Industrial-Internet vision 'relied on a software ecosystem that didn't really exist yet—operating systems and apps, data protocols and standards, troubleshooting tools for the inevitable early hiccups, and clouds and server farms to hold the massive volume of data that GE hoped to analyse'.[127] If GE and Immelt had been more technically knowledgeable, they may have been less overconfident about the task that lay ahead.

Immelt seems to have been overconfident, too, about his 'digital-industrial' business growth potential. Predix software and the Industrial Internet could not convert his industrial businesses, such as GE Healthcare, into growth engines. Their products still lacked the potential to be the basis of rapid, large-scale growth. And without a cultural transformation, these businesses still lacked the potential to create truly innovative, breakthrough products. Yet Immelt's mid-2010s redevelopment of GE was relying mainly on a prioritizing reorientation towards such businesses and their industrial products.

His prioritization included, however, some prioritizing *within* GE's array of industrial products. The conglomerate's assortment of products had already been pruned a few years earlier. NBC and other media or entertainment ventures had been sold off to strengthen GE's cash reserves as it emerged from the global financial crisis.[128] Now, in the mid-2010s, two of the industrial business groups were divested as part of the redevelopment. The sale of GE Appliances to Electrolux was stopped by regulators, but the Appliances group was successfully divested to the Chinese firm Haier in 2016.[129] That year also saw a partial divestment of GE Oil & Gas, which made oil and gas equipment and had once been GE's third-largest group of businesses. After years of expansion, Oil & Gas had been hit by collapsing oil prices and was downsized in 2015.[130] Then the group was merged with an oil-field services provider, Baker Hughes, and was spun off as a separate company, known as 'Baker Hughes, a GE Company'.[131]

In addition to these divestments, there was some prioritizing among GE's remaining industrial groups. The prioritizing was of course based on growth prospects, which excluded such small groups as GE Lighting. The three biggest groups varied markedly in their prospects. GE Healthcare, the third-largest, had good long-term prospects, especially in the bio-tech area. The group was troubled, though, and facing difficult market conditions, so it was not worth prioritizing.[132] GE's second-largest group, GE Aviation, was thriving and was a leader in the aircraft-engine industry.[133] But jet engines were a specialized product sold in a mature market, without much potential for growth. Hence GE Power, the largest group, was the focus of the corporation's redevelopment.

GE Power supplied and serviced the machinery that generated electric power. The group was the world number one in its field: its 'power turbines generated about 25 percent of the world's electricity and about 45 percent' of America's.[134] Although GE Power's growth prospects were good, they were also somewhat uncertain. As Immelt explains, the global market for electricity had promising long-term prospects, but the electric-power industry could be cyclical, and the power-equipment market could be volatile.[135]

However, GE Power had an opportunity for reliable and large-scale expansion through acquisition. The opportunity arose when GE was offered the chance to buy one of GE Power's major global competitors. In January 2014, GE was offered the chance to buy the French power firm Alstom: the world's fourth-largest power-generation and transmission company.[136] Within a few months, a deal had been agreed and publicly announced, though the acquisition of Alstom did not clear all the regulatory and other hurdles until late 2015. Adding Alstom to GE Power created a 'behemoth', with more than 65,000 employees and annual revenue of some $30 billion.[137] This expansion was the key step in Immelt's prioritizing of industrial products and, in particular, GE Power's products. Upsized GE Power was 'the centrepiece of Immelt's new GE' of the mid-2010s.[138]

From a broader perspective, the Alstom acquisition marked the beginning of Immelt's attempt to redevelop GE. With this huge 2014 acquisition, he had clearly begun to reorient GE's product range towards industrial products—to prioritize them—and to reduce the role of financial services in the firm's product range. In the early 2010s, GE Capital's financial services had still been producing a large proportion of GE's earnings. But Immelt 'had promised he would reduce to 30 per cent, from 45 percent, the percentage of earnings that came from GE Capital'.[139] The Alstom acquisition reduced the GE Capital percentage by boosting the industrial contribution to GE's earnings. Thanks to the Alstom acquisition, GE Capital's contribution was reduced to only 25 per cent of the corporation's earnings in 2015.[140] GE was no longer a *financial*-industrial conglomerate.

Immelt's prioritizing through acquisition had therefore quickly reshaped the corporation. He followed this up with a divestment that downsized GE Capital's financial services. Early in 2015, GE decided that much of GE Capital would be divested: 'we'd be hanging on to our aircraft leasing operation, as well as financing for the energy and healthcare businesses—all lending lines that supported our industrial base. But the bulk of the Capital businesses would be sold over the next two years'.[141] Immelt was therefore putting an end to almost the whole of the financial-services legacy that he had inherited from Welch. After this divestment was completed, 'financial services would contribute less than 10 percent of our income, down from 25 percent at the time of the [divestment's] announcement and as compared to 50 per cent when I became CEO in 2001'.[142] In the mid-2010s his sweeping industrial prioritization had reshaped GE into a predominantly industrial corporation. He had achieved this change in just a few years by adding to GE Power through acquisition and then removing financial services from GE Capital through divestment.

GE's stagnation problem remained unsolved, however, and the firm had not yet been given a bright new future. Prioritizing industrial products had not turned them into breakthrough products. Neither had it turned the industrial businesses into growth engines, able to take on the role that GE Capital had played in the 1990s–2000s. For instance, the businesses had not been greatly helped by the firm's divestment of financial services. GE 'said that its decision to sell off Capital would focus and energize the already promised reorientation to its industrial operations', and the divestment was also projected to have a cash yield of $35 billion.[143] The cash did not, though, provide extra funds for industrial products, such as funding new investments or acquisitions. Instead, there was a stock/share buyback that reduced the number of GE shares to compensate for the loss of financial-services earnings.[144] Hence GE's earnings-per-share ratio remained the same as before the GE Capital divestment, but earnings and the corporation had been more downsized than developed. The share price, however, rose by more than 10 per cent when the divestment was announced.[145] After all, GE's financial-services earnings had been disliked by investors ever since the 2008/9 crisis, and Immelt indicates that the underlying reason for the GE Capital divestment was that 'investors would give GE no credit for financial services earnings. Only industrial EPS [earnings per share] growth would move the stock' price.[146] His industrial prioritization therefore may have been aimed largely at the stock-price problem that had been troubling his corporation.

GE had been troubled by its stock-price's poor recovery from the global financial crisis of 2008/9. Other corporations' shares—and the stock market—had recovered much more strongly than GE's shares.[147] This problem may even have helped motivate his redevelopment of the corporation. 'GE's stock price and its miserable performance were a constant cloud over Immelt's head', and indeed the stock price did not recover to a pre-crisis $30 level until the end of 2015.[148] Earlier in the year he had publicly committed GE to a long-term rise in earnings per share: to reach $2 per share in 2018. Immelt was apparently wanting to 'assure investors that they would all be rewarded for their patience', and certainly this encouraging long-term projection should have underpinned the stock price.[149] By making a hostage-to-fortune commitment, however, he had created a new opportunity for his luck to run out—and this duly occurred.

Immelt's bad luck resulted in him dramatically failing to solve the stock-price problem. Unluckily for him and the firm, their key industrial business—GE Power—was hit by a downturn in its market.[150] The $2 earnings-per-share target therefore appeared increasingly unrealistic. In 2016 GE Power badly missed its numbers and, by the end of the year, 'it was increasingly clear that GE would not make the numbers it had promised investors it would make'.[151] In 2017, matters went from bad to worse. Investors' faith in GE Power was undermined in April by news of cash flow problems, and the stock price was falling by the time Immelt addressed a May conference of investors and analysts.[152] He did not perform well when handling questions about the $2 earnings-per-share target and other difficult issues. 'I was uncharacteristically jittery. I had a sense that the end was near for me' and indeed on the following day GE's chairman told him that the board wanted to choose his successor as soon as possible.[153] His pending retirement was announced soon afterwards. He felt that 'I hadn't gotten the company where I wanted it to be' and he notes that GE's share price went up after the announcement: 'Apparently, investors thought my impending departure was good for the company. The press coverage was brutal' in its assessment of his tenure.[154]

These negative attitudes are hardly surprising. Similarly, GE's employees, investors, and other stakeholders would by now presumably have lost rational confidence in the redevelopment of GE. Its leader had obviously failed to solve the stock-price problem. More importantly, the GE Power debacle showed that he had failed to solve the stagnation problem. His prioritizing had not led to any of GE's industrial businesses taking on the growth-engine role that GE Capital had performed so powerfully in the Welch era. By the time Immelt retired in August 2017, GE's market capitalization had fallen to less than a quarter of its Welch-era peak, and the firm's value fell a further $140 billion in the year after Immelt's departure:

> In the weeks and months after Immelt left GE in 2017, a parade of negative stories and embarrassing disclosures revealed major problems that sent the company's stock into a long decline. Conversations about what happened inevitably shifted to blame, and Immelt was the obvious target. He had spent sixteen years at the top and, regardless of what Welch had left for him, he'd had plenty of time to fix it.[155]

He had tried to 'fix it' but had not used the right combination of tools. As Comstock shows, there needed to be a preceding cultural transformation as well as the use of prioritization and diversification.[156] Without this innovation-encouraging cultural transformation, GE was very unlikely to create breakthrough products. And there were indeed 'no breakthrough new products', as Gelles observes in his book on GE.[157] This absence of breakthrough products meant that, in turn, the firm's industrial businesses had no hope of becoming growth engines.

Immelt had therefore risked a redevelopment that in hindsight appears to have had no real chance of success. And the failed attempt had tipped GE into decline. In 2021, CEO Culp announced that GE was to be split into three separate companies. 'Culp would spin off the power division and the healthcare division as new public companies, leaving General Electric—a company that practically invented the modern American economy as we know it—as nothing more than a supplier of airplane engines'.[158] GE had missed its chance in the 2010s for a successful rational redevelopment. Its leader had used two appropriate rational means but not the necessary third one, cultural transformation, which was so crucial in GE's circumstances. Without this crucial rational means, the redevelopment had no real chance of success. GE's leader had shown too little discernment when selecting appropriate rational means, and this insufficiently rational leadership had foredoomed his corporation to a failed redevelopment.

Conclusion

The rational type of leadership inspires people with confidence by capably using the appropriate rational means of achieving the objective. The version of rational leadership that develops business corporations was highlighted and illustrated in an earlier edition; now an expanded edition has added a similar survey of a version that *re*develops business corporations. These two versions of rational leadership have different and distinctive objectives. The development version establishes and enhances corporations. It establishes them by developing start-ups into large-scale public companies; it enhances existing corporations by developing them further, even occasionally achieving iconic status. The *re*development version has a more specialized objective: a remedial renewal. A redevelopment aims to solve the problems of a troubled, stagnant, or declining corporation and give it a bright new future, propelling it forward to perhaps even iconic status.

Both these versions of rational leadership also have distinctive rational means of achieving their objectives. The development version has a set of seven appropriate rational means. They are generic rational methods, such as diverse deliberation, that shape decision-making about the development of a corporation. Leaders select the methods that are appropriate for the circumstances they are facing (and they may emphasize a favourite or key method). The *re*development version of rational leadership uses a specialized 'tool kit' that contains five tools. They are change-making organizational processes, such as a structural transformation. Each of the five tools is—potentially—an appropriate rational means of redeveloping a corporation. Leaders select the tools that are appropriate for dealing with the problems and other circumstances of their corporation.

Parts I and II have presented many cases of rational leaders using these rational means to develop or redevelop corporations. The cases usually included a 'leader's-eye view' of the development or redevelopment, as usually the leader had later written a memoir or partly autobiographical account of his or her achievement. Part I presented best-practice cases, showing brilliant leaders developing iconic corporations. The seven main cases were Sloan at General Motors, Ohno at Toyota, Kroc at McDonald's, Walton at Wal-Mart, Grove at Intel, Whitman at e-Bay, and Bezos at Amazon. Five other leader's-view examples were added to illustrate particular methods and issues. Two of these examples also extended the range of industries being covered, with Sandberg enhancing social-media Facebook and Packard establishing a remarkably diversified high-tech corporation. The other three examples broadened the range of countries and industries by describing Armani's Italian fashion, Roddick's British cosmetics, and Dassault's French aircraft construction.

Rational Leadership. Paul Brooker and Margaret Hayward, Oxford University Press. © Paul Brooker & Margaret Hayward (2023). DOI: 10.1093/oso/9780198894643.003.0017

Part II on redeveloping presented almost as many cases and examples. Only a few of them were iconic cases, such as Jobs at Apple, but they were all classic cases of high-quality leaders redeveloping well-known corporations. In addition to Jobs at Apple, the main cases were Knight at Nike, Iacocca at Chrysler, Gerstner at IBM, and Immelt at General Electric. Other examples were added to illustrate particular aspects or means of redevelopment. The leader's-view examples of Ollila at Nokia and Fiorina at Hewlett-Packard were used in the chapter on charismatic aspects of redevelopment. And the means of redevelopment were illustrated by the leader's-view examples of Nadella at Microsoft, Siilasmaa at Nokia, and Fiorina at Hewlett-Packard. Two examples were added to show the problems and background to redevelopment. The Mayer at Yahoo example illustrated the problems facing a redeveloper in the 2010s, while the leader's-view example of Welch at General Electric provided the background to his successor's attempt at redeveloping this corporation in the 2010s.

Summing Up

The various cases provided a wealth of information about rational leaders' use of appropriate rational means to achieve development or redevelopment. In Part I they were means of development and, specifically, were generic rational methods that shaped decision-making about development. The basic set of six appropriate methods comprised: rapid or innovative adaptation, quantitative or strategic calculation, and diverse or institutionalized deliberation. The seven main cases of Part I each showed which of the six methods were selected by 'its' leader as appropriate to use in that case—and which of these selected methods he or she emphasized.

There was a surprising amount of uniformity in the seven leaders' selection of methods. Sloan, Kroc, Walton, Whitman, and Bezos used the whole basic set of six methods in their developing of General Motors, McDonald's, Wal-Mart, eBay, and Amazon. The two other leaders, namely Ohno at Toyota and Grove at Intel, used only three of the six methods. Ohno's book described him using innovative adaptation plus both the calculative methods; Grove's book espoused an analytical framework which involved rapid adaptation plus both the deliberative methods. But their autobiographical writings were more narrowly focused than those of the other leaders. Grove was intent on recounting how he handled adaptive crises—strategic inflection points—and did not refer to the methods he used when dealing with other aspects of Intel's development. Similarly, Ohno was intent on describing his innovative production system and did not refer to the methods used by his leadership teammates, first Ishida and then Nakagawa. So the Grove and Ohno cases may in fact have involved a selection of rational methods that was little or no different from the six-method selections made by the other five leaders.

There was much less uniformity, however, in the leaders' choice of methods to *emphasize*. Innovative adaptation was emphasized by Sloan, Ohno, Kroc, and Bezos; rapid adaptation by Grove; quantitative calculation by Walton and Whitman; strategic calculation by Sloan, Kroc, Walton, Whitman, and Bezos; diverse deliberation by Kroc; and institutionalized deliberation by Sloan. It had been expected that leaders' selection of methods to emphasize would be largely a matter of personal preferences (and aptitudes) but actually in these cases it was more often due to the circumstances that the leaders were facing. For example, circumstances required Grove to emphasize rapid adaptation and required Sloan to emphasize innovative adaptation.

The most unexpected feature of the seven cases was that four of them used learning as an additional, seventh appropriate means of developing a corporation. Walton, Grove, Whitman, and Bezos used and indeed emphasized this generic rational method. In all four cases, too, learning was emphasized as a both key and favourite method: both because of personal preferences and because of the circumstances that each leader was facing. Furthermore, the Whitman case highlighted the importance of learning quickly, and the Walton case showed that learning has several different forms and contexts. The active forms of learning were highlighted by the Bezos case. The distinctive aspect of his emphasis on learning was the role of iteration, invention, experimentation, and other active learning processes—plus showing a positive attitude towards their accompanying failures. There was much to be learnt from Bezos's and other leaders' emphasis on learning.

A second unexpected feature of the seven cases was the prevalence of dual-leadership teams. They appeared in the Toyota, McDonald's, Walmart, and Intel cases. There were important appearances by all three versions of the dual-leadership team: the two-roles, the two-generations, and the innovation-introducing team. The Toyota case saw the innovation-introducing teams of Ohno and Ishida and then Ohno and Nakagawa. At McDonald's, the two-role team of Kroc and Sonneborn led the firm through a crucial period in its development. Then the two-generation team of Kroc and Turner led McDonald's into a further period of expansion and the new, globalized era of international joint ventures. Similarly, the two-generation team of Walton and Glass took Wal-Mart in important new directions, including the Supercentre, in the years before Walton's death. At Intel, the two-role team of Noyce and Moore established the corporation and then it was enhanced by the Grove and Moore two-role team. Furthermore, the Intel chapter examined some corporate development by perhaps the greatest ever dual-leadership team: Hewlett and Packard.

The dual form of leadership is not, however, a distinctive characteristic of development; dual leadership also appeared in the cases of *re*development that were presented in Part II. In two of its five main cases there were periods of dual leadership. Nike's team of Strasser and Knight launched its redevelopment. And Chrysler had a dual-leadership team in the second stage of its redevelopment, when Lutz helped Iacocca exploit the hybridizing with AMC (American Motors Corporation).

The Part II chapters were looking at the version of rational leadership that redevelops corporations. This version of rational leadership has a 'tool kit' of five appropriate rational means, each of them a change-making organizational process. The five tools are cultural or structural transformation, a diversifying or prioritizing reorientation of the product range, and hybridization through a merger with another company. A rational leader of redevelopment uses the tools that are appropriate for dealing with the problems and other circumstances of his or her corporation.

In Part II the most frequently used tool was diversification, which was used in four of the five main cases. Prioritization was a close second, though, used in three of the five cases. The least popular tool was hybridization, which appeared only when Chrysler hybridized with AMC. Each of the kit's five tools was used in one or more of the main cases, so all the tools were confirmed to be potentially appropriate. And no *other* tools were shown to be similarly appropriate. There was no equivalent of what occurred in Part I, which discovered that an additional method—learning—should be included in development's set of appropriate rational means.

In the Part II cases a leader tended to use only about half of the tools in redevelopment's tool kit. These rational leaders, as expected, were therefore not overloading their firms with too many change-making processes. None of the leaders used more than three of the five organizational processes and indeed none used more than two at the same time—simultaneously. Immelt simultaneously diversified and prioritized at General Electric. Gerstner used cultural and structural transformations simultaneously at IBM and then prioritized IT services. Iacocca prioritized and diversified in the first stage of Chrysler's redevelopment and then hybridized with AMC in the second stage. Jobs transformed Apple culturally and structurally in the first stage of redevelopment and then used diversification in the second and third stages. Such multiple stages were not pre-planned however. Chrysler's second stage was largely due to an oversight in the first stage, while Apple's second stage was largely due to a recession sending the firm back into decline.

An unexpected feature of the five cases was that redeveloping had often been combined with a cost-cutting turnaround. The Chrysler and IBM redevelopments were preceded or accompanied by a cost-cutting turnaround carried out by the redeveloping leader. In Apple's case, the previous leader had carried out a turnaround. IBM's previous leader had even attempted a rectification of mistakes made before he took charge.

A not surprising feature of redevelopment is that often the leader was an outside CEO. Iacocca at Chrysler and Gerstner at IBM had been brought in from outside the firm. Similarly, although Jobs was a co-founder of Apple, he had pursued his career elsewhere for many years before he was asked back in the late 1990s. The same tendency appeared among the six 'minor' cases that were used to illustrate particular aspects of redevelopment. Mayer at Yahoo was an outside CEO and so was Fiorina at Hewlett-Packard. Siilasmaa at Nokia was another outsider, who had been a board-member for only a few years before leading a redevelopment. This tendency for redevelopment to be led by outsiders is not surprising, as redevelopment is such a specialized version of rational leadership. And an outsider is perhaps better placed to discern how a remedial renewal can be achieved.

Broadening the Perspective

The Part II chapters on redevelopment broadened the Part I perspective on rational leadership and the development of corporations. Redeveloping is a special and specialized form of corporation development, requiring a specialized version of rational leadership. However, the specialized tools for redevelopment—the five change-making organizational processes in the redeveloper's tool kit—may also be used to implement decisions by leaders of corporation development. This was pointed out in Chapter 10 and was illustrated by Chapter 14. It showed how Google's diversification into smartphone software had implemented a strategically calculated decision about development. Here the change-making organizational process of diversifying the product range had been used for development rather than redevelopment's remedial renewal.

Other examples can be found among the cases presented in Part I. A structural transformation was needed to implement Sloan's decision to centralize General Motors into operational divisions. Likewise, a structural transformation was needed to carry out Ohno's decisions about creating a 'lean' just-in-time production system at Toyota. At Walmart, Walton culturally transformed labour relations and later diversified into subdiscounting and groceries. Kroc diversified McDonald's by adding sit-down options to its drive-in restaurants. Whitman diversified eBay by adding fixed-price options to its online auction platform. Bezos frequently diversified, as part of his grand strategy for Amazon. And Grove prioritized microprocessor chips at Intel. As for the other cases, Armani diversified his product pyramid, Dassault diversified from military airplanes into business jets, and Roddick culturally transformed The Body Shop into a prominent example of a socially responsible business.

Another broadening of perspective is that rational leadership appears—not surprisingly—to have various kinds of capability. As Chapter 10 observed, the redevelopment version of rational leadership relies on discernment as well as such business capability as adept acquisition of firms to supplement a diversification or prioritization. Other Part II chapters, particularly Chapter 16, confirmed that the level of discernment can be crucial in achieving a successful redevelopment.

The highest level of discernment/capability was shown by Jobs at Apple. Yet that case also highlighted the importance of having highly capable executives—and in this case, designers and programmers—help the leader carry out a redevelopment. The extraordinary success of Apple was due to the extraordinary capability of both the leader and the led. Clearly the capability of a corporation's employees is one of the factors that the leader must take into account when assessing circumstances and discerning which rational means are appropriate in these circumstances.

Finally, a warning should be given about the limits of capability. Chapter 13 pointed out that even Jobs could not have successfully redeveloped Yahoo in the 2010s. An objective may be so difficult that the appropriate rational means will not be enough to achieve it. Capability is also limited by the effects of bad luck, whether redeveloping or developing. Chapter 14 recounted the devastating effect that the 2000/1 high-tech recession had on Jobs's redevelopment of Apple, requiring him to start again with a new stage of redevelopment. That recession also destroyed a swathe of new high-tech firms, especially new Internet-related firms. Among the casualties there were doubtless some companies that might have developed into corporations if this bad luck had not denied them their opportunity. Luck is perhaps the biggest challenge facing rational leaders.

The Next Generation: 2020–50

What does the future hold for the development and redevelopment of corporations? In 2020–50 redeveloping will likely become more notable because of an overall reduction in corporation development: specifically, a reduction in the development of start-ups into corporations. There are three trends that will likely reduce this kind of corporation development. The first trend is the petering out of the 1980–2010 torrent of technologically based commercial innovation, which produced a series of new opportunities for development. For example, there were personal computers and their software, then the Internet and e-commerce, and, finally, the smartphone and its apps. By comparison, the 2010s was an aftermath era with declining opportunities and that trend seems likely to continue until the return of major technological innovation.

A second trend is the decline in new geographical sources of corporation development. East Asian countries' economic development has long provided the world with a succession of new corporations, such as Japan's Toyota, Korea's Samsung, and China's Alibaba. But these countries now have mature economies, and no other region of the world seems ready to take over this role of producing a series of high-growth economies and corporations.

A third trend is the 'big fish' tendency for corporations to acquire start-ups and small firms that might otherwise have developed into corporations. These are small-scale acquisitions that do not involve hybridization and are more like foraging or feeding. The motivation is typically not anti-competitive and defensive but, on the contrary, an attempt to keep the corporation competitive and expanding. As Chapter 13 observed, such an acquisition may even be aimed at gaining clever new personnel rather than a clever new product idea. Whatever the motive, however, the effect of the 'big fish' tendency is that new corporations are likely to develop only in niche markets or poorer countries that do not attract existing corporations. And the prospects for this peripheral kind of corporate development seem rather dim, considering the lack of new technological and geographical sources of development.

The future therefore lies with the existing corporations. Redeveloping will hence be proportionately more common, even though it is such a specialized form of development. And if the future is relatively humdrum, redevelopment may become more of a standard than specialized form of development. A corporation's long-term future may depend upon its potential to be a remedially renewable organization. Many corporations should be able to renew themselves through redevelopment, preferably when only troubled and not yet facing the threat of stagnation or decline. However, the leader of a redevelopment will inspire people with confidence only if he or she employs the redevelopment version of rational leadership. He or she will have to be using the appropriate rational means—from the specialized tool kit—for achieving that redevelopment.

Addendum: Reconstructive Development

Post-Nazi Volkswagen

This Addendum looks at rational leadership in the reconstructive development of corporations. It is called 'reconstructive' development because it is analogous to reconstructive surgery being used to solve the physical development problems of a baby or child. In business terms, it is the start-up equivalent of the problem-solving redevelopment discussed in Part II. Unlike with redevelopment, the problem-solving occurs before a corporation has been established, when it is still only a start-up and not yet a public company. The objective of reconstructive development is to solve a start-up's development problems so successfully that it develops into a corporation. Such success is a major achievement, as many start-ups *without* obvious development problems nevertheless fail to develop into corporations: success is more the exception than the rule. But how would a rational leader carry out the reconstructive development that would establish this corporation? What are the appropriate rational means of achieving a successful result?

There is some evidence that a rational leader would have used one or more of the five organizational processes discussed in Part II. Those processes are part of a 'tool kit' that is used to *re*develop corporations *after* they had been established, but there is evidence of them also having been used as the 'surgical instruments' of reconstructive development. In fact the most famous and successful case of reconstructive development, post-Nazi Volkswagen, used four of these five organizational processes as instruments for reconstructive surgery on its development problems.

This Addendum's following four sections will therefore examine this classic case of reconstructive development. It arose after the Second World War, when the ex-Nazi Volkswagen factory was developed into 'one of the world's preeminent carmakers and a symbol of Germany's rebirth'.[1] Volkswagen was Germany's equivalent of General Motors and Toyota, whose development was described in Chapters 2 and 3. All three firms became iconic corporations and they epitomized the automobile era of the global economy. Volkswagen's development has some similarities with Toyota's, as both firms had to develop in post-war economies that had been devastated by aerial bombing and then had experienced a military occupation by foreign armies. In the Volkswagen case, however, the firm was not a public company and it was reconstructively developed by two rational leaders in the 1940s–50s.

The rational leadership was provided initially by a British army officer, Ivan Hirst, and then by a German business executive, Heinrich Nordhoff. They used four of the five organizational processes that this book's Part II has identified as potentially—depending upon the circumstances—appropriate rational means of redevelopment. Both leaders culturally as well as structurally transformed their ex-Nazi factory, and Nordhoff reoriented its product range by prioritizing as well as diversifying.

The prioritized product was a small car, nicknamed 'the Beetle' because of its beetle-like body shape. The Beetle sold around the world in the 1950s–60s and eventually overtook the Model T Ford as the most-produced car ever made. The nickname 'Beetle' had appeared as early as 1938 but did not become the official name until 1968, even though in Germany it had increasingly replaced the names 'Volkswagen' and 'VW'.[2] In America, the car was often called 'the Bug', as in the 1960s comedy film *The Love Bug*.[3] Under whatever name, though, the Beetle was one of the greatest ever automobile products and, like the Volkswagen factory, had been started up during the Nazi era.

The Nazi Start-Up

The Beetle car and Volkswagen factory originated as an attempt to create an affordable car that would bring mass motoring to Germany. In the early 1930s, the country had fewer than half a million cars, compared to America's more than twenty million, and there were attempts at creating a car that could be afforded by many people rather than just a privileged few.[4] In 1933, Hitler came to power and pressured the automobile industry to fulfil this aspiration by producing an affordable 'people's car' (*Volkswagen*). The resulting venture hired Ferdinand Porsche's design firm, which went on to create the first Beetle.

The new car's most obvious and distinctive feature was its beetle-like body shape. This streamlined shape was designed to reduce drag at higher speed, especially through having a sloping rather than blunt hood at the front of the car. The Beetle's body benefited, too, from structural innovations that reduced its weight and increased the space available inside, allowing this small car to seat a family of five and to be less cramped than other small cars. The Beetle's streamlining and light weight enabled its small, four-cylinder engine to power the car to the high cruising speeds expected on the new *Autobahn* expressways. Yet the Beetle could also readily use inferior roads—and even farm tracks—thanks to its innovative suspension system and its rear-engine design: with the engine in the rear of the car, power was delivered directly to the rear wheels and the engine's weight improved the wheels' grip on difficult surfaces. The engine was not liquid-cooled by a radiator system but instead air-cooled by a fan, which reduced weight and lessened the likelihood of the engine being frozen up in wintery conditions. Consequently, the car did not need to be garaged, unlike most other German cars of the time. Another cost-saving feature was the relatively low maintenance requirements and costs, such as giving the owner or repairer easy access to the engine. And the owner would be saving substantially on fuel costs, as the Beetle had markedly less fuel consumption than other cars of its era and capabilities. This was an economical, affordable car to run as well as to buy.

In 1930s Germany, though, the Beetle was not sufficiently affordable to be a people's car—within the reach of all social classes. So in 1938 this private-sector venture was taken over by a Nazi political organization, the German Labour Front. It was the Nazi regime's version of a labour-union movement and was a practically compulsory organization that included employers as well as employees. The Labour Front officially referred to the Beetle as the 'KdF-Wagen', named after the Front's leisure organization: 'Strength through Joy' (KdF). And it created a new company, the Volkswagenwerk GmbH, to produce the Beetle for members of the Front.

The *Volkswagen* venture had therefore been converted into an enterprise that was not commercially owned and operated. The Beetle could be purchased only by Labour Front members and only by paying in advance through weekly instalments: the car would be delivered to buyers after they had paid its price through weekly deposits into a savings account that they had to open with the KdF.[5] More importantly, the car's price was set too low to be profitable and yet too high to stimulate the massive demand—from the working class as well as the middle class—originally envisaged by the Nazis and their Volkswagenwerk company.[6] Indeed, the car-buying savings scheme had attracted only about 250,000 people by the time the company's factory was nearing completion in 1939, though this huge state-of-the-art factory had been designed to produce up to 450,000 cars a year and there were plans to extend it into a gigantic facility that would produce as many as a *million* cars a year.[7] Such high levels of production could have been sustained only by exports and indeed German automobile exports surged dramatically in the latter half of the 1930s.[8] But military conquest, not an export drive, was on Hitler's agenda.

The Second World War led to the shelving of the Nazi car-making venture—the largest start-up ever not to be started. Its huge new factory never began mass production of the KdF Beetle. During the war, the factory produced war-related material and was badly damaged by aerial bombing. At war's end, all that remained of the Nazi Volkswagenwerk company was a bomb-damaged factory that was more of a liability than an asset to a country devastated by war and occupied by foreign armies.

Hirst's Structural and Cultural Transformations

In 1945, the four big powers that had defeated and occupied Germany—the US, Britain, France, and Russia—each established a zone of military occupation ruled by a military government. The ex-Nazi Volkswagenwerk factory was in the British occupation zone and therefore under the control of its British military government until 1949. Specifically, it was under the control of Major Ivan Hirst, an officer in the army's Royal Electrical and Mechanical Engineers. When Hirst took charge of the bomb-damaged factory in August 1945, he found that 70 per cent of the buildings and over 90 per cent of the machinery were still standing.[9] Hirst decided to start up production at the factory by making Beetles for the British army occupying that part of Germany. As he later recalled, a Beetle 'that had been built at the beginning of the war was sprayed Khaki green and driven to H.Q. 21 Army Group as a demonstration model. The resulting order for the first batch of saloons was taken as the signal to go ahead' and begin production.[10] In 1946, some 10,000 Beetles were produced for the soldiers of the British occupation army—and the factory was employing several thousands of German workers.[11] Already, it was a very sizeable start-up.

There were serious limits, though, to its expansion. The production target of 1,000 cars per month 'represented the absolute maximum for a long time and it was a target that was often not reached.'[12] For example, the severe winter in 1947 crippled production and led to a new round of repair work aimed at weather-proofing the factory.[13] Furthermore, production was hampered by the incapacities of Germany's still war-devastated economy. In 1947, German industry was still only 'a third of the size that it had been' and could not readily supply parts or materials for Beetle production.[14] These supply shortages stymied Hirst's plan to raise monthly car production from 1,000 to 2,500 by the end of the year.[15] However, he was able to take the crucial step of offering the Beetle to German consumers as well as British soldiers, and during 1947 about a quarter of his production had been snapped up by German car-buyers.[16] The limited number of Beetles allocated to German buyers had been so much in demand that the black-market price for the cars had far exceeded their official price.[17] Clearly the Beetle had the potential to succeed in the car market that was gradually re-emerging in Germany.

Hirst had begun a structural transformation that would enable the Volkswagenwerk factory to compete effectively in this re-emerging car market. In particular, he created a sales department and an accompanying organization of distributors and dealerships: there were some forty Beetle dealerships in Germany by 1948.[18] This new sales apparatus developed a 'Volkswagen way' philosophy, whose central tenet was that customer service was more important than sales.[19] For example, the factory set up a training school to teach dealership and service-station staff how to service the Beetle. Soon 'any dealership that sold a Volkswagen would be equipped to service it too, or at least be in proximity to a station that could.'[20] In addition to the new sales apparatus, an extensive administrative bureaucracy was being created. By mid-1948 there was not just a sales department and a general-office department but also a collection of separate departments for accounting, tax, insurance, legal matters, purchasing, personnel, organization, statistics, and planning.[21] So the Volkswagenwerk factory had been given sales and administrative capacities similar to those of the car-making companies it would compete against in the re-emerging car market.

This structural transformation obviously was not about *re*structuring an existing organization. Instead, it was creating sales and administrative organizations that would normally be developed *along with* the development of production facilities, such as starting up a new factory. In the Volkswagenwerk case, a huge factory had been developed without these accompanying organizations. However, Hirst's reconstructive 'surgery'—using the organizational process of structural transformation—had created the missing organizations and capacities. Thanks to this reconstructive development, the Volkswagenwerk enterprise was fully equipped to compete successfully against the companies that had dominated the German car market before the war.

When these companies re-entered the car market in 1947/8, they therefore did not pose much of a competitive threat to the Volkswagenwerk enterprise. Opel, Ford, and Mercedes-Benz resumed production in the second half of 1947, but they lacked anything comparable to the Beetle or to the huge state-of-the-art factory that produced the Beetle.[22] Before the war, Opel had been a subsidiary of General Motors and the leader of the German automobile industry; in 1948, the company produced fewer than 6,000 cars while nearly 20,000 Beetles emerged from the Volkswagenwerk factory.[23]

The second half of 1948 was a turning point for the German car market and the Beetle. Economic reforms had led to a rapid improvement in the supply of parts and materials, as 'almost every article was available again' (at the right price).[24] And there were no longer any restrictions on how many Beetles could be bought by German consumers, who that year purchased some 60 per cent of its factory's production.[25] Freed of supply and demand constraints, the monthly production of Beetles began a steady rise that took it from the standard *c*.1,000 in August 1948 to nearly 5,000 a month in October 1949.[26] This remarkable increase in production and sales—far outstripping its competitors' figures—confirmed that the Volkswagenwerk factory had been reconstructively developed into a very successful commercial enterprise, even if officially it was still operated by the British army and owned by the Nazis' defunct Labour Front!

However, the British army's representative had included an anti-Nazi cultural transformation in his reconstructive development of the Volkswagenwerk factory. Soon after Hirst took charge of the factory, he began this organizational process of transforming its Nazi-influenced culture. He believed that the authoritarian Nazi mentality was at least partly responsible for the fact that the workers 'had to have orders to do things and had no initiative'.[27] So the 'authoritarian management style of former years was replaced by a new one. Direct contact with workers was now desirable and colleagues were encouraged to follow open door arrangements'.[28] Hirst's policy was to meet and talk with workers face to face, hoping 'to give the workers a sense of independence and a chance to make decisions for themselves'.[29]

He also sought to change industrial-relations attitudes and practices that had been inherited from the Nazis' Labour Front. For example, in November 1945 the factory's elected works council had bewildered Hirst by asking him to sign the minutes of a council meeting *before* it had been held.[30] This was explained to him as a legacy from the Nazi era, when a Labour Front works council had to have its minutes pre-approved by the factory's boss. In Hirst's words, 'we got that straightened out and it worked better. They still had much to learn'.[31] Not long after, however, independent labour unions emerged and were allowed by him to hold on-site meetings at the factory.[32] The workers eventually even wanted to have a say in management policy-making, which led him to ask his army headquarters for help. It sent him a British trade-union official, who restored the workers' faith in British-style 'them and us' industrial relations: 'he listened to what they wanted, a seat on the management, and he said ... if you have a seat on the management who are you going to fight with?'[33]

Hirst's tenure as leader of the Volkswagenwerk factory came to an end in late 1949. It was time for the British to hand the factory back to German control, namely control by the post-war Federal Republic of Germany. The enterprise's new leader would be Heinrich Nordhoff, who was a 50-year-old veteran of the automobile industry. He had joined Opel in 1930 as an engineer, risen rapidly to senior-executive status, joined the board of directors in 1936, and managed Opel's big truck-making factory in 1942–5.[34] He even had American experience, as part of his executive training had been a study trip to Detroit to look at the production and marketing techniques of General Motors. He was therefore well qualified to take over from Hirst as leader of the now German-controlled Volkswagenwerk enterprise.

Nordhoff had in fact for years been leading the enterprise as part of a dual-leadership team with Hirst. In January 1948, Nordhoff had been appointed general director of the enterprise, becoming Hirst's second in command. Although officially a subordinate, the new appointee had soon made himself 'the centre of company affairs'.[35] Hirst was left with what he later described as the 'awkward task of monitoring Nordhoff's performance'.[36] But this performance was of a high quality and he went on to complete the reconstructive development initiated by Hirst.

Nordhoff Continues the Reconstructive Development

Nordhoff had already been helping structurally transform the Volkswagenwerk enterprise in 1948/9, as part of a dual-leadership team with Hirst. 'In the early months of 1948 Nord-hoff established a hierarchical management structure to tighten his control of the plant'.[37] His new structure also tightened control over the specialized departments being spawned by the factory's administration, which might otherwise have become an unwieldy and splintered bureaucracy. Nordhoff grouped these numerous departments into six management divisions: Technical, Personnel, Purchasing, Sales, Financial, and Costing.[38] For example, the Personnel management division contained not only the personnel department but also the depart-ments for catering, housing, hygiene, and welfare. Nordhoff's management divisions were his equivalent of the operating divisions pioneered by Sloan at General Motors and described in Chapter 2.[39] But instead of making a particular brand or type of car, the management divisions were carrying out a particular administrative function, such as a personnel or financial func-tion. As with operating divisions, minor decision-making was decentralized to the divisional leaders while major decisions were made higher up the hierarchy: in this case, by Nordhoff. 'In this new structure, much of the decision-making power was located with him, the general manager', and indeed his combination of personal power and divisional decentralization has been described as 'industrial feudalism'.[40]

More importantly, the new management structure and administrative departments played a key role in the reconstructive development—they 'revolutionized the Volkswagen factory'.[41] They boosted even the factory's technical capabilities. For instance, two crucial capabilities were promoted by the Technical management division, specifically its departments for design and production layout.[42] Improving the Beetle car's 'inner workings' was one of Nordhoff's main concerns and, as the next section recounts, the Technical design team would pro-vide many enhancements in the years ahead.[43] Improving the factory's production layout was another of Nordhoff's main concerns, for the limited-production layout of 1946/7 left much to be desired: 'there was no standardization of the actual assembly procedure, with the machines laid out chaotically on the factory floor'.[44] Now though, the factory had the ben-efit of a production-layout team in the Technical management division. It helped Nordhoff slowly restore and augment the mass-production system of assembly lines and production shops that the factory had been designed to use.[45] With mass production back in place, the factory could handle the fivefold increase in production in 1948/9 and without having to take on many thousands of new workers.[46]

Productivity had also been improved by the Costing management division, with its depart-ments for budget, organization, statistics, and cost control.[47] For example, the budgeting projections and controls in the fiscal plan for 1949 had significantly reduced the cost of produc-ing a Beetle.[48] In the next decade, heavy investment in new machinery would enable the factory to achieve a threefold increase in output per worker.[49] But it was under the Hirst-Nordhoff dual leadership that the factory had become a productivity-oriented enterprise.

Nordhoff had also helped structurally transform the selling of its products. He had 'expanded the dealership network that the British had started in October 1946'.[50] And his Sales management division included a separate sales department for exports: the Beetle's export potential had already begun to be promoted and institutionalized.[51] By late 1949, more than 10,000 Beetles had been exported to neighbouring countries, and the factory had begun pro-ducing an upgraded Export version of the Beetle.[52] The car and the factory were ready for the decades of export success that lay ahead.

In addition to his structural transformation, Nordhoff had aided and completed the anti-Nazi cultural transformation of the firm. As late as the 1950s, he had to keep Nazi ideology in mind when he talked about bridging social divisions in the workplace.

> Nordhoff took great care to point out that his ideas were different from the notions of social har-mony the Nazis had propounded under the label of the 'people's community', declaring that in the context of industrial relations [the Nazis'] National Socialism offered nothing but 'politically coloured cant'.[53]

In contrast, he was pursuing an American-style capitalist collaborative relationship with the labour unions of his factory's workforce. 'While the management benefited from the absence of disruptive strikes, the trade union seized opportunities to demonstrate its efficacy to the workforce by taking the lead in negotiations for beneficial contracts'.[54] This industrial-relations system was a step in the same direction taken by Hirst when dealing with the independent labour unions that emerged in post-war Germany. Nordhoff, however, had now fully replaced the industrial-relations ideas inherited from the Nazi era and, more broadly, was completing the anti-Nazi cultural transformation.

His continuation of Hirst's reconstructive development also used a new 'surgical' instrument—prioritizing within the product range. But Nordhoff was not using this organi-zational process in the usual manner of focusing on a particular product within a range of products and eliminating or cutting back on the others. Instead, he was focusing on improve-ments to the only product available, the Beetle, and was not seeking either to replace it or to widen the range of products by adding new car designs.

In Nordhoff's early years as leader he was pressured to abandon the 1930s Beetle design and introduce newer car products. 'The pressure Nordhoff came under to abandon the [Beetle] design was terrific', and some of the pressure came 'from within the Volkswagenwerk's own ranks'.[55] But he was determined not to either replace the Beetle or even to supplement it by introducing other car products aimed at other segments of the car market. Several years later a sports-car version was introduced, but it was not until the 1960s that a new family-car design was introduced to supplement the Beetle.[56]

Although improvements would be made to the Beetle, the design's distinctive features would be preserved—along with its official name of 'Volkswagen Type 1'.[57] In Nordhoff's words:

> I brushed away all temptation to change model and design ... Offering people an honest value, a product of the highest quality, with low original cost and incomparable resale value, appealed more to me than being driven around by a bunch of hysterical stylists trying to sell people something they really do not want to have.[58]

He was intent on 'organically' improving the car 'from the inside out, without touching the basically sound Porsche design' developed in the 1930s.[59] Hence a new model of the Bee-tle would appear each year with barely noticeable but significant improvements to the car's mechanical parts and interior fittings.[60] As early as 1953, the 'organic redesign' of the Beetle through annual model changes had created a car 'which contained not a single screw that exactly corresponded to its Porsche-designed forerunner' yet still looked much the same as its earliest versions.[61]

However, Nordhoff had carried out much more drastic surgery elsewhere by diversifying into vans—and thereby was creating a non-car range of vehicle products. The diversification into vans occurred as early as 1949, with a design called the Transporter. It originated as an innovative design for a light delivery van: a 'simple boxy vehicle with the driver sitting above the front axle and a pusher Volkswagen engine at the rear'.[62] In the years and decades ahead, the van would appear in a wide variety of guises and was even used as a camper van. The two most famous models would be the many-windowed Microbus, with seating for nine passengers, and the dual-purpose Kombi van, which could be used as a cargo van or converted into an eight-passenger microbus.[63] By 1954, it was clear that the diversification into vans had been very successful: more than 40,000 were produced that year—a sixth of the Volkswagenwerk enterprise's production—and the vans were already an export success in Europe and America.[64]

That the enterprise was producing over 240,000 vehicles a year by 1954 was partly due to another form of diversification—the export orientation created by Nordhoff. As noted earlier, he had introduced an export version of the Beetle as early as 1949: an upmarket model priced 12 per cent higher than the Standard Beetle.[65] 'The Export Sedan was identifiable by its chrome bumpers, bright hubcaps, chrome headlight rims and shiny door handles. The Export interior appointments were also of better quality'.[66] This upgrading paid off handsomely. The Beetle 'charmed its way abroad', as customers appreciated its looks as well as its practicality and reliability.[67] Indeed, no other car at the low end of the market could match the Beetle. However, the product was only half the story; the other half was the market opportunity. For the Beetle was being exported to 'the burgeoning middle classes of Europe'.[68] They were benefiting from an economic boom in the 1950s and were also more likely than their German equivalents to buy a car: only one in four German middle-class households owned a car at the end of the booming, income-doubling 1950s.[69] So exports played a crucial role in the almost miraculous expansion of Beetle production during that decade:

> As early as 1955, the [Volkswagenwerk] company was retailing more vehicles abroad (177,657) than at home (150,397). Over the next years, exports remained at the heart of VW's expansion, and it shipped over 620,000 cars, or more than 55 per cent of its annual output, to destinations beyond West Germany in 1963.[70]

In the 1960s, the growth in production slowed and relied increasingly on exports to America rather than Europe. By the end of the decade, production had yet to reach 1.5 million vehicles a year, but exports to America had increased dramatically, with now nearly 40 per cent of VW's vehicle production being exported to the US.[71] Annual Beetle sales in America had increased to over 230,000 by 1963, and by the time Nordhoff retired in 1968 they had reached their peak of some 420,000.[72]

The Beetle's American success was partly due to its distinctive charm. It stood out as something unconventional and aroused surprisingly affectionate emotions. 'Many drivers established a deep emotional attachment' to a small car that 'possessed a charm that cast a uniquely enchanting spell over drivers, leaving them infatuated with an inanimate object whose shape contrasted sharply with America's automotive mainstream'.[73] Its charm was highlighted by an advertising campaign that has been ranked as the best ever in the twentieth century.[74] In the early 1960s, an American ad agency produced a series of witty magazine and television advertisements that focused on the Beetle's distinctive features, such as the car's smallness and the firm's stringent quality control.[75] (The Beetle was in a sense a forerunner of the small, reliable, and economical Japanese cars that would hit the American market some twenty years later.) Its brilliant advertising campaign also helped the Beetle gain a unique status—and market niche—among youthful Americans. 'It was the college kids who first understood the VW ad campaign', and soon the Beetle acquired a 'sort of cult following among the young'.[76] In the second half of the 1960s, this youthful following increasingly consisted of rebellious or unconventional young people. Indeed the Beetle became 'a symbol of the counterculture'.[77]

> As protests against the Vietnam War gathered force, Volkswagen tapped into the backlash against consumerism and the military industrial complex, with which the Detroit automakers were identified …The transformation of the Volkswagen [Beetle] from Nazi propaganda project to counterculture phenomenon was one of the most spectacular examples of rebranding in the history of marketing.[78]

Similarly, one of the most spectacular examples of corporation development was how an ex-Nazi factory had been developed into democratic Germany's iconic corporation, producing more than a million vehicles a year and exporting hundreds of thousands of them to America.

The success had been due to a reconstructive development carried out by its two leaders, Hirst and Nordhoff. They had solved the factory's stark development problems by using four different organizational processes: a structural transformation and a cultural transformation plus a prioritizing and a diversifying of the products made by the factory. These four instruments had proved to be appropriate rational means of achieving the objective, and indeed had been used to carry out the most famous case of reconstructive development of a business corporation.

An Incongruous as well as Famous Case

Yet although the development of the Volkswagenwerk factory had been remarkably successful, there had been one huge anomaly or incongruity. The enterprise did not become a public company until 1960: only then did it become the 'Volkswagenwerk AG', with the abbreviation AG referring to its new status as a 'stock company'.[79] By then it was one of the largest industrial firms in the country, with a workforce of over 60,000 and with production approaching a million vehicles a year.[80] So it had been developed into a large-scale firm before it had been converted into a public company—and hence acquired the status of a business *corporation*.

Why had it not been converted into a public company a decade earlier, when the British occupation army had handed the enterprise over to German federal and state governments? The British had specified that the local state of Lower Saxony was to be 'responsible for control of the Volkswagenwerk, but on behalf of and under the direction of the Federal Government until such time as the responsible German authorities issue other directions'.[81] However, no such 'other directions' emerged during the 1950s. As the German governments stuck to the makeshift arrangement inherited from the British, the nominal owner of the factory continued to be the defunct Nazi-era Labour Front! Trusteeship had passed from the British army to Germany's new democratic institutions, but their politicians could not decide how to deal with the ownership issue.[82]

Even when the politicians finally privatized the Volkswagenwerk enterprise, they created an unusual and rather dubious form of public-company ownership. The 1960 privatization was only partial and it limited the power of the private-sector shareowners, for the Federal Republic and its state of Lower Saxony retained 40 per cent of the shares, while the other 60 per cent were sold to a multitude of shareholders (some 1.5 million), with restrictions on their ownership rights.[83] In particular, no individual or institutional shareholder was allowed to own more than 20 per cent of the shares or, more specifically, more than 20 per cent of shareowners' voting rights.[84] So the newly created Volkswagen corporation was wholly protected against a domestic or foreign takeover. But another effect of this unusual form of privatization was that the private shareholders had 'essentially no say' in the corporation's policy-making.[85]

The politicians' dithering and dubious privatization arrangement therefore may have been because they did not want to disrupt Nordhoff's successful leadership of this important enterprise. He and his Beetles had even appeared on the cover of *Time* magazine's special issue in 1954 about Germany's economic recovery.[86] Within Germany, Nordhoff was publicly identified with his firm's success. He gained a national reputation as 'an economic miracle worker' and became 'somewhat of a legend'.[87] This was partly because of his performance on the public stage. He had 'a charismatic persona, commanding and charming crowds with ease' as he 'celebrated' his firm's impressive production and sales figures.[88] His personal prominence and power in fact led to him being nicknamed 'King Nordhoff' by journalists, but most of the public saw his regal role in a positive light, as being 'lord over an enviable empire of production'.[89]

Nordhoff certainly had achieved far more than might have been expected in 1948 when he arrived at the Volkswagenwerk factory. By the time his tenure (and life) ended in 1968, the Volkswagen corporation was the most important company in Germany and perhaps the whole of Europe. Furthermore, his twenty years of leadership had made a lasting contribution. The Volkswagen corporation is, to this day, a leading player in the global automobile industry, comparable to such titans as Toyota and General Motors. The Volkswagen case was therefore a remarkable instance of the application of rational leadership in the development of an iconic corporation.

The Theory of Rational Leadership

This Appendix examines the theory of rational leadership that originated in the 1920s–30s and has been developed in two different ways by later generations of theorists. Such renowned theorists as Burns and Christensen have enhanced the theory by showing how it can be expanded to incorporate new areas and issues, as will be discussed in the third section of the Appendix. However, the latest generation of theorists, namely the present authors, are enhancing the theory in a different way. They are instead restructuring the original, 1920s–30s contributions into a highly focused but flexible analysis of an early identified variety of rational leadership—the rational type of inspirational leadership.

This restructuring will be described in the first and second sections of the Appendix, which examine the original contributions made by Weber 'the prophet' and Barnard 'the theorist'. However, first there will be an introductory summary of their contributions and of how these have been restructured into an analysis of the rational type of inspirational leadership. The summary will include, too, some comparisons between this rational leadership and other modern varieties of leadership.

The most well-known varieties are charismatic leadership and the transformational-transactional leadership dimensions identified by Burns. However, modern leadership appears in many different forms, types, and versions.[1] What all these varieties of leadership have in common is that they are setting a direction, giving a lead, in some way or another. In fact there are forms of leadership which do little more than give a lead, as in the cases of transactional and deliberative leadership. But more is expected of an inspirational form of leadership. In this case a leader is expected to inspire people as well as give a lead or set a direction. For example, the charismatic and transformational types of leadership inspire followers with an emotional or moral confidence and commitment. In contrast, the rational type of inspirational leadership does not inspire followers with commitment, only with confidence, and it inspires them with a confidence that is not emotional or moral but rational.

Nonetheless, this rational leadership is the most appropriate type of inspirational leadership for the modern times and circumstances of the twenty-first century. As Weber pointed out in the early 1920s, the increasing modernity of societies in the West and then other parts of the globe has been exemplified by the increasing rationality of their institutions, processes, and attitudes. It is true that this rationality has been more a matter of form than content and has not always produced rational behaviour.

But in an increasingly rational world a rational type of leadership becomes increasingly appropriate, if only because people's more rational attitudes have made them more discerning followers, who are less likely to be swayed by tradition or emotion and more likely to be sceptical. Only in unusual circumstances, such as religious revivals or ideological politics, will the rational type of inspirational leadership be less appropriate than other types.

Furthermore, this tendency towards 'rationalization' affects not only attitudes but also all a society's institutions and processes. So sooner or later, to a lesser or greater degree, society's *leadership* institutions and processes will be affected by rationalization, as in the political case of a ruling monarchy evolving into a constitutional monarchy or being replaced by a presidential democracy. Likewise, a society's various forms and types of leadership will eventually be 'rationalized' to some degree, as in the case of the charismatic type evolving into a rationalized version of charismatic leadership.

Weber should therefore be viewed as the 'prophet' of rational leadership. But he did not foresee that the tendency to rationalize leadership would actually produce a whole new type of inspirational leadership. This new type was identified in the 1930s by a pioneering analyst of organizations, Chester Barnard. In his book *The Functions of the Executive* he pointed to the 'technical' aspect of the leadership provided by organizations' executives. The technical aspect inspires followers with confidence because their leader (1) has the ability to use technological means to accomplish the organization's objective; and (2) has the ability to select the *appropriate* technological means of accomplishing the objective, such as selecting the 'better' method under the conditions that the organization will be facing as it pursues this objective.

Barnard's theory of technical leadership can be restructured into a more focused and more flexible, widely applicable analysis. It becomes more focused when the leader is described as inspiring followers with confidence through the capable use of the appropriate technological means of achieving a particular objective. And the analysis becomes more widely applicable when the technological means are described in broader terms. Barnard employed a peculiarly broad definition of 'technological'—which included technical systems and organizational schemes—but an even broader term is needed to encompass such methods as devising a strategy to achieve a particular objective. Such methods are used at the higher levels of leadership and in many different fields, including political and even religious leadership.

So there is good reason to integrate Barnard's theory of technical leadership into Weber's theory of rationalization, as a new extension or branch covering a key development in the rationalization of leadership. Then Barnard's technical aspect is categorized as a *rational type* of inspirational leadership, which inspires followers with *rational* confidence through the capable use of the appropriate *rational* means of achieving a particular objective. The broad term 'rational means' includes a wide range of technological and other means, even such general, generic-level rational methods as quantitative calculation or rapid adaptation. Furthermore, the term 'particular objective' is so variable that rational leadership has to be viewed as having many different versions: each version with the particular rational means that are appropriate for achieving its particular objective.

Weber—The Prophet

The rise of rational leadership was prophetically foreshadowed by Max Weber in the early 1920s in his great sociological treatise *Economy and Society*. It identified the historical process of rationalization through which various fields and spheres of social life were being increasingly dominated by what Weber termed 'formally' rational—in the sense of rational in form—processes and institutions, such as quantitative calculation and administrative rules. Now authority was being rationally legitimated by legal rules, now the administration of states and large businesses was being rationally carried out by modern bureaucracies, now politics was being rationally organized by constitutional democracy's rules and numbers, and now economic activities were being rationally directed by modern market capitalism. In fact Weber argued that 'thorough market freedom'—being free of business cartels as well as state distortions—was the pre-condition for 'the highest level of rationality' in accounting and its calculating approach to economic activities.[2]

Weber did not refer to a similar rationalization of *leadership* but his theory implied that leadership would sooner or later succumb to the spread of formal rationality. In fact leader-follower relations were already being affected by the rationalization of cultural attitudes. Weber believed that this change in attitudes was due to rationality becoming a 'revolutionary force' that was felt in two different ways: it 'intellectualizes the individual' and it changes attitudes through 'altering the situations of life and hence its problems.'[3] Intellectualization was a cultural process that had been going on for thousands of years but the most important part of the process was modern scientific progress and the accompanying use of technical means and calculations.[4]

The other way in which attitudes were being rationalized was through a social process—changes in people's life situations and problems. For example, there were the changes that had been instigated by Taylorism's scientific-management approach to organizing the workplace. Weber noted that 'organizational discipline in the factory has a completely rational basis' and that the 'American' scientific-management system also brought about the 'rational conditioning and training of work performances'.[5] This scientific-management system had been invented by the American management theorist Frederick Taylor. Weber and Taylor have been described by Taylor's biographer as embodying 'the implacable currents of rationalism that swirled through early twentieth century life' and pre-dated Ford's introduction of assembly-line mass production.[6] Taylor's definitive 1911 text *The Principles of Scientific Management* presented a very wide-ranging, comprehensive system for managerially maximizing workers' productivity.[7] It included selecting the best-suited workers', training them in recuperative work habits and efficient work methods, discovering the most efficient work methods through time-and-motion studies, motivating workers through a task-and-bonus approach, and, most importantly, increasing management's control over the workplace: 'all of the planning which under the old system was done by the workman, as a result of his personal experience, must of necessity under the new system be done by the management in accordance with the laws of the science'.[8]

Clearly this scientific-management system was rationalizing the attitudes of managers as well as workers. Like workers, managers were experiencing new, rationalized working life situations and problems. In addition, managers were being culturally intellectualized by a supposedly 'scientific' management system that emphasized technical means and calculations. And this rationalization of both managers' and workers' attitudes would soon affect their leader-follower relations.

Already Weber had noticed how a rationalizing of attitudes was changing *military* leader-follower relationships. Military leaders now 'rationally calculated' how to inspire soldiers to fight: 'everything is rationally calculated, especially those seemingly imponderable and irrational emotional factors'.[9] The military was developing rationally calculated methods of leadership that would inspire soldiers to fight with an emotional commitment and confidence. Soon the civilians, too, would develop what Burns has labelled the 'how to' approach to leadership. He argued that 'how to' manuals on leadership 'may be useful for gaining and exercising leadership in highly predictable and structured situations' but 'the manuals treat persons [followers] as *things*, as tools to be used or objects to be stormed like a castle'.[10]

Indeed Weber's account of military leaders' rationalized attitudes and leadership had highlighted two crucial distinctions. The first is the difference between (1) uncalculated, 'natural' leadership; and (2) calculated, 'how to' inspirational leadership, in which leaders use rationally calculated methods of inspiring followers with emotional commitment and confidence. The second distinction is between (1) this partly rational type of inspirational leadership; and (2) the *wholly* rational type, in which leaders inspire their followers with rational confidence because the leader is using the appropriate rational means of achieving the organization's objective. Weber had identified only the first of these two distinctions but in doing so he had highlighted the importance of the second distinction, even though he had not foreseen the appearance of a wholly rational type of inspirational leadership.

Some twenty years later, however, military leaders were moving from the partly to the wholly rational type of inspirational leadership—because by then their *followers'* attitudes, too, had been rationalized. This development was noted by a military historian when discussing the military leadership of the British army fighting in North Africa in 1942. The 'tough, deferential, uncomplaining privates who had died like lemmings on the Western Front in an earlier war had not bred their kind to replace them. These men wanted to stay alive, wanted to get home, wanted to know what was happening and why'.[11] These conscript soldiers had such a rational attitude to military service and leadership that they were discerning or even sceptical 'followers' of their commanders. So it is not surprising that the commander of this army, General Montgomery, presented his soldiers with an image of himself as:

> a professional giving reliable reassurances; one who did not promise more than he could perform, and one who was thoroughly, almost insolently on top of his job. There would inevitably be casualties, he indicated, but no more than strictly necessary to achieve the objective.[12]

Montgomery had therefore invented a method of inspiring confidence among soldiers who had a rational, discerning, and possibly sceptical attitude to military service and leadership. He had come close to the wholly rational type of inspirational leadership that had recently been identified in the pioneering theory of rational leadership presented in 1938 by Chester Barnard.

Barnard—The Theorist

Like Montgomery, Barnard had practical experience of high-level leadership of an organization. Since 1927, he had been president of New Jersey Bell Telephone, a company associated with Bell-ATT.[13] However, his 1938 monograph *The Functions of the Executive* was also based on his familiarity with a wide range of academic sources, including major works in philosophy and sociology.[14] He therefore epitomizes the rationalization of managers' attitudes through what Weber termed 'intellectualization'. Furthermore, Barnard's broad intellectual interests may be why he presented his arguments in a theoretical and general way that would be applicable not just to business firms but to *all* formal organizations, even churches and armies. In fact his book is widely recognized as a landmark in the theory of organizations—and a very influential landmark. For example, a 1990s collection of articles on organization theory was entitled *Organization Theory: From Chester Barnard to the Present and Beyond*, and a celebrated institutional economist declared that the 'incipient science of organization' is 'inspired, directly and indirectly, by Chester Barnard's classic book'.[15]

Barnard's work included innovative theories about organizational leadership, such as its role in creating the culture of the organization. In fact, Barnard foreshadowed the concept of 'corporate culture' that became prominent in business-management theory several decades later.[16] He stressed the importance of organizational culture, as when he described the 'creation of organization morality' as the thing that 'gives common meaning to common purpose, that creates the incentive that makes other incentives effective, that infuses the subjective aspect of countless decisions with consistency in a changing environment'.[17] And apparently this cultural, moral aspect of the organization is created through the *responsibility* aspect of organizational leadership, as it involves a 'moral creativeness' that encompasses 'the creation of moral codes for others' and also 'securing, creating, inspiring "morale" within the organization'.[18]

This morally creative, responsibility aspect of organizational leadership is very similar to what Weber had called 'charismatic' leadership. For example, creating moral codes for others is a feature and concern of religious leaders with charismatic authority.[19] They and secular charismatic leaders are also capable of 'securing, creating, inspiring' morale, if only through their followers' emotional devotion to the leader and to 'the normative patterns or order revealed or ordained by him'.[20] But Barnard's morally creative, responsibility aspect of leadership was not a typical example of charismatic leadership and in fact it seems more like a calculated, partly rational type of inspirational leadership. For when Barnard discussed—and apparently prescribed—creating moral codes and inspiring morale, he implied that it was premeditated and instrumental: a means to an organizational end. It seems therefore to be a calculated, partly rational version of charismatic leadership and a new example of the partly rational type of inspirational leadership that Weber had identified when he described the changes in military leader-follower relationships.

However, Barnard's study of organizational leadership had also identified a *wholly* rational type of inspirational leadership. He argued that in addition to the morally creative, responsibility aspect of leadership there is also what he termed the 'technical' aspect of leadership. This aspect involves individual superiority in skill, knowledge, perception, imagination, and other personal qualities or abilities.[21] Among them is a superiority in what Barnard described as *technology*, which he viewed in peculiarly broad terms. For example, technology included 'schemes of organization' and 'technical systems, as well as the techniques of the applied sciences where they are pertinent'.[22] But these schemes, systems, and techniques are all formally rational and in this sense the superiority in technology is the 'rational' component of leaders' individual superiority and, furthermore, of the technical aspect of their leadership.

More importantly, this rational component of leadership inspires followers with confidence—it is an inspirational form of leadership. For Barnard noted that confidence is 'engendered' by executives who combine their hierarchical authority with a technical 'authority of leadership' arising from their superior ability, knowledge, and understanding.[23] As this superiority will include the technological, rational component of leadership, the executives will at times be inspiring confidence through their superiority in using rational schemes, systems, techniques, and other technology. Their followers will therefore at times be inspired with a rational confidence that is based on the leader's use of rational means to an end. In that case the followers will be showing the kind of rational attitudes to work and leadership that makes them rational, discerning followers—like the conscript soldiers led by General Montgomery. So Barnard is here referring to a wholly rational type of inspirational leadership in which both leader and follower have a rational attitude to their relationship and the follower is inspired with rational confidence by the leader's 'superiority' in using rational means to a particular end.

Such superiority includes the leader's selection of the *appropriate* rational means to achieve an end. For example, when Barnard described organizational effectiveness, he pointed out that the use of technology—of rational means—includes selecting the appropriate rational means of accomplishing the organization's objective.

> [Effectiveness] relates exclusively to the *appropriateness* of the means selected under the conditions as a whole for the accomplishment of the final objective. This is a matter of *technology* in a very broad sense of the term ... At a given time, for a given end, under given conditions, which specific technology is to be selected is the variable factor. We select which is the 'better' method under the conditions.[24]

The technological, rational component of leadership therefore inspires followers with confidence because their leader is *selecting* the appropriate rational means—the 'better' method—as well as *using* it to accomplish the organization's objective. In other words, they are being inspired with confidence because their leader has the ability not only to use rational means but also to select the appropriate rational means of accomplishing an objective at a given time and under given conditions.[25]

In fact Barnard's theorizing about a 'technical' aspect of organizational leadership explored the key features of a new, wholly rational type of inspirational leadership. It inspires followers with only a rational confidence rather than the emotional—and possibly moral—confidence and commitment that charismatic leaders inspired in their followers. Nonetheless, it is the most effective way of inspiring employees whose rationalized attitudes have made them rational, discerning followers—who might become sceptical and even cynical about the leadership. So although this rational type of inspirational leadership emerged long ago, it is still very 'modern' and is the appropriate type for our twenty-first-century world.

As was argued at the beginning of this Appendix, Barnard's theory of technical-rational leadership can be restructured into a highly focused and flexible analysis of the rational type of inspirational leadership. The analysis becomes highly focused when the leader is described as inspiring followers with confidence through the capable use of the appropriate technological means of achieving a particular objective. And the analysis becomes highly flexible, widely applicable, when his theory is combined with Weber's theory of rationalization. For then Barnard's notion of 'technological' means is replaced by the broader Weberian concept of 'rational' means, which covers a wider range of formally rational means—and includes generic rational methods.

This combination of Barnard and Weber is best viewed as a restructuring of their contributions to the theory of rational leadership. Barnard's technical-rational leadership has been integrated into Weber's theory of rationalization as a new extension or branch that applies to a rationalization which Weber did not foresee—the emergence of a wholly rational type of inspirational leadership. More importantly, these 1920s–30s contributions have now been restructured into a new, twenty-first-century analysis of the rational type of inspirational leadership.

Later Theorists: Burns and Christensen

But of course after the 1920s–30s, there were other major contributions to the theory of rational leadership. Forty years after Barnard's book, a political scientist presented a more widely applicable equivalent of its dualistic, moral/rational conception of leadership. In his 1978 *Leadership*, Burns presented a moral-transformational and rational-transactional dualistic conception of leadership that could be applied to a much wider range of social contexts than just the leadership of organizations. And his conception of rational-transactional leadership had expanded the theory of rational leadership by incorporating a new and very wide area of leader-follower relationships.

On the other hand, Burns had eclipsed the rational type of inspirational leadership by stressing what he referred to as the 'transformational' type. It transforms both leader and followers as 'leaders and followers raise one another to higher levels of motivation and morality'.[26] In fact followers may be inspired with new sources of motivation, if they have a leader who can 'mobilize within them newer motivations and aspirations'.[27] More importantly, the followers are being inspired with a *moral* motivation, whether it is something new or an existing source of motivation being used in a new way. For instance, Gandhi 'aroused and [morally] elevated the hopes and demands of millions of Indians'.[28]

This morally inspirational leadership can be readily contrasted with the form of *rational* leadership—the transactional form—that was identified and described by Burns. Transactional leadership is rational rather than moral and is pragmatic rather than inspirational.

> Such leadership occurs when one person takes the initiative in making contact with others for the purpose of an *exchange* of valued things. The exchange could be economic or political or psychological in nature: a swap of goods or of one good for money; a trading of votes between candidate and citizen or between legislators; hospitality to another person in exchange for willingness to listen to one's troubles. Each party to the *bargain* is conscious of the power, resources and attitudes of the other.[29]

Each party to this pragmatic bargain has presumably calculated the pay-off in a formally rational fashion. Indeed, Burns depicted transactional leadership in the marketplace of public opinion as 'dominated by quick calculations of cost-benefits' by leaders and followers, whom he characterized here as 'sellers' and 'buyers'.[30] These rational leaders and followers also have a relatively tenuous and temporary leader-follower relationship. Unlike transformational leadership, the transactional leadership act 'is not one that binds leader and follower together in a mutual and continuing pursuit of a higher purpose'; they may 'have no enduring purpose that holds them together' and 'may go their separate ways' after the bargaining and exchange.[31]

As Burns acknowledged, there was a marked similarity between his theory of transactional leadership and sociology's exchange theory.[32] Another marked similarity is with psychology's transactional-analysis theory, which was made famous in the 1960s by Berne's *Games People Play* and Harris's best-selling *I'm OK—You're OK.* This theory viewed the transaction as the basic unit of social interaction and defined it as one person acknowledging the presence of another in some way (transactional stimulus) and the other person then saying or doing something that is related to this stimulus (transactional response).[33] Such a broad definition can be applied to a very wide range of social contexts and in fact Harris ended his book by applying transactional analysis to international relations and to the relationship between American voters and public officials.[34]

Similarly, the transactional form of rational leadership occurs in a very wide range of social contexts—much wider than any other variety of rational leadership. From this perspective it seems surprising that Burns's book focused on transactional leadership in political contexts and had so little to say about how it operated in other social contexts, such as within business organizations. A similar political focus or bias was evident when another political scientist, Brooker, identified in 2010 another pragmatic form of rational leadership—the deliberative leadership that is discussed in the second section of Chapter 1.

However, a business theorist made the most important post-Burns contribution to the theory of rational leadership. Christensen's 1997 *The Innovator's Dilemma: When New Technologies Cause Great Firms to Fail* became famous for its contribution to management theory and practice, but it should also be celebrated for expanding the theory of rational leadership. For in this book a Barnard-like concern with using the 'better' method—the appropriate rational means—was applied to a new issue or problem that exemplified the technologically driven market economy of the 1980s–2010s.

Christensen's book was 'about the failure of companies to stay atop their industries when they confront certain types of market and technological change'.[35] These changes are caused by what he termed 'disruptive' technologies.[36] They have a very different economic and commercial effect than the 'sustaining' technologies that 'improve the performance of established products'.[37] Disruptive technologies lead to products, such as the desktop personal computer, which have lower performance than established products but are 'typically cheaper, simpler, smaller, and, frequently, more convenient to use'.[38] The new products generally 'underperform established products in mainstream markets' but their new features are valued by 'a few fringe (and generally new) customers' who are the basis of a new market and a new marketing challenge.[39]

Firms that fail to adapt rapidly enough to this situation will be overtaken by competitors, often new firms, which have seized the opportunities offered by the new market.[40] Furthermore, Christensen argued that an industry's *leading* firms are especially vulnerable to this challenge. For the highly focused management effort and skills that bring success when dealing with *sustaining* technology also produce a tunnel vision that prevents the firm from seeing the opportunities and threats presented by disruptive technology.[41]

Like Barnard, Christensen emphasized that management methods are appropriate only for given ends, times, and conditions. He pointed out that 'many of what are now widely accepted principles of good management are, in fact, only *situationally appropriate*' and that an alternative set of principles is sometimes appropriate: 'times at which it is right to invest in developing lower-performance products that promise lower margins, and right to aggressively pursue small, rather than substantial, markets'.[42] Executives therefore have to be flexible enough to adopt whichever set of management principles—the widely accepted or the disruptive alternative—are appropriate for the situation they are facing at the time. Fortunately, Christensen gave them some rules for judging when it was appropriate to adopt the alternative set of management principles. He provided rational, research-based rules 'that managers can use to judge when the widely accepted principles of good management should be followed and when alternative principles are appropriate'.[43]

This would be a twenty-first-century version of what Barnard described as selecting the 'better' method under given conditions—and thereby inspiring employee-followers with confidence. Christensen did not explore the confidence-inspiring implications of leaders' selecting the appropriate set of management principles. But by expanding the theory of rational leadership to deal with a very modern business issue, he had very convincingly illustrated why using the *appropriate* rational means is such a crucial element of the rational type of inspirational leadership.

Machiavelli and Rational Leadership

This Appendix will end by looking back some 500 years to a book that was a pre-modern precursor of the theory of rational leadership. Machiavelli's *The Prince* presented an analysis of princely rule that became more notorious than famous, and led to the term Machiavellian being used to characterize devious and deceitful strategies or policies.[44] But his book includes passages that are a pre-modern precursor of both the theory of rational leadership and, more specifically, the analysis of corporation-developing rational leadership presented in Chapter 1. In particular, Machiavelli advised princes (1) to select the *appropriate methods* for the times and circumstances; and (2) evaluated these methods in terms of effectiveness and success in *achieving an objective* that was the pre-modern political equivalent of establishing or enhancing a business corporation.

The best modern interpretation of *The Prince* has pointed out that Machiavelli was describing princes who are operating 'in the context of innovation and in the role of innovator'.[45] They are *new* princes, who are establishing a new state or regime through conquest, coup, or rebellion, and therefore lack the legitimacy enjoyed by hereditary, traditional monarchs. The new prince therefore seeks to increase the loyalty of his subjects through innovations that enhance the new state or regime, as it is 'in the world of innovation' that 'the new prince can outshine the hereditary and evoke more loyalty'.[46] These innovations to enhance a newly established state or regime are pre-modern political equivalents of high-level business leaders establishing and enhancing corporations. And the princes' politically innovative leadership is a pre-modern political equivalent of the corporate-developing version of rational leadership discussed in Chapter 1.

Machiavelli even identified the methods that princes used to make these political innovations. He noted that 'men proceed in different ways: one man cautiously, another impetuously; one man forcefully, another cunningly; one man patiently, another impatiently, and each of these different ways of acting can be effective' if it is appropriate for the times and circumstances, because 'we are successful when our ways are suited to the times and circumstances'.[47] In other words, he had identified a three-pair set of six methods (cautiously-impetuously, forcefully-cunningly, and patiently-impatiently) which were potentially appropriate ways of achieving the objective. He also drew the obvious conclusion that princes should be flexible enough to change their methods to fit changes in the times and circumstances, as princes are more successful if their 'methods are appropriate'.[48] A less obvious conclusion was that princes should be ready to alternate quickly between the contrasting methods of fox-like cunning and lion-like forcefulness. A prince 'should imitate both the fox and the lion, for the lion is liable to be trapped, whereas the fox cannot ward off wolves. One needs, then, to be a fox to recognise traps, and a lion to frighten away wolves'.[49]

Machiavelli's set of methods is therefore similar in form but not in content to the three-pair set of rational methods delineated in Chapter 1.[50] His three-pair set does not contain generic rational methods or indeed methods that seem very rational at all to a modern reader. Furthermore, Machiavelli is well known for preferring the method of 'impetuosity' to the highly generic rational method of 'calculation'. For *The Prince* included the notoriously sexist remark that 'fortune is a woman' and 'is more inclined to yield to men who are impetuous than to those who are calculating'.[51] Whether or not this assessment was ever correct, it would now have to be reversed: success is more likely to be achieved by calculating leaders than by those who are impetuous. Machiavelli's political analysis of the appropriate methods is therefore almost a *pre-rational* precursor of the analysis of corporate-developing leadership presented in Chapter 1.

From IT Services to Cloud Services

This Appendix has two aims. One is to deal with an issue raised briefly in Chapter 13, namely why did Gerstner's redevelopment of IBM not include a second-stage diversification into cloud services. The other, broader aim is to provide a brief history of the rise of cloud services in the 1990s–2000s. By the late 2000s, they were challenging the older form of IT-associated services. As Chapter 13 explained, these 'IT services' involved consultancy contracts and/or outsourcing arrangements. IBM supplied consultants to handle a business's IT problems and/or personnel to run a business's IT system. In contrast, cloud services were connectional services, like those provided by an Internet service provider (ISP) connecting customers to the Internet. A *cloud* services provider (CSP) offered the next step. It provided customers with Internet access to the computing services, such as software, offered by the CSP's server computers.

The Coming of the Cloud in the 1990s

Cloud services were the most sophisticated product of the Internet high-tech revolution that began in the mid-1990s. However, cloud services were not technologically practical until the late 1990s, because CSPs had to piggyback on the ISP connection in order to make their Internet connection to a customer's computer. Piggybacking cloud services 'wasn't practical with traditional, low-speed dial-up connections' to the Internet and there was not yet 'a critical mass of people' with higher speed, broadband connections.[1] Broadband required the fibre-optic cable that was used only 'in high-capacity, intercity and corporate phone lines'.[2] Although corporations were not as dependent as consumers on copper-wire phone lines, smaller businesses and corporations' retail outlets were relying on this traditional wiring for their connections to the Internet. The technology was soon improved however. The late 1990s upgrade to the US telephone system (through Digital Subscriber Line technology) enabled the copper-wire phone lines to carry digital data at broadband speed—thereby making cloud services technologically practical.[3]

What was Gerstner's IBM doing about cloud services during the 1990s? His book mentions that he may have been introduced to 'the cloud' as early as 1993.

> The cloud would be shown in the middle. To one side there would be little icons representing people using PCs, cell phones, and other kinds of network-connected devices. On the other side of the cloud were businesses, governments, universities, and institutions also connected to the network ... [And] the massive, global connectivity that the cloud depicted would create a revolution in the interactions among millions of businesses, schools, governments, and consumers.[4]

However, the cloud concept presented to him 'was not primarily an Internet strategy', as 'this was back in the days when few people outside of universities and government labs had heard of the Internet. Fewer still believed that the Internet could be a mass-market communications medium', let alone a medium for providing computing-related services.[5] Yet even if the cloud was being envisioned as a non-Internet network, this network concept had huge implications that were already foreseen by Gerstner. He saw that the cloud 'would change computing because it would shift the workload from PCs and other so-called client devices to larger enterprise systems inside companies and to the cloud—the network—itself. This would reverse the trend that had made the PC the center of innovation and investment' since the early 1980s.[6] The cloud would in a sense *reverse* the desktop PC's challenge to the big mainframe computer, for the cloud was shifting the emphasis back from the PCs to the *central* computers, which could well be mainframes. So IBM might be expected to have pioneered what came to be known as the 'company' cloud, where a company provides its employees' PCs with Internet access to services offered by the company's central computers. But IBM did not pioneer the 'company cloud' when Internet cloud services became technologically practical in the late 1990s.

The company-cloud pioneering was instead done by Oracle corporation, the largest and most diverse business-software firm. By 1999, it had created an Internet-centralized company database that also had a suite of software applications that could be Internet-accessed and used by the company's PCs. Founder-leader Larry Ellison had claimed that Oracle's 'first Internet database' could be developed into a platform for 'Internet computing', because 'it was all that companies needed to deploy business applications that could be accessed using a standard Web browser' on a PC.[7] The browser was used to request the company's central servers to give the user's PC on-screen access to these business apps. As the access was by way of the Internet, the user could be on the other side of the world from the company's servers or could be nearby but using a home desktop for work purposes. Another advantage was that software upgrades could be carried out centrally, without having to modify a company's hundreds or thousands of PCs.[8] To mix metaphors, this pioneering company cloud was a form of hub-and-spokes system (see Table A2.1). The 'hub' was the company's central cluster of server computers and the 'spokes' were the Internet connections that radiated out from the hub to employees' PCs.

Ellison employed his pioneering company cloud to carry out a late 1990s rectification programme within Oracle. He aimed to rectify his mistake of having let Oracle become too functionally and geographically decentralized. It had developed a 'feudal structure' in which 'I was a weak king surrounded by a bunch of strong and fiercely independent dukes. I would sit in my capital in California and make policy decisions—which the dukes promptly ignored'.[9] Rectification was based on 'king' Ellison's capital having a hub cluster of servers that hosted an integrated suite of software apps and a centralized database (CDB). Its Internet spokes meant that 'dukes' and other employees could use this suite of apps but, in return, the employees' data was absorbed by the CDB, enabling Ellison to monitor how his policy decisions were being implemented around the world. The result was described as 'an Internet-based business transformation' that had centralized, standardized, and automated the company's operations.[10] This Internet-based rectification was therefore comparable to Gerstner's redeveloping structural transformation, aimed at the country-level 'barons' of IBM. But a more important comparison is with Gerstner's mid-1990s expectation that the cloud would downgrade the role of PCs. Oracle's company cloud meant that apps were no longer installed on PCs or even downloaded to them; the PCs were merely a device for remote-controlled working of the apps installed on the central servers. And this aspect of the cloud became more obvious with the late 1990s emergence of cloud service providers (CSPs).

The CSPs used a hub-and-spokes system that differed from the company clouds' system. A CSP's spokes radiated out to the PCs not of the company's employees but those of customer firms (see Table A2.1). The firms had paid the CSP a rental for their PCs to be provided with access to its hub servers' apps. CSPs' servers offered relatively specialized apps, not an overall and integrated suite of apps like Oracle's. Yet the arrival of CSPs was the most significant effect of the broadband breakthrough created by Digital Subscriber Line technology in the late 1990s.

The two pioneering CSPs were the NetLedger and Salesforce start-ups of 1998/9. NetLedger, as its name implies, used the Internet to provide customer firms with access to accounting software. This CSP's apps were aimed at small businesses, and the service was termed 'online software'.[11] Another pioneering CSP was Salesforce.com, which provided small businesses with access to software for customer-relations management (CRM). Like

Table A2.1 Cloud Hub-and-Spokes

(1) company cloud (Oracle, etc.)
company's hub servers > Internet spokes > employees' desktop PCs PCs provided with access in return for data absorbed by central database
(2) cloud service provider (Salesforce, etc.)
CSP's hub servers > Internet spokes > customer firms' desktop PCs PCs provided with access in return for customer paying rental to CSP

NetLedger, Salesforce was described as offering an 'online' service: the term 'cloud' was not yet widely used.

When Salesforce founder-leader Marc Benioff published *Behind the Cloud* in 2009, he pointed to how the terminology had changed. His firm's pioneering 'delivery model seems so obvious now. Today we call it on-demand, Software-as-a-Service (SaaS), multitenant (shared infrastructure), *or cloud computing*'.[12] Salesforce's delivery model had used the Internet to provide customer firms with an on-demand software service, available 'on a Web site that they could access from any device anywhere in the world, 24/7. This CSP model made software similar to a utility, akin to paying a monthly electric bill'.[13] The customer firms handed over 'proprietary data to be housed on our server—and then "rented" access to our software'.[14] Although different firms' data had been 'housed' on the same server computer, this was analogous to multiple tenants sharing an apartment building and each of them having a private, secure, and personally furnished apartment: a 'multitenant' server had ensured that 'each customer [firm] received a securely partitioned, highly personalized experience with their own data, logic, and end-user experience'.[15]

By the time Benioff's book appeared, Salesforce had been joined by many other CSPs. Carr noted that hundreds of start-ups had launched 'software-as-a-service [SaaS] businesses':

> Some, like Right Now Technologies, compete with Salesforce in the CRM market. Others apply the new model to different kinds of popular business programs. Employease offers a system for managing personnel. LeanLogistics has one for scheduling transportation. Oco provides a 'business intelligence' service, allowing executives to analyse corporate information and create planning reports. Digital Insight supplies a range of services to banks. Workday and Netsuite [ex-NetLedger] offer online versions of complete 'enterprise resource planning' packages.[16]

SaaS was therefore providing either specialized apps or a broader software package aimed at small businesses and offered at very affordable monthly rentals. Such software was indeed much less costly to rent from a CSP than to buy from a software company.[17] But where was IBM? Why had the leader in IT services not taken the lead in cloud services?

Gerstner's Missing Second Stage?

With the benefit of hindsight, it seems clear that Gerstner could and should have diversified into cloud services—as a second stage to his redevelopment of IBM. By the final years of Gerstner's tenure as CEO, namely 2000/1, the SaaS start-ups had confirmed that being a CSP was both technologically and commercially feasible. Gerstner may have disregarded SaaS because it did not threaten a vital source of his firm's revenue. In 2001, software contributed only 15 per cent of IBM's annual revenue of nearly $82 billion.[18] Yet software's nearly $13 billion was a sizeable amount of revenue, and furthermore might have been markedly increased by IBM taking the lead in SaaS.

Gerstner had reason to doubt, however, whether SaaS had much potential. The CSPs took several years to gain some momentum. As late as 2005, SaaS start-ups had yet to account for more than 5 per cent of the business software market in the US.[19] By then the largest CSP, Salesforce, had an annual revenue of only some $300 million, despite having expanded beyond the small-business market.[20] And cloud services were generating little revenue when compared to the amount coming from IT services. In 2006, cloud services were globally generating revenue that was 'well short of 4 percent of the overall IT services industry' revenue.[21]

Back in 2001, Gerstner therefore had good reason to be sceptical about SaaS—and to be more interested in a cloud service called the E-Business Suite. Oracle was developing the E-Business Suite as a company-cloud product that could eventually threaten IT consultancy services.[22] The new product offered customers an integrated range of apps that was broad enough to meet most of any customer's software requirements, no matter how large and complex the customer company.[23] The remainder of the company's requirements could then be met by 'reengineering business practices to fit the software instead of rewriting code to produce customized systems.'[24] A Suite might not be the best available solution for a company's software needs, but Oracle CEO Ellison argued that companies were far better off buying a software system that quickly delivered '80 percent of the benefits of a "perfect" system at 20 percent of the cost.'[25]

Oracle's E-Business Suite therefore posed a threat to the 'perfect' systems offered by IT consultancy services. IBM's consultants offered the service of made-to-measure selection, integration, and customization of software (see Table A2.2). The consultants and IBM were fortunate that the E-Business Suite had teething troubles and did not fulfil its potential until the mid-2000s.[26] But its challenge to IT consultancy services—and specifically to IBM's consultants—had been publicized by Oracle as early as 2001.[27] So even while Gerstner was CEO, he had reason to view this company-cloud Suite as a threat to an important source of his vital IT-services revenue.

The E-Business Suite was also a potential threat to the IT-services revenue that IBM derived from outsourcing (see Table A2.3), for Oracle was developing what would become its E-Business Suite Outsourcing venture.[28] And CEO Ellison wanted this new business to imitate IBM's outsourcing arrangements.

> I want us to imitate the one brilliant thing IBM has done over the last decade. They got more money from their huge installed base of mainframe customers by selling them a much broader range of services, including taking over and running their customers' data centers ... We need to grow to thousands of outsourcing customers. It's a great new business for us.[29]

IBM was therefore facing a multipronged threat from cloud services: the company-cloud Suite threatened the outsourcing and consultancy IT services, while SaaS threatened the software products.

In these circumstances a proactive second stage of redevelopment seems appropriate. Gerstner did not retire as CEO until March 2002, so he had time to begin a second-stage redevelopment—diversifying his firm into cloud services. IBM had the capability to develop a wide range of cloud services, not only company-cloud services and SaaS but also new services that were not yet envisioned or were only just appearing on the horizon. The corporation had the potential to lead the emerging cloud services industry and hence play an important role in the evolution of the IT sector.

However, in 2001/2, IBM was still suffering from the recession brought on by the 'dot-com' stock-market crash. The devastating effects of the dot-com crash have often been described in this book. And the crash blighted the credibility of Internet-based firms. 'Corporate America assured itself that it had been right all along: there was little money to made on the Internet.'[30] IBM's CEO was therefore hardly likely to end his tenure in 2001/2 by taking the firm into

Table A2.2 IT Services' Comprehensive Consultancy Relationship

---

IBM consultants provide customer with:
(1) selection and integration of software as well as hardware
[NB 'best of kind' selection and middleware integrating software]
(2) customizing software to suit a company's business peculiarities
(3) several-year service contract to help solve a company's IT problems

---

Table A2.3 IT Services' Full Outsourcing Arrangement

IBM personnel provide customer with several-year:
(1) running of mainframes and/or other server computers
(2) maintenance of servers and the numerous PCs
(3) addition or upgrading of software when required

Internet-based cloud services. Neither could he be expected to foresee that this missed opportunity would leave his firm vulnerable to a new cloud threat, Infrastructure as a Service (IaaS), which would emerge several years later.

From SaaS to IaaS

In the mid-2000s, a new cloud service emerged, Infrastructure as a Service. At the time, however, it was also termed 'hardware-as-a-service'. This term indicates more starkly why it posed a threat to IT services' outsourcing arrangements,[31] for now some CSPs would be 'setting up big data centers and then letting customers tap directly into them over the Net'.[32] The customer firms could therefore avoid the cost of having big data centres and of paying to have them run by IBM or any other provider of an IT-service outsourcing arrangement.

The IaaS cloud service did not originate as a start-up or as a diversification by a provider of SaaS. Rather, it was an innovative adaptation by the online retailer Amazon.com, as was described in Chapter 8. In the mid-2000s, Amazon created a new cloud service that sold 'basic computer *infrastructure* like storage, databases, and raw computing power', and was later termed 'Infrastructure as a Service'.[33] Like SaaS, this was an on-demand online service with a multitenant sharing of the server computers. Customers could buy exactly as much computing power as they needed, and start-ups could 'run their operations over the Internet as if the high-powered servers were sitting in the backs of their own offices'.[34]

Amazon had its own names for the new service. Amazon Web Services (AWS) was the unit title and Elastic Compute Cloud was the name of its flexible on-demand supply of computing power. The latter's use of the word 'Cloud' foreshadowed the popularity of such terms as 'cloud computing' and 'cloud services' and may also explain why the term would sometimes be applied only to IaaS. For instance, IBM's historian refers to cloud computing as 'a form of mainframe outsourced processing'.[35] Another tendency was to apply the term 'cloud' only to IaaS and Platform as a Service, an emerging cloud service that helped small-scale developers of software applications.

All cloud services expanded rapidly and globally from 2006 to 2008, with global revenue more than doubling to almost $47 billion.[36] Although the main market was still small firms, larger businesses were seeing the advantages of paying for the use of someone else's computers and furthermore paying on an electricity-like basis, based on how much use was made of the service. The arrival of a recession in 2008 led even big businesses to shift to cloud services as a way of reducing their computing costs.[37]

IBM responded too slowly to this growing threat to its IT outsourcing services. As IBM's historian points out, the firm 'arrived late to cloud computing' and was still seeking to 'catch up in cloud computing' in the *mid-2010s*.[38] Although he is referring to IaaS, one reason for this delay was the missed opportunity to take the lead in SaaS and company cloud in the early 2000s. If IBM had become a leader in cloud services, the firm would have been cloud-minded enough to have recognized the potential for IaaS. Even if it had not led the way into this new cloud service, the firm would at least have been more aware of the threat and have been less likely to have arrived late to IaaS.

Similarly, IBM was unlikely to have under-estimated a new form of server cluster. Now a cluster of servers could share 'the same short-term memory or "cache"', allowing them effectively to operate as one computer' and also allowing more servers to be added to the cluster 'without making any configuration changes or rewriting the code in any of their applications'.[39] This shared-memory form of clustering meant that data centres could be cheaper, more flexible, and more reliable than when they relied on the big mainframe computers. A cluster of small server computers was much less expensive than a mainframe. The cluster could also flexibly respond to increases in demand by adding however many small servers were required. And the cluster was very reliable, because the failure of one server did not bring down the others; the cluster would instead slow down or be bolstered by a back-up server.

Another advantage was that the cluster could create a division of labour, as in the notable case of Google's Web Index. Google was handling innumerable search requests and had server computers ranking Web pages according to their relevance to words entered into its search engine. These Web Index server computers were each allocated only a small 'shard' of the total Index. So when a user entered a keyword into the search engine, each shard server in a cluster would compare the word to only a small part of the Web Index: 'this kind of "parallel processing" proceeds much faster than if a single computer had to compare the keyword to the entire index'.[40] By the late 2000s, Google's server clusters were housed in data centres that were often called 'server farms'. Each farm housed thousands of small servers, with different 'herds' of servers each having their distinctive functions, such as the index servers or the ad servers (which selected relevant advertisements to include with a user's search result).[41] And Google's dozens of server farms were linked together as a global cluster of more than half a million servers.[42]

Server farms were set up, too, by other big e-business firms. Amazon's server farms had the beneficial side-effect of helping its Web Services unit win IaaS contracts. For instance, it won the bidding for a CIA (Central Intelligence Agency) contract because IBM could not match the Amazon server farms:

> Amazon.com had made the case that because e-commerce was very much like cloud computing, involving millions of individuals accessing server farms to process data (orders), it could support the CIA's large number of employees ... IBM protested, since it was the low-cost bidder, but government auditors responded that CIA officials had 'grave' doubts that IBM could provide reliable technology and cloud computing.[43]

This 2013 setback epitomized IBM's problems as a latecomer to IaaS. Its historian describes IBM as struggling to adapt to the 'cloud era'.[44] But it had to adapt, as customers wanted 'subscriptions to cloud-based offerings' and there were 'a growing number of cloud service providers' offering IaaS.[45]

Furthermore, in the 2010s the cloud-service providers included a growing number of large high-tech corporations pursuing a new diversification. Microsoft is the most notable example. As Chapter 10 mentioned, Microsoft boosted its cloud services effort from 2011 onwards to become the well-established number two in the industry. By 2019, Microsoft's Azure cloud service used 'more than one hundred data centers—giant buildings filled with millions of servers—located in places like Sao Paulo and Marseille, Canberra and Doha'.[46]

But Amazon's veteran Web Services continued to be the biggest battalion in the field. In 2015, AWS had reached $10 billion in annual sales and continued to dominate the global market for IaaS, having expanded to 'ten times the computing capacity of the next fourteen cloud companies combined'.[47] By 2019, AWS still had some 47 per cent of the market and had reached $35 billion in revenue.[48] Another successful veteran was Salesforce, the SaaS pioneer. The firm was earning over $5 billion in revenue by 2015 and had the number-four position in the whole cloud services industry: 'a notch higher than IBM'.[49] The redeveloped IBM had therefore missed a lucrative opportunity with SaaS as well as having been too slow to move into IaaS.

Cloud services were booming in the 2010s. If cloud services are viewed as part of the IT-services sector, they accounted for less than 15 per cent of its revenue in the mid-2010s, but their portion was the growing part of an otherwise stagnant sector.[50] Plus, cloud services' competitive position was benefiting from continual improvements to Internet technology. Fibre-optic cable had been greatly extended—bringing a faster broadband—and wireless had moved on to 4G (fourth generation) wireless broadband, with 5G (fifth generation) in the pipeline.[51]

IBM's 2010s CEO, Virginia Rometty, therefore had to carry out a rectification programme. She 'doubled down' on cloud services, created a specialized cloud-services business, and ensured IBM extended 'its presence among large enterprises in 2015 and 2016 with combinations of cloud services'.[52] Rometty's rectification programme might also be seen as the long-delayed second stage in the redevelopment of IBM. In Rometty's recent memoir she acknowledges that 'other companies had a huge start' in the cloud area.[53] She tried to catch up through a 2013 acquisition and by hiring 'more cloud talent', but she eventually decided to rectify by specializing, namely specializing in *hybrid*-cloud services that 'connect a client's applications and data across their public clouds, private clouds, and on-premise systems'.[54] In 2018, she made a $34 billion acquisition of Red Hat to speed up IBM's progress in this hybrid-cloud direction.

Notes

Chapter 1

1. Drucker 1993 [1946]: 5, and see also 7, 8, 15.
2. Weber 1978 [1922]: 152 and 1394, which comes from an article he wrote in 1917.
3. Weber 1978 [1922]: 85.
4. Chandler 1990 [1962]: 322.
5. Thorndike 2012: 44, 90–1, 163.
6. Michell 2010: 97, 39, 102. Sony was then ranked at eighteenth, with an estimated brand value of $16 billion, while Samsung was ranked only forty-third thanks to its brand value of only $5 billion (Michell 2010: 102). But O'Boyle describes how in a corporation suffering from 'the tyranny of numbers' these numbers 'take on a life of their own' and management is expected to accept quantitative assessments even when their conclusions seem to defy logic (1999: 210, 214–15).
7. Knight 2014 [1921]: 231–2. Similarly, the humorous *How to Lie with Statistics* long ago provided a pithy warning about the unreliability of quantitatively calculated predictions. 'The trend-to-now may be a fact, but the future trend represents no more than an educated guess. Implicit in it is "everything else being equal" and "present trends continuing". And somehow *everything else refuses to remain equal*' (Huff 1954: 140).
8. Christensen 2000: xxii.
9. Clausewitz 1984 [1832]: 95, 128.
10. Clausewitz 1984 [1832]: 119–20.
11. Clausewitz 1984 [1832]: 139.
12. Clausewitz 1984 [1832]: 177.
13. Welch 2003: 448. In this and the latter case, Welch was referring to post-Clausewitz Prussian military thinkers who were applying and developing Clausewitz's concepts.
14. Welch 2003: 390.
15. In fact Welch's theory of a central idea evolving through continually changing circumstances is referring to what could be a grand strategy. For his example was an idea that he presented at the beginning of the 1980s. He predicted that the decade would see 'slower world-wide growth' and that the winning companies would be 'those who search out and participate in the real growth industries and insist upon being number one or number two in every business they are in' (2003: 449). In practice, this meant what he terms the 'No. 1 or No. 2, "fix, sell or close" strategy' of fixing, selling, or closing down any division, subsidiary, or associated company that was not the number-one or number-two firm in a growth industry or business (2003: 109). Although he describes it as a strategy, it is more like a grand strategy or indeed an innovative adaptation to the expected low-growth economic environment!
16. Burgelman et al. 2017.
17. McCraw 2007: 44.
18. Schumpeter 1961 [1934]: 61–7, 81, 92–3; Brooker 2010: 39–41, 210–12.
19. Schumpeter 1974 [1947]: 132.

20. Drucker 2007 [1985]: 25, 31, 160.
21. Drucker 2007 [1985]: xv, 127.
22. Drucker 2007 [1985]: 25, 31.
23. Schumpeter 1989 [1947]: 222. He defined the creative response as having three essential features: (1) the content of the response could not have been predicted beforehand; (2) the response has a significant and lasting effect; and (3) the frequency of such creative responses has something to do with the quality of the available personnel and their individual patterns of behaviour (Brooker 2010: 221 n. 27).
24. Schumpeter 1974 [1947]: 105.
25. Schumpeter 1974 [1947]: 105. It is true that he seems to be referring to the loss and reduced output suffered by an economy rather than by firms resisting adaptation, but resisting adaptation was likely to have similarly negative effects on a firm.
26. Cohen and Gooch 2006: 161, and see also 139 for an example of failing to take full advantage.
27. Machiavelli 2012 [1532]: 82.
28. Allison 1971: 179.
29. George 1972: 753.
30. Allison 2007: 138. This may have been because Neustadt, like Machiavelli, had been a 'practical man' in administration and politics before he had become a scholar. He had worked for four years in the Bureau of the Budget's legislative division and then for three years on the White House staff of President Truman (Dickinson 2007).
31. Neustadt 1990: 132. Similarly, George's classic article on 'multiple advocacy' among presidential advisers argued for central intervention 'to maintain and make use of internal competitive processes' within the bureaucracy (1972: 760).
32. Kroc 1987: 191–2.
33. Machiavelli 2012 [1532]: 81–2.
34. Strayer 2005 [1970]: 74.
35. Brooker 2010: 4–5.
36. Brooker 2010: 4. Similarly, Drucker's classic 1954 text on management noted how the president/CEO of a company has to deal with managers who 'want to "sell" him their ideas' (2006 [1954]: 168).
37. Marder 2015 [1974]: 177, citing a member of Pound's personal staff.
38. Walton 1993: 314.
39. According to Zuckerberg, a CEO's basic roles are recruiting a team and setting a vision for the firm (Beahm 2012: 111). He and his board of directors wanted Sandberg for the post of COO because of 'her willingness to be number two' as well as because of 'her role developing Google's ad business, and her experience as a manager' (Kirkpatrick 2011: 254).
40. Kirkpatrick 2011: 256.
41. Kirkpatrick 2011: 256–7. He notes that Zuckerberg was 'on a month-long around-the-world-trip, now that he'd completed his search for his number two' and could entrust her with such a key task as leading the firm in the direction of exploiting its advertising opportunity (2011: 257). Their long-lasting leadership makes a dramatic contrast with the problems experienced by Twitter, the other social media phenomenon of the 2000s. The firm was established in 2007, with three official co-founders and with one of them, Jack Dorsey, as CEO; but in 2008 he was replaced by another co-founder, Evan Williams, who was himself replaced in 2010 by the firm's COO, the non-founder, Dick Costolo (Bilton 2013: 105, 4).

42. Kirkpatrick 2011: 257–8.
43. Kirkpatrick 2011: 273.
44. Sandberg 2013: 74, 82.
45. Sandberg 2013: 83.
46. Sandberg 2013: 85.
47. Sandberg 2013: 77, but she pointed out that reticence is often caused by people backing away from honesty 'to protect themselves and others'.
48. Sandberg 2013: 81–2.
49. Sandberg 2013: 82.
50. Khurana 2002: 152.
51. Grove 1999: 152.
52. Walton 1993: 147.
53. Walton 1993: 253.
54. Walton 1993: 253–4.
55. Tedlow 2003: 1. The seven individuals were Carnegie, Eastman, Ford, Watson, Revson, Walton, and Noyce.
56. Tedlow 2003: 4.
57. It might even be argued that the more ordinary cases are in a sense more modern. The president of Sony noted in the 2000s that a modernized company 'means a company that stands independent from past glories, and the founders; a company that can be managed [and developed] by ordinary people like myself' (quoted by Chang 2008: 163).
58. Drucker noted in his discussion of management teams that 'if two men [sic] can work together closely, they form an ideal team. But two people like this are rarely found' (2006 [1954]: 177). However, in the case of *leadership* teams this phenomenon is not as rare as finding *three* people who can work together closely.

Chapter 2

1. Pelfrey 2006: 1.
2. Farber 2004: 198.
3. Tedlow 2003: 171; Sloan 1990 [1964]: xxi.
4. Pelfrey 2006: 246.
5. Pelfrey 2006: 236; Sloan 1990 [1964]: 437.
6. McDonald 2003: 41–2. He describes it as a 'remarkable team of professionals—altogether twenty-some persons at one time or another' (42). McDonald's book about his experiences with the project explains why it was so protracted, beginning in 1954 and finishing in 1959, and why the book's publication was then held up for another four years!
7. Drucker in Sloan 1990 [1964]: x. Gates's endorsement was originally quoted in the 16 January 1995 issue of *Fortune* magazine, according to McDonald 2003: 189.
8. Sloan 1990 [1964]: xxiii.
9. Farber 2004: 243.
10. Chandler 1990 [1962]: 12, 390.
11. Sloan 1990 [1964]: xxi, 4, 429.
12. Sloan 1990 [1964]: 4, 46. For example, 'all the units in the General Motors empire were still structured and managed the way they had been before Billy bought them, and the heads of each unit all reported directly to him' (Pelfrey 2006: 215).
13. Sloan 1990 [1964]: 429–30.

14. Sloan 1990 [1964]: 48.
15. Sloan 1990 [1964]: 31. Sloan dated his drafting of the Organization Study to 'after December 5 [1919] and before January 19, 1920' (45 n. 2).
16. Pelfrey 2006: 13, 221.
17. Pelfrey 2006: 13, 224, 236.
18. Pelfrey 2006: 224.
19. Pelfrey 2006: 228; Sloan 1990 [1964]: 41, graph on stock prices adjusted for a 10 for 1 split in March.
20. Chandler 1990 [1962]: 130; Farber 2004: 50; Sloan 1990 [1964]: 51–2. Chandler described this restructuring in Schumpeterian terms as an innovative 'creative' response rather than a merely adaptive response: it was 'a creative response to new needs and new conditions' (1990 [1962]: 284).
21. Sloan 1990 [1964]: 52, 55, 56. Farber 2004: 72, 214, 240 details the various high offices and positions held by Sloan during his years with General Motors.
22. Farber 2004: 51.
23. Sloan 1990 [1964]: 113. He gave the divisional managers some representation at central level by combining them with the members of the executive committee to form the large operations committee. However, Sloan acknowledged that it 'was not a policy-making body but a forum for the discussion of policy or the need for policy' (113).
24. Chandler 1990 [1962]: 158, 160.
25. Drucker 1993 [1946]: 42.
26. Sloan 1990 [1964]: 55. See Snow 2014: 313 on Sloan apparently copying the military model of a headquarters' general staff.
27. Chandler 1990 [1962]: 138–9.
28. Chandler 1990 [1962]: 154, 160.
29. Sloan 1990 [1964]: 431, emphases added.
30. Chandler 1990 [1962]: 135.
31. Sloan 1990 [1964]: 54.
32. Chandler 1990 [1962]: 135–7.
33. Sloan 1990 [1964]: 52.
34. Chandler 1990 [1962]: 135.
35. Chandler 1990 [1962]: 133, 135.
36. Drucker 1993 [1946]: 52. Drucker also noted that a 'vice-president in charge of a group of divisions acts as a constant liaison on policy and performance between head office and division' (60).
37. Chandler 1990 [1962]: 138.
38. Chandler 1990 [1962]: 158.
39. Sloan 1990 [1964]: 30, 121, 140–1.
40. Chandler 1990 [1962]: 147. In 1921, central management moved to 'co-ordinate financial organizations of the divisions and the central Financial Staff' and reaffirmed the principle of dual responsibility for the divisional comptrollers, that is, their responsibility to the corporation comptroller as well as to their divisional managers (Sloan 1990 [1964]: 143).
41. Chandler 1990 [1962]: 152. The financial data from the divisions was used to analyse 'the critical revenue and cost factors determining the rate of return on investment', which was the key quantitative calculation 'used to measure the effectiveness of each division's operation' and 'to evaluate divisional performance' (Chandler 1990 [1962]: 152; Sloan 1990 [1964]: 141).

42. Sloan 1990 [1964]: 140.
43. Sloan 1990 [1964]: 140.
44. Sloan 1990 [1964]: 429; Farber 2004: 59.
45. Sloan 1990 [1964]: 30.
46. Sloan 1990 [1964]: 124–7.
47. Sloan 1990 [1964]: 138. As Sloan pointed out, the accuracy of the forecasts was less important than 'the sensitivity to actual market changes through prompt reports and adjustment' (138).
48. Sloan 1990 [1964]: 176.
49. Sloan 1990 [1964]: 176–7, 148; Pelfrey 2006: 265 on being the only car-maker to operate profitably throughout. Pelfrey also points out that, apart from 1932, during the Depression 'it showed a profit margin of at least 10 per cent (high by even today's standards), despite slow sales and reduced volume' (265).
50. Sloan 1990 [1964]: 199.
51. Pelfrey 2006: 265, and 262 on number of employees.
52. Tedlow 2003: 167. Sloan pointed out that his new marketing strategy had been 'formulated before its time. It took a number of events in the automobile market to give full substance to its principles' (1990 [1964]: 69–70). It was therefore more of a *pre*-adaptation than an adaptation to market conditions or changes (Gould 2002: 1231–2).
53. Sloan 1990 [1964]: 59, 60, 62.
54. Sloan 1990 [1964]: 59.
55. Sloan 1990 [1964]: 62–3.
56. Sloan 1990 [1964]: 65.
57. Farber 2004: 64.
58. Sloan 1990 [1964]: 67–9.
59. Sloan 1990 [1964]: 69, 68.
60. Sloan 1990 [1964]: 67.
61. Sloan 1990 [1964]: 155, and 155–60 on the replacement. The founder of modern military thinking pointed out in the 1830s that war could be compared to commerce, 'which is also a conflict of human interests and activities' (Clausewitz 1984: 149).
62. Sloan 1990 [1964]: 442.
63. Sloan 1990 [1964]: 441–2.
64. Farber 2004: 101.
65. Sloan 1990 [1964]: 269, 274.
66. Sloan 1990 [1964]: 272; Pelfrey 2006: 255.
67. Farber 2004: 103.
68. Farber 2004: 103. In addition to this concern with market communication, he improved the corporation's product distribution by including GM's franchised car retailers in his marketing strategy and overall administrative rationalization. Favouring, of course, 'a rational approach to the problem of distribution', Sloan established a new approach—enlightened and exemplary—to relations with the franchised car dealers (1990 [1964]: 284–5). His achievements in this area led Drucker to suggest that GM's principles of inter-business federalism and harmonious resolution of conflicts could provide a model for relations between big business and small business in other branches of the economy (1993 [1946]: 114).
69. Farber 2004: 103–4.
70. Pelfrey 2006: 40.

71. Sloan 1990 [1964]: 60.
72. Sloan 1990 [1964]: 25.
73. Chandler 1990 [1962]: 125. In 1919, the ever-expanding corporation 'was still largely run and coordinated on a day-to-day basis by Billy [Durant] himself. By the end of the year, he was overseeing more than seventy factories in forty cities' and 'with no fewer than fifty senior operating executives reporting directly to him' (Pelfrey 2006: 223).
74. Sloan 1990 [1964]: 433.
75. Pelfrey 2006: 271.
76. Sloan 1990 [1964]: 433.
77. Sloan 1990 [1964]: xviii.
78. Sloan 1990 [1964]: 434–5. Managers were still 'allowed and encouraged to offer new ideas on their own, but the concepts would be thoroughly vetted before being acted on' (Pelfrey 2006: 236).
79. Farber 2004: 90.
80. For example, it was in response to the 1924 downturn in the car market that 'I issued one of the few flat orders I ever gave to the division managers', namely 'to curtail production schedules immediately', and his memoirs also declared: 'I never minimized the administrative power of the chief executive officer in principle when I occupied that position. I simply exercised that power with discretion; I got better results by selling my ideas than by telling people what to do' (Sloan 1990 [1964]: 131, 54).
81. Farber 2004: 86, 88. Farber describes Sloan as the first public representative of a new kind of corporate organization, which required the new kind of leadership provided by a professional corporate manager (90).
82. Farber 2004: 91–2.
83. Brooker 2010: 28.
84. Farber 2004: 87.
85. Sloan 1990 [1964]: 100.
86. Farber 2004: 67.
87. Sloan 1990 [1964]: 186, 188.
88. Sloan 1990 [1964]: 188.
89. Sloan 1990 [1964]: 187. Sloan later restructured and renamed the two governing committees—which became the policy committee and the administration committee—to embody his principle of distinguishing between policy and administration (185). The new structure was eventually abandoned, nearly ten years later, and the committees were renamed the financial policy committee and the operations policy committee—returning to their traditional titles of finance committee and executive committee some two years after Sloan's retirement (186). The administration committee continued to exist but was apparently demoted to the role of making recommendations to the CEO about manufacturing, selling, or any other matters that he referred to it for consideration (435).
90. Chandler 1990 [1962]: 155–6.
91. Chandler 1990 [1962]: 156, 157.
92. Sloan 1990 [1964]: 182–3. Pelfrey notes that this 'policy committee structure' survived until the 1990s (2006: 246).
93. Drucker 1993 [1946]: 51–2.
94. Chandler 1990 [1962]: 158, quoting Brown.
95. Farber 2004: 81.
96. Sloan 1990 [1964]: 433, emphases added.

97. Pelfrey 2006: 272.
98. Whyte 1961: 8, 11.
99. Shapley 1993: 70. But McNamara also implies that the careerist pressures towards reticence could be neutralized by Machiavellian dexterity, as he notes that 'it also takes a certain dexterity to espouse an unpopular view and still keep your place in the pecking order certain' (70).
100. Sloan 1990 [1964]: xx.
101. Sloan 1990 [1964]: xxii.
102. Sloan 1990 [1964]: xxii, 4.
103. Sloan 1990 [1964]: 3; Farber 2004: 104.
104. Curcio 2013: 69–72.
105. Curcio 2013: 72–3.
106. Curcio 2013: 123. His fixation on production hardware even included a tendency to gigantism. In the 1920s he built the gigantic Rouge River plant, which was so vertically integrated that it was 'capable of taking in iron ore and other raw materials at one end and putting out fully finished vehicles at the other end' (116).
107. Sloan 1990 [1964]: 4; Tedlow 2003: 128.
108. Drucker 2006 [1954]: 114. Other owner-managers had rarely been so concerned about extending and displaying personal control of their firm. For example, the most famous owner-manager of the previous century, John D. Rockefeller of Standard Oil, was a believer in 'management by consensus' and would tolerate long committee debates about a pet project instead of imposing his views upon the opposing minority (Chernow 2004: 285).
109. Curcio 2013: 93.
110. Curcio 2013: 205, 240. However, when Ford realized that his production prejudices were leading to serious financial losses in the making of his new Model A, he returned to his insistence 'on saving money, as he always had in the past, by using the best production methods available' (205).
111. Tedlow 2003: 145, 139.
112. Snow 2014: 288.
113. Curcio 2013: 240; Tedlow 2003: 172.
114. Curcio 2013: 241, 121. Again, there is a marked contrast with Rockefeller's owner-manager management style in the 1870s–80s. He had a 'special affinity for accounting' and used his era's number-crunching as 'an objective yardstick to compare his far-flung operations' and to extend 'rationality from the top of his organization down to the lowest rung' (Chernow 2004: 46, 179).
115. Tedlow 2003: 167; Farber 2004: 103.
116. Snow 2014: 300.
117. Snow 2014: 312. In the 1920s, Ford actually concealed changes in the Model T, 'some of which were substantive', even though General Motors 'was exploiting to the hilt the idea of change in the automobile' (Tedlow 2003: 166).
118. Curcio 2013: 197–8.
119. Pelfrey 2006: 253–4.
120. Sloan 1990 [1964]: 163.
121. Sloan 1990 [1964]: 163.
122. Sloan 1990 [1964]: 163; Snow 2014: 315.
123. Womack et al. 1991: 41–2.

124. Farber 2004: 97.
125. Sloan 1990 [1964]: 163, 164–5. In fact the car-making divisions had initially opposed the idea of an annual model change and, in contrast to Ford's management style, Sloan had allowed this new policy 'to evolve into a consensus' (Pelfrey 2006: 256).
126. Farber 2004: 104.
127. Farber 2004: 104; Curcio 2013: 197–8.
128. Curcio 2013: 200–1. The price was more than 10 per cent lower than GM's comparable Chevrolet.
129. Snow 2014: 325. Tedlow believes the Model A brought Ford 'technological parity' with General Motors but it also revealed the gap or difference in their production flexibility (2003: 168). Nearly all of the 5,580 parts that were assembled to create a Model A were new parts and were made by specialized machine tools, unlike GM's use of standardized parts and flexible machine tools, and therefore Ford had to shut down his factories for six months in order to switch production from Model T to Model A: 'In business terms this was a disaster' (168).
130. Curcio 2013: 205; Snow 2014: 324; Sloan 1990 [1964]: 167.
131. Chandler 1990 [1962]: 160, comparing 1921 with 1940.
132. Curcio 2013: 209, 240.
133. Chandler 1990 [1962]: 373.
134. Shapley 1993: 68, 45, 48, 54. McNamara was a graduate of Harvard Business School, where in the late 1930s he had been taught the financial and other quantitative controls that Sloan had established at General Motors (24).

Chapter 3

1. Cole 1979: 157–8.
2. Togo and Wartman 1993: 203–4; Fujimoto 1999: 43.
3. Womack et al. 1991: 13. The term 'lean production' was coined by John Krafcik.
4. Miller 2013: 154. But another exponent argues that most organizations seeking Ohno's ideal of continuous flow have found it 'elusive' and that this 'illustrates how challenging it is for leaders to adapt' (Emiliani 2013: 158).
5. Ohno 1988: 119.
6. Ohno 1988: 76; Togo and Wartman 1993: 115.
7. Ohno 1988: 75.
8. The Toyoda-family presidents have been Risaburo Toyoda and then his brother Kiichiro in 1937–50, their cousin Eiji Toyoda in 1967–82, Kiichiro's sons Shoichiro and then Tatsuro in 1982–95, and Shoichiro's son Akio from 2009 onwards. The post-war occupation authorities' policies led to Toyoda family-owned stock being 'released to the market' after 1945, and in 1950 the family 'held only a minor financial share' in the company (Togo and Wartman 1993: 90, 105). In 1984, its chairman Eiji Toyoda and its president Shoichiro Toyoda 'together held less than 1 percent of the corporation's shares; banks were the principal owners' (Cusumano 1985: 182).
9. Togo and Wartman 1993.
10. Togo and Wartman 1993: chs. 3–5 on diversification and 74–6 on spinning off. They note that initially 240,000 shares of stock were sold to 'twenty-six stockholders, primarily family members, company directors and the Mitsui Trading Company' but by 1939 the

company's shares were also being bought by institutional investors (1993: 76, 81). According to Wada and Yui, the new company's shares were bought by 'firms in the Toyoda group and people with close ties with these firms' (2002: 275).

11. Togo and Wartman 1993: 73 on the public competition and why the name was changed. According to Cusumano, the new name of 'Toyota' rather than Toyoda was 'an alternate reading of the two ideographs that make up the family name [Toyoda]' and was chosen 'for its clarity in sound and potential advertising appeal' (1985: 59).
12. Togo and Wartman 1993: 102. The relationship was complicated by the fact that Risaburo was initially Kiichiro's brother-in-law but had been adopted by Kiichiro's father as his elder son and was therefore successor as head of the family (28–9).
13. Ohno 1988: 123.
14. Ohno 1988: 91.
15. Fujimoto 1999: 67.
16. Togo and Wartman 1993: 79–80.
17. His biographers also relate how Kiichiro explained the just-in-time concept in the media—all parts were to be made and delivered to the assembly line 'just at the right time'—and they describe how retired employees still remember him trying 'to get the idea of "just in time" to permeate everything done on the production site' (Wada and Yui 2002: 279, and see also 289).
18. Wada and Yui 2002: 274, 294. Togo and Wartman point out that the war in China benefited Toyota by boosting the government's orders for trucks but it also led to more government control of the economy (1993: 77).
19. Wada and Yui 2002: 283–5, 294–6.
20. Togo and Wartman 1993: 83.
21. Risaburo retired to the position of chairman of the company (Togo and Wartman 1993: 82).
22. Togo and Wartman 1993: 83.
23. Wada and Yui 2002: 290, 291.
24. Wada and Yui 2002: 290–1, emphases added.
25. The post-war problems included not only reconstruction in a war-devastated country but also dealing with the occupation authorities' policies and, as described in the next section, adjusting to unionization and the new labour-relations situation.
26. Wada and Yui 2002: 304–5; Togo and Wartman 1993: 101–6.
27. Togo and Wartman 1993: 104.
28. Ohno 1988: 79.
29. Fujimoto 1999: 61.
30. Cusumano 1985: 278.
31. Togo and Wartman 1993: 131.
32. Ohno 1988: 32.
33. Cusumano 1985: 278–9.
34. Cusumano 1985: 269.
35. Cusumano 1985: 269, 298; Ohno 1988: 32.
36. Cusumano 1985: 269; Shimokawa and Fujimoto 2009: 6; Ohno 1988: 135.
37. Ohno 1988: 31. Togo and Wartman note that Ohno's assembly-line innovations were being greeted with some scepticism and even passive resistance (1993: 131).
38. See, for example, Womack et al. 1991: 11, 49. According to Togo and Wartman, 'Eiji Toyoda, in particular, was supportive of Ohno's work' in the mid-1950s (1993: 131).

Nonetheless, Eiji published an English-language autobiography in 1987 which claimed that Ohno merely 'revived and further refined' the just-in-time production system that was put into practice in the late 1930s (Toyoda 1987: 58). However, this view is not widely held and the modern tendency is to emphasize Ohno's role as 'the father of the Toyota Production System' (Shimokawa and Fujimoto 2009: 5).

39. Togo and Wartman refer to Ishida's 'rational business plans' and to him being a 'realist whose life was ruled by numbers and calculations' in the financial context of ensuring the firm would 'remain solvent so it could pay its employees and its bills' (1993: 112–13, 127).

40. Togo and Wartman 1993: 114, 128, 142, 146, 160.

41. Fujimoto 1999: 68.

42. Togo and Wartman 1993: 114.

43. Nemoto in Shimokawa and Fujimoto 2009: 177, 210–11; Togo and Wartman 1993: 160. Fujimoto contrasts the 1961 introduction of Total Quality Control (TQC) with the diffusion of just-in-time production processes in the 1950s: 'TQC was diffused in a top-down manner and quickly' (1999: 71). However, TQC was a well-established programme that had already been introduced by other firms; just-in-time production had to be developed virtually from scratch before it could be introduced by Toyota and later by other firms.

44. Nemoto in Shimokawa and Fujimoto 2009: 210.

45. Toyota company history 1988: 155.

46. Toyota company history 1988: 461. By the early 1960s Toyota was producing 'close to twenty vehicles per employee' as compared to just 'two per employee in 1950' (Togo and Wartman 1993: 156).

47. Togo and Wartman 1993: 172. Eiji Toyoda's autobiography notes that 'Ishida had worked with two executive vice-presidents under him. Our duties were clearly divided, with Nakagawa in charge of business, and me handling the technical side of things' (1987: 128).

48. Cusumano 1985: 269; Shimokawa and Fujimoto 2009: 6.

49. For example, Togo and Wartman mention only how Nakagawa supported the development of the Corolla but 'mindful of the company's finances' stipulated that the new design 'would have to use the existing 1,000-cc engine used in the second-generation Corona' (1993: 172).

50. Togo and Wartman 1993: 147 mentions a figure of 70 per cent for 1959, and the firm's production was skewed even more heavily towards trucks earlier in the 1950s. They point out that in 1965 'Toyota was close to being an automobile manufacturer that also made trucks' because cars now comprised 49 per cent of its production (1993: 170).

51. Togo and Wartman 1993: 148–9, 167, 180.

52. Toyota company history 1988: 461.

53. Togo and Wartman 1993: 175.

54. Toyota company history 1988: 461.

55. Togo and Wartman 1993: 190 says merely that he 'died suddenly in 1967'.

56. Toyota company history 1988: 461.

57. Cusumano 1985: 196. This figure had been adjusted for differences in the amount of vertical integration and therefore the extent to which parts production had been outsourced.

58. Cusumano 1985: 196.

59. Togo and Wartman 1993: 156.

60. Cusumano 1985: 379.
61. Fujimoto 1999: 50.
62. Cusumano 1985: 266. He also notes that 'the Japanese market was small and companies wanted to produce a variety of models but were unable to afford large supplies of parts or specialized assembly lines before the 1960s' (1985: 285).
63. Ohno 1988: 37–8.
64. Fujimoto 1999: 52.
65. Fujimoto 1999: 53.
66. Cole 1979: 98–9. The familial solidarity of the work group also increased productivity by strengthening motivation (209).
67. Ohno 1988: 3; Cole 1989: 96–7.
68. Cole 1989: 97.
69. Cole 1989: 57, 87, 97, 112. A workshop quality-control circle typically comprised five to eight workers of similar status who voluntarily met for about an hour each week to learn statistical and other problem-solving methods and to examine job-related quality and production problems (18–19). Although the circles were imitated in America, resistance at the office and factory-floor levels led to the Japanese origin of the circles being downplayed and to the development of new, local variations of what was generally known as a 'quality circle' (19, 112–13).
70. Ohno 1988: 23, 24.
71. Womack et al. 1991: 13, emphasis added.
72. Cole 1979: 99.
73. Cole 1979: 119.
74. Ohno 1988: 125, 128. Togo and Wartman 1993: 116–18 provides an in-depth description of how Ohno developed this continuous-flow innovation.
75. Ohno 1988: 125, 128.
76. Ohno 1988: 11. Fujimoto points out that here traditional craft jobs were being replaced not through 'American Taylor-Ford approaches that essentially created single-skilled workers' but instead through a shift to multiskilled jobs (1999: 64).
77. Ohno 1988: 14.
78. Cusumano 1985: 306. Togo and Wartman 1993: 118 have a different perspective on how this issue was handled by the union leaders and Ohno but agree that his innovation aroused protests from 'some senior workmen in the machine shop' who had become 'highly skilled craftsmen on their individual machines'.
79. Cusumano 1985: 307.
80. Ohno 1988: 10, 13–14. In Germany, this function-oriented approach extended far beyond the labour unions and the factory environment; there was a social, educational, and even legal emphasis on workers having specialized and nationally standardized occupational skills (Streeck 1996: 145–7).
81. Cusumano 1985: 137.
82. Cusumano 1985: 272, 307.
83. Cusumano 1985: 171.
84. Ohno 1988: 14.
85. Brooker 1991: 274.
86. Brooker 1991: 275. Even when it reached its peak membership in 1936, the pre-war labour movement represented less than 10 per cent of the country's industrial workforce.
87. Brooker 1991: 275–7.

88. Togo and Wartman 1993: 92, 99 describe the creation of Toyota's first union in 1946 and how in 1948 the union joined the new, American-style Japanese Automobile Manufacturers Labour Union. Cusumano notes that Toyota not only granted 'workers "lifetime" employment in exchange for their loyalty' in the contentious early 1950s but also treated these permanent workers in a privileged manner that 'tended to reduce opposition from union members' (1985: 182). According to Cole, the large firms' revival of familial paternalism succeeded in eliciting some feelings of obligation to management and to the company 'as a community' (1979: 243).
89. Cole 1979: 245. Some firms shifted in the 1960s from the *nenkō* system to a job-related system of wage differentials, but they implicitly retained much of the older system, and when many firms cut production in the mid-1970s, they improvised ways of avoiding lay-offs or redundancies (130, 176–7, 220, 256, 261).
90. Cusumano 1985: xix.
91. Cusumano 1985: 379.
92. Togo and Wartman 1993: 92.
93. Ohno 1988: 4, emphases added. Even Toyota has only been able to approach, not attain, 'zero' inventory (Fujimoto 1999: 63).
94. Ohno 1988: 5, emphasis added.
95. Ohno 1988: 26. In an interview with Cusumano, Ohno recalled how he had read in a Japanese newspaper about the 'supermarket method' adopted by American aircraft producers in the Second World War to deal with the component problems that arose when they rapidly and drastically increased production to meet wartime needs (1985: 277–8).
96. Cusumano 1985: 289.
97. Ohno 1988: 27–8.
98. Cusumano 1985: 292, table 73.
99. Cusumano 1985: 298, 317–18.
100. Cusumano 1985: 298.
101. Ohno 1988: 35; Fujimoto 1999: 61.
102. Womack et al. 1991: 58.
103. Womack et al. 1991: 58. However, General Motors later changed the mixture to favour out-sourcing and by the early twenty-first century its 'payroll' of blue-collar and white-collar employees was 'about half the size it was in 1970' (Lichtenstein 2006: 10).
104. Womack et al. 1991: 60–1 describes the structure and workings of this two-tier alliance, such as the first-tier suppliers' cross-holdings of shares and the second-tier suppliers' information-sharing associations. Beneath these two tiers of suppliers there was a third and even fourth tier of less significant parts suppliers (Fujimoto 1999: 42).
105. Womack et al. 1991: 155.
106. Togo and Wartman 1993: 147; Ohno 1988: 32. See also Cusumano 1985: 291, 298 and Fujimoto 1999: 69 on extending the system to suppliers.
107. Ohno 1988: 32.
108. Ohno 1988: 34.
109. Cusumano 1985: 192. When Kiichiro began dealing with organized suppliers in 1939, there were only twenty firms in the Cooperation Association, but by 1958 there were already 160 members (252).
110. Toyota company history 1988: 461.
111. Ohno 1988: 36.
112. Ohno 1988: 37, emphases added.

113. Ohno 1988: 37, 126.
114. Ohno 1988: 38. See also Togo and Wartman 1993: 156.
115. Cusumano 1985: 287; Womack et al. 1991: 52–3; Togo and Wartman 1993: 155–6.
116. Ohno 1988: 39.
117. Cusumano 1985: 232.
118. Womack et al. 1991: 13.
119. Ohno 1988: 9, 54. Waste reduction was nothing new in the sense that Henry Ford's 'abhor-
    rence of waste' was actually 'one of the cornerstones of his business philosophy and his
    personality', but Ford's 'mania' for the adage 'waste not, want not' was focused on *by-
    products* of the production process rather than on reducing waste *within* the process itself
    (Curcio 2013: 80–1, 219).
120. Ohno 1988: 19–20.
121. Cusumano 1985: 305.
122. Ohno 1988: 67.
123. Ohno 1988: 69.
124. Ohno 1988: 46.
125. Ohno 1988: 45.
126. Ohno 1988: 74, 80.
127. Fujimoto 1999: 27, 50.
128. Ohno 1988: 100.
129. Curcio 2013: 74, 77; Snow 2014: 210 and ch. 13.
130. Curcio 2013: xii, 128.
131. Snow 2014: 209.
132. Curcio 2013: 160.
133. Curcio 2013: 128.
134. Beynon 1984: 25.
135. Cusumano 1985: 284.
136. Cole 1979: 160. He notes how this line-stopping policy contrasted with American car-
    producing firms' tendency to undertake line stoppages only 'with great reluctance' and to
    allow only plant managers and other 'select individuals' to stop the line (1979: 160). He
    also refers to the policy being adopted by Toyota from 1968 onwards, though Cusumano
    describes Ohno using line-stopping in parts of the main plant in the 1950s (1979: 160;
    1985: 280).
137. Ohno 1988: 7, 122.
138. Ohno 1988: 104–5; and 95 on large Fordist versus small Toyotaist batch lots.
139. Ohno 1988: 97.
140. Ohno 1988: 97.
141. Curcio 2013: 248.
142. Ohno 1988: 103–4.
143. Ohno 1988: 104.
144. Cusumano 1985: 299, 301–2.
145. Fujimoto 1999: 43.
146. Togo and Wartman 1993: 204, 207.
147. Fujimoto 1999: 45.
148. Togo and Wartman 1993: 218–19.
149. Togo and Wartman 1993: 219. Creating a network of parts suppliers was a longer term
    problem but Japanese parts suppliers, too, were setting up manufacturing operations

in America—more than 200 suppliers had done so by the mid-1980s (Fujimoto 1999: 45).

150. Ohno 1988: 109.

151. Womack et al. 1991: 241.

152. Womack et al. 1991: 86. This assessment was based on the authors' 1989 world survey of car-assembly-plant performance. Other imitators of Japanese production advantages had been less successful because these companies had lacked a less tangible feature of the Japanese approach: 'workers respond only when there exists some sense of reciprocal obligation' and therefore just 'changing the organization chart to show "teams" and introducing quality circles to find ways to improve production processes are unlikely to make much difference' (Womack et al. 1991: 99).

Chapter 4

1. Ritzer 1996: 33. He was describing a 'more extreme' version of formal rationalization than Weber's 1920s version (see Appendix 1) and Ritzer identified McDonaldization's four dimensions as emphases on (1) efficiency, (2) quantitative calculation, (3) predictability, and (4) 'control over people through the replacement of human with nonhuman technology' (1996: 19, 33). His initial, 1983, article on 'The McDonaldization of Society' had appeared in *Journal of American Culture* 6: 100–6.

2. Barber 2001 [1995]: 12, 17. Barber's preceding article on 'Jihad vs. McWorld' had appeared in *The Atlantic Monthly*, March 1992: 53–63. Ritzer noted that this article had expressed a viewpoint similar to but 'narrower' than his viewpoint on the impact of McDonald's (1996: 205 n. 1).

3. Napoli 2016.

4. However, this book will be using the posthumous 1987 edition with the afterword by Robert Anderson, who had written the book 'with' Kroc. See Napoli 2016: 166–7 on the origins of Kroc's memoirs and Anderson's role in preparing them for publication.

5. Kroc 1987: 13.

6. Watson 2006: 25; Kroc 1987: 103. Watson acknowledged that 'McDonald's was certainly not the first enterprise to follow Fordist methods of food production': these had been 'followed by various American enterprises that predated McDonald's, including railway dining cars and the Howard Johnson restaurant chain' (2006: 25).

7. Watson 2006: 20, 26.

8. Anderson in Kroc 1987: 208.

9. Kroc 1987: 70–1. The origins and development of the McDonald brothers' business is described in some detail in Napoli 2016: 15–26.

10. Kroc 1987: 71–2. See also Napoli on the contract and the McDonald brothers' pre-Kroc franchising of their business (2016: 24–6, 36–7).

11. Anderson in Kroc 1987: 208.

12. Kroc 1987: 202–3.

13. Kroc 1987: 150. The shift from drive-in to sit-down restaurant did not mean a shift away from drive-*through* operations, in which customers bought their food in their cars but consumed it elsewhere. In the 1980s the average McDonald's restaurant was still earning half its revenue from drive-through sales (Leidner 1993: 61).

14. Napoli 2016: 85.

15. Kroc 1987: 88.

16. Kroc 1987: 87, 108–9. The supplier aspect of the franchising system was also a case of adapting to a potential threat as well as exploiting an opportunity. 'Many franchise systems came along after us and tried to be suppliers, and they got into severe business and financial difficulty' (84). Instead McDonald's 'set the standards for quality' and also recommended methods through which a supplier could reduce costs and 'afford to sell to McDonald's for less' (100).
17. Napoli 2016: 55; Kroc 1987: 86, emphases added.
18. Love 1995: 144.
19. Love 1995: 145. McDonald's 'field service operation' has often been imitated by competitors but 'while they copied the chain's field service methods' they 'did not demonstrate the same zeal in enforcing their standards' (146).
20. Love 1995: 140.
21. Love 1995: 147.
22. Kroc 1987: 126, 167, 178.
23. Love 1995: 140.
24. Leidner 1993: 49, 50.
25. Leidner 1993: 29.
26. Love 1995: 150, emphasis added.
27. Sloan allowed his divisional managers some control over the advertising of their division's cars but it was his central headquarters' staff that came up with the styling changes for each car's annual model change (Sloan 1990 [1964]: 104–5, 241–2; Farber 2004: 103).
28. Kroc 1987: 172.
29. Love 1995: 225, and see also 225 and 318 on the Quarter Pounder and Chicken McNuggets.
30. Love 1995: 220–2. Napoli provides a different perspective on these Washington origins of Ronald McDonald and his eventual adoption by the corporation (2016: 102–3, 112).
31. Love 1995: 213.
32. Kroc 1987: 109.
33. Kroc notes that 'it would be unwieldy and counterproductive for the corporation to own [rather than franchise] more than about thirty percent of all stores' (1987: 109). In 1967–76, Kroc and Turner greatly increased the number of company-operated restaurants by buying out hundreds of franchisees, but the expansion was reined in when the advantages of franchising became clear: 'Lacking the incentive and drive of entrepreneurial owner/operators, company-run stores rarely equaled the profit margins of franchised units' and in difficult markets 'it was becoming clear that the above-average dedication of an owner/operator was critical to profitability' (Love 1995: 290).
34. Kroc 1987: 172, 173.
35. Love 1995: 218–21. See also Napoli 2016: 102–3.
36. Napoli 2016: 101.
37. Kroc 1987: 84; Love 1995: 142.
38. Kroc 1987: 84; Love 1995: 142.
39. Kroc 1987: 138–9, 150, 160; Love 1995: 222, 303. Eventually, 96 per cent of American children would be familiar with Ronald McDonald (Watson 2006: vi).
40. Watson 2006: 33.
41. Love 1995: 145.
42. Love 1995: 145.

43. Kroc 1987: 139. 'My way of fighting the competition is to emphasize *quality, service, cleanliness, and value*, and the competition will wear itself out trying to keep up'—it can be defeated 'simply by giving the public the old McDonald's QSC and V' (Kroc 1987: 115, 116).
44. Leidner 1993: 53.
45. Love 1995: 308.
46. Love 1995: 148.
47. Leidner 1993: 50.
48. Yan 2006: 44.
49. Yan 2006: 71.
50. Love 1995: 143; Napoli 2016: 75. Love noted that even McDonald's competitors conceded that its 'uncommon dedication to running a clean restaurant set a standard in the industry that others aimed for but seldom hit' (1995: 142).
51. Watson 2006: 31, 36.
52. Kroc 1987: 102, 145.
53. Kroc 1987: 159.
54. Napoli 2016: 99. See Love 1995: 274 on the 1970s.
55. Kroc 1987: 72, 87–8; Love 1995: 154, 157; Napoli 2016: 86.
56. Kroc 1987: 88; and another advantage of the income from leasing rentals was that, unlike income from franchisee royalties, it did not have to be split with the McDonald brothers (72).
57. Love argues that without Sonneborn's new financing formula, 'McDonald's would never have become a viable competitor in fast food' and that Sonneborn 'must be credited for converting the flawless Kroc–Turner operating system into a highly profitable corporation' (1995: 152, 153).
58. Farber 2004: 56–8.
59. Farber 2004: 56.
60. Kroc 1987: 147, 191–2.
61. Love 1995: 6, 7.
62. Kroc 1987: 124–5, 151.
63. Kroc 1987: 172.
64. Kroc 1987: 96, 98. In effect, Kroc was the 'people' person, Sonneborn the 'numbers' person, and Turner the 'rules' person.
65. Kroc 1987: 108–9, 121–2. See also Napoli 2016: 93 on buying out the McDonald brothers.
66. Kroc 1987: 132; Napoli 2016: 87–8.
67. As Chapter 1's note 58 pointed out, Drucker argued that two-person teams rarely worked but that when they did, they made an ideal team (2006 [1954]: 177).
68. Brandt 2011a: 8.
69. Kroc1987: 132, 133. Love describes the geographical division of labour as 'McDonald's East, McDonald's West' (1995: 252).
70. Napoli 2016: 111; Love 1995: 264.
71. Love 1995: 254. 'Ray favored an aggressive growth strategy, while Harry pushed for more measured, deliberate expansion' (Napoli 2016: 113).
72. Napoli 2016: 181. Kroc 1987: 155, 160, and 166 describes the 1967–8 origins and 1977 retirement ending of their dual leadership.
73. Kroc 1987: 147, 166.
74. Kroc 1987: 143.

75. Chapter 2 contains a detailed survey and analysis of Sloan's committee-based system of deliberation.
76. Love 1995: 7.
77. Sloan 1990 [1964]: xviii, 433.
78. Kroc 1987: 191.
79. Love 1995: 7.
80. Kroc 1987: 170.
81. Napoli 2016: 103, 107.
82. Kroc 1987: 138.
83. Love 1995: 8.
84. Kroc 1987: 202–3.
85. Watson 2006: 185.
86. Kroc 1987: 203.
87. Leidner 1993: 47.
88. Watson 2006: 38.
89. Kroc 1987: 206, referring to the situation in 1976. By then McDonald's global expansion included Germany, Britain, France, and Sweden in Europe; Japan and Hong Kong in Asia; and both Australia and New Zealand in Australasia (Watson 2006: 15, table 2).
90. Love 1995: 428. Love acknowledged that 'no two foreign partners have similar backgrounds or even similar arrangements with McDonald's' but it had 'entered most countries by forming a joint venture which involves 50 percent ownership by McDonald's and 50 per cent by a local entrepreneur', who in some cases owns and operates the stores through his/her joint-venture company and in other cases licences them to local franchisees in typical McDonald's fashion (1995: 428).
91. Love 1995: 428, emphases added.
92. Watson 2006: 12, ix. Watson also noted that McDonald's preferred to describe itself as multilocal rather than multinational (12).
93. Watson 2006: 13, 14, 204 n. 28.
94. Watson 2006: 13–14.
95. Love 1995: 434. His exception that proves the rule is the German experience with adapting the menu and restaurant décor to local conditions. The German operation was a commercial failure until it switched to the standard, American-style menu and design and confined its innovations to marketing changes, especially in its advertising—which was unusually humorous and also emphasized that it was 'not a typical American multinational operation but rather the product of German franchisees, German workers, and homegrown food' (433–6).
96. Watson 2006: 23.
97. Watson 2006: 24.
98. Love 1995: 437–8. An innovative television advertising campaign also emphasized McDonald's quality and its menu's 'crisp fries' and 'thick shakes', which differed in form or quality from anything its fast-food competitors could offer (438).
99. Ohnuki-Tierney 2006: 162–3.
100. Ohnuki-Tierney 2006: 162, 170, 172–3.
101. Ohnuki-Tierney 2006: 164–5, 173. The experiments with adding rice-based items to the menu were partly due to the fact that the absence of rice is the 'deciding factor that makes hamburgers a snack in Japanese eyes' and therefore limits their appeal as an alternative to traditional restaurant options (168).

102. Watson 2006: 7.
103. Ohnuki-Tierney 2006: 170–1.
104. Yan 2006: 47, 50, 55–6, 58. School students appear to have been less attracted to McDonald's restaurants, perhaps because they had not yet been built in favourable locations, and it was not only young people who liked to use McDonald's as a place for socializing (56).
105. Yan 2006: 45, 74.
106. Yan 2006: 50–1.
107. Yan 2006: 62, 65. The children's families therefore go to McDonald's not only for birthday parties and other celebrations but also to give the children 'a special treat', even though the parents and grandparents in many cases 'dislike or cannot afford the foreign food' (52, 65).
108. Yan 2006: 60–1.
109. Kroc 1987: 205.

Chapter 5

1. Walton's autobiography was written with John Huey in the early 1990s (Walton 1993: 329–30, 333–4).
2. The book begins by describing how his life was disrupted after *Forbes* magazine named him the 'richest man in America' in 1985 (Walton 1993: 1–3). In 1989, he dropped from number one to number twenty on the *Forbes* list, having transferred more than $7 billion of assets to his children (Moreton 2006: 75). If he had lived another decade and had not transferred any of his fortune, 'his net worth of $100 billion would have made him twice as rich as Bill Gates, with his measly $50 billion' (Hoopes 2006: 96).
3. Tedlow 2003: 355.
4. Soderquist 2005: 29. In 1992, the year Walton died, there were only five Wal-Mart stores outside the US, specifically a joint venture in Mexico, and Walmart International was not established until 1993 (Berg and Roberts 2012: 196–7, 217).
5. Soderquist 2005: 29.
6. Berg and Roberts 2012: 2–3.
7. Tedlow 2003: 340, quoting Walton 1993: 53. See Tedlow 2003: 341 on Walton having fifteen variety stores by 1960.
8. Walton 1993: 63.
9. Walton 1993: 27.
10. Walton 1993: 53; Vance and Scott 1994: 14.
11. Vance and Scott 1994: 15.
12. Vance and Scott 1994: 26.
13. Vance and Scott 1994: 38, emphasis added.
14. Walton 1993: 55, 57.
15. Moreton 2009: 38.
16. Walton 1993: 64.
17. Walton 1993: 59.
18. Vance and Scott 1994: 47.
19. Vance and Scott 1994: 54; Ortega 1999: 68–71; Walton 1993: 121–5, 153, 154. 'Wal-Mart blew right through the stagflation "malaise" of the 1970s that was so hard on so many other retailers' (Tedlow 2003: 313).

20. Walton 1993: 112, 116. The firm ordered merchandise from manufacturers on behalf of its stores, the merchandise was delivered by manufacturers to the firm's warehouse distribution centres, and there the merchandise was assembled into store-by-store orders that were delivered to each store by the firm's fleet of trucks. Wal-Mart's reliance on its own fleet of trucks was an unusual and lasting feature that was in marked contrast to its competitors' preference for contracting out the delivery of merchandise from their distribution centres (266–7).
21. Vance and Scott 1994: 158–9.
22. Walton 1993: 113–14, 264; Vance and Scott 1994: 70–1.
23. Ortega 1999: 110, 111.
24. Ortega 1999: 75.
25. Berg and Roberts 2012: 122 on the 'hub and spoke model'.
26. Walton 1993: 140.
27. Walton 1993: 140–1. The saturation strategy also deterred competition from other discounting retailers. For example, there were eventually forty Wal-Mart stores within 100 miles of Springfield, Missouri, and so any competing firm entering the territory would have 'a rough time going up against our kind of strength' (142).
28. Walton 1993: 264–5.
29. See Vance and Scott 1994: 82–3, 85, and 156–8.
30. Vance and Scott 1994: 85, 86.
31. It became the number-one retailer after a year of more than 20 per cent growth in net sales and net income (Vance and Scott 1994: 158).
32. Walton 1993: 141.
33. Ortega 1999: 75.
34. Vance and Scott 1994: 84.
35. Vance and Scott 1994: 84.
36. Walton 1993: 142. The firm's expansion in the 1980s had also been aided by acquisitions, notably the 1981 takeover of Kuhn's Big K Stores through which Wal-Mart acquired more than a hundred discount department stores located in nine different states in the southeast of the country (Walton 1993: 251–3; Vance and Scott 1994: 82; Ortega 1999: 103–5).
37. Vance and Scott 1994: 113, 115; Ortega 1999: 140–4; Walton 1993: 255–6.
38. Trimble 1990: 209; Ortega 1999: 148; Vance and Scott 1994: 118–19; Walton 1993: 256–7. Originally, they had been called Sam's Wholesale Clubs but in 1990 the name was changed to Sam's Clubs: Members Only, after a legal challenge to the use of the word 'wholesale' to describe a store selling goods to customers for their own use rather than for on-selling (Vance and Scott 1994: 118).
39. Walton 1993: 260.
40. Walton 1993: 254. The first Wal-Mart hypermarket opened in December 1987 and the final, fourth example in 1990; the first supercenter opened as early as 1988 and only eleven had been added by 1992 (Vance and Scott 1994: 129–32, 166).
41. Ortega 1999: 164; Vance and Scott 1994: 133. The addition of groceries also meant that Wal-Mart was becoming more of a convenient one-stop shop for its customers (Strasser 2006: 55).
42. Berg and Roberts 2012: 161, 164, fig. 10.1. More than half of the new Supercenters had been created through a modernization programme that converted many ageing discount stores into the new hybrid discount/grocery Supercenter (Vance and Scott 1994: 134; Berg and Roberts 2012: 162).

43. See Appendix 1 on Barnard's distinction between technical, rational leadership and the *moral* leadership involved in creating and maintaining a corporate culture.

44. Walton 1993: 216. Years earlier he had told an interviewer that one of his assets 'is my willingness to try something new, to change. I think that is a concept we carry throughout the company. We have a low resistance to change' (quoted by Trimble 1990: 142).

45. See how innovative adaptation is defined in Chapter 1 in terms of Schumpeter's concept of creative response.

46. Fishman 2011: 24.

47. Walton 1993: 147.

48. Walton 1993: 147.

49. Walton 1993: 148.

50. Soderquist 2005: 148.

51. See Walton 1993: 193 on mismanagement; 151 on concepts getting out of control; and 318 on the next trouble spot.

52. Walton 1993: 271, 272.

53. Slater 2003: 54.

54. Lichtenstein 2010: 34–5.

55. Walton 1993: 64.

56. Vance and Scott 1994: 69–70. See also Trimble 1990: 151.

57. Vance and Scott 1994: 69; Trimble 1990: 118; Walton 1993: 64.

58. Even in the 2010s global Wal-Mart was pursuing an 'Everyday Low Cost' (EDLC) grand strategy: 'saving money (or pursuing an EDLC strategy) is at the heart of most Walmart strategies' (Berg and Roberts 2012: 56, 132).

59. Walton 1993: 295. However, he then remarks that 'I think we came to work earlier and stayed later', which is *not* the waste-eliminating way in which Ohno reduced the number of workers and 'operated with fewer people'!

60. Walton 1993: 295.

61. Walton 1993: 317. For example, when describing his innovative distribution network, he noted that 'cost savings alone would make the investment worthwhile' and that it was costing Wal-Mart markedly less than its competitors to distribute goods to stores (265). Vance and Scott point out that the 'expansion of Wal-Mart's sophisticated distribution system during the 1980s was central to its costcutting strategy' and in fact by the end of the 1980s its distribution costs were down to 1.3 per cent of sales, compared to the 3.5 per cent and 5 per cent of its two main competitors (1994: 92).

62. Walton 1993: 317.

63. Vance and Scott 1994: 90. In the 1990s, too, Wal-Mart's percentage of sales revenue spent on selling and general expenses was markedly lower than that of its competitors (Hoopes 2006: 93).

64. Walton 1993: 294. See Trimble 1990: 152 on being 'far below industry norms' for office expenses.

65. Ortega 1999: xv, xxv. See also Vance and Scott 1994: 108 on political criticism of Wal-Mart's employment policies. However, even one of the critics of Wal-Mart's labour policies acknowledges that the firm was 'lowering prices and raising the standard of living of the working-class and middle-class customers who are its main clientele' (Hoopes 2006: 88).

66. Walton 1993: 164, 162.

67. Walton 1993: 165, 169. The share-buying and bonus programmes gave employees the chance to buy Wal-Mart shares at a discount and to earn bonuses for boosting their store's

sales and for reducing its 'shrinkage' of merchandise due to theft or damage (Ortega 1999: 90–1; Trimble 1990: 234, 274). The profit-sharing plan used a formula based on profit growth to calculate the percentage of every eligible worker's wages that the firm would contribute to his or her personal account within the firm's overall profit-sharing plan (Walton 1993: 169). In 1976, workers' eligibility for participating in the profit-sharing plan was reduced from two years to one year's employment (Ortega 1999: 93).

68. Ortega 1999: 90.
69. Walton 1993: 168, 173, 181, 200 on new features, and 166–7 on opposition to unionization; Ortega 1999: 91 on the 1973 renaming employees as 'associates' and 93, 105, and 230–3 on the continuing fight against unionization; Vance and Scott 1994: 107 on informal use of first names—and also the apparent 'sense of family' in the firm, if only because many employees felt they were part of Walton's extended family. See also Trimble's chapter 'Labor Unions Not Wanted' (1990: ch. 22).
70. Moreton 2009: 185.
71. Moreton 2009: 185.
72. Tedlow 2003: 343.
73. Fishman 2011: 62, 227. Walton was also not monopolistic and in fact seems to have enjoyed the challenge of competition.
74. Ortega 1999: 126.
75. He acknowledged that if he had not recruited these technocrats, 'we would have come apart somewhere there in the seventies, or we certainly wouldn't have been able to pull off our really incredible expansion in the eighties' (Walton 1993: 157–8).
76. Walton 1993: 263.
77. Walton 1993: 270. See also Ortega 1999: 78 and 99 on how they and the earlier generation of technocratic executives pushed for technological investment during the pivotal 1970s phase of Wal-Mart's development.
78. Ortega 1999: 131. It is not clear whether Walton was in fact told that the technology 'wasn't there yet' and a 'million different things could go wrong with something so untested' (131).
79. Ortega 1999: 131–2, 133. Wal-Mart signed the contract for a satellite system in 1984 but the installation of the system was not completed until 1987 (Berg and Roberts 2012: 141–3).
80. Ortega 1999: 104. Similarly, retired chief operating officer (COO) Arend said, 'I always knew when it was time to stop arguing a point when Walton thundered, "By golly, I still own most of the stock in this company, and this is the way we are going to do it"' (quoted by Trimble 1990: 143).
81. Ortega 1999: 211, 135.
82. Hillary Clinton was also the wife of Arkansas Governor Bill Clinton. She lobbied Walton and the board about involving Wal-Mart in environmental affairs, sold Walton the proposal to establish an environmental advisory board, and eventually saw her efforts rewarded when the corporation launched 'its green effort' in 1989 (Ortega 1999: 215, 216). See Vance and Scott 1994: 111–12 on this environmentally friendly 'green' campaign, such as Wal-Mart stores switching to shopping bags made of recycled paper rather than non-biodegradable plastic.
83. Walton 1993: 278. Ortega confirms that Walton 'encouraged those lower down to debate and challenge ideas' (1999: 122). Vance and Scott confirm that his efforts had some success, as a 'tendency to encourage independent thinking permeated every level of the organization, from top managers down to hourly associates' (1994: 100).

84. Vance and Scott 1994: 99.
85. Vance and Scott 1994; Ortega 1999: 136; Walton 1993: 198.
86. Walton 1993: 259, 216.
87. Vance and Scott 1994: 99.
88. Walton 1993: 259 and Ortega 1999: 136 on Glass as the preferred successor, even though after the job swapping these two executives were officially equal in status. Shewmaker resigned soon after his rival became CEO in 1988, 'leaving Glass, along with Walton, to lead the company' (Vance and Scott 1994: 99).
89. Walton 1993: 263.
90. Berg and Roberts 2012: 138. Walton's attitude to technology has also been described as embracing the new technology 'but always with a heathy dose of skepticism. He knew how to put technology in its place. It was a means to an end' (Tedlow 2003: 312).
91. Walton 1993: 117.
92. The introduction of barcode scanning in the 1980s required 'testing the system for a couple of years to get the bugs out' (Ortega 1999: 130). In the late 1970s, the mechanization of the Searcy distribution centre became 'such a nightmare that Sam began to question the whole idea of mechanized distribution' (Glass quoted in Walton 1993: 264). Earlier in the decade, the introduction of electric cash registers ran into unforeseen problems that one of the victims later blamed on a technocrat's choice of equipment: 'right idea but the wrong register' (quoted in Walton 1993: 159).
93. Ortega 1999: 125.
94. Walton 1993: 252; Ortega 1999: 103. Ortega describes how debates about the acquisition had dominated board meetings for more than a year beforehand, and he argues that Walton would not have 'quietly acceded to the majority' if the vote in the executive committee had been four-to-two against the acquisition (1999: 103).
95. Vance and Scott 1994: 98; Ortega 1999: 104, 73, 166; and see 214 on membership of the dual- leadership executive committee.
96. Trimble mentioned not only a finance committee but also a real-estate committee and personnel committees (1990: 138–9).
97. Walton 1993: 97, 199. See also Vance and Scott 1994: 68, 101 on the size of meetings and who attended them. The regional managers spent several days each week in their regions, commuting weekly by small plane from an airport near Bentonville (Walton 1993: 286–7; Trimble 1990: 278).
98. In Walton's book, Soderquist said that the meetings did not really have an agenda but 'the chairman always has his yellow legal pad with notes scribbled on it of things he wants to discuss' (quoted in Walton 1993: 211–12).
99. Walton 1993: 209.
100. Vance and Scott 1994: 101.
101. Vance and Scott 1994: 68, 101.
102. Learning about a problem may lead to an adaptive response that solves the problem, as learning about a change, threat, or opportunity is usually the first part of an adaptive process that produces a rapid or innovative adaptation.
103. Walton 1993: 209, 291.
104. Ortega 1999: xxiv and it was only one of several occasions that he refers to Walton learning something (80, 85, 117, 140).
105. Tedlow 2003: 312, 332.
106. Learning and adaptation should be viewed as separate business processes and methods even though learning is usually included in the first part of an adaptive process. The distinction between learning and adaptation is also found in military analysis, such as

Cohen and Gooch's chapter on 'Failure to Learn: American Antisubmarine Warfare in 1942'. It analyses the failure of the US Navy to learn organizational lessons from how the British fought Germany's U-boat submarines in 1939–41. This failure to *learn* proved costly in 1942, when America was targeted by the U-boats; but the Navy eventually *adapted* organizationally to the problems and environment of anti-submarine warfare in the Atlantic (Cohen and Gooch 2006: 94).

107. In addition to Dassault, Grove and Whitman will be described in Chapters 6 and 7 as emphasizing learning.
108. Walton 1993: 29, 289.
109. Walton 1993: 57, 102, 104–5.
110. Walton 1993: 191, 192.
111. Walton 1993: 254.
112. Kroc 1987: 191.
113. Tedlow 2003: 340, 341.
114. Tedlow 2003: 340.
115. Tedlow 2003: 344.
116. Walton 1993: 53–4.
117. Walton 1993: 59.
118. Walton 1993: 59.
119. Walton 1993: 200–2.
120. Vance and Scott 1994: 78.
121. Walton 1993: 47. One of the lessons he learnt from his early training in retailing 'was not to be so smug you ignored your competitors, especially their successful policies and practices' (Trimble 1990: 91).
122. Walton 1993: 102, 255.
123. Walton 1993: 243. Kmart's stores were so superior 'back then that sometimes I felt we couldn't compete' (104). But, as he told Trimble, 'we were protected by our small-town market. It would have been unthinkable for them to have tried to put a competing store in a small town. They gave us a ten-year period to grow, and finally we were able to hold our own' (quoted by Trimble 1990: 93).
124. Trimble 1990: 148.
125. Walton 1993: 293.
126. Ortega 1999: 193. See also Trimble 1990: 146–7.
127. Walton 1993: 293 and see also 316.
128. Walton 1993: 285; and see also 267 on a similar learning-monitoring by talking to Wal-Mart's truck drivers.
129. Soderquist 2005: 118.
130. He changed his name from Marcel Bloch to Marcel Dassault after the Second World War, as 'Dassault' had been the pseudonym used by his brother when fighting with the Resistance insurgency against France's occupation by Nazi Germany.
131. He was estimated to have the 'largest fortune in France in 1985' (Villette and Vuillermot 2009: 121).
132. The talisman mentioned by his book's title was a four-leaf clover that he had discovered in 1939 and kept in his wallet ever since (Dassault 1971: 126–7).
133. Dassault 1971: 32–3.
134. Dassault 1971: 32–3.
135. Dassault 1971: 32–3. His firm's official history describes it as a 'two-seat combat aircraft' (Carlier and Berger 1996: 11–12).
136. Dassault 1971: 34–5.

137. Dassault 1971: 38.
138. Dassault 1971: 41–2.
139. Dassault 1971: 43; and 43–4 on the later government order for planes to be used in the colonies.
140. See Dassault 1971: 44–7 on this period. Villette and Vuillermot 2009: 124–7 provides a different perspective on this period.
141. Dassault 1971: 47, 106; Carlier and Berger 1996: 22–4.
142. Villette and Vuillermot 2009: 127, emphases added.
143. Bergerud 2000: 179–81.
144. Carlier and Berger 1996: 25.
145. Carlier and Berger 1996: 28. However, this method of technological development involved the risk of being leap-frogged by a less derivative, more innovative aircraft. A very relevant case is the American F-16 fighter that defeated Dassault's F 1E in the mid-1970s 'contract of the century' to sell a new fighter to the air forces of Belgium, Denmark, the Netherlands, and Norway. The innovative F-16 not only had a more powerful engine but also was constructed of composite materials as well as metal and was pioneering fly-by-wire, computerized flight controls (Carlier and Berger 1996: 119).
146. Dassault 1971: 113.
147. Dassault 1971: 113.
148. Dassault 1971: 105.
149. Waterton 2012 [1956]: 197, 165.
150. Carlier and Berger 1996: 37.
151. Waterton 2012 [1956]: 167. A British test pilot from a later era confirms that the flight characteristics of prototypes were less predictable in Waterton's era, which lacked sophisticated computer-assisted design techniques, and that there was indeed 'always a tendency then, without the multitude of recorders now fitted to test aircraft, for the firm to prefer not to believe their own test pilot and take no action until the certification pilot or the customer criticised the product' (Blackman in Waterton 2012 [1956]: x–xi).
152. Waterton 2012 [1956]: 166.
153. On the importance of exports, see Carlier and Berger 1996: 64, 68, 71, 84–5, 132–3; exports in fact averaged 58 per cent of sales in the period from 1952 to 1977 (133).
154. Dassault 1971: 108–9. The Falcons had been sold in more than twenty countries on five continents.
155. Dassault 1971: 109.
156. Carlier and Berger 1996: 29, 161.
157. Carlier and Berger 1996: 85, 148.

Chapter 6

1. Tedlow 2007: 121.
2. Tedlow 2007: xiv–xv.
3. Tedlow 2007: 385, 278.
4. Grove's concern with adaptive crises was part of his wider concern with business survival and guardianship. He argued that 'when it comes to business, I believe in the value of paranoia. I believe that the prime responsibility of a manager is to guard constantly against other people's attacks' (1999: 3). Bill Gates experienced a similar anxiety about

the future of his corporation Microsoft. His 'concern that Microsoft could always be surpassed and made irrelevant is a constant theme for Gates' (Becraft 2014: 117).

5. Grove's facility with concepts and conceptualization is one of the reasons why he might be considered a business equivalent of Plato's philosopher-king rulers, in the sense of kings who 'genuinely and adequately philosophize' (Strauss 1972: 29).

6. Grove 1999: 32, and he explains that the term 'inflection point' was used in mathematics to describe a change in sign from negative to positive or vice versa and to describe where a curve changes from convex to concave or vice versa.

7. Grove 1999: 4, 5, 20.

8. Grove 1999: 5, 6, 7.

9. Grove 1999: 95.

10. Grove 1999: 88.

11. Jackson 1998: 253.

12. Jackson 1998: 253–4, citing Grove's own assessment, which acknowledges that the adaptive response 'took us a total of three years': the firm's 'performance started to slump when the entire industry weakened in mid-1984', but the decision to get out of memory chips was not made until mid-1985, took 'until mid-1986 to implement', and then 'took another year before we returned to profitability' (Grove 1999: 95).

13. Jackson 1998: 358.

14. Grove 1999: 22.

15. Grove 1999: 66–7. Tedlow notes that 'the Intel Inside program had succeeded to a remarkable degree' in creating a consumer-recognized brand *but* 'no one at Intel had any experience at brand management' (2007: 332–3).

16. Grove 1999: 90. Two intellectual prejudices 'that were as strong as religious dogmas' were that 'our salesmen needed a full product line [including memory-chip products] to do a good job in front of our customers' and that memory chips were 'technology drivers' because 'we always developed and refined our technologies on our memory products first because they were easier to test' (90, 91).

17. Grove 1999: 92–3.

18. It might be argued that Intel was indirectly benefiting from an innovative adaptation because in 1985 it was able to fall back on a microprocessor business created largely by IBM's innovative adaptation to disruptive technology, namely the IBM PC's exploitation of new markets for desktop computers (Christensen 2000: 109–10, 217).

19. Grove 1999: 143.

20. Grove 1999: 94; Berlin 2005: 64.

21. Thackray et al. 2015: 441, 439.

22. Tedlow 2007: 224.

23. Malone 2014: 364. Grove's account of second-sourcing notes that once a second source is in production, 'multiple companies now compete for the same business. This may please the customer but [it] certainly hurts the wallet of the prime source' (1999: 70). Yet when he then describes the 'enormous' impact on the PC industry of Intel's shift from second-sourcing to sole-sourcing, he mentions that 'our influence on customers increased' but fails to note that this increased influence included being a monopolistic supplier and price-setter (70).

24. Thackray et al. 2015: 437; and 436 on Windows being designed for Intel's microprocessors. But the first, 1985 version of Windows was actually a 'flop' and not until the third, 1990, version would it meet the great expectations (Wallace and Erickson 1993:

314, 362–3). Nonetheless, 'Wintel' was an effective 'bilateral monopoly' when compared to the highly competitive market of IBM/clone PC manufacturers (Tedlow 2007: 305). 'What really mattered from Intel's point of view was the birth of the IBM "clones." A clone worked just like an IBM PC' and so when 'IBM wanted to hold off on its purchase of the 386' microprocessor, Intel found ready customers among the clone-makers, who were able to gain a competitive advantage over IBM by manufacturing 386-equipped PCs which were more capable and popular than IBM's non-386 version (227, 228).

25. Thackray et al. 2015: 439.
26. Thackray et al. 2015: 439.
27. Tedlow 2007: 395; and 230 on how the sole-sourcing strategy had put Intel 'in a position to print money'.
28. Grove 1999: 4.
29. Tedlow 2007: 369; and 282 on being described by *Fortune* as the world's most profitable firm.
30. Moore's Law was first formulated by Gordon Moore in a 1965 magazine article, where he had predicted that the number of transistors being chemically imprinted on a microchip would double every year and therefore in ten years' time would total 65,000 transistors per chip (Thackray et al. 2015: xix–xx).
31. Thackray et al. 2015: 375. Furthermore, he phrased Moore's Law in economic as well as technological terms by phrasing in terms of a doubling of the capability that it would be *economical* to produce in a microchip (507, 381, 460). In other words, there would have to be a market for these continually updated, exponentially more capable microchips: there would need to be sufficient customers willing to pay for the research, development, and manufacturing costs involved in maintaining Moore's Law.
32. Thackray et al. 2015: 377; and see 277, 310, 329, 348 on the treadmill strategy, and 325–6, 462–4 on Moore's strategic role. Similarly, Malone's history of Intel's triple leadership describes how Moore devised 'an incredibly powerful business strategy' based on Moore's Law (2014: 375).
33. Malone 2014: 435.
34. Malone 2014: 436. Malone prefers the analogy with a spiral rather than a treadmill but his analysis is applicable to both conceptions of Intel's strategy. Because Intel had set the rate of the spiral/treadmill 'at the pace of Moore's Law, its competitors had to maintain that breakneck pace always or risk falling back' and 'it was almost impossible for competitors to gain ground on Intel as long as it hewed to the law': that is, to Moore's Law (436). Cringely simply suggested that Grove's strategy was to outspend Intel's competitors in order to speed up its product development and 'result in Intel's building the very profitable leading-edge chips, leaving its competitors to slug it out in the market for commodity processors' (1996: 354).
35. Grove 1999: 28. Substitution would include what Christensen termed 'disruptive' new technologies, which pose a threat to the leading firms in an industry (see Chapter 1 and Appendix 1).
36. Grove 1999: 30.
37. Grove 1999: 56–7, 66. These two examples were mentioned in Chapters 2, 5, and 6.
38. Grove 1999: 181–2.
39. Grove 1999: 182, 183.
40. Malone 2014: 430.

41. Malone 2014: 431.
42. Grove 1999: 7; see 153 and 164 for two different descriptions of the three stages.
43. Grove 1999: 108. Grove's term 'Cassandras' comes from the Trojan priestess in *The Iliad* who prophesied the destruction of Troy. Most strategic inflection points are hard to identify: 'instead of coming in with a bang, [they] approach on little cat feet. They are often not clear until you can look at the events in retrospect' (107).
44. Grove 1999: 109–10.
45. Grove 1999: 110, 119.
46. Grove 1999: 117.
47. Grove 1999: 35.
48. Tedlow 2007: 190; Thackray et al. 2015: 387.
49. Grove 1999: 146–7, 149–50.
50. He even co-taught a course on strategic management at Stanford University's Graduate School of Business in the 1990s (Grove 1999: xi).
51. Grove 1999: 114, 162. Moore's biographers note that debates among Intel's management could be very vigorous: 'macho and combative posturing often preceded "rational judgment." Andy Grove set the tone, frequently shouting and hurling insults at opponents' (Thackray et al. 2015: 387). This was likely an example of what Intel's corporate culture called 'constructive confrontation', which was described by Grove as 'a style of ferociously arguing with one another while remaining friends' (1999: 84).
52. Grove 1999: 157.
53. Grove 1999: 155.
54. Grove 1999: 153, 154.
55. Grove 1999: 155, 156.
56. Tedlow 2007: 335. General Electric's CEO, Jack Welch, acknowledges that he was 'late' in adopting email in 1999 (2003: 341–2).
57. Tedlow 2007: 334.
58. Welch 2003: 349.
59. Grove 1999: 156; and 157 on worldwide firms.
60. Packard 2005 [1995]: 155.
61. Grove 1999: 153; and 130 on experimenting with new products or other new things.
62. Grove 1999: 130.
63. Berlin 2005: 217, 203.
64. Berlin 2005: 183.
65. Berlin 2005: 227.
66. Berlin 2005: 227; Tedlow 2007: 241.
67. Tedlow 2007: 407.
68. Malone 2014: 482.
69. Malone 2014: 482, where he also describes how Intel 'had developed a new, very-low-power processor family called Atom but had designed it for laptops and netbooks, not tablets and smartphones. Intel had blown it'.
70. Berlin 2005: 185–6.
71. Berlin 2005: 193. Berlin notes that another feature of Noyce's deliberative style was that he 'spoke of "hierarchy power" and "knowledge power" and firmly believed that when it came to technical decisions, the word of the person with the most knowledge ought to trump the opinion of the one with the higher title' (191).
72. Packard 2005 [1995]: 96.

73. Packard 2005 [1995]: 97. Another factor involved in the selection of new ideas for further development was of course the likelihood of high profits or rate of return: 'we often used to select projects on the basis of a six-to-one engineering return. That is, the profit we expected to derive over the lifetime of a product should be at least six times the cost of developing the product' (97–8). Furthermore, Packard later referred to HP's selecting new ideas for products that 'will meet *latent* needs of *future* importance to our customers' (110, emphases added).

74. Packard 2005 [1995]: 100.

75. Packard 2005 [1995]: 100.

76. Packard 2005 [1995]: 100.

77. Packard 2005 [1995]: 100–1. The deliberative process's informal rules gave inventors and Hewlett reciprocal rights and duties, such as the right to / duty of initial encouragement and then 'inquisitorial' questioning.

78. Malone 2007: 139.

79. Packard 2005 [1995]: 141–2.

80. Packard 2005 [1995]: 140.

81. Packard 2005 [1995]: 140–1. However, HP soon discovered that operating divisions' focus on their divisional profit-and-loss statements led them to focus on their existing markets rather than seeking opportunities to diversify into new markets; in contrast, its eventual company-wide experimentation system encouraged cooperative cross-divisional efforts at innovation and diversification (House and Price 2009: 99).

82. Malone 2007: 144–5.

83. Malone believes that the primary reason was the leaders' desire to strengthen their firm's corporate culture: 'the primary reason was cultural' and, specifically, 'retaining the company's innovative, and already well-established, "[HP] Way" of doing business' (2007: 145).

84. Packard 2005 [1995]: 146. An organizational structure containing many small-sized divisions had already been pioneered by Cordiner at General Electric in the 1950s (Chandler 1990 [1962]: 368).

85. House and Price 2009: 4–5, 142.

86. A relatively recent example of these treadmill-like strategies is the printer upgrading treadmill of the 1980s–90s. HP 'upgraded its printer generations so quickly that [its] competitors barely had time to react before its superior replacement arrived' (Malone 2007: 332–3).

87. House and Price 2009: 86.

88. Packard 2005 [1995]: 140–1; Malone 2007: 211.

89. Packard 2005 [1995]: 147.

90. House and Price 2009: 264; Malone 2007: 212.

91. Malone 2007: 212. The need for inter-divisional coordination was highlighted by the failure of HP's entry into the 1980s personal-computer market, namely its HP150, which 'opened everyone's eyes at HP to problems of cooperation across divisions' (Bowen et al. 1994: 418).

92. House and Price 2009: 90.

93. House and Price 2009: 90.

94. Packard 2005 [1995]: 142.

95. House and Price 2009: 113.

96. House and Price 2009: 308–11; Bowen et al. 1994: 418–25.

97. House and Price 2009: 5, 33.
98. House and Price 2009: 150–1.
99. House and Price 2009: 151. The desktop calculator was the HP9100A, introduced in 1968, the hand-held calculator was the pioneering HP-35, introduced in 1972, and the small computer was the HP3000, especially the highly successful Series II introduced in 1975 (Malone 2007: 291).
100. House and Price 2009: 518, fig. A. 4.
101. House and Price 2009: 518, fig. A. 5.
102. Burgelman et al. 2017: 124, 126.
103. Burgelman et al. 2017: 138–9.
104. Burgelman et al. 2017: 139.
105. Burgelman et al. 2017: 154–5. Young's efforts took HP from number seventeen to number three in the field of business computing (149).
106. Burgelman et al. 2017: 154. HP became the number-four provider of PCs and was actually number one in the home personal-computer market (154).
107. Burgelman et al. 2017: 158, 170.
108. Burgelman et al. 2017: 152, 158–9.
109. House and Price 2009: 518, fig. A. 6.
110. In addition, the experimentation system was affected by such new moves as the reduction in divisional R&D budgets and the reduced funding of HP Labs (Burgelman et al. 2017: 174–5).
111. Burgelman et al. 2017: 170–1, 176.
112. Burgelman et al. 2017: 175. Malone pointed out that inkjet printing 'was the last great technical breakthrough at Hewlett-Packard in the twentieth century' (2007: 330).
113. Burgelman et al. 2017: 175.
114. Isaacson 2013: xxi.
115. Speech at Stanford University 2005, quoted by Lee 2011: 7.
116. Isaacson 2013: 375.
117. Isaacson 2013: 424.
118. Young and Simon 2005: 276.
119. Young and Simon 2005: 277.
120. Young and Simon 2005: 278–9.
121. Young and Simon 2005: 280.
122. Stone 2014: 232–4 on top-down experimentation; and 236, 238–9, 248 on a hands-on approach.
123. Young and Simon 2005: 285. A key factor in the iPod's success was Jobs's negotiation of agreements with music firms that allowed Apple to sell their music through the online iTunes Music Store (290).
124. Isaacson 2013: 429. His anxiety may have been fuelled by his knowledge of Grove's book, as was described at the beginning of this chapter, and also by his knowledge of Christensen's concept of disruptive technology, as 'Jobs was deeply influenced by his book *The Innovator's Dilemma*' (376).
125. Isaacson 2013: 430.
126. Isaacson 2013: 433.
127. Isaacson 2013: 433, 434, 436.
128. Isaacson 2013: 438. Another diversification was that the iPhone earned huge, continuing revenues from the non-phoning activities, the applications, which could be performed

with this portable IT platform. Apple's online App Store opened in July 2008 and, less than two years later, was offering 185,000 different applications for sale—thanks in part to an innovative policy of allowing independent apps designers to sell their products through Apple (463).

129. Isaacson 2013: 431–2, 452–3.
130. Isaacson 2013: 453. However, it was apparently not Jobs but one of his key team members who wanted to change from an Intel to an ARM-based microprocessor—and persuaded Jobs to make the change (454).
131. Isaacson 2013: 455, 459.
132. Sloan 1990 [1964]: 433–4.
133. Brandt 2011a: 177.
134. Brandt 2011a: 177.
135. Brandt 2011a: 178.
136. Brandt 2011a: 178.
137. Malone 2014: 338. Grove made these remarks in a 2004 interview. The management book was Drucker's 1954 classic *The Practice of Management* (Drucker 2006 [1954]).
138. Malone 2014: 448.
139. Jackson 1998: 377.

Chapter 7

1. Cohen 2003: 9, 314.
2. Cohen 2003: 8–9.
3. Whitman 2010: 9–10.
4. Van Dijck 2013: 62.
5. Whitman 2010: 3–4.
6. Whitman 2010: 9. Details of her pre-eBay career can be found in her book and in Horvitz 2006: 11–17.
7. Whitman 2010: 248.
8. Viegas 2007: 11. These statistics include only individuals over 16 years old but, on the other hand, they include Canadians as well as residents of the US.
9. Viegas 2007: 65.
10. Bunnell 2000: 46. He also describes the advantages of online auctions for small-business dealers in used goods (42–3). But later he points out that the high-volume sellers on eBay 'face daunting back-office chores that effectively limit their potential revenues and profits' and indeed 'many volume sellers of low-priced items must find themselves working for very low hourly wages' (52).
11. Horvitz 2006: 360. By the time Whitman retired, there were more than a million (Whitman 2010: 9).
12. Bunnell 2000: 10, 36.
13. Cohen 2003: 117.
14. Cohen 2003: 25, 58. But many auctions did not result in a final-sale fee. For sellers could also include a reserve price, known to eBay but not the bidders, and Bunnell pointed out that many auctions were not 'consummated' because the bidding failed to reach the secret reserve price (Bunnell 2000: 49).
15. Bunnell 2000: 120; Viegas 2007: 48, 56.

16. Whitman 2010: 8. On the other hand, once eBay became a public company, Whitman had to deal with the tension between the user community's needs and the revenue needs of stockholders. 'We really lived in la-la land with our community for two wonderful years', Whitman said in an interview, but then went on to acknowledge that 'once you go public the pressures are completely different. You've got investors and analysts looking at you, you've got the media looking at you, you've got to worry about shares and stockholders and revenue' (Horvitz 2006: 60).

17. Cohen 2003: 28–9. According to Cohen, too, Omidyar had tried to register 'Auction-Web.com' but it had already been registered by another online-auction pioneer, so the site continued to have the online address of 'eBay.com', which Omidyar had chosen when he found that his first-preference 'EchoBay.com' had already been registered by another company (n. 79).

18. Cohen 2003: 28; Viegas 2007: 46.

19. Cohen 2003: 50.

20. Bunnell 2000: 64–5. 'The users who posted and lurked in the eBay Café were for the most part middle-aged, middle-class, and lived in Middle America, and they chatted as if they had known each other all their lives' (Cohen 2003: 50). Amazon, too, had moved in this direction in 1996 by not only inviting readers to post reviews of books but also enabling browsers to communicate with one another: 'it became an early social network site for book fans' (Brandt 2011b: 86).

21. Kirkpatrick 2011: 67. In fact Usenet's social messaging began in 1979 (66).

22. Kirkpatrick 2011: 67, 69.

23. Van Dijck 2013: 57; Kirkpatrick 2011: 71–5, 145, 151–2.

24. Bilton 2013: 62, 67, 174. Twitter might well be categorized as a 'microblogging' information network rather than some form of e-socializing, especially as most tweeting is not reciprocal or interactive but merely providing information to a prominent tweeter's following of fans, admirers, supporters, and so forth (Van Dijck 2013: 74, 78–9).

25. Bunnell 2000: 105; Cohen 2003: 59, 93.

26. Cohen 2003: 56, 59.

27. Cohen 2003: 30–2.

28. Viegas 2007: 76; Cohen 2003: 79–80.

29. Cohen 2003: 126. Omidyar and Skoll began to disengage from the firm in 1999 (303–4).

30. Cohen 2003: 186, 189.

31. Cohen 2003: 147–8. Even in 1997, Whitman had never come across 'a young enterprise' with such impressive numbers as, for example, eBay's profit margin: 'their costs were so low that their profits were 85 percent of revenues' (Whitman 2010: 19).

32. Whitman 2010: 4.

33. Whitman 2010: 46.

34. Whitman 2010: 68–9, emphases added. She also seems to share Grove's preference for an early-mover strategy. There is something Grove-like about her maxim that 'the price of inaction is far greater than the cost of making a mistake' and her warning that no matter how 'confusing or hard or even paralyzing your circumstances might feel, the price you'll pay for treading water, dithering, not moving forward, is far higher than the cost of making a mistake' (46, 72). There is a very similar warning in Grove's analytical framework for dealing with inflection points (Grove 1999: 152).

35. 'When you operate in a technology-driven space, everything can change overnight and you have to change with it' (Whitman 2010: 260).

36. Cohen 2003: 183.
37. Cohen 2003: 181; Whitman 2010: 206–7. Her longer term response included hiring the best technical expert that 'money could buy', and in her book she noted that hiring and retaining him, with the highest salary paid to any of the firm's managers, was 'the best money we ever spent' (121).
38. Whitman 2010: 211; Cohen 2003: 184. A week after the outage ended, listings on the eBay site were almost back to the pre-outage level (Horvitz 2006: 58).
39. Global expansion was the other source or area of innovative adaptation, as in the case of the joint-venture relationship that was pioneered in China in 2003 (Whitman 2010: 70–1).
40. Horvitz 2006: 40.
41. Whitman 2010: 167.
42. Whitman 2010: 251.
43. Whitman 2010: 88.
44. Cohen 2003: 131–2. Another example of her use of diverse deliberation was the recruitment of outside directors who had developed new firms in other industries, such as the chairman/CEO of Starbucks and the chairman of Intuit software (Bunnell 2000: 32).
45. Horvitz 2006: 34.
46. Whitman 2010: 169.
47. Cohen 2003: 209.
48. Bunnell 2000: 100.
49. The board was also helped to perform its auditing (rather than deliberative) role by her informal rule that all senior executives were to attend board meetings so that directors 'could ask them questions' (Whitman 2010: 97).
50. Whitman 2010: 91.
51. Whitman 2010: 90.
52. Whitman 2010: 90, emphasis added.
53. Burgelman et al. 2017: 287–8, 296.
54. Burgelman et al. 2017: 297, 326–7.
55. Whitman 2010: 137, emphasis added.
56. Cohen 2003: 126.
57. Whitman 2010: 138; Horvitz 2006: 46.
58. Horvitz 2006: 45, 48.
59. Whitman 2010: 140.
60. Whitman 2010: 187–8.
61. Whitman 2010: 188. The collectibles-focused strategy might well be viewed as a niche-market strategy, but Bunnell preferred to describe it in terms of market segmentation and concentrating the firm's marketing resources on the 20 per cent of registered users who accounted for 80 per cent of its revenues (Bunnell 2000: 124).
62. Cohen 2003: 132.
63. Cohen 2003: 132, 138.
64. Viegas 2007: 70.
65. Bunnell 2000: vii, 5. He noted that the figure for registered users is nothing like the number of *active* users, which may be only half or a third of the official count (120).
66. Cohen 2003: 132. Bunnell noted that in 1998 trading in Beanie Babies accounted for some 6 per cent of eBay's revenue (2000: 25).
67. Horvitz 2006: 63.

68. Cohen 2003: 208, and 279 quoting Whitman.
69. Cohen 2003: 279.
70. Cohen 2003: 200.
71. Bunnell 2000: 121; and 188 n. 1 on the 1999 move towards globalization.
72. Bunnell 2000: 75–6. Later he describes this as a land-grab approach and mentions the 'positive network effect' that eBay enjoyed as a 'first mover' (134).
73. Whitman 2010: 226–8.
74. Horvitz 2006: 2. The figures for users and countries are for 2004.
75. Horvitz 2006: 48; Whitman 2010: 228.
76. Stone 2014: 264, 265.
77. Stone 2014: 263, 264.
78. Bunnell 2000: 15. In 2000, most analysts were predicting that eBay would keep on growing at its current rapid rate 'for two or three more years, and then experience the usual tapering off that comes with market maturation' in the mid-2000s (181).
79. Stone 2014: 263–4.
80. Whitman 2010: 44.
81. Cohen 2003: 235. 'We were about to start experimenting with our own "buy it now" [fixed-price] format' (Whitman 2010: 44).
82. Whitman 2010: 258.
83. Whitman 2010: 69.
84. Cohen 2003: 155.
85. See Whitman 2010: 60–2; and 218–19 on the learning part of iteration; 212, 216 on validating; and 168–9 on feedback. Unlike Walton, she has little to say about copying others' ideas but she does mention 'borrowing' good ideas and following 'best practice' (219, 221).
86. Whitman 2010: 156.
87. Whitman 2010: 72.
88. Burgelman et al. 2017: 296.
89. Bunnell 2000: 22, 101.
90. Cohen 2003: 188.
91. Whitman 2010: 258.
92. Born in 1964, he was a Princeton graduate in computer science and electrical engineering who had worked in three Wall Street financial-computing firms, where he had managed computer programmers, an engineering department, and then a large team exploring new opportunities, such as those offered by the burgeoning Internet (Brandt 2011b: 31, 35–9).
93. Bezos's use of three of these rational methods is mentioned in this section: his learning on the job, his Kindle rapid adaptive response, and his Web Services innovative adaptation. There is also plenty of evidence of him using the other four methods. In the case of strategic calculation there is, for example, his 1999 strategy of not 'working toward a profit' until the Internet's 'cone of opportunity' had narrowed enough 'to make it difficult for newcomers to squeeze through ahead of him' in the markets he desired for Amazon (Brandt 2011b: 128–9). In the case of quantitative calculation there is, for example, his 'vision of an Amazon with data at its heart', which meant in practice that it 'relies on metrics to make almost every important decision' (Stone 2014: 204, 327). In the case of the deliberative methods there is, for example, his belief that 'truth springs forth when ideas and perspectives are banged together', which in practice meant policy-making arguments

'backed by numbers and passion' (Stone 2014: 326, 328), and his formal rule that policy-making discussions were to be based on written 'narratives' similar to an essay or to a press release—if a new feature or product was being proposed (Stone 2014: 175–6).

94. Whitman 2010: 268.
95. Stone 2014: 24–6; Brandt 2011b: 5.
96. Whitman 2010: 247.
97. Cohen 2003: 136.
98. Brandt 2011b: 107 on new high-tech warehouses as well as quadrupled computer capacity; 121, 124 on heavy losses; 129–30 on efficiency campaign; 122–3 on making a profit; Stone 2014: 101, 120, 168 on efficiency campaign and lay-offs.
99. Stone 2014: 340.
100. Whitman 2010: 247.
101. Making the customer happy included both ensuring 'that people left the site happy' and ensuring that they were happy with their post-site experiences: even the packaging was redesigned to make it easier for people to open (Brandt 2011b: 10). Furthermore, Amazon's customer obsession included the notion that the customers might not be aware of what would make them happy until the company showed it to them (Brandt 2011b: 185).
102. Stone 2014: 107.
103. Bunnell 2000: 159; and 158–9 on how they operated. Stone, however, presents the zShops as a failure (2014: 80, 107, 114).
104. Stone 2014: 107–11.
105. Stone 2014: 115. Marketplace earned 'a flat 6 to 15 percent commission on each sale' (303).
106. Stone 2014: 116. In fact Marketplace would be used by Amazon as a way of learning about a category of goods before it began selling items in that category. 'If you don't know anything about a business, launch it through Marketplace, bring retailers in, watch what they do and what they sell, understand it, and then get into it' (182, quoting an Amazon retail manager). However, this did not prevent Marketplace becoming an increasingly important part of Amazon's business. In late 2001, 'sales from third-party sellers on the vaunted Amazon platform made up 15 percent of company's orders' but ten years later some 36 per cent of the goods sold on Amazon 'were brokered over its third-party marketplace' (134, 301).
107. Stone 2014: 194.
108. Brandt 2011b: 119.
109. Brandt 2011b: 109, 113, 118, 130.
110. Stone 2014: 67, 123.
111. Bunnell 2000: 115.
112. Stone 2014: 277.
113. Whitman 2010: 44, 63.
114. Whitman 2010: 63.
115. Van Dijck 2013: 68, 186 n. 2.
116. In 1998, Amazon claimed that the majority of its customers came to its site 'because of positive word-of-mouth' rather than advertising, but by the end of the year it was spending nearly a quarter of its revenue on advertising (Brandt 2011b: 10, 100). In 2000, however, it completely abandoned television advertising and by 2003 was relying on word of mouth and lower prices to attract customers to Amazon.com (Stone 2014: 128–9, 368 n. 12). But of course even this involved a costly emphasis on customer happiness: continuing to be

'obsessed with the customer experience' and 'to cater obsessively for its customers' (Stone 2014: 111, 355).

117. Cohen 2003: 101.
118. Cohen 2003: 101.
119. Cohen 2003: 100, 101.
120. Van Dijck 2013: 57.
121. Bunnell 2000: 161. In fact 'some 800 auction sites popped up between 1995 and 2000, many inspired by eBay's success' (161–2).
122. Cohen 2003: 101, emphasis added.
123. Bunnell 2000: 156–7.
124. Bunnell 2000: 157. Stone, too, ascribes the failure of Amazon Auctions to 'the dynamics of network effects' and notes that 'eBay already had an insurmountable advantage' (2014: 79–80).
125. Stone 2014: 262, 263.
126. Brandt 2011b: 140–1, 145.
127. Stone 2014: 231. Bezos believed that 'if Amazon didn't lead the world into the age of digital reading, then Apple or Google would' (234).
128. Stone 2014: 211; Brandt 2011b: 180.
129. Stone 2014: 211. Some two years after its July 2002 launch there were said to be 65,000 such 'developers' using Amazon Web Services (Brandt 2011b: 179).
130. Brandt 2011b: 182. Web Services enjoyed 'up to 23 percent operating margins compared to 5 percent in the rest of the business' (180–1). Its growth was so rapid that only two years later, in 2012, it was earning an estimated $2.2 billion in annual revenue (Stone 2014: 211). And by 2016 it was earning some $12 billion in annual revenue (see note 134).
131. Stone 2014: 293.
132. Whitman 2010: 260.
133. Stone 2014: 265.
134. Stone 2014: 354. By 2015, too, it would employ more than 120,000 people and would have more than 200 million customers (354). A 2017 *Economist* article on 'Amazon's empire' noted that the firm's 'e-commerce site accounts for about 5% of retail spending in America, roughly half the share of Walmart, the biggest firm in the sector' (25–31 March 2017: 17). Presumably this figure of 5 per cent included the third-party sellers who used Amazon as a platform and in 2016 paid it $23 billion in fees, as compared to the $12 billion Amazon was earning from its Web Services (18).
135. Stone 2014: 285, 286. Amazon was mentioned alongside Wal-Mart and Exxon as well as Apple and Google in a 2016 *Economist* article, 'The Rise of the Superstars', about the domination of the global economy by a small group of giant companies (17–23 September 2016: 3–16). Amazon had the group's sixth largest market capitalization, approaching $400 billion, and Apple was top of the group with a market capitalization of nearly $600 billion.

Chapter 8

1. Bezos 2021: 208–9.
2. Stone 2014: 106.
3. Bezos 2021: 200. See also Brandt 2011b: 31, 34–9 on 1986–94.

4. Bezos 2021: 201.

5. Brandt 2011b: 47–9. There was certainly sufficient demand for the product, as that year some $19 billion worth of books had been sold in America. Shipping was not problematic: books were relatively small and durable items that could be shipped cheaply and quickly through the mail. Competition from other online book retailers was not too serious. Although a Books.com had been started up two years earlier, it did not provide the sort of selection envisaged by Bezos. And the big chainstore booksellers had not yet grasped the online opportunity.

6. Bezos 2021: 201.

7. Brandt 2011b: 1, 3; and see 87 on the website adding book reviews and suggesting books to customers based on their past buying patterns.

8. Bezos 2021: 78; Stone 2014: 56–7 on booksellers Barnes & Noble in 2016/17.

9. Bezos 2021: 34–5.

10. Marcus 2005: 215.

11. Bezos 2021: 260. Marcus, who was then an Amazon employee, confirms that 'many people' had been persuaded by expert opinion that Amazon 'was now on the ropes' (Marcus 2005: 221). However, Bezos rose to the occasion. At a meeting with employees, 'his famous, goofy charm' was still evident as he briefed them on future initiatives and left them feeling at least 'slightly' encouraged (238–9). Throughout the crisis, 'Bezos never showed anxiety or appeared to worry' (Stone 2014: 102).

12. Marcus 2005: 236–7; Bezos 2021: 54–5; Brandt 2011b, 131–3.

13. The two authors had joined Amazon in 1998/9. In 2003, Bryar became Bezos's 'technical advisor' or 'shadow', comparable to a chief of staff; and in 2004, Carr became a vice-president and deputy head of the digital division (2021: xii, xv). They left Amazon, respectively, in 2010 and 2014.

14. Bryar and Carr 2021: 240.

15. Bryar and Carr 2021: 166. See also Brandt 2011b: 136.

16. Bryar and Carr 2021: 166, 177.

17. Bryar and Carr 2021: 178. Bezos 'chose the path of invention by looking beyond the music category', which led him to begin Amazon's foray into digital by focusing on e-books and an e-reader device' (171).

18. Bezos 2021: 85.

19. Bezos wanted to keep the project hidden from Amazon's rivals, and so it 'was kept very quiet for years' (Brandt 2011b: 136). Indeed, it was 'top-secret' even within Amazon but eventually 'became the subject of persistent rumours inside Amazon, even though no one was supposed to know of the project's existence' (Stone 2014: 239). Secrecy, however, was not the main reason for locating the Lab126 unit far from Seattle. According to Stone, Bezos was following a project strategy recommended in Christensen's *The Innovator's Dilemma* (234, 235). Bezos had in fact already established a 'remote development centre' in Silicon Valley in 2003 and had called this unit 'A9' (199). And Silicon Valley had a large pool of hardware-development talent for Lab126 to draw from as it proceeded with the Kindle project (Bryar and Carr 2021: 180).

20. Bryar and Carr 2021: 182.

21. Bryar and Carr 2021: 183–5.

22. Brandt 2011b: 138–41; Stone 2014; 256, 278. Bezos's pricing strategy for e-books had also strengthened Amazon's hold on the digital-book markets (Brandt 2011b: 142–3).

23. By early 2011, Apple's iPad had won nearly a third of the market for e-book readers, leaving Amazon with only 47 per cent (Brandt 2011b: 144). And Amazon's share of the e-book market 'fell from 90 percent in 2010 to around 60 percent in 2012', thanks to Apple's iBookstore and other competitors (Stone 2014: 312).

24. Bryar and Carr 2021: 192; and see 191–2 on decelerating sales growth and expansion of e-commerce.

25. Bezos asked senior executives in October for a 'shipping membership programme' to be launched by the end of the year, and later was 'adamant' about a February launch for Prime (Bryar and Carr 2021: 188; Stone 2014: 187).

26. Bryar and Carr 2021: 195–200.

27. Stone 2014: 185–6; Bezos 2021: 86; Bryar and Carr 2021: 201–2.

28. Bezos 2021: 86.

29. Bezos 2021: 206–7.

30. Stone 2014: 188. 'Amazon customers who joined Prime doubled, on average, their spending on the site, according to a person familiar with the company's finances at the time' (262). And 'they bought more products across more categories' of product (263). Obviously not all products were eligible for such super-fast shipping, but Prime began with a million eligible products and had increased that to twenty million by 2013 (Bezos 2021: 108).

31. Stone 2014: 188; see also 263 on Amazon's dramatically accelerating sales growth in 2006/7; and 274 on Amazon navigating the 2008/9 recession more effectively than the 'offline' retailers.

32. Bryar and Carr 2021: 241.

33. Brandt 2011b: 178; Bryar and Carr 2021: 242–6. Amazon had numerous allied firms or 'affiliates', whose websites included links to relevant Amazon products.

34. Brandt 2011b: 179, quoting Bezos and citing mid-2004 user numbers. Bryar and Carr 2021: 249 on over 25,000 developers enrolling with AWS within a year of its July 2002 launch, creating 'a new customer set—the software developers'.

35. On 'building blocks', see Stone 2014: 213; Bryar and Carr 2021: 251. Bezos was pushing for this new kind of product partly because of his experiences with Amazon's own problems regarding software development and IT infrastructure (Stone 2014: 213, 217).

36. See Stone 2014: 213–14 on S3's difficult creation in Seattle and on EC2's creation by a 'remote developer centre' in Cape Town, South Africa.

37. Bezos 2021: 77.

38. Stone 2014: 221, quoting Bezos from a PBS interview on 26 February 2009.

39. Brandt 2011b: 79; Stone 2014: 355.

40. Bezos 'decided that rather than trying to run the company at a profit, he would invest heavily' in the race to capture market share, as whichever firm captured market share first would establish the pole position and would be difficult to pass' (Brandt 2011b: 95).

41. Stone 2014: 48–9.

42. Bezos 2021: 53, in his 2000 letter to shareholders.

43. Stone 2014: 48; Brandt 2011b: 95.

44. See Brandt 2011b: 109, 113 on the 1998 diversification into CDs and then DVDs. The 1999 onward partnerships with retailers varied in two ways. One was the level or lack of ownership, as when Amazon acquired Tool Crib, invested in Pets.com, and allied itself with Toys 'R' Us. The other variation was that Amazon might sell a partner's products or

instead allow the partner—for a fee—to have a place on Amazon's website and thereby have access to Amazon customers (Marcus 2005: 131).

45. See Chapter 7 on Walmart and other retailers taking their businesses online. It is not surprising that 'Jeff wanted to get into every market at once' and by 2000 'really felt it was expand or die' (Marcus 2005: 276).

46. Marketplace was launched in November 2000 and was soon 'far surpassing our expectations' (Bezos 2021: 56).

47. Marcus 2005: 264.

48. Marcus 2005: 264.

49. See Brandt 2011b: 184–5 on shoe-seller Zappos, which became an independent subsidiary; and see Stone 2014: 295–9 on diaper-selling Quidsi, which was likewise allowed to operate independently.

50. Stone 2021: 169. 'Bezos supervised the project closely at first' (169).

51. Stone 2021: 165. Launched in 2007, the FBA service had shipped more than three million units in the fourth quarter of 2008 (Bezos 2021: 86–7). Bezos 'managed FBA closely during the late 2000s' and it was strongly supported by him even though it did not become profitable until 2014 (Stone 2021: 166, 167). He wanted to keep the seller fees low and to aim for scale rather than income, even if that meant losing money (166, 168).

52. Bezos 2021: 89.

53. Bezos 2021: 88.

54. Bezos 2021: 73n., describing a 1976 paper's distinction between strategic 'unstructured' decisions and the more quantifiable, 'operating' decisions.

55. Bezos 2021: 72; and see 72–3 for his examples.

56. Marcus 2005: 51. Marcus was one of Bezos's early employees and was present when he promised this Culture of Metrics.

57. Bryar and Carr 2021: 122.

58. Marcus 2005: 51–2.

59. Stone 2014: 327. 'Yet random customer anecdotes, the opposite of cold, hard data, also carry tremendous weight', for Bezos often assumed that one customer's bad experience reflected a larger problem (327).

60. Stone 2014: 163–5.

61. Stone 2014: 162–3, 164.

62. Bryar and Carr 2021: 123, which also describes how the WBR originated in the early 2000s. Stone 2014: 332 describes them as 'metrics meetings' and this seems an apt description in light of Bryar and Carr's descriptions of the WSB in their Chapter 6, entitled 'Metrics: Manage Your Inputs, Not Your Outputs'. For example, a meeting typically begins with 'visual or printed distribution of the data package which contains the weekly snapshot of graphs, tables, and occasional explanatory notes for all your metrics' (134). Of course, if there is 'a surprise or a perplexing problem with the data', the meeting looks for the root cause and presumably this might require more than 'metrics thinking' (131–2).

63. Bryar and Carr 2021: 123; and 99 on Bezos attending a WBR as one of the three 'recurring' meetings that he attended every week. At the departmental and other large-unit meetings, not all the personnel would attend, only senior managers and anyone who 'owned' or was speaking about some part of the data package (136).

64. Bezos 2021: 150; and see also 143.

65. Bezos 2021: 143.

66. Bezos 2021: 143. See also Bryar and Carr 2021: 160.

67. Some decisions might even be made by just one person: a 'high-judgment' individual (Bezos 2021: 143, 228). Furthermore, a firm can afford to make two-way-door decisions even when it has only 70 per cent of the desired information (150). This would certainly speed up the decision-making and perhaps the deliberations too.

68. Bezos 2021: 150. As an example, he describes his meeting with a team of Amazon's video-streaming specialists. There was 'a genuine disagreement of opinion, a candid expression of my view, a chance for the team to weigh my view, and a quick, sincere commitment to go their way': a much quicker decision than 'if the team had actually had to *convince* me rather than simply get my commitment' (151).

69. Bezos 2021: 227–8.

70. See Bryar and Carr 2021: 11–13. Initially there were only ten Leadership Principles, developed largely by human-resources executive Robin Andrulevich in 2004, and then later endorsed by Bezos through his formal announcement of the Principles in an email in early 2005.

71. Bryar and Carr 2021: 15.

72. Bryar and Carr 2021: 16.

73. Stone 2014: 328. 'Amazon's culture is notoriously confrontational', and while some employees 'love this confrontational culture', some who have left Amazon 'call the internal culture "a gladiator culture"' (328).

74. The only mention is by Isaacson in the introduction to the book (Bezos 2021: 14–15). Stone noted that Bezos's board rarely resisted his 'will', so presumably there was little argumentative deliberation (Stone 2014: 217).

75. Bryar and Carr 2021: 17. It originated in 1999 after Bezos acquired a chief operating officer (COO) and allowed him to take over the J-Team, which was now renamed the S[enior]-Team (Stone 2014: 91–2). The COO departed in 2000 and Bezos 'regained' the senior leadership team, but he kept the name 'S-Team' (99).

76. Bryar and Carr 2021: 99.

77. Bezos 2021: 90. Bryar and Carr note some 80 per cent of the weekly S-Team meeting 'was focused on how the company was making progress towards achieving the S-team goals' (Bryar and Carr 2021: 80). They also point out that S-Team's concern with goal achievement was a distinctive feature of Amazon's leadership. 'At many companies, when the senior leadership team meets, they tend to focus more on the big-picture, high-level strategy issues than on execution' (20). However, Stone notes that the S-Team's monitoring of units' progress towards their goals 'was a crucial way that the S-team managed a sprawling amalgamation of loosely affiliated business units' (Stone 2021: 200). It was also a centralized version of the 'management by objectives' approach that Drucker had promoted back in the 1950s (2006 [1954]: ch. 11).

78. Bryar and Carr 2021: 19.

79. His 2004 move from PowerPoint presentations to discussion documents marked a change that Stone described as 'perhaps unique in corporate history' (2014: 175). Certainly no corporate leader had shifted to discussion documents as a way of institutionalizing deliberation.

80. Bezos 2021: 156.

81. Bryar and Carr 2021: 93.

82. See Bryar and Carr 2021: ch. 4, entitled 'Communicating: Narratives and the Six-Pager'.

83. Bezos 2021: 156.

84. Bryar and Carr 2021: 95.

85. Bryar and Carr 2021: 94.
86. Bezos 2021: 157.
87. Amazon's market capitalization of $1 trillion did not last for long in 2018 but returned in early 2020, on a more permanent basis (Stone 2021: 14).
88. This business model is 'a potent cocktail of customer obsession, crazy innovation, and long-term thinking driven by a relentless AI flywheel' (Dumaine 2020: 269).
89. Bezos 2021: 133, 139; Bryar and Carr 2021: xi. There was good commercial reason for businesses to outsource their computing needs to a cloud-computing provider. 'Traditionally, if you were a company and needed computation, you would build a data center, and you'd fill that data center with servers, and you'd have to upgrade the operating systems of those servers and keep everything running, and so on. None of that added any value to what the business was doing' (Bezos 2021: 210). Furthermore, AWS's cloud-computing was 'inherently more efficient than the traditional in-house data center. That's primarily due to two things—higher utilization and the fact that our servers and facilities are more efficient than what most companies can achieve running their own data centers' (183).
90. Stone 2014: 211. AWS won the CIA contract in 2013, and as late as 2018 'controlled a commanding 47.8 percent share of the cloud market' (Stone 2021: 359).
91. Bezos 2021: 211.
92. Bryar and Carr 2021: 258; Dumaine 2020: 64.
93. Dumaine 2020: 94, 99.
94. Bezos 2021: 107–8, 159. Prime members spent 'on average $1,300 a year on Amazon, compared to $700 for non-Prime members. The company says it sees a big ramp-up in spending right after a customer signs up for Prime' (Dumaine 2020: 100).
95. Bezos 2021: 125.
96. Bezos 2021: 125. See Dumaine 2020: ch. 8 'Warehouses that Run in the Dark'.
97. Bryar and Carr 2021: 209.
98. See Bryar and Carr 2021: 211–12, 216–17; 223 on Unbox's problems downloading movies to PCs and, in 2007, to TV set-top boxes. See 224–7 on the launch of video streaming in 2007 by Netflix and its service being available by 2008 on not only televisions but also game consoles and other devices. Netflix started its video streaming as a free add-on for subscribers to its DVD-rental-by-mail service, as Bezos pointed out in 2010 when he decided to offer video streaming as a free add-on to Prime membership (224–5, 233). Amazon switched to video streaming in 2008 with its new television service 'Amazon Video on Demand' (226–7).
99. Bryar and Carr 2021: 227, 231, 232. Two of the studios also launched their own video-streaming service, the Fox-NBC venture 'Hulu', which was initially funded by advertising and eventually became a subscription service controlled by Disney (225–6).
100. Stone 2021: 137–8.
101. Stone 2021: 138; Bryar and Carr 2021: 233–4. Stone describes Prime Instant Video as an 'ingenious' solution to Amazon's video-streaming problems: customers were not inclined to pay for a subscription service 'that was inferior to Netflix's more established offering', so the service was instead being used as free add-on that made Prime membership more attractive (Stone 2021: 138). He describes the increased attractiveness as a way of retaining existing members but, likewise, it was a way of attracting new members to the Prime programme. Dumaine describes it as 'a great way to attract and retain' (2020: 25). Bezos's aims were apparently to attract new members and to give Prime an added distinctiveness

that could not be copied by any retail competitors tempted to launch their own version of Prime (Bryar and Carr 2021: 234).

102. Dumaine 2020: 102, citing evidence from within Amazon that came to light in 2018. And Bezos's 2017 letter to shareholders noted that 'Prime Video continues to drive Prime member adoption and retention' (Bezos 2021: 161).

103. Prime Video's profitability was assisted by the annual membership fees paid by Prime's ever-increasing membership of many millions: the fees were raised from $79 annually per person to $99 in 2014 and then again to $119 in 2018 (Stone 2021: 139). Furthermore, both Netflix and Amazon were paying fixed fees, not usage fees, to 'the studios' for licences to stream films and television series: this was a fixed cost that meant video streamers would make large profits once they had a sufficiently large set of subscribers (233–4).

104. Stone 2021: 148. 'Video was the introductory product for new markets, as books had once been' (148).

105. Stone 2021: 141; Bryar and Carr 2021: 237.

106. Bezos 2021: 109. He points out that it had grown to more than 40,000 movies and episodes by the end of 2013.

107. Bryar and Carr 2021: 237.

108. Two other RILD cases were discussed in section one: the Kindle and the AWS cloud computing.

109. Stone 2021: 142.

110. Bryar and Carr 2021: 239; Stone 2021: 142. *The Man in the High Castle* series was credited with attracting over a million new Prime members (Dumaine 2020: 103).

111. Stone 2021: 401.

112. Bryar and Carr 2021: 237.

113. Bezos 2021: 109–10.

114. The strategy still seemed partly defensive, though now just defending against stagnation or the threat of stagnation. He may have seen it as a way of preventing what he calls 'Day 2'. His 2016 letter to shareholders described a company's Day 2 as 'stasis. Followed by irrelevance. Followed by excruciating, painful decline. Followed by death', presumably through the firm being broken up, taken over, or wound up (Bezos 2021: 146).

115. Bezos 2021: 144.

116. Stone 2021: 163.

117. Stone 2021: 285.

118. During the 2010s, Marketplace's third-party sellers had actually out-sold Amazon's own retail efforts. The 'share of physical gross merchandise sales sold on Amazon by independent third-party sellers' had grown from 31 per cent of the total in 2009 to 58 per cent in 2018. (Bezos 2021: 167–8). And this was mainly due to an increase in the sales per seller, not simply to an increase in the number of sellers 'joining' Marketplace (see Stone 2021: 170). However, it had managed to attract an impressive number and variety of third-party sellers. Most Marketplace sellers, some two million, were small or medium-sized businesses and could be found in over a hundred countries but particularly America and China (Bezos 2021: 168; Dumaine 2020: 10, 150; Stone 2021: 172–9).

119. Stone 2021: 73–9.

120. Ultimately, it is a matter of striking a balance based on the benefits expected from each strategy, but often it is simpler to view the calculation in terms of needs/benefits or needs/needs.

121. Marcus 2005: 264. Marcus's analysis of Amazon in the mid-2000s was discussed in section two.
122. Marcus 2005: 295; Stone 2014: 208; Stone 2021: 255.
123. Auletta 2010: 88–90. In 2003, Google introduced a third-party version, AdSense (91). Here Google acted as a 'matchmaker', matching advertisers with third-party websites or blogs in exchange for a share of their revenue from the advertisers. By 2004, Google was earning about half of its revenue from this third-party AdSense (91).
124. Auletta 2010: 88–90.
125. Auletta 2010: 89.
126. Auletta 2010: 90.
127. Stone 2021: 252–3; 257 points out that Bezos's concern for the 'customer experience' meant that he was ambivalent about even the limited amount of *display* advertising that he allowed on his websites. And Stone describes the mid-2010s shift to *search-based* advertising as converting 'the relative meritocracy of search results into a domain that prioritized Amazon's commercial interests' (257). As for Dumaine, he notes that the present advertising policy is a change from the years when 'Bezos's rock-solid tenet of always pleasing customers made the company wary of annoying them or overwhelming them with ads on its site' (Dumaine 2020: 219).
128. Stone 2021: 246, 254–6.
129. Stone 2021: 255.
130. Dumaine 2020: 220. He is citing a prediction by Juniper Research. He also notes that Amazon was 'generating little or no advertising revenue' before the addition of search-based advertising (220). Stone, too, notes that display advertising had been disappointing and that by 2014 Amazon had 'been close to retiring' its display advertising (Stone 2021: 253). The shift to Google-style search-based ads had been the 'answer' to its advertising problems (254).
131. Bryar and Carr 2021: 236. The 'Kindle' part of its name was dropped in 2014 (236).
132. Stone 2021: 39. He also describes the phone's three-year development, software shortcomings, pricing issues, and cancellation (39–41).
133. Dumaine 2020: 65; and 64 on its software shortcomings.
134. Stone 2021: 23, 25.
135. Lashinsky 2013: 2. However, there was still a long way to go with the new VIT. 'At first Siri was notorious for misinterpreting commands and the novelty of a voice-activated AI perhaps overpowered its utility. In 2014, Apple plugged Siri into a neural net, allowing it to harness machine learning techniques ... and it slowly improved its performance' (Merchant 2017: 279).
136. See Merchant 2017: 279 on the Siri software app and its acquisition by Apple. Google was the third biggest player in VIT, along with Apple and Amazon. Google had added voice commands to its Android smartphone software by 2010 and would develop increasingly impressive 'search' VIT (Stone 2021: 24; Vogelstein 2014: 222).
137. Stone 2021: 27, quoting one of the device's early developers.
138. Stone 2021: 27–8.
139. Stone 2021: 45. The shopping-list assistance may be especially important, as apparently Amazon hopes that Alexa 'will boost its retail business' by helping consumers with their shopping (Dumaine 2020: 115).
140. Bezos 2021: 212–13.

141. Stone 2021: 47. However, when Google Home appeared in 2016, it had a stylish speaker and its VIT searched the Internet 'with aplomb' (50).
142. Bezos 2021: 173.
143. Dumaine 2020: 109, 110.
144. Dumaine 2020: 113: Stone 2021: 36–7.
145. Bezos 2021: 94.
146. As the second section described, this 'metrifying' logistics upgrade had begun with Wilke's recruitment in 1999. In 2006, Bezos shifted him to retailing, to head up Amazon's North American retailing, and Stone describes him as running the weekly business review of Amazon's whole retailing operation in the early 2010s (Stone 2014: 189, 255, 332).
147. Dumaine 2020: 85; and 84 on Wilke's role as CEO of e-commerce. This example also has a comparative aspect, as Wilke's pre-AI weekly meetings had been 'similar to Walmart's famous Saturday-morning meetings' (85). Chapter 5 recounted that Sam Walton ran his firm's Saturday-morning meetings and that, before a meeting, he would spend hours studying its metrics—'the numbers'—in a typical example of his emphasis on quantitative calculation. In contrast, Bezos had delegated this role to a numbers-man lieutenant. Wilke, not Bezos, ran Amazon's equivalent of Saturday-morning meetings. However, Bezos was leading not just a retail operation but a multifaceted high-tech firm—requiring some multifaceted leadership. Chapter 6 pointed out that Bezos had a Jobs-like hands-on approach to developing high-tech products, as he had shown with the Kindle project. This hands-on approach was also evident in the 2010s, especially with the Echo/Alexa and Fire Phone devices (Stone 2021: 25, 39). In fact he was 'running' two or more projects simultaneously, as befitting a leader of a *multifaceted* high-tech corporation.
148. Dumaine 2020: 54–6.
149. Stone 2021: 147, 158.
150. For example, see Dumaine 2020: 44–5.
151. Bryar and Carr 2021: 106, and 104, 106–7 113–18. The PR page was meant to show how the new product would benefit customers. The FAQ section was meant to provide, in particular, 'a clear-eyed and thorough assessment of how expensive and challenging it will be to build the product' (107). Even products instigated by Amazon's leaders had to be fitted within the PR/FAQ format, as Stone describes in the case of the Echo/Alexa project, code-named Doppler. 'Dozens of versions of Doppler's PR FAQ were written, presented, debated, obsessed over, rewritten, and scrapped' during the device's development: this was 'a hallowed part of Amazon's rituals around innovation' (Stone 2021: 31).
152. Bryar and Carr 2021: 119, emphasis added. They point out that 'during our time with Amazon, most PR/FAQs never made it to a stage where they were launched as actual products' (119).
153. See the second section and its description of bottom-up diverse deliberation as subordinates providing their leaders with policy proposals, product ideas, or other items for deliberation.
154. Stone 2021: 404.
155. His book also contends that 'Bezonomics, a potent cocktail of customer obsession, crazy innovation, and long-term thinking driven by a relentless AI flywheel, is the business model of the twenty-first century' (Dumaine 2020: 269).
156. Dumaine 2020: 219; see also 88.

157. Dumaine 2020: 24, 165.
158. Dumaine 2020: 24.
159. See Stone 2021: 57–66 on the difficult development process, which began in 2013. And there were cost/revenue problems when the technology was launched in the first Amazon Go store in 2018 (66–7).
160. Bezos 2021: 217. See also Dumaine 2020: 24, 163 and Stone 2021: 184–5, 208–11 on the acquisition of this distinctive chain of supermarkets. Both authors also point to commercial reasons for the acquisition, such as problems with Amazon Fresh's online grocery business (Dumaine 2020: 170–1; Stone 2021: 208–9 2011–12).
161. Mackey, et. al. 2020: 81 and 95–8; but also 72 on his now subordinate position.
162. Dumaine 2020: 20–1. Amazon's sales of its private-label brands reached $7.5 billion in 2018 (21). See also Stone 2021: 199–204 on this private-label initiative. Each private-label brand of course sold a range of different items: the Amazon Basics sold a range of more than 500 by 2019 (258).
163. For example, Amazon markedly increased its full-time and part-time workforce, reaching the remarkable figure of a million employees (Stone 2021: 401).
164. Brandt 2011b: 173.
165. Bezos 2021: 169.
166. Bezos 2021: 169.
167. Bezos 2021: 171; see 173 on the Echo device.
168. Brandt 2011b: 190.
169. Bezos 2021: 121.
170. Bezos 2021: 134. 'We all know that if you swing for the fences, you're going to strike out a lot, but you're also going to hit some home runs. The difference between baseball and business, however, is that baseball has a truncated outcome distribution. When you swing … the most runs you can get is four. In business … you can score one thousand runs. This long-tailed distribution of returns is why it's important to be bold' (134–5).
171. Brandt 2011b: 178.
172. Dumaine 2020: 81. Dumaine notes that this R&D 'number, however, is somewhat deceiving because it includes not just R&D but what the company's annual report describes as costs for "maintaining its existing products and services, its server farms, stores, website displays"—costs most businesses would report as operating expenses, not R&D. What this means is that Bezos doesn't think about R&D as being separate from the business. R&D *is* the business' (81).
173. Dumaine 2020: 236. Stone provides some comparisons from 2017, when Amazon's R&D spending was $22.6 billion, Alphabet/Google's was $16.6 billion, and Microsoft's was $12.3 billion (Stone 2021: 67).
174. This attitude is evident not only in the case recounted later in the section but also in some of Bryar and Carr's descriptions of Amazon's working-backwards technique.
175. Bezos 2021: 260. However, he has been careful to distinguish experimental failure from the operational kind of failure. The operational kind is 'not good failure'; only the experimental kind is 'failure you should be happy with' in business (230–1).
176. Bryar and Carr 2021: 218. The 'I' in the quotation refers to Carr.
177. Bryar and Carr 2021: 218.
178. The great 1940s–60s aerospace era culminated in a supersonic airliner and a moon landing; the great 1980s–2000s IT era in cloud computing and a computer-like smartphone.
179. See the first section of Chapter 6.

180. Advances in any scientifically sophisticated technology will sooner or later be outdated. More than a century ago, Weber pointed out that whatever is accomplished in science 'will be antiquated in ten, twenty, fifty years. That is the fate to which science is subjected; it is the very *meaning* of scientific work ... it *asks* to be "surpassed" and outdated' (Weber 1970 [1919]: 138).
181. See the first two sections of Chapter 6.

Chapter 9

1. Armani 2015: 272d.
2. Armani 2015: 272d.
3. Armani 2015: 28k.
4. Roddick 2000: 14.
5. Agins 2000: 8–14. The fourth 'megatrend' was that 'top designers stopped gambling on fashion' as public companies, in particular, 'can't afford to gamble on fashion whims' (13–14). But fashion had become a 'gamble' only because of the megatrend changes in fashion preferences, which meant that customers could no longer be relied upon to follow the directions of designers and their publicists. Agins subtitled her book *How Marketing Changed the Clothing Business Forever* but the marketing changes were responding to earlier changes in preferences created by socioeconomic and cultural factors, such as the growing number of career women.
6. Agins 2000: 6, 7, 9.
7. Agins 2000: 8, emphases added.
8. Armani 2015: 28k–l.
9. Molho 2007: 53. She suggests that Armani began designing for the Hitman line in 1962 or 1963, but he mentions 1965 in his book (Molho 2007: 33, 39; Armani 2015: 28h).
10. Molho 2007: 60–1.
11. White 2000: 17, 19.
12. White 2000: 17, 19; Molho 2007: 63.
13. Armani 2015: 28m, 96a. He also refers to his designs being known for 'a certain sartorial androgyny' and notes that 'I invented the unstructured jacket for both men and women' (133a, 96c).
14. Armani 2015: 28k; Molho 2007: 69–71. Some idea of the difference in costs between the traditional haute couture production methods and Armani's manufactured ready-to-wear is that by the 2000s a haute couture suit started at $25,000 but a top-line Armani suit at only about $2,000 (Thomas 2008: 29; White 2000: 13).
15. Agins 2000: 131.
16. Fraser 1981: 91.
17. White 2000: 17, 24. She acknowledges that he had also 'recognized the shift in the socioeconomic position of women' as another opportunity (24).
18. Armani 2015: 28k, 400d.
19. Molho 2007: 65, 69; Thomas 2008: 115.
20. Molho 2007: 97. This was referring to his menswear as well as womenswear designs and indeed the previous year he had won two international menswear design awards (92–3).
21. Molho 2007: 65, 124–5.
22. Grove 1999: 65, 66.

23. Kapferer and Bastien 2012: 176–7, 305–8, and 309 discusses vertical and horizontal stretching, compares examples of the 'pyramid business model', and analyses the distinctive Armani pyramid.
24. Thomas 2008: 33.
25. Thomas 2008: 33.
26. The 'Armani power suit' had as dramatic an effect on menswear as on womenswear: its success 'would transfer the locus of tailored fashion southward from London to Milan' (Ball 2010: 87).
27. White 2000: 10.
28. White 2000: 13; Molho 2007: 81.
29. Armani 2015: 68d.
30. White 2000: 13.
31. Kapferer and Bastien 2012: 309.
32. Kapferer and Bastien 2012: 178. However, the glasses, cosmetics, and perfumes were licensed to other firms (191).
33. Kapferer and Bastien 2012: 178.
34. Armani 2015: 352a.
35. Ball 2010: 75.
36. Molho 2007: 93.
37. Kapferer and Bastien 2012: 178, 191.
38. Agins 2000: 136; White 2000: 22.
39. Molho 2007: 163, 264.
40. Molho 2007: 232. From 1994 to 2000, Brusone had been Armani's managing director and had supervised the 'gradual process of industrial acquisitions' (125, 215).
41. Molho 2007: 128, 214–15. In contrast to his out-sourcing in the 1970s–80s, 'all formal apparel was produced directly by Armani himself' by 2001 (215). This reversal was similar to what happened in the luxury company Louis Vuitton, where Arnault and Carcelle reversed the previous policy of out-sourcing. 'Carcelle pulled it all back in-house and increased the number of factories from five to fourteen' and Arnault explained that 'If you control your factories, you control your quality' (Thomas 2008: 51–2).
42. Molho 2007: 232.
43. White 1999: 10. She published a similar book on Armani in 2000.
44. White 1999: 15.
45. White 1999: 22. Turner declares simply that Versace 'sold sex and glamour' (1997: 35).
46. Molho 2007: 158–9.
47. Ball 2010: 118.
48. Ball 2010: 77.
49. Ball 2010: 190; Gastel 2008: 168.
50. Gastel 2008: 73–4.
51. White 1999: 17.
52. By 1995 'about 18 per cent of Versace's sales' were in North America (Gastel 2008: 204). Ball describes Versace's problems in the early 1980s with department-store retailers who 'felt that American women, just entering the workplace in force, wanted to be taken seriously; they wouldn't want to sport black leather biker jackets, peekaboo black lace gowns with beading applied like clusters of caviar, and skirts so short they were little more than belts' (Ball 2010: 85).
53. Ball 2010: 121.

54. Ball 2010: 121.
55. Ball 2010: 175.
56. Ball 2010: 175.
57. Versace depicted the exclusive Couture line as focused on 'daytime wear, on clothes dedicated to the active, successful working woman' (quoted by Gastel 2008: 117).
58. Gastel 2008: 122, 140. The Versus line was introduced in 1989, by which time Donatella had become her brother's 'muse, sounding board and first assistant' (Ball 2010: 99). Furthermore, she performed the crucial role of keeping him on the novelty treadmill: 'she wouldn't let him repeat himself or rest on the laurels of previously successful design ideas' (100).
59. Agins 2000: 14.
60. Ball 2010: 121, 176; Gastel 2008: 175–6, quoting a boutique owner in Palermo.
61. Turner 1997: 53–4. She listed the diffusion lines as 'Versus, Istante, Versace Jeans Couture, Signature, Versace Sport, Versatile and Versace Classic V2' (54).
62. Turner 1997: 55–6.
63. Turner 1997: 54. There were also Versace watches (Gastel 2008: 47).
64. Turner 1997: 54. The homeware category encompassed 'everything from china, glass, quilts and cushions, vases, picture frames, lamps and tiles to furnishing fabrics, beds, tables, and bath linen: a Versacian can furnish an entire home with Versace items' (54).
65. His massive advertising in fashion and other magazines is described by White 1999: 20; Gastel 2008: 217–18; and Ball 2010: 143–4. His dramatic modernizing of fashion shows is described by Gastel 2008: 135–8. His creation and use of the 'supermodel' is extensively described by Turner 1997: ch. 4 and Ball 2010: ch. 9. Versace's and Armani's use of celebrities is extensively described by Turner 1997: ch. 5; Ball 2010: ch. 8; Agins 2000: ch. 4; and Thomas 2008: ch. 4.
66. There seems to be some doubt or dispute about when the haute couture line was launched. According to Turner, the Atelier haute couture line was launched in 1989; Gastel mentions Atelier Versace haute couture debuting in Paris in January 1990; Ball, too, mentions a January 1990 haute couture show in Paris; and White refers to the 'atelier' line haute couture collection being introduced in 1993 (Turner 1997: 51; Gastel 2008: 142; Ball 2010: 116; White 1999: 21).
67. For example, menswear accounted for nearly half of Armani's clothing sales in 1997–8 (White 2000: 23). Versace presented separate menswear collections and clothing lines, as well as including menswear in a few of his diffusion lines, but his menswear designs were characterized by Turner as 'if not an acquired taste, aimed a niche market' (1997: 53).
68. Gastel 2008: 46; Ball 2010: 75.
69. Ball 2010: 76.
70. Gastel 2008: 108, 227; Turner 1997: 43. Ball, too, notes that by 1997 'Versace products sold in three hundred boutiques around the world, as well as four thousand department stores' (Ball 2010: 190).
71. Santo's business difficulties included (1) relying too much on licensing for sales growth in the 1990s, (2) problems with diffusion lines that were not clearly identified as Versace and were cannibalizing one another's sales, and (3) the cost of the firm's new strategy of owning rather than franchising its retail network, which meant opening its own stores and buying back franchises (Ball 2010: 176–7). Santo believed that going public would provide the funds to deal with such problems and he had won Gianni's approval for a planned

initial public offering (IPO) that would 'sell as much as 40 percent of the company to stock market investors' (190).
72. Agins 2000: 7.
73. Gastel 2008: 237, quoting Versace.
74. Ball 2010: 314.
75. Turner 1997: 47.
76. Agins 2000: 135–6.
77. Agins 2000: 136.
78. Molho 2007: 213.
79. White 2000: 18–19. The mid-1990s Versacian change led to sequinned hot-pants by 2000, but Armani 'explained this [change] as a reflection of socio-economic change, expressing the belief that women no longer need to "dress like a man to be taken seriously"' (18).
80. White 2000: 18.
81. Armani 2015: 400d.
82. Gastel 2008: 64, 119.
83. Gastel 2008: 174–5, 183, 216, and 221 quoting Versace.
84. Gastel 2008: 117, 247. There seems to be no comprehensive analysis of Versace's stylistic variations, but there is enough descriptive material in Gastel's *The Versace Legend* to make a partial analysis of the 1987–97 collections. At least thirteen changes in style can be identified: (1) from Optical to mini-skirted Armanian jackets, (2) to targeted prints, (3) neo-Baroque, (4) sadomasochist, (5) country style, (6) punk, (7) grunge, (8) space-galactic, (9) demure women, (10) Armanian, (11) white-out, (12) modern art, and (13) Ravenna mosaics.
85. Ball 2010: 245.
86. Thomas 2008: 50–4, 59–60, 66–7, 192; Agins 2000: 19–20, 41, 278.
87. One of the firm's business problems was Santo's continuing pursuit of his pre-1997 strategy of increasing the number of owned rather than franchised stores. 'He had tripled the number of Versace-controlled stores since Gianni's death, but the strategy ... was a costly mistake, perhaps born from a refusal to accept that his sister's work would never sell well enough to support such a grand store network' (Ball 2010: 269).
88. Ball 2010: 219.
89. Ball 2010: 265.
90. Ball 2010: 292–5.
91. Davis 2011: 75, 79, 88.
92. Davis 2011: 75, 81–2, 90.
93. Ball points out that going public 'not only brought in a wave of fresh money, but [also] a company's stock options were juicy bait in recruiting talented executives', as when Gucci went public in the mid-1990s and 'succeeded in attracting some of the best managers in the business' (Ball 2010: 240).
94. The Roddick biographies published by Alcraft in 1999 and by Paprocki in 2010 are brief accounts and were apparently aimed at what the libraries categorized as 'juvenile' readers. Jones's 2010 magisterial history of the beauty industry contains some material on Roddick, but it is based largely on her *Body and Soul*.
95. Roddick 2000: 36.
96. Roddick 2000: 247.
97. Jones's history of the beauty industry defines it as 'including fragrances; hair and skin care products; sun care; color cosmetics, including make-up and other products for

the face, eyes, lips, and nails; men's grooming products, including shaving creams; bath and shower products, including toilet soap; deodorants; oral care; and baby care' (2011: 9 n. 2).

98. Roddick 1991: 71.

99. Roddick 1991: 73. Roddick also lacked business training and experience. She had been trained as a teacher and her business experience was largely confined to having run a small hotel with her husband. In contrast, the famous American cosmetics entrepreneur, Mary Kay Ash, started her direct-sales cosmetics business after years of experience in the 1960s as national sales director for a large direct-sales company (Brands 1999: 249–50).

100. Roddick 1991: 73.

101. Roddick 1991: 73.

102. Roddick 2000: 37, emphasis added.

103. Roddick 1991: 82.

104. Jones 2011: 283, 285.

105. Roddick 1991: 92.

106. Jones 2011: 282.

107. Roddick 1991: 90, 230, 235–6.

108. Roddick 1991: 132.

109. Roddick 1991: 111–13. These green 'political' campaigns had begun in 1985 with a Greenpeace-linked Body Shop campaign against acid rain (111). A rather different approach was adopted by the 'green' clothing company Patagonia in California. In the mid-1980s it was making 'regular donations to smaller groups working to save or restore habitat' (Chouinard 2006: 61). It later adopted the idea of an environmental 'tax' that took the form of donating to these small groups an 'annual one percent of sales, or 10 percent of profits, whichever is greater' (Chouinard and Stanley 2012: 45).

110. Alcraft 1999: 50.

111. Roddick 2000: 14, emphasis added.

112. Roddick 1991: 131.

113. Jones 2011: 285.

114. Paprocki 2010: 62, 64.

115. Roddick 2000: 141.

116. Roddick 2000: 141. Roddick refers to the first B&BW being opened in 1990, not 1988, and being opened by 'retail mogul Leslie Wexner' rather than being founded by Limited Brands. Furthermore, Paprocki notes that when The Body Shop came to America, 'cosmetics company Estee Lauder *had* opened an environmentally conscious division called Origins, and The Limited, a clothing company, was *about to* open a line of stores called Bath & Body Works' (Paprocki 2010: 60–2, emphases added).

117. Roddick 2000: 141, 143–4, 154, 156 on marketing details, discounting, politics, humour, advertising, pricing promotions, and shopping malls.

118. Roddick 2000: 139, 141. In her earlier book she noted 'we managed to get twenty-three franchises open that first year [1990]. Another fifty-plus are scheduled to open in 1991, and probably double that number in 1992' (Roddick 1991: 139).

119. Roddick 2000: 151, 154. 'For every 100 customers, we were losing five' (154).

120. Roddick 2000: 154; Alcraft 1999: 38.

121. Roddick 2000: 157.

122. Roddick 2000: 67–70. This social audit included an environmental audit and an 'ethical' audit that assessed the social impact and behaviour of the firm in relation to its

stakeholders, which included the communities in which it operated. Boyle cited Roddick and The Body Shop as an example of social auditing in *The Tyranny of Numbers* (Boyle 2001: 145). And indeed the social audit was another example of her moving away from rational business leadership, in this case from the method of quantitative calculation. In 2004, she and Boyle co-authored the brief *Numbers*, which included criticism of management being 'done by numbers' and of modern life being 'reduced to numbers' (Boyle and Roddick 2004: 80, 82).

123. Roddick 2000: 244.
124. Roddick 2000: 253; Paprocki 2010: 76. An *Economist* article of 14 May 1998 described the co-chair positions as Roddick serving alongside Gordon as 'executive co-chairman' and it also declared that 'Ms Roddick deserves much of the blame for the decline' in the fortunes of the corporation, whose share price had fallen 'from a peak of 370 pence ($6.50) in 1992 to 111 pence in March [1998]'.
125. Roddick 2000: 254, 259, 260, and 261.
126. Paprocki 2010: 76, 86.
127. Paprocki 2010: 89; Jones 2011: 330.

Chapter 10

1. Hargrove 1998: vi; Johansson 2005: 84, 225.
2. Gerstner 2003: 237–8.
3. Nadella 2019: 90.
4. See Wallace and Erickson 1993: 233–4; Becraft 2014, 69–70, and 49–59 on the development of Windows as the second-generation operating system for PCs.
5. McCullough 2018: 165.
6. McCullough 2018: 165.
7. Wallace and Erickson 1993: 428; Nadella 2019: 244 on becoming the most valuable company in 1998 and keeping that position until 2000, when Jack Welch's General Electric returned to the number-one position. Microsoft's stock-market value peaked at the end of 1999 at almost $619 billion and did not reach this figure again until 2018 (McCullough 2018: 164–5).
8. Nadella 2019: 45.
9. Woyke 2014: 54, 68.
10. Nadella 2019: 54, referring to his assessment in 2011.
11. In 2002, Microsoft 'was getting up to speed with its smartphone software' and launched a joint-venture smartphone, the Orange SPV, but not until 2003 was Microsoft's smartphone software given the name 'Windows Mobile' (Woyke 2014: 29, 32).
12. See Chapter 15. Nokia was a Finnish corporation, not an American company, and in fact Motorola was the only US firm that played a major role in the first wave of the mobile-tech revolution: the other major players were European, Asian, or Canadian (BlackBerry). By contrast, the personal-computer revolution had been initiated and led by American firms, which may partly explain why Microsoft dominated that high-tech revolution but not the first wave of the subsequent mobile-tech revolution.
13. Woyke 2014: 53. The arrival of the iPhone and Android software will be described in detail in Chapter 14. The third stage of the mobile-tech revolution occurred in early 2010s with the arrival of tablet computers, such as the Apple iPad described in Chapter 6 and the Amazon Kindle Fire described in Chapter 8.

14. Woyke 2014: 60.
15. McCracken 2017: 52, emphasis added.
16. Woyke 2014: 53, 67–9; Good 2020: 131.
17. These events are described in the next section; and the preceding creation of the Microsoft-Nokia alliance is described in Chapter 15.
18. Nadella 2019: 66.
19. Nadella 2019: 13.
20. Nadella 2019: 90.
21. Good 2020: 128.
22. Nadella 2019: 57. See Chapter 8 and Appendix 2 on the origins of the cloud-computing revolution.
23. Nadella 2019: 105.
24. Nadella 2019: 101–2.
25. Nadella 2019: 11.
26. Nadella 2019: 103. He also instituted such culture-changing activities and gatherings as One Week: a series of events that the media described as 'designed to inform employees about, and inspire them to engage in, the company's vision and strategy' (Good 2020: 147, quoting the *Seattle Times* of 30 July 2014).
27. Nadella 2019: 54–61. See Chapter 8 on Amazon's unsurmountable lead in cloud services.
28. Woyke 2014: 69; Nadella 2019: 90. This target 'took us from a defensive frame amid falling PC and phone share to an offensive mindset … to ownership of our future' (Nadella 2019: 90).
29. Good 2020: 170.
30. Good 2020: 155.
31. Good 2020: 149.
32. Good 2020: 149. The 2014 lay-offs 'marked a departure from hardware and a pivot away from projects like low-priced Nokia Asha phones' (149). Most of the lay-offs were therefore from the Nokia mobile-phone business that had been divested to Microsoft in 2013 as part of the Nokia redevelopment recounted in the next section (149).
33. Nadella 2019: 105. He mentions, too, that because he had 'made cultural change at Microsoft such a high priority, people often ask how it's going' (105).
34. Nadella 2019: 244. 'In 1998, when we first achieved the milestone of highest market cap in the world, a lot of us interpreted the success as our own brilliance. By 2018, twenty years later, I think we have all come to realize how temporal—how fleeting—these moments can be. By the time you read this, it's anyone's guess what the stock market will do' (244).
35. An *Economist* magazine article of 24–30 October 2020 on Microsoft pointed out that Azure 'drives its share price. Azure is estimated to make up only a tenth of Microsoft's $53bn in annual operating profit. But every quarter Wall Street fixates on how fast the cloud is growing' (58). The article also points to the importance of Nadella putting Azure 'at the heart of the business. The result has been double-digit revenue growth … and the firm's shares have more than quintupled in value since Mr Nadella took over' (57).
36. Doz and Wilson 2018: 64, 89.
37. Doz and Wilson 2018: 138.
38. Siilasmaa 2019: 13.
39. See Chapter 15.
40. See Siilasmaa 2019: 132 on falling behind Samsung.
41. On the operating losses, see Siilasmaa 2019: 116, 133; and Doz and Wilson 2018: 139.

42. Siilasmaa 2019: 113, 133. The 2011 lay-offs, however, were largely due to redundancies created by the alliance with Microsoft (113).
43. Doz and Wilson 2018: 172–3. Nokia had a 'chairman-centric history' and so the chairman, not the CEO, was seen as the leader of the corporation (Siilasmaa 2019: 148).
44. See Siilasmaa 2019, 115–6, 126, 132; on the Lumia models, 720, 800, and 900.
45. Siilasmaa 2019: 166. The Lumia phones' software offered a full digital 'ecosystem' of operating system, applications, and platform for third-party sellers, but this would be competing against the formidable iPhone and Android ecosystems, described in Chapters 14 and 15.
46. Doz and Wilson 2018: 139. As Siilasmaa admits, 'we just couldn't seem to break through with consumers' and indeed after a few months of 'respectable growth' in 2012, Lumia 920 sales actually fell back in the first half of 2013 (Siilasmaa 2019: 171). 'Opening a third ecosystem was proving more difficult than we expected. Android and Apple had started spinning their virtuous circle so much earlier that it felt almost impossible to match their velocity, let alone catch up with them. Their head start boosted them far ahead on the growth curve, with volume shares of 75 percent and 15 percent respectively, with [Microsoft's] Windows Phone OS at just 2 per cent ... Lumia activations declined to roughly 300,000 per week. Android activations were over a million. Every day' (170–1).
47. Siilasmaa 2019: 187.
48. By 1997 mobile phones were bringing in 51 per cent of Nokia's revenue, compared to network infrastructure's 35 per cent; and by 2000 the mobile phones were bringing in 72 per cent (Doz and Wilson 2018: 60, 63).
49. See Ollila and Saukkomaa 2016: 325; see 324–5 on the origins and creation of NSN.
50. Siilasmaa 2019: 199–200.
51. Siilasmaa 2019: 200, 202.
52. Siilasmaa 2019: 199.
53. Siilasmaa 2019: 205; Doz and Wilson 2018: 140–1.
54. Siilasmaa 2019: 211. Nokia had sold 'all of its Devices & Services business and the required IP license' for $7.17 billion in cash. Nokia's board of directors did not resist the sale: 'the fall of its phone business had been so severe that, to save the rest of the company, Nokia's board agreed its sale' (Doz and Wilson 2018: 140).
55. Siilasmaa 2019: xv–xvi.
56. Siilasmaa 2019: 252.
57. Siilasmaa: 2019: 205. The price was so low that 'we felt that we had made out like bandits'.
58. Siilasmaa 2019: 208. He 'made it a precondition of his continuing negotiations with Microsoft that the US firm provide a commercial loan to Nokia of US$1.5 billion to fund the buy-out' of Siemens (Doz and Wilson 2018: 140–1).
59. Siilasmaa 2019: 211; and 170, 185 on him being the lead negotiator with Microsoft. See 179–211 on the months of negotiations, lasting from April to August.
60. These regulatory delays meant that the sale was not finally completed until April 2014 (Siilasmaa 2019: 258–9). In May, the head of NSN, Rajeev Suri, was appointed CEO of the whole Nokia corporation (Doz and Wilson 2018: 141). Although Nokia was still led by chairman Siilasmaa, promoting Suri to CEO was another sign of Nokia's reorientation towards NSN's network-infrastructure products.
61. Doz and Wilson 2018: 141. In addition, there was more prioritizing divestment in 2015. Nokia sold its mapping business, once known as Navteq, to a consortium of German car-makers for some $2 billion (141).

62. Burgelman et al. 2017: 201.
63. Fiorina 2007: 150, 153. For example, although HP had become a major producer of PCs, these were hardly profitable versions of the industry's standard PC (Burgelman et al. 2017: 199). HP's operating profit margin on PCs was estimated in 2001 as 'breakeven at best', while Compaq's was less than 2 per cent and Dell's a remarkable 7 per cent (199).
64. Anders 2003: 41.
65. Anders 2003: 40, 43.
66. Anders 2003: 46–8, 52–3.
67. Fiorina 2007: 151.
68. Her book contains a long, forceful complaint about these weaknesses in sales and marketing (Fiorina 2007: 175–6).
69. Fiorina 2007: 196. The two other of the four groups would be product-based groups (one for computers, one for printers), which were to design and supply the products marketed and sold by the two customer-based groups. Fiorina also instituted a structural centralization that reduced the power of the four group leaders. They had to adjust to 'new roles' and to 'new collaboration and accountability for improved performance' (Fiorina 2007: 198). See also Burgelman et al. 2017: 194. The centralization led to HP headquarters monitoring the groups and divisions more closely but also helping to reduce their costs by providing centralized services and purchasing (Fiorina 2007: 179, 196–7).
70. Burrows 2003: 142, 160. See also Anders 2003: 75; Burgelman et al. 2017: 193–4. This new structure can be viewed as a front-end and back-end arrangement, with two units at the customer-interacting front end and two units at the product-supplying back end. The new structure had some disadvantages, though, which Fiorina tried to remedy during the hybridizing with Compaq: 'her front-end/back-end system' was restructured into a new model that revived features of the pre-Fiorina system (Anders 2003: 76). Burgelman et al. 2017: 202 observes that Fiorina in fact 'abandoned' her front-end/back-end structure.
71. However, Burrows noted that this increase was accompanied by what seemed to be 'channel stuffing', that is, pushing through more sales to retailers by offering them discounts or other incentives (Burrows 2003: 169). He also points to the lack of concern for profitability when making sales and to the failure to expand beyond selling personal-computers and other low-margin (old-era) products (170). Anders, too, pointed to problems with the growth figures. In particular, 'some salespeople raced to beat their quotas, only to saddle HP with what ultimately turned out to be unprofitable new orders' (Anders 2003: 75–6). Such problems came home to roost when the high-tech sector of the economy started to feel the first effects of its 2000/1 recession.
72. Fiorina 2007: 227.
73. See Chapter 13.
74. It seems that she had identified the right or likely target company as early as December 1999 but 'also knew that the organization [HP] wasn't yet capable of executing the move' (Fiorina 2007: 229).
75. On Compaq, see Anders 2003: 130–1; Burgelman et al. 2017: 199; Burrows 2003: 177–9.
76. Thanks to these diversifications, by 2001 less than half of Compaq's revenue came from PCs (Burgelman et al. 2017: 199).
77. Burgelman et al. 2017: 200.
78. Fiorina 2007: 239. She points out, too, that Compaq was bettering HP in the business-use PC market and in the fastest growing part of the server market (229).

79. Anders used the biological-hybridizing analogy to describe the HP-Compaq merger. 'The new HP was mixing up its gene pool, hybridizing what it hoped would be the best elements of both its predecessor companies' (Anders 2003: 216). Fiorina uses the biological analogy too. 'We needed the DNA of both companies to form a new company that could compete and win in the twenty-first century' (Fiorina 2007: 246). She took the analogy further by referring to two different strands of DNA. 'We needed two strands of DNA to adapt to the changing industry landscape' and in fact the 'explicit goal was to use two strands of DNA to create a stronger, better company' (246, 265).
80. Anders 2003: 128, 130; Burrows 2003: 179.
81. Burrows 2003: 178–9, citing one of the 'key players' in the negotiations.
82. Fiorina 2007: 246, emphasis added. The importance of the firms' cultural differences was highlighted by the merger's cultural version of due diligence. 'We pioneered something we called cultural due diligence ... to examine in detail how these two cultures differed. We conducted in-depth interviews with more than 100 executives and 2,000 employees from both companies' (265).
83. Burgelman et al. 2017: 208. Even before the merger was completed, Anders and Burrows had noted the prevalence and influence of ex-Compaq executives in the new HP. They were increasingly prominent in the sales organization, while in the computer units there was 'something of a reverse takeover, say many insiders, with Compaq people taking many of the important jobs' and setting the direction for the future (Anders 2003: 216; Burrows 2003: 262).
84. House and Price 2009: 471.
85. House and Price 2009: 471.
86. Burgelman et al. 2017: 214.
87. House and Price 2009: 470.
88. Malone 2007: 384 makes favourable comments about the mechanics of the merger, and Burrows favourably describes the merger's integration plan and its cost-cutting (Burrows 2003: 179, 261).
89. Burgelman et al. 2017: 202.
90. Burgelman et al. 2017: 214. Fiorina 2007: 278 and 286 acknowledges that in September 2004 the stock price was still disappointing shareholders, and that in January 2005 it was a matter of legitimate concern. Another aspect of the share-price problem was HP's vulnerability to takeover. 'There was particular urgency to improve the share price, because the company's weak stock price could have subjected HP to a takeover by any of several leveraged buyout firms reportedly then circling around the company. This was a prospect that nobody on the board wished for the venerable company' (Burgelman et al. 2017: 218).
91. See Fiorina 2007: 302–3. House and Price 2009: 472 points to a sales shortfall in third-quarter 2004 as the defining issue. But the authors also mention two other explanations for Fiorina's demise. One was a possible gender bias by the board; and the other was that boards like HP's had often discarded CEOs who were failing to live up to expectations or to their previous achievements (472, 477).
92. Burgelman et al. 2017: 221.
93. Malone 2007: 389; Burgelman et al. 2017: 231.
94. Fiorina 2007: 286.
95. Burgelman et al. 2017: 225.
96. Burgelman et al. 2017: 241.
97. Siilasmaa 2019: xv–xvi.
98. Machiavelli 2012 [1532]: 85.

Chapter 11

1. These are the Nike figures for 2022.
2. Nike employees felt that it was a matter of company loyalty to say that they had not read the book: 'co-authored by Rob Strasser's wife, [it] was said to reflect Strasser's viewpoint' (Katz 1994: 88). *Swoosh* has been described as 'two books in one', namely 'the genesis and early days of Nike, and *The Rob Strasser Story* with benchmarks along the way of what Adidas was doing as Nike went through its mercurial growth' (Hollister 2008: 275–6). Hollister's own book described Nike's development from the perspective of one of its earliest employers and managers—providing a manager's-eye view of the firm from start-up to the 2000s.
3. The German sports-and-fitness firms Adidas and Puma had begun their rise to prominence after the Second World War. The two Dassler brothers had divided their athletic-shoe firm into two separate companies: Adi Dassler established 'Adidas'; brother Rudolf established 'Ruda' before settling on the name 'Puma' (Smit 2006: 39).
4. Knight 2018: 9–10. 'Being a runner, I knew something about running shoes. Being a business buff, I knew that Japanese cameras had made deep cuts into the camera market, which had once been dominated by the Germans. Thus, I argued in my paper that Japanese running shoes might do the same thing' (9).
5. Knight 2018: 10.
6. Bowerman had been Knight's running coach at the University of Oregon. Moore's 2006 *Bowerman and the Men of Oregon* provides a biography of this remarkable man.
7. It was a useful learning experience 'about what made companies tick, what made them fail' (Knight 2018: 81).
8. Knight 2018: 117–18.
9. Knight 2018: 86–7.
10. Knight 2018: 110–11. See also Moore 2006: 182–3. Moore claims that the Cortez made Blue Ribbon 'a viable company', if only because 'people bought them in great numbers' (183).
11. Knight 2018: 195–7; Semmelhack 2015: 83.
12. Knight 2018: 113. Bowerman had co-authored the book with a medical doctor, W. E. Harris.
13. Semmelhack 2015: 83.
14. Knight 2018: 165, 177, 187–8.
15. Knight 2018: 207–8. Strasser later viewed this and the Nissho adaptation as examples of Knight at his best (Strasser and Becklund 1993: 392).
16. Knight 2018: 180. According to Moore, however, it was a shipment of shoes from a new Japanese supplier, Nippon Rubber Company, that led to Knight's innovative adaptation of a new logo and brand name (Moore 2006; 267–8).
17. Knight 2018: 181. Her name was Carolyn Davidson.
18. Jeff Johnson suggested 'Nike'. Knight's early employees, such as 'first employee' Jeff Johnson and 'wheelchair driver' Bob Woodell, made a big contribution to the start-up's success and became the firm's first generation of managers.
19. Knight 2018: 184.
20. Knight 2018: 313. As well as being an accountant, Knight had been a competitive runner. 'Running track gives you a fierce respect for numbers, because you *are* what your numbers say you are' (82).
21. Knight 2018: 327. This an example of the development combination of diversification and strategic calculation that was mentioned in Chapter 10.

22. Vanderbilt 1998: 142; Hollister 2008: 193; Knight 2018: 363.
23. Knight 2018: 297, 299. A yet more informal forum was the resort's bar, where the company's senior managers would 'continue laying into each other about some problem or idea or hare-brained scheme' (300).
24. Knight 2018: 347. It was decided, too, that there would be a system of class A and class B shares which left control with Knight and his inner circle.
25. This difference is readily apparent when Bowerman's book on jogging is compared with Jim Fixx's book on running.
26. Fixx 1977: 134–7, 177.
27. The inventor was Frank Rudy. His air bags were so revolutionary that at first the idea sounded to Knight 'like jet packs and moving sidewalks. Comic book stuff' (Knight 2018: 306).
28. Knight 2018: 331–2.
29. Knight 2018: 332. A different sort of product-development problem was experienced by Puma in 1992. It introduced a disc-like tightening mechanism that replaced shoelaces on Puma's latest sports shoe. But 'what had initially appeared to be a huge success ended as a flop' because 'the mechanism kept jamming in the mass-market version', unlike with the version endorsed by celebrity athletes in Puma's advertising campaign (Peters 2008: 95–6).
30. Knight 2018: 332.
31. Smith 2018: 137.
32. Smith 2018: 138.
33. Katz 1994: 134.
34. Katz 1994: 136.
35. Strasser and Becklund 1993: 481–2.
36. Smith 2018: 139–40.
37. Smith 2018: 140; Katz 1994: 106. Soon Reebok had the clever marketing idea of giving the Freestyle to aerobics instructors as a free gift: 'those ordinary endorsers provided a level of trust not present with a celebrity athlete' (Smith 2018: 141).
38. Katz 1994: 106–7; Strasser and Becklund 1993: 456, 462.
39. Strasser and Becklund 1993: 478; Katz 1994: 107.
40. Strasser and Becklund 1993: 365, 367.
41. Strasser and Becklund 1993: 393, 438, 449.
42. Katz 1994: 7; Strasser and Becklund 1993: 414, 449.
43. Katz 1994: 107. Katz later mentioned that the total 1980s lay-offs 'culled' 600 employees from a 'community of 2,000', which indicates that the initial 400 job losses were a dramatic downsizing of the workforce (297). However, *Swoosh* observed that by the end of 1984 Nike had laid off 400 people, 'about 10 percent of its work force', which indicates that Nike had employed as many as 4,000 people before the crisis emerged (Strasser and Becklund 1993: 449). Similarly, Hollister's book noted that Nike had 3,600 employees in 1982 (Hollister 2008: 189).
44. Knight 2018: 381.
45. Moore 2006: 342.
46. Moore 2006: 381. 'Bowerman, by his own account hadn't been listened to since 1975' (Strasser and Becklund 1993: 532). He often attempted to resign from the board of directors, but Knight refused to accept his resignation until in 1999 Bowerman was finally allowed to leave the company, at the age of 88, and he died later that year (Moore 2006: 416).

47. Hollister 2008: 169. Hollister mentioned, too, that Knight was 'always reluctant to show his cards, Knight kept you guessing' (226).

48. Carbasho 2010: 118, quoting the Nike website. According to Hollister, 'Knight had appointed Bob Woodell as president. A little burned out, Phil was spending more time at his place at Sunriver' (Hollister 2008: 267). *Swoosh* described the context in which Knight asked Woodell to take over the post of president. 'The change in Nike's fortunes seemed to hit Knight hard. He appeared increasingly agitated, tired and out of sorts' (Strasser and Becklund 1993: 393). After Woodell suggested Knight rethink the idea, he returned and confirmed that he still wanted Woodell to be president, while Knight 'would do long-range planning and remain chairman of the board' (394). See also 403–5 on Knight's activities and role during Woodell's time as president.

49. Strasser and Becklund 1993: 401–2; 404 on Woodell's administrative changes; 405–6 on his apparel strategy; and 438 on its failure.

50. Strasser and Becklund 1993: 439–41, 444. Woodell was reassigned to a lesser role, and left Nike at the end of 1985 (470).

51. Strasser and Becklund 1993: 505, 524, 528.

52. Strasser and Becklund 1993: 529.

53. Strasser and Becklund 1993: 481–2.

54. Strasser and Becklund 1993: 483–4. The Air Max was apparently part of an overall Nike Air development and marketing package that also included the cross-training Air Trainer (484–5). In the 2010s, however, Tinker Hatfield was being personally credited with visible Air and the cross-trainer. See for example the Air Trainer entry in the Exhibition Checklist of Semmelhack 2015, plus Smith 2018: 178–9, and Le Maux 2016: 57.

55. Katz 1994: 135.

56. Katz 1994: 135.

57. Smith 2018: 194–5.

58. Strasser and Becklund 1993: 482–3.

59. Vanderbilt 1998: 134.

60. Vanderbilt 1998: 134; Katz 1994: 144.

61. Vanderbilt 1998: 55, fig. 5.

62. Rothenberg 1995: 215; Katz 1994: 9, 274.

63. Katz 1994: 8, 229.

64. Katz 1994: 146; Vanderbilt 1998: xi, fig. 1.

65. Strasser and Becklund 1993: 409–10. In 1983, Nike had set the goal of 'rejuvenating the brand' (409).

66. Strasser and Becklund 1993: 410–13, 426.

67. Nike was producing good basketball sneakers, though, particularly the 1982 design 'Air Force 1' that became a fashionable sneaker in the 1990s' (Le Maux 2016: 89). Smith sees the basketball prioritizing as beginning with a 1984 Buttface meeting, and with Knight having decided that Nike 'needed to make a big play in the basketball market lest it be relegated to just being a running shoe company' (Smith 2018: 159–60). But he also mentions that Strasser was pursuing 'something that he had summed up in a 1983 memo. "Individual athletes, even more than teams, will be the heroes; symbols more and more of what real people can't do anymore—risk and win" ... Strasser was on the lookout for the basketball version—someone with outsized talent plus that something extra' (161).

68. Vanderbilt 1998: 31.

69. In the 1990s, US research indicated that 80 per cent of the wearers of 'athletic shoes' did not use them for sporting pursuits but instead for other purposes: 'usually they were used for walking around' (Vanderbilt 1998: 52; Katz 1994: 100).
70. Vanderbilt 1998: 31.
71. Le Maux 2016: 81.
72. Sonny Vaccaro not only spotted but also championed Jordan's potential (Lazenby 2015: 238–9).
73. See Lazenby 2015: 241 on Jordan's preference for Adidas; and 242–3 on him not wanting to negotiate with Nike. Apparently, Jordan tried to get Adidas to match Nike's offer, but they would only offer him about $100,000 a year and 'wouldn't do a special Jordan shoe' (Strasser and Becklund 1993: 435).
74. Lazenby 2015: 238, 242.
75. See Strasser and Becklund 1993: 430; 433 on the distinctive Air Jordan logo and the red-and-black colour scheme for the sneakers.
76. Strasser and Becklund 1993: 432. Lazenby 2015: 242 mentions, too, 'the 25 percent royalty that Jordan would get on each Air Jordan shoe sold'.
77. Smith 2018: 166–7.
78. Lazenby 2015: 240.
79. Lazenby 2015: 242, 245. 'Phil Knight supposedly never officially sanctioned or gave his approval to the deal. But he didn't move to stop it either, as Rob Strasser seized on Vaccaro's idea and made it happen. As a result, Knight's silence became his tacit approval' (245).
80. Smith 2018: 169. Another indication that Strasser had got it right was that Nike's annual US sales of running shoes had fallen from $240 million in 1983/4 to $161 million in 1984/5, but the equivalent basketball sales had already risen from $125 million to $141 million (Strasser and Becklund 1993: 462).
81. Strasser and Becklund 1993: 459.
82. Lazenby 2015: 382, quoting reporter David Alridge.
83. Hollister 2008: 251.
84. Kawamura 2017: 43, 84.
85. Kawamura 2017: 60 and 73, emphasis added.
86. The shoes' success increased the tendency for sneakers to be worn by young males. Research in the 1990s showed that more than half the customers for 'athletic shoes' in general, including basketball sneakers, were 'young men under eighteen', and they typically owned multiple pairs of sneakers (Katz 1994: 199, 260–1).
87. Smith 2018: 175. A Nike spokesman told the *Sports Illustrated* magazine that this new design 'would look great' with a tuxedo (175).
88. Strasser and Becklund 1993: 508.
89. Smith 2018: 179. This was Tinker Hatfield's first design for the Air Jordan series of sneakers.
90. Le Maux 2016: 44.
91. Knight 2018: 313. The nearest thing to advertising that he had favoured was paying for product endorsements by high-level players or coaches. Even that minimal product promotion was merely his trying to keep up with Nike's competitors in this area of marketing. On Nike's product endorsements, see 215, 309, 310.
92. See Rothenberg 1995: 200–8. The watershed was Nike's 1977 superb poster ad of a lone runner and the memorable message: 'there is no finish line' (200).

93. Vanderbilt 1998: 125.
94. Goldman and Papson 1998: 47. See also Katz 1994: 7, which credits the commercial for a 'nationwide Air Jordan basketball shoe shopping spree'.
95. Katz 1994: 7.
96. Bradshaw and Scott 2017: 11.
97. Bradshaw and Scott 2017: 71–2. See also Smith 2018: 196; Katz 1994: 138; and Rothenberg 1995: 215.
98. Katz 1994: 141. See also Smith 2018: 198–9.
99. Strasser and Becklund 1993: 460, 464–5.
100. Katz 1994: 135. The injury occurred in the third game of the 1985/6 season and meant that Jordan had to miss games or play for only a short time in a game (Lazenby 2015: 288–9, 293).
101. Strasser and Becklund 1993: 506–7; Katz 1994: 297.
102. 'The Air Jordan line hummed along with sales of $200 million each year' in 1988/9, but Nike's annual sales had by then reached $1.7 billion (Katz 1994: 147; Rothenberg 1995: 215). Just the new Air Trainer and other cross-training products were generating $400 million in annual revenue by 1990 (Strasser and Becklund 1993: 537).
103. Katz 1994: 55. A Nike designer pointed out in the mid-1990s that its competitor Adidas still regarded athletic footwear as equipment and still failed to 'understand how to go beyond that and design in romance and imagery and all of those subliminal characteristics that make an object important to people in less utilitarian ways': in other words, important to them as a fashion item (130).
104. Knight 2018: 372.
105. Strasser and Becklund 1993: 530.
106. Knight acknowledges Strasser's role in the Air Jordan diversification, but Strasser's working for Adidas was 'an intolerable betrayal' (Knight 2018: 371, 372).
107. Goldman and Papson 1998: 48. Although the Mars Blackmon character was African-American, the commercials appealed not just to 'a black audience. The ads would also engage a larger swathe of young Americans, who would be attracted by the use of an avant-garde director and the spot's jabs at commercialism' (Rothenberg 1995: 215).
108. Rothenberg 1995: 215.
109. Goldman and Papson 1998: 49. The punchline was spoken in the 1989 commercial in the Mars-Michael series (Smith 2018: 1).
110. Peters 2008: 66; Katz 1994: 8. The Nike strain of coolness was heavily influenced by the inner-city African-American youth culture. A Nike employee confirmed that the target consumer was 'the black, urban teen' and that this was due to 'the coolness factor—if they wear it, the others will follow' (quoted by Goldman and Papson 1998: 176). As Vanderbilt observed, here was an interesting twist on aspirational brand theory: affluent suburban youth were emulating youths living in socioeconomically deprived inner-city areas (Vanderbilt 1998: 34). Furthermore, 'African American youth in the largest urban markets became the foot soldiers for a sneaker's success in mostly white suburban and rural areas', as Nike estimated in 1991 that 'about 87 percent of its products were purchased by whites' (31). Nike was not the only sneaker company to adopt this approach. Its competitors, too, were 'methodically cultivating' a vanguard market that the sneaker industry called 'urban' as a code word for 'black' (33).
111. Vanderbilt 1998: 31; Le Maux 2016: 27. On the Clyde's heritage, see also Vanderbilt 1998: 20; Le Maux 2016: 27; Smith 2018: 166.

112. Le Maux 2016: 39; Smith 2018: 157.
113. Le Maux 2016: 39; Smit 2006: 218, quoting the Adidas representative who arranged the endorsement deal with the group Run-DMC.
114. Le Maux 2016: 57. Basketball sneakers, though, eventually made up some 60 per cent of annual sneaker sales in the US (Smit 2006 220).
115. Peters 2008: 182.
116. Vanderbilt 1998: 66, 70.
117. Vanderbilt 1998: 116.
118. In other words, 'the creation and strong marketing of these [sneaker] technologies' helped 'give a specific brand an aura of being an authentic athletic brand' (Vanderbilt 1998: 52, quoting a Wall Street analysis of the sneaker industry).
119. Vanderbilt 1998: 50.
120. Vanderbilt 1998: 50. Nike's rivals, too, were turning out multiple new lines each year.
121. 'The design, in theory, flows from the athletic core outward, though fashion is never absent from the design process of even the most advanced athletic shoes' (Vanderbilt 1998: 52).
122. Katz 1994: 260.
123. Vanderbilt 1998: 142. Goldman and Papson 1998: 13, gives a non-US revenue figure of over $2 billion from a total of over $6 billion in 1996, compared to only a few hundred million from a total of over $2 billion in 1990.
124. LaFeber 2002: 135.
125. LaFeber 2002: 139, 150.
126. Vanderbilt 1998: viii.
127. Vanderbilt 1998: xi.
128. Carbasho 2010: ii.
129. Knight 2018: 111.
130. See Smit 2006: 348, 353–6 on the Adidas takeover of Reebok. On the fall and rise of Adidas in the late-1980s to mid-1990s era, see 269–70, 334–5, 347; and Le Maux 2016: 118. Puma went through a fall and rise during these years too, as described by Peters 2008: 105–6, 126–30, 157–9, 162–3, 177, 182.
131. Smit 2006: 357.

Chapter 12

1. Ingrassia and White 1995: 24.
2. The Chapter 10 example of hybridization shows why it is difficult to use this tool successfully.
3. 'The book was a bestseller for thirty-seven consecutive weeks, all but one week at number one. In less than a year, bookstores sold more than two million hardback copies, which put *Iacocca* in a league with *Gone with the Wind*' (Levin 1995: 84). Another reason for his fame was his role in television commercials promoting the new cars produced by Chrysler in the early 1980s. According to Iacocca's book, he was persuaded to do the commercials by an ad-agency executive, who saw it as the best means of showing the public that Chrysler was now a new, different sort of company (Iacocca 1986: 283). Iacocca takes the credit, though, for the commercials' famous punchline: 'if you can find a better car—buy it', he says to the camera and public with impressive conviction (284).

4. Iacocca had not been recruited directly from Ford, as in 1978 he had been fired by the firm's CEO, Henry Ford II, despite the fact that Iacocca had apparently been a successful president of the firm (Iacocca 1986: 132–5).
5. See Chapter 10 for an account of how the change-making organizational processes of diversifying/prioritizing may be internal or may instead add/remove organizations through acquisitions or divestments.
6. Lutz 2014: 147. He makes this assessment in his 2014 *Icons and Idiots: Straight Talk on Leadership*.
7. Chrysler was producing poor-quality car products and its share of the car market had fallen from 12.2 per cent to 11.1 per cent in 1978 (Iacocca 1986: 168, 170).
8. Levin 1995: 44, 52–3.
9. Iacocca 1986: 293. Due to the recession, the 'annual rate of car sales in this country dropped to almost half of what it had been' (195).
10. See Lutz 2011: 177 on Iacocca's strong performance at the congressional hearings.
11. Hyde 2003: 258.
12. Iacocca 1986: 298.
13. Iacocca 1986: 298.
14. Hyde 2003: 258.
15. Iacocca 1986: 248.
16. Hyde 2003: 261.
17. Hyde 2003: 261.
18. Moritz and Seaman 1984: 291.
19. Hyde 2003: 258, which also notes that most of Chrysler's parts came from non-union low-wage plants.
20. Moritz and Seaman 1984: 291. The new emphasis on quality control was typical of how in the 1980s US car companies were imitating Japanese practices. 'The industry as a whole turned to the Japanese during the early Eighties in search of whatever it was that allowed them to win so much of the world's market' (291).
21. For example, the Robogate body assemblers would 'pinch the pieces of the frame together accurately and consistently' (Moritz and Seaman 1984: 280).
22. Hyde 2003: 234.
23. An example of the new leanness and efficiency was that Chrysler had 'reduced its break-even sales volume from 2.4 million units in 1979 to 1 million in 1982' (Hyde 2003: 234).
24. Moritz and Seaman 1984: 290–1. The profit was artificially boosted by the lucrative sell-off of Chrysler's tank-making division, but the profit was also artificially *reduced* by a damaging strike in Canada.
25. Moritz and Seaman 1984: 291.
26. Moritz and Seaman 1984: 291. Sales were down to some six million units a year.
27. Iacocca 1986: 294. Production in the 1982 trough had been fewer than one million units, 'down 4 per cent from 1981', but 'sales of 1.3 million vehicles in 1983, combined with company's lean cost structure, brought large profits' (Hyde 2003: 253).
28. Moritz and Seaman 1984: 291, 296.
29. Iacocca 1986: 294; Hyde: 2003: 255.
30. Hyde 2003: 233. He also declares that 'this monumental recovery was the work of one remarkable man' (233).
31. Iacocca 1986: 294. The official corporate decision to change to front-wheel drive was made in February 1980 (Hyde 2003: 266).

32. Hyde 2003: 254.
33. Moritz and Seaman 1984: 288, referring to the production capacity in 1980. On the Omni and Horizon cars, launched in 1978, see 4–5, 14–15; and Hyde 2003: 225.
34. These were the rear-wheel drive Chrysler Fifth Avenue, Dodge Diplomat, and Plymouth Fury, which all survived until 1989 (Hyde 2003: 265).
35. Moritz and Seaman 1984: 288; Hyde 2003: 254–5. Chrysler had already used this four-cylinder type of engine in the Omni and Horizon cars.
36. Moritz and Seaman 1984: 288.
37. Iacocca 1986: 264–5. In its advertising, Chrysler 'pointed out that the K-car was roomy enough to hold "six Americans"—a little shot at our Japanese competitors' (265).
38. Moritz and Seaman 1984: 212.
39. Iacocca 1986: 264. Moritz and Seaman 1984: 224 confirm that the K-car became the 'rallying point for Chrysler throughout 1979 and 1980'.
40. Iacocca 1986: 265.
41. Hyde 2003: 249.
42. Iacocca 1986: 267–8; Hyde 2003: 249–50. The K-cars in the showrooms were often more than 50 per cent more expensive than the price set for the basic models (Hyde 2003: 249).
43. Hyde 2003: 250.
44. Hyde 2003: 251.
45. Moritz and Seaman 1984: 297.
46. Hyde 2003: 265.
47. Moritz and Seaman 1984: 298. The minivan could also be 'ordered without seating for passengers and used as a light delivery vehicle for florists or other tradespeople' (Levin 1995: 83).
48. See Hyde 2003: 266–7; and Iacocca 1986: 296–7.
49. Iacocca 1986: 296.
50. Levin 1995: 83.
51. Hyde 2003: 265.
52. Iacocca 1986: 297.
53. Hyde 2003: 266–7.
54. Hyde 2003: 267.
55. Iacocca 1986: 296.
56. Hyde 2003: 265.
57. Production in 1984 amounted to more than 190,500 units, then increased to some 220,000 in 1985 and some 226,000 in 1986 before production was markedly increased by the opening of a second plant in 1987 (Hyde 2003: 267–8).
58. Iacocca 1986: 296.
59. Levin 1995: 83. This was indeed an astonishing margin, as apparently the minivans 'sold briskly at prices ranging from $8,000 to $11,000 fully equipped' (83). He calculated that with sales of '200,000 units annually, minivans promised a potential gross profit of $1 billion' (83–4).
60. Levin 1995: 84.
61. Lutz 2014: 144.
62. Iacocca 1986: 290.
63. Ingrassia and White 1995: 203.
64. A decline in rationality is evident as early as 1984, when he initiated a sports car joint venture with Maserati. This two-seat convertible finally appeared in showrooms five years

later and failed to sell in anything like the numbers envisioned by Iacocca. 'He squandered $500 million on a vehicle that was supposed to create a new image for Chrysler, but utterly failed to do so' (Hyde 2003: 272).

65. Ingrassia and White 1995: 203.
66. Hyde 2003: 272.
67. GM bought Hughes Aircraft and Electronic Data Systems, while Ford bought Hertz rental cars and a consumer-finance company (Hyde 2003: 272).
68. Hyde 2003: 273–5. Iacocca went even further and in November 1985 announced a restructuring that converted the corporation into a holding company with four subsidiaries: Chrysler Motors and three *non*-automotive entities, such as Chrysler Aerospace (Ingrassia and White 1995: 81). He later admitted that the restructuring had been a mistake, as the holding company 'made us top-heavy. If we went astray—you know, people do go astray now and then in many areas—man, we got focused in a hurry' (203). The getting 'focused in a hurry' is referring to the 1990/1 turnaround, but there had already been a return to rationality in 1988/9, as is recounted in the next section.
69. Inefficiencies and costs had increased markedly, and by 1987 the sales break-even point was 1.9 million units when it should have been only about 1.5 million in vehicle sales (Ingrassia and White 1995: 189).
70. The ultimate objective of Iacocca's business mission is unclear. But if he was attempting a second-stage redevelopment, he was not using the appropriate rational means and therefore lacked discernment. If, on the other hand, he was attempting an enhancing development, he was not using the appropriate rational method of strategic calculation and presumably had not used diverse deliberation when deciding to undertake this mission. In fact his new business mission seems to be an example of irrationality, to add to those mentioned in Chapter 10.
71. The failure to finish off the redevelopment might well be viewed as an example of irrationality, like his new business mission (see note 70). Similarly, Iacocca's decision to write a second book might be viewed as an irrational use of his time and energy while still in the midst of a new business mission and with the redevelopment not yet finished. His new book, *Straight Talking*, was published in 1988 and seems more concerned with how to run the country than with describing how he was running Chrysler. Of its seventeen chapters, only three are specifically about Chrysler and business. There are three chapters on his family and personal life, eight chapters on America's various problems or policy issues, a chapter on his view of history, a chapter on 'if I were President', and a chapter looking towards the twenty-first century.
72. Hyde 2003: 251. These new vehicles could be 'done on the cheap' because they were based on a pre-existing platform (254).
73. Iacocca 1986: 266.
74. Ingrassia and White 1995: 188.
75. Ingrassia and White 1995: 188; Levin 1995: 234. In Hyde's words, the '"look" of Chrysler's cars reflected Iacocca's styling preferences and prejudices—and these were increasingly out of touch with the tastes of the car-buying public' (Hyde 2003: 272).
76. Hyde 2003: 271–2.
77. Yates 1996: 11–12.
78. Ingrassia and White 1995: 196, 207; Yates 1996: 12.
79. Lutz 1998: 48.

80. Hyde 2003: 293 describes Iacocca's decision to buy AMC as 'against the advice of his lieutenants', while Lutz 2014: 131 notes that most of the 'senior management was opposed to the AMC acquisition, including me'.
81. Bradsher 2002: 4; and see 4 for a detailed definition of the SUV type of vehicle.
82. Bradsher 2002: 51. In contrast, 'minivans had become quickly stereotyped as "mom-mobiles" that older children would not want to be caught dead in, and that formerly rebellious boomers saw as an acknowledgment of domestic responsibilities' (51).
83. Foster 2013: 199. These SUVs were the Jeep-brand Cherokee model.
84. Hyde 2003: 266–7 suggests that a larger model of the minivan 'had to await the availability' of a Mitsubishi-made six-cylinder engine. But this model was produced with an improved four-cylinder engine months before the option of a six-cylinder engine was available (Zatz 2019: 17, 52–4).
85. Hyde 2003: 268.
86. Lutz 2014: 130.
87. Ingrassia and White 1995: 196.
88. Hyde 2003: 268–9. The minivan continued to be a 'cash cow of almost unbelievable proportions' (Lutz 1998: 10).
89. Hyde 2003: 269.
90. Hyde 2003: 282–3. This was the Grand Cherokee model.
91. Bradsher 2002: xvi.
92. Levin 1995: 102; Foster 2013: 199. As mentioned earlier, it had sold some 221,000 Jeeps. Foster distinguishes between Jeeps and cars. For instance, when referring to AMC's 1986 sales outside the US, he says: '16,331 cars and 37,375 Jeeps were sold, for a grand total of 287,734 cars and Jeeps worldwide' (Foster 2013: 199).
93. Lutz 2014: 131–2. Yates referred to 'a nucleus of about a dozen top AMC executives and engineers who were to play major roles in Chrysler's future' (Yates 1996: 58).
94. Levin 1995: 231, 234. Lutz was also promoted to one of the two newly created posts of co-president. After being recruited from Ford in 1986, he was appointed Chrysler's executive vice-president for trucks and international, with a seat on the board of directors.
95. Lutz 1998: 31.
96. Hyde 2003: 280.
97. Lutz 1998: 32. A new Chrysler division, the Jeep-Eagle Division, was created from the 'remnants' of AMC (Yates 1996: 58). And 'Iacocca had permitted Jeep engineering under Castaing to absorb Dodge truck engineering as an exercise to see whether Jeep's spartan habits might rub off on Dodge' (Levin 1995: 238).
98. Hyde 2003: 179.
99. Lutz 1998: 32. See also Hyde 2003: 179.
100. Lutz 1998: 33. Chrysler's then president, Sperlich, later asserted that the main reason for the project having lain dormant was Iacocca 'having lost focus' (Yates 1996: 68). But Levin's account of what had gone wrong in 1986/7 implies that Sperlich himself was responsible (as overall director of product development) for 'the process turning into an expensive, time-consuming spiral: engineering problem, followed by compromise, followed by new engineering problem, and new compromise' (Levin 1995: 236).
101. Lutz 1998: 34.
102. Yates 1996: 14. Hyde points out that the windscreen was 'located directly above the front wheels' as well as creating a relatively 'enormous' driver and passengers' compartment (Hyde 2003: 281).

103. Levin 1995: 240.
104. Hyde 2003: 281. Hyde dates this official announcement as February 1989, but other writers imply that the decision occurred in 1990. See Ingrassia and White 1995: 439; Yates 1996: 74.
105. Lutz 1998: 32.
106. Lutz 1998: 27–8.
107. The manufacturing advisors or 'factory rats' were manufacturing engineers and plant foremen, and there was even a new programme called DFM (design for manufacture) that aimed to design parts for ease of assembly (Levin 1995: 258).
108. Hyde 2003: 281. Iacocca had already committed Chrysler to a product-development plan and schedule that included having the LH-car finished by mid-1992 (Levin 1995: 236).
109. Hyde 2003: 281.
110. Ingrassia and White 1995: 274.
111. Hyde 2003: 283.
112. Hyde 2003: 297.
113. Hyde 2003: 297.
114. Lutz 1998: 44.
115. Lutz 1998: 48.
116. Lutz 1998: 47–8.
117. Ingrassia and White 1995: 452.
118. Ingrassia and White 1995: 452. The teams were no longer centred on a particular vehicle project but instead on a particular type of product: they became the small-car team, the large-car team, the minivan team, and so forth (Lutz 1998: 40). 'Platform teams, in essence, are the company today' as even the finance and public-relations staff had been 'platformized' and the 'old mother ship exists only as a secondary support function' (40).
119. Vlasic and Stertz 2001: 29, 157.
120. Lutz 1998: 41.
121. Lutz 1998: 57–8.
122. Ingrassia and White 1995: 447.
123. Hyde 2003: 298–9; Ingrassia and White 1995: 448.
124. Ingrassia and White 1995: 455.
125. Lutz 1998: 32.
126. Vlasic and Stertz 2001: 156.
127. Vlasic and Stertz 2001: 156, 157. Chrysler 'hummed like a Viper V10 engine at full throttle', with most of its assembly plants running heavily overtime (156).
128. Vlasic and Stertz 2001: 156, 168–71.
129. Lutz 2014: 165. He retired from Chrysler in 1998, aged 66, moving on to an impressive career in other companies, including General Motors.
130. Hyde 2003: 309. He therefore describes the new company as a 'German corporation'.

Chapter 13

1. Cortada 2019: 440.
2. Gerstner 2003: 84.
3. Gerstner was not in Iacocca's position of having to convince Congress as well as bankers that his firm had a possible future and was worth saving.
4. Gerstner 2003: 68–9.

5. Christensen, 2000: ix.
6. Christensen, 2000: x.
7. Christensen, 2000: x.
8. IBM had already shown that it could deal with the threat of disruptive new technology. Although IBM had missed the minicomputer wave of the 1960s–70s, the corporation had not suffered much because its mainframe market was still expanding and lucrative. Furthermore, after seeing the minicomputers' success, IBM had entered the market and by 1979 it had won a third of the minicomputer market, not far behind leader DEC (Cortada 2019: 264–5). Cortada points out that IBM was producing minicomputers by 1970 and that the S/38 introduced in 1979 'proved massively popular, wiping out the majority of its competitors in the 1980s and leaving others crippled survivors (such as DEC)' (265).
9. Christensen, 2000: 110.
10. Christensen, 2000: 110.
11. Wallace and Erickson 1993: 168.
12. Cortada 2019: 393.
13. Cortada 2019: 395–401, 414.
14. Cortada 2019: 397. Microsoft and the clone-makers had been the big winners of the PC revolution. As Chapter 10 noted, Microsoft was valued more highly than IBM on the post-1993 Wall Street stock market. One of the stock-market analysts observed that this was 'an unbelievable reversal of fortune', considering that Microsoft had been a tiny company when 'IBM ruled the world' in the early 1980s (Wallace and Erickson 1993: 429).
15. The desktop had an even more severely disruptive effect on makers of minicomputers. 'The missile-like attack of the desktop computer from below severely wounded every minicomputer maker', for 'stand-alone workstations and networked desktop computers obviated most customers' needs for minicomputers almost overnight' (Christensen, 2000: 109).
16. Cortada 2019: 382.
17. Cortada 2019: 401.
18. Cortada 2019: 401. As late as 1993, a survey found that corporations 'expected one out of every three computer terminals running on a mainframe system to be replaced by a desktop computer' (Wallace and Erickson 1993: 437).
19. Wallace and Erickson 1993: 166, 403. See also Gerstner 2003: 203 on the halving of its market share.
20. Cortada 2019: 455; and 431–2 on unrealistic growth projections in 1982 that supported this strategy.
21. Cortada 2019: 436. See also 431–4 on the misguided growth strategy.
22. Garr, 2000: 20. According to Slater, Akers closed nineteen factories in 1986–91 (Slater 1999: 24).
23. Cortada 2019: 442.
24. Garr, 2000: 63. IBM's global workforce shrank from 403,000 in 1986 to 373,000 in 1990, and then fell more sharply to 301,000 by the end of 1992 (Cortada 2019: 427, tables 15.2 and 15.3). Slater points out, however, that the loss of jobs was not due to mass lay-offs but to 'highly attractive' early-retirement packages and to 'normal attrition', which presumably means not replacing those people reaching retirement age or with some other normal reason for leaving their IBM job (Slater 1999: 24).
25. Cortada 2019: 450–2.
26. Cortada 2019: 452.

27. Cortada 2019: 427–8 on these one-off costs, especially 'the huge write-offs it took to cover the cost of severance for the tens of thousands of employees pushed out of the company'. In 1991–3 IBM 'claimed $24 billion in restructuring costs', which gave an appearance of massive losses, but operating earnings did not decline until 1993 (428).
28. Slater 1999: 63, 67.
29. 'Sales of mainframes dropped 50 percent between 1991 and 1993' (Slater 1999: 55).
30. Slater 1999: 55.
31. Slater 1999: 80. However, 'Akers faced a great deal of opposition within his own IBM ranks' to the idea of breaking up the company (80).
32. See Cortada 2019: 422 on Akers being blamed for the firm's problems and on IBM announcing in January 1993 that he would retire in April, a year earlier than expected. He had resigned after a 25 January board meeting (453).
33. It was this 'precipitous decline' in operating earnings that 'set off alarms' (Cortada 2019: 428). Operating earnings in 1991/2 had been about $3 billion a year, but they fell to only $300 million in 1993 (427). Whereas a 1992 quarter had brought in $734 million profits on revenue of $16.2 billion, the same quarter in 1993 would be reporting a loss of $40 million on revenue of $15.5 billion (Slater 1999: 66–7).
34. Gerstner 2003: 61. Such thinking led eventually to a prioritizing of the firm's IT services. He refers later in his book to the 'powerful logic' of keeping IBM intact because 'this services-led model was IBM's unique competitive advantage' and would have been lost if the corporation had been split up (130).
35. Gerstner 2003: 61. He knew that 'in every industry there's an integrator' and knew from his past experience of IT 'that all this complicated, difficult-to-integrate, proprietary collection of technologies was [not] going to be purchased by customers who would be willing to be their own general contractors' and put the pieces and technologies together like someone building a new house that required electrical systems, plumbing, roofing, windows, and so forth (60–1). Furthermore, 'Gerstner came to his decision to keep the company intact after listening to customers who wasted little time in conveying their wishes' for an IT form of 'one-stop shopping' that would take care of all their computer needs (Slater 1999: 83)
36. Gerstner 2003: 66. The cashflow crisis in fact led to an emergency cash-raising programme that sold off unproductive assets, including the corporation's real estate, airplanes, and fine-art collection (66; Cortada 2019: 491. Gerstner's most controversial cash-raising measure was his $1.5 billion sale of the Federal Systems Division, which serviced the federal government's computer requirements (Cortada 2019: 491).
37. Gerstner 2003: 63. The uncompetitive nature of IBM's expenses had been revealed by an investigation showing that IBM had a 42 per cent expense-to-revenue ratio compared to the 31 per cent ratio of its competitors (Gerstner 2003: 63; Garr, 2000: 60).
38. Gerstner 2003: 63.
39. Slater 1999: 67, 75–6. Profitability had returned by the first quarter of 1994, with earnings of $392 million, and earnings grew to $689 million in the second quarter of 1994 (Garr, 2000: 132).
40. Gerstner 2003: 108.
41. Gerstner 2003: 189. 'IBM even had a language of its own', including the now widely used term 'pushback'.
42. Cortada 2019: 468. Akers had attempted to change the culture, by introducing a programme called Market-Driven Quality, but the change was not successfully implemented (445–7).

43. Gerstner 2003: 206, 210. As early as 1993 he had sent all IBM employees a list of eight principles that 'I thought ought to be the underpinnings of IBM's new culture' (201). But he acknowledges that there was no follow-up to this long list of suggested principles, which also had analyses or explanations accompanying each principle (203).
44. Gerstner 2003: 210.
45. Gerstner 2003: 182.
46. Gerstner 2003: 211.
47. Gerstner 2003: 211–12. He already had been using incentives at the executive level. 'I made it a high priority to promote and reward executives who embraced the new culture. It sent a message to all the up-and-coming managers' (209). Enforcement had been used too. 'Nothing can stop a cultural transformation quicker than a CEO who permits a high-level executive—even a very successful one—to disregard the new behavior model' (208).
48. Gerstner 2003: 188.
49. Gerstner 2003: 249.
50. Garr, 2000: 287, 289.
51. Garr, 2000: 287.
52. Gerstner 2003: 86.
53. Gerstner 2003: 86. He was following a model that had been adopted by banking corporations.
54. Gerstner 2003: 86, 251. A country manager in Europe 'simply refused to recognize that the vast majority of the people in his country had been reassigned to specialized units reporting to global leaders' (87).
55. Gerstner 2003: 87. One of the reasons why the restructuring was worth the effort is that it also helped to solve another of IBM's problems. The product-based organizations created by Akers's decentralization had since been converted into nothing more than operating divisions, and are called 'product divisions' or 'technological divisions' in Gerstner's book (84–5). But Gerstner was not happy with their performance. For they were primarily interested in 'what they thought could be built, or what they wanted to build, with little concern about customer needs or priorities' (85). The new customer-based groups, however, helped push the product-based operating divisions into being more concerned about customer needs and priorities.
56. See Chapter 10 on how rational leaders need to show discernment in not overloading a redevelopment and in how they sequence their use of redeveloping tools.
57. Gerstner 2003: 134.
58. Slater 1999: 235.
59. See Cortada 2019: 513 on hardware maintenance; 511 on the mid-1980s outsourcing deals, where IBM 'learned the business' of outsourcing; and 512 on the Consulting Group, which provided 'management consulting' on IT issues.
60. Cortada 2019: 513. Services were providing more revenue than IBM's software sales (509, fig. 18.1).
61. Gerstner 2003: 129. The idea was presented to Gerstner by Dennie Welch. He warned Gerstner, however, about two aspects of this envisioned unit that could be problematic. In particular, (1) the unit had to be allowed—despite the feelings of those in other parts of the firm—to recommend the products of IBM's competitors when this was in a customer's best interests; and (2) the unit's contract to provide services to a customer might last seven years and actually lose money in the first year (130).
62. Slater noted that 'during his first two years at the helm', Gerstner 'did not boost the services arm', let alone prioritize it through a new organization (Slater 1999: 227).

63. Gerstner 2003: 124.
64. Gerstner 2003: 132. See 131–2 on creating the prototype unit. Gerstner was also dealing with the prospect of organizational rivalry, as product units 'that had been the traditional base of a company more often than not resisted (overtly or silently) the emergence of a new sibling' (131). The prioritizing of services was indeed very likely to be seen as a threat—to be resisted—by the product units, such as the mainframe unit, which had traditionally been the most important. When the new services unit finally appeared in 1996, the change 'was still traumatic for some managers, but it was eventually accepted as inevitable by most of our colleagues' (132). Similarly, during the new unit's 'critical early days, it seemed there was a crisis a week between services and some other unit. Many of our brand executives or sales leaders went ballistic every time the services unit proposed a product solution that incorporated a competitor's product' (131). Eventually, however, professional working relationships were duly established between services and the other units.
65. Gerstner 2003: 132. According to Cortada, the Global Services unit was created in 1995 rather than 1996 (2019: 513). But Cortada may be dating Global Services back to the creation of the prototype unit or referring to the creation of Global Services having been announced in 1995.
66. Cortada 2019: 516, 517.
67. Slater 1999: 230–1.
68. Symonds 2004: 124.
69. Cortada 2019: 521; Symonds 2004: 225.
70. Symonds 2004: 45, 125. Customization also made it more difficult to update particular components in the software suite. 'The fact that every computer system was more or less unique meant that it was either frozen in time or required almost constant attention from teams of ever-helpful consultants to keep it up to date' (47).
71. As Ellison noted in the case of system integration, consultancy had the advantage of being 'the gift that keeps on giving' (Symonds 2004: 47).
72. Gerstner 2003: 285, app. B.
73. Cortada 2019: 514.
74. Cortada 2019: 514. For example, Garr's book had relatively little to say about the growth of IBM's IT services, despite noting that Global Services was 'Gerstner's most successful business unit' and that he had achieved 'glittering success with services' (Garr, 2000: 256, 329).
75. Gerstner 2003: 132.
76. Burgelman et al. 2017: 197.
77. Cortada 2019: 521–2 notes that customers' outsourcing in the early 1990s was often a way of lowering costs, but by 2001 the main reason for outsourcing was that customers lacked the staff or time to deal with the rapidly expanding IT world. Gerstner, too, mentions that 'skilled IT professionals were in such short supply that millions of IT jobs went unfilled. Customers simply couldn't staff up to do what needed to be done' (Gerstner 2003: 132).
78. Gerstner 2003: 134. 'Even in an economic downturn, many services—outsourcing is the leading example—hold strong appeal as customers look for ways to reduce expenses' (134).
79. See Cortada 2019: 524–6; 531 on Gerstner's transitional leadership with his successor as CEO, Sam Palmisano. However, 'the executive most responsible for the acquisition of PwC's consulting arm' was the leader of IBM's IT consulting services, Virginia 'Ginni' Rometty (513).

80. See Chapters 10 and 15. HP CEO Carly Fiorina and her services lieutenant Ann Livermore had begun pursuing the acquisition in September 2000, but the negotiations were hampered by bad luck and concerns about risk as well as price; by November, Fiorina had decided that even a renegotiated price was too high and that the acquisition should be forgone (Anders 2003: 93–4; Fiorina 2007: 228–9). In 2002, IBM was able to negotiate a much lower price for the acquisition, thanks largely to the subsequent recession in the high-tech sector.
81. 'IBM bought it for $3.5 billion in stock and cash, a bargain given that in 2000 H-P tried to acquire it for $17 billion' (Cortada 2019: 513).
82. Cortada 2019: 517.
83. Although the business was still generating $13 billion in annual revenue, selling a commoditized product in mature markets had become 'barely profitable' (Cortada 2019: 408–9).
84. Cortada 2019: 509, fig. 18.1.
85. House and Price 2009: 499–501, 507. HP also aimed to improve the acquisition's competitiveness through cost-cutting and operational improvements (Burgelman et al. 2017: 254–5).
86. Burgelman et al. 2017: 255.
87. Burgelman et al. 2017: 255.
88. Carlson 2015: 128.
89. See Kupperberg 2010: 12, which gives a more detailed account.
90. Hempel 2014: 83.
91. Ring 2017: 208–9.
92. Ring 2017: 209–11. See Chapters 6 and 14 on the Apple case.
93. Ring 2017: 101–2.
94. Carlson 2015: 318. He also compares Mayer to the 'extraordinary' people who had preceded her as CEO of Yahoo. 'If Marissa Mayer were to lose the fight to save Yahoo, she would not be the first extraordinary person to do so' (318).
95. Carlson 2015: 319.
96. Weston has pictorials of the Mosaic browser website and of an early Yahoo home page, with its directory headings and search button (Weston 2007: 40, 44).
97. Ring 2017: 105. By 1999, 'being a "portal" was all the rage. Keep users on Yahoo! for all of their needs. Be the one place to go for all of your online needs—be all things to all people' (105).
98. Kupperberg 2010: 13, 66.
99. Carlson 2015: 57.
100. Ring 2017: 137. Yahoo had missed two opportunities to acquire Google, first in 1998 and then in 2002 (104, 138–9).
101. Carlson 2015: 70, 123. In fact during 2005, Google had extended its hold to nearly half of all search-oriented advertising business (Kupperberg 2010: 88).
102. Neither of the co-founders had previously served as CEO of Yahoo. From 1995 to 2001, the CEO had been Tim Koogle; and from 2001 to 2007, Terry Semel.
103. Ring 2017: 192. He gives the deal a grade of C- from Yahoo's perspective (193). He also points out that Yahoo's share of the US search market continued to decline, to less than 13 per cent in 2015; while the share of Microsoft's Bing search engine increased from 8 per cent to 20 per cent in 2009–15 (191, 194). See also Carlson 2015: 122–3 on the deal and the continuing decline in Yahoo's share of the market.

104. Carlson 2015: 123. See 124 on Facebook's effect on advertising; and see Chapter 1 for Facebook's and Sheryl Sandberg's perspective on the issue.

105. Carlson 2015: 124–5; 'US Internet traffic to web-based email providers peaked in December 2009 at 140 million-plus unique visitors, and quickly declined from there. By September 2010, it was down to 125 million. It kept shrinking, and Yahoo took the brunt of the damage' (125). The smartphones' effects on web-based emails would have been followed by similar but lesser effects from the arrival in the early 2010s of Apple's iPad and the Android tablet computers.

106. Even after the Microsoft search-business deal, Bartz was under pressure to revive Yahoo. A *Forbes* magazine's story about her was subtitled 'After the Microsoft Deal, She Is Under the Gun to Remake Yahoo—Quickly'. *Forbes* 184/4, 7 September 2009: 84.

107. Carlson 2015: 194 on the share price fall; 127–8 on the 'awful' miss in expected quarterly results, and on the firing of Bartz.

108. CEO Scott Thompson was hired in January and resigned in May. When informing the board of his resignation, the still new CEO indicated that 'he was being treated for thyroid cancer': he was also facing issues related to the education part of his CV (Ring 2017: 204). See Carlson 2015: 208–17 on Thompson; and 246 on the shrinking revenues.

109. Ring 2017: 205.

110. Ring 2017: 211. Even a critic of Mayer's appointment framed his criticism in terms of her product-centred career and brilliance: 'It will be a struggle. She's never managed more than ten to twenty people. She's a product person who hasn't managed sales, business development, human resources and all that. Her problem is not product innovation— she's a great innovator' (anonymous Google executive quoted by Carlson 2015: 238).

111. The deal had been arranged largely by Yahoo co-founder Yang and gave Yahoo a 40 per cent stake in Alibaba in exchange for $1 billion and ownership of Yahoo's China business (Clark 2018: 196–7).

112. Clark 2018: 229.

113. Carlson 2015: 218. Yahoo's share price in fact increased steeply during Mayer's initial years, for Yahoo was 'just about the only way for investors around the world to invest in a humongous, fast-growing Chinese Internet company ahead of its imminent IPO' in the US in 2014 (218).

114. Ring 2017: 214. Mayer's announcement that there would be 'no company-wide layoffs' was apparently 'against the wishes of the board, industry observers, and analysts' (214).

115. Hempel 2014: 84.

116. Carlson 2015: 250.

117. Carlson 2015: 250–1.

118. McCracken 2015: 77, 78. See also Carlson 2015: 250 on the newly arrived Mayer's dismay when she found so few Yahoo staff were working on mobile apps.

119. Carlson 2015: 251–2. Mayer eventually spent about $1 billion acquiring 'at least fifty small companies. None were noteworthy and her history as a dealmaker is certainly underwhelming' (Ring 2017: 219). But these acquisitions were presumably being bought as acqui-hires and would have been too expensive to buy if they had been 'noteworthy'.

120. McCracken 2015: 76.

121. McCracken 2015: 80. Annual revenue in 2012 was just under $5 billion, in 2013 almost $4.7 billion, in 2014 over $4.6 billion, in 2015 just under $5 billion, and in 2016 over $5.1 billion (Ring 2017: 227).

122. Carlson 2015: 274–5; Ring 2017: 217.

123. Ring 2017: 217–8. 'The second challenge, according to Cohan, was for marketers to be able to advertise on Tumblr [blogs], permission was required by the owner of the blog, which was not Tumblr' (218).

124. Ring 2017: 217. Although the Tumblr network was eventually ranked eighth in the world, by mid-2016 'more than half the acquisition had been written down, and analysts believed its value to be zero' (217, 218). Carlson had still been hopeful about Tumblr in 2015. 'Tumblr is growing. Though its user base is smaller than Facebook's or Twitter's, the Tumblr users spend more time with the product' (Carlson 2015: 320). But he did not explain how Tumblr would boost Yahoo's revenue. 'The revenue figures for Tumblr were never released, but Yahoo! and industry statements indicate that Tumblr has underperformed for the company' (Ring 2017: 218).

125. McCracken 2015: 76.

126. See Carlson 2015: 287–9 on video. See Ring 2017: 220 on native advertising; and 222–4 on video.

127. Carlson 2015: 274.

128. Ring 2017: 219.

129. McCracken 2015: 78.

130. Alibaba had its IPO (initial public offering) in September 2014 (Clark 2018: 209). Yahoo had originally intended to sell off half of its Alibaba stake, specifically over 261 million shares, but it now decided to sell only 140 million (Carlson 2015: 316). So Yahoo continued to have the support of a sizeable Alibaba investment, 'worth more than $30 billion', which was later spun off as a separate company (McCracken 2015: 80).

131. Ring 2017: 227.

132. Ring 2017: 231.

133. McMurray 2018: 310. AOL had been acquired by Verizon in 2015, but AOL's leader Tim Armstrong remained as CEO and later became head of the newly created 'Oath' combination of AOL and Yahoo (309–10).

Chapter 14

1. Although he sold his near 10 per cent shareholding, he retained one share so that he could still attend the annual shareholder meetings (Blumenthal 2012: 135).

2. Lashinsky 2013: 22.

3. Lashinsky 2013: 19; Pisano 2021 [2019]: 78.

4. Schlender and Tetzeli 2016: 220.

5. Linzmayer 2004: 175.

6. Young and Simon 2005: 212. Isaacson 2013: 272, describes the fall as from a 16 per cent high in the late 1980s to just 4 per cent by 1996.

7. Recent acknowledgements of the role played by charisma in Jobs's leadership success can be found in Mickle 2022: 13, 96.

8. These numbers should be kept in mind when reading such descriptions of Jobs as: 'an autocrat who has remade a big, dysfunctional corporation into a tight, disciplined ship that executes on his demanding product schedules' (Kahney 2009: 12).

9. Amelio had a reputation as 'a transformation manager', especially from his time as CEO of National Semiconductor, and has been described as a 'great business manager' (Linzmayer 2004: 263; Young and Simon 2005: 214, 215). Amelio's financial lieutenant, Fred

Anderson, has been described as a 'great CFO' (chief financial officer) (Schlender and Tetzeli 2016: 191).

10. Linzmayer 2004: 235, 239.
11. Schlender and Tetzeli 2016: 194. See also Linzmayer 2004: 265, 267.
12. Linzmayer 2004: 265; Young and Simon 2005: 263.
13. Linzmayer 2004: 265–6.
14. Isaacson 2013: 278–9, 281.
15. Linzmayer 2004: 289–90.
16. Isaacson 2013: 306.
17. Schlender and Tetzeli 2016: 217; Linzmayer 2004: 265, 267. 'Amelio laid the groundwork for getting Apple back on its feet by replacing ineffectual executives, hoarding cash, simplifying the product line, releasing the world's fastest laptop and desktop, improving quality, spinning off Newton, and establishing a bold new operating system strategy' (Linzmayer 2004: 269). In addition, Amelio had been willing to ask Jobs to return to help with the turnaround. Although his replacement by Jobs has sometimes been seen as a stab in the back, it was more a case of the old adage that 'no good deed goes unpunished'. Furthermore, during Amelio's short tenure Apple had suffered over $1.6 billion in losses, so he was in weak position to ask for more time to finish his turnaround (268).
18. Schlender and Tetzeli 2016: 223. This meant that Jobs had only to make another 400 lay-offs.
19. Isaacson 2013: 311. For a different perspective on shutting down Apple's laser printers, see Kahney 2009: 30–1.
20. For example, there were still a dozen versions of the Mac computer, despite Amelio's simplification of the product range and lines (Isaacson 2013: 310).
21. Isaacson 2013: 310–11.
22. Hancock had been recruited by Amelio and, apparently, she resigned on the same day as him (Linzmayer 2004: 266, 270).
23. Linzmayer 2004: 292–3.
24. Schlender and Tetzeli 2016: 237.
25. Schlender and Tetzeli 2016: 237.
26. Isaacson 2013: 518.
27. Kahney 2014: 122–8.
28. Kahney 2014: 122.
29. Isaacson 2013: 301–2. The agency was TBWA/Chiat/Day and was led by the renowned Lee Clow.
30. Isaacson 2013: 302.
31. Schlender and Tetzeli 2016: 240.
32. Schlender and Tetzeli 2016: 238. The iMac was also given its own comprehensive advertising campaign, costing $100 million (Kahney 2014: 132–3).
33. Kahney 2014: 131–2; Isaacson 2013: 326.
34. Kahney 2009: 273–4.
35. Kahney 2009: 275.
36. For instance, the value of aesthetic design was emphasized when Jobs ignored engineering advice that an aesthetic feature of the iMac computer was simply not practical—was 'an ergonomic nightmare' (Kahney 2014: 126). Another instance of Jobs prioritizing the aesthetic was his objection to the iMac having a CD tray with an eject/close button, rather than a slot for insertion of a CD. Jobs ensured that the next model of the iMac would

change from tray to slot, despite an engineer having warned him that this would leave the iMac at a disadvantage when new technology enabled desktop computers to burn music onto CDs (Isaacson 2013: 324–5, 328–9).

37. Schlender and Tetzeli 2016: 234; Isaacson 2013: 318.
38. Mickle 2022: 75.
39. See Isaacson 2013: 408, 474 quoting Jobs on wanting to make great products.
40. Mickle 2022: 19. One of the unit's prodigies, a New Zealander named Daniel Coster, was appointed design leader of the iMac project (Kahney 2014: 71, 123).
41. Mickle 2022: 83.
42. Mickle 2022: 72.
43. Lashinsky 2013: 3, 20.
44. To what extent, though, was Jobs playing a part that gave him the right to be an autocratic and micromanaging 'different breed' of CEO?
45. Linzmayer 2004: 267. See Young and Simon 2005: 215 on CEO Amelio's powerlessness.
46. Lashinsky 2013: 65, 68; Young and Simon 2005: 262. 'A crucial step was to create single marketing, sales, manufacturing, and finance groups that operated across the company' (Young and Simon 2005: 262).
47. Lashinsky 2013: 65, 67.
48. Lashinsky 2013: 109–11, 118; Schlender and Tetzeli 2016: 383; Isaacson 2013: 412, 414.
49. Isaacson 2013: 305–6.
50. Isaacson 2013: 306.
51. Mickle 2022: 14.
52. Mickle 2022: 127–8.
53. Mickle 2022: 16–17.
54. Linzmayer 2004: 296, 298.
55. Linzmayer 2004: 295, 298.
56. Linzmayer 2004: 297. Market research showed that well over a quarter of iMac buyers had never previously bought a computer, while an eighth had previously bought one of the Apple-competing PCs (295).
57. Kahney 2014: 138, 139–40, citing Doug Satzger. However, Jobs wanted a pink colour added to cater for female consumers.
58. Kahney 2014: 140.
59. See Kahney 2014: ch. 6; Linzmayer 2004: 296–7.
60. Quoted by Schlender and Tetzeli 2016: 240.
61. Malone 2007: 376; Kahney 2009: 181.
62. Linzmayer 2004: 298–9. The board's chairman praised Jobs for Apple's market capitalization having increased from less than $2 billion to more than $16 billion in the two and a half years under his leadership.
63. Linzmayer 2004: 280; Schlender and Tetzeli 2016: 247. 'The radical new operating system would be the flywheel of all the extraordinary developments that would follow over the next decade, from Apple's suite of iLife applications, to iOS—the slimmed-down operating system that would give life to the iPhone and the iPad—to the entirely new software industry that emerged to produce the millions of apps written for those devices' (Schlender and Tetzeli 2016: 243).
64. See Kahney 2014: 155–6 on the Cube. Kahney 2009: 169–171, is particularly scathing about the Cube, and Jobs's role in its design and market failure.
65. Schlender and Tetzeli 2016: 241; Kahney 2014: 157.

66. See Schlender and Tetzeli 2016: 241 on the aesthetic-engineering trade-off. As for the expense-versus-performance issues, potential buyers 'viewed the Cube as basically a mid-range Power Mac G4 tower at a higher price. It was $200 more expensive than a comparable G4 and didn't come with a monitor' (Kahney 2014: 156).
67. Kahney 2014: 144; Schlender and Tetzeli 2016: 239. Similarly, Apple's computer-design masterpiece of 2001 was aimed at professionals rather than consumers. This Titanium PowerBook G4 portable/laptop was so thin and light that it 'did a lot for rehabilitating Apple's reputation among movers and shakers in the tech industry. The iMac had been great, but it was a cute plastic toy for consumers' rather than 'a serious machine for professionals' (Kahney 2014: 150, 153).
68. Schlender and Tetzeli 2016: 240.
69. Kahney 2014: 157; Linzmayer 2004: 299; Kahney 2009: 218; Schlender and Tetzeli 2016: 248.
70. Isaacson 2013: 410.
71. Kahney 2009: 203; Blumenthal 2012: 242.
72. Blumenthal 2012: 217; Kahney 2009: 203. The iMac was undergoing a redesign that would take it into the PowerBook G4 league, but this new-generation iMac G4 would not be available for another year.
73. Isaacson 2013: 354; Kahney 2009: 8.
74. Isaacson 2013: 353; Young and Simon 2005: 274.
75. Isaacson 2013: 353–4. There were dozens of models of portable music-player on the market (Mickle 2022: 81).
76. The name may have originated from an analogy with the spaceship pod that appeared in the science-fiction film *2001: A Space Odyssey* (Kahney 2009: 227).
77. Mickle 2022: 81.
78. Mickle 2022: 80.
79. Blumenthal 2012: 214–15; Isaacson 2013: 358–9; Young and Simon 2005: 278–9.
80. Kahney 2009: 194.
81. Kahney 2009: 195. Until then the iPad had needed a FireWire connection, 'which was rare on Windows computers', but now it had the widely used USB 2 connection.
82. Isaacson 2013: 372–3 on Jobs being persuaded to make the iPod compatible with Windows.
83. Kahney 2009: 195; Blumenthal 2012: 220; Mickle 2022: 81.
84. Kahney 2014: 194–5; Isaacson 2013: 377.
85. Mickle 2022: 101. Jobs had expected 'the Nano model, with its colourful, lightweight aluminium cover, to trigger a surge in demand', and he ensured that Apple's supply chain was 'able to fulfil demand when it spiked as Jobs predicted' (103).
86. Kahney 2009: 39.
87. Linzmayer 2004: 302–3.
88. He employed a mixture of carrot and stick in negotiating the deals. The carrot was the 70 per cent of each sale's proceeds that Apple would pass on to the music companies; the stick was the likelihood that music companies would end up with little or nothing if consumers were not given a legitimate means of downloading the songs they wanted to hear (Schlender and Tetzeli 2016: 288–9). Isaacson's account of the negotiations puts more emphasis on Jobs's ability to persuade and even charm these other business leaders (Isaacson 2013: 365–70).
89. Young and Simon 2005: 295.

90. Mickle 2022: 81; Blumenthal 2012: 242.
91. Isaacson 2013: 429.
92. Blumenthal 2012: 241.
93. The 'mobile' designation could also fit the portable/laptop computers that contributed a large fraction of Apple's computer sales. In fact for a few months in 2003 portables comprised almost half of all Apple's computer sales (Linzmayer 2004: 302).
94. The term 'luxury goods' can be applied to handbags and other leather accessories (as well as a range of other personal items) when they are produced for the luxury market. Kapferer and Bastien's text on luxury goods, brands, and strategies has included Apple as an example of following a luxury strategy (2012: 342–5).
95. Isaacson 2013: 429. See also Kahney 2014: 215 and also Merchant 2017: 235 on the iPod being deemed vulnerable 'as early as 2004' and the mobile phone being 'seen as a threat because it could play [digital-music] MP3s'.
96. Isaacson 2013: 429–30; Schlender and Tetzeli 2016: 307. When Jobs publicly demonstrated the ROKR in September 2005, he was so disappointed with the device that 'he was resolving to make it obsolete' with an Apple-built phone (Merchant 2017: 252). Furthermore, the smartphone threat was becoming ever more real. In 2005, 'Nokia announced its intention to sell music phones branded XpressMusic, showing Jobs he was right to be wary of phone makers' (Woyke 2014: 36–7).
97. Lashinsky 2013: 116.
98. Isaacson 2013: 430.
99. Isaacson 2013: 352.
100. Kahney 2009: 189.
101. Kahney 2014: 222.
102. Kahney 2014: 222, 224–5.
103. Vogelstein 2014: 66; Schlender and Tetzeli 2016: 359.
104. Kahney 2014: 227–8. See also Isaacson 2013: 434–5; Mickle 2022: 104–5.
105. Kahney 2014: 229.
106. Mickle 2022: 7.
107. Merchant 2017: 1, quoting from Jobs's keynote speech introducing the iPhone in January 2007. See also Schlender and Tetzeli 2016: 359–60 on the presentation.
108. Woyke 2014: 17, 29.
109. Mickle describes the iPhone software as 'transformational' and as having 'ignited the smartphone revolution' (Mickle 2022: 86, 117).
110. Furthermore, software experts helped to create the new phone's crucial piece of hardware, the multifinger touchscreen that replaced the need for a keyboard. The touchscreen was being developed as part of a tablet-computer project, but software experts came up with an app that enabled the touchscreen to work with a device of pocket-size, phone dimensions (Kahney 2014: 216).
111. See Becraft 2014: 38 on Microsoft's desire to recruit and retain 'very good programmers', and on the importance of such 'stars' as Charles Simonyi: 'regarded as the father of Microsoft Word'.
112. Woyke 2014: 43.
113. Woyke 2014: 44, and 43 on the apps-selling companies.
114. Merchant 2017: 425–6.
115. Isaacson 2013: 462.
116. Isaacson 2013: 462–3. See also Mickle 2022: 117.

117. Woyke 2014: 43. Jobs was announcing that Apple would soon be releasing a software development kit for app developers who wanted to sell their apps to iPhone users (43).
118. Woyke 2014: 44.
119. Doz and Wilson 2018: 126, fig. 7.2.
120. Woyke 2014: 43. Apple's fee of 30 per cent of the app's sales price was standard for major apps platforms, then and later (90). See also Doz and Wilson: 2018: 126, fig.7.2.
121. Woyke 2014: 45. See Schlender and Tetzeli 2016: 365 on it being a new form of computer that was 'more intimate' than the personal computer. Jobs himself had acknowledged privately, even before he unveiled the iPhone, that it would be able to do much of what was done on a desktop computer (352).
122. Doz and Wilson: 2018: 6.
123. Doz and Wilson: 2018: 6. In late 2008, Jobs told the leading mobile-phone firm, Nokia, that it was not an iPhone competitor because it was not a platform company. The Finnish firm's CEO 'came away from that encounter realizing that the change wasn't just about technology, it was a complete shift from one business to another' (Doz and Wilson: 2018: 117).
124. Isaacson 2013: 455, 459; Mickle 2022: 88–9. Apple sold twenty-five million iPads 'in little more than a year' (Mickle 2022: 108).
125. Blumenthal 2012: 264–5.
126. Blumenthal 2012: 244.
127. Blumenthal 2012: 257.
128. Schlender and Tetzeli 2016: 384. Jobs retired from the post of CEO in August 2011 due to his terminal illness, but he remained chairman of Apple until his death in October (Mickle 2022: 106).
129. Mickle 2022, 108; Blumenthal 2012: 257, 264. Apple had replaced Microsoft as the most valuable high-tech corporation on the world's stock markets. 'In May 2000 Apple's market value was one-twentieth that of Microsoft. In May 2010 Apple surpassed Microsoft as the world's most valuable technology company, and by September 2011 it was worth 70 per cent more than Microsoft' (Isaacson 2013: 518).
130. Lashinsky 2013: 132. And Apple's investor-relations unit, staffed by just two people, supplied 'precious little information to Wall Street analysts and shareholders' (132).
131. Kahney 2009: 220.
132. Mickle 2022: 14.
133. See the introduction to this chapter and the first two sections.
134. Mickle 2022: 22.
135. Auletta 2010: ch. 4.
136. Auletta 2010: 197.
137. Levy 2011: 214; Vogelstein 2014: 52.
138. Vogelstein 2014: 53. However, Android's pitch was not well received by such phone-makers as Samsung (Levy 2011: 214).
139. Vogelstein 2014: 53. The deal was for $50 million 'plus incentives'. Google co-founder Larry Page seems to have been the prime mover in making the acquisition (53).
140. Vogelstein 2014: 53.
141. See the section in Chapter 10 on Microsoft.
142. Vogelstein 2014: 50.
143. Vogelstein 2014: 51.
144. Woyke 2014: 62.

145. Schmidt and Rosenberg 2017: 202.
146. When discussing open systems in general, Schmidt and Rosenberg describe opting for an open system as a 'strategic tactic' (Schmidt and Rosenberg 2017: 89).
147. Schmidt and Rosenberg 2017: 89–90.
148. Woyke 2014: 62.
149. Vogelstein 2014: 47. Google's initial prototype, the Sooner phone, was not only 'ugly' but also had a 'traditional keyboard and small screen that wasn't touch-enabled' (47).
150. Woyke 2014: 50.
151. Woyke 2014: 50.
152. Vogelstein 2014: 119.
153. Vogelstein 2014: 132; Woyke 2014: 62.
154. Levy 2011: 217. Although Google freely licensed Android to any smartphone-maker, the licences included rules about Google apps and services. 'Device makers that reject these conditions can use the open-source version of Android but will have to find their own replacements for Google's signature services and software tools' (Woyke 2014: 63).
155. Woyke 2014: 63, quoting Steven Levy.
156. Vogelstein 2014: 132.
157. Schlender and Tetzeli 2016: 370.
158. Schlender and Tetzeli 2016: 370–1. Two American companies were also sued by Apple. Jobs's litigation was part of a wider and deeper opposition to Android. 'Clearly, Steve believed, Google's intent in offering a free operating system was to propagate a standard across all cell phones and mobile devices, leading to nothing less than a replay of what Gates had done to Apple's Macintosh with the release of Windows two decades before' (370).
159. Schlender and Tetzeli 2016: 371; Vogelstein 2014: 5–6.
160. Woyke 2014: 61.
161. Woyke 2014: 70.
162. Woyke 2014: 61.
163. Schmidt and Rosenberg 2017: 51.

Chapter 15

1. Weber 1978 [1922]: 241, emphases added.
2. Weber 1978 [1922]: 1114. But the issues of proof and success can be contentious. For in the less clear-cut cases, a sceptic might argue that the success proves nothing because the leader's efforts made little or no difference to the outcome. Or the success itself might be viewed sceptically, as just a temporary triumph or as failing to bring real well-being to the leader's followers.
3. It is true that German sociologist Weber could have looked further back in history and with a global perspective, but even in America the leaders of business corporations lacked the leadership prestige that they would enjoy later in the century.
4. Doz and Kosonen 2008: 5; Doz and Wilson 2018: 14–15.
5. Doz and Wilson 2018: 18. So Nokia was making mobile phones in the 1970s and in fact had 13 per cent of the world market in the 1980s (Ollila and Saukkomaa 2016: 120). But the American firm Motorola dominated the market by the end of the 1980s, with 22 per cent of the market and with Nokia reduced to only 10 per cent (120).
6. Ollila and Saukkomaa 2016: 103–4, 173–6.

7. Doz and Wilson 2018: 25.
8. Doz and Wilson 2018: 35; and see 36 on Ollila's pre-CEO career.
9. Ollila and Saukkomaa 2016, 149.
10. Ollila and Saukkomaa 2016: 120, 121, 127; Doz and Wilson 2018: 35.
11. Ollila and Saukkomaa 2016: 163; see chs. 26–9 on his experience as head of the mobile-phone business.
12. Ollila and Saukkomaa 2016: 161. At that time Nokia's workforce numbered some 25,000, so a lot of people would no longer have jobs at Nokia (166). But from Ollila's prioritizing perspective, Nokia 'needed to concentrate on an area where we would be one of the world's best, and it had to be in a growing market. Only this combination could save us' (161–2).
13. Ollila and Saukkomaa 2016: 173, 99–100.
14. Ollila and Saukkomaa 2016: 189, 193. Ollila notes that it was only in 1994 that Nokia's board 'decided to sell everything except telecommunications' (163). As Chapter 10 described, Ollila retained Nokia's longstanding mobile-infrastructure network business, which had been a greater source of revenue than mobile phones and would return to prominence after Siilasmaa's redeveloping in the 2010s.
15. Ollila and Saukkomaa 2016: 143, 179.
16. Doz and Wilson 2018: 44. By 1994, Nokia was in good enough shape to be listed on the Wall Street stock exchange.
17. Ollila and Saukkomaa 2016: 253.
18. Doz and Wilson 2018: 70, 77.
19. Ollila and Saukkomaa 2016: 252.
20. Ollila and Saukkomaa 2016: 228. Doz and Wilson 2018: 39–40 describe how Motorola did not see the potential for a mass-consumer market and focused for too long on analogue phones aimed at the top end of the market. Indeed Nokia's shift to digital technology has been seen as more of a marketing than a technological innovation, with Nokia being the first to see that mobile phones could be a mass-consumer rather than niche product (Doz and Kosonen 2008: 3).
21. Another feature of this digitalization is the influence of infrastructure issues, which were decided by countries rather than corporations. A smartphone expert has pointed to the significance of when and how countries adopted digital 2G wireless network technology. Finland and other European countries had adopted it as early as 1987, but the US delayed until 1995 and did not shift uniformly to the version of 2G that was standard in Europe and much of the world: the version called GSM (Global System for Mobile communications) (Woyke 2014: 11) Such a belated, fragmented shift to 2G in its home market obviously did not encourage industry leader Motorola to keep up with the times and the global market.
22. Woyke 2014: 8.
23. Woyke 2014: 12–13; Doz and Kosonen: 2008: 157.
24. By 2013, 'a billion new smartphones shipped to retailers annually' and they 'accounted for 55 percent of all cellphone shipments' (Woyke 2014: 60, 61).
25. Doz and Wilson 2018: 38; Ollila and Saukkomaa 2016: 179.
26. Ollila and Saukkomaa 2016: 179.
27. Ollila and Saukkomaa 2016: 179. Global sales of mobile phones grew by '51 percent in 1998, 65 percent in 1999, and 46 percent in 2000', reaching annual sales of over 400 million in 2000 (Doz and Wilson 2018: 77).

28. Doz and Wilson 2018: 64. In 1995–2000, its revenues had increased by more than 500 per cent and its operating profit 'by a staggering 1,924 percent', reaching more than an annual 4,500 million euros in 2000 (77). By 2001, Nokia had 35 per cent of the global market and its closest competitor was still Motorola, which had just under 15 per cent of the market (77).

29. Doz and Wilson 2018: 5, 64.

30. Ollila and Saukkomaa 2016: 309; Doz and Wilson 2018: 94–5, 108.

31. Ollila and Saukkomaa 2016: 295–6, 298–9.

32. Doz and Wilson 2018: 76.

33. Ollila and Saukkomaa 2016: 266. For example, see 300, 302 on Motorola's 'clamshell' folding mobile phones and Doz and Kosonen 2008: 20, on design problems that delayed Nokia's response to the clamshell challenge.

34. Ollila and Saukkomaa 2016: 335. As they point out, however, Nokia had 'peaked around this time' (335).

35. Siilasmaa 2019: 14. The charismatic Steve Jobs had a very different sort of relationship with Apple's board of directors. His board has been described as handpicked and doting on Jobs but also as engaging in freewheeling discussions led by Jobs standing at a whiteboard (Isaacson 2013: 412, 414).

36. Doz and Wilson 2018: 156.

37. 'Ollila's concern with the overreliance on two businesses' was understandable, but his 'yearning for a "third leg"' was unrealistic' (Doz and Wilson 2018: 65). See Doz and Kosonen 2008: 153 on how 'the quest for a third big "leg"' was gradually abandoned' in the 2000s.

38. Siilasmaa 2019: 16, 50–1, 199–200.

39. Ollila and Saukkomaa 2016: 354.

40. Doz and Wilson 2018: 98. Nokia's cultural bias in favour of hardware has also been noted by Siilasmaa. See his quoted remark in Chapter 1 and Siilasmaa 2019: 21.

41. Doz and Kosonen point out that it had also been 'strategically important to stop Microsoft alone taking the lead in [mobile] software development, and to stop others capturing the value from [mobile] software development' (Doz and Kosonen 2008: 161).

42. Siilasmaa 2019: 20.

43. Ollila and Saukkomaa 2016: 314.

44. Ollila and Saukkomaa 2016: 351–2.

45. Siilasmaa 2019: 59. Nokia also created a separate group for basic mobile phones so that a new group, Mobile Solutions, could focus on smartphones and software.

46. Ollila and Saukkomaa 2016: 347 has a superb photograph of the two leaders operating together at a microphone.

47. Woyke 2014: 53; Doz and Wilson 2018: 96–7.

48. Doz and Wilson 2018: 77–8.

49. The supplementary apps had to be as good as Google's, and the third-party platform had to match Android's Market. However, by the end of 2010, Android's Market boasted 130,000 third-party apps and 270 million downloads a month, while Nokia's equivalent had only 25,000 apps and ninety million downloads (Doz and Wilson 2018: 126, fig. 7.2).

50. See Doz and Wilson 2018: 133–4 on CEO Elop's skilful presentation of the move.

51. Siilasmaa 2019: 111.

52. Ollila does not discuss the Microsoft alliance in his book—his final chapter deals with the replacement of the CEO in 2010. However, neither *Ringtone* nor Siilasmaa indicate that

Ollila did anything else but support the new alliance. Ollila's book offers relatively limited coverage of Nokia's fate between his retirement as CEO in 2006 and then as chairman in 2012. Only the last five of the seventy-five chapters cover the post-2006 period, and not in great detail. For example, he hardly mentions Android except in the chapter on China: he observes there that the tide turned against Nokia in its China market when the iPhone arrived and when the 'Android operating system was adopted for use in Chinese mobile phones' (Ollila and Saukkomaa 2016: 333).

53. Weber 1978 [1922]: 36. See also Weber 1978 [1922]: 1121 on routinization.
54. Weber 1978 [1922]: 243 on prophet creating new obligations; 446 on prophetic messages with relatively rational doctrinal content; and 632–3 on Jesus's message.
55. Citing and quoting Kahney 2009: 273–5.
56. Ollila and Saukkomaa 2016: 167. 'I knew that only a common culture and common values could bring Nokia back to growth and a new resurgence' (170).
57. Ollila and Saukkomaa 2016: 170.
58. Ollila and Saukkomaa 2016: 171.
59. Siilasmaa 2019: 262.
60. Kahney 2009: 275.
61. Gerstner 2003: 182–3. He refers specifically to adaptations, but the point also applies to other changes, such as a redevelopment. 'The cultures of large institutions reflect the environment in which they emerged. When that environment shifts, it is very hard for the culture to change. In fact, it becomes an enormous impediment to the institution's ability to adapt. This is doubly true when the company is the creation of a visionary leader' (182).
62. Gerstner 2003: 183.
63. Weber gave some warning of these sorts of problem when he noted that post-founder routinization could be shaped by followers' self-interest, could be a long-term process, and would have a conservative effect (Weber 1978 [1922]: 246–8, 254).
64. Gerstner 2003: 185–6.
65. Gerstner 2003: 186–7. However, Gerstner later felt that this attitude of entitlement was less problematic than employees having 'become accustomed to immunity to things like recessions, price wars, and technology changes': an immunity that had helped create the everyday cultural features that he had mentioned (186). The accustomed immunity also contributed, though, to the distortion of the third belief into an attitude of entitlement and also further distortion of the other two Basic Beliefs.
66. Gerstner 2003: 184–5.
67. Cringely 2014: x, 14.
68. See the chapter's earlier citing and quoting of Weber's theory of charismatic leadership.
69. Malone 2007: 145.
70. See Packard 2005 [1995]: 80–1.
71. Packard 2005 [1995]: 81–2.
72. Gerstner 2003: 187, 188.
73. House and Price 2009: 517–18.
74. The suggestion was made when discussing the tenure of her successor, Mark Hurd: 'it is questionable whether he, like Fiorina before him, really understood and appreciated the nature of the HP innovation process, which was deeply rooted in serendipity and some redundancy' (Burgelman et al. 2017: 262).
75. Anders 2003: 222.
76. Khurana 2002: 66.

77. Anders 2003: 52.
78. Fiorina 2007: 154.
79. Fiorina 2007: 165. She used the term for the first time in her first, informal meeting with the board of directors: it 'seemed to resonate with the Board, and I would use it over and over again' (165).
80. HP was a company 'known for its lifetime employment record' (Burrows: 2003: 263). The full definition of the objective 'Employees' reads: 'To provide employment opportunities for HP people that include opportunities to share in the company's success, which they help make possible. To provide for them job security based on performance, and to provide the personal satisfaction that comes from a sense of accomplishment in their work' (Packard 2005 [1995]: 81).
81. Fiorina 2007: 232.
82. Fiorina 2007: 159.
83. It committed HP to 'continual improvement in the quality, usefulness, and value of the products and services we offer our customers' (Packard 2005 [1995]: 81).
84. Fiorina 2007: 175–6.
85. Burrows 2003: 170. She apologized to HP's board, 'took full responsibility for the miss, and told the board she had ended talks to buy PwC' (170). As Chapter 13 mentions, she had been interested in buying the PwC computer-services business. The acquisition would have greatly expanded HP's offering in computer services: a line of products in which HP was competitive and would grow impressively during Fiorina's tenure (House and Price 2009: 500).
86. Burrows 2003: 172.
87. Weber 1978 [1922]: 242.
88. Fiorina 2007: 227, 231, 235.
89. Fiorina 2007: 231.
90. Malone 2007: 251: Anders 2003: 121. Specifically, he had asked 'every HP employee, from himself to the grave-yard-shift janitors, to take off work every other Friday' (Malone 2007: 251).
91. Anders 2003: 120. Burgelman et al. 2017: 197 notes that on taking the job Fiorina had expected to make large cost savings in the first three years through, among other things, 'the first broad-based layoffs at HP since the end of World War II'. See Burrows: 2003: 167 on the problems she faced, though, in cutting back even the obvious labour surplus created by her centralizing of marketing services.
92. Fiorina 2007: 234, emphases added.
93. See the account given by Burrows 2003: 173.
94. Fiorina 2007: 237. 'Perhaps in my quest for speed I sacrificed broader-based acceptance of the decision' (237).
95. Fiorina 2007: 235–6.
96. Anders 2003: 180 on the effectiveness of this argument in dealing with opposition to the merger.
97. Anders 2003: 206, 222.
98. Anders 2003: 164. By November 2002, the lay-offs had increased by nearly 3,000 beyond the pre-merger estimate of some 15,000 (Burrows 2003: 263).
99. Anders 2003: 200–1. The HP board's overall margin of victory in the proxy vote was 51.4 per cent to 48.6 per cent (285).
100. Malone 2007: 381.

101. Anders 2003: 206–7. Malone 2007: 382 suggests that hardly any voted in favour.
102. House and Price 2009: 459.
103. House and Price 2009: 476. The preponderant view among the latter two groups was 'profoundly negative about Fiorina'.
104. House and Price 2009: 485. These post-Compaq numbers did not include the huge number of employees added later through Hurd's EDS acquisition.
105. Fiorina 2007: 237.

Chapter 16

1. Cohan's history of GE is a massive work of twenty-eight chapters and more than 700 pages, covering GE from the 1890s to the early 2020s. The book is particularly concerned, though, with the Welch and Immelt leadership eras of 1981–2001 and 2001–17 (Cohan 2022: chs. 8–17, chs. 18–25).
2. See Chapters 6 and 8. On GE's development into a *multifaceted* high-tech corporation, see Slater 1993: ch. 1 and Gelles 2022: 21–2.
3. Immelt 2021: 1.
4. Gelles 2022: 25.
5. Gelles 2022: 8.
6. Gelles 2022: 9; and 8–9 on Welchism. He describes downsizing, deal-making, and financialization in more detail in 2–4 in the case of GE; and 57, 67 for America generally.
7. Gelles 2022: 3, 68.
8. 'GE's shareholders prospered mightily during Welch's tenure, with a compound annual return of 20.9 percent' (Thorndike 2012: vii). The *Economist* magazine, 7–13 March 2020: 56 has a graph that displays this steadily growing and indeed accelerating increase in annual shareholder returns. Welch delivered these increases on a quarterly basis and was able to 'meet or beat analysts' estimates for nearly eighty quarters in a row, an unprecedented run' (Gelles 2022: 6).
9. Gelles 2022: 163.
10. See the discussion in Chapter 10 on the need for discernment when choosing appropriate products for diversification, and on discerning that diversification should not be internal but instead external: through diversifying acquisitions as external change-making organizational processes.
11. The *Economist* magazine, 7–13 March 2020: 55. See also Gelles 2022: 91 on these plaudits, including how the Harvard Business School 'practically deified Welch, its professors churning out more than a dozen case studies that lionized his exploits'.
12. See Slater 1993: ch. 3.
13. Welch 2003: 125–6.
14. Welch 2003: 139. 'The Asian assault had been coming for many years, swamping one industry after another: radios, cameras, televisions, steel, ships, and finally autos … We had several vulnerable businesses, including housewares and consumer electronics' (108). Gelles, too, notes that GE was 'particularly vulnerable' to global competitors, as many of GE's industrial product lines were Edison era and therefore relatively low-tech by the 1980s (Gelles 2022: 19). This particular vulnerability may be why Welch was one of the first business leaders to take serious notice of the threat from foreign competition (Gelles 2022: 18; Slater 1993: xviii).

15. Slater 1993: xviii, xix, xx. Welch has been described as the 'first CEO to take a healthy company and treat it like a turnaround job' (Gelles 2022: 229). But some experts would disagree with Gelles's view that GE was a 'healthy' company when Welch took charge in 1981. For instance, see the *Economist* magazine, 7–13 March 2020: 55, 56.

16. Welch 2003: 126. 'We gave our employees significant notice and good severance pay, and our good reputation helped many of them find new jobs' (126).

17. Welch 2003: 108–11, 129. See also 92–6, 156–62. The downsizing sell-offs were based on Welch's criteria of 'No.1 or No.2' and 'fix, sell, or close'. If any GE business was not No. 1 or No. 2 in its line of business (in a high-margin growth market), then that business should be fixed, sold, or closed down (108–9).

18. Cohan quotes a former Welch-era executive: 'Making your earnings [numbers] was just life to us' and was 'part of the company culture, clearly. Make your numbers. Make your numbers. And stretch. The guys did it' (quoted by Cohan 2022: 256). In the mid-1990s Immelt failed to hit his numbers and 'found himself in Jack's [Welch's] doghouse as the numbers got worse' (319). But in the late 1990s, Immelt was more than hitting his numbers and benefited from the rewards aspect of the performance-numbers culture. By 2000, he was earning a bonus of $1.2 million, in addition to his salary of over $616,000 (321).

19. Slater 1993: 13.

20. The third section of the chapter points out that this performance-numbers culture did in fact discourage innovation.

21. Kuykendall 2015: 131. For instance, he spent $8 billion on plant automation and robotics in 1981–5 (Gryta and Mann 2020: 17–18). Gelles does not acknowledge this part of the rectification programme. He describes Welch's remedial actions in more sweeping terms. 'Instead of trying to fix American manufacturing, he effectively abandoned it, and would soon start shuttering factories around the country and shipping jobs overseas' (Gelles 2022: 19).

22. Kuykendall 2015: 131.

23. O'Boyle 1999: 122–3, 128. Cohan describes Welch's 'desire to create the "Factory of the Future", where networked computers tell machines what to do and when to do it. Creating the next generation of factories became the a "holy grail" inside Jack's GE. But it failed' (Cohan 2022: 159). Welch also acquired 'microelectronics manufacturing plants' and began joint-venture production of robots (159).

24. As Chapter 10 described, in the 1990s Hewlett-Packard stagnated and declined after it lost its ability to add new high-tech facets.

25. Welch 2003: 140, 144. He also mentions that the 'Japanese threat' led to the RCA deal (140). He again mentioned the Japanese-competition threat in a later interview with Cohan (2022: 200). GE divested itself of the non-NBC components of RCA, such as the music records/recording business and then the television-manufacturing business. The latter and GE's television-manufacturing arm were divested in 1987 through a deal with a French firm that provoked some media criticism: these critics 'claimed we were bowing to Japanese competition by selling out. Some attacked the deal as un-American. I even got called a chicken for running away from a fight' (Welch 2003: 150).

26. Gelles 2022: 56.

27. Such acquisitions are therefore external substitutes for internal diversifying, as discussed in earlier chapters and especially Chapter 10.

28. Welch admits that although NBC's 'ratings were strong in 1985, cable television had started to eat into its network audience', and so his question to doubters had to be: 'Ten

years from now, would you rather be in appliances or in network television?' (Welch 2003: 142). Rather than choosing between these alternatives, the question might have been framed as whether it would be better to be in network television or PC products in 1995. However, Cohan believes that the RCA acquisition was one of Welch's 'best deals, if not his very best' (Cohan 2022: 201).

29. See Chapters 6, 10, and 14.
30. See Chapters 10 and 13.
31. Welch 2003: 74, 233; O'Boyle 1999: 40.
32. Welch 2003: 71.
33. Welch 2003: 233–4.
34. O'Boyle 1999: 128.
35. Welch 2003: 235. The biggest financial-services growth before 1985–9 was the 1984 acquisition of Employers Reinsurance Corporation (ERC) for over $1 billion (235). However, ERC was not incorporated into the newly renamed GE Capital. Instead, GE Financial Services was formed to be the parent for both these organizations (Slater 1993: 104).
36. Indeed his Chapter 16 was titled 'GE Capital: The Growth Engine'.
37. Gelles 2022: 60. For instance, in 1991–6, GE Capital more than doubled GE's revenue growth, from an otherwise only 4 per cent a year to an impressive 9 per cent a year (59). By the beginning of the 1990s, GE Capital was providing more than a fifth of GE's total net income (Cohan 2022: 247). And in 1981–91, GE Capital's assets grew from $11 billion to $70 billion (Gelles 2022: 58). In 1992–2000, GE Capital went on to expand its assets from this $70 billion to no less than $370 billion, as described later in this section. GE Capital was also 'providing nearly 40 percent of GE's pre-tax net income' by the end of the 1990s (Cohan 2022: 217).
38. O'Boyle 1999: 40n. Cohan describes GE Capital as 'the nation's first, and biggest, non-bank bank', which 'got the money it needed by borrowing it on the cheap—leveraging GE's AAA credit rating—from the commercial paper market or from other pools of cheap capital around the world. It made money by borrowing short and cheaply and lending long and expensively' (Cohan 2022: 216). GE Capital also enjoyed an extra source of cash, as GE's industrial businesses provided their finance arm with extra cash for investment (Tichy and Sherman 1993: 25).
39. Gelles 2022: 59. Such flexibility was also evident in its finetuning of earnings to help GE meet or beat expected quarterly earnings. In the final days of a quarter, GE Capital 'would often unleash a flurry of activity, adding profits and taking restructuring charges as needed to help the parent company meet Wall Street's expectations' (60). For example, a $1.4 billion profit from the sale of a business could be 'offset' by a '$1 billion charge to cover the cost of closing various facilities worldwide' (Cohan 2022: 254–5). After all, if the earnings beat expectations by too high a margin, this would be setting a new, higher standard of what was to be expected of GE. Such finetuning of earnings was feasible because 'accounting rules were relatively lax and neither investors nor regulators asked too many questions'; the rules and questions became much tougher after the Enron debacle in the 2000s, and even more so after America was hit by a financial crisis in 2008 (Gelles 2022: 62, 124, 147–8).
40. Welch 2003: 235, 237.
41. Welch 2003: 244. This seems to be an underestimate, as GE made 125 acquisition deals 'in 1999 alone' (Cohan 2022: 363–4).

42. 'Sometimes Welch quickly sliced up the companies he bought, then sold them off for parts' (Gelles 2022: 5).
43. Gelles 2022: 5. The acquisitions cost some $130 billion, while the divestments brought in less than $11 billion.
44. Welch 2003: 241. See Chapters 10 and 13 on how such acquisitions are an external change-making organizational process that supplement an internal prioritization: in the GE cases, they were supplementing the internal prioritizing of GE Capital's financial services.
45. Gelles 2022: 59.
46. Welch 2003: 237, 250. Gelles, too, does not mention any Internet businesses in his account of GE Capital's wide range of businesses (Gelles 2022: 59).
47. Immelt 2021: 14.
48. Immelt 2021: 9. He points out that 'until 1986, GE had more patents than any other corporation. But the corporation had deemphasized technology, and GE was not even in the top-twenty ranking of companies holding patents. Instead of innovation, Jack [Welch] had been focused more on management techniques such as Six Sigma' (9). Welch had only 'three or four initiatives in twenty years—Six Sigma, going global [financially], and developing more [financial] service revenue' (Cohan 2022: 457–8). There were no *high-tech* initiatives from the mid-1980s to the 1999/2000 internal initiative to catch up with the Internet revolution.
49. Welch 2003: 349 on emails; and 341 on the Internet. He had begun taking the Internet seriously in late 1998, when 'I began to hear about people at work doing their Christmas shopping on-line' (341).
50. Welch. 2003: ch. 22, 'E-Business'.
51. However, there is at least one indication that he was not entirely satisfied with the results of his redevelopment. In 2000, he made a merger-like share deal to acquire the Honeywell industrial corporation, though intervention by EU regulators led him to abandon the deal (Welch 2003: 361–74). Immelt notes that 'diluting GE Capital's dominance by making our industrial arm bigger' was Welch's main argument for pursuing the acquisition: it would 'reset the company at 70 percent industrial, 30 percent financial—a worthy goal' (Immelt: 2021: 52, 55). But if Welch was seeking to reduce GE Capital's dominant role in GE, he presumably was not happy with that result of his redevelopment.
52. Welch 2003: 74, 233; Gelles 2022: 59. These are the figures for the year 2000. See also Welch 2003; 250 and its pie-graph information, which shows the new emphasis on consumer financial services.
53. GE Capital's 'easy profits during the long economic expansion of the 1990s masked plenty of sins, including mounting troubles at GE's core industrial units', according to the *Economist* magazine, 7–13 March 2020: 56.
54. Immelt 2021: 119. GE had allowed Plastics to stick 'to the status quo' while its competitor DuPont moved into agricultural chemicals in the late 1990s: GE Plastics was 'sitting on the sidelines as its competitors—Dow, DuPont, and Monsanto—responded to stagnating markets by moving into the agriculture business' (81, 119–120).
55. Gelles 2022: 116.
56. He had joined GE in 1982 as a sales consultant within the marketing department at GE headquarters, and then became a GE Plastics regional sales manager (Magee 2009: 12, 15). In 1989 he shifted to customer services for Appliances before going on in the 1990s to become general manager of Plastics and then CEO of Medical Systems (192, 327, 29).

57. Immelt 2021: 126–7. The GE inherited by Immelt was 'a bank attached to a huge, slow-growth industrial company' (Cohan 2022: 379).
58. Immelt 2021: 59, emphasis added.
59. Immelt 2021: 62.
60. In particular, there were the effects of the 2001 Enron scandal and resulting 2002 Sarbanes-Oxley Act (Gryta and Mann 2020: 54, 57). See also Cohan 2022: 380–1 on the media's and investors' new scepticism about corporate disclosure and accounting. There was 'a change in the zeitgeist' (381).
61. Gelles 2022: 115. Immelt apparently agrees that he should have taken the post-9/11 opportunity. Interviewed by Gelles shortly before *Hot Seat* was published, Immelt acknowledged that 'he had a chance to reset GE after 9/11, and regretted not acting with a sense of urgency. "I thought I had the luxury of time", he admitted. "I thought we could do this a little bit at a time, and do it over a period of five or eight years". But ... "You're with the most admired company, with the most admired team, right after a crisis like 9/11", he said. "Standing up and saying, 'Hey, the place is broken'—I had no foundation for that"' (228). Immelt also told Cohan that 'I wish I had reset the company in 2002' (quoted by Cohan 2022: 380).
62. Gellles 2022: 136.
63. Gryta and Mann 2020: 59. See Cohan 2022: 382–91 for detailed background on this criticism of GE and on the prudential problems of GE Capital, especially with regards to its massive commercial-paper borrowing.
64. Gryta and Mann 2020: 81. The stock market's change in attitude to GE was partly due to increasing scepticism about Welch's success. There was 'a small but growing movement to reconsider Welch's success. How much of his nine years of double-digit earnings growth had simply reflected the careful management—if not outright manipulation—of the numbers?' (56).
65. Immelt 2021: 63–71. Gelles 2022: 8, 114, 165 points to the Welch era's underinvestment in R&D.
66. Immelt 2021: 66–7.
67. Immelt 2021: 61.
68. Immelt 2021: 77–80. The bio-tech 20 per cent of Amersham's business 'would, in time, prove very valuable' (Cohan 2022: 425). In 2003, GE also acquired 'a Finnish medical devices maker, for $2.4 billion, as it sought to move its Health-care business deeper into technology and patient monitoring' (Gryta and Mann 2020: 66).
69. Immelt 2021: 119–20; Gryta and Mann 2020: 89.
70. Immelt 2021: 152. In 2003, NBC was expanded by a $14 billion acquisition of film, television, and other media/entertainment assets, creating NBC Universal, but this produced no profit growth from 2005 to 2008 (Gryta and Mann 2020: 66, 134).
71. Immelt 2021: 87.
72. The divestment of insurance businesses began in 2003, with the sale of three insurance businesses for nearly $5 billion (Cohan 2022: 423). The later divestments included the mortgage-insurance and bond-guarantee businesses. Immelt believes that if they had not been divested, 'GE wouldn't have survived' the global financial crisis in 2008/9 (Immelt 2021: 88). The reinsurance business was not sold until 2005/6 and then at a $3 billion loss: in Immelt's words, 'I couldn't have been happier' (89). Cohan describes why Immelt was rightly pleased to be rid of the Employers Reinsurance Corporation (Cohan 2022: 423). Gryta and Mann 2020: 69–70 acknowledge Immelt's success in taking GE Capital

out of insurance but also point to his failure to get out of the long-term-care insurance business (70).

73. Gryta and Mann 2020: 104. Another example of GE Capital's flexibility and voraciousness was its move into the housing mortgage market. GE Capital acquired WMC (Weyerhaeuser Mortgage Company) in 2004 and, through WMC, became in 2005–7 'one of the top producers of subprime mortgages' (82, 99). In 2007, however, GE exited from the housing-mortgage business, before the subprime-mortgage crisis hit the market (89). Immelt later remarked that, 'I wish we'd never gotten into the business' (Immelt 2021: 122).

74. Gryta and Mann 2020, 83; Magee 2009: 214.

75. Tichy and Bennis 2007: 174.

76. Magee 2009: 213.

77. Immelt: 2021: 122. Gelles argues that GE had actually become more, not less, dependent on GE Capital. 'Financial services had never contributed more than 41 percent of GE's profits under Welch. Under Immelt, that figure soared to nearly 60 percent' (Gelles 2022: 138).

78. Immelt 2021: 145.

79. For instance, these more radical measures could have been the cultural transformation and high-tech diversifying acquisitions that are mentioned at the end of this section. As Cohan points out, the Internet and mobile-tech revolutions were well underway in the 2000s, but the high-tech 'inventions that had been GE's bread and butter for the first fifty years of its existence now seemed to be happening elsewhere' (Cohan 2022: 457). Although this failure was an inheritance from the Welch era, Immelt does not seem to have realized that radical measures were needed to 'update' GE.

80. 'He was already working to reduce GE's reliance on its finance division to 40 per cent of annual revenues through a variety of moves, including the sale of its Japanese consumer finance arm' (Magee 2009: 219).

81. Immelt 2021: 124; Gryta and Mann 2020: 108; Cohan 2022: 487–8.

82. Gelles 2022: 146.

83. What the investment analyst 'had warned about in 2002 was now coming to a head' (Gryta and Mann 2020: 116). GE's very short-term, commercial-paper borrowing was no longer viewed by investors as an acceptable risk, not in a crisis that was bringing down famous Wall Street financial houses (124).

84. Immelt 2021: 142. Although the federal government would have prevented GE from collapsing, there was always the danger of the government or someone else breaking the conglomerate up into smaller parts—of collapse by disassembly rather than disintegration (Gryta and Mann 2020: 109, 120).

85. Cohan 2022: 520; Gryta and Mann 2020: 124–6; Immelt 2021: 138–140. The new guarantee programme was the Temporary Liquidity Guarantee Programme (TLGP) of the Federal Deposit Insurance Corporation. However, although the TLGP had been established in October, GE was not given the necessary access to the programme until 12 November (Cohan 2022: 513–20).

86. Gryta and Mann 2020: 127, 128. Soon after February 2009, the share price bottomed out at $7 and then recovered to over $10 (129).

87. Immelt 2021: 151.

88. See Gryta and Mann 2020: 138–40 on how the 2010 Dodd-Frank Wall Street Reform and Consumer Protection Act restricted GE Capital, and on how the unit now came under

the scrutiny of the Federal Reserve. The latter's officials even 'set up shop in GE Capital's offices' (139).

89. Immelt 2021: 151; Cohan 2022: 590–1.
90. Immelt 2021: 111.
91. See Immelt 2021: 77–8 on the Amersham bio-tech products being a diversification, but the med-tech products being at best a development of existing GE Healthcare scanning/imaging technology. The Chapter 10 analysis of supplementary acquisitions was focused on prioritized products, but of course it can be applied to cases that are not part of a redevelopment. Hence GE's 2003 acquisition of Universal Studios for $14 billion may appear to have been a high-tech supplement to NBC's television-broadcast products, as 'cable offerings were beginning to outshine traditional network fare' and Universal had four cable channels (81). However, cable television was not a new high-tech product; nation-wide cable networks had been operating in America since HBO in the 1970s. By contrast, a truly high-tech supplement was the 2006/7 acquisition of IDX Systems, a healthcare software company, and 'we'd failed to capitalize on the $1.2 billion deal', according to Immelt (109).
92. The acquisitions problem was pointed out at the end of the previous section and was discussed in the Yahoo case covered in Chapter 13.
93. As the first section described, the performance-numbers emphasis was Welch's revival of a 1960s aspect of GE's culture. Welch's revived version was more 'positive' than the original version, as he supported the performance-numbers culture with rewards as well as sanctions. He even rewarded them with 'lots of handwritten notes, and there were stock grants and bonuses' (Comstock 2018: 40).
94. Gryta and Mann 2020: 29; Comstock 2018: 41.
95. As Welch wrote, 'Beth is a star. I found her at NBC, where she headed up public relations for news and then served as PR head of the network', before becoming GE's head of PR (Welch 2003: 362).
96. Comstock 2018: 43.
97. Comstock 2018: 43. She points out that 'it's hard to enlist risky new ideas from people who are expected to do everything perfectly. A society that glorifies numbers—and fears mistakes—leaves little room for human imperfections' (43). By contrast, toleration of imperfect and even bad ideas seems to be part of an innovation-encouraging culture. A 2016 study of how to build a culture of originality has argued that 'conformity will begin to rear its ugly head' if there is not 'some degree of tolerance in the organization for bad ideas' (Grant 2020 [2016]: 121).
98. Immelt 2021: 64. The previous section described how he boosted the funding and role of R&D.
99. Magee 2009: 25; Gryta and Mann: 2020. 90. As in the Welch era, the key numbers were those linked to quarterly earnings. 'Managers were expected to hit those targets at the end of every quarter, and anyone who came up short scrambled to cover their required contribution to feeding Wall Street's expectations. Since the Welch years, GE had rarely missed a quarter's projections' (Gryta and Mann 2020: 90).
100. See Chapters 8 and 14. In logicians' language, such innovation-encouraging culture is 'not a sufficient condition' for innovation but may well be a 'necessary condition': without it, there may be no chance of creating these products.
101. Gryta and Mann 2020: 152. Immelt recalls being 'impressed by how she threw herself into problems, no matter how intractable' (Immelt 2021: 97).

102. Comstock 2018: 305. During the Welch era, the pressure for cost-cutting meant that 'managers cut back on R&D and stayed out of risky new sectors' (53). In the 2000s, Immelt had boosted the R&D spending but had also sought 'very ambitious growth targets' for his industrial businesses: 'there was no way to optimize or cost-cut your way to those kinds of numbers' (86). So it is not surprising that GE's managers had difficulty meeting those targets, as described in the previous section.

103. Comstock 2018: 344.

104. Comstock 2018: 344. She stayed on not only because her new appointment was a capstone to her GE career but also because her new position recognized the role of innovation and marketing; she was the first woman to achieve such a high position in GE; and she had a sense of loyalty to Immelt and GE (344).

105. Comstock describes how an innovative project was under pressure in 2016 after it had a poor quarter and failed to meet its expected sales numbers (Comstock 2018: 349–50). She also mentions that GE in 2017 was experiencing cultural change: 'we were becoming more entrepreneurial, willing to take more, smaller risks' (352). But her reference to 'smaller' risks suggests that any cultural change was not in the direction of radical innovations.

106. Christensen, 2000: xv.

107. Christensen, 2000: xv.

108. Christensen, 2000: xv.

109. Gryta and Mann 2020: 152.

110. Immelt 2021: 64. It is hard to understand how the CEO of an American corporation in the 2000s–10s could not have been fully aware of the 'link between innovation and value creation inside companies'.

111. Comstock 2018: 367.

112. Comstock 2018: 195.

113. The chapter's introduction quoted his remark about 'too often' being neither brilliant nor lucky. And he makes the point in his speeches that he is neither lucky nor a genius (Immelt 2021: 6).

114. Immelt 2021: 287.

115. Gryta and Mann 2020: 98.

116. Comstock 2018: 367.

117. GE was reversing the Welch-era's negative attitude towards internally developing and/or diversifying into new high-tech products.

118. 'GE bought an office building in San Ramon, California, on the outskirts of Silicon Valley, gutted it to make it hipster friendly, and began a hiring spree of some three hundred expensive Silicon Valley engineers, about one third of the way to its goal of having a thousand engineers in Silicon Valley' (Cohan 2022: 561). But quality is more important than quantity when it comes to software programmers, as was pointed out in Chapters 14 and 15.

119. Comstock 2018: 254–6. She ascribes the term to Steve Liguori, the executive director of global marketing.

120. Comstock 2018: 255–6. 'Predix was a cloud-based platform' and created 'a computerized model, or "digital twin", of each machine that showed in real time how it was performing and when its parts were wearing out' (Immelt 2021: 111).

121. Comstock 2018: 263. Immelt refers to Christensen's *The Innovator's Dilemma* when describing GE's need to innovate digitally and consequently lose some spare-part

revenue: otherwise, 'one of our competitors will capture all these revenues' (Immelt 2021: 113–14).

122. Gryta and Mann 2020: 189, 190.

123. Gryta and Mann 2020: 210, 216.

124. See Gryta and Mann 2020: 190, 216–17, 221 on problems with software, recruitment, and implementation. Immelt highlights the recruitment problem. GE 'had a difficult time hiring top-flight software engineers. And we needed them' (Immelt 2021: 112). He notes that GE's software 'expertise deficit' was partly due to its long history of outsourcing to software-provider firms, which 'left us with a talent gap' (109, 112). He admits that 'I probably underestimated GE's digital deficit from years of outsourcing' (118). There was also an innovation deficit, which was at least partly due to the performance-numbers culture. Immelt acknowledges that executives 'focused on making their quarterly numbers' were not happy about GE Digital, and 'I'll admit that I was asking people to support uncertain, long-term innovation while also making their short-term numbers' (114).

125. Immelt 2021: 117. Acquisition was another possibility. Back in 2006, GE had spent more than $1 billion to acquire a healthcare software company (109). And there was plenty of money available for digital acquisitions: in the mid-2010s more than $5 billion was spent on the digital diversification (Gryta and Mann 2020: 218).

126. See Chapter 10 on discernment and internal diversification versus diversification through acquisition.

127. Gryta and Mann 2020: 215.

128. Immelt 2021: 152; Cohan 2022: 535–45.

129. Cohan 2022: 620; Comstock 2018: 299.

130. Gryta and Mann 2020: 209–13. By 2014, Oil & Gas was GE's third-largest group in terms of sales revenue and was generating a quarter of GE's total industrial revenue (210).

131. Immelt 2021, 214–15; Gryta and Mann 2020: 213–14.

132. Gryta and Mann 2020: 219–20.

133. See Immelt 2021: 74–5 on the very successful GEnx engine.

134. Cohan 2022: 576.

135. Immelt 2021: 262–4.

136. Cohan 2022: 570; see 579, 581, 608 on the deal and its eventual completion in late 2015.

137. Cohan 2022: 608; Immelt 2021: 276.

138. Gryta and Mann 2020: 257. They point out, however, that the acquisition was later viewed as a bad deal and that some lower level GE executives had even thought so at the time but had not spoken up (231–2).

139. Cohan 2022: 570.

140. Cohan 2022; 582; Gryta and Mann 2020: 203.

141. Immelt 2021: 250. See 242–3, on the February–March 2015 decisions by him, the leadership team, and the board of directors to divest GE Capital. His book indicates that the decision was precipitated by three factors (237, 240–1). First, the government regulation of GE Capital had become more burdensome; second, experts had found a way of reducing the tax bill of a GE Capital divestment; third, other experts had found a way of selling off GE Capital's huge amount of assets. The global financial crisis had led to the assets being markedly reduced, from $660 billion at the end of 2008 to only $400 billion in 2013, but that was still a huge amount of assets to sell off (235).

142. Immelt 2021: 251.

143. Gryta and Mann 2020: 184.

144. Cohan 2022: 595–6; Immelt 2021: 251. The stock/share buyback produced a 20 per cent reduction in the number of shares (Cohan 2022: 595). As Immelt describes, the goal of the buyback 'was to make our GE Capital divestment an EPS-neutral proposition—to reduce the denominator (the number of outstanding shares) in proportion to how much the numerator had been shrunk by the GE Capital sell-off' (Immelt 2021: 258). So GE did not have to create new earnings to replace the financial-services earnings that it had lost through the GE Capital divestment.

145. 'Shares jumped nearly 11 percent that day, closing at $28.51. It was the stock's largest one-day percentage gain in five years' (Immelt 2021: 251).

146. Immelt 2021: 232. Cohan, too, mentions the problem of analysts and investors' valuation of GE Capital's earnings (Cohan 2022: 590).

147. Cohan 2022: 590 on the rise of the S&P index and of the share price of such industrial corporations as Honeywell.

148. Gryta and Mann 2020: 186, 240. They refer to the mid-2010s redevelopment as 'the project of reviving GE's lame stock price' (256).

149. Gryta and Mann 2020: 218.

150. Not only was there a market downturn but also GE Power had failed to see the downturn coming and had therefore been too optimistic when predicting sales and earnings (Cohan 2022: 624; Gryta and Mann 2020: 231, 245–6).

151. GE Power earned less than $5 billion rather than the projected $5.4 billion (Cohan 2022: 628–9), even while resorting to 'aggressive' accounting, especially about service contracts, in a vain attempt to reach its overly optimistic targets (Gryta and Mann 2020: 245–6, 249–50).

152. Gryta and Mann 2020: 258–60.

153. Immelt 2021: 294. He was presenting PowerPoint slides and answering questions that included queries about GE's earnings-per-share target, GE Power's cash flow, and whether the Alstom deal was working: 'his credibility on Wall Street [was] battered as much by his besieged tone as his shaky assurances' (Gryta and Mann 2020: 260, 261).

154. Immelt 2021: 298.

155. Gryta and Mann 2020: 314, 319.

156. If not a cultural transformation, what other redeveloping tools might have been used? Hybridization was not a realistic option for a conglomerate, so the only remaining possible redevelopment tool was a structural transformation of some kind. Specifically, GE might have been energized by a decentralizing structural transformation, as the firm had been an unusually centralized conglomerate for more than forty years. But even a radical decentralization might not have been enough of a change to overcome GE's innovation-inhibiting culture. A recent study of innovative cultures points out that decentralizing a firm into smaller units has seldom led to the creation of an 'innovative start-up culture'; instead, 'these offspring units tend to inherit the culture of the parent organization that spawned them' (Pisano 2021 [2019]: 79–80). In GE's case, the parent's innovation-inhibiting culture might well have been inherited and maintained by the offspring divisional units.

157. Gelles 2022: 165.

158. Gelles 2022: 226. The break-up was planned for 2023/4. The healthcare company was 'to be spun off in early 2023, with GE retaining a 19.9 percent stake'; the energy company 'would comprise GE's power, renewable energy, and digital monitoring businesses, to be spun off in 2024 (and renamed, absurdly, GE Vernova); and a jet engine business ... would keep the GE name' (Cohan 2022: 718–9).

Addendum

1. Ewing 2017: 33.
2. Rieger 2013: 72, 226. It seems that the nickname 'Beetle' was first used in 1938 when the *New York Times* mentioned the prospect of 'thousands and thousands of shiny little beetles' crawling over the *Autobahn* (motorway) network being constructed in Germany by the Nazi regime (72).
3. Rieger 2013: 221.
4. Rieger 2013: 29. On the origins of the Beetle, see Ludvigsen 2012: ch. 1; and Hiott 2012: part one.
5. Rieger 2013: 75, 78; Ludvigsen 2012: 34.
6. Rieger 2013: 79–80; Ludvigsen 2012: 36, 373; and 36 on attracting only about 250,000 people by 1939.
7. Ludvigsen 2012: 37.
8. See Ludvigsen 2012: 373–4 on the export opportunity. Germany's exports of cars and trucks had almost tripled in 1935/6 and almost doubled in 1937 (24).
9. Rieger 2013: 97.
10. Nelson 1998 [1970]: 97, quoting Hirst.
11. Nelson 1998 [1970]: 100.
12. Richter 2003: 60.
13. Ludvigsen 2012: 116.
14. Hiott 2012: 212. Hirst's factory could not outsource the supply of parts and had to make them in the factory (Ludvigsen 2012: 111).
15. Richter 2003: 85, 86.
16. Rieger 2013: 113.
17. Ludvigsen 2012: 114–15.
18. Hiott 2012: 207; Ludvigsen 2012: 115.
19. Hiott: 2012: 207–8.
20. Hiott 2012: 208. After referring to the factory's service training school she notes: 'it's amazing that Feuereissen and the British were able to focus on the bigger picture in such a direct way' despite the 'chaotic and unstable conditions' of that era (208).
21. Richter 2003: 92.
22. Rieger 2013: 122.
23. Rieger 2013: 122.
24. Richter 2003: 93. There had been a deregulation of the economy as well as a currency reform.
25. Rieger 2013: 113.
26. Richter 2003: 93, text and graph.
27. Richter 2003: 43, quoting Hirst. See also Ewing 2017: 20.
28. Richter 2003: 44.
29. Hiott 2012: 203.
30. Richter 2003: 46.
31. Richter 2003: 46, quoting Hirst.
32. Richter 2003: 45.
33. Richter 2003: 46, quoting Hirst.
34. See Nelson 1998 [1970]: 120–2 on Nordhoff's origins and career with Opel.
35. Richter 2003: 90. Nordhoff had actually been offered the general-director position by Hirst after applying for a lesser, technical position at the factory (89).

36. Richter 2003: 90.
37. Rieger 2013: 111.
38. Richter 2003: 92.
39. Hiott 2012: 260.
40. Hiott 2012: 260, citing German historians' description of Nordhoff's system as being 'a kind of industrial feudalism'.
41. Hiott 2012: 260.
42. Richter 2003: 92.
43. Hiott 2012: 258–9.
44. Hiott 2012: 258.
45. Hiott 2012, 258.
46. Richter, 2003: 93.
47. Richter 2003: 92.
48. Hiott 2012: 259.
49. Rieger 2013: 132–3; and 134 on the shift towards automation.
50. Rieger 2013: 111.
51. Richter 2003: 92.
52. Ludvigsen 2012: 362. The main export destinations were Holland, Belgium, and Switzerland.
53. Rieger 2013: 138.
54. Rieger 2013: 138.
55. Nelson 1998 [1970]: 145.
56. In the mid-1950s, Nordhoff's designers reclothed the Beetle in a stylish Italian-designed body that gave it a sports-car look. The resulting 'Karmann Ghia' was described by an advertisement as 'a Volkswagen in an Italian sports jacket', but this a two-seater rather than a family car (Nelson 1998 [1970]: 152). Some 445,000 were made during its seventeen-year production life, from 1956 to 1973, and the car was an export success in America, where more than 15,000 were sold annually by the late 1960s (Gunnell 2017: 203; Nelson 1998 [1970]: 211). In 1961, Nordhoff then introduced a new family-car design aimed at supplementing—not replacing—the Beetle. The new design was slightly bigger than the Beetle but the main difference was the switch to an orthodox square-ish body shape that made the '1500', officially the Type 3, hard to distinguish from other cars of its era: it 'never caught on with the car-buying public' and was not exported to America until 1965 (Gunnell 2017: 242, 244).
57. As was pointed out earlier, Volkswagen did not officially adopt the name Beetle until 1968.
58. Quoted by Nelson 1998 [1970]: 145–6.
59. Nelson 1998 [1970]: 145. Hiott describes Nordhoff's notion of 'organic' redesign in rather different terms. 'He wanted to keep improving the mechanics, but without changing the design itself: He wanted it done *organically*, he said, as though on a cellular level, step by step' (Hiott 2012: 298).
60. See, for example, the description of annual model changes in Gunnell: 2017.
61. Nelson 1998 [1970]: 146. 'Between 1948 and 1954, every single part of the People's Car was inspected and improved' (Hiott 2012: 298).
62. Gunnell: 2017: 133.
63. Nelson 1998 [1970]: 149.
64. Nelson 1998 [1970]: 149; Ewing 2017: 33.
65. Ludvigsen 2012: 368.

66. Gunnell 2017: 20–1. The Export version was also sold as a more expensive version of the Beetle within Germany and therefore by the end of 1949 it comprised nearly two-thirds of Volkswagen's production (Ludvigsen 2012: 368).

67. Ewing 2017: 22.

68. Ewing 2017: 22.

69. Rieger 2013: 148. Until the late 1950s, the majority of Beetles were bought as commercial, company cars rather than as private cars owned by individuals or families (148). And average real incomes doubled in the 1950s, as the German economy grew at an average annual rate of 8 per cent in the 1950s: followed by growth of more than 6 per cent in the 1960s (128-9).

70. Rieger 2013: 192.

71. Rieger 2013: 199. In addition to the Beetle and the Ghia, there were some 50,000 vans and over 90,000 of the Type 3 1500/1600 family cars (Gunnell 2017: 81).

72. Rieger 2013: 241. Exporting Beetles to America was a different challenge from exporting them within Europe. In America there was a mature mass market for cars and further-more the market had long been dominated by US car-makers, leaving only a few niches to be exploited by the Beetle and other foreign imports. The most important market niche was middle-class suburban households' desire for a smallish second car, smaller than the standard models and reliable as well as inexpensive (Rieger: 2013: 200–4). By 1960, US car-makers had seen the potential of the smaller car niche and had 'entered the market with their so-called compact cars', but the Beetle would survive and prosper (Nelson 1998 [1970]: 212). 'Detroit's compact cars had a disastrous impact on most European imports, cutting sales in half' but 'the VW survived, captured the bulk of the remaining foreign-car market, and eventually outsold the compacts themselves' (213).

73. Rieger 2013: 201.

74. Hiott 2012: 367. At the end of the 1990s, *Advertising Age* ranked it the century's number-one campaign.

75. Hiott 2012: 365–7.

76. Hiott 2012: 366. For example, college students were 'tacking the ads to their dorm walls'.

77. Both Hiott: 2012: 371 and Ewing 2017: 34 describe it as 'a symbol of the counterculture'.

78. Ewing 2017: 35. However, the youthful counterculture did not provide the Beetle with an enduring market niche. The Beetle's US sales peaked in 1968/9 at about 420,000 and then went into increasingly rapid decline: to some 360,000 in 1972, below 244,000 in 1974, and fewer than 20,000 in 1977, when the Beetle was withdrawn from sale in America (Rieger 2013: 199, 245, 253; Gunnell 2017: 81, 85, 93, 97, 105, 111).

79. Ludvigsen 2012: 378; Nelson 1998 [1970]: 135.

80. Rieger 2013: 130.

81. Ludvigsen 2012: 368, which also quotes Ordinance 202.

82. Ludvigsen 2012: 377 quoting from an article in *The Observer* in 1956.

83. Ludvigsen 2012: 378.

84. Ludvigsen 2012: 378.

85. Ewing 2017: 25–6.

86. 'A hand-drawn picture of Nordhoff is on the cover of that issue, alongside a VW sign with sunbursts of Beetles streaming out' (Hiott 2012: 343).

87. Rieger 2013: 132; Nelson 1998 [1970]: 169.

88. Rieger 2013: 132.

89. Rieger 2013: 132. See also Hiott: 2012: 326 on Nordhoff being described as a king.

Appendix 1

1. See, for example, the extensive survey of theories and varieties of leadership presented by Bass and Bass 2008 or Northouse 2016.

2. Weber 1978 [1922]: 108. Political rationalization, too, needed free competition as well as calculation, rules, and numbers (Brooker 2014: ch. 8). The rules included constitutions, electoral laws, legislative procedures, and the internal rules of political parties; the numbers included the voting figures and majorities in elections, parliaments, congresses, committees, and political parties. When combined with free competition, they produced the highest level of rationality in politics—modern democracy.

3. Weber 1978 [1922]: 245.

4. Weber 1970 [1919]: 138–9. Intellectualization was described by Weber in a speech entitled 'Science as a Vocation' which he gave in 1918 and was published the following year.

5. Weber 1978 [1922]: 1156. Although he described it here as the 'American' system of 'scientific management', Weber referred to it as 'the Taylor system' in other rationalizing contexts in *Economy and Society*, such as the rational specialization and selection of workers on the basis of their personal aptitudes (150).

6. Kanigel 2005: 530.

7. Taylor's fundamental thesis was that the productivity of any system of production could be maximized by selecting and training workers so that 'at the fastest pace and with the maximum of efficiency' they could do the highest class of work for which their 'natural abilities' suited them (Taylor 1998 [1911]: 2–3).

8. Taylor 1998 [1911]: 16.

9. Weber 1978 [1922]: 1150.

10. Burns 1978: 446, 446–7.

11. Howard 1984: 254–5.

12. Howard 1984: 254–5. A similar approach was shown by the commander of a British army in Burma in 1943 when he analysed the 'intellectual' foundations of morale. The soldier must be convinced that the objective is attainable, must be convinced that the organization is efficient, and must have confidence in his leader—must be convinced that 'whatever dangers and hardships he is called upon to suffer, his life will not be lightly thrown away' (Slim 2006 [1956]: 208).

13. Barnard stayed in that post until his retirement in 1947 but he also had a distinguished post-1938 career of public service as head of the wartime United Services Organizations, the Rockefeller Foundation charity, and the National Science Foundation (Scott 1992: ch. 4).

14. Scott 1992: ch. 5.

15. Williamson 1995: 172.

16. Scott 1992: 112–13 and 116–17. See also 113, 117 on how the famous business book *In Search of Excellence* (Peters and Waterman 1982) pointed out that Barnard had discussed corporate culture and value shaping more than forty years earlier.

17. Barnard 1968 [1938]: 283.

18. Barnard 1968 [1938]: 261, 279, 283; and see also 259 on 'creating faith'.

19. However, charismatic leadership may well be secular rather than religious, as in the case of military charismatic leadership. 'In primitive circumstances this peculiar kind of quality [charisma] is thought of as resting on magical powers, whether of prophets, persons

with a reputation for therapeutic or legal wisdom, leaders in the hunt, or heroes in war'
(Weber 1978 [1922]: 241).
20. Weber 1978 [1922]: 215.
21. Barnard 1968 [1938]: 260. Presumably the superiority in skill and perception includes
superiority in what Barnard had characterized earlier as 'executive' processes, namely
the 'logical processes of analysis and the discrimination of the strategic factors' (233).
22. Barnard 1968 [1938]: 236, emphasis added.
23. Barnard 1968 [1938]: 173, 174.
24. Barnard 1968 [1938]: 236, emphases added. The rational type of leadership that he is
describing has similarities with what Northouse's recent leadership textbook refers to as
the 'skills' approach, which is 'a leader-centered perspective that emphasizes the competencies of leaders' and has developed a 'capability' model of leadership (Northouse 2016:
47, 69). It also has similarities with what Northouse describes as the typical twenty-first-
century perspective on defining leadership, 'whereby an individual influences a group of
individuals to achieve a common goal' (4).
25. However, the purpose of this technical-rational leadership was not to inspire confidence
but to perform the executive's adaptive function, which Barnard compared to that of 'the
nervous system, including the brain, in relation to the rest of the body. It exists to maintain
the bodily system by directing those actions which are necessary more effectively to adjust
to the environment' (Barnard 1968 [1938]: 217). The survival of a formal organization
depends upon its relationship with a 'continuously fluctuating environment' and upon
the accompanying 'readjustment of processes internal to the organization' (6; and see
also 35, 61).
26. Burns 1978: 20.
27. Burns 1978: 254.
28. Burns 1978: 20.
29. Burns 1978: 19, emphases added.
30. Burns 1978: 258. The reference to sellers and buyers is one reason why transactional
leadership seems similar to the deliberative form of leadership discussed in Chapter 1.
However, deliberative leadership's selling and buying of leads is not 'an exchange of valued things' but instead the seller convincing the buyer that the lead *is* a valuable thing
that is worth accepting and also is more valuable than any other lead being offered.
31. Burns 1978: 20.
32. Burns 1978: 258. There are also similarities between transactional leadership and
Neustadt's 1960 theory of presidential power, which has been described as presenting
'an early example of an exchange theory of politics' (Brooker 2010: 141). The obvious
similarity is with Neustadt's famous pair of maxims that presidential leaders' power 'is
the power to persuade' and 'the power to persuade is the power to bargain' (Neustadt
1990: 11, 32).
33. Harris 2004 [1967]: 13–14, quoting Berne's definition.
34. Harris 2004 [1967]: 262–5.
35. Christensen 2000: ix.
36. This term is reminiscent of Schumpeter's famous concept of Creative Destruction, which
described the revolutionary restructuring of industries that is caused by the introduction
of new commodities, markets, methods of production, forms of organization, or sources
of supply (Schumpeter 1974 [1947]: 83, 68). However, Christensen's conception of disruptive technology is solely concerned with technologically new commodities and the
new markets which they open up.

37. Christensen 2000: xv.
38. Christensen 2000: xv.
39. Christensen 2000: xv, 227.
40. Christensen 2000: x; xi and especially 108–9 on new entrants.
41. For 'the logical, competent decisions of management that are critical to the success of their companies are also the reasons why they lose their positions of leadership' when they face the challenge of disruptive technologies (Christensen 2000: xiii). In this situation, management decisions logically derived from listening to customers and tracking competitors' activities will not bring success if these customers and competitors prefer sustaining, not disruptive, technological innovations (98). In this situation, too, decisions logically aimed at designing and building higher performance products that offer greater profit will not bring success if disruptive technologies underperform existing technologies, offer lower profit, and can be sold only in what *appear* to be insignificant markets, whose growth and profit opportunities have not yet been identified (98).
42. Christensen 2000: xii, emphasis added. Steve Jobs apparently 'was deeply influenced' by Christensen's book and in a 2010 interview referred to 'what Clayton Christensen calls "the innovator's dilemma"' (Isaacson 2013: 376, 490).
43. Christensen 2000: xii–xiii.
44. Modern students of leadership have created a 'Mach' scale that measures 'the extent to which respondents subscribe to Machiavelli's dictums' and 'a high score on the Mach scale was seen as an indication of a predisposition to maximize self-interest using *deceit and manipulation* at the expense of others' (Bass and Bass 2008: 161, emphasis added).
45. Pocock 2003 [1975]: 154, 167; and see ch. 6 on *The Prince*. Machiavelli's 'great originality is that of a student of delegitimized politics' in an era where legitimacy is still based on tradition rather than rational-legal sources and where charismatic legitimacy is problematic: 'the new prince can outshine the hereditary and evoke more loyalty; his *virtu*—functioning where rational and traditional authority are both absent—is a kind of charisma' (163, 179). The great originality of Machiavelli's thinking is also pointed out in Isaiah Berlin's landmark essay 'The Originality of Machiavelli', which highlights Machiavelli's distinction between Christian-private morality and classical-public morality (Berlin 2013 [1972]: 299–324).
46. Pocock 2003 [1975]: 178–9.
47. Machiavelli 2012 [1532]: 85–6.
48. Machiavelli 2012 [1532]: 86.
49. Machiavelli 2012 [1532]: 61. Machiavelli's famous analogy with the lion and the fox was borrowed from the Roman writer Cicero, who had written that the use of force and fraud reduces men to the level of beasts, respectively the lion and the fox (Skinner 2012: xix–xx).
50. This similarity in form is very different from any similarity in terms of actual application of Machiavellian methods to modern times, which many theorists have attempted. During the First World War, Pareto published a theory of political elites with an updated version of Machiavelli's contrast of fox-like cunning and lion-like forcefulness (Parry 1971: 47, 60–1). Nearly thirty years later, Burnham's famous *The Machiavellians* described Pareto as well as Mosca, Sorel, and Michels as 'modern Machiavellians' (Burnham 1987 [1943]). In the twenty-first century, too, Ledeen presented Machiavelli's ideas as still relevant for leaders in politics and other fields; Morris updated *The Prince* for twenty-first-century politics; and, more recently, Lisch applied Machiavelli's ideas to modern business management (Ledeen 2000; Morris 2000; Lisch 2012).
51. Machiavelli 2012 [1532]: 87.

Appendix 2

1. Carr 2008: 19.
2. McMurray 2018: 188.
3. McMurray 2018: 187, 189.
4. Gerstner 2003: 167–8. Gerstner notes that the cloud was introduced to him as 'a graphic' used on IBM charts (167). His memories of his first introduction to 'the cloud' may therefore be affected by the way in which the term 'cloud' was first applied to computing. The computing term 'cloud' had originated from computer-network diagrams, which depicted each server computer as a symbol surrounded by a circle. 'A cluster of servers in a network diagram had several overlapping circles, which resembled a cloud' (Schmidt and Rosenberg 2017: 11 n. 10).
5. Gerstner 2003: 168.
6. Gerstner 2003: 168.
7. Symonds 2004: 185.
8. Symonds 2004: 186.
9. Quoted by Symonds 2004: 167.
10. This assessment is quoted by Symonds 2004: 178. Oracle had been transformed 'into a disciplined machine capable of responding very quickly to inputs from the top', and the top was now capable of realizing very quickly if a part of the machine needed fixing or improving (181).
11. Symonds 2004: 241–2.
12. Benioff and Adler 2009: 4, emphasis added.
13. Benioff and Adler 2009: 4.
14. Benioff and Adler 2009: 105.
15. Benioff and Adler 2009: 104.
16. Carr 2008: 71.
17. Carr 2008: 70.
18. Gerstner 2003: 285, app. B.
19. Carr 2008: 72. Microsoft seems not to have been worried about SaaS until 2005/6, even though this PC-software corporation seemed to have been threatened by the SaaS tendency to 'replace' PC apps with cloud app services. A 2005 Microsoft memo and plan warned senior managers and engineers of the 'disruptive potential' of what it termed 'Internet' services (63, 81). By 2006, Microsoft was delivering an 'array' of software services 'to businesses and consumers, through its Windows Live, Office Live, and MSN brands' (82).
20. Yost 2017: 265; Carr 2008: 71.
21. Yost 2017: 265.
22. The previous section described the 'company' cloud and how Oracle had pioneered this version of cloud services.
23. There were some 140 modules 'designed to run nearly every aspect of even the biggest and most complex multinational company's operations' (Symonds 2004: 188).
24. Symonds 2004: 476.
25. Symonds 2004: 223.
26. Symonds 2004: 493.
27. Symonds 2004: 200.
28. Symonds 2004: 193. By 2003, E-Business Suite Outsourcing was Oracle's fastest growing business (193, quoting Ellison).

29. Symonds 2004: 480.
30. McCullough 2018: 178.
31. Carr 2008: 72.
32. Carr 2008: 72.
33. Stone 2014: 211, emphasis added.
34. Stone 2014: 211.
35. Cortada 2019: 558.
36. Yost 2017: 265.
37. See the point about HP's service contracts cited in the third section of Chapter 13.
38. Cortada 2019: 571.
39. Symonds 2004: 254.
40. Carr 2008: 67.
41. Brandt 2011a: 174–5.
42. Carr 2008: 65.
43. Cortada 2019: 558.
44. Cortada 2019: 558.
45. Cortada 2019: 558, 559; Yost 2017: 264.
46. Good 2020: 156.
47. Bezos 2021: 133. Although AWS remained focused on IaaS basics, it was also offering more sophisticated services, such as encryption and 'machine learning' (Yost 2017: 266).
48. Bryar and Carr 2021: 258.
49. Yost 2017: 268.
50. Yost 2017: 264. In 2014, IBM found that its Global Services business was actually shrinking (Cortada 2019: 565).
51. McMurray 2018: 177, 202–3, 226–7, 282, 288.
52. Cortada 2019: 562, 563, 571.
53. Rometty 2023: 135.
54. Rometty 2023: 135, 136.

References

Agins, T. (2000) *The End of Fashion: How Marketing Changed the Clothing Business Forever* (New York: HarperCollins).

Alcraft, R. (1999) *Anita Roddick* (Oxford: Heinemann).

Allison, G. (1971) *Essence of Decision: Explaining the Cuban Missile Crisis* (Boston, MA: Little, Brown).

Allison, G. (2007) 'Institution Builder', in M. J. Dickinson and E. A. Neustadt (eds.), *Guardian of the Presidency: The Legacy of Richard E. Neustadt* (Washington, DC: Brookings Institute).

Anders, G. (2003) *Perfect Enough: Carly Fiorina and the Reinvention of Hewlett-Packard* (New York: Portfolio).

Armani, G. (2015) *Giorgio Armani* (New York: Rizzoli International Publications).

Auletta, K. (2010) *Googled: The End of the World As We Know It* (London: Virgin Books).

Ball, D. (2010) *House of Versace* (New York: Three Rivers Press).

Barber, B. B. (2001 [1995]) *Jihad vs. McWorld* (New York: Ballantine Books).

Barnard, C. I. (1968 [1938]) *The Functions of the Executive* (Cambridge, MA: Harvard University Press).

Bass, B. M. and Bass, B. (2008) *The Bass Handbook of Leadership* (New York: Free Press).

Beahm, G. (2012) *The Boy Billionaire: Mark Zuckerberg in His Own Words* (Chicago: Agate).

Becraft, M. B. (2014) *Bill Gates: A Biography* (Santa Barbara, CA: Greenwood).

Benioff, M. and Adler, C. (2009) *Behind the Cloud* (San Francisco, CA: Jossey-Bass).

Berg, N. and Roberts, B. (2012) *Walmart* (London: Kogan Page).

Bergerud, E. M. (2000) *Fire in the Sky: The Air War in the South Pacific* (Boulder, CO: Westview).

Berlin, I. (2013 [1972]) 'The Originality of Machiavelli', *The Proper Study of Mankind: An Anthology of Essays* (London: Vintage).

Berlin, L. (2005) *The Man behind the Microchip: Robert Noyce and the Invention of Silicon Valley* (New York: Oxford University Press).

Beynon, H. (1984) *Working for Ford* (Harmondsworth: Penguin).

Bezos, J. (2021) *Invent & Wander: The Collected Writings of Jeff Bezos* (Boston, MA: Harvard Business Review Press).

Bilton, N. (2013) *Hatching Twitter* (New York: Portfolio).

Blumenthal, K. (2012) *Steve Jobs: The Man Who Thought Different* (London: Bloomsbury).

Bowen, H. K., Clark, K. B., Holloway, C. A., and Wheelwright, S. C. (eds.) (1994) *The Perpetual Enterprise Machine* (New York: Oxford University Press).

Boyle, D. (2001) *The Tyranny of Numbers: Why Counting Can't Make Us Happy* (London: Flamingo).

Boyle, D. and Roddick, A. (2004) *Numbers* (Chichester: Anita Roddick Publications).

Bradshaw, A. and Scott, L. (2017) *Advertising Revolution: The Story of a Song, from Beetles Hit to Nike Slogan* (London: Repeater).

Bradsher, K. (2002) *High and Mighty: SUVs—The World's Most Dangerous Vehicles and How They Got That Way* (New York: Public Affairs).

Brands, H. W. (1999) *Masters of Enterprise: Giants of American Business* (New York: Free Press).

Brandt, R. L. (2011a) *The Google Guys* (London: Portfolio).

Brandt, R. L. (2011b) *One Click: Jeff Bezos and the Rise of Amazon.com* (London: Portfolio Penguin).

Brooker, P. (1991) *The Faces of Fraternalism: Nazi Germany, Fascist Italy, and Imperial Japan* (Oxford: Oxford University Press).

Brooker, P. (2010) *Leadership in Democracy* (Basingstoke: Palgrave).

Brooker, P. (2014) *Non-Democratic Regimes* (Basingstoke: Palgrave).

Brooker, P. and Hayward, M. (2018) *Rational Leadership: Developing Iconic Corporations* (Oxford: Oxford University Press).

Bryar, C. and Carr, B. (2021) *Working Backwards: Insights, Stories, and Secrets from Inside Amazon* (New York: St. Martin's Press).

Bunnell D. with Luecke, R. A. (2000) *The eBay Phenomenon* (New York: John Wiley and Sons).

Burgelman, R. A., McKinney, W., and Meza, P. E. (2017) *Becoming Hewlett Packard: Why Strategic Leadership Matters* (New York: Oxford University Press).

Burnham, J. (1987 [1943]) *The Machiavellians: Defenders of Freedom* (Washington, DC: Gateway).

Burns, J. M. (1978) *Leadership* (New York: Harper and Row).

Burrows, P. (2003) *Backfire: Carly Fiorina's High-Stakes Battle for the Soul of Hewlett-Packard* (Hoboken, NJ: Wiley).

Carbasho, T. (2010) *Nike* (Santa Barbara, CA: Greenwood).

Carlier, C. and Berger, L. (1996) *Dassault: The Corporation* (Paris: Editions du Chene)

Carlson, N. (2015) *Marissa Mayer and the Fight to Save Yahoo!* (New York: Twelve).

Carr, N. (2008) *The Big Switch: Rewiring the World, from Edison to Google* (New York: W. W. Norton).

Chandler, A. D. (1990 [1962]) *Strategy and Structure: Chapters in the History of the American Industrial Enterprise* (Cambridge, MA: MIT Press).

Chang, S.-J. (2008) *Sony vs. Samsung* (Singapore: Wiley).

Chernow, R. (2004) *Titan: The Life of John D. Rockefeller, Sr* (New York: Vintage Books).

Chouinard, Y. (2006) *Let My People Go Surfing; The Education of a Reluctant Businessman* (New York: Penguin).

Chouinard, Y. and Stanley, V. (2012) *The Responsible Company: What We Have Learned from Patagonia's First 40 Years* (Ventura, CA: Patagonia).

Christensen, C. M. (2000) *The Innovator's Dilemma: When New Technologies Cause Great Firms to Fail* (Boston, MA: Harvard Business Review Press).

Clark, D. (2018) *Alibaba: The House That Jack Built* (New York: Ecco).

Clausewitz von, C. (1984 [1832]) *On War* (Princeton, NJ: Princeton University Press).

Cohan, W. D. (2022) *Power Failure: The Rise and Fall of an American Icon* (New York: Portfolio/Penguin).

Cohen, A. (2003) *The Perfect Store: Inside eBay* (New York: Back Bay).

Cohen, E. A. and Gooch, J. (2006) *Military Misfortunes: The Anatomy of Failure in War* (New York: Free Press).

Cole, R. E. (1979) *Work, Mobility and Participation* (Berkeley, CA: University of California Press).

Cole, R. E. (1989) *Strategies for Learning: Small-Group Activities in American, Japanese and Swedish Industry* (Berkeley, CA: University of California Press).

Comstock, B. with Raz, T. (2018) *Imagine It Forward: Courage, Creativity, and the Power of Change* (New York: Currency).

Cortada, J. W. (2019) *IBM: The Rise and Fall and Reinvention of a Global Icon* (Cambridge, MA: The MIT Press).

Cringely, R. X. (1996) *Accidental Empires* (New York: HarperCollins).

Cringely, R. X. (2014) *The Decline and Fall of IBM* (Memphis, TN: NeDRTV, LLC).

Curcio, V. (2013) *Henry Ford* (New York: Oxford University Press).

Cusumano, M. A. (1985) *The Japanese Automobile Industry* (Cambridge, MA: Harvard University Press).

Dassault, M. (1971) *The Talisman: The Autobiography of Marcel Dassault* (New Rochelle, NY: Arlington House).

Davis, D. K. (2011) *Versace* (New York: Chelsea House).

Dickinson, M. J. (2007) 'Practicum on the Presidency, 1946 to 1953', in M. J. Dickinson and E. A. Neustadt (eds.), *Guardian of the Presidency: The Legacy of Richard E. Neustadt* (Washington, DC: Brookings Institute).

Doz, Y. L. and Kosonen, M. (2008) *Fast Strategy: How Strategic Agility Will Help You Stay Ahead of the Game* (Harlow: Pearson Educational).

Doz, Y. L. and Wilson, K. (2018) *Ringtone: Exploring the Rise and Fall of Nokia in Mobile Phones* (Oxford: Oxford University Press).

Drucker, P. F. (1993 [1946]) *Concept of the Corporation* (New Brunswick, NJ: Transaction).

Drucker, P. F. (2006 [1954]) *The Practice of Management* (New York: Harper).

Drucker, P. F. (2007 [1985]) *Innovation and Entrepreneurship: Practice and Principles* (Oxford: Elsevier).

Dumaine, B. (2020) *Bezonomics: How Amazon Is Changing Our Lives and What the World's Best Companies Are Learning from It* (New York: Scribner).

Emiliani, B. (2013) 'Ohno's Insights on Human Nature', *Taiichi Ohno's Workplace Management* (New York: McGraw-Hill).

Ewing, J. (2017) *Faster, Higher, Farther: The Volkswagen Scandal* (New York: Norton).

Farber, D. (2004) *Sloan Rules: Alfred P. Sloan and the Triumph of General Motors* (Chicago: University of Chicago Press).

Fiorina, C. (2007) *Tough Choices: A Memoir* (New York: Portfolio).

Fishman, C. (2011) *The Wal-Mart Effect* (London: Penguin).

Fixx, J. F. (1977) *The Complete Book of Running* (New York: Random House).

Foster, P. R. (2013) *American Motors Corporation* (New York: Motorbooks).

Fraser, K. (1981) *The Fashionable Mind: Reflections on Fashion 1970–1981* (New York: Alfred A. Knopf).

Fujimoto, T. (1999) *The Evolution of a Manufacturing System at Toyota* (New York: Oxford University Press).

Garr, D. (2000) *IBM Redux: Lou Gerstner and the Business Turnaround of the Decade* (New York: Harper Business).

Gastel, M. (2008) *The Versace Legend* (Milan: Baldini Castoldi Dalai).

Gelles, D. (2022) *The Man Who Broke Capitalism* (New York: Simon & Schuster).

George, A. I. (1972) 'The Case for Multiple Advocacy in Making Foreign Policy', *American Political Science Review*, 66/3, 751–85.

Gerstner, L. V. (2003) *Who Says Elephants Can't Dance? Leading a Great Enterprise through Dramatic Change* (New York: Harper Business).

Goldman, R. and Papson, S. (1998) *Nike Culture: The Sign of the Swoosh* (London: Sage).

Good, D. (2020) *The Microsoft Story* (New York: HarperCollins).

Gould, S. J. (2002) *The Structure of Evolutionary Theory* (Cambridge, MA: Harvard University Press).

Grant, A. (2020 [2016]) 'How to Build a Culture of Originality', *HBR's Ten Must Reads: On Building a Great Culture* (Boston, MA: Harvard Business Review Press).

Grove, A. S. (1999) *Only the Paranoid Survive* (New York: Crown).

Gryta, T. and Mann, T. (2020) *Lights Out: Pride, Delusion, and the Fall of General Electric* (New York: Houghton Mifflin Harcourt).

Gunnell, J. (2017) *The Complete Book of Classic Volkswagens* (Minneapolis, MN: Quarto).

Hargrove, E. (1998) *The President as Leader* (Kansas City, KA: Kansas University Press).

Harris, T. A. (2004 [1967]) *I'm OK—You're OK* (New York: HarperCollins)

Hempel, J. (2014) 'Marissa's Moment of Truth', *Fortune*, 169/7 (19 May), 83.

Hiott, A. (2012) *Thinking Small: The Long, Strange Trip of the Volkswagen Beetle* (New York: Ballantine).

Hollister, G. (2008) *Out of Nowhere: The Inside Story of How Nike Marketed the Culture of Running* (Maidenhead: Meyer & Meyer Sport).

Hoopes, J. (2006) 'Growth through Knowledge: Wal-Mart, High-Technology, and the Ever Less Visible Hand of the Manager', in N. Lichtenstein (ed.), *Wal-Mart: The Face of Twenty-First Century Capitalism* (New York: The New Press).

Horvitz, L. A. (2006) *Meg Whitman: President and CEO of eBay* (New York: Ferguson).

House, C. H. and Price, R. L. (2009) *The HP Phenomenon: Innovation and Business Transformation* (Stanford, CA: Stanford University Press).

Howard, M. (1984) *The Causes of Wars* (London: Unwin).

Huff, D. (1954) *How To Lie With Statistics* (London: Gollancz).

Hyde, C. K. (2003) *Riding the Roller Coaster: A History of the Chrysler Corporation* (Detroit: Wayne State University Press).

Iacocca, L. with Novak, W. (1986) *Iacocca: An Autobiography* (New York: Bantam).

Immelt, J. with Wallace, A. (2021) *Hot Seat: What I Learned Leading a Great American Company* (New York: Avid Reader).

Ingrassia, P. and White, J. B. (1995) *Comeback: The Fall and Rise of the American Automobile Industry* (New York: Touchstone).

Isaacson, W. (2013) *Steve Jobs* (London: Little, Brown).

Jackson, T. (1998) *Inside Intel: Andy Grove and the Rise of the World's Most Powerful Chip Company* (New York: Plume).

Johansson, J. (2005) *Two Titans: Muldoon, Lange and Leadership* (Wellington, NZ: Dunmore).

Jones, G. (2011) *Beauty Imagined: A History of the Global Beauty Industry* (New York: Oxford University Press).

Kahney, L. (2009) *Inside Steve's Brain* (London: Portfolio).

Kahney, L. (2014) *Jony Ive: The Genius behind Apple's Greatest Products* (London: Portfolio).

Kanigel, R. (2005) *The One Best Way: Frederick Winslow Taylor and the Enigma of Efficiency* (Cambridge, MA: MIT Press).

Kapferer, J. N. and Bastien, V. (2012) *The Luxury Strategy* (London: Kogan Page).

Katz, D. (1994) *Just Do It: The Nike Spirit in the Corporate World* (Holbrook, MA: Adams).

Kawamura, Y. (2017) *Sneakers: Fashion, Gender, and Subculture* (London: Bloomsbury).

Khurana, R. (2002) *Searching for a Corporate Savior: The Irrational Quest for Charismatic CEOs* (Princeton, NJ: Princeton University Press).

Kirkpatrick, D. (2011) *The Facebook Effect* (New York: Simon & Schuster).

Knight, F. H. (2014 [1921]) *Risk, Uncertainty and Profit* (Mansfield Centre, CT: Martino).

Knight, P. (2018) *Shoe Dog: A Memoir by the Creator of Nike* (London: Simon & Schuster).

Kroc, R. with Anderson, R. (1987) *Grinding It Out: The Making of McDonald's* (New York: St Martin's).

Kupperberg, P. (2010) *Jerry Yang* (New York: Chelsea House).

Kuykendall, M. (2015) *Rebuilding the GE House Jack Blew Down* (Seattle, WA: CreateSpace).

LaFeber, W. (2002) *Michael Jordan and the New Global Capitalism* (New York: W. W. Norton).

Lashinsky, A. (2013) *Inside Apple: How America's Most Admired—and Secretive—Company Really Works* (New York: Business Plus).

Lazenby, R. (2015) *Michael Jordan: The Life* (New York: Back Bay).

Le Maux, M. (2016) *1000 Sneakers: A Guide to the World's Greatest Kicks, from Sport to Street* (New York: Universe).

Ledeen, M. A. (2000) *Machiavelli on Modern Leadership* (New York: St Martins Griffin).

Lee, S. W. (2011) *The Legacy of Steve Jobs: 92 Inspirational Quotes of Steve Jobs* (Seattle, WA: Create Space).

Leidner, R. (1993) *Fast Food, Fast Talk: Service Work and the Routinization of Everyday Life* (Berkeley, CA: University of California Press).

Levin, D. P. (1995) *Behind the Wheel at Chrysler: The Iacocca Legacy* (New York: Harcourt Brace).

Levy, S. (2011) *In the Plex: How Google Thinks, Works, and Shapes Our Lives* (New York: Simon & Schuster).

Lichtenstein, N. (ed.) (2006) 'Wal-Mart: A Template for Twenty-First Century Capitalism', *Wal-Mart: The Face of Twenty-First Century Capitalism* (New York: The New Press).

Lichtenstein, N. (2010) *The Retail Revolution: How Wal-Mart Created a Brave New World of Business* (New York: Picador).

Linzmayer, O. W. (2004) *Apple Confidential 2.0* (San Francisco, CA: No Starch Press).

Lisch, R. (2012) *Ancient Wisdom for Modern Management: Machiavelli at 500* (Farnham: Gower).

Love, J. F. (1995) *McDonald's: Behind the Arches* (New York: Bantam).

Ludvigsen, K. (2012) *Battle for the Beetle* (Cambridge, MA: Bentley).

Lutz, R. A. (1998) *Guts: The Seven Laws of Business that Made Chrysler the World's Hottest Car Company* (New York: John Wiley & Sons).

Lutz, R. A. (2011) *Car Guys vs. Bean Counters: The Battle for the Soul of American Business* (New York: Portfolio).

Lutz, R. A. (2014) *Icons and Idiots: Straight Talk on Leadership* (New York: Portfolio).

Machiavelli, N. (2012 [1532]) *The Prince* (Cambridge: Cambridge University Press).

Mackey, J., McIntosh, S., and Phipps, C. (2020) *Conscious Leadership: Elevating Humanity through Business* (New York: Portfolio).

Magee, D. (2009) *Jeff Immelt and the New GE Way* (New York: McGraw-Hill).

Malone, M. S. (2007) *Bill & Dave: How Hewlett and Packard Built the World's Greatest Company* (New York, Portfolio).

Malone, M. S. (2014) *The Intel Trinity* (New York: HarperCollins).

Marcus, J. (2005) *Amazonia: Five Years at the Epicenter of the Dot.Com Juggernaut* (New York: The New Press).

Marder, A. J. (2015 [1974]) *From the Dardanelles to Oran: Studies of the Royal Navy in War and Peace* (Barnsley: Seaforth).

McCraw, T. K. (2007) *Prophet of Innovation: Joseph Schumpeter and Creative Destruction* (Cambridge, MA: Harvard University Press).

McCracken, H. (2015) 'The Marissa Mayer Project', *Fast Company* 195 (May), 77–80.

McCracken, H. (2017) 'Microsoft Rewrites the Code', *Fast Company*, October: 52.

McCullough, B. (2018) *How the Internet Happened: From Netscape to the iPhone* (New York: Liveright).

McDonald, J. (2003) *A Ghost's Memoir: The Making of Alfred P. Sloan's 'My Years with General Motors'* (Cambridge, MA: MIT Press).

McMurray, S. (2018) *Verizon Untethered: An Insider's Story of Innovation and Disruption* (New York: Post Hill Press).

Merchant, B. (2017) *The One Device: The Secret History of the iPhone* (London: Corgi).

Michell, T. (2010) *Samsung Electronics and the Struggle for Leadership of the Electronics Industry* (Singapore: Wiley).

Mickle, T. (2022) *After Steve: How Apple Became a Trillion-Dollar Company and Lost Its Soul* (New York: HarperCollins).

Miller, J. (2013) 'Seeking What Taiichi Ohno Sought', *Taiichi Ohno's Workplace Management* (New York: McGraw Hill).

Molho R. (2007) *Being Armani* (Milan: Baldini Castoldi Dala).

Moore, K. (2006) *Bowerman and the Men of Oregon* (New York: Rodale).

Moreton, B. E. (2006) 'It Came from Bentonville: The Agrarian Origins of Wal-Mart Culture', in N. Lichtenstein (ed.), *Wal-Mart: The Face of Twenty-First Century Capitalism* (New York: The New Press).

Moreton, B E. (2009) *To Serve God and Wal-Mart: The Making of Christian Free Enterprise* (Cambridge, MA: Harvard University Press).

Moritz, M. and Seaman, B. (1984) *Going for Broke: Lee Iacocca's Battle to Save Chrysler* (Garden City, NY: Anchor).

Morris, D. (2000) *The New Prince: Machiavelli Updated for the Twenty-First Century* (New York: Renaissance Books).

Nadella, S. with Shaw, G. and Nichols, J. T. (2019) *Hit Refresh: The Quest to Rediscover Microsoft's Soul and Imagine a Better Future for Everyone* (New York: Harper Business).

Napoli, L. (2016) *Ray & Joan: The Man Who Made the McDonald's Fortune and the Woman Who Gave It All Away* (New York: Dutton).

Nelson, W. H. (1998 [1970]) *Small Wonder: The Amazing Story of the Volkswagen Beetle* (Cambridge, MA: Bentley).

Neustadt, R. E. (1990) *Presidential Power and the Modern Presidents: The Politics of Leadership from Roosevelt to Reagan* (New York: The Free Press).

Northouse P. G. (2016) *Leadership: Theory and Practice* (Los Angeles: Sage).

O'Boyle, T. F. (1999) *At Any Cost: Jack Welch, General Electric, and the Pursuit of Profit* (New York: Vintage).

Ohno, T. (1988) *Toyota Production System: Beyond Large-Scale Production* (Boca Raton, FL: CRC Press).

Ohnuki-Tierney E. (2006) 'McDonald's in Japan: Changing Manners and Etiquette', in J. L. Watson (ed.), *Golden Arches East: McDonald's in East Asia* (Stanford, CA: Stanford University Press).

Ollila, J. and Saukkomaa, H. (2016) *Against All Odds: Leading Nokia from Near Catastrophe to Global Success* (Palmyra, VA: Maven House).

Ortega, B. (1999) *In Sam We Trust: The Untold Story of Sam Walton and How Wal-Mart is Devouring the World* (London: Kogan Page).

Packard, D. (2005 [1995]) *The HP Way: How Bill Hewlett and I Built Our Company* (New York: HarperCollins).

Paprocki, S. B. (2010) *Anita Roddick: Entrepreneur* (New York: Chelsea House).

Parry, G. (1971) *Political Elites* (London: George Allen & Unwin).

Pelfrey, W. (2006) *Billy, Alfred, and General Motors* (New York: AMACOM).

Peters, R.-H. (2008) *The Puma Story* (London: Marshall Cavendish).

Peters, T. J. and Waterman, R. H. (1982) *In Search of Excellence* (New York: Harper and Row).

Pisano, G. (2021 [2019]) 'The Hard Truth about Innovative Cultures', *HBR's Must Reads 2021* (Boston, MA: Harvard Business Review Press).

Pocock, P. G. A. (2003 [1975]) *The Machiavellian Moment: Florentine Political Thought and the Atlantic Republican Tradition* (Princeton, NJ: Princeton University Press).

Quinn, R. E. and Thakor, A. V. (2020 [2018]) 'Creating a Purpose-Driven Organization', *Building a Great Culture* (Boston, MA: Harvard Business Review Press).

Richter, R. (2003) *Ivan Hirst: British Officer and Manager of Volkswagen's Post-War Recovery* (Wolfsburg: Volkswagen).

Rieger, B. (2013) *The People's Car: A Global History of the Volkswagen Beetle* (Cambridge, MA: Harvard University Press).

Ring, J. (2017) *We Were Yahoo! From Internet Pioneer to the Trillion Dollar Loss of Google and Facebook* (New York: Post Hill Press).

Ritzer, G. (1996) *The McDonaldization of Society* (Thousand Oaks, CA: Pine Forge Press).

Roddick, A. (1991) *Body and Soul: Profits with Principles—The Amazing Success Story of Anita Roddick & The Body Shop* (New York: Crown Publishers).

Roddick, A. (2000) *Business as Unusual* (London: Thorsons).

Rometty, G. (2023) *Good Power: Leading Positive Change in Our Lives, Work, and World* (Boston, MA: Harvard Business Review Press).

Rothenberg, R. (1995) *Where the Suckers Moon: The Life and Death of an Advertising Campaign* (New York: Vintage).

Sandberg, S. with Scovell, N. (2013) *Lean in: Women, Work, and the Will to Lead* (New York: Alfred A. Knopf).

Schlender, B. and Tetzeli, R. (2016) *Becoming Steve Jobs: The Evolution of a Reckless Upstart into a Visionary Leader* (New York: Crown Business).

Schmidt, E. and Rosenberg, J. with Eagle, A. (2017) *How Google Works* (London: John Murray).

Schumpeter, J. A. (1961 [1934]) *The Theory of Economic Development* (New York: Oxford University Press).

Schumpeter, J. A. (1974 [1947]) *Capitalism, Socialism and Democracy* (London: Allen and Unwin).

Schumpeter, J. A. (1989 [1947]) 'The Creative Response in Economic History', *Essays on Entrepreneurs, Innovations, Business Cycles and the Evolution of Capitalism* (New Brunswick, NJ: Transaction Publishers).

Scott, W. G. (1992) *Chester I: Barnard and the Guardians of the Managerial State* (Kansas: University Press of Kansas).

Semmelhack, E. (2015) *Out of the Box: The Rise of Sneaker Culture* (New York: Rizzoli).

Shapley, D. (1993) *Promise and Power: The Life and Times of Robert McNamara* (Boston: Little, Brown).

Shimokawa, K. and Fujimoto, T. (2009) *The Birth of Lean* (Cambridge, MA: Lean Enterprise Unit).

Siilasmaa, R. with Fredman C. (2019) *Transforming Nokia* (New York: McGraw-Hill).

Skinner, Q. (2012) 'Introduction', *The Prince* (Cambridge: Cambridge University Press).

Slater, R. (1993) *The New GE: How Jack Welch Revived an American Institution* (Homewood, IL: Business One Irwin).

Slater, R. (1999) *Saving Big Blue: Leadership Lessons and Turnaround Tactics of IBM's Lou Gerstner* (New York: McGraw Hill).

Slater, R. (2003) *The Wal-Mart Decade* (New York: Portfolio).

Slim, W. J. (2006 [1956]) *Defeat into Victory* (London: Pan Macmillan).

Sloan, A. P. (1990 [1964]) *My Years with General Motors* (New York: Doubleday).

Smit, B. (2006) *Pitch Invasion: Adidas, Puma and the Making of Modern Sport* (London: Allen Lane).

Smith, N. (2018) *Kicks: The Great American Story of Sneakers* (New York: Crown).

Snow, R. (2014) *I Invented the Modern Age: The Rise of Henry Ford* (New York: Scribner).

Soderquist, D. (2005) *The Wal-Mart Way* (Nashville: Nelson).

Stone, B. (2014) *The Everything Store: Jeff Bezos and the Age of Amazon* (New York: Back Bay).

Stone, B. (2021) *Amazon Unbound: Jeff Bezos and the Invention of a Global Empire* (London: Simon & Schuster).

Strasser, J. B. and Becklund, L. (1993) *Swoosh: The Unauthorized Story of Nike and the Men Who Played There* (New York: Harper Business).

Strasser, S. (2006) 'Woolworth to Wal-Mart: Mass Merchandising and the Changing Culture of Consumption', in N. Lichtenstein (ed.), *Wal-Mart: The Face of Twenty-First Century Capitalism* (New York: The New Press).

Strauss, L. (1972) 'Plato', in L. Strauss and J. Cropsey (eds.), *History of Political Philosophy* (Chicago: Rand McNally).

Strayer, J. R. (2005 [1970]) *On the Medieval Origins of the Modern State* (Princeton, NJ: Princeton University Press).

Streeck, W. (1996) 'Lean Production in the German Automobile Industry: A Test Case for Convergence Theory', in S. Berger and R. Dore (eds.), *National Diversity and Global Capitalism* (Ithaca, NJ: Cornell University Press).

Symonds, M. (2004) *Softwar: An Intimate Portrait of Larry Ellison and Oracle* (New York: Simon & Schuster).

Taylor, F. W. (1998 [1911]) *The Principles of Scientific Management* (Mineola, NY: Dover).

Tedlow, R. S. (2003) *Giants of Enterprise: Seven Business Innovators and the Empires They Built* (New York: HarperCollins).

Tedlow, R. S. (2007) *Andy Grove: The Life and Times of an American Business Icon* (New York: Portfolio).

Thackray, A., Brock, D. C., and Jones, R. (2015) *Moore's Law: The Life of Gordon Moore, Silicon Valley's Quiet Revolutionary* (New York: Basic Books).

Thomas, D. (2008) *Deluxe: How Luxury Lost Its Luster* (New York: Penguin).

Thorndike, W. N. (2012) *Outsiders: Eight Unconventional CEOs and Their Radically Rational Blueprint for Success* (Boston, MA: Harvard Business Review Press).

Tichy, N. M. and Bennis, W. G. (2007) *Judgment: How Winning Leaders Make Great Calls* (New York: Portfolio).

Tichy, N. M. and Sherman, S. (1993) *Control Your Destiny or Someone Else Will* (New York: Currency).

Togo, Y. and Wartman, W. (1993) *Against All Odds: The Story of the Toyota Corporation and the Family That Created It* (New York: St Martin's Press).

Toyoda, E. (1987) *Toyota: Fifty Years in Motion* (Tokyo and New York: Kodansha International).

Toyota company history (1988) *Toyota: A History of the First 50 Years* (Toyota City: Toyota Motor Corporation).

Trimble, V. H. (1990) *Sam Walton: The Inside Story of America's Richest Man* (New York: Dutton).

Turner, L. (1997) *Gianni Versace: Fashion's Last Emperor* (London: Essential).

Van Dijck, J. (2013) *The Culture of Connectivity: A Critical History of Social Media* (New York: Oxford University Press).

Vance, S. S. and Scott, R. V. (1994) *Wal-Mart: A History of Sam Walton's Retail Phenomenon* (New York: Twayne).

Vanderbilt, T. (1998) *The Sneaker Book: Anatomy of an Industry and an Icon* (New York: New Press).

Viegas, J. (2007) *Pierre Omidyar: The Founder of eBay* (New York: Rosen).

Villette, M. and Vuillermot, C. (2009) *From Predators to Icons: Exposing the Myth of the Business Hero* (Ithaca, NJ: Cornell University Press).

Vlasic, B. and Stertz, B. A. (2001) *Taken for a Ride: How Daimler-Benz Drove off with Chrysler* (New York: Harper Business).

Vogelstein, F. (2014) *Battle of the Titans: How the Fight to the Death between Apple and Google Is Transforming Our Lives* (London: William Collins).

Wada, K. and Yui, T. (2002) *Courage and Change: The Life of Kiichiro Toyoda* (Toyota City: Toyota Motor Corporation).

Wallace, J. and Erickson, J. (1993) *Hard Drive: Bill Gates and the Making of the Microsoft Empire* (Chichester: John Wiley & Sons).

Walton, S. with Huey, J. (1993) *Sam Walton: Made in America, My Story* (New York: Bantam).

Waterton, W. A. (2012 [1956]) *The Quick and the Dead: The Perils of Post-War Test Flying* (London: Grub Street).

Watson, J. L. (ed.) (2006) 'Introduction', *Golden Arches East: McDonald's in East Asia* (Stanford, CA: Stanford University Press).

Weber, M. (1970 [1919]) 'Science as a Vocation', in H. H. Gerth and C. Wright Mills (eds.), *From Max Weber: Essays in Sociology* (London: Routledge & Kegan Paul).

Weber, M. (1978 [1922]) *Economy and Society* (Berkeley, CA: University of California Press).

Weber, M. (2001 [1904–5]) *The Protestant Ethic and the Spirit of Capitalism* (London: Routledge).

Welch, J. with Byrne J. A. (2003) *Jack: Straight from the Gut* (London: Headline).

Weston, M. R. (2007) *Jerry Yang and David Filo: The Founders of Yahoo* (New York: Rosen).

White, N. (1999) *Versace* (London: Carlton).

White, N. (2000) *Giorgio Armani* (London: Carlton).

Whitman, M. with Hamilton, J. (2010) *The Power of Many: Values for Success in Business and in Life* (New York: Three Rivers Press).

Whyte, W. H. (1961) *The Organization Man* (Harmondsworth: Penguin).

Williamson, O. E. (ed.) (1995) 'Chester Barnard and the Incipient Science of Organization', *Organization Theory: From Chester Barnard to the Present and Beyond* (New York: Oxford University Press).

Womack, J. P., Jones, D. T., and Roos, D. (1991) *The Machine that Changed the World: The Story of Lean Production* (New York: Harper Collins).

Woyke, E. (2014) *The Smartphone: Anatomy of an Industry* (New York: The New Press).

Yan, Y. (2006) 'McDonald's in Beijing', in J. L. Watson (ed.), *Golden Arches East: McDonald's in East Asia* (Stanford, CA: Stanford University Press).

Yates, B. (1996) *The Critical Path: Inventing an Automobile and Reinventing a Corporation* (Boston, MA: Little, Brown and Company).

Yost, J. R. (2017) *Making IT Work: A History of the Computer Services Industry* (Cambridge: MA: The MIT Press).

Young, J. S. and Simon, W. L. (2005) *iCon: Steve Jobs, the Greatest Second Act in the History of Business* (Hoboken, NJ: Wiley).

Zatz, D. (2019) *Mopar Minivans: Creating the First 20 Years of Chrysler, Dodge, and Plymouth 'Magic Wagons'* (New York: BusiStories).

Index

For the benefit of digital users, indexed terms that span two pages (e.g., 52–53) may, on occasion, appear on only one of those pages.